Property of
Charles A. Owen, Jr.
Medieval Studies Library

THE HEADS OF RELIGIOUS HOUSES
ENGLAND AND WALES
940–1216

THE
HEADS OF RELIGIOUS HOUSES
ENGLAND AND WALES
940–1216

Edited by

PROFESSOR DOM DAVID KNOWLES
Emeritus Regius Professor of Modern History
University of Cambridge

PROFESSOR C. N. L. BROOKE
Professor of History
Westfield College, University of London

VERA C. M. LONDON

CAMBRIDGE
AT THE UNIVERSITY PRESS
1972

Published by the Syndics of the Cambridge University Press
Bentley House, 200 Euston Road, London NW1 2DB
American Branch: 32 East 57th Street, New York, N.Y.10022

© Cambridge University Press 1972

Library of Congress Catalogue Card Number: 79-171676

ISBN: 0 521 08367 2

Printed in Great Britain
at the University Printing House, Cambridge
(Brooke Crutchley, University Printer)

CONTENTS

PREFACE

This book has been long in the making. When one of the authors (M.D.K.) first began to study English monastic records in 1929 he adopted the practice, for his own interest and information, of noting any contemporary reference to an abbot or prior. He took for his limiting dates 1066 and 1216. In the event, the opening date has been pushed back to 940, the refoundation of Glastonbury which heralded the great revival. The entries were made in a series of large note-books, divided among the orders with a page for each house. When, about 1931, the names had already accumulated in some strength, the compiler, on a visit to Cambridge, called upon Dr (later Professor) Z. N. Brooke in his house in Milton Road to tell him of this and other projects which were under way. Dr Brooke was, as always, courteous and helpful, but did not appear to take any special interest in the lists. In due course, however, when correspondence passed, he began to send notes of abbots he had come across in his own reading. At last in May, 1942, a formal suggestion of collaboration was made by M.D.K. and accepted by Dr Brooke. This was followed by a meeting in London, which was attended by C.N.L.B., still a schoolboy, but already interested in problems of chronology. The Brookes carried off the notebooks to transcribe them, and C.N.L.B. left them on the top of a bus. Fortunately, a swift pursuit on foot led to their recovery; and the pursuit has continued ever since, though rarely at the original pace or with the same hazard. Transcripts of the notebooks were made by Z. N. Brooke with his son's help, and the lists continued to grow until Dr Brooke's death in October 1946. After 1946, M.D.K. (now resident at Peterhouse, Cambridge) and C.N.L.B. (from 1950 to 1956 a Fellow of Gonville and Caius College, Cambridge) continued the collection, and a beginning was made in the pillaging of manuscript material.

So far, there had been no thought of proximate publication, if only because the time spent in checking references and examining the many sources still untapped was more than two academic historians, fairly busy with other work, could afford. In 1956 C.N.L.B. moved to Liverpool, and in due course the Secretaries in the School of History there (and later, in Westfield College, University of London) gave valuable help in typing lists and notes. The event, however, which made publication possible was the entry into the collaboration of Vera London in 1962. It has been her contribution to introduce system into the plan, to put the lists first into something approaching final shape, and then, after further revision by all three editors, to prepare for the printer and type the large majority of them; also to complete the sifting of documentary areas only partly covered, especially public records and printed and unprinted fines.

In early days M.D.K. worked alone: in the later years a greater part of the task has fallen on C.N.L.B. and V.L.; but the collaboration has been very close throughout, and information has been thrown into the pool by all three when it came to hand. The pre-Conquest sections of the lists have been mainly the work of C.N.L.B.; otherwise our shares cannot now be distinguished. Thus gradually the work, from being desultory and occasional, became more thorough and methodical; but we are all aware, even so, that without unstinting help from many others this book could never have been effectively completed.

At the base of our enterprise lies a collection of notes originally made entirely from primary sources. In the sequel, we have made full use of the work of innumerable predecessors in this work as well as of the generous collaborators listed below. This we gladly and fully acknowledge (see p. ix); the value of the book, such as it may have, depends on the very extensive collaborative effort over many centuries which lies behind it. Yet it also depends in a great measure on the accuracy and completeness of its reference to essential primary sources (see p. 19). Even where we have depended most on others' work, we have always tried to cite the original source, so as to make clear the foundation of all the lists, and to save needless recourse to secondary literature – though we have also tried to make clear when the secondary literature is especially useful and necessary. The ultimate responsibility for all the references is ours; we are only too fully aware that this book will prove to have many shortcomings – omissions and errors, and even the continued existence of some 'ghost' heads of whom it has been our task to eliminate as many as possible. We have neither sought nor desired perfection; we have tried to lay out for the use of other scholars the best lists that we could provide, without further, and possibly indefinite, delay.

First among our fellow-workers must be named the late Professor Z. N. Brooke, partner in the first collaboration, whose work in the early years added considerably to the value of many lists, and whose inspiration has been with us throughout the enterprise. Next, Sir Charles Clay, who has already published lists for many Yorkshire houses, and who added to an already considerable weight of debt by providing draft lists of almost all the others, checking various versions of our own lists and answering numerous queries. We have had a similar collaboration with Dr Diana Greenway, who has prepared lists of the Cathedral priors for the new edition of Le Neve; with Dr Marjorie Chibnall, with whom we exchanged drafts when she was preparing lists for the *Victoria History of Shropshire*; and with Mrs Vivien Brown and Dr Christopher Holdsworth, who are editing the cartulary of Eye priory and the charters of Rufford abbey. Our list for Tavistock is based on Professor H. P. R. Finberg's. These names must be singled out, since although we contributed much to these lists independently, these scholars provided the basis for the lists of these houses printed here (see p. 17); and with them Professor Dorothy Whitelock, who generously undertook to read the pre-Conquest sections, and provided us with invaluable notes and advice. Yet scarcely less is the debt we owe to Professor R. B. Pugh, Editor of the *Victoria County Histories*, since he and his colleagues readily arranged exchange of information for lists under way for volumes of the *VCH Middlesex* and *Staffordshire* (since published); for help with the Staffordshire houses we owe our thanks too to Mr M. W. Greenslade, Mr C. R. Elrington, and Dr Chibnall, and the Reverend J. C. Dickinson, also our helper in many other ways. For all Premonstratensian houses, we had a basis in Mr H. M. Colvin's *White Canons in England*. For Burscough, Buckfast, Quarr and St Mary's York we have had the benefit of help from Mr A. N. Webb, Dom John Stephan, Dom S. F. Hockey, and Dom Alberic Stacpoole. Mrs G. Keir and Dr David Smith have devoted much time to providing notes and checking references for us; they have given us new evidence and saved us from many errors; and Dr Smith and Professor Kathleen Major have been generous in providing notes for Lincolnshire houses and Lincoln Cathedral dignitaries. Professor Francis Wormald gave us much help in pursuit of calendars and the like. Generous help and advice have come too from Mr H. N. Blakiston, Dr Rosalind Brooke, Professor C. R. Cheney, Mrs M. G. Cheney, Dr G. R. C. Davis, Miss J. Foster, Dr B. R. Kemp, Dr J. Lally, Dr D. J. A. Matthew, Dom Adrian Morey, Mr R. G. Parker, Mrs U. Rees, Dr M. Richter, Mr John Saltmarsh, Professor P. H. Sawyer, Miss M. Screech, Miss B. SoRelle, Dom Aelred Watkin, and, in sorting and arranging the lists, from C.N.L.B.'s youngest son, Patrick Brooke. To the staff the Cambridge University Press we are greatly indebted for their skill and help. Dr R. N. Hadcock has collaborated with M.D.K. over many years in successive editions of *Medieval Religious Houses, England and Wales*: in innumerable ways his ready help has been given to this book too. Dr D. Oschinsky and Dr Greenway have most generously helped with the proofs.

Finally, many Librarians and Archivists have helped us in crucial ways: among these particular mention should be made of Mrs Cotterill (formerly of the Hampshire Record Office, Winchester), Miss Penelope Morgan (Hereford Cathedral), Mrs Dorothy Owen (Ely Diocesan Records), Mrs Joan Varley (formerly of the Lincolnshire Archives Office), Mrs M. E. Welch (Nottingham University), M. I. Cloulas (Archives Départementales, Eure), Dr F. G. Emmison (former County Archivist of Essex), Mr Peter Gwynn (Winchester College), Mr B. C. Jones (Cumberland, Westmorland and Carlisle Record Office), Mr M. F. Messenger (Shrewsbury Borough Library), Mr David Michelmore (Yorkshire Archaeological Society, Leeds), Miss A. Oakley (formerly Kent Record Office, now Canterbury Cathedral), Dr L. A. Parker (Leicestershire Record Office), Dr F. Taylor (John Rylands Library); and Dr W. Urry (formerly Canterbury Cathedral).

M.D.K.   C.N.L.B.   V.L.

January 1972

MANUSCRIPTS REFERRED TO

This list omits MSS used only for Anglo-Saxon chts. in Appendix III.

Aberdeen University Library, MS 137: Gregory the Great, etc., from London, St Paul's.
Aberystwyth, National Library of Wales, MS 7851 D: Ctl. Shrewsbury, Davis, no. 895.
    Peniarth MS 390: Ctl. Burton, Davis, no. 93.
Belvoir Castle, Add. MS 71: Ctl. Croxton, Davis, no. 292.
Berkeley Castle Muniments, Trustees of the Berkeley Estates, Ctl. Bristol (Microfilm in
    Bodleian Library), Davis, no. 77.
Boughton House, Kettering, Duke of Buccleuch: Ctl. Peterborough (Reg. Fraunceys), Davis,
    no. 764.[1]
Cambridge, Corpus Christi College, MSS 59: Ann. Merton.
    111: Miscellany including Ctl. Bath, Davis, no. 23, and Ann. ? Wenlock.
    391: Worcester Cathedral Psalter.
Cambridge, Gonville and Caius College, MS 314/376: Ctl. Spalding, Davis, no. 922.
Cambridge, King's College Muniments 2. W/2, 6, 7, 11, 15–18.
    B. 9.
Cambridge, St John's College, MS 236: Council of 1075.
Cambridge, Sidney Sussex College, MS 95: Miracles of the Blessed Virgin Mary.
Cambridge, Trinity College, MSS O. 2. 1 (1105): Ctl. Ely, Davis, no. 366.
    O. 9. 25 (1437): Martyrology of Belvoir Priory.
    R. 5. 33 (724): Miscellany Glastonbury, Davis, no. 438.
    R. 14. 9 (884): Ann. Horsham and Norwich.
Cambridge University Library (CUL) MSS Dd. iii. 87, art. 20: Ctl. Owston, Davis, no.
    738.
    Dd. viii. 2: Calendar of Kington St Michael.
    Ee. iii. 60: Ctl. Bury St Edmunds, Davis, no. 119.
    Gg. iii. 21: Missal and calendar of Tewkesbury.
    Kk. i. 22: Martyrology of Abingdon.
    Mm. ii. 20: Ctl. Bromholm, Davis, no. 79.
    Mm. iv. 19: Ctl. Bury St Edmunds, Davis, no. 118.
    Add. MSS 3020–1: Ctl. Thorney (Red Book), Davis, no. 964.
        4220: Ctl. Bury St Edmunds, Davis, no. 110.
    Ely Diocesan Records, G. 3. 27: Liber 'R.', Davis, no. 362.
        G. 3. 28: Liber 'M.', Davis, no. 369.
Canterbury Cathedral, Dean and Chapter Muniments, Chartae Antiquae, M. 20, R. 50.
    Eastry Correspondence, Group III, no. 25.
    Reg. E, Davis, no. 168.
Carlisle Cathedral, Dean and Chapter Library: 17th cent. transcript of Ctl. Lanercost,
    Davis, no. 526.
Chelmsford, Essex Record Office, MSS: D/DBy Q 19: Ctl. Eye, Davis, no. 397.
    T/B3: Ctl. Tilty, cf. Davis, no. 971.
Dublin, Trinity College Library, MS E. 5. 15: Ctl. Torre, Davis, no. 978.

---

[1] Photostats in Peterborough Cathedral Library (Mellows Collection).

Durham Cathedral, Dean and Chapter Muniments, 1. 1. Arch. 8; 2. 2. 4. Ebor. 57–61, 63; 2. 4. Ebor. 41; 3. 1. Pont. 11a; 3. 2. 4. Ebor. 45; 4. 2. 4. Ebor. 4; 4. 1. Pont. 5.
    Cartularium 11, 111, Davis, nos. 328–30.
    Misc. Charters 5828/14.
    Reg. 11, 111.
Durham Cathedral Library, MSS B. 11. 35: Ch. Durham.
    B. 1v. 24: Martyrology of Durham.
Ely, *see* Cambridge University Library.
Eton College Muniments, *see* Modbury, p. 105.
Eure, Archives Départementales, 11. F. 2463: Ctl. Wootton Wawen.
Exeter Cathedral Library, MS 3518: Exeter Martyrology.
Exeter City Archives, Muniment Book 53A: Ctl. Exeter, St John's, Davis, no. 393.
Forde Abbey, MS of G. D. Roper, Esq.: Ctl. Forde, Davis, no. 409.
Glasgow University Library, Hunterian MS U. 2. 6: Ctl. London, Holy Trinity, Aldgate, Davis, no. 610 (= *Ctl. London, Holy Trinity, Aldgate*).
Gloucester Cathedral Library, Reg. A, Davis, no. 455.
    Reg. B, Davis, no. 456.
    Seals and Documents, v. 1.
Hereford Cathedral, Dean and Chapter Archives, no. 1894.
Leeds, Yorkshire Archaeological Society, MS 542; Ctl. Hexham, Davis, no. 485.
Lexington, Kentucky, MS 091-M. 313 (photostat in Ipswich Borough Reference Library): Ctl. Ipswich, St Peter and St Paul, Davis, no. 500.
Lincoln Cathedral, Dean and Chapter Muniments, Dij/74/1/1.
Lincolnshire Archives Office, 2 Anc. 1/1/7; 2 Anc. 1/1/10; 3 Anc. 2/1; 5 Anc. 1/1/3.
    Transcript of Ctl. Newhouse (earl of Yarborough), Davis, no. 690.
    And see Spalding.
London, British Museum (BM)
    Additional Charters: 6104; 6109; 10,594; 15,185; 15,470; 15,694; 20,512; 21,205; 21,278; 22,380; 22,563; 28,323; 28,353–4; 28,360; 28,362; 28,364; 28,396; 28,398; 47,483–4; 47,601; 47,629; 47,631; 47,638; 47,640; 47,645–6; 47,854; 47,954; 47,958; 48,145; 48,490; 49,068; 49,117–18; 74,470.
    Additional MSS: 4797: extract from Ann. Hyde.
        4934: Peck transcripts, esp. part of *Collectanea Anglo-Praemonstratensia* (ed. Gasquet).
        5804: Cole transcript, Cole MS 3.
        5827: Cole transcript, Cole MS 26.
        5849: Cole transcript, Cole MS 48.
        5948: Ctl. Langley, Davis, no. 528.
        6118: Collections of Gervase Holles (17th cent.), esp. Thornton list.
        6671: One of A. Wolley's collections for Derbyshire (18th and 19th cent.).
        8177: Collections for History of Suffolk, presented by Hudson Gurney (1830).
        9822: Reg. Ely, Davis, no. 378.
        15,314: Ctl. St Denys, Southampton, Davis, no. 906.
        15,350: Ctl. Winchester, Davis, no. 1042.
        18,461: Ctl. Newent, Davis, no. 689.
        19,090: Collections for the History of Suffolk of D. E. Davy.
        29,436: Ctl. Winchester Cathedral, Davis, no. 1043 (with fragment of calendar).
        33,354: 18th cent. transcript of Ctl. Haughmond.
        35,285: Calendar of Guisborough.
        35,295: Collection of historical works etc., by a canon of Kenilworth (15th cent.).
        35,296: Ctl. Spalding, Davis, no. 920.

36,872: Ctl. Felley, Davis, no. 402.

40,000: Liber Vitae of Thorney, including Ann.

40,725: Ctl. Blythburgh, Davis, no. 60.

46,353: Ctl. West Dereham, Davis, no. 307.

46,362 (T): Ctl. Royston, Davis, no. 826.

47,677: Ctl. Kenilworth, Davis, no. 502.

47,784: Ctl. Coxford, Davis, no. 281.

Arundel MSS: 29: Ch. Walden, cf. Davis, no. 985.

   68: Martyrology of Canterbury Cathedral, Davis, no. 187.

   155: Calendar of Canterbury Cathedral.

   326: Ann. Abingdon.

Campbell Charters, x, 7; xv, 2.

Cotton Charters, v, 6 (2); viii, 10; xi, 10; xxi, 5; xxvii, 65.

   Rolls, iv, 57; xiii, 6, 26.

Cotton MSS: Appendix xxi: Ctl. Stoke by Clare, Davis, no. 933.

   Augustus ii, 6, 136 (charters).

   Calig. A. viii: Calendar and obituary of Beauchief.

   Calig. A. xii: Ctl. Pipewell, Davis, no. 776.

   Calig. A. xiii: Ctl. Pipewell, Davis, no. 777.

   Claud. A. viii: Extracts from Ctl. Bermondsey, Davis, no. 45.

   Claud. B. iii: Ctl. York Minster, Davis, no. 1086.

   Claud. B. iv: Ch. Durham.

   Claud. C. vi: Fragment of Canterbury obituary.

   Claud. D. iii: Obituary of Wintney.

   Claud. D. xi: Ctl. Malton, Davis, no. 648.

   Claud. D. xii: Ctl. Daventry, Davis, no. 302.

   Claud. D. xiii: Ctl. Binham, Davis, no. 56.

   Cleop. C. iii: Collections of F. Thynne, Ann. Little Dunmow.

   Cleop. C. vii: Ctl. and list Merton, Davis, no. 662.

   Domit. A. i: Ann. St Davids.

   Domit. A. iii: Ctl. Leominster, Davis, no. 552.

   Domit. A. x: Ctl. Rochester, Davis, no. 818.

   Faust. A. ii: Compotus etc., with historical notes from Sherborne.

   Faust. A. iii: Ctl. Westminster, Davis, no. 1011.

   Faust. A. iv: Ctl. St Neots, Davis, no. 859.

   Faust. A. viii: Ann. Southwark, Ctl. Southwark and Ann. Merton, Davis, no. 909.

   Faust. B. i: Ann. Winchcombe, Ctl. Barlings, Davis, no. 19.

   Faust. B. vi: Ann. and list Croxden; Reg. Canterbury Cathedral, Davis, no. 178.

   Faust. C. i: Ctl. Huntingdon, Davis, no. 499.

   Galba E. ii: Ctl. Hulme, Davis, no. 497.

   Julius A. i: Ctl. Chatteris, Davis, no. 221.

   Julius A. x: Miracula S. Oswini.

   Julius D. ii: Ctl. and list Canterbury, St Augustine, Davis, no. 192.

   Julius D. iii: Ctl. St Albans, Davis, no. 837.

   Julius D. v: Ann. Dover.

   Julius D. vii: Collection from St Albans (John of Wallingford, etc.).

   Julius D. x: Ch. Llanthony.

   Nero C. vii: Ann. Thorney.

   Nero C. ix: Obituary of Canterbury Cathedral.

London, British Museum, Cotton MSS (*cont.*)
 Nero D. ii: Ch. Rochester, Ann. Battle.
 Nero D. iii: Ctl. York, St Leonard, Davis, no. 1106.
 Nero D. viii: List Colchester.
 Nero E. vi: Ctl. Hospitallers, Davis, no. 852.
 Nero E. vii: Ctl. Walsingham, Davis, no. 988.
 Otho A. ii: Ctl. Bayham, Davis, no. 38.
 Otho A. v: Calendar Barking.
 Otho B. xiv: Ctl. Pipewell, Davis, no. 778.
 Tiberius A. x: Ann. Dunstable and Montacute, cf. Davis, no. 322.
 Tiberius B. ii: Ely Miscellany, Davis, no. 358.
 Tiberius B. v: Calendar etc. Battle.
 Tiberius C. ix: Ctl. Waltham, Davis, no. 990.
 Tiberius D. vi: Ctl. Christchurch (Hants), Davis, no. 252.
 Tiberius E. iv: Ann. Winchcombe.
 Tiberius E. v: Ctl. and list Northampton, St James, Davis, no. 698.
 Titus C. viii: Ctl. Wymondham, Davis, no. 1082.
 Titus D. xx: Ch. Walden.
 Titus D. xxvii: 11th cent. Liber Precum from Hyde Abbey.
 Titus F. iii: Miscellaneous transcripts.
 Vespasian A. v: Transcript of ch. of Gregory of Caerwent.
 Vespasian A. vi: Ctl. Ely, Davis, no. 373.
 Vespasian A. xxii: Ann. Rochester.
 Vespasian B. xi: Crowland list, Ch. Hagnaby.
 Vespasian B. xxiv: Ctl. Evesham, Davis, no. 381.
 Vespasian E. ii: Ctl. Ramsey, Davis, no. 787.
 Vespasian E. v: Calendar Reading.
 Vespasian E. vi: Ch. Walden, cf. Davis, no. 985.
 Vespasian E. xiv: Ctl. Leiston, Davis, no. 550.
 Vespasian E. xvii: Ctl. Northampton, St Andrew, Davis, no. 700.
 Vespasian E. xviii: Ctl. Kirkstead, Davis, no. 519.
 Vespasian E. xix: Ctl. Nostell, Davis, no. 721.
 Vespasian E. xx: Ctl. Bardney, Davis, no. 18.
 Vespasian E. xxii: Reg. Peterborough, Davis, no. 766.
 Vespasian E. xxiii: Ctl. Durford, Davis, no. 323.
 Vitellius A. i: Ctl. Combe, Davis, no. 274.
 Vitellius A. x: De abbatibus, Malmesbury.
 Vitellius A. xi: Ctl. Bradenstoke, Davis, no. 66.
 Vitellius C. xii: Martyrology of Canterbury, St Augustine's.
 Vitellius D. ix: Ctl. (and list) Exeter, St Nicholas, Davis, no. 392.
 Vitellius D. xviii: Ctl. Combe, Davis, no. 273.
 Vitellius E. xii: Obituary of Evesham.
 Vitellius F. viii: Collection of transcripts (see p. 215, London, Haliwell).
 Vitellius F. xvii: Ctl. Leicester (with list), Davis, no. 549.
Egerton Charters: 382, 515.
Egerton MSS: 2104: Ctl. Wherwell, Davis, no. 1031.
 2823: Ctl. Byland, Davis, no. 142.
 2827: Ctl. Easby, Davis, no. 354.
 2849: Mortuary roll of Lucy, prioress of Castle Hedingham.
 3031: Ctl. Reading, Davis, no. 801.

3033: Ctl. Canons Ashby, Davis, no. 157.

3088: Ann. Dore.

3126: Ctl. Stanlow, Davis, no. 1028.

3137: Ctl. Blackborough, Davis, no. 57.

3140: Calendar and Ctl. Eye, Davis, no. 398.

3316: Ctl. Bath, Davis, no. 24.

3667: Ctl. Carisbrooke, Davis, no. 213.

3712: Ctl. Wombridge, Davis, no. 1066.

Harleian Charters: 43. I. 18; 44. B. 38; 44. I. 24–5; 47. F. 49; 50. I. 4; 52. E. 48; 52. G. 20; 53. D. 10; 53. G. 55; 54. B. 9; 54. C. 47; 75. C. 28; 83. A. 4; 83. B. 2; 83. B. 12; 112. C. 12.

Harleian MSS: 209: Miscellanea, mostly theological, from Abingdon.

229: Ann. Evesham.

391: Ctl. Waltham, Davis, no. 989.

544: List Southwark.

622: Ctl. Little Dunmow, Davis, no. 318.

742: Ctl. Spalding, Davis, no. 921.

743: Ctl. Bury St Edmunds, Davis, no. 97.

1616: Ctl. Winchester, St Cross, Davis, no. 1053.

1761: Ann. and Ctl. Hyde, Davis, no. 1048.

1804: Calendar Durham.

2071: Ctl. Chester, Davis, no. 228.

2110: Ctl. Castle Acre, Davis, no. 215.

2188: Notes from Ctl. Haughmond.

3586: Ctl. Wormesley, Davis, no. 1081.

3640: Ctl. Welbeck, Davis, no. 1002.

3650: Ctl. Kenilworth, Davis, no. 501.

3658: Ctl. East Deeping, Davis, no. 304.

3697: Ctl. Walden, Davis, no. 984.

3759: Ctl. Blyth, Davis, no. 58.

3763: Ann. and Ctl. Evesham, Davis, no. 382.

3868: Ctl. Lichfield Cathedral, Davis, no. 562.

3950: Calendar Norwich.

4664: Calendar Durham.

4714: Ctl. Biddlesden, Davis, no. 54.

4757: Transcripts: extract from Ctl. Bermondsey, Davis, no. 45.

6068: Miscellaneous collection of Welsh records.

6952, 6974, 6976: Matthew Hutton's transcripts (17th cent.).

Lansdowne Charter, 679.

Lansdowne MSS: 207 A–C: Collections and transcripts of Gervase Holles (early 17th cent.) – esp. (in 207A) extracts from Ctl. Haverholme (cf. Davis, no. 477).

375: Ctl. St Albans, Davis, no. 836.

402: Ctl. York archdiocese, Davis, no. 1085.

427: Copy of obituary of Evesham.

436: Vitae sanctorum from Romsey.

863: Collections of Sir Richard St George, vol. III (early 17th cent.).

Loans: 30 (Marquess of Anglesey): Ctl. Burton, Davis, no. 91.

Royal MSS: 2. B. vi: Psalter from St Albans.

5. A. iv: Ctl. Rochester, Davis, no. 819.

8. C. vii: Calendar Tewkesbury.

London, British Museum, Royal MSS (*cont.*)
    11. B. ix: Ctl. Northampton, St Andrew, Davis, no. 699.
  Sloane Roll xxxi. 4: Ctl. Basset of Weldon, Davis, no. 1188A.
  Stowe Charter 504.
  Stowe MSS: 882: Ctl. of John Blaunchard, Davis, no. 1196.
    925: Ctl. Bradenstoke, Davis, no. 67.
    937: Ctl. Pipewell, Davis, no. 775.
    941: Ctl. St Neots, Davis, no. 860.
  Topham Charter 13.
  Wolley Charter i. 43.
London, Lambeth Palace Library MSS 20: Martyrology of Canterbury Cathedral.
  42: MS of Florence (John of Worcester), from Abingdon.
  198a: Custumal and calendar, Peterborough.
  241: Ctl. Dover, Davis, no. 312.
  585: Henry Wharton's transcripts (17th cent.): list and Ann. Merton; list, Dover.
  719: Ctl. Launceston, Davis, no. 542.
  1106: Ann. Peterborough-Huntingdon.
  1131: Ctl. Harbledown, Davis, no. 470.
  1212: Ctl. see of Canterbury, Davis, no. 159.
London, Public Record Office (PRO)
  Assize Rolls, (JI) 23, 167, 229, 560, 912.
  31/8/169–170F: Transcripts of Fines.
  31/9/16: Ch. Sempringham, in Transcripts from Rome.
  C53/81: Charter roll, 23 Edward I.
  C115: Cartularies of Llanthony, A1: K2/6683 and A2: K1/6681 (Davis, no. 531, 2 vols., not foliated).
    A9: K1/6679 (Davis, no. 530).
  C146 (Anc. Deeds, Series C, Chancery)/3038.
  CP25(1)/203/File 2, 30.
  DL 25/273, 449, 1223 (Deeds).
  DL 27/3 (Deed).
  DL 42 (Misc. Books)/5: Ctl. Bury St Edmunds, Davis, no. 108.
  E 40 (Anc. Deeds, Series A, Exchequer, T.R.)/217, 241, 2383, 2389, 2907, 3013, 3316, 3357, 3529, 3706, 5273, 5785, 8897, 13,850(6), 14,021, 14,208.
  E 164 (Misc. Books, Series I, Exchequer K.R.)/1: Domesday Breviate.
  E164/20: Ctl. Godstow, Davis, no. 462.
  E164/22: Ctl. Warwick, St Mary, Davis, no. 1001.
  E164/29: Ctl. Langdon, Davis, no. 527.
  E315/49/83, 277; E315/53/223 (Exchequer, Augmentations, books of deeds).
  E326 (Anc. Deeds, Series B, Exchequer Augmentations)/2836, 3905, 4610, 8494, 8548, 8649, 8776, 8887, 8901, 11,550.
  E327 (ditto)/78.
  Le Neve's Indexes, xxiv, 5.
  Transcripts of Fines, *see* 31/8/169–170F above.
London, St Bartholomew's Hospital, Archives, Cok's Cartulary, Davis, no. 617.
London, St Paul's Cathedral Library, Muniments, A25/1109.
  W.D.1 Liber A: Davis, no. 597.
London, Society of Antiquaries, MSS: 59: Peterborough (Robert of Lindsey's) Psalter.
  60: Ctl. Peterborough, Davis, no. 754.

London, Westminster Abbey Muniments, Charters 2154, 2185, 2203, 2222, 2238, 2251, 2265, 2270, 2280, 3551, 3746, 3763, 3779.

Muniment Book 11, 'Domesday' Ctl. Westminster, Davis, no. 1013.

Maidstone, Kent Archives Office, Rochester Dean and Chapter Muniments (deposited): A. 3. 5, Textus Roffensis: *see* Printed Books.

DRc/T193/1; DRc/T389/1 (charters).

Manchester, John Rylands Library, Arley Charters, I, 11.

Latin MSS: 215: Ann. Wigmore.

Norwich Cathedral, Dean and Chapter Muniments (Charters), 839, 1686, 4067, 4194.

Reg. I, Davis, no. 702.

Sacrist's Book, Davis, no. 712.

Norwich Central Library, Norfolk and Norwich Record Office, Diocesan Records SUN/8: Ctl. Coxford, Davis, no. 280.

Nottingham University Library, Manuscript Department, Middleton Collections, Mid. 1.

Orne, Archives Départementales, H. 937.

Oxford, Balliol College MS 271: Ctl. Hereford, St Guthlac, Davis, no. 484.

Oxford, Bodleian Library (Bodl.) MSS

Barlow 22(6461): Calendar Peterborough.

Bodley 297 (2468): MS of Florence (John of Worcester).

Digby 81: Ann. Tavistock.

227: Abingdon missal and calendar.

Dodsworth 76(5018), 96(5037): Dodsworth's collections and transcripts.

Douce 296(21,870): Psalter from (?) Lewes.

Dugdale 12(6502): Dugdale's transcripts.

Fairfax 9(3889): Ctl. Warter, Davis, no. 1000.

Gough Norfolk 18(18,074): Ctl. Thetford, St Mary, Davis, no. 962.

Lat. liturg. e. 6 (32,558): Chertsey breviary and calendar.

Laud Lat. 5: Guisborough Psalter.

Laud Misc. 625: Reg. Leicester, Davis, no. 548.

642: Ctl. Alvingham, Davis, no. 12.

723: Ann. Merton.

Lyell 15: Ctl. Abingdon, Davis, no. 5.

Rawlinson B. 329: Ctl. Hereford Cathedral, Davis, nos. 481-2.

B. 421: Ctl. Sibton, Davis, no. 899.

B. 461: 18th cent. transcripts.

C. 939: Ordinale from Oseney Abbey with Oseney list.

Tanner 166: Thornton Curtis list.

169: Calendar Chester.

425: Ctl. Hickling, Davis, no. 487.

Top. Glouc. c. 5(27,630): 18th cent. History of Gloucester, vol. II (from Archdeacon Furney's papers).

Top. Lincs d. 1(29,005): Ctl. Nun Cotham, Davis, no. 726.

Top. Northants c. 5(16,622): transcript of Ctl. Northampton, St James (cf. Davis, no. 698: for 'e. 5' read 'c. 5').

Top. Suffolk d. 15(29,006): Ctl. South Elmham, Davis, no. 356.

Top. Yorks c. 72: Ctl. Drax, Davis, no. 315.

Wood Empt. 5(8593): Ctl. Malmesbury, Davis, no. 641.

Oxford, Magdalen College MS lat. 53: De electione priorum Wymondham, with St Albans and Wymondham lists.

Oxford, New College, Reg. Secundum, Davis, no. 745.

Swalcliffe Charters, 127

Oxford, Queen's College Muniments (deposited in Bodl.) (Monk Sherborne), 284–5, 945, 955.

Oxford, St John's College, MSS 17: Bede with historical notes, Thorney.

126: Florilegium of Guy, prior of Southwick.

Peterborough Cathedral, Dean and Chapter MSS, 1: Ctl. Peterborough, Davis, no. 757 (Liber R. de Swaffham).

5: Ctl. Peterborough, Davis, no. 756 (Liber Cartarum of Henry of Pytchley).

Rochester, *see* Maidstone.

Rome, *see* Vatican.

Shrewsbury Borough Library, Ctl. Haughmond, Davis, no. 476.

Spalding Gentlemen's Society, Ctl. Crowland, transcript in Lincs Archives Office, Davis, no. 294.

Stafford, William Salt Library, S. MS 237/M: Collections of the Rev. Thomas Loxdale.

Vatican City, Biblioteca Apostolica Vaticana, Barberini MS xliii. 74(2689): Ch. Sempringham.

Lat. 6024: 'Register of Master David'.[1]

Reginensis 470: Giraldus Cambrensis, *Speculum Duorum* (see p. 107).

Wilton House Charters: cited from *VCH Wilts.*

Winchester College Muniments, nos. 2125–6, 2131, 2792, 2794, 2798, 2818, 2834, 10,631, 17,213.

Winchester, Hants Record Office, Southwick, Reg. 1, Davis, no. 913.

Worcester Cathedral, Dean and Chapter Library, charter B. 167.

Reg. A. 8, Davis, no. 1072 (= *Ctl. Worcester*).

York, Dean and Chapter Muniments, Magnum Registrum Album, Davis, no. 1087.

---

[1] Imperfectly printed in F. Liverani, *Spicilegium Liberianum*, 1 (Florence, 1863); see Z. N. Brooke, in *Essays in History presented to R. L. Poole*, ed. H. W. C. Davis (Oxford, 1927), pp. 227–45.

PRINTED BOOKS AND ARTICLES CITED, WITH ABBREVIATED REFERENCES

Most annals, chronicles and cartularies have references starting *Ann.*, *Ch.*, and *Ctl.*; most collections of fines and lives of saints, etc., are under the headings FINES and VITAE.

AB: Analecta Bollandiana.
'Abbot Newland's Roll', ed. I. H. Jeayes, *BGAS*, XIV (1889–90), 117–30.
Abb. Plac.: Abbreviatio Placitorum (Richard I–Edward II), ed. W. Illingworth, RC, 1811.
Acta Chichester: The Acta of the Bishops of Chichester, 1075–1207, ed. H. Mayr-Harting, Canterbury and York Society, 1964.
Acta Lanfranci: in Earle and Plummer, I, 287–92.
Acta Sanctorum: Acta Sanctorum Bollandiana (Brussels and elsewhere, 1643–   ).
Acta Stephani Langton: Acta Stephani Langton, Cantuariensis archiepiscopi, A.D. 1207–1228, ed. Kathleen Major, Canterbury and York Society, 1950.
Ad. Dom.:Adami de Domerham, Historia de rebus gestis Glastoniensibus, ed. T. Hearne, 2 vols., London, 1727.
Addy, S. O., *Historical Memorial of Beauchief Abbey*, Oxford, London and Sheffield, 1878.
Aelfric, Homilies in *Liber Sermonum Catholicorum*, ed. B. Thorpe, 2 vols., Aelfric Society, London, 1844.
Anc. Chts.: Ancient Charters, royal and private, prior to A.D. 1200, ed. J. H. Round, PRS, X, 1888.
Andrews, H. C., 'Two twelfth-century charters of Reading Abbey', *Antiquaries' Journal*, XIV (1934), 7–12.
Ann. Bermondsey, in *Ann. Mon.*, III.
Ann. Burton, in *Ann. Mon.*, I.
Ann. Cambriae: Annales Cambriae, ed. Rev. J. Williams ab Ithel, RS, 1860.
Ann. Chester: Annales Cestrienses: the chronicle of the abbey of St Werburg, Chester, ed. R. C. Christie, Record Society of Lancashire and Cheshire, London, 1887.
Ann. Colchester: Annales Colecestrienses, ed. F. Liebermann in *UGQ*.
Ann. Dunstable, in *Ann. Mon.*, III.
Ann. Durham: Durham Annals and Documents of the Thirteenth Century, ed. F. Barlow, Surtees Society, CLV (1945).
Ann. Lewes: 'The annals of Lewes priory', *see* Liebermann.
Ann. Little Dunmow in *Mon.*, VI, 147.
Ann. Margam, in *Ann. Mon.*, I.
Ann. Merton (1) in *Flor. Hist.*, I.
Ann. Mon.: Annales Monastici, ed. H. R. Luard, 5 vols., RS, 1864–9.
Ann. Oseney, in *Ann. Mon.*, IV.
Ann. Plympton, ed. F. Liebermann in *UGQ*.
Ann. Ramsey in *Ch. Ramsey*, ed. W. D. Macray, RS., 1886, pp. 339ff.
Ann. Reading: (1) 'Annales Radingenses', ed. F. Liebermann in *UGQ*.
   (2), *see* Previté-Orton.
Ann. Tavistock, in Newburgh, ed. Hearne, III, 709–10.
Ann. Tewkesbury, in *Ann. Mon.*, I.

Ann. Waverley, in *Ann. Mon.*, II.

Ann. Winchcombe: 'Winchcombe Annals 1049–1181', ed. R. R. Darlington in *Misc. D. M. Stenton*, pp. 111–37; see also p. xiii.

Ann. Winchester, in *Ann. Mon.*, II.

Ann. Worcester, in *Ann. Mon.*, IV.

Anonimalle Chronicle, 1333 to 1381, The, ed. V. H. Galbraith, Manchester, 1927.

Anselm Epp.: in S. Anselmi, *Opera Omnia*, ed. F. S. Schmitt, 6 vols., Edinburgh, 1946–61 (*Epistolae* in vols. III–V).

Appleby, J. T., 'Richard of Devizes and the Annals of Winchester', *BIHR*, XXXVI (1963), 70–7.

Arnulf of Lisieux, Letters of, ed. F. Barlow, Camden 3rd series, LXI, 1939.

AS: Anglia sacra sive collectio historiarum de archiepiscopis et episcopis Angliae ad annum 1540, ed. H. Wharton, 2 vols., London, 1691.

ASC: Anglo-Saxon Chronicle (the dates given are as corrected in *EHD*, I, ed. D. Whitelock, and II, ed. D. C. Douglas and G. W. Greenaway, London, 1955, 1953). See also Earle and Plummer.

AS Chts.: Anglo-Saxon Charters, ed. A. J. Robertson, Cambridge, 1939.

AS Wills: Anglo-Saxon Wills, ed. D. Whitelock, Cambridge, 1930.

AS Writs: Anglo-Saxon Writs, ed. F. E. Harmer, Manchester, 1952.

Asser: Asser's *Life of King Alfred*, ed. W. H. Stevenson, Oxford, 1904.

Atkins: Atkins, Sir Ivor, 'The Church of Worcester from the eighth to the twelfth century', *Antiquaries' Journal*, XVII (1937), 371–91; XX (1940), 1–38, 203–29.

Auvry: C. Auvry, *Histoire de la Congrégation de Savigny*, ed. A. Laveille, 3 vols., Société de l'Histoire de Normandie, Rouen–Paris, 1896–8.

Backmund, N., O.Praem., *Monasticon Praemonstratense*, 3 vols., Straubing, 1949–56.

Baddeley, W. St Clair, *History of Cirencester*, Cirencester, 1924.

Baildon: *Notes on the religious and secular houses of Yorkshire*. Extracted from the public records by W. P. Baildon, 2 vols., Yorkshire Archaeological Society, XVII, LXXXI, 1895, 1931.

Baker, L. G. D., 'The Foundation of Fountains Abbey', *Northern History*, IV (1969), 29–43. 'The Genesis of English Cistercian Chronicles. The Foundation History of Fountains, I', *Analecta Cisterciensia*, XXV (1969), 14–41.

Baluze, *Misc.*, II: S. Baluze (Baluzius), *Miscellaneorum Liber Secundus*, 1st edn., Paris, 1679.

Barker (1949): Barker, E. E., 'Sussex Anglo-Saxon Charters, part III', *Sussex Archaeological Collections*, LXXXVIII (1949), 51–113.

Barlow (1963): Barlow, F., *The English Church, 1000–1066: a constitutional history*, London, 1963.
The Life of King Edward who rests at Westminster, NMT, 1962.

Barraclough, G., 'Some charters of the Earls of Chester' in *Misc. D. M. Stenton*, pp. 25–43.

Bart. Cotton: *Bartholomaei de Cotton, monachi Norwicensis, historia Anglicana (A.D. 449–1298)...*, ed. H. R. Luard, RS, 1859.

Bateson, Mary, 'The Register of Crabhouse Nunnery', *Norfolk Archaeology*, XI (1892), 1–71.

Bec Documents: Select Documents of the English Lands of the Abbey of Bec, ed. M. Chibnall, Camden 3rd Series, LXXIII (1951).

Bede, his Life, Times and Writings, ed. A. H. Thompson, Oxford, 1935.

Beds Eyre: Roll of the justices in eyre at Bedford, 1227, ed. G. H. Fowler, BHRS, III, 1916, 1–206.

Bentham, *Ely*: Bentham, James, *The history and antiquities of the Conventual and Cathedral Church of Ely*, 2 vols., Cambridge, 1771; 2nd edn. 1 vol., Norwich, 1812. Supplement by W. Stevenson, Norwich, 1817.

Berkeley Chts.: Descriptive catalogue of charters and muniments in the possession of the Right Hon. Lord FitzHardinge at Berkeley Castle, ed. I. H. Jeayes, Bristol, 1892.

Bethell, D., 'The Foundation of Fountains Abbey and the State of St Mary's, York in 1132', *Journal of Ecclesiastical History*, XVII (1966), 11–27.

BGAS: Transactions of the Bristol and Gloucestershire Archaeological Society.

BHRS: Bedfordshire Historical Record Society.

BIHR: Bulletin of the Institute of Historical Research.

Birch: Birch, W. de G., *Cartularium Saxonicum: a collection of charters relating to Anglo-Saxon History*, 3 vols., London, 1885–93. (Index, 1899.)

A History of Margam Abbey, London, 1897.

A History of Neath Abbey, Neath, 1902.

Bishop, T. A. M., *Scriptores Regis*, Oxford, 1961.

Bishop and Chaplais: *Facsimiles of English royal writs to A.D. 1100, presented to V.H. Galbraith*, ed. T. A. M. Bishop and Pierre Chaplais, Oxford, 1957.

BJRL: Bulletin of the John Rylands Library.

Bk. Seals: Sir Christopher Hatton's Book of Seals, ed. L. C. Loyd and D. M. Stenton, Oxford, and Northamptonshire Record Society, XV, 1950.

Blaauw, W. H., 'On the early history of Lewes Priory and its Seals', *Sussex Archaeological Collections*, II (1849), 7–37.

Blomefield, Blomefield, *Norfolk*: Blomefield, F., *An essay towards a topographical history of the county of Norfolk*, 2nd edn., 11 vols., London, 1805–10.

'Blyborough Charters', ed. K. Major in *Misc. D. M. Stenton*, pp. 203–19.

BM Facs.: Facsimiles of Ancient Charters in the British Museum, ed. E. A. Bond, 4 vols., London, 1873–8.

Book of Fees: Liber feodorum. The book of fees commonly called Testa de Nevill, PRO Texts and Calendars, 2 vols. in 3, 1920–31.

Bracton's Note Book, ed. F. W. Maitland, 3 vols., London, 1887.

Bridges, J., *The History and Antiquities of Northamptonshire*, 2 vols., Oxford, 1791.

Brooke, C. N. L., 'Approaches to Medieval Forgery', *Journal of the Society of Archivists*, III (1965–9), 377–86.

'Archbishop Lanfranc, the English Bishops, and the Council of London of 1075', *Studia Gratiana*, XII (Bologna, 1967), 41–59.

'Episcopal Charters for Wix Priory', in *Misc. D. M. Stenton*, pp. 45–63.

Review of '*Regesta Regum Anglo-Normannorum*, II' in *EHR*, LXXII (1957), 687–95.

(Short note in) *EHR*, LXXVII (1962), 554.

Brooke, Z. N., 'The register of Master David of London and the part he played in the Becket crisis' in *Essays in History presented to R. L. Poole*, ed. H. W. C. Davis, Oxford, 1927, pp. 227–45.

Brooke, Z. N. and C. N. L., 'Hereford Cathedral Dignitaries in the twelfth century', *CHJ*, VIII, i (1944), 1–21; 'Supplement', *CHJ*, VIII, iii (1946), 179–85.

Brut y Tywysogion, Red book of Hergest Version, ed. and trans. T. Jones, Board of Celtic Studies of the University of Wales, History and Law Series, XVI, 1955.

Peniarth, MS 20 Version, ed. T. Jones, ibid., VI, 1941, XI, 1952 (references are to pages of vol. XI, translation).

Burton Chts.: Descriptive catalogue of the charters and muniments belonging to the Marquis of Anglesey..., ed. I. H. Jeayes, *SHC*, 3rd Series, 1937.

Butler, Alban, *Lives of the Saints*, 4 vols., edition of London, 1956.

Butler, H. E., *The Autobiography of Giraldus Cambrensis*, London, 1937.

Cal. Docts. Ireland: Calendar of Documents relating to Ireland..., I, *1171–1251*, ed. H. S. Sweetman, London, 1875.

Calendar of Charters and Rolls preserved in the Bodleian Library (Oxford), ed. W. H. Turner and H. O. Coxe, Oxford, 1878.

Candidus: *The Chronicle of Hugh Candidus, a monk of Peterborough*, ed. W. T. Mellows, London, 1949.

Canivez, I: *Statuta Capitulorum Generalium Ordinis Cisterciensis*, Bibliothèque de la Revue d'Histoire Ecclésiastique, Fasc. 9, ed. J.-M. Canivez, I, Louvain, 1933.

CAP: Collectanea Anglo-Praemonstratensia, arranged and ed. F. A. Gasquet, 3 vols., Camden 3rd Series, VI, X, XII, 1904–6.

Cart. Antiq.: The Cartae Antiquae rolls 1–10, ed. L. Landon, PRS, LV, 1938.

Cat. Anc. D., Deeds: A Descriptive Catalogue of Ancient Deeds in the Public Record Office, 6 vols., PRO Texts and Calendars, 1890–1915.

CChR: Calendar of the Charter Rolls preserved in the Public Record Office, 6 vols., PRO Texts and Calendars, 1903–27.

CCR: Calendar of the Close Rolls preserved in the Public Record Office, ibid., 1896– .

CDF: Calendar of Documents preserved in France illustrative of the History of Great Britain and Ireland, I, A.D. 918–1206, ed. J. H. Round, PRO Texts and Calendars, 1899.

Ch. Abingdon: Chronicon monasterii de Abingdon, ed. J. Stevenson, 2 vols., RS, 1858.

Ch. Ang. Pet.: Chronicon Angliae Petriburgense, ed. J. A. Giles, Caxton Society, II, 1845.

Ch. Barnwell in *Walt. Cov.*

Ch. Barnwell (J. W. Clark): *Liber memorandorum ecclesie de Bernewelle*, ed. J. W. Clark, Cambridge, 1907.

Ch. Battle: Chronicon Monasterii de Bello, ed. J. S. Brewer, Anglia Christiana Society, 1846.

Ch. Bec: Chronique du Bec, ed. A. A. Porée, Société de l'Histoire de Normandie, 1883.

Ch. Bristol: *see* 'Abbot Newland's Roll'.

Ch. Clairvaux: *Chronicon Clarevallense* in *PL*, CLXXXV, cols. 1247–52.

Ch. Dale: 'Chronicle of the Abbey of St Mary de Parco Stanley, or Dale, Derbyshire', ed. W. H. St John Hope, *Journal of the Derbyshire Archaeological and Nat. Hist. Society*, V (1883), 1–29, also medieval list, 'The Abbots of the Monastery of...Dale, Derbyshire', ib., 81–100; new edition by A. Saltman, see Saltman.

Ch. Edward I and II: Chronicles of...Edward I and Edward II, ed. W. Stubbs, 2 vols., RS, 1882–3.

Ch. Evesham: Chronicon abbatiae de Evesham..., ed. W. D. Macray, RS, 1863.

Ch. Gloucester, see Ctl. Gloucester.

Ch. Lanercost: Chronicon de Lanercost, ed. J. Stevenson, Bannatyne Club, Edinburgh, 1839.

Ch. Louth Park: Chronicon abbatie de Parco Lude, ed. E. Venables, Lincolnshire Record Society, I, 1891.

Ch. Man: Chronica regum Manniae et insularum, ed. P. A. Munch, Manx Society, XXII, 1874.

Ch. Meaux: Chronica monasterii de Melsa a fundatione usque ad annum 1396..., ed. E. A. Bond, 3 vols., RS, 1866–8.

Ch. Melrose: The Chronicle of Melrose, facsimile ed. by A. O. and M. O. Anderson, London, 1936.

Ch. Peterborough: Chronicon Petroburgense, ed. T. Stapleton, Camden Old Series, XLVII, 1849.

Chs. Peterborough: *see* Sparke.

Chronicles of the Picts, chronicles of the Scots and other early memorials of Scottish history, ed. W. F. Skene, Scottish Record Office, Texts and Calendars, I, 1867.

Ch. Ramsey: Chronicon abbatiae Rameseiensis..., ed. W. D. Macray, RS, 1886.

Ch. Ste Barbe: Chronique de Sainte Barbe-en-Auge, ed. R. N. Sauvage in *Mémoires de l'Académie de Caen*, 1906.

Ch. Stephen, etc.: Chronicles of the Reigns of Stephen, Henry II and Richard I, ed. R. Howlett, 4 vols., RS, 1884–9.

Ch. Walden: 'The Book of the Foundation of Walden Abbey', translated H. Collar, *Essex Review*, XLV (1936), 73–236 *passim*, XLVI (1937), 12–234 *passim*, XLVII (1938), 36–220 *passim*.

Ch. Wigmore: Chronicle of Wigmore, ed. T. Wright, *The History of Ludlow and its neighbour-hood...*, Ludlow, 1852, pp. 102–32. Also in *Mon.*, VI, 344–8. [See p. 190.]

Ch. Witham: E. M. Thompson, 'A fragment of a Witham Charterhouse Chronicle and Adam of Dryburgh, Premonstratensian, and Carthusian of Witham', *BJRL*, XVI (1932), 482–506; see also Wilmart.

Ch. York: The Chronicle of St Mary's abbey, York, ed. H. H. E. Craster and M. E. Thornton, Surtees Society, CXLVIII, 1934.

Chaplais (1965): Chaplais, P., 'The Origin and Authenticity of the Royal Anglo-Saxon Diploma', *Journal of the Society of Archivists*, III (1965–9), 48–61.

'The original charters of Herbert and Gervase, abbots of Westminster (1121–1157)', in *Misc. D. M. Stenton*, pp. 89–110.

(1968): 'Some early Anglo-Saxon Diplomas on Single Sheets: Originals or Copies?', *Journal of the Society of Archivists*, III (1965–9), 315–36.

Charlton, *Hist. Whitby*: Charlton, L., *The History of Whitby and of Whitby Abbey*, York, 1779.

'Charters of Combwell Priory, 1166–1270', *Archaeologia Cantiana*, V (1863), 194–222; VI (1866), 190–222; VIII (1872), 271–93.

Chartes de Cluny: Recueil des chartes de l'abbaye de Cluny, ed. A. Bernard and A. Bruel (Collection de documents inédits sur l'histoire de France), 6 vols., Paris, 1876–1903.

Cheney, C. R., *English Bishops' Chanceries, 1100–1250*, Manchester, 1950.

'Gervase, abbot of Prémontré: a medieval letter writer', *BJRL*, XXXIII (1950–1), 25–56.

'Harrold priory: a twelfth-century dispute', *BHRS*, XXXII (1952), 1–26.

The Records of Medieval England, Cambridge, 1956.

Cheney, *Inn. III: The Letters of Pope Innocent III (1198–1216) concerning England and Wales*, ed. C. R. and M. G. Cheney, Oxford, 1967.

Cheney, C. R. and M. G., 'The Letters of Pope Innocent III...: Additions and Corrections', *BIHR*, XLIV (1971), 98–115.

Cheney, M. G., 'The recognition of Pope Alexander III: some neglected evidence', *EHR*, LXXXIV (1969), 474–97.

Ches. Chts.: Facsimiles of early Cheshire charters, ed. G. Barraclough, Lancashire and Cheshire Record Society, CVII, 1957.

(Chibnall), M. Morgan (Mrs Chibnall), *The English Lands of the Abbey of Bec*, Oxford, 1946.

Chicksands Chts.: 'Early charters of the priory of Chicksands', ed. G. H. Fowler, *BHRS*, I (1913), 101–28.

CHJ: Cambridge Historical Journal.

Christina of Markyate, The Life of, ed. and translated C. H. Talbot, Oxford, 1959.

Chronicles, see Ch.

Clapham, A. W., *English Romanesque Architecture after the Conquest*, Oxford, 1934.

Clark, Cecily, '"This ecclesiastical adventurer": Henry of Saint-Jean d'Angely', *EHR*, LXXXIV (1969), 548–60.

Clark, G. T., 'Contributions towards a cartulary of Margam', *Archaeologia Cambrensis*, 3rd Series, XIII (1867), 311–34; XIV (1868), 24–59, 182–96, 345–82.

Clay, Sir Charles T., 'An Unauthenticated Prior of Pontefract', *YAJ*, XLI (1963–6), 740.

(1952): 'The early abbots of the Yorkshire Cistercian houses', *YAJ*, XXXVIII (1952–5), 8–43.

'The early precentors and chancellors of York', *YAJ*, XXV (1940–3), 116–38.

'The early priors of Pontefract', *YAJ*, XXXVIII (1952–5), 456–64.

'The early treasurers of York', *YAJ*, XXV (1940–3), 7–34.

(with N. K. M. Gurney) *Fasti Parochiales*, IV. Yorkshire Archaeological Society, Record Series, CXXXIII, 1971 for 1970.

Fasti: York Minster Fasti, 2 vols., Yorkshire Archaeological Society, Record Series, CXXIII, CXXIV, 1958–9.

Clay, Sir Charles T., 'Notes on the early archdeacons in the Church of York', *YAJ*, XXXVI (1944–7), 269–87, 409–34.

Clemoes, P., 'Aelfric' in *Continuations and Beginnings* (see below), pp. 176–209.

Clover, Helen, 'Alexander II's Letter *Accepimus a quibusdam* and its relationship with the Canterbury Forgeries', in *La Normandie Bénédictine*, pp. 417–42.

Cluny Chts.: Charters and Records illustrative of the English foundations of the Ancient Abbey of Cluni, ed. G. F. Duckett, 2 vols., London, 1888.

Cohn, E. S., 'The Manuscript evidence for the Letters of Peter of Blois', *EHR*, XLI (1926), 43–60.

Collinson, J., *The History and Antiquities of the County of Somerset . . .*, 3 vols., Bath, 1791.

Colvin: Colvin, H. M., *The White Canons in England*, Oxford, 1951.

Continuations and Beginnings: Studies in Old English Literature, ed. E. G. Stanley, London, 1966.

Councils and Synods, II: Councils and Synods, with other documents relating to the English Church, II, 1205–1313, ed. F. M. Powicke and C. R. Cheney, 2 parts, Oxford, 1964. (Vol. I forthcoming.)

CP: The Complete Peerage by G. E. C., revised edn. V. Gibbs, H. A. Doubleday, Lord Howard de Walden, G. H. White and R. S. Lea, London, 1910–59.

CPL: Calendar of entries in the papal registers relating to Great Britain and Ireland, PRO Calendars, I, 1894.

CPR: Calendar of the Patent Rolls preserved in the Public Record Office, PRO Calendars, 1891– .

CR: Close Rolls of the Reign of Henry III preserved in the Public Record Office, 14 vols., PRO Calendars, 1902–38.

Crawford Chts.: The Crawford Collection of Early Charters and Documents now in the Bodleian Library, ed. A. S. Napier and W. H. Stevenson, Oxford, 1895.

Croke, A., *The Genealogical History of the Croke Family . . .*, 2 vols., Oxford, 1823.

Cronne, H. A., 'An agreement between Simon, bishop of Worcester, and Waleran, earl of Worcester', *University of Birmingham Historical Journal*, II (1949–50), 149–50, 201–7.

Crook, B. M., 'General History of Lewes Priory in the Twelfth and Thirteenth Centuries', *Sussex Archaeological Collections*, LXXXI (1940), 68–96.

CRR: Curia Regis Rolls, PRO Calendars, I– , 1922– .

CS: Celt and Saxon: K. Jackson, P. Hunter Blair, B. Colgrave, B. Dickins, J. and H. M. Taylor, C. Brooke, N. K. Chadwick, *Celt and Saxon: Studies in the early British Border*, Cambridge, 1963.

CTG: Collectanea topographica et genealogica, ed. J. G. Nichols, 8 vols., London, 1834–43.

Ctl. Athelney: Two cartularies of the Benedictine abbeys of Muchelney and Athelney in the county of Somerset, ed. E. H. Bates, Somerset Record Society, XIV, 1899.

Ctl. Bath: Two Chartularies of the Priory of St Peter at Bath, ed. W. Hunt, Somerset Record Society, VII, 1893.

Ctl. Bayeux: Antiquus Cartularius Ecclesiae Baiocensis, ed. V. Bourrienne, 2 vols., Société de l'Histoire de Normandie, 1902–3.

Ctl. Beauchamp: Two registers formerly belonging to the family of Beauchamp of Hatch, ed. Sir H. C. Maxwell Lyte, Somerset Record Society, XXXV, 1920.

Ctl. Boxgrove: The Cartulary of Boxgrove Priory, ed. L. Fleming, Sussex Record Society, LIX, 1960.

Ctl. Brecon: 'Cartularium Prioratus S. Johannis Evang. de Brecon', ed. R. W. Banks, *Archaeologia Cambrensis*, 4th Series, XIII (1882), 275–308; XIV (1883), 18–311.

Ctl. Breedon: 'The Cartulary of Breedon Priory', ed. R. A. McKinley, M.A. Thesis, Manchester, 1950.

Ctl. Bridlington: Abstract of the Charters . . . of Bridlington Priory, ed. W. T. Lancaster, Leeds, 1912.

Ctl. Brinkburn: The Chartulary of Brinkburn priory, ed. W. Page, Surtees Society, XC for 1892, 1893.

Ctl. Bristol, St Mark's: The cartulary of St Mark's Hospital, Bristol, ed. C. D. Ross, Bristol Record Society, Publications, XXI, 1959.

Ctl. Bruton: Two Cartularies of the Augustinian Priory of Bruton and the Cluniac Priory of Montacute..., Somerset Record Society, VIII, 1894.

Ctl. Buckfast: Register of J. de Grandisson, Bishop of Exeter, ed. F. C. Hingeston-Randolph, pt. III (1899), 1563–1610.

Ctl. Buckland: A cartulary of Buckland priory in the county of Somerset, ed. F. W. Weaver, Somerset Record Society, XXV, 1909.

Ctl. Burscough: An edition of the Cartulary of Burscough Priory, ed. A. N. Webb, Chetham Society, 3rd Series, XVIII, 1970.

Ctl. Burton: 'The Burton Chartulary', ed. G. Wrottesley, in *Collections for a History of Staffordshire*, V, i, 1–101, William Salt Archaeological Society, 1884. (For MS, see p. xv.)

Ctl. Bushmead: The cartulary of Bushmead priory, ed. G. H. Fowler and J. Godber, Bedfordshire Historical Record Society, XXII, 1945.

Ctl. Canonsleigh: The cartulary of Canonsleigh Abbey, ed. V. C. M. London, Devon and Cornwall Record Society, New Series, VIII, 1965 for 1962.

Ctl. Canterbury, St Augustine's: The register of St Augustine's abbey, Canterbury, commonly called the Black Book, ed. G. J. Turner and H. E. Salter, 2 vols., British Academy, 1915–24.

Ctl. Canterbury, St Gregory's: Cartulary of the Priory of St Gregory, Canterbury, ed. Audrey M. Woodcock, Camden 3rd Series, LXXXVIII, 1956.

Ctl. Carmarthen: Cartularium S. Johannis Baptiste de Carmarthen..., ed. Sir T. Phillipps, Cheltenham, 1865.

Ctl. Cerne: 'The Cartulary of Cerne Abbey', ed. B. F. Lock, *Proc. Dorset Nat. Hist. and Antiq. Field Club*, XXVIII (1907), 65–95; XXIX (1908), 195–223.

Ctl. Chertsey: Chertsey (Abbey) Cartularies, vols. I, II, Surrey Record Society, XII, 1915–63.

Ctl. Chester: The Chartulary or Register of the Abbey of St Werburgh, Chester, ed. J. Tait, 2 vols., Chetham Society, New Series, LXXIX, LXXXII, 1920–3.

Ctl. Chichester: The Chartulary of the High Church of Chichester, ed. W. D. Peckham, Sussex Record Society, XLVI, 1946, for 1942–3.

Ctl. Cirencester: The Cartulary of Cirencester Abbey, Gloucestershire, ed. C. D. Ross, vols. I, II (III to come), London, 1964.

Ctl. Clerkenwell: The Cartulary of St Mary, Clerkenwell, ed. W. O. Hassall, Camden 3rd Series, LXXI, 1949.

Ctl. Cockersand: The Chartulary of Cockersand Abbey, ed. W. Farrer, 3 vols. in 7 parts, Chetham Society, New Series, XXXVIII–XL, XLIII, LVI–LVII, LXIV, 1898–1909.

Ctl. Colchester: Cartularium monasterii S. Johannis Baptiste de Colecestria, ed. S. A. Moore, 2 vols., Roxburghe Club, 1897.

Ctl. Colne: Cartularium Prioratus de Colne, ed. J. L. Fisher, Essex Archaeological Society, Occasional Publications, I, 1946.

Ctl. Coxford: 'A history of Coxford Priory', ed. H. W. Saunders, *Norfolk Archaeology*, XVII (1910), 284–370 (extracts, pp. 330ff.; calendar, pp. 355ff.).

Ctl. Crabhouse: 'The Register of Crabhouse Nunnery', ed. Mary Bateson, *Norfolk Archaeology*, XI, 1892, 1–71.

Ctl. Dale: The Cartulary of Dale Abbey, ed. A. Saltman, Derbyshire Archaeological Society, Record Series, II (1967 for 1966).

Ctl. Darley: The Cartulary of Darley Abbey, ed. R. R. Darlington, 2 vols., Kendal for the Derbyshire Archaeological Society, 1945.

Ctl. Dieulacres: 'Chartulary of Dieulacres Abbey', ed. G. Wrottesley, in *SHC*, New Series, IX, 310–62, 1906.

Ctl. Dryburgh: Liber S. Marie de Dryburgh, ed. J. Spottiswoode, Bannatyne Club, 1847.

Ctl. Dublin, St Thomas's: Register of the Abbey of St Thomas the Martyr, Dublin, ed. J. T. Gilbert, RS, 1889.

Ctl. Dunstable: A digest of the Charters preserved in the Cartulary of the Priory of Dunstable, ed. G. H. Fowler, Bedfordshire Historical Record Society, X, 1926.

Ctl. Exeter, St Nicholas: 'List of charters in the cartulary of St Nicholas Priory at Exeter', *CTG*, I (1834), 60–5, 184–9, 250–4, 374–88.

Ctl. Eynsham: Eynsham Cartulary, ed. H. E. Salter, 2 vols., Oxford Historical Society, XLIX, LI, 1907–8.

Ctl. Flaxley: The Cartulary and Historical Notes of the Cistercian Abbey of Flaxley, . . ., ed. A. W. Crawley-Boevey, Exeter, 1887.

Ctl. Fountains: Abstracts of the charters and other documents contained in the chartulary of the Cistercian abbey of Fountains, ed. W. T. Lancaster, 2 vols., Leeds, 1915.

Ctl. Furness: The Coucher Book of Furness Abbey, ed. J. C. Atkinson and J. Brownbill, 2 vols. in 6 parts, Chetham Society, New Series, IX, XI, XIV, LXXIV, LXXVI, LXXVIII, 1886–1919.

Ctl. Glastonbury: The Great Chartulary of Glastonbury, ed. Dom Aelred Watkin, 3 vols., Somerset Record Society, LIX, LXIII, LXIV, 1947–56.

Ctl. Gloucester: Historia et cartularium monasterii sancti Petri Gloucestriae, ed. W. H. Hart, 3 vols., RS, 1863–7.

Ctl. Godstow: The English Register of Godstow Nunnery, ed. A. Clark, 3 vols., *EETS*, Original Series, CXXIX, CXXX, CXLII, 1905–11.

Ctl. Guisborough: Cartularium Prioratus de Gyseburne, ed. W. Brown, 2 vols., Surtees Society, LXXXVI, LXXXIX, 1889, 1894 for 1891.

Ctl. Harrold: Records of Harrold Priory . . ., ed. G. H. Fowler, *BHRS*, XVII, 1935.

Ctl. Haughmond: 'Extracts from the cartulary of Haughmond Abbey', ed. W. A. Leighton, *CTG*, I (1834), 362–74.

'Extracts from the Cartulary of Haghmon Abbey, Co. Salop', ed. W. A. Leighton, *Transactions of the Salop Archaeological . . . Society*, I (1878), 173–216.

Ctl. Haverholme: 'Haverholme Priory Charters', *Lincolnshire Notes and Queries*, XVII (1923), 7–48, 65–74, 89–98.

Ctl. Healaugh Park: The Chartulary of Healaugh Park, ed. J. S. Purvis, Yorkshire Archaeological Society, Record Series, XCII, 1936 for 1935.

Ctl. Holm Cultram: The Register and Records of Holm Cultram, ed. F. Grainger and W. G. Collingwood, Cumberland and Westmorland Antiquarian and Archaeological Society, Record Series, VII, 1929.

Ctl. Hospitallers: Cartulaire général de l'ordre des hospitaliers de S. Jean de Jérusalem (1100–1310), ed. J. Delaville Le Roulx, 4 vols., Paris, 1894–1906.

Ctl. Hulme: St Benet of Holme, 1020–1210, ed. J. R. West, 2 vols., Norfolk Record Society, II, III, 1932.

Ctl. Huntingdon: 'The cartulary of the priory of St Mary, Huntingdon', ed. W. M. Noble, *Transactions of the Cambridgeshire and Huntingdonshire Archaeological Society*, IV (1930), 89–280 *passim*.

Ctl. Kirkstall: Coucher Book of the Cistercian abbey of Kirkstall, ed. W. T. Lancaster and W. P. Baildon, Thoresby Society, VIII, 1904.

Ctl. Lanercost: 'Breviate of the Cartulary of Lanercost', ed. M. E. C. Walcott, *Transactions of the Royal Society of Literature*, 2nd Series, VIII (1866), 434–524.

Ctl. Leeds: 'The Cartulary of Leeds Priory', ed. L. Sherwood, *Archaeologia Cantiana*, LXIV (1951), 23–34.

Ctl. Lewes, I, II: *The chartulary of the priory of St Pancras of Lewes*, ed. L. F. Salzman, 2 vols., Sussex Record Society, XXXVIII, XL, 1933–5.

III: 'The Wiltshire, Devonshire and Dorset portion of the Lewes chartulary, with London and Essex documents from the Surrey portion', ed. W. Budgen and L. F. Salzman, *The chartulary of Lewes priory. The portions relating to counties other than Sussex*, Sussex Record Society, Additional volume, 1943.

Ctl. Lewes, Norfolk: The Norfolk portion of the Chartulary of the priory of St Pancras of Lewes, ed. J. H. Bullock, Norfolk Record Society, XII, 1939.

Ctl. Llanthony (Irish): The Irish Cartularies of Llanthony Prima and Secunda, ed. E. St J. Brooks, Irish Manuscripts Commission, 1953.

Ctl. Loders: Cartulaire de Loders: prieuré dépendant de l'abbaye de Montebourg, ed. Léon Guilloreau, Evreux, 1908.

Ctl. London, Holy Trinity, Aldgate: The Cartulary of Holy Trinity Aldgate, ed. G. A. J. Hodgett, London Record Society, VII, 1971.

Ctl. Malmesbury: Registrum Malmesburiense, ed. J. S. Brewer and C. T. Martin, 2 vols., RS, 1879–80.

Ctl. Missenden: The Cartulary of Missenden Abbey, ed. J. G. Jenkins, 3 vols., Buckinghamshire Record Society, II, X, XII, 1938–62.

Ctl. Monk Bretton: Abstracts of the Chartularies of the Priory of Monkbretton, ed. J. W. Walker, Yorkshire Archaeological Society, Record Series, LXVI, 1924.

Ctl. Montacute: Two Cartularies of the Augustinian Priory of Bruton and the Cluniac Priory of Montacute..., Somerset Record Society, VIII, 1894.

Ctl. Muchelney: Two cartularies of the Benedictine abbeys of Muchelney and Athelney in the county of Somerset, ed. E. H. Bates, Somerset Record Society, XIV, 1899.

Ctl. Newminster: Chartularium abbathiae de novo monasterio, ed. J. T. Fowler, Surtees Society, LXVI, 1878 for 1876.

Ctl. Newnham: The Cartulary of Newnham Priory, ed. Joyce Godber, 1 vol. in 2, Bedfordshire Historical Record Society, XLIII, 1964.

Ctl. Oseney: Cartulary of Oseney Abbey, ed. H. E. Salter, 6 vols., Oxford Historical Society, LXXXIX–XCI, XCVII–XCVIII, CI, 1929–36.

Ctl. Oxford, St Frideswide: Cartulary of the monastery of St Frideswide at Oxford, ed. S. R. Wigram, 2 vols., Oxford Historical Society, XXVIII, XXXI, 1895–6.

Ctl. Peterborough: Carte Nativorum: a Peterborough Abbey Cartulary of the Fourteenth Century, ed. C. N. L. Brooke and M. M. Postan, Northamptonshire Record Society, XX, 1960.

Ctl. Pontefract: Chartulary of St John of Pontefract, ed. R. Holmes, 2 vols., Yorkshire Archaeological Society, Record Series, XXV, XXX, 1899–1902.

Ctl. Ramsey: Cartularium monasterii de Rameseia, ed. W. H. Hart and P. A. Lyons, 3 vols., RS, 1884–93.

Ctl. Rievaulx: Cartularium abbathiae de Rievalle, ed. J. C. Atkinson, Surtees Society, LXXXIII, 1889 for 1887.

Ctl. Rouen, Ste-Trinité: Cartulaire de l'abbaye de la Ste-Trinité du Mont de Rouen, ed. A. Deville, in Collection des cartulaires de France, ed. B. Guérard, III, Paris, 1840.

Ctl. Rydeware: 'The Rydeware Chartulary', ed. I. H. Jeayes and G. Wrottesley, *SHC*, XVI (1895), 229–302.

Ctl. St Bees: The Register of the priory of St Bees, ed. J. Wilson, Surtees Society, CXXVI, 1915.

Ctl. St Michael's Mount: The Cartulary of St Michael's Mount, ed. P. L. Hull, Devon and Cornwall Record Society, New Series, V, 1962 for 1958.

Ctl. Sallay: The Chartulary of the Cistercian Abbey of St Mary of Sallay in Craven, ed. J. McNulty, 2 vols., Yorkshire Archaeological Society, Record Series, LXXXVII, XC, 1933–4.

Ctl. Sandford: The Sandford Cartulary, ed. A. M. Leys, 2 vols., Oxfordshire Record Society, XIX, XXII, 1938–41.

Ctl. Selby: The Coucher Book of Selby, ed. J. T. Fowler, 2 vols., Yorkshire Archaeological Society, Record Series, X, XIII, 1891–3.

Ctl. Sele: Chartulary of the priory of St Peter at Sele, ed. L. F. Salzman, Cambridge, 1923.

Ctl. Stone: 'The Stone chartulary', ed. G. Wrottesley, *SHC*, VI, pt. i (1885), 1–28.

Ctl. Stoneleigh: The Stoneleigh Leger Book, ed. R. H. Hilton, Publications of the Dugdale Society, XXIV, 1960.

Ctl. Thame: The Thame Cartulary, ed. H. E. Salter, 2 vols., Oxfordshire Record Society, XXV, XXVI, 1947–8.

Ctl. Trentham: 'A chartulary of the Augustine priory of Trentham', ed. F. Parker, in *SHC*, XI, 1890.

Ctl. Tutbury: The Cartulary of Tutbury Priory, ed. A. Saltman, *SHC*, 4th Series, IV, 1962 (Historical Manuscripts Commission, JP 2).

Ctl. Wardon: Cartulary of the Abbey of Old Wardon, ed. G. H. Fowler, Bedfordshire Historical Record Society, XIII, 1930.

Ctl. Wetheral: Register of the priory of Wetherhal, ed. J. E. Prescott, Cumberland and Westmorland Antiquarian and Archaeological Society, Record Series, I, 1897.

Ctl. Whalley: The Coucher Book...of Whalley Abbey, ed. W. A. Hulton, 4 vols., Chetham Society, X, XI, XVI, XX, 1847–9.

Ctl. Whitby: Cartularium abbathiae de Whiteby, ed. J. C. Atkinson, 2 vols., Surtees Society, LXIX, LXXII, 1879–81.

Ctl. Wilton: Registrum Wiltunense, ed. R. C. Hoare and others, London, 1827.

Ctl. Winchcombe: Landboc sive Registrum monasterii B.M. Virginis et Sancti Cenhelmi de Winchelcumba..., ed. D. Royce, 2 vols., Exeter, 1892–3.

Ctl. Winchester: Chartulary of Winchester Cathedral, ed. A. W. Goodman, Winchester, 1927.

Ctl. Wombridge: 'Abstracts of...the Chartulary of Wombridge', ed. G. Morris, *Transactions of the Shropshire Archaeological and Natural History Society*, First Series, IX, 305ff.; XI, 325ff.; Second Series, I, 294ff.; IX, 96ff.; X, 180ff.; XI, 331ff.; XII, 205ff., 1886–1900.

Ctl. Worcester: The Cartulary of Worcester Cathedral Priory, ed. R. R. Darlington, PRS, LXXVI, 1968 for 1962–3.

Curia Regis Roll for 1196, ed. R. A. Brown, PRS, LXIX, 1956.

Darlington, R. R., 'Aethelwig, abbot of Evesham', *EHR*, XLVIII (1933), 1–22, 177–98.

    'Ecclesiastical Reform in the Late Old English Period', *EHR*, LI (1936), 385–428.

    And see Ann. Winchcombe.

Dart: Dart, J., *The History and Antiquities of the Cathedral Church of Canterbury...*, London, 1726.

Davies, J. Conway, 'Ewenny Priory, some recently found records', *JNLW*, III (1943–4), 107–37.

    'The Records of the Abbey of Ystrad Marchell', *Montgomeryshire Collections*, LI (1949), 3–22.

    'Strata Marcella Documents', *Montgomeryshire Collections*, LI (1949), 164–87.

Davis: Davis, G. R. C., *Medieval Cartularies of Great Britain: a Short Catalogue*, London, 1958.

Davis, H. W. C., 'The Chronicle of Battle Abbey', *EHR*, XXIX (1914), 426–34.

Davis, R. H. C., 'The Authorship of the *Gesta Stephani*', *EHR*, LXXVII (1962), 209–32.

DB: Domesday Book: Liber censualis vocatus Domesday-Book, 4 vols., RC, 1783–1816.

DC: Documents illustrative of the Social and Economic History of the Danelaw from various collections, ed. F. M. Stenton, British Academy, London, 1920.

Delisle–Berger: *Recueil des actes de Henri II...concernant les provinces françaises et les affaires de France*. Introduction and 3 vols., ed. L. Delisle and E. Berger, Académie des Inscriptions et Belles Lettres, Chartes et Diplômes, Paris, 1909–27.

Delisle, L., 'Documents relative to the abbey of Furness, extracted from the archives of Savigny', *Journal of the British Archaeological Association*, VI (1851), 419–24.

Dep. Keeper's Rept.: Reports of the Deputy Keeper of the Public Records.

Derbys Chts.: Descriptive catalogue of Derbyshire charters in public and private libraries and muniment rooms, ed. I. H. Jeayes, London, 1906.

Devizes: *The Chronicle of Richard of Devizes of the time of King Richard the First*, translated and ed. J. T. Appleby, NMT, 1963.

DHG: Dictionnaire d'histoire et de géographie ecclésiastiques, ed. A. Baudrillart, etc., Paris, 1912– .

Diceto: *Radulfi de Diceto decani Londoniensis opera historica...*, ed. W. Stubbs, 2 vols., RS, 1876.

Dickins, B., 'The Day of Byrhtnoth's Death and Other Obits from a Twelfth-Century Ely Calendar', *Leeds Studies in English*, VI (1937), 14–24.

Dickinson: Dickinson, J. C., *The Origins of the Austin Canons and their Introduction into England*, London, 1950.

'The English regular canons and the continent in the twelfth century', *TRHS*, 5th Series, I (1951), 71–89.

The Shrine of Our Lady at Walsingham, Cambridge, 1956.

DNB: Dictionary of National Biography, ed. L. Stephen and S. Lee, 66 vols., London, 1885–1901, repr. 22 vols., Oxford, 1921–2.

Doble, G. H., 'The Relics of St Petroc', *Antiquity*, XIII (1939), 403–15.

Dodwell, B., 'The foundation of Norwich Cathedral', *TRHS*, 5th Series, VII (1957), 1–18.

'Some charters relating to the honour of Bacton', in *Misc. D. M. Stenton*, pp. 147–65.

Douglas, *Bury: Feudal documents from the abbey of Bury St Edmunds*, ed. D. C. Douglas, British Academy, 1932.

Douglas, *Social Structure*: Douglas, D. C., *The Social Structure of medieval East Anglia*, Oxford, 1927.

Dowden, J., *The Bishops of Scotland*, Glasgow, 1912.

Du Cange, C. D., *Glossarium mediae et infimae Latinitatis*, ed. G. A. L. Henschel, 7 vols., Paris, 1840–50.

Dugdale, W., *The Antiquities of Warwickshire illustrated*, London, 1656, repr. Coventry, 1765; 2nd edn. by W. Thomas, 2 vols., London, 1730.

Durham Episcopal Charters 1071–1152, ed. H. S. Offler, Surtees Society, CLXXIX, 1968.

E, *see* Elmham, p. xxx below.

Eadmer, (*HN*): Eadmer, *Historia novorum in Anglia...*, ed. M. Rule, RS, 1884.

Eadmer *VA*: Eadmer..., *Vita Sancti Anselmi...*, ed. R. W. Southern, NMT, 1962.

Earldom of Hereford Chts.: Charters of the Earldom of Hereford, 1095–1201, ed. D. Walker, *Camden Miscellany*, XXII, Camden 4th Series, I, 1964, 1–75.

Earle: Earle, J., *A Handbook to the Land Charters and other Saxonic Documents*, Oxford, 1888.

Earle and Plummer: *Two of the Saxon chronicles parallel*, ed. J. Earle and C. Plummer, 2 vols., Oxford, 1892–9. See also *ASC*.

Easterling, R. C., 'List of Civic Officials of Exeter in the 12th and 13th centuries', *Transactions of the Devonshire Association*, LXX (1938), 455–94.

Eccles. Docts.: Ecclesiastical Documents, viz. I, A brief history of the bishoprick of Somerset from its foundation to the year 1174, II, Charters from the library of Dr Cox Macro. Now first published by J. Hunter, Camden Society, Old Series, VII, 1840.

EETS: Early English Text Society.

EHD: English Historical Documents, I, *c.* 500–1042, ed. D. Whitelock, London, 1955; II, 1042–1189, ed. D. C. Douglas and G. W. Greenaway, 1953.

EHR: English Historical Review.

Elmham, E: Thomas of Elmham, *Historia monasterii S. Augustini Cantuariensis*, ed. C. Hardwick, RS, 1858.

Epp. Cant.: Epistolae Cantuarienses, ed. W. Stubbs, RS, 1865.

Erdeswick, S., *A Survey of Staffordshire*, ed. Thomas Harwood, London, 1844.

Essays in Medieval History presented to Bertie Wilkinson, ed. T. A. Sandquist and M. R. Powicke, Toronto, 1969.

Exon DB = DB, III: *Libri censualis vocati Domesday-book, additamenta ex codic. antiquiss. Exon' Domesday, etc.* (ed. H. Ellis), RC, 1816.

EYC: Early Yorkshire Charters, I–III, ed. W. Farrer, Edinburgh, 1914–16; IV–XII, ed. Sir C. T. Clay, Yorkshire Archaeological Society, Record Series, Extra Series, I–III, V–X, 1935–65 (Extra Series vol. IV is Index to *EYC*, I–III, ed. C. T. and E. M. Clay, 1942).

Eyton, *Itinerary*: Eyton, R. W., *Court, Household and Itinerary of King Henry II*, London and Dorchester, 1878.

Eyton, *Salop*: Eyton, R. W., *Antiquities of Shropshire*, 12 vols., London and Shifnal, 1854–60.

F, FF: *see* FINES.

Farnham, G. F., *Leicestershire Medieval Village Notes*, 6 vols., Leicester, 1929–33.

Feltoe, C. L., *Three Canterbury Kalendars*, London, n.d. (1922).

Feodarium Dun.: Feodarium prioratus Dunelmensis: A survey of the estates of the prior and convent of Durham compiled in the fifteenth century, illustrated by the original grants and other evidences, ed. W. Greenwell, Surtees Society, LVIII, 1872.

Finberg, H. P. R., 'The House of Ordgar and the Foundation of Tavistock Abbey', *EHR*, LVIII (1943), 190–201.

'Abbots of Tavistock', *Devon and Cornwall Notes and Queries*, XXII (1942–6), 159–62, 174–5, 186–8, 194–7.

Tavistock Abbey, Cambridge, 1951.

FINES:

Beds F.: A calendar of the feet of fines for Bedfordshire preserved in the Public Record Office, of the reigns of Richard I, John and Henry III, ed. G. H. Fowler, BHRS, VI (1919).

Bucks F.: A calendar of the feet of fines for the county of Buckingham, 7 Richard I – 44 Henry III, ed. M. W. Hughes, Buckinghamshire Record Society, IV, 1940 (1942).

Cambs. F.: Pedes finium...relating to the county of Cambridge (calendar 7 Richard I – 1485), ed. W. Rye, Cambridge Antiquarian Society, Octavo Series, XXVI, 1891.

Cornwall F.: Cornwall feet of fines, Richard I – Edward III, 1195–1377, ed. J. H. Rowe, Devon and Cornwall Record Society, 1914.

Derbys F.: 'A calendar of the fines in the county of Derby (1196–1324)', ed. W. H. Hart and C. Kerry, *Derbyshire Archaeological and Nat. Hist. Society Journal*, VII, 195–217, VIII, 15–64, IX, 84–93, X, 151–8, XI, 93–106, XII, 23–42, XIII, 9–31, XIV, 1–15, XV, 1–19, XVII, 93–113, XVIII, 1–17, London, 1885–96.

Devon F.: Devon feet of fines, I, Richard I –Henry III, 1196–1272, ed. O. J. Reichel, Devon and Cornwall Record Society, 1912.

Dorset F.: Full abstracts of the Feet of Fines relating to the county of Dorset..., 1195–1485, ed. E. A. Fry and G. S. Fry, 2 vols., Dorset Record Society, V, X (1896–1910).

Essex F.: Feet of Fines for Essex (abstracts, 1182–1281), ed. R. E. G. Kirk and E. F. Kirk, I, Essex Archaeological Society, Colchester, 1899.

*Feet of Fines of the reign of Henry II and of the first seven years of the reign of Richard I,
A.D. 1182–A.D. 1196*, PRS, XVII, 1894.

Feet of Fines of the seventh and eighth years of the reign of Richard I, A.D. 1196–A.D. 1197,
PRS, XX, 1896.

Feet of Fines of the ninth year of King Richard I, A.D. 1197–1198, PRS, XXIII, 1898 (repr. 1929).

Feet of Fines of the tenth year of King Richard I, A.D. 1198–1199..., PRS, XXIV, 1900 (repr.
1929).

Glos F.: 'Pedes finium: or excerpts from the feet of fines for the county of Gloucester,
7 John – 57 Henry III', ed. J. Maclean, *BGAS*, XVI (1892), 183–95.

Hunts F.: Huntingdonshire Fines, 1194–1603, ed. G. J. Turner, Cambridge Antiquarian
Society, Octavo Series, XXXVII, 1913.

Kent F.: Calendar of Kent feet of fines to the end of Henry III's reign. Prepared in collaboration by I. J. Churchill, R. Griffin, F. W. Hardman, with introduction by F. W.
Jessup, Kent Archaeological Society, XV, 1956.

*Lancs F.: Final Concords of the county of Lancaster from the original chirographs, or feet of
fines, preserved in the Public Record Office, London, Part i, 7 Richard I – 35 Edward I,
A.D. 1196–A.D. 1307.* Transcribed, translated and annotated by W. Farrer, Lancashire and Cheshire Record Society, XXXIX, 1899.

Lincs F., I: *Abstracts of Final Concords, temp. Richard I, John and Henry III* (1193–1244),
ed. W. K. Boyd and W. O. Massingberd, I (in 2 parts), 1896.

Lincs F., II: *Final concords of the county of Lincoln from the feet of fines preserved in the
Public Record Office, A.D. 1244–1272, with additions from various sources, A.D. 1176–
1250*, ed. C. W. Foster, Lincoln Record Society, XVII, 1920.

*Lincs F., PRS LXVII: Feet of fines for the county of Lincoln for the reign of King John,
1199–1216*, ed. M. S. Walker, PRS, LXVII, 1953.

*London and Middlesex F.: A calendar of the feet of fines for London and Middlesex, Richard I –
12 Elizabeth*, ed. W. J. Hardy and W. Page, 2 vols., London, 1892–3.

*Norfolk F., PRS LXV: Feet of fines for the county of Norfolk for the tenth year of the reign of
King Richard the First, 1198–1199, and for the first four years of the reign of King John,
1199–1202*, ed. B. Dodwell, PRS, LXV, 1952.

*Norfolk F., PRS LXX: Feet of fines for the county of Norfolk for the reign of King John,
1201–15...*, ed. B. Dodwell, PRS, LXX, 1959 for 1956.

Norfolk F. (Rye): A short calendar of the feet of fines for Norfolk (Richard I – Richard III),
ed. Walter Rye, 2 parts, Norwich, 1885–6.

Northumberland and Durham F.: Feet of fines, Northumberland and Durham (abstracts
1196–1228), ed. A. M. Oliver and C. Johnson from transcripts by P. Oliver, Newcastle upon Tyne Records Committee, Publications, X, 1931 (1933).

Oxford F.: The Feet of Fines for Oxfordshire, 1195–1291. Transcribed and calendared by
H. E. Salter, Oxfordshire Record Society, XII, 1930.

*Ped. Fin.: Fines sive Pedes Finium sive Finales Concordiae in Curia Domini Regis, 7 Richard I–
16 John, 1195–1214.* Bedford to Dorset in counties, ed. J. Hunter, 2 vols., RC, 1835,
1844.

*Soms F.: Pedes finium, commonly called feet of fines, for the county of Somerset, Richard I –
Edward I, A.D. 1196–A.D. 1307*, ed. E. Green, Somerset Record Society, VI, 1892.

Staffs F.: 'Calendar of final concords or pedes finium, Staffordshire, temp. Richard I –
Henry III', ed. G. Wrottesley, *SHC*, III, i, 165–77; IV, i, 217–63, 1882–3.

Suffolk F., PRS LXX: Feet of fines...for the county of Suffolk, 1199–1214, ed. B. Dodwell,
PRS, LXX, 1959 for 1956, nos. 280–565.

Suffolk F. (Rye): A calendar of the feet of fines for Suffolk (1 Richard I – 3 Richard III), ed.
W. Rye, Suffolk Institute of Archaeology and Natural History, 1900.

FINES (*cont.*):

Surrey F.: (Calendar of) *Pedes Finium, or fines relating to…Surrey* (*Richard I – Henry VII*), ed. F. B. Lewis, Surrey Archaeological Collections, Extra vol. I, 1894.

Sussex F.: *An abstract of feet of fines relating to the county of Sussex, from Richard I to 33 Henry III*, compiled L. F. Salzman, Sussex Record Society, II, 1903.

Warws F.: *Warwickshire feet of fines, 7 Richard I, 1195 – 12 Edward I, 1284.* Abstracted by E. Stokes and ed. F. C. Wellstood, with introduction and indexes by F. T. S. Houghton, Dugdale Society, XI, 1932.

Wilts F.: *A calendar of the feet of fines relating to the county of Wiltshire, remaining in the Public Record Office, London. From their commencement in the reign of Richard I (1195) to the end of Henry III (1272).* Compiled by E. A. Fry, Wiltshire Archaeological and Nat. Hist. Society, 1930.

Yorks F. Ric. I: 'Pedes Finium Ebor., tempore Ricardi Primi', ed. W. Brown, *YAJ*, XI (1891), 174–88.

Yorks F., John: *Pedes finium Ebor., regnante Johanne, A.D. MCXCIX – A.D. MCCXIV*, ed. W. Brown, Surtees Society, XCIV, 1897.

Yorks F., 1218–31: *Feet of Fines for the county of York from 1218 to 1231*, ed. J. Parker, Yorkshire Archaeological Society, Record Series, LXII, 1921.

Yorks F., 1232–46: *Feet of Fines for the county of York from 1232 to 1246*, ed. J. Parker, Yorkshire Archaeological Society, Record Series, LXVII, 1925.

Flete: *Flete's History of Westminster Abbey*, ed. J. Armitage Robinson, Cambridge, 1909.

Florence: Florence of Worcester, *Chronica ex chronicis*, ed. B. Thorpe, 2 vols., English Historical Society, London, 1848–9.

Flor. Hist.: (Matthew Paris) *Flores Historiarum per Mattheum Westmonasteriensem collecti*, ed. H. R. Luard, 3 vols., RS, 1890.

Floyer and Hamilton: *Catalogue of MSS preserved in the Chapter Library of Worcester Cathedral*, ed. J. K. Floyer and S. G. Hamilton, Worcestershire Historical Society, 1906.

Foreville, S. Gilbert: Foreville, R., *Un procès de canonisation à l'aube du xiiie siècle (1201–1202): Le livre de saint Gilbert de Sempringham*, Paris, 1943.

Fowler, J., 'Dean Azo of Sarum', *Somerset and Dorset Notes and Queries*, XXIII (1942), 319–20.

Fowler, R. C. and A. W. Clapham, *Beeleigh Abbey*, London, 1942.

Fox, J. C., 'Marie de France', *EHR*, XXV (1910), 303–6.

'Mary, abbess of Shaftesbury', *EHR*, XXVI (1911), 317–26.

Freeman, NC: Freeman, E. A., *The Norman Conquest*, 6 vols., Oxford, 1867–79; 2nd edn., vols. I–IV, 1870–6; 3rd edn., vols. I–II, 1877; revised American edn., vols. I–V, New York, 1873–6; VI, Index, 1879.

Fulman, I: 'Historiae Croylandensis continuatio' in *Rerum Anglicarum Scriptores*, I, ed. W. Fulman, Oxford, 1684.

Fundacio: 'Fundacio Abbathiae de Kyrkestall', ed. and translated E. K. Clark, 'The Foundation of Kirkstall Abbey', *Miscellanea*, Thoresby Society, IV (1895), 169–208.

Galbraith, V. H., 'Monastic Foundation Charters of the Eleventh and Twelfth centuries', *CHJ*, IV, iii (1934), 205–22, 296–8.

'Osbert, dean of Lewes', *EHR*, LXIX (1954), 289–302.

GASA: *Gesta Abbatum S. Albani*, ed. H. T. Riley, 3 vols., RS, 1867–9.

GC: *Gallia Christiana*, 16 vols., Paris, 1715–1865.

Gentleman's Magazine, Letter in, LXXVIII, ii (1808), 969.

Geoffrey of Coldingham in *Historiae Dunelmensis scriptores tres*, ed. J. Raine, Surtees Society, IX, 1839.

Gervase: *The Historical Works of Gervase of Canterbury*, ed. W. Stubbs, 2 vols., RS, 1879–80.

Gesta Henrici II: Gesta regis Henrici secundi Benedicti abbatis. The chronicle of the reigns of Henry II and Richard I, A.D. 1169–1192, known commonly under the name of Benedict of Peterborough, ed. W. Stubbs, 2 vols., RS, 1867.

GF: Morey, A. and C. N. L. Brooke, *Gilbert Foliot and his Letters*, Cambridge Studies in Medieval Life and Thought, New Series, XI, Cambridge, 1965.

GFL: The Letters and Charters of Gilbert Foliot, ed. A. Morey and C. N. L. Brooke, Cambridge, 1967.

Gibbs: *Early Charters of the Cathedral Church of St Paul, London*, ed. M. Gibbs, Camden 3rd Series, LVIII, London, 1939.

Gilbert Crispin: J. Armitage Robinson, *Gilbert Crispin, abbot of Westminster*, Cambridge, 1911.

Gilbert of Swineshead, *Sermons on the Canticle, PL*, CLXXXIV, cols. 11–298.

Gilbertine Chts.: Transcripts of charters relating to the Gilbertine houses of Sixle, Ormsby, Catley, Bullington and Alvingham, ed. with a translation, from the King's Remembrancer Memoranda rolls nos. 183, 185, and 187, by F. M. Stenton, Lincoln Record Society, XVIII, 1922.

Gir. Camb.: Giraldi Cambrensis Opera, ed. J. S. Brewer, J. F. Dimock and G. F. Warner, 8 vols., RS, 1861–91 (full bibliography by E. A. Williams, *JNLW*, XII (1961–2), 97–140).

Gir. Camb., *De invectionibus*, ed. W. S. Davies, *Y Cymmrodor*, XXX, 1920.

Gir. Camb., *Speculum Duorum: see* Pembroke, p. 107 below.

Glapwell Chts.: The Glapwell Charters, ed. R. R. Darlington, Derbyshire Archaeological and Nat. Hist. Society, 1957–9.

Godric of Finchale: *Libellus de vita et miraculis S. Godrici heremitae de Finchale, auctore Reginaldo monacho Dunelmensi. Adjicitur appendix miraculorum* (ed. J. Stevenson), Surtees Society, XX, 1847.

Gorham, I: Gorham, G. C., *The History and Antiquities of Eynesbury and St Neots...*, I, London, 1824.

Gorham, II: idem, *A Supplement to the History and Antiquities of Eynesbury and St Neots*, London, 1824 (vol. II = *Appendix* and *Supplement*, separately paged).

Goring Chts.: A collection of charters relating to Goring, Streatley and the neighbourhood, 1181–1546, preserved in the Bodleian Library, with a supplement, ed. T. R. Gambier-Parry, 2 vols., Oxfordshire Record Society, XIII, XIV, 1931–2.

Goscelin (Gocelin), *De miraculis* and *Historia translationis S. Augustini, Acta Sanctorum*, Maii, VI, 393–426.

'La Légende de Ste Edith en prose et vers par le moine Goscelin', ed. A. Wilmart, *Analecta Bollandiana*, LVI (1938), 5–101, 265–307.

'Miracula S. Ivonis' in *Ch. Ramsey*, ed. W. H. Macray, RS, 1886, pp. lix–lxxxiv.

'La vie de Sainte Vulfhilde par Goscelin de Cantorbéry', ed. M. Esposito, *Analecta Bollandiana*, XXXII (1913), 10–26.

And see Talbot, C. H.

Gough: Gough, R., *The History and Antiquities of Croyland Abbey...* (J. Nichols, Bibliotheca Topographica Britannica, III, 1780).

Goulburn, E. M. and H. Symonds, *The Life, Letters and Sermons of Bishop Herbert de Losinga*, 2 vols., Oxford, London, 1878.

Graham, Rose, *English Ecclesiastical Studies: being some essays in research in medieval history*, London, 1929.

Graham, *St Gilbert*: idem, *S. Gilbert of Sempringham and the Gilbertines*, London, 1901.

Gray, *St Radegund*: Gray, A., *Priory of St Radegund, Cambridge*, Cambridge Antiquarian Society, Octavo Series, XXXI, 1898.

Grierson, P., 'Les livres de l'abbé Seiwold de Bath', *Revue Bénédictine*, LII (1940), 96–116.

Hackett, M. B., *The original Statutes of Cambridge University*, Cambridge, 1970.

Haddan and Stubbs: *Councils and ecclesiastical documents relating to Great Britain and Ireland*, ed. A. W. Haddan and W. Stubbs, 3 vols., Oxford, 1869–78.

Haines: Haines, C. R., *Dover Priory*, Cambridge, 1930.

Handbook: The Handbook of British Chronology, 2nd edn., ed. F. M. Powicke and E. B. Fryde, Royal Historical Society, Guides and Handbooks, II, London, 1961.

Hardy, *Catalogue: Descriptive catalogue of materials relating to the history of Great Britain and Ireland, to the end of the reign of Henry VII*, ed. T. D. Hardy, 3 vols. in 4, RS, 1862–71.

Hart (1957): Hart, C. R., *The Early Charters of Essex: The Norman Period*, Leicester, 1957.

Hart (1966): idem, *The Early Charters of Eastern England*, Leicester, 1966.

Haskins, *Med. Science*: Haskins, C. H., *Studies in the history of Medieval Science*, 2nd edn., Cambridge, Mass., 1927.

Hassall, W. O., 'Two papal bulls for St Mary, Clerkenwell', *EHR*, LVII (1942), 97–101.

Heales, A. C., *Records of Merton Priory*, London, 1898.

Heinriquez, C., *Menologium Cistertiense*, Antwerp, 1630.

Hemming: *Hemingi Chartularium ecclesiae Wigornensis*, ed. T. Hearne, 2 vols., Oxford, 1723.

Henderson, C., *Essays in Cornish History*, Oxford, 1935.

Henry of Pytchley's Book of Fees, ed. W. T. Mellows, Northamptonshire Record Society, II, 1927.

Herbert Losinga, *Epp.: Epistolae Herberti de Losinga, primi episcopi Norwicensis...*, ed. R. Anstruther, Caxton Society, Brussels, 1846.

HF: Recueil des historiens des Gaules et de la France, ed. M. Bouquet *et al.*, nouv. édn., ed. L. Delisle, 24 vols., Paris, 1869–1904.

Hist. Northumberland: A History of Northumberland. Issued under the direction of the Northumberland County History Committee, vols. I– , Newcastle upon Tyne, 1893– .

Histoire de l'Ordre de Fontevrault, par les religieuses de Sainte-Marie de Fontevrault, 3 vols., Auch, 1911–15.

Hist. Selby: Historia Selebiensis Monasterii, in *Ctl. Selby*, I, [1]–[54].

Hist. York: The historians of the church of York and its archbishops, ed. J. Raine, 3 vols., RS, 1879–94.

HMC: Royal Commission on Historical Manuscripts. Appendices to Reports and Calendars, London, 1870– .

HMC Ancaster: Report on the manuscripts of the Earl of Ancaster preserved at Grimsthorpe, 1907.

HMC De L'Isle and Dudley: Report on the manuscripts of Lord De L'Isle and Dudley, preserved at Penshurst Place, 4 vols., 1925–42.

HMC Hastings: Report on the manuscripts of the late Reginald Rawdon Hastings, Esq., of the Manor House, Ashby de la Zouche, 4 vols., 1928–47.

HMC Lothian: Report on the manuscripts of the Marquess of Lothian (formerly) preserved at Blickling Hall, Norfolk, 1905.

HMC Middleton: Report on the manuscripts of Lord Middleton (formerly) preserved at Wollaton Hall, Nottinghamshire, 1911.

HMC Rutland: The manuscripts of his Grace the Duke of Rutland, G.C.B., preserved at Belvoir Castle, 4 vols., 1888–1905.

HMC Var. Coll.: Report on manuscripts in various collections, 8 vols., 1901–14.

HMC Wells: Calendar of the manuscripts of the Dean and Chapter of Wells, 2 vols., 1907–14.

Hockey, S. F., *Quarr Abbey and its Lands, 1132–1631*, Leicester, 1970.

Hodgson, J. F., 'Eggleston Abbey', *YAJ*, XVIII (1905), 129–82.

Holdsworth, C. J., 'John of Ford and English Cistercian writing, 1167–1214', *TRHS*, 5th Series, XI (1961), 117–36.

Holland, T. E., 'The University of Oxford in the twelfth century', *Collectanea*, II, Oxford Historical Society, XVI (1890), 137–92.

Hope, W. H. St John and H. Brakspear, 'Jervaulx Abbey', *YAJ*, XXI (1911), 303–44.

Howden: *Chronica Rogeri de Houedene*, ed. W. Stubbs, 4 vols., RS, 1868–71.

Hugh the Chanter (Chantor): *The History of the Church of York, 1066–1127*, ed. and translated C. Johnson, NMT, 1961.

Hugo, C. L., *Sacra Antiquitatis Monumenta*, Stivagii, 1725.

Hundred Rolls: Rotuli Hundredorum temp. Henrici III et Edwardi I in turr' Lond' et in curia receptae scaccarii West. asservati (ed. W. Illingworth), 2 vols., RC, 1812–18.

Hunt, R. W., 'English learning in the late twelfth century', *TRHS*, 4th Series, XIX (1936), 19–42; reprinted in *Essays in Medieval History*, ed. R. W. Southern, London, 1968, pp. 106–28.

    'The Disputation of Peter of Cornwall against Symon the Jew', in *Studies in Medieval History presented to F. M. Powicke*, ed. R. W. Hunt, W. A. Pantin and R. W. Southern, Oxford, 1948, pp. 143–56.

Hurry, J. B., *Reading Abbey*, 2 vols., London, 1901.

Hutchins, *Dorset*: Hutchins, J., *The history and antiquities of the county of Dorset*, 2 vols., London, 1774, 3rd edn. by W. Shipp and J. W. Hodson, 4 vols., Westminster, 1861–70.

Incledon, B., 'Account of the Hospital of St Margaret at Pilton in Devonshire', *Archaeologia*, XII (1796), 211–14.

Ivo, bishop of Chartres, *Epp.*: *Epistolae* in *PL*, CLXII, cols. 11–288 (new edn. by J. Leclercq, vol. 1 only so far, *Classiques de l'Histoire de France au Moyen Age*, Paris, 1949).

Jackson, J. E., 'Kington St Michael', *Wiltshire Archaeological Magazine*, IV (1858), 36–124.

Jahncke, R., *Guilelmus Neubrigensis*, Bonn, 1912.

James, M. R., *Descriptive catalogue of the Manuscripts in the Library of Gonville and Caius College, Cambridge*, 2 vols., Cambridge, 1907–14.

    Descriptive catalogue of the Western Manuscripts in the Library of Trinity College, Cambridge, 4 vols., Cambridge, 1900–4.

JL: Jaffé, P., *Regesta Pontificum Romanorum ad annum 1198*, ed. W. Wattenbach, S. Loewenfeld, F. Kaltenbrunner and P. Ewald, 2 vols., Leipzig, 1885–8.

JNLW: Journal of the National Library of Wales.

Jocelin of Brakelond, *Brak.*: *The Chronicle of Jocelin of Brakelond*, ed. and translated H. E. Butler, NMT, 1949.

John, E., 'The Beginning of the Benedictine Reform in England', *Revue Bénédictine*, LXXIII (1963), 73–87.

    'St Oswald and the tenth-century Reformation', *Journal of Ecclesiastical History*, IX (1958), 159–72.

John of Hexham: John of Hexham's continuation to the *Historia Regum* attributed to Symeon of Durham in *Symeonis monachi opera omnia*, ed. T. Arnold, II, RS, 1885.

John of Salisbury: *see also JS below.*

John of Salisbury, ed. Giles: *Johannis Sareberiensis...opera omnia*, ed. J. A. Giles (Patres Ecclesiae Anglicanae), 5 vols., London, Oxford, 1848.

John of Tynemouth, *Nova Legenda Anglie*, ed. C. Horstmann, Oxford, 1901.

Jones, M. C., 'The Abbey of Ystrad Marchell', *Montgomeryshire Collections*, IV (1871), 16–34, 293–322; V (1872), 109–48; VI (1873), 347–86.

JS Epp: The Letters of John of Salisbury, I, *The Early Letters*, ed. and translated W. J. Millor and H. E. Butler, revised by C. N. L. Brooke, NMT, 1955; vols. II and III forthcoming.

JS Epp., ed. Giles: in John of Salisbury, ed. Giles, I, II; also *PL*, CXCIX.

JS, *HP*: John of Salisbury, *Historia Pontificalis*, ed. and translated M. Chibnall, NMT, 1956.

JW: The Chronicle of John of Worcester, 1118–1140, ed. J. R. H. Weaver, Anecdota Oxoniensia, Mediaeval and Modern Series, XIII, Oxford, 1908 (also in Florence of Worcester q.v.).

Kalendar of Abbot Samson of Bury St Edmunds and related documents, The, ed. R. H. C. Davis, Camden 3rd Series, LXXXIV, 1954.

Kemble: *Codex Diplomaticus Aevi Saxonici*, ed. J. M. Kemble, 6 vols., English Historical Society, London, 1839–48.

Kemp, B. R., 'The Churches of Berkeley Hernesse', *BGAS*, LXXXVII (1968), 96–110.

'The Foundation of Reading Abbey and the growth of its possessions and privileges in England in the twelfth century', University of Reading, Ph.D. thesis, 1966.

'The monastic dean of Leominster', *EHR*, LXXXIII (1968), 505–15.

Kennett, White, *Parochial antiquities...in the counties of Oxford and Buckingham*, Oxford, 1695, new edn., 2 vols., 1818.

Ker, N. R., *Catalogue of Manuscripts containing Anglo-Saxon*, Oxford, 1957.

'Hemming's Cartulary: a description of two Worcester Cartularies in Cotton Tiberius A. xiii', in *Studies in Medieval History presented to F. M. Powicke* (see Hunt), pp. 49–75.

Medieval Libraries of Great Britain: a list of surviving books, Royal Historical Society, Guides and Handbooks, III, 2nd edn., 1964.

KH: Knowles, D. and R. N. Hadcock, *Medieval Religious Houses: England and Wales*, London, 1st edn., 1953, 2nd edn., 1971 (all refs. to 2nd edn.).

Kirby, D. P., 'Bede and Northumbrian Chronology', *EHR*, LXXVIII (1963), 514–27.

Kirby, T. F., 'Records of the Manor of Dunnington, Wilts', *Archaeologia*, LIX, i (1904), 75–82.

Knowles, Dom David, *The Historian and Character and other Essays*, Cambridge, 1963.

Knowles, *EC*: idem, *The Episcopal Colleagues of Archbishop Thomas Becket*, Cambridge, 1951.

Knowles, *MO: see MO*.

Kuttner, S. and Rathbone, E., 'Anglo-Norman canonists of the twelfth century', *Traditio*, VII (1949–51), 279–358.

Lally, J., 'The Court and Household of King Henry II', University of Liverpool, Ph.D. Thesis, 1969.

Lancaster Hist.: Materials for the History of the church of Lancaster, ed. W. O. Roper, 4 vols., Chetham Society, New Series, XXVI, XXXI, LVIII, LIX, 1892–1906.

Lancaster, J. C., 'The Coventry forged charters: a reconsideration', *BIHR*, XXVII (1954), 113–40.

Lancs PR: The Lancashire Pipe Rolls, 1130–1216, ed. W. Farrer, Liverpool, 1902.

Langston, J. N., 'The Priors of Lanthony by Gloucester', *BGAS*, LXIII (1942), 1–144.

Laurence of Durham: *Dialogi Laurentii Dunelmensis monachi ac prioris*, ed. J. Raine, Surtees Society, LXX, 1880.

Lawrie: *Early Scottish Charters*, ed. A. C. Lawrie, Glasgow, 1905.

Le Couteulx, C., *Annales Ordinis Cartusiensis*, 8 vols., Montreal, 1887–91.

Lees, *Templars: Records of the Templars in England in the Twelfth Century*, ed. B. A. Lees, Records of the Social and Economic History of England and Wales, IX, British Academy, London, 1935.

Leighton, W. A., *see Ctl. Haughmond*.

Le Keux, *Memorials of Cambridge*, ed. T. Wright and H. Longueville Jones, II, London, 1842.

Leland, *Coll.*: J. Leland, *Collectanea*, ed. T. Hearne, 2nd edn., 6 vols., London, 1770.

Leland, *Itin.*: *The Itinerary of J. Leland*, ed. L. T. Smith, 5 vols., Oxford, 1907–10.

Le Neve: John Le Neve, *Fasti Ecclesiae Anglicanae, 1066–1300* (revised edn.), I, St Paul's, London, ed. D. E. Greenway, London, 1968; II, *Monastic Cathedrals* (Northern and Southern Provinces), ed. D. E. Greenway, London, 1971.

Leofric Collectar: *The Leofric Collectar*, ed. E. S. Dewick and W. H. Frere, 2 vols., Henry Bradshaw Society, XLV, LVI, 1914–21.

Le Roulx, J. Delaville, 'Des sceaux des prieurs anglais de l'ordre de l'Hôpital aux XIIe et XIIIe siècles', *Mélanges d'archéologie et d'histoire*, Ecole Française de Rome, I (1881), 369–80.

'Des sceaux des prieurs anglais de l'ordre de l'Hôpital aux XIIe et XIIIe siècles. Note complémentaire', ibid., VII (1887), 59–61.

Levison, W., 'Bede as Historian' in *Bede, his Life, Times and Writings*, ed. A. Hamilton Thompson, Oxford, 1935, pp. 111–51.

Lib. El.: *Liber Eliensis*, ed. E. O. Blake, Camden 3rd Series, XCII, 1962.

Liber de Hyda: *Liber Monasterii de Hyda. A Chronicle and Chartulary of Hyde Abbey, Winchester, 455–1023*, ed. E. Edwards, RS, 1866.

Liber Landav.: *The Text of the Book of Llan Dâv*, ed. J. G. Evans and J. Rhys, Oxford, 1893.

Liber Luciani: *Liber Luciani de laude Cestrie*, ed. M. V. Taylor, Lancashire and Cheshire Record Society, LXIV, 1912.

Liebermann, F., 'The annals of Lewes priory', *EHR*, XVII (1902), 83–9.

Lincs Ass. Roll: *The earliest Lincolnshire assize rolls, A.D. 1202–1209*, ed. D. M. Stenton, Lincoln Record Society, XXII, 1926.

Lincs Domesday: *The Lincolnshire Domesday and the Lindsey survey*, ed. C. W. Foster and T. Longley, Lincoln Record Society, XIX, 1924.

Lit. Cant.: *Literae Cantuarienses, The letter books of the monastery of Christ Church, Canterbury*, ed. J. B. Sheppard, 3 vols., RS, 1887–9.

Lit. Wallie: *Littere Wallie*, ed. J. G. Edwards, Board of Celtic Studies of the University of Wales, History and Law Series, V, 1940.

Liverani: *Spicilegium Liberianum*, ed. F. Liverani, I, Florence, 1863.

Lloyd: Lloyd, Sir J. E., *A History of Wales from the Earliest Times to the Edwardian Conquest*, 3rd edn., 2 vols., London, 1939.

London Letter Books: *Calendar of letter books of the city of London*, ed. R. R. Sharpe. Letter books A–L, 11 vols., London, 1899–1912.

Lot, *St-Wandrille*: Lot, F., *Études critiques sur l'abbaye de Saint-Wandrille*, Bibliothèque de l'École des Hautes Études, CCIV, Paris, 1913.

Loyd: Loyd, L. C., *The Origins of some Anglo-Norman Families*, ed. C. T. Clay and D. C. Douglas. Publications of the Harleian Society, CIII, Leeds, 1951.

Luffield Chts.: *Luffield Priory Charters*, Part I, ed. G. R. Elvey, Buckinghamshire Record Society, XV, 1968; Northamptonshire Record Society, XXII, 1968.

LV Durham, 1st edn.: *Liber vitae ecclesiae Dunelmensis; nec non obituaria duo ejusdem ecclesiae*, ed. J. Stevenson, Surtees Society, XIII, 1841.

LV Durham, LVD: *Liber vitae ecclesiae Dunelmensis*, facsimile edn., ed. A. Hamilton Thompson, ibid., CXXXVI, 1923.

LVH: *Liber Vitae: register and martyrology of New Minster and Hyde abbey, Winchester*, ed. W. de G. Birch, Hampshire Record Society, 1892.

Macray, W. D., *Notes from the Muniments of St Mary Magdalen College, Oxford...*, Oxford and London, 1882.

Madan, F., 'The Greslels of Drakelowe: an account of the family and notes of its connexions by marriage and descent from the Norman Conquest to the present day', *SHC*, New Series, I, 1898.

Madox, *Form.*: *Formulare Anglicanum*, ed. T. Madox, London, 1702.

Mander, G. P., 'The Priory of the Black Ladies of Brewood, Co. Stafford', *SHC*, 3rd Series, 1939 (1940), pp. 177–220.

Marshall, E., *The Early History of Woodstock Manor and its Environs...*, Oxford, London, 1873.

Matthew: Matthew, D. J. A., *The Norman Monasteries and their English possessions*, Oxford, 1962.

Mayr-Harting, H., *The Bishops of Chichester, 1075–1207: biographical notes and problems.* The Chichester Papers, XL, Chichester, 1963.

MB: Materials for the History of Thomas Becket, Archbishop of Canterbury..., ed. J. C. Robertson and J. B. Sheppard, 7 vols., RS, 1875–85.

MB Epp.: ibid., vols. V–VII. Letters cited by number.

Mem. Bury: Memorials of St Edmund's Abbey, ed. T. Arnold, RS, 3 vols., 1890–6.

Mem. Dunstan: Memorials of St Dunstan, Archbishop of Canterbury, ed. W. Stubbs, RS, 1874.

Mem. Fountains: Memorials of the abbey of St Mary of Fountains, ed. J. R. Walbran and J. T. Fowler, 3 vols., Surtees Society, XLII, LXVII, CXXX, 1863–1918.

Mem. St Giles, Durham: Memorials of St Giles's, Durham, being grassmen's accounts and other parish records, together with documents relating to the hospitals of Kepier and St Mary Magdalene (ed. J. Barmby), Surtees Society, XCV, 1896.

Miller, E., *The Abbey and Bishopric of Ely*, Cambridge Studies in Medieval Life and Thought, I, 1951.

'Miracula S. Oswini', in *Misc. Biographica*, ed. J. Raine, Surtees Society, VIII, 1838.

Misc. Biographica: Miscellanea biographica: Oswinus, rex Northumbriae; Cuthbertus, episcopus Lindisfarnensis; Eata, episcopus Haugustaldensis, ed. J. Raine, Surtees Society, VIII, 1838.

Misc. D. M. Stenton: A Medieval Miscellany for Doris Mary Stenton, ed. P. M. Barnes and C. F. Slade, PRS, LXXVI, 1962.

MO: Knowles, Dom David, *The Monastic Order in England*, Cambridge, 1940 (2nd edn. 1963, pagination unaltered).

Moir, A. L., *Bromfield Priory*, Chester, 1947.

Mon.: Dugdale, W., *Monasticon Anglicanum*, rev. edn. J. Caley, H. Ellis and B. Bandinel, 6 vols. in 8, London, 1817–30, repr. 1846.

Mon. Ebor.: Burton, J., *Monasticon Eboracense*, York, 1758.

Mont. Coll.: Montgomeryshire Collections.

Montfaucon, B. de, *Bibliotheca Bibliothecarum Manuscriptorum Nova*, 2 vols., Paris, 1739.

Moore, Norman Moore, I: Moore, Sir Norman, *The History of St Bartholomew's Hospital*, 2 vols., London, 1918.

Moore, Sir Norman, *The Book of the Foundation of St Bartholomew's Church in London*, ed. Sir Norman Moore, *EETS*, Original Series, CLXIII, 1923.

Morey: Morey, Dom Adrian, *Bartholomew of Exeter, Bishop and Canonist*, Cambridge, 1937.

Morgan, *see* Chibnall.

Morris, G., 'Abstract of the grants and charters contained in the chartulary of Wombridge Priory', *Transactions of the Shropshire Archaeological and Nat. Hist. Society*, 1st Series, IX (1886), 305–80; XI (1888), 325–48.

Mowbray: *Charters of the Honour of Mowbray, 1107–1191*, ed. D. E. Greenway, British Academy, 1972.

Mozley, J. H., 'The Collection of Mediaeval Latin Verse in MS Cotton Titus D. xxiv', *Medium Aevum*, XI (1942), 1–45.

MPCM: Matthaei Parisiensis Chronica Majora, ed. H. R. Luard, 7 vols., RS, 1872–84.

MPHA: Matthaei Parisiensis Historia Anglorum, 1067–1235, ed. F. Madden, 3 vols., RS, 1886–9.

MVH: Magna Vita S. Hugonis, ed. and translated D. L. Douie and H. Farmer, 2 vols., NMT, 1961–2.

Newburgh, William of Newburgh: *Stephen*, etc., I, II; also *Guilielmi Neubrigensis Historia sive Chronica Rerum Anglicarum*, ed. T. Hearne, 3 vols., Oxford, 1719.

Newcourt: Newcourt, R., *Repertorium ecclesiasticum parochiale Londinense*, 2 vols., London, 1708–10.

Newington Longeville Charters, ed. H. E. Salter, Oxfordshire Record Society, III, 1921.

Nicholl, D., *Thurstan, Archbishop of York, 1114–1140*, York, 1964.

Nichols, *Leics*: Nichols, J., *The history and antiquities of the county of Leicester*, 4 vols. in 8, London, 1795–1815.

Nightingale, J. E., *Memorials of Wilton...*, Devizes, 1906.

NMT: Nelson's Medieval Texts (later Oxford Medieval Texts).

Norman Moore, *see* Moore.

Normandie Bénédictine, La, Lille, 1967.

Northants Ass. Roll: The Earliest Northamptonshire assize rolls, A.D. 1202 and 1203, ed. D. M. Stenton, Northamptonshire Record Society, V, 1930.

Northants Chts.: Facsimiles of early charters from Northamptonshire collections, ed. F. M. Stenton, Northamptonshire Record Society, IV, 1930.

Northumberland pleas from the curia regis and assize rolls, 1198–1272, ed. A. Hamilton Thompson, Newcastle upon Tyne Records Committee, Publications, II, 1922.

Norwich Customary: The customary of the cathedral priory church of Norwich, ed. J. B. L. Tolhurst, Henry Bradshaw Society, LXXXII, 1948.

Nott, J., *Some of the Antiquities of 'Moche Malverne'*, Malvern, 1885.

Nottingham Borough Recs.: Records of the borough of Nottingham, ed. W. H. Stevenson, 5 vols., London, etc., 1882–1900.

NRA: National Register of Archives.

Obit. Sens: Obituaires de la Province de Sens, ed. A. Molinier, A. Longnon, etc., I– . *Recueil des Historiens de la France: Obituaires*, I– . Paris, 1902– .

Offler: see *Durham Episcopal Charters*.

Oliver: Oliver, G., *Monasticon Dioecesis Exoniensis*, Exeter and London, 1846–54.

Oliver, A. M., 'A list of the Abbots of Alnwick', *Proceedings of the Society of Antiquaries of Newcastle upon Tyne*, 3rd Series, IX (1919–20), 42–4.

'A list of the abbots of Newminster', *Archaeologia Aeliana*, 3rd Series, XII (1915), 206–25.

Orderic: Orderic Vitalis, *Historiae ecclesiasticae libri tredecim*, ed. A. Le Prévost and L. Delisle, 5 vols., Paris, 1838–55.

Orderic, ed. Chibnall: *The Ecclesiastical History of Orderic Vitalis*, II, ed. and translated M. Chibnall, Oxford Medieval Texts, 1968.

Ormerod, G., *The History of the county palatine and city of Chester*, 2nd edn., ed. T. Helsby, 3 vols., 1875–82.

Osbert of Clare, prior of Westminster, The Letters of, ed. E. W. Williamson, London, 1929.

OS Facs.: Facsimiles of Anglo-Saxon Manuscripts, ed. W. B. Sanders, 3 vols., Ordnance Survey, Southampton, 1878–84.

Oxenedes: *Chronica Johannis de Oxenedes*, ed. Sir H. Ellis, RS, 1859.

Oxford Chts.: Facsimiles of Early Charters in Oxford Muniment Rooms, ed. H. E. Salter, Oxford, 1929.

Palmer, W. M. and C. Parsons, 'Swavesey Priory', *Transactions of the Cambridgeshire and Huntingdonshire Archaeological Society*, I (1904), 29–48.

Peck, F., *Academia Tertia Anglicana, or the Antiquarian Annals of Stamford*, 1727.

Peers, C., 'Rievaulx Abbey: the Shrine in the Chapter House', *Archaeological Journal*, LXXXVI (1929), 20–8.

Penrice and Margam MSS: A descriptive catalogue of the Penrice and Margam Abbey manuscripts in the possession of Miss Talbot of Margam, ed. W. de G. Birch, Series 1–4, London, 1893–1904.

Penwortham Docts.: Documents relating to the priory of Penwortham and other possessions in Lancashire of the abbey of Evesham, ed. W. A. Hulton, Chetham Society, Old Series, XXX, 1853.

Peter of Celle, *Epp.* in *PL*, CCII.

Peter the Venerable, *Epp.: The Letters of Peter the Venerable*, ed. G. Constable, 2 vols., Cambridge, Mass., 1967.

PL: Patrologiae cursus completus, series Latina, ed. J. P. Migne, 221 vols., Paris, 1844–64.

Placita de Quo Warranto, ed. W. Illingworth, RC, 1818.

Pleas before the King or his Justices, 1198–1202, ed. D. M. Stenton, 3 vols., Selden Society, LXVII, LXVIII, LXXXIII, 1953–67.

Poynton, E. M., 'Charters relating to the Priory of Sempringham', *Genealogist*, New Series, XV (1899), 158–61, 221–7; XVI (1900), 30–5, 76–83, 153–8, 223–8; XVII (1901), 29–35, 164–8, 232–9.

PR: Pipe Rolls, cited by the regnal year, ed. in *PRS*.

Previté-Orton, C. W., 'Annales Radingenses posteriores, 1135–1264', *EHR*, XXXVII (1922), 400–3.

Price, G. V., *Valle Crucis Abbey*, Liverpool, 1952.

PRS: *Pipe Roll Society*, London, 1884– .

Prynne, *Records*: Prynne, W., *An exact Chronological vindication of our kings' supreme ecclesiastical jurisdiction over all religious affairs...*, 3 vols. in 6, London, 1666–8.

PUE: Papsturkunden in England, W. Holtzmann, 3 vols., Abhandlungen der Gesellschaft der Wissenschaften in Göttingen, phil.-hist. Klasse, Berlin, Göttingen, I = neue Folge XXV (1930–1), II = 3 Folge XIV–XV (1935–6), III = 3 Folge XXXIII (1952).

Raine, *Finchale: The charters of endowment, inventories and account rolls of the priory of Finchale in the county of Durham*, ed. J. Raine, Surtees Society, VI, 1837.

Raine, *Hexham Priory: The Priory of Hexham*, ed. J. Raine, 2 vols., Surtees Society, XLIV, XLVI, 1864–5.

Raine, J., *The History and Antiquities of the Parish of Blyth*, Westminster, 1860.

Raine, *North Durham*: Raine, J., *The History and Antiquities of North Durham*, London, 1852.

Ralph Cogg.: Chronicon Anglicanum Radulphi de Coggeshall, ed. J. Stevenson, RS, 1875.

RC: Record Commissions.

Red Book: The Red Book of the Exchequer, ed. H. Hall, 3 vols., RS, 1896.

Rees, W., 'The Possessions of the Abbey of Tewkesbury in Glamorgan', *South Wales and Monmouth Record Society*, II (1960), 148–64.

Reg.: Regesta Regum Anglo-Normannorum, 1066–1154: I, 1066–1100, *Regesta Willelmi Conquestoris et Willelmi Rufi*, ed. H. W. C. Davis, Oxford, 1913; II, 1100–35, *Regesta Henrici Primi*, ed. C. Johnson and H. A. Cronne, Oxford, 1956; III, IV, 1135–54, *Regesta Stephani... and Facsimiles...*, ed. H. A. Cronne and R. H. C. Davis, Oxford, 1968–9.

Reg. Bronescombe: The Register of Walter Bronescombe, 1257–80, ed. F. C. Hingeston-Randolph, London, 1889.

Reg. Concordia: Regularis Concordia, ed. and translated T. Symons, NMT, 1953.

Reg. Godfrey Giffard: Episcopal registers, diocese of Worcester. Register of Bishop Godfrey Giffard, September 23rd 1268 to August 15th 1301, ed. J. W. Willis Bund, 2 vols., Worcester Historical Society, 1902 (1898–1902).

Reg. Grandisson: The Register of John de Grandisson, 1327–69, ed. F. C. Hingeston-Randolph, 3 vols., London, 1894–9.

Reg. Gravesend: Rotuli Ricardi Gravesend, diocesis Lincolniensis, ed. F. N. Davis, additions by C. W. Foster and A. Hamilton Thompson, Canterbury and York Society, XXXI, 1925.

Reg. Gray: The register, or rolls, of Walter Gray, lord archbishop of York, ed. J. Raine, Surtees Society, LVI, 1872.

Reg. Greenfield: The register of William Greenfield, lord archbishop of York, 1306–15, transcribed by W. Brown, ed. A. Hamilton Thompson, 5 vols., Surtees Society, CXLV, CXLIX, CLI, CLII, CLIII, 1931–40.

Reg. Grosseteste: Rotuli Roberti Grosseteste, episcopi Lincolniensis A.D. MCCXXXV–MCCLIII, ed. F. N. Davis, Canterbury and York Society, X, 1913 (1910–13).

Reg. Hamonis Hethe: Registrum Hamonis Hethe, diocesis Roffensis, A.D. 1319–1352, transcribed and ed. C. Johnson, 2 vols., Canterbury and York Society, XLVIII, XLIX, 1948.

Reg. Lichfield: The Great Register of Lichfield Cathedral, known as Magnum Registrum Album, ed. H. E. Savage, *SHC*, 3rd Series, 1924 (1926).

Reg. Lincoln: The Registrum Antiquissimum of the Cathedral Church of Lincoln, ed. C. W. Foster and K. Major, I– , Lincoln Record Society, 1931– .

Reg. Master David: see Brooke, Z. N.

Reg. Norwich, I: *The first register of Norwich cathedral priory*, ed. H. W. Saunders, Norfolk Record Society, XI, 1939.

Reg. palatinum Dunelmense: The register of Richard de Kellawe, lord palatine and bishop of Durham, 1314–1316, ed. T. D. Hardy, 4 vols., RS, 1873–8.

Reg. Pinchbeck: The Pinchbeck Register, ed. Lord Francis Hervey, 2 vols., Brighton, 1925.

Reg. Pontissara: Registrum Johannis de Pontissara, episcopi Wyntoniensis A.D. MCCLXXXII–MCCCIV, translated and ed. C. Deedes, 2 vols., Canterbury and York Society, XIX, XXX, 1915–24.

Reg. Reg. Scot., I: *Regesta Regum Scottorum*, I: *The Acts of Malcolm IV, King of Scots, 1153–1165...*, ed. G. W. S. Barrow, Edinburgh, 1960.

Reg. Rochester: Registrum Roffense..., ed. J. Thorpe, London, 1769.

Reg. St Osmund: Vetus registrum Sarisberiense alias dictum registrum S. Osmundi episcopi..., ed. W. H. R. Jones, 2 vols., RS, 1883–4.

Reg. Swinfield: Registrum Ricardi Swinfield..., ed. W. W. Capes, Cantilupe Society and Canterbury and York Society, 1909.

Reg. Wells: Rotuli Hugonis de Welles, episcopi Lincolniensis A.D. MCCXXIX–MCCXXXV, ed. W. P. W. Phillimore and F. N. Davis, Canterbury and York Society, 3 vols., London, 1907 (1905)–1909.

Reginald Dun.: Reginaldi monachi Dunelmensis libellus de admirandis beati Cuthberti virtutibus quae novellis patratae sunt temporibus, ed. J. Raine, Surtees Society, I, 1835.

Revesby Chts.: Abstracts of the deeds and charters relating to Revesby Abbey, 1142–1539, ed. E. Stanhope, privately printed, Horncastle, 1889.

'Ribston and the knights templars', ed. R. V. Taylor, *YAJ*, VII (1882), 429–52; VIII (1884), 259–99; IX (1886), 71–98.

Richard of Hexham in *Ch. Stephen*, etc., III, ed. R. Howlett, RS, 1886.

Richardson, H. G., 'The Letters and Charters of Eleanor of Aquitaine', *EHR*, LXXIV (1959), 193–213.

Richardson and Sayles, *Governance*: H. G. Richardson and G. O. Sayles, *The Governance of Medieval England from the Conquest to Magna Carta*, Edinburgh, 1963.

Roberts, G., 'Llanthony Priory, Monmouthshire', *Archaeologia Cambrensis*, I (1846), 201–45.

Robertsbridge Chts.: Calendar of charters and documents relating to the abbey of Robertsbridge..., London, 1873.

Robinson, J. A. (1911), *see Gilbert Crispin*.
    (1918): Robinson, J. Armitage, *The Saxon Bishops of Wells. A Historical Study in the Tenth Century*, British Academy Supplemental Papers, IV, 1918.
    (1919): *St Oswald and the Church of Worcester*, British Academy Supplemental Papers, V, 1919.
    (1921): *Somerset Historical Essays*, British Academy, London, 1921.
    (1923): *The Times of St Dunstan*, Oxford, 1923.
Rolls of the justices in Eyre, being the rolls of pleas and assizes for Gloucestershire, Warwickshire and Staffordshire (recte Shropshire) 1221, 1222, ed. D. M. Stenton, Selden Society, LIX, 1940.
Rolls of the king's court in the reign of King Richard the First, A.D. 1194–1195. Introduction and notes by F. W. Maitland, PRS, XIV, 1891.
Romsey Records: Liveing, H. G. D., *Records of Romsey Abbey*, Winchester, 1906.
Rot. Chart., Cht.: Rotuli Chartarum in Turri Londinensi asservati, 1199–1216, ed. T. D. Hardy, RC, 1837.
Rot. Cur. Reg.: Rotuli Curiae Regis: Rolls and Records of the Court held before the King's Justiciars or Justices, 6 Richard I – 1 John, ed. F. Palgrave, 2 vols., RC, 1835.
Rot. de Finibus: Rotuli de Oblatis et Finibus in Turri Londinensi asservati temp. Regis Johannis, ed. T. D. Hardy, RC, 1835.
Rot. Lit. Claus.: Rotuli Litterarum Clausarum in Turri Londinensi asservati, ed. T. D. Hardy, 2 vols., RC, 1833–4.
Rot. Lit. Pat.: Rotuli Litterarum Patentium in Turri Londinensi asservati, 1201–16, ed. T. D. Hardy, RC, 1835.
Roul. Morts: Rouleaux des Morts du IX au XV siècle, ed. L. V. Delisle, Société de l'Histoire de France, Paris, 1866.
Round, J. H., *The Commune of London and other studies*, Westminster, 1899.
    'The Families of St John and of Port', *Genealogist*, New Series, XVI (1900), 1–13.
    Feudal England, London, 1895, repr. 1964.
    'The Foundation of the Priories of St Mary and St John, Clerkenwell', *Archaeologia*, LVI (1899), 223–8.
    'The Ports of Basing and their priory', *Genealogist*, New Series, XVIII (1902), 137–9.
    Studies in Peerage and Family History, Westminster, 1901.
RS: Rolls Series.
RTAM: Recherches de théologie ancienne et médiévale.
Rud: Rud, T., *Codicum Manuscriptorum Ecclesiae Cathedralis Dunelmensis Catalogus Classicus*, Durham, 1825.
Rufford Chts.: The Charters of Rufford Abbey, ed. C. J. Holdsworth, Thoroton Society, forthcoming.
Russell, J. C., 'Alexander Neckam in England', *EHR*, XLVII (1932), 260–8.
    'Attestation of Charters in the Reign of John', *Speculum*, XV (1940), 480–98.
Rye, W., *Carrow Abbey*, Norwich, 1889.
— and E. A. Tillett, 'Carrow Abbey', *Norfolk Archaeological Miscellany*, II (1883), 465–508.
Rymer, *Foedera: Foedera, conventiones...*Accurante Thoma Rymer, 2nd edn., 20 vols., London, 1727–35.
St Albans Psalter, The, ed. O. Pächt, C. R. Dodwell, F. Wormald, London, 1960.
Salter, H. E., *Chapters of the Augustinian Canons*, Canterbury and York Society, XXIX, 1922.
    'Geoffrey of Monmouth and Oxford', *EHR*, XXXIV (1919), 382–5.
    'William of Newburgh', *EHR*, XXII (1907), 510–14.
Saltman: Saltman, A., *Theobald, Archbishop of Canterbury*, University of London Historical Studies, II, London, 1956.

'The History of the Foundation of Dale Abbey, or the so-called Chronicle of Dale', *Derbyshire Archaeological Journal*, LXXXVII (1967), 18–38.

'John II, Bishop of Rochester', *EHR*, LXVI (1951), 71–5.

Sarum Chts.: Charters and Documents illustrating the history of the cathedral, city and diocese of Salisbury in the twelfth and thirteenth centuries, ed. W. (H.) R. Jones and W. D. Macray, RS, 1891.

Sawyer: *Anglo-Saxon Charters. An annotated list and bibliography*, ed. P. H. Sawyer, Royal Historical Society, Guides and Handbooks, VIII, 1968.

Scammell: Scammell, G. V., *Hugh du Puiset, Bishop of Durham*, Cambridge, 1956.

'A note on the chronology of the Priors, Archdeacons and Sheriffs of Durham during the episcopate of Hugh du Puiset', *Archaeologia Aeliana*, 4th Series, XXXIII (1955), 61–9.

Scott, J. R., 'Charters of Monks Horton priory', *Archaeologia Cantiana*, X (1876), 269–81.

Scriptores Tres: Historiae Dunelmensis scriptores tres: Gaufridus de Coldingham, Robertus de Graystanes et Willelmus de Chambre, ed. J. Raine, Surtees Society, IX, 1839.

Searle (1899): Searle, W. G., *Anglo-Saxon Bishops, Kings and Nobles*, Cambridge, 1899.

Christ Church, Canterbury, Cambridge Antiquarian Society, Octavo Series, XXXIV, 1902.

(1897): *Onomasticon Anglo-Saxonicum*, Cambridge, 1897.

Select cases of procedure without writ under Henry III, ed. H. G. Richardson and G. O. Sayles, Selden Society, LX, 1941.

Shaw, *Staffs*: Shaw, Stebbing, *The History and Antiquities of Staffordshire*, 2 vols., London, 1798–1801.

SHC: Staffordshire Historical Collections, William Salt Archaeological Society, now Staffs. Record Society. Vols.: II, i (1881), 178–276 (*Ctl. Staffordshire*, ed. R. W. Eyton); III, i (1882), 165–77 (see *Staffs F.*), 178–231 (*Ctl. Staffs*, ed. G. Wrottesley); IV, i (1883), 1–215 (*Plea Rolls*, ed. G. Wrottesley), 217–63 (see *Staffs F.*), 267–95 (*Ctl. Ronton*); V, i (1884), 1–101 (see *Ctl. Burton*); VI, i (1885), 1–28 (see *Ctl. Stone*); VII, i (1886), 1–191 (*Plea Rolls, 1294–1307*); VIII, i (1887), 125–201 (*Ctl. Stafford, St Thomas*); XI, i (1890), 295–336 (see *Ctl. Trentham*); XVII (1896), 237–98 (see *Shenstone Chts.*); New Series, VII (1904), 1–187 (see Wrottesley, G.); 3rd Series, (1911), 416–48 (*Ctl. Staffs*, ed. J. C. Wedgwood); (1913), pp. 1–178 (Inquisitions post mortem, Edward III); (1937) (see *Burton Chts.*); (1939), 177–220 (see Mander, G. P.).

Shenstone Chts.: The Shenstone charters, copied from the chartulary or great coucher book of the Duchy of Lancaster, ed. G. Grazebrook, *SHC*, XVII (1896), 237–98.

Sim. Dur.: Symeonis monachi opera omnia, ed. T. Arnold, 2 vols., RS, 1882–5.

Sim. Dur., ed. Hinde: *Symeonis Dunelmensis opera et collectanea*, I, ed. J. H. Hinde, Surtees Society, LI, 1868.

Smalley, B., 'Andrew of St Victor, Abbot of Wigmore: a twelfth-century Hebraist', *RTAM*, X (1938), 358–73.

'Gilbertus Universalis, bishop of London (1128–34) and the problem of the "Glossa Ordinaria"', ib., VII (1935), 235–62; VIII (1936), 24–60.

'La Glossa Ordinaria. Quelques prédécesseurs d'Anselme de Laon', ib., IX (1937), 365–400.

The Study of the Bible in the Middle Ages, 2nd edn., Oxford, 1952.

Smith, *Bede*: Beda, *Historiae Ecclesiasticae Gentis Anglorum Libri Quinque*, ed. J. Smith, Cambridge, 1722.

Smith, R. A. L., *Collected Papers*, London, 1947.

Smith of Nibley, J., *The Berkeley Manuscripts: The lives of the Berkeleys*, ed. Sir J. Maclean, 3 vols., Gloucester, 1883–5.

Solloway, J., *The Alien Benedictines of York: being a complete history of Holy Trinity Priory, York*, Leeds, 1910.

Somner: *The Antiquities of Canterbury*, 2nd edn., ed. W. Somner, 2 parts, ed. N. Battely, London, 1703.

Southern, R. W., 'The English origins of the miracles of the Virgin', *Mediaeval and Renaissance Studies*, IV (1958), 176–216.

Medieval Humanism and other Studies, Oxford, 1970.

St Anselm and his biographer: a study of monastic life and thought, 1059–c. 1130, Cambridge, 1963.

'St Anselm and Gilbert Crispin, abbot of Westminster', *Mediaeval and Renaissance Studies*, III (1954), 78–115.

Sparke: *Historiae Coenobii Burgensis Scriptores varii* (Chs. Peterborough), ed. J. Sparke in *Historiae Anglicanae Scriptores Varii*, 2 vols. in 3, London, 1723.

Stapleton, T., *Holy Trinity Priory, York*; section separately paged of the (Royal) Archaeological Institute of Great Britain and Ireland's *Memoirs illustrative of. . . York* (1846), London, 1847.

Stenton, Sir F. M., *Anglo-Saxon England*, Oxford History of England, II, 2nd edn., Oxford, 1947.

The First Century of English Feudalism, 1066–1166, 1st edn., Oxford, 1932; 2nd edn., Oxford, 1961.

'St Benet of Holme and the Norman Conquest', *EHR*, XXXVII (1922), 225–35.

Stephan, Dom J., *Buckfast Abbey*, Buckfast, 1962.

Stewart-Brown, R., *Birkenhead Priory and the Mersey Ferry*, Liverpool, 1925.

'Oliver, prior of Birkenhead', *Cheshire Sheaf*, XX (1923), 60–1, note 4830.

Stogursey Chts.: Stogursey Charters, ed. T. D. Tremlett and N. Blakiston, Somerset Record Society, LXI, 1949 for 1946.

Styles, D., 'The Early History of Alcester Abbey', *Transactions of the Birmingham Archaeological Society*, LXIV (1941–2), 20–38.

Tait: *see Ctl. Chester.*

Talbot, C. H., 'The Testament of Gervase of Louth Park', *Analecta Sacri Ordinis Cisterciensis*, VII (1951), 32–45.

'The Life of St Wulsin of Sherborne by Goscelin', *Revue Bénédictine*, LXIX (1959), 68–85.

Taylor, C. S., 'Berkeley Minster', *BGAS*, XIX (1894–5), 70–84.

Taylor, F., 'Hand-list of the Crutchley MSS in the John Rylands Library', *BJRL*, XXXIII (1950–1), 138–87, 327–72.

Taylor, T., *St Michael's Mount*, Cambridge, 1932.

Text. Roff.: Textus Roffensis, pt. II, ed. P. Sawyer, *Early English Manuscripts in Facsimile*, vol. XI, Copenhagen, 1962.

Thomas of Monmouth, *The Life and Miracles of St William of Norwich*, ed. A. Jessopp and M. R. James, Cambridge, 1896.

Thomas, W., *Descriptio ecclesiae Majoris Malverne* in *Antiquitates Prioratus Majoris Malverne*, London, 1725.

Thompson, A. Hamilton, 'The Monastic Settlement at Hackness and its relation to the Abbey of Whitby', *YAJ*, XXVII (1923–4), 388–405.

The Premonstratensian Abbey of Welbeck, London, 1938.

Thompson, E. M. (1930): Thompson, E. M., *The Carthusian Order in England*, London, 1930.

Thorne: William Thorne, *Chronica de rebus gestis abbatum sancti Augustini Cantuariae*, ed. R. Twysden, *Historiae Anglicanae Scriptores X*, London, 1652, cols. 1753–2202 (also translation by A. H. Davis, *William Thorne's Chronicle. . .*, Oxford, 1934, with pages of Twysden noted).

Thoroton, ed. Throsby: Thoroton, R., *The Antiquities of Nottinghamshire*, with additions by J. Throsby, 3 vols., Nottingham, 1797.

Thorpe: *Diplomatarium Anglicum aevi Saxonici*, ed. B. Thorpe, London, 1865.

Thurston, H., 'The Legend of Abbot Elsi', *Month*, CIV (1904), 1–15.

Tierney, M. A., *The History and Antiquities of the Castle and Town of Arundel...*, London, 1834.

Tillmann: Tillmann, H., *Die päpstlichen Legaten in England bis zur Beendigung der Legation Gualas (1218)*, Bonn, 1926.

Torigny: *The chronicle of Robert of Torigny, abbot of Mont St Michel...*, in *Ch. Stephen*, etc., ed. R. Howlett, IV, RS, 1889.

Torigny, ed. Delisle: *Chronique de Robert de Torigni...*, ed. L. Delisle, 2 vols., Société de l'Histoire de Normandie, Rouen, 1872–3.

TRHS: Transactions of the Royal Historical Society.

Trokelowe, ed. Hearne: *Johannis de Trokelowe, Annales Edwardi II*, etc., ed. T. Hearne, Oxford, 1729.

Twysden, Roger, *Historiae Anglicanae scriptores X*, London, 1652.

UGQ : Ungedruckte anglo-normannische Geschichtsquellen, ed. F. Liebermann, Strassburg, 1879 (repr. Ridgewood, N.J., 1966).

Ullmann, W., 'A forgotten Dispute at Bridlington Priory and its Canonistic Setting', *YAJ*, XXXVII (1948–51), 456–73.

Urry: Urry, W., *Canterbury under the Angevin Kings*, London, 1967.

Vaughan, R., 'The Chronicle of John of Wallingford', *EHR*, LXXIII (1958), 66–77.

Matthew Paris, Cambridge Studies in Medieval Life and Thought, New Series, VI, Cambridge, 1958.

VCH: Victoria History of the Counties of England.

Visio Monachi Eynsham in *Ctl. Eynsham*, II, pp. 255–371.

VITAE: of

St Ælfheah (Osbern), in *Acta Sanctorum*, Apr. II, 628–41.

Sts Æthelfleda and Merewenna in *Romsey Records*, pp. 19 ff.

St Æthelwold (Ælfric) in *Ch. Abingdon*, II, 253–66; (Wulfstan) in *PL*, CXXXVII, col. 79–114.

Vita Ailredi, see Walter Daniel.

St Gilbert of Sempringham, in *Mon.*, VI, ii, pp. *v–*xxix (between pp. 946 and 947).

St Godric, see Godric of Finchale.

'Vita S. Gaufridi Saviniacensis', ed. E. P. Sauvage, *Analecta Bollandiana*, I (1882), 390–409.

'Vita Gundulfi', in *PL*, CLIX, 813–36.

'Vita Herluini' (abb. Bec) in *Gilbert Crispin*, pp. 87–110.

'Vita Lanfranci' (Milo Crispin) in *PL*, CL, col. 29–58.

'Vita S. Margarete' (Turgot of Durham) in *Sim. Dur.*, ed. Hinde, I, 234–54.

'Vita Roberti Betun' (William of Wycombe), *AS*, II, 293–322.

'Vita S. Roberti Novi Monasterii in Anglia abbatis', ed. P. Grosjean, S.J., *Analecta Bollandiana*, LVI (1938), 334–60.

'Vita S. Waltheni' (St Waltheof) in *Acta Sanctorum*, Aug., I, 249–78.

Vita Wulfrici: see Wulfric of Haselbury.

And see Goscelin.

Voss: Voss, L., *Heinrich von Blois, Bischof von Winchester, 1129–71*, Historische Studien, CCX, Berlin, 1932.

Walberg, E., *La tradition hagiographique de S. Thomas Becket*, Paris, 1929.

xlv

Walker, J. W., *An historical and architectural description of the priory of St Mary Magdalene of Monk Bretton in the West Riding of the county of Yorkshire*, Yorkshire Archaeological Society, Extra Series, 1926.

Walt. Cov.: Memoriale fratris Walteri de Coventria. The historical collections of Walter of Coventry, ed. W. Stubbs, 2 vols., RS, 1872–3.

Walter Daniel, *Vita Ailredi*, ed. and translated F. M. Powicke, NMT, 1950.

WAM: Wiltshire Archaeological Magazine.

Welsh Epis. Acts: Episcopal Acts and cognate documents relating to Welsh dioceses, 1066–1272, ed. J. Conway Davies, Historical Society of the Church in Wales, nos. 1, 3–4, 2 vols., Cardiff, 1946–8.

Wendover: Roger of Wendover, *Chronica*, ed. H. O. Coxe, 4 vols., English Historical Society, 1841–2; ed. H. G. Hewlett, 3 vols., RS, 1886–9; but cited from *MPCM*, II.

Wethered (1898): Wethered, F. T., *St Mary's, Hurley in the Middle Ages*, Hurley, 1898.
(1909): idem, *The Last Days of Hurley Priory*, Reading, 1909.

White, R., *Dukery Records*, Worksop, 1904.

Whitelock, D., 'The conversion of the Eastern Danelaw', *Saga Book of the Viking Society*, XII, iii (1941), 159–76.
'Scandinavian personal names in the Liber Vitae of Thorney Abbey', ib., XII, ii (1940), 127–53.
'Two Notes on Ælfric and Wulfstan', *Modern Languages Review*, XXXVIII (1943), 122–6.
(1955): *English Historical Documents*, I, *c*. 500–1042, ed. D. Whitelock, London, 1955.

Widmore, R., *History of Westminster Abbey*, London, 1751.

Wightman, W. E., *The Lacy Family in England and Normandy, 1066–1194*, Oxford, 1966.

Wilkins, *Concilia*: Wilkins, D., *Concilia Magnae Britanniae et Hiberniae...*, 4 vols., London, 1737.

Will of Æthelgifu, The, ed. D. Whitelock, Roxburghe Club, 1968.

William of Canterbury, *Miracula S. Thomae*, in *MB*, I.

Williams, Gwyn, *Medieval London*, London, 1963.

Williams, S. W., *The Cistercian Abbey of Strata Florida*, London, 1889.

Wilmart, A., 'Maître Adam chanoine Prémontré devenu Chartreux à Witham', *Analecta Praemonstratensia*, IX (1933), 209–32 (eds. Ch. Witham on pp. 215–32).
'Un opuscule sur la confession composé par Guy de Southwick vers la fin du XIIe siècle', *RTAM*, VII (1935), 337–52.

WMAG: (William of Malmesbury) *De antiquitate Glastoniensis ecclesiae* in *Ad. Dom.*, I, 1–122.

WMGP: Willelmi Malmesbiriensis, *De gestis Pontificum Anglorum*, ed. N. E. S. A. Hamilton, RS, 1870.

WMGR: idem, *De gestis Regum*, ed. W. Stubbs, 2 vols., RS, 1887–9.

WMHN: idem, *Historia Novella*, ed. K. R. Potter, NMT, 1955.

WMVW: idem, *The Vita Wulfstani... and The Miracles and Translation of St Wulfstan*, ed. R. R. Darlington, Camden 3rd Series, XL, 1928.

Woodruff, C. E., 'Some early professions of canonical obedience to the see of Canterbury by heads of religious houses', *Archaeologia Cantiana*, XXXVII (1925), 53–72.

Worcestre, William, *Itineraries*, ed. J. H. Harvey, Oxford Medieval Texts, 1969.

Wormald, F., *English Benedictine Kalendars after A.D. 1100*, 2 vols., Henry Bradshaw Society, LXXVII, LXXXI, 1939–46.
English Kalendars before 1100, ib., LXXII, 1934.
'Liturgical Calendar from Guisborough Priory', *YAJ*, XXXI (1932–4), 5–35.

Wright, T., *History of Ludlow and its neighbourhood*, London, 1852.

Wrottesley, G., 'An account of the family of Okeover of Okeover, Co. Stafford, with transcripts of the ancient deeds at Okeover', *SHC*, New Series, VII (1904), 4–187.

Wulfric of Haselbury by John abbot of Ford, ed. M. Bell, Somerset Record Society, XLVII, 1933.

Wulfstan's *Sermo Lupi*, ed. D. Whitelock, London, 1939, 3rd edn., London, 1963.

YAJ: *Yorkshire Archaeological Journal*.

York Fasti: *see* Clay, *Fasti*.

Yorks Deeds: *Yorkshire Deeds*, ed. W. Brown, C. T. Clay, M. J. Hebditch (Mrs Stanley Price), 10 vols., Yorkshire Archaeological Society, XXXIX, L, LXIII, LXV, LXIX, LXXVI, LXXXIII, CII, CXI, CXX, 1909–55.

OTHER ABBREVIATIONS

abb.: abbacy, abbess, abbey, abbot
abp., Archbp.: archbishop
acc.: accession
Ann., ann.: annals
app.: appointed, appointment
archd.: archdeacon
bl.: blessed, blessing
bp.: bishop
can.: canon
cent.: century
Ch., ch.: chronicle
chapl.: chaplain
Cht., cht.: charter
consec.: consecrated, consecration
Ctl., ctl.: cartulary, chartulary
d.: death, died
dep.: deposed, deposition
el.: elect, elected, election
f.: foundation, founded
F.: Fine(s)
FF.: Feet of Fines
freq.: frequent, frequently
j.d.: (papal) judge delegate
lic.: licence
m.: monk
n.d.: no date
obit, obit.: obit, obituary
occ.: occur(s), occurred, occurrence
pal.: palaeographical evidence
pr., prs.: prior(s), prioress(es), priory
prev.: previously
ref.: refoundation, refounded; also references
res.: resignation, resigned
s.a.: sub anno
ss.: subscriptions (to pre-Conquest chts.)
subpr.: subprior

INTRODUCTION

I. *The purpose and scope of this book*

This book aims at providing lists of all the known superiors of the religious houses that existed in England and Wales between 940 and 1216. The term religious house is understood as covering all establishments of monks, regular canons and nuns, whether of abbatial or lower rank and whether autonomous or dependent. Roughly speaking, therefore, it comprises all the houses existing between these dates that are listed in the relevant sections of *Medieval Religious Houses: England and Wales* – all, that is, save those of whose heads we know nothing – but the military orders are not included, nor are hospitals. Similarly, the groups of nuns staffing hospitals or serving guests or pilgrims on the outskirts of an abbey are not included unless they ranked as a religious community possessed of an income and domestic autonomy.

Four classes of establishment are represented: the autonomous abbey; the autonomous priory; the dependent priory with regular life; and smaller houses, priories or cells, whose exact status it is often difficult to define. Our lists make no claim to classify or divide the last group, as *Medieval Religious Houses* attempts to do; our concern is solely with the heads of all houses (save hospitals and the like) who are called in the documents abbots and priors. The exact distinction, in terms of authority and prestige, between the classes of abbots and priors, and the *raison d'être* of the status of a given house, are by no means as easy to define as might be expected. As a rule of thumb, Benedictine autonomous houses normally, but not always, had abbots, and size and wealth are a rough criterion; dependent houses are always priories, as were also Cluniac monasteries, however wealthy and important (e.g. Lewes). Cistercian monks and Premonstratensian canons, save in the rare cases of small dependencies, always had an abbot as superior. Augustinian canons, on the other hand, normally had priors, but during our period some 25 out of 180 had abbots, and though the majority of the abbeys are the largest and wealthiest houses (e.g. Cirencester), a few (e.g. Notley and Wigmore) are not. The reason for the distinction must often be sought in historical circumstances. It might be that a founder's intentions for endowment, upon which abbatial rank was assumed, failed to materialise. The Gilbertine canons had priors, but the head of the order, normally resident at Sempringham, was Master. Among the nuns a similar lack of uniformity prevailed. Abbesses were uncommon among Benedictine nuns save in the pre-Conquest houses; they are scanty among the Austin

(Augustinian) canonesses, rare among the Cistercians and non-existent among the Premonstratensians. Sometimes the status of the house changed; more often, especially among the Austin canons, contemporaries used the wrong term. In any case, our lists record status; we do not ordinarily explain it.

The contents of our lists are explained in detail on pp. 16–20. We took c. 940 as the year when monastic life was revived in England by Dunstan at Glastonbury. For practical purposes of chronology, King John's death in 1216 is the most convenient date in the early thirteenth century; it was chosen also because the years round about mark an epoch in the history of the religious orders. The Fourth Lateran Council in the previous year (1215), the death of Innocent III (1216) and the birth of the two orders of friars all help to change the picture. From about that date, too, the survival of so many governmental and episcopal records and other religious documents give more plentiful information, and render many of the lists of superiors already in print fuller and more reliable.

The value of such lists, which vary in completeness, will be clear at once to a practising medievalist. Many events, great and small, bear no date in the normal narrative sources, but can often be dated, at least within a few years, by charters of foundation, of gifts, and of agreements. There is a mass of undated charters in this period; but they were usually witnessed or approved by a group of worthies, varying in dignity according to the importance of the occasion, and often containing heads of neighbouring monasteries. If the limiting dates of the term of office or life of one or more of these is known, and if also some names are common to other similar documents, the date of compilation of the document itself can often be ascertained within a narrow margin. This in turn may give us greater precision for a totally different occasion, and so a mass of information gradually builds up for the whole period. There are many other uses of these lists. Thus, taken as a whole, they will present for the first time a record as full as the evidence allows of the number and provenance of superiors from overseas in English houses from c. 1050 onwards. They reveal cases of pluralism, and of the practice in some orders of an able superior passing through several houses. They show the gradual elimination of superiors of Anglo-Saxon nationality or nomenclature; and also the affiliations of the early houses of Austin canons. Indeed, all precise factual information extends our knowledge of a religious community, and on the lowest and widest level there is a satisfaction in knowing what abbot was ruling a house when this or that event or building took place, and in being able to see his relationship in the past to this or another community. A medievalist will find in these lists many a glimpse of the world that he is trying to recover and to understand. The bare statement that many Norman and French abbots were appointed to English monasteries may be illuminated by a glance at three or four of the greatest houses.

Westminster from 1076 to *c.* 1158 had the following abbots: Geoffrey, an unsuccessful Norman; Vitalis, a monk of Fécamp and abbot of Bernay; Gilbert Crispin the writer, a monk of Bec; Herbert, a monk of Westminster of unknown origin; and Gervase of Blois, a natural son of King Stephen, deposed *c.* 1158. Glastonbury between *c.* 1077/8 and 1171 had the following: Thurstan, a monk of Caen; Herluin, another monk from Caen; Seffrid, a monk of Séez; Henry of Blois, the royal Cluniac, who held the abbacy for forty-five years, putting in as prior Robert, a Cluniac from Lewes. St Albans between 1077 and 1166 had: Paul, a monk of Caen and a nephew of Lanfranc; Richard, of Norman (possibly baronial) family; Geoffrey de Gorron, another Norman of baronial family; Ralph, an Englishman; and Robert de Gorron, a nephew of Geoffrey. Peterborough, from 1069 to 1155 had: Turold, a warlike monk of Fécamp moved from Malmesbury to contain Hereward; Matthew, a monk of Mont-S.-Michel; Ernulf, a monk of Beauvais, before becoming prior of Canterbury; John, a monk of Séez; Henry of Poitou, monk and prior of Cluny, bishop-elect of several sees and an ecclesiastical adventurer on a unique scale; and Martin, a monk of Bec and prior of St Neots. Some such pattern can be found in many of the monasteries and in almost every case the line of overseas abbots came to an end in the first half of the reign of Henry II, which implies that appointments from abroad lessened during the latter half of the reign of Stephen.

A few houses stand out as particularly fortunate or unlucky in their superiors. In the first class stands St Albans. During the whole of our period after the arrival of Abbot Paul in 1077 the house was governed by a succession of men who, whatever may have been their personal failings as seen through the eyes of critical chroniclers, were individuals of personality who were also monks by vocation. At the other extreme the equally wealthy and celebrated abbey of Glastonbury had a series of irregular happenings. After the deposition of the last English abbot by Lanfranc *c.* 1077 × 8, the house was ruled on and off for twenty years by the tactless and ruthless Thurstan. Then, after twenty-five years of regular rule, broken at least once for some years by a long vacancy, the monks had for forty-five years as titular abbot the magnificent Henry of Blois, bishop of Winchester. Henry doubtless kept the place solvent, under a Cluniac prior, but it is perhaps no accident that the history of the house is virtually a blank for those years. Henry's death was followed by a vacancy of eighteen months, and another vacancy extending over nine years occurred soon after. Finally, in the last decades of our period, Glastonbury was harassed by the attempts, temporarily successful, of Bishop Savaric to engross the abbey.

Somewhat unexpectedly, a summary glance at a number of houses shows that many abbots were long-lived. Given the common disinclination of a conservative community to elect a young man this is somewhat surprising, yet for many of the largest houses there were no more than eight or ten abbacies between the first appointment after the Conquest and the end of John's reign, giving an average tenure of over twelve years. This figure, however, is modest compared with the still more striking figure of eighteen years, the average for bishops of the age. These figures are a warning that the frequent emphasis by historians on the short expectation of life in the middle ages is only valid with certain qualifications; but on the other hand we must remember that in both classes of appointment there were numerous intermissions of a year or even longer between a demise and the subsequent appointment.

The term of office of cathedral priors was notably shorter than that of abbots, as may be seen at a glance at the two large Canterbury houses. The priors lacked the cachet bestowed in the abbatial blessing, which grew liturgically till it resembled an episcopal consecration, and had not, like an abbot, security for life. They were vulnerable to domestic revolts and to episcopal acts of power, and resignations and depositions were not rare. In addition they were candidates ready to hand for abbeys in search of a superior; Winchester in particular lost several of its priors in this way. Finally, a popular prior was the obvious choice for the monks who formed the chapter of their cathedral and though several such choices were refused by the king or other interested parties, one would now and again get home.

Equally short, in some cases, was the term of office of a Cluniac prior. In some cases, this was because the abbot of Cluny, or some mediate superior, replaced the priors from time to time; it was also because the leading Cluniac houses, Bermondsey and Lewes in particular, were favourite recruiting grounds from which abbots were taken to Reading, Faversham, Evesham, Glastonbury and even further afield. The list for Bermondsey has a special interest, since it raises too in an extreme form the critical problem of how the house preserved its records. The relation between these lists and the documents is discussed on pp. 6 ff.; cf. pp. 114 ff.

We give here deliberately only a selection of some of the points which may be noted in the lists: our purpose is to offer them for others' use, not to anticipate what that use may be. Clearly the compilation of such lists provides many aperçus into social and religious history, and the most substantial ground for a survey of monastic recruitment in the period. It also reveals points of interest which may not be anticipated. Thus at first sight the Gilbertine Order gives only lists of names of men who can never (save the founder himself, St Gilbert of Sempringham) be more than names. But the repetition of the same names in different lists – including some of exceptional rarity – suggests that it was a common practice to move a prior from house to house after a few years (p. 200), and that this was done on a scale without parallel elsewhere.

4

The Cistercians, who did not spread widely over England until the fifth decade of the twelfth century, show generally no influx of overseas superiors after the first abbot of a colony from the continent. Here the chief interest of the lists is to reveal the progress of a successful abbot from house to house, or the frequency of elections of a stranger, often a sign that the abbey, or a visiting abbot, felt the need of new blood.

Among the Austin canons, the provenance of priors or abbots sometimes gives welcome evidence of the filiation of one house from another. It shows also, as we have seen with the black monks, that certain houses were more distinguished or fortunate than others. Thus the London priory of Aldgate had a succession of long-lived priors who were also theologians and chroniclers of note. Dunstable, Merton and St Osyth's (Essex) were equally distinguished, and a prior of the last-named became archbishop of Canterbury in 1123. The imagination lingers over the name of Andrew of St Victor, a celebrated biblical scholar of English birth, who had two spells of office at Wigmore, deep in rural Herefordshire. His presence is partly explained by the interest previously taken in Wigmore by the bishop of Hereford, Robert of Bethune, a distinguished teacher, but it is one more instance of the cultural unity of western Europe in this century.

II. *The materials*

At one time it was fashionable to argue about the relative merits of the chronicle and the charter as historical evidence: some scholars held up the charter to our admiration as an authentic, contemporary and objective witness; the chronicle as biassed, subjective, liable to every wind of human error. The contrast no longer seems so clear: the authenticity of the charter is a matter for investigation, not assertion; it often needs careful interpretation; contrariwise, it has always been recognised that chronicles and annals contain a mass of authentic information.[1] Every kind of evidence is grist to the historian's mill: none of it can be accepted without critical enquiry. The lists contained in this book are based mainly on the evidence of chronicles and annals and charters; with copious help from obituaries and calendars, and occasional help from mortuary rolls, saints' lives, biographies, inscriptions, and other evidence. No detailed study of the nature of each type of evidence can be attempted here; but a brief analysis of the problems of using chronicle, calendar and charter evidence is a necessary introduction to the lists themselves; and the pre-Conquest sections, though not a large part of the whole, raise peculiar problems and demand a special explanation, which will be given in section III.

---

[1] See especially the wise comments of C. R. Cheney, *The Records of Medieval England* (Cambridge, 1956). Reference for individual chronicles, and, in some cases, discussion of their value, are given at the head of the lists. For a general survey of monastic chronicles, see the forthcoming book by Mrs A. Gransden.

Monastic communities had long and tenacious memories. A fifteenth-century chronicle can retail entirely reliable information about eleventh-century abbots. Unfortunately, it can also, obviously enough, provide entirely unreliable evidence, and it can be a delicate matter to decide the status of many late entries. It is clear that there is a world of difference between the value of a contemporary entry in one of the eleventh-century versions of the *Anglo-Saxon Chronicle*, and the fifteenth-century annals of Bermondsey, which Rose Graham investigated in a well known article and rejected altogether as evidence.[1] To help distinguish the value of local chronicles a note is given, where appropriate, of the date (and sometimes the nature) of these at the head of the lists. Where appropriate, we also note useful discussions of chronicles of wider range in the bibliography. But in many cases judgement is more subtle and difficult than this, and the present book can be no substitute for a critical survey of monastic annals.

Miss Graham's strictures on the Bermondsey annals were primarily due to the hopeless discrepancies between their lists of priors of Bermondsey and other evidence, especially for the thirteenth century; and the inveterate habit of the scribe who compiled them of converting one prior into two or three. Further study has established the fact that they are more reliable for the eleventh and twelfth centuries than for the thirteenth and fourteenth. This is at first sight paradoxical; but a little reflection readily explains how this can happen, and there are indeed several analogies. The author of the annals (if he can be dignified by the word) made incompetent use of varied materials: he seems to have worked from a mixture of earlier annals and lists of priors. It seems likely that there was an early and good set of annals which provided less opportunity for error in the period down to *c.* 1200 than the later material. Even in the twelfth century there is a slight tendency to multiply priors, and we have relegated obvious duplicates to footnotes; we have also indicated clearly where dates or names depend wholly on the annals; but with the aid of other evidence and by making judicious use of the annals a reliable list for the period can be compiled.

We are on safer ground with the Evesham and the Gloucester chronicles. The Evesham chronicle as we have it was compiled by Thomas of Marlborough at the outset of the thirteenth century; but it has been shown that the section relating to the eminent Abbot Æthelwig in the mid-eleventh century is a notice written perhaps by Prior Dominic *c.* 1110 and incorporated in the later compilation. For Gloucester we have thirteenth and early fifteenth-century witnesses from which an excellent contemporary record of the late eleventh and twelfth centuries can be reconstructed with some confidence, although the reconstruction is complicated by the fact that the Gloucester chronicle bore some relation to

[1] See p. 114.

6

the spider's web of west country annals with its centre in John of Worcester's compilation.[1]

These chronicles and their satellites provide information locally preserved of local abbots. There is abundant evidence that it was normal for monastic houses to be well provided with records of this kind, even though later scribes might quite often misunderstand the evidence before them. There are occasional astonishing lapses. Thus St Albans, famous for its historical tradition in the late twelfth and thirteenth centuries, seems to have retained only the haziest memory of its pre-Conquest history,[2] a memory perhaps affected by loss of documents (a common difficulty, made worse in many cases for the modern scholar by the practice of filling the gaps by fabrication), perhaps too by controversy as to the situation of St Alban's relics. The converse of this is the case of a chronicler like William of Malmesbury, who was interested in many houses, and whose *Gesta Pontificum* contains a wealth of information which almost makes us claim him as a fellow-author of this book.

Even William offers difficulties. If the scribe at Bermondsey was careless, William, in a sense, was too scholarly. Armitage Robinson showed[3] that Hearne's edition of the *De Antiquitate* of Glastonbury represented an interpolated and confused version of what William wrote; and even when allowance has been made for this, that William had dated the pre-Conquest abbots, not in the main from annals, but by comparison of an earlier list of abbots with dated charters, often of doubtful authenticity. William's book represents a peak in historical research for its period; but his results are commonly of little critical value. Where the charters survive, however, they can be used directly; and it is possible to deduce the list of abbots with which he worked and compare it with an earlier surviving version, of the late tenth century.

Lists of abbots and priors are common; they provide valuable but treacherous evidence: treacherous, because they brought out the worst in careless scribes, because we often do not know how they were compiled, and because the chronological data can be ambiguous. The practice of keeping lists of kings and bishops, sometimes with notes of the length of their reigns, was ancient, and king-lists formed the most important chronological foundations for Bede's *Historia*.[4] Many surviving lists of monastic superiors were based on notes made from time to time as abbots came and went, and are as reliable as contemporary annals. Commonly, however, they were not kept up consistently, and gaps were left,

---

[1] See R. R. Darlington in *EHR*, XLVIII (1933), 1–10; *MO*, pp. 704–5 (Evesham); on Ch. Gloucester, see p. 52; also R. R. Darlington in *WMVW*, pp. xvff., on John of Worcester.

[2] See pp. 64 ff.

[3] J. A. Robinson (1921), chaps. I, II.

[4] See D. P. Kirby in *EHR*, LXXVIII (1963), 514–27, and references cited; W. Levison, 'Bede as Historian', in *Bede, his Life, Times and Writings*, ed. A. Hamilton Thompson (Oxford, 1935), pp. 111–51, esp. p. 130.

or were filled from memory or conjecture; or by injudicious use of the monastic calendars. Thus the fourteenth-century list of the abbots of Furness seems to have been drawn at conjecture from a calendar or obituary, and its early sections contain duplications, or abbots (maybe) of other houses, or abbots of Furness of other centuries. The order of abbots is of almost no authority, and can never be accepted without other evidence. The abbatial list for Fountains in the fifteenth-century 'President Book', however, contains precise information of the years, months and days of each abbacy, and it has been shown that in the large majority of cases they are precisely right;[1] though only if one appreciates that the list works on two eccentric principles: that a month is not a calendar month but a period of 28 days, and that each reign is calculated from the previous abbot's death, as if no vacancies occurred. This list implies a warning: the author was evidently a mathematician of some competence who took pains to make his data consistent. The scribes of many lists were content to copy entries written at different times and on different assumptions; and they normally failed to check if the numbers they quoted added up correctly. Furness and Fountains represent the extremes: every list has to be judged on its own merits – its date, source, relation to other evidence, and to any indication one can find of its authors' access to sound materials.

A useful supplement to the evidence of annals and lists is provided by entries in calendars and obituaries. Occasionally they give years as well as days of death; but for the most part they give (in their nature) only months and days; since liturgical books were more readily discarded than chronicles and charters, they had less chance of survival and are, comparatively speaking, rare; and bare names – especially for the late Saxon period or the early Norman when a handful of English or Scandinavian and French names made up the modest range of choice brought to the font – identification can be hazardous. But obits have one great advantage over entries of day and month of death in chronicles, and that is that they are less subject to the major vagaries of scribal error. Within a few days they can seldom be relied on to be precise: the lists in this book provide copious examples of obits recorded over the range of several days. The calendar, strictly speaking, recorded when a man was minded, not when he died; and liturgical convenience, space in the calendar, scribal care or the reverse dictated within limits where the name was placed. There are a few cases in which a bishop (for one reason or another) was commemorated at quite a different time of year from his death; but in these lists, out of very numerous cases in which we can check a calendar or the like against other evidence, there are only a handful of discrepancies of more than a few days, and these seem mostly due to scribal error – in the majority of cases in the chronicle. St Francis of Assisi died on

[1] See note on p. 132.

3 October 1226 – though towards midnight; but he was immediately, and universally, commemorated on 4 October. We can never assume, unless we have the most precise information (as in Francis's case) from other sources, that we know the exact day of a man's death; nor would medieval computations of midnight satisfy a modern chronologer. Nor again can we assume that entries in chronicles (where no scribal error has altered the month or changed 'ides' to 'nones') are more reliable than entries in calendars, since clearly the former were often based on the latter. The editors of this book have therefore felt that it was misleading to draw too sharp a distinction between evidence drawn from chronicles and obituaries, and have used the shorthand 'd.' = 'died', rather than some periphrasis, with calendar evidence;[1] this is one of many cases where the shorthand used in lists of this kind can itself mislead unless interpreted in the light of the type of evidence available.

For all its inequalities and the problems that it raises, the evidence of chronicles, annals, abbatial lists and other directly chronological materials provides the bone structure on which lists of this kind must be based. The most copious sources of names for these lists are charters, but between 1066 and 1200 charters are commonly undated, and twenty or thirty charters may not tell us as much as one soundly based annal. Episcopal charters were not commonly dated in the twelfth century; private charters seldom before the reign of Edward I, and not regularly until the time of Edward II. At the very end of our period royal writs and charters began to be regularly dated, and dated final concords first appeared and then became prolific. The early chancery rolls, early collections of fines, and the one bishop's 'register' – the roll of Hugh of Wells, bishop of Lincoln – to survive from our period, are a very fruitful source of precisely dated information for the closing decades. For the rest, the copious evidence of charters can only be used when the charters have been interpreted and dated.

These processes are full of hazards. Forgery was common in the twelfth century, and far from unknown in the centuries which followed.[2] Fortunately one may reasonably presume of the large majority of the charters used in this book that they are not in any ordinary sense forgeries. To use them for the present purpose, however, it is necessary also to assume, broadly speaking, that all the witnesses were alive when the transaction described took place; that a man will be called 'bone memorie' when he is dead; 'quondam' when he has resigned his office; that whether he be earl or abbot or archdeacon, a man will be given his title if he has one, but cannot be given it before it was inherited or

---

[1] The alternative is the practice of the new Le Neve, of using the word 'commemorated': this is unobjectionable, although it may suggest a degree of scepticism not justified by the evidence, and would add somewhat to the length of entries in lists of monastic superiors where such evidence is copious.

[2] For a general survey, with bibliography, *GF*, chap. VIII, see also Brooke in *Journal of the Society of Archivists*, III (1965–9), 377–86.

earned. On such assumptions one must work if charters are to be dated at all; but none of them is watertight. We rarely know what relation a twelfth-century charter bore to the transaction it described. It is a reasonable assumption that it was normally written very soon after, and when the symbolic act of a grant or the like took the form of laying a charter on the altar, the charter must already have been written. But there are cases, especially the monastic foundation charters studied by Professor Galbraith in a well known article, in which 'authentic' charters were drawn up years after the event, with many anachronisms.[1] We have almost no information as to how witness lists were compiled: thirteenth-century evidence shows that witnesses did not necessarily have to be present at any stage in the transaction;[2] the formulas used in the twelfth century and the precision with which the witnesses to particular stages in a transaction are sometimes noted, suggests the normal assumption of physical presence. Even so, there is plenty of room for error – scribal error in later copies, and even from time to time errors made by scribes in originals. Unfortunately, charters were often written after the event, and always written with the idea that they would be read by posterity; thus a living pope may be called 'beate memorie';[3] a royal clerk who collected patronage might frequently witness royal charters without any reference to his archdeaconry – while his neighbour, also an habitual absentee, could be regularly given his title. When a charter was drawn up later than the event it described, anachronisms could enter in, and a man might appear to have received a title some years before the accepted date. Finally, in the early twelfth century, surprising though it seems, it has been shown[4] that the title 'comes' was commonly left out even with men whose earldom was perfectly well recognized; and in Stephen's reign, when the use of the title was becoming more stable, its tenure was often in dispute.

It is a delicate matter to balance the probabilities in using these criteria. Some must be ignored: the pious aim of a charter can be expressed as 'pro salute anime' of a donor's family and overlords; or 'pro anima'; no doubt there was a tendency to use the latter formula for the dead, the former for the living. The exceptions were too numerous for this criterion ever to be used.[5] Similarly, the appearance or absence of 'comes' down to the death of Henry I gives no reliable guidance. On the other hand abuse of 'bone memorie' seems to have been rare; and it is sometimes possible to deduce whether a particular charter is likely or most unlikely to contain informalities or anachronisms of this kind.

---

[1] *Cambridge Historical Journal*, IV, iii (1934), 205–22, 296–8.

[2] See the well-known document quoted e.g. by J. C. Russell in *Speculum*, XV (1940), 492–3.

[3] Innocent II is 'beate memorie' in an original of *Regesta Regum Anglo-Normannorum*, II, no. 1687 (CCXLVIII). Cf. Brooke in *EHR*, LXXII (1957), 690 where a later date for the text is suggested; but see P. Chaplais in *EHR*, LXXV (1960), 266, who shows it to be the work of a chancery scribe. See, however, *Reg.* III, p. xiii and n.

[4] By Sir Charles Clay, *EYC*, VIII, pp. 46–7.   [5] See idem, *EYC*, IV, pp. xxvii–xxx.

A charter which names Peter of Blois but not his archdeaconry may safely be dated before he acquired it – when that happened is not so easily determined;[1] no such criterion works with William de Sainte-Mère-Eglise until he becomes a bishop. Problems abound; hopeless inconsistencies are, however, comparatively rare. There is a document naming Richard de Belmeis II, bishop of London, as dean of St Alcmund's Shrewsbury, but not as bishop, and on its date turn the dates of several Shropshire and Staffordshire dignitaries; it seems probable that he was already bishop when it was drawn up, and if so, it is in our experience a unique case of a bishop not carrying his order. Fortunately, such lapses are rare.[2]

Fortunately, too, much of the spade work has already been done. The work of many scholars, from Bishop Stubbs to Professor Cheney, makes the lists of bishops in the *Handbook of British Chronology* (2nd edn.) thoroughly reliable; the same work contains lists of earls and other magnates distilled from the *Complete Peerage*. The new Le Neve has now embarked on the period before 1300: the volumes for the London diocese and the monastic cathedrals have appeared, and close collaboration beyond the printed page has happily been possible. Many of our lists are obviously based on the work of other scholars.[3] We are surrounded by a cloud of witness in our study of twelfth-century chronology. This does not mean that we have abdicated responsibility: the date proposed for a charter in our lists has in every case been checked.[4] Many will be subsequently improved by other scholars; all are offered with the provisos implicit in this survey of the problems of twelfth-century chronology. None the less, the dating of charters is not a morass: so far as they go, with all allowance for error, we believe that most of our dates are tolerably reliable.

In this survey, many incidental sources of evidence, many sources of truth and error, have been omitted; they will speak for themselves as they appear in the lists. As a final instance of a document peculiarly reliable, if discreetly handled, yet occasionally most misleading, the Pipe Rolls have a special claim to be selected. The central contemporary records of the Exchequer, virtually complete from 1155,[5] carry many references to the revenues of vacant monastic houses which were tenants in chief; and these entries often specify the approxi-

---

[1] See J. A. Robinson (1921), pp. 113–14, corrected by E. Cohn in *EHR*, XLI (1926), 58f. In very numerous cases Peter witnesses charters of Archbishop Richard with William of Northolt, archdeacon of Gloucester. In all that we have seen they are always either both without title or both archdeacons. This confirms the date *c.* 1177 for Peter's promotion (for William, see *GF*, p. 284; Le Neve, revised edn., II, 107).

[2] See *Mon.*, VI, 263.

[3] See pp. viii–ix, 17 on Sir Charles Clay and others who have particularly helped us; the *EYC* has also provided extensive help in dating charters, both from its notes on documents and from its exceptionally helpful notes on lay barons and knights of the twelfth century.

[4] See pp. 18–19.

[5] The series of Pipe Rolls includes, of course, an isolated survivor from 1130. The sifting of the early Pipe Rolls was one of Z. N. Brooke's many contributions to the book.

mate length of the vacancy. They cannot be used as negative evidence: a vacant house could be administered without any direct reference in the Pipe Roll. But the positive evidence is exceedingly reliable. Yet even the Pipe Rolls lay traps for the historian. Some are well known. A debt may be recorded year after year, even after the debtor has died. Somewhere in the series 'sed mortuus est' may appear; but even this can be a scribe's error and if correct may first be noted some years after the event. Such traps rarely affect records of vacancies, but they may affect mentions of apparently living abbots and priors. The oddest error, noted independently by Professor Finberg and the late Professor Z. N. Brooke, is due neither to the normal conventions of the Exchequer nor to carelessness. About 1158 Walter, abbot of Tavistock, died; yet years later his name continued to appear on the Pipe Rolls, not only in relation to old trans-actions, but to new scutages, thought of long after his death. This may have originated in an error: it is clear that in the long run it became a standing joke among the Exchequer clerks – if an abbot of Tavistock was mentioned, he must be called 'Walter'.

Even Exchequer clerks were human; and even in sifting such apparently mechanical materials as make up these lists, the final lesson of diplomatic has always to be borne in mind: that all our documents were the products of human agency; they are subject to human error and to the human circumstances which produced them.

III. *Special problems of the period 940–1066*

We have started our lists in 940; and this has involved us in facing the special problems of pre-Conquest evidence. We would like, however, to say at the outset that this is also a field admirably prepared by a succession of scholars – and that without the foundations laid long ago by W. G. Searle, and more recently in such works as Professor Whitelock's *Anglo-Saxon Wills*, Miss Robert-son's *Anglo-Saxon Charters* and Miss Harmer's *Anglo-Saxon Writs*, this part of our enterprise would have been exceedingly hazardous and far more difficult.

The long lists of signatories to Anglo-Saxon diplomas give many names of abbots. In all but a handful the abbey is not named; in many cases the abbeys cannot be identified, or identified with anything approaching certainty; in numerous cases the authenticity of the diploma is questionable. Since a sub-stantial amount of vital information has to be taken from these documents, the entries for pre-Conquest abbots have both to be more elaborate and to use a different formula from the rest of our lists. Chronicle and other precise evi-dence is given as elsewhere; likely identifications in the charters follow, covered by a variety of phrases such as 'presumably', 'probably' and 'possibly'. We have tried to be generous in giving cross-references to other abbots with whom confusion is possible or easy; and unidentified abbots and abbesses are gathered in Appendix I – which does not, however, include abbots identified with any degree of probability in the main lists.

To state in every case where a charter is used the extent of our faith in it would be quite impractical; it is equally impossible, however, to cite the diplomas without any discrimination between them. We have therefore included in Appendix III a list of all the diplomas to which reference has been made. For a number of years one of us has kept a note-book with references to serious discussions of the authenticity of pre-Conquest charters; recently Professor P. H. Sawyer has put all students of such documents heavily in his debt by publishing his *Anglo-Saxon Charters: an annotated List and Bibliography*;[1] and by his kindness we were able to study the book in proof, and with its aid very much to simplify Appendix III. *Anglo-Saxon Charters* is the first step towards the full new edition of the collections by Kemble and Birch which is now under way. This will take many years; in the meantime Professor Sawyer's book has made it possible for us to check in a large majority of cases one or more of the best manuscripts of the charters we use, so that our lists are not dependent on Kemble's or Birch's texts; and also to be sure that we had made a tolerably full inspection of known charters not printed by either.[2]

It is now widely recognised that authenticity is not simply a matter of distinguishing genuine from forged, but of establishing the status of a particular text in a much wider and subtler range of possibilities. In the present state of knowledge, it would be impossible to describe the precise status as evidence of all the charters we have used: many have not been subjected to detailed analysis by experts, and for those which have there is a range of possibilities – from outright forgery, through interpolation or tendentious alteration, to innocent re-writing and careless copying – and a range of disagreement which would make any attempt at a sophisticated indication within our lists meaningless. It would be unduly sceptical, however, to claim on this account that there was no merit in constructing such lists: the cumulative effect of most of the information given here is tolerably reliable; and we hope that as an analysis and index of the material we have sifted, our lists may help in clearing the ground for the new edition and fuller analysis of the charters which is to come.

Our task is at once complicated and simplified by the fact that our concern is not primarily with the authenticity of the charters in the full sense, but with the reliability of their lists of *signa*. It is clearly true that we shall have most con-

[1] Royal Historical Society Guides and Handbooks, no. 8, 1968.

[2] We have referred throughout – save for documents in *AS Chts.*, *AS Wills* and *AS Writs* – to Kemble and Birch, since these remain the most accessible *corpora*; we note in Appendix III which texts have in fact been used. Where a reliable modern edition exists, this has of course been followed.

fidence in *signa* from an authentic original,[1] and that we shall always be uneasy about using *signa* from a document known to have been forged or rewritten. But it is clear that in many cases a forger used a genuine list of *signa*; and it is a theoretical possibility that the scribe of an original – who in pre-Conquest England invariably (so far as our information goes) wrote all the *signa* himself – could be more careless than a later forger copying the work of a better scribe. This means that every list must be considered on its merits; and since many of them are very long – and the chronological data for the bishops especially is relatively copious – we can reckon to have fair confidence in any list which cannot be proved to be chronologically inconsistent; and this has been our main criterion, although we have naturally placed more reliance on documents probably genuine than on those probably forged. Inconsistency can take two forms: the accumulation of names clearly not contemporary with one another, and the appearance of one or two signatories dead or not yet in office at the time when the bulk of the *signa* could reasonably have been gathered. The first case usually occurs in arrant forgeries, and they have been little used here – occasional reference is made to such lists, to establish that a particular name occurred among the materials available to eleventh and twelfth-century forgers, which doubtless included much genuine evidence not now surviving. In the more numerous cases where there are minor discrepancies in long lists of *signa*, it is clear that an early, genuine list of some sort must lie behind the document as we have it: no forger could or would have reconstructed such lists with so near an approximation to consistency, before the publication of Kemble's *Codex*, without in the main using earlier lists. On these lists we can rely in a general way; but not, of course, in detail when they can be shown to be faulty in detail. In such cases we put a query before the date in our lists.

Two qualifications, however, need to be emphasised. First, we have almost no information as to how lists of *signa* were compiled; but since *diplomata* could clearly be drawn up some time after the events they described, we need not be unduly surprised by the occasional occurrence in an apparently authentic list of a minor anachronism. This is, however, a hazard quite distinct from the practice of some medieval scribes of giving artistic verisimilitude to a list by adding a few names from other documents – which is the probable explanation of some of the minor inconsistencies, and perhaps of a few of the major.

The second relates to our criterion of consistency. Broadly speaking, this is based on the lists of bishops, who can usually be identified and dated with more precision than the abbots – though princes, ealdormen, earls and thegns can help; and we have of course made use of the abbots themselves wherever possible. But since abbots are very rarely, and bishops comparatively rarely,

---

[1] On the meaning of the word in this context, see Chaplais (1965), (1968). On the general problem of authenticity, see esp. *AS Writs*; Whitelock in *EHD*, I, 337ff.

given the titles of their abbeys and sees in authentic documents, the basis of evidence is somewhat less than might at first appear. We have to assume, too, that we know the dates of bishops: for this purpose, we have used the evidence cited in Searle's *Anglo-Saxon Bishops, Kings and Nobles*, revised by modern studies, where they exist – such as Armitage Robinson's *Saxon Bishops of Wells*, and the notes to *AS Chts.*, *Wills* and *Writs* – and corrected by our own observations. In due course these lists will be further revised, and this will affect our work; but we hope in the process our own lists may be of some use. The criterion of consistency is further weakened by the possibility of abbeys, and even bishoprics, having two heads at a time. There is no doubt that some abbeys had two abbots simultaneously, especially in those cases where a great monastic paladin like Leofric of Peterborough had accumulated offices under his hand: the evidence is discussed at length in our list for Bath, the best documented example. There are three cases in this period in which there is reason to suspect that a see had two bishops. A Bishop Wulfric of unidentified see occurs from 958 to 970.[1] He may have been an assistant to another bishop, or to an archbishop, like Siward of Abingdon, assistant (later called 'chorepiscopus') to the archbishop of Canterbury, 1044–8; his existence seems clearly proved and he has not been used to bring charters into question. The third example is the puzzling case of Bishop Brihtwine. This name occurs in the bishops' lists of both Sherborne (twice) and Wells in the early eleventh century, although there is hardly space in the Wells list for such a bishop. William of Malmesbury makes two bishops of Wells, Brihtwine and Æthelwine, play Cox and Box – each twice ejected, twice restored – in a manner which is hardly credible;[2] and Armitage Robinson suggested that Brihtwine of Wells was due to confusion between Brihtwine of Sherborne and Brihtwig of Wells. It seems clear that Sherborne had two bishops of the name: the first occ. 1018–22, the second 1031–45; the presence of the shadowy Brihtwine of Wells in the episcopal list of Wells and in William of Malmesbury may indicate a tradition that the bishop of Sherborne had acted as coadjutor in the neighbouring see. Whatever the explanation, Brihtwine's *signum* can neither be used to call a charter in question nor to lend precision to its date.

In preparing these lists we have wandered among the manuscripts to a fair degree; but not sufficiently, nor with sufficient philological knowledge, to have any independent or precise information to offer about the spelling of pre-Conquest abbots. We have followed the advice and the practice of recent experts in this field, and only occasionally have we thought it right to indicate early variants. Although variants are very numerous, the confusion they cause cannot be cleared up by mere lists, and it would be a very elaborate exercise to dis-

[1] See below, p. 230, n. 1.
[2] *WMGP*, p. 194; cf. Robinson (1918), pp. 68–9.

tinguish those which come from early texts and those due to the corruptions and changes of later centuries. We believe that for present, practical purposes the reasonably intelligible, normal spellings we use are best for the purpose; but it is essential for anyone using these lists for detailed research to be aware of the confusions that easily arise; in particular, that some names normally distinct – such as Æthelric and Ælric, Æthelwine and Ælfwine – may be treated by scribes as a single name, especially in late and poor texts.

IV. *The arrangement of the lists*

It should be emphasised at the outset that complete consistency in the layout of the entries in each list proved neither desirable nor possible. Within each list the abbots or priors are in chronological order, wherever this is known; within each entry the occurrences etc. are normally in chronological order. But there are many cases where the order is not precisely known; where the nature of the evidence or convenience of reference demands some grouping of items. Thus many houses have chronicles whose evidence is most conveniently summarised at the beginning of each entry; many have abbatial lists giving the numbers of years of an abbot's tenure: this can sometimes be explained only if evidence for accession and death or resignation are brought together, before the occurrences and other evidence.

Where possible, each list has the following items.

1. Name, county and dedication. The dedications are not the result of an elaborate investigation, but are mainly based on documentary evidence observed in the course of our work.[1] For Cistercians and dependencies we give also the names of the mother house; and in all cases, under or immediately after the name of the house, alternative names.[2]

2. Date of foundation, from *KH*:[3] where a community moved from one place to another, the moves are noted; in many cases the earlier places are found as the heads' titles in the texts; and it is no uncommon thing for a name to last after a move has taken place. A particularly confusing case is Kingswood (Cistercian), which began and ended a prolonged exodus at Kingswood, and was sometimes called by that name, sometimes by others, in the interim. Normally a later name (like Stoneleigh) cannot be anticipated; though an earlier

---

[1] Cistercian houses were all dedicated to the Blessed Virgin, so only those which had an additional dedication are noted, otherwise a blank means that we have not found solid or early evidence. We are much indebted to Dr Hadcock, and also to Miss Barbara SoRelle of Cornell University, for providing us with notes of a number of dedications.

[2] See below for houses which moved. These alternatives are vital for the identification of heads, and a variety of medieval forms are sometimes noted in the Index.

[3] Where we wished to give a different date from that in *KH*, 1st edn., we have given references; but see now, p. 20. We gladly acknowledge the help of Dr Hadcock, who has been at work *pari passu*, with MDK, in the preparation of *KH*, 2nd ed.

(like Stoneleigh's predecessor, Radmore) may linger for a time after the move.

3. A note of former lists.[1] In every case, we include a *VCH* list where one exists. The lists noted vary enormously in usefulness, ranging from those for many Yorkshire houses by Sir Charles Clay – or by Dr Greenway, in the revised Le Neve for Cathedral priories, or in a number of recent volumes of the *VCH* and elsewhere – to which we have rarely been able to make any significant addition, to those in some of the early *VCH* volumes, which are of no critical value. Apart from this, we only give lists where they have some critical value. Our debts are innumerable; we have, however, listed as many as we could in the Preface. In the following cases, collaboration has been so close that it seemed impossible not to give another author's initials at the head of the list – though for its present form and for its errors we are wholly responsible:

C.T.C. Sir Charles Clay (virtually all Yorkshire houses).

M.C. Dr Marjorie Chibnall (all Shropshire houses).

D.G. Dr Diana Greenway (all monastic cathedrals, except Bath and Coventry).

V.B. Mrs Vivien Brown (Eye Priory).

C.J.H. Dr Christopher Holdsworth (Rufford Abbey).

H.P.R.F. Prof. H. P. R. Finberg (Tavistock Abbey).

This paragraph also includes a note of important annals, lists of abbots and priors, and calendars etc., containing obits, for the house.

4. An entry for each head known, in chronological order wherever possible; interspersed with occasional notes on vacancies, or discussing special problems by the way (see especially Bermondsey, Cluniac). Each list ends, in principle, with the first death or resignation after 1216. Frequently, and in particular when no precise date can be attached to this, the first occurrence of the next head is noted; in some cases it is necessary to carry the list further to tidy up some problem of succession. Obit lists and undated charters produce many names which may really belong to a somewhat later epoch, but are noted to save confusion. No systematic attempt has been made to note all cases of 'ghost' heads – names in old lists for which no evidence can be found or which are due to confusion; but a number have been noted, especially where they can either be confidently dismissed or are likely to be based on evidence no longer available.

The entries for individual heads frequently consist solely of one or more occurrences; where there is fuller information, they may consist of the following.

---

[1] Lists by the seventeenth and eighteenth-century antiquaries are commonly not specifically mentioned – it would be a very laborious and expensive task to include every list made by Browne Willis or Blomefield or Nichols, or every list in the new *Monasticon*, and they are now almost valueless for critical purposes. But this means no disrespect for the generations of pioneers; our own work has taught us great respect for them – they have often wasted our time by making us search to no purpose; far more often they have anticipated what we found, or shown us what we might have missed.

17

i. Name and outside dates; and surnames when known.[1]

ii. Brief summary of previous history and family (if known).

iii. Date of election and blessing; also length of tenure (if specified by the sources). All independent evidence from sources in which any credence can be placed is included; though occasionally, for events richly documented, we give only a selection.

iv. Occurrences. Where a head's career is well documented, occurrences are only very selectively noted – to support a date of accession or death, to fill a gap, to help establish that a long tenure was indeed continuous; but never to give a comprehensive impression of the documentary evidence. No strictly consistent principles can be established in such cases, and it must frankly be admitted that over the years during which the lists have been compiled, some differences of practice have made unavoidable a certain degree of inconsistency in the book itself. We have tried to give what was useful, but not too burdensome. With pre-Conquest heads, we have the special difficulty that they normally appear without the name of their houses: the special arrangements of these parts of the lists are explained above, pp. 12–16; grouping of dates and references, normally avoided elsewhere, has seemed appropriate in this case. The use of an initial (before a date)[2] indicates that the head is identified by an initial only in that particular case; in all others, before or after such an initial, the full Christian name is given – though the surname can only be assumed to be in a source when this is specified.[3] Christian names are given in their modern form, where such exists, rationalised where it is safe to do so – Osbern and Osbert were identical names by *c.* 1100 and are given as Osbert; Ranulf and Ralph distinct, though frequently confused – and Randulf can do service for either.

The *dating* of undated documents has, needless to say, been one of the major problems in compiling this book. All the dates offered have been checked, and a majority represent our own calculations based on the dates of bishops, abbots, priors, earls, archdeacons and the like. In a fair number of cases reference is made to a modern edition of a charter or a cartulary whose editor has provided an adequate explanation for a date; in such cases we give no note. Where the date depends on the mention of a bishop,[4] a royal official or an earl,[5] readily checked in the *Handbook of British Chronology*, or an abbot or a prior, to be found elsewhere in this book, we give no note; where it is based on evidence provided by Sir Charles Clay in *York Fasti* or by Dr Greenway in the new

---

[1] For toponymics, we use 'of' before an English place-name, where readily identifiable in its modern form; 'de' before a continental name or the medieval form of an English name not clearly identifiable.   [2] An initial is occasionally used elsewhere simply to save space.

[3] When no source is specified for a surname, the first reference may be presumed to give it.

[4] For Archbishop Theobald's titles, see *GFL*, App. II, pp. 505–6, whose findings are assumed in this book.

[5] For the difficulty that earls can appear, at least in the early twelfth century, without the title, see above p. 10 and n. 4.

Le Neve, 1066–1300, I, *St Paul's London* (London, 1968), or II, *Monastic Cathedrals* (London, 1971), or (for sheriffs) in the *PRO List of Sheriffs*, or (for papal legates) in Tillmann, again, we give no note. In some cases editors have provided dates which seem plausible, but whose precise grounds we have not been able to check – in such cases we sometimes quote their date in *italics*. Originals can sometimes only be dated very approximately on palaeographical grounds, and in such cases 'pal.' is noted. In all other cases we have given the evidence for the date in notes. Our dates are not definitive – the book would never have been published had we attempted to make them so; but we have tried to ensure that any scholar using the book can readily check the dates. In all cases we use the modern convention of dating a year from 1 January.

' + ' attached to dates means in or after; '–' means in or before; ' × ' links the limiting dates of an undated charter or the like.

References in nearly all cases are given to all essential primary sources; those to secondary literature are much more selective (see p. viii). We have not attempted a ruthless consistency in referring, e.g. to cartularies or fines by page or number; but in all cases where ambiguity could arise, 'p.' or 'no.' is specified – and we have tried on the whole to give convenient reference in each case.

In a number of cases, the problem of *identification* is very difficult. Insoluble references are collected in Appendix II. Cases in which confusion is easy have sometimes been noted in the lists. Thus for 'De Insula' among the Gilbertines, see Haverholme; for 'Novus Locus' – Newark, Newhouse, Newstead – see especially Newark. A characteristic example is Kir(k)by – priors of 'Kirkby' have been identified by editors as of Kirby Bellars, Leics, which was founded in 1315, and of Kirkby, Lincs, which seems never to have existed (see references under Monks Kirby, Warws).

A number of houses have been excluded because we have found no evidence of priors before 1216; and whereas we have included any Benedictine house whose head claimed to be a 'prior', we have excluded all hospitals not themselves conventual. Thus Tunstall has a list starting in 1164 in *VCH Lincs*, II, 197; but the twelfth-century prior probably belongs to Haverholme (q.v.). Walter Rye (*Suffolk F.* (Rye), p. 7; cf. p. 25) described one Thomas as prior of St Peter, Dunwich; but this was an error for parson (*personam* in *Suffolk F.*, PRS LXX, no. 303).

Finally, the *order of lists* broadly follows *KH*; and to save difficulty for those who use the two books together, we have given the same (Ordnance Survey) forms for all but a handful of houses, and reckoned their prefixes as part of the alphabet – thus Great Malvern appears under G; but cross-references are given in such cases, to reduce such inconvenience as this may cause. In this book, however, it has seemed desirable for convenience of reference to eliminate some smaller pockets and to re-divide the Benedictines in a manner suited to the special circumstances of the period before 1216 and of the likely use of the book. Thus the Benedictine lists are in three sections: the independent houses – all but a handful great houses whose lists are fullest and likely to be most frequently used; their dependencies; and the alien priories. The aliens include dependencies of Fontevrault (male) and Tiron, but lesser Cluniac and Augustinian houses have all been included in the alphabetical sequence within those orders; and the nuns have been gathered into a single alphabet, which includes the double houses of Fontevrault, but not the Gilbertines. This treatment of the nuns has the incidental advantage of resolving the uncertain cases, in which we cannot be sure to which order a community belonged, in one or two cases because the nuns themselves seem to have been in doubt.

NOTE

The revision of *KH*, 2nd edn., and of this book were completed in close collaboration; this involved a number of changes in our headings, so that the principle enunciated in p. 16, n. 3 could not be consistently applied; some minor differences of statement or interpretation remain between our dates and those in *KH*. References to *KH* are to the 2nd edn.

THE HEADS OF RELIGIOUS HOUSES
ENGLAND AND WALES
940–1216

THE BENEDICTINE HOUSES:
INDEPENDENT HOUSES

ABBOTSBURY (Dorset), St Peter f. *c.* 1044
  List in *VCH Dorset*, II, 53.

Æsuuerdus Occ. 1075 (Wilkins, *Concilia*, I, 364; signatories to this document have been checked by Cambridge, St John's Coll., MS 236. Cf. Brooke in *Studia Gratiana*, XII (Bologna, 1967), pp. 56ff.).

1107–1139: abbey held by Roger, bp. Salisbury (*Red Book*, I, 211; cf. *JW*, p. 59).

Geoffrey 1140– M. of S. 'Floscello',[1] app. 1140 (Florence, II, 122 = *JW*, p. 59 and n.).

Roger Occ. (R.) 1129 × 50 (Voss, p. 175; see Quarr); ?1148 (*Ctl. Eynsham*, I, no. 114; cf. no. 115: see Luffield).

Geoffrey II Occ. 1166 (*Red Book*, I, 211).

1–8 July 1175 abbey vacant (Diceto, I, 401; *Gesta Hen. II*, I, 91–3).

?Ralph Occ. in late 12th cent. context in BM Cott. MS Claud. C. vi, f. 172 (167); possibly the Ralph who d. 21 May (see below).

Roger II Occ. 3 June 1201 (*Ped. Fin.*, II, pp. 78, 81).

Hugh Occ. 1204 × 5 (14th cent. note in *CPR*, *1313–17*, p. 299); early 13th cent. (*Reg. St Osmund*, I, p. 373).

Vacant, 15 July 1213: abbey ordered to send candidates for the king's choice (*Rot. Lit. Claus.*, I, 150).

The next recorded abb., Hugh II, occ. 1216 × 20 (*Ctl. Loders*, pp. 62–4: see Axmouth). An Abb. Ralph d. 21 May in Cambridge, Trinity Coll. MS O. 9. 25, f. 158v (?13th cent.), and BM Arundel MS 68, f. 28.

ABINGDON (Berks), St Mary ref. *c.* 954
  List in *VCH Berks*, II, 61; basis in Florence, MS Lambeth 42, cited by Thorpe in notes to his edn. (also in *AS*, I, 166–8); and in *Ch. Abingdon*; Ann. in BM Arundel MS 326, ff. 10–22 (only cited + 1066); bare list of little value in BM Harl. MS 209, f. 1v. Obits in CUL MS Kk. i. 22, ff. 1vff. (obit 1); Bodl. Digby MS 227 (obit 2).

St Æthelwold *c.* 954–963 Prev. m. Glastonbury; first abb. *c.* 954, res. 963 bp. Winchester, d. 984 (commemorated 8 Aug., obit). See also Thorney (*Ch. Abingdon*, I, 123–4, 348; *Vita*, ib. II, 257ff.; *PL*, CXXXVII, 88ff.). Occ. frequently 956–63 (Birch, nos. 919, 924 etc., 1101, 1120). *DNB*.

Osgar 963–984 M. Glastonbury and Abingdon, el. 963 (*Ch. Abingdon*, I, 124, 348; cf. *PL*, CXXXVII, 91; *WMGP*, p. 191); bl. 28 Dec. 963; d. 984 (Florence, I, 140n., 147n.), 24 May (obit 2). Presumably the abb. O. who occ. frequently 964–79 (*Ctl. Muchelney*, no. 3; Birch, nos. 1135, 1143; Kemble, nos. 621–2). *DNB*.

Eadwine 985–990 Son of Ælfhere ealdorman of Mercia (*Ch. Abingdon*, I, 357); bl. 985 (*ASC* C, the Abingdon version; also Florence, I, 147; E gives 984); d. 990 (*ASC* C;

---

[1] Not identified: the saint should be S. Floceau of Beaune (*Acta Sanctorum*, Sept., V, 478–81), but there was no abbey dedicated to him there.

[ABINGDON]

989, E, with other events of 990). An abb. E. occ. 987, 988, 990(x 1) (*Liber de Hyda*, pp. 231–6, 238–42; Kemble, nos. 663, 712).[1]

Wulfgar 990–1016 Succeeded 990 (*ASC* C, 989 E); d. 18 Sept. (obit 1, 2) 1016 (*ASC* C, E; 1017, Florence, I, 182n.: 28th year). Occ. 993, 997 and presumably the W. who occ. frequently 990 × 2 to 1014 (Kemble, nos. 684, 696; *AS Chts.*, no. 66; Kemble, no. 1309). Cf. *Ch. Abingdon*, I, 357–8, 433; *AS Wills*, p. 150; *AS Chts.*, p. 381.

Æthelsige 1016–1018 Acc. 1016 (*ASC* C, E); d. 1018 (*ASC* E). See *Ch. Abingdon*, I, 433–4: the Abingdon lists seem to have conflated Æ. and his successor into one man (Earle and Plummer, *ASC*, II, 202, however, suggests that *ASC* E has divided one into two; but this seems somewhat less likely). An Æ. occ. ?1018, 1019, ?1026 (Kemble, no. 728 and *OS Facs.*, II, Exeter 10; *EHD*, I, 553ff.; Kemble, no. 743) – but he was probably Ælfsige of St Benet of Hulme.

Æthelwine 1018–1030 See above.

Siward 1030–1044 M. of Glastonbury; succeeded 1030 (Florence, I, 185n.); occ. 1034; assistant to abp. Canterbury 1044, returned to Abingdon and d. 23 Oct. 1048 (*Ch. Abingdon*, I, 434–5, 443–4, 451–2; 461–2; *ASC* C; Florence, I, 185n., 199n.). See *AS Writs*, pp. 571–2. A Siward (Sigeward) occ. 1032; two in 1042 × 4; see Chertsey and cf. Thorney (Kemble, nos. 746, 769).

Æthelstan Prob. 1044–1047 M. and sacrist Abingdon; d. year before Siward (*Ch. Abingdon*, I, 452, 462; s.a. 1048, Florence, I, 199n., 201n.). An Abb. Æ. occ. 1044, 1045 (*OS Facs.*, II, Exeter 12; Kemble, nos. 776, 778, 781). Cf. Ramsey (and Ælfstan, Canterbury, St Augustine).

Spearhafoc *c.* 1047–1051 M. Bury (s.a. 1048, without name, Florence, I, 201n.); el. bp. London in 1051, but dep. before consecration (*Ch. Abingdon*, I, 463; Florence, I, 204 (s.a. 1050); for the date cf. *ASC* D; C, F, s.a. 1050). An Abb. Spearhafoc occ. ?1050 (Kemble, no. 793).[2] A noted craftsman: see Goscelin, *Hist. translationis S. Augustini* (*Acta Sanctorum*, Maii, VI, 438) – apparently occ. temp. Ælfstan abb. St Augustine's, Canterbury, i.e. –1045.

Rodulf 1051–1052 An elderly Norwegian bp., said to be related to Edward the Confessor, d. 'annis haud duobus integris transactis' (*Ch. Abingdon*, I, 463–4; Florence, I, 207n., s.a. 1052).

Ordric 1052–1066 M. Abingdon (1052, Florence, I, 207n.); d. 23 Jan. 1066 (23 Jan., obit 1; *c.* 22 Jan. 1066 in *Ch. Abingdon*, I, 464–82; II, 119, 281–2). An Abb. Ordric occ. 1050,[2] 1061, 1061 × 5 (Kemble, nos. 792, 810; *AS Chts.*, no. 117). See *AS Writs*, p. 569.

Ealdred 1066–1071 M. and provost ('exteriorum preposituram...agens') Abingdon; succ. 1066; deprived because of his part in the conspiracy of Bp. Æthelwine of Durham (and so presumably 1071; 1071, Florence, II, 9n.); d. in custody of Walkelin, bp. Winchester (*Ch. Abingdon*, I, 482, II, 282–3, 493; for the conspiracy cf. *ASC* D (s.a. 1072), E (1071)).

Adelelm (Ethelelm) 1071–1083 M. of Jumièges (*Ch. Abingdon*, II, 283; Florence, II, 9n.); occ. 1072, 1075 (Bishop and Chaplais, facing pl. xxix; Wilkins, I, 364); d. 10 Sept. 1083 (*Ch. Abingdon*, II, 11–12); cf. Ann., f. 20v; s.a. 1084 in *AS*, I, 168 (omitted in Florence, ed. Thorpe).

Reginald (Rainald) 1084–1097 M. of Jumièges, once chaplain of William I (*Ch. Abingdon*, II, 15; cf. *AS*, I, 168); app. by William I, 19 June 1084 (*Ch.*, II, 15–16); occ. 27 Jan. 1091 (*Reg.*, I, no. 315); d. 4 Feb. (obit 1) 1097 (*Ch.*, II, 42; Florence, II, 41n.; Ann., f. 20v).

[1] *WMGP*, p. 32, makes Ælfric, later bp. Ramsbury and abp. Canterbury, abb. Abingdon: this is probably a mistake for St Albans, q.v.

[2] Cf. Barlow (1963), pp. 154–5.

Abbey in the king's hands, 1097–1100 (*Ch. Abingdon* II, 42, 44; cf. Florence, II, 46n.).

Faricius **1100–1117** M. of Malmesbury; prev. citizen of Arezzo; physician (*Ch. Abingdon*, II, 44; *WMGP*, p. 192; Florence, II, 47n.; cf. Orderic, IV, 94; 1100 (?1101)–17, in Ann., f. 20v); app. by Henry I (*Ch. Abingdon*, II, 44); d. 23 Feb. 1117 (*ASC* E; *Ann. Oseney*, p. 17; 23 Feb. in his 17th year, *Ch. Abingdon*, II, 158; Florence, II, 70n., s.a. 1117; 23 Feb. also in obit 1, Mont-St-Michel obit, *HF*, XXIII, 577 – his house not specified).[1]

Abbey vacant 1117–1121: 4 years, *Ch. Abingdon*, II, 159, 161.

Vincent **1121–1130** M. of Jumièges (*Ch. Abingdon*, II, 161; Florence, II, 75n.; Ann., f. 20v); app. by Henry I (*Ch.*, II, 161–2, 1121; *Ann. Winchester*, p. 46; cf. *Reg.*, II, no. 1259). Occ. 1123; *c.* 1126 × 7 (ib. nos. 1391, 1477); d. 29 Mar. 1130 (Florence, II, 91n.; obit 1; *PR 31 Henry I*, p. 123; cf. *Ch. Abingdon*, II, 172: in his 10th year; 1130, Ann., f. 21. Cf. *Ch. Abingdon*, II, 315; prob. before 11 Apr.).

Ingulph **1130–1159** Pr. of Winchester (q.v.; *Ch. Abingdon*, II, 173; 1130, Ann., f. 21r; 1130, Florence, II, 92 = *JW*, p. 30; cf. *Reg.*, II, no. 1641); bl. by Roger bp. of Salisbury (Florence), dates as Ann., f. 21r. Occ. 8 Sept. 1131 (*Sarum Chts.*, p. 7; cf. Tillmann, p. 37); 1149 (*Reg.*, III, no. 455); 7 Apr. 1152 (Bodl. Lyell MS 15, ff. 13v–14v); d. 19 Sept. 1158 (*Ch. Abingdon*, II, 215: 4 Henry II, 29th year of abb., i.e. 1158; 19 Sept. also obit 1; 1159 in Ann., f. 21v; *Ann. Winchester*, p. 56).

Walkelin[2] **1159–1164** M. of Evesham (*Ch. Abingdon*, II, 215–16); el. or app. 1159, Ann., f. 21v; d. 10 Apr. (obit 1) 1164 (*Ann. Winchester*, p. 58; cf. *Ch. Abingdon*, II, 315; prob. before 11 Apr.).

Abb. vacant in the king's hand for half year in 1164–5 (*PR 11 Henry II*, p. 77). From 1165 to 1175 it was held *in commendam* (for 9½ years) by Godfrey, bp. St Asaph (*Ch. Abingdon*, II, 34). Vacant on 8 Aug. 1175 (Diceto, I, 401).

Roger **1175–1185** Pr. of Bermondsey (q.v.); el. 1175 ('Reginald', *Ann. Tewkesbury*, p. 51). Occ. 1175 (*Ch. Abingdon*, II, 236–7);[3] (R.) 1179 × 85 (*Ctl. Harrold*, pp. 55–6); held office 9½ years (*Ch. Abingdon*, II, 235); d. 30 Mar. (obit 1 – shortly before 11 Apr., *Ch. Abingdon*, II, 315; 1184 in Ann., f. 21v).

Abb. vacant for half year 1185 and half year 1186, i.e. *c.* Easter 1185 to *c.* Easter 1186: *PR 31 Henry II*, p.29; *32 Henry II*, pp. 116–17 – in custody of Thomas of Hurstbourne (cf. *Ch. Abingdon*, II, 237).

Alvred **1186–1189** Pr. of Rochester (q.v.; *Ch. Abingdon*, II, 244; 'Reading', *Ann. Chester*, p. 34, s.a. 1186); app. 1186 by Henry II (ib.; Gervase, I, 335); d. Sept. 1189 (*Ch. Abingdon*, II, 245). Dates 1186–9 in Ann., f. 21v.

Hugh **1189/90–c. 1221** M. Abingdon (*Ch. Abingdon*, II, 293); el. 1189/90 (ib., II, 245; Ann. ff. 21v–22); occ. 13 June 1197 (Westminster Abb., Domesday Ctl., ff. 378v–9); 17 June 1202 (*Ped. Fin.*, I, p. 118); *c.* Jan. 1209 (*Essex F.*, p. 43); (H.) *c.* Easter 1216 (Wendover in *MPCM*, II, 649); 10 July 1220 (Bodl. Lyell MS 15, ff. 16–17v). D. 14 July (obits 1, 2) 1221 (Ann., f. 22).

The el. of the next abb., Robert, received the royal assent on 29 July 1221 (*CPR, 1216–25*, p. 298).

ALCESTER (de Insula; Oversley) (Warws), St Mary, St Joseph, St Anne, and St John the Baptist f. 1140.[4]

---

[1] *Reg.* II, no. 825 (cf. n.) has 'Roger' abb. Abingdon occ. Aug. 1107. This is clearly an error.
[2] The Abb. William who occ. in *HMC 4th Rept*, p. 468, was abb. Eynsham – the charter is in *Oxford Chts.*, no. 60.
[3] Cht. of Henry II witnessed by the bp. elect of Norwich ('G.' for 'J.'), i.e. 24 Nov. × 14 Dec. 1175.
[4] Cf. D. Styles in *Trans. Birmingham Arch. Soc.*, LXIV (1941–2), 27–9, arguing for 1139; but 1140 is confirmed in *Reg.*, III, no. 16n.

[ALC   TER]

List in *VCH Warws* II, 60.

Robert 1140– Alleged to have been m. Worcester in spurious f. cht. dated 1140[1] (*Mon.,* IV, 175; cf. Styles, art. cit. (p. 25 n. 4), pp. 30ff.); occ. 1139 × 53 (*CChR,* V, 102); 1145 × 53 (*Ctl. Gloucester,* II, p. 111).

Hugh Prob. el. 1158 × 60; occ. 1158 × 61 (Saltman, pp. 233–5, nos. 1–2. No. 1 settles a dispute between Alcester and Worcester on the election of the abb., presumably referring to a time when such an el. was pending; no. 2 takes Abb. Hugh and the abbey into Archbp. Theobald's protection and confirms its possessions).

?Thomas Prob. 1153 × 84[2] (BM Harl. MS 3650, f. 21r–v).

H.[3] Occ. 1196 × 8 (ib. f. 77v); –1199, ?1198 × 9 (Cheney, *Inn. III,* no. 175).

O. Occ. +27 June 1200 (BM Add. Cht. 6109; cf. Cheney, *Inn. III,* no. 247).

Matthew 1216–1232 Prev. sacrist, el. 1216 (*Ann. Worcester,* p. 407, called Maurice);[4] royal assent to el. 1 Jan 1217 (*CPR 1216–25,* p. 18); occ. 17 or 20 Aug. 1220 (*Ctl. Winchcombe,* II, pp. 552–4); d. –8 Oct. 1232 (*CPR, 1225–32,* p. 505).

ATHELNEY (Soms) (St Saviour), St Peter, St Paul and St Ethelwin   ref. *c.* 960

List in *VCH Soms,* II, 102.

(Abb. 'Seignus' occ. 937 (*Ctl. Athelney,* no. 98); this is before the ref. and the name seems corrupt).

Æthelric Occ. 993 (Kemble, no. 684); he was probably the Æ. who occ. ?995, 25 July 997, just possibly the Ætheric who occ. ?early 11th cent.; just possibly, also, the same as Ælfric, below (and if so, he may be one of the Ælfrics who occ. in the 990s. *Mon.,* VI, 1443–6; *OS Facs.,* III, no. 35; N. R. Ker in *Powicke Studies,* p. 75; *AS Chts.,* p. 380). Cf. Malmesbury, St Albans (and Crowland, 'Ægelric').

Ælfric Occ. 1009 (*Ctl. Athelney,* no. 64 = Kemble, no. 1306); possibly at other dates, but he is difficult to distinguish from the homilist, abb. Eynsham; possibly the Æ. who occ. 1012, 1018 – but see below[5] (Kemble, no. 1307; *OS Facs.,* III, no. 39).

VCH, following J. Collinson, *History . . . of Somerset,* I (1791), 87, which cites a Reg. Athelney, gives here 'Alfward, Simon, Æthelweard' for which no other evidence can be found. The names may have come from a list in a lost medieval ctl. Cf. Appendix 1; Davis, no. 15.

Æthelwine Occ. 1024 × 32 (Kemble, no. 1324 = *Ctl. Athelney,* no. 57), and as 'Egelwius' *c. temp.* Cnut in Goscelin's *De miraculis S. Augustini* (*Acta Sanctorum, Maii,* VI, 397); presumably to be identified with the Æ. who occ. ?1012 (but see Evesham), ?1019, ?1022, 1023 to 1031 (Kemble, nos. 1307, 729, 734, 739, etc., 744; *OS Facs.,* II, Exeter 11).

?Wulfgeat: *see* Appendix 1.

Ralph Mauduit Occ. 1125 (*Ctl. Athelney,* no. 26).

Simon Crassus *c.* 1136–*c.* 1138 Occ. 1136 × 7[6] (*Ctl. Bath,* I, p. 59); sacrist of Abingdon, appointed by King Stephen, d. in third year of abbacy (*Ch. Abingdon,* II, 292; called abb. of 'Alignia' – presumably for 'Adelingia' or the like, i.e. of Athelney).

---

[1] Forged not much later, when the facts must have been known, but in the interest of Worcester pr., which wished to claim Alcester as a dependency.

[2] In a cht. of William Giffard confirmed by William earl of Warwick (1153–84) (ff. 21v–22). Dr J. Lally informs us that Giffard occ. 1161–76, but these are not exclusive dates.

[3] Presumably too late to be identified with Hugh; certainly so if Thomas is correctly placed.

[4] After an unsuccessful attempt to el. William, subpr. Worcester.

[5] Two Ælfrics occ. in Kemble, no. 714, but in Salter's ed. (*Ctl. Eynsham,* I, pp. 19–28) both are Ælfsiges.

[6] Dated '1135' 1 Bp. Robert (Mar. 1136 × Mar. 1137); prob. 1136 × 7, in spite of J. A. Robinson (1921), pp. 56ff., who argues that Ivo dean of Wells, who also witnesses, was not appointed till *c.* 1140.

Benedict I Occ. 1159 (*HMC Wells*, I, p. 27); *c.* 1155 × 64 (*Ctl. Beauchamp*, p. 57; cf. Montacute).

Roger I Occ. 8 Nov. 1186 (*Ctl. Buckland*, no. 11); 1174 × 91 (*HMC Wells*, I, 45).

Benedict II Occ. 1197[1] × 1205 (*HMC Wells*, I, 57); 1200 × 5 (*CDF*, no. 770); 1213 × 14 (*Ctl. Athelney*, no. 99); 25 Nov. 1220 (ib., no. 7); 1225 (ib., no. 84).

The next abb., Roger, then pr. of Athelney was el. 1227 – royal assent Apr., *CPR, 1225–32*, p. 123.

BARDNEY (Lincs), St Peter, St Paul and St Oswald f. –697; 1087 (dependent on Charroux); 1115 × 16 (independent abb.; cf. Cheney, *Inn. III*, no. 891).
 List in *VCH Lincs*, II, 103.

PRIORS

Ralph 1087–1115 M. Charroux, pr. Bardney, made abb. in 1115 (*Mon.*, I, 629 = *CChR*, IV, 235 = *Reg.* II, no. 1097; cf. Cheney, loc. cit.).

ABBOTS

Ralph 1115– See above.

Ivo 1134– M. of Bardney, app. by Henry I (*Reg.*, II, no. 1895: for date see eds.' note).

John of Ghent Occ. 14 Aug. 1147 (*PUE*, I, no. 40); 1145 × 50 (Saltman, p. 237, no. 40); 28 Feb. 1150 (*Mon.*, V, 420); recently dead in writ of 1155+ (BM Cott. MS Vesp. E. xx, f. 42v).

Walter de Howest For name see *Reg. Lincoln*, IV, no. 1200; occ. 22 Jan. 1155 (Lees, *Templars*, p. 242); 1 Feb. 1157; 15, 16, 18 Jan. 1159 (*PUE*, I, nos. 66, 76–8); Aug. 1162, 1163 (*DC*, nos. 172, 186); 25 July 1163 (Bodl. Dodsworth MS 76, f. 18).

Ralph of Stainfield Occ. 30 June × 6 July 1177 (BM Cott. MS Vesp. E. xx, f. 95); 8 Dec. 1178 (*PUE*, I, no. 155); 9 Dec. 1180 (*Lincs F.*, LRS XVII, p. 313); 8 May 1182 (*Ctl. Bridlington*, pp. 355–6, 434–5).

The abbey was vacant and in the king's hands for 1½ years, 1184–5 (*PR, 31 Henry II*, p. 117).

Robert Occ. 11 July 1192 (*EYC*, II, no. 1205); 1185 × 1200 (*EYC*, II, no. 1196).

Ralph de Rand –1214 Occ. 1203 × 6 (*Reg. Lincoln*, I, no. 216; cf. no. 218); 25 Nov. 1207 (*Lincs. F*, PRS, LXVII, no. 232); 3 Dec. 1208 (ib., no. 296); dep. 1213/14 by legate Nicholas (*Walt. Cov.*, II, 217; *Gir. Camb.*, IV, 92–3).

Peter of Lenton 1214– Pr. of Lenton; received temporalities 26 June 1214 (*Rot. Lit. Claus.*, I, 207b); cf. *Walt. Cov.*, II, 217; *Ann. Dunstable*, p. 40, s.a. 1213; *Ch. Ramsey*, p. 342 (not named); occ. in j.d. case+27 Apr. 1217 (PRO Anc. Deed, E 326/8548).

The next recorded abb., Matthew, occ. 4 March 1218 (BM Cott. MS Vesp. E. xx, ff. 33v–34).

BATH (Soms), St Peter ref. *c.* 963 as abb.; Cathedral pr. from 1090
 List in *VCH Soms*, II, 80.

ABBOTS

Note: Bath presents a peculiar problem, in that both in the 960s and 970s and in the period –1061–1084 there is evidence of two abbs. in office concurrently. In the latter case, it seems clear that Wulfwold, as a pluralist, had the title abb. Bath as well as abb. Chertsey, but that the title was also held by an abb. on the spot;[2] and this is paralleled in some of the abbeys held by the arch-pluralist Leofric of Peterborough in the 1050s and 1060s. It is possible that Ælfheah did not bear the title abb. till Æscwig's departure (and that the early references to an Abb. Ælfheah are to another Æ.). Ælfheah's *Vita* clearly treats him as the founder; but it is not contemporary (late 11th cent.), and may not be good evidence to establish the office he

---

[1] See Taunton.   [2] See p. 15; and P. Grierson in *Rev. Bénédictine*, LII (1940), 97f.

[BATH]

held.[1] It is even possible that there were for a time two houses in Bath. Perhaps the most likely solution is that in early days Æscwig was the active, Ælfheah the hermit or contemplative abb.

St Ælfheah *c.* 963–984 Prev. m. Deerhurst, became a recluse at Bath, where he gathered disciples and became abb. (Osbern's Vita in *Acta Sanctorum*, Apr., II, 629–30; also called abb. in *Mem. Dunstan*, pp. 116, 217, 312, cf. 61; Florence, I, 147; *WMAG*, p. 92, where he is said to have been m. and pr. Glastonbury). Bp. Winchester, 984–1005; abp. Canterbury, 1005–12. Prob. the Æ. who occ. ?968, 970, 972, 974, 982 (*AS Chts.*, no. 45, cf. p. 342; Birch, nos. 1257, 1268–9, 1282 (see p. 230), 1284, 1303–4; Kemble, no. 1278).

Æscwig *c.* 963–?*c.* 977 Occ. as abb. Bath 965, 970 (Birch, nos. 1164, 1257), and was presumably the Æ. who occ. 963, 964, 965, etc., 975+ (Birch, nos. 1120, 1124, 1143 (and *Ctl. Muchelney*, no. 3), 1169, etc., cf. 1135; Kemble, no. 1277). He may have been the Æ. who was bp. Dorchester *c.* 977–1002 (cf. *AS Chts.*, p. 342; *AS Wills*, p. 125); but there is no evidence for this identification except the coincidence of dates – and the fact that Æ. is not a common name – and the bp. is known to have been a m. of the Old Minster, Winchester (*LVH*, p. 23), refounded the year after Æ. first occ. as abb. Either there were two abbs. Æ. or the abb. and the bp. were different men.

Ælfhere (**Ælfuere**, etc.) Occ. 993, 997 (Kemble, nos. 684, 698), and was presumably the Æ. who occ. from 985 to 1005, 1007 (Kemble, nos. 648, 1283, etc., 714, 1301, 1303–4). An abb. of the same name occ. from 1018 to 1031 (see Appendix I), and some of the references may be to the abb. Bath; but it is hardly likely that one abb. covered the whole span from 980s to 1031.

Wulfwold held Bath and Chertsey in plurality, presumably from 1061 or before to his death in 1084 (see Chertsey; occ. abb. Bath 1061, Kemble no. 811 = *Ctl. Bath*, II, pp. 33–5, 65–6; cf. p. 37; also occ. in *AS Writs*, p. 580, and Exon DB, *DB*, IV, 171–3). See P. Grierson in *Rev. Bénédictine*, LII (1940), 97f., who shows that Ælfwig, Sæwold and prob. Ælfsige were also called abbs. during Wulfwold's rule.

Ælfwig Occ. 1061 × 5 (*AS Chts.*, no. 117); he may very likely be one of the two Æs. who occ. ?1033, 1035, ?1044, 1045, possibly the Æ. who occ. 1024 (see Westminster), and 1042, ?1062, ?1065 (Kemble, nos. 1318, 1322, 772, 778, 741, 762, 813 (spurious), 817; but the last two may refer to the abb. Evesham). See Appendix I.

Sæwold Occ. 4 May 1065, in or before 1066 and in undated manumissions (*HMC Wells*, I, 428–9; *Exon DB*, loc. cit.; Kemble, no. 1351). He res., went to Arras, and gave his books to St-Vaast: on him see Grierson, art. cit., pp. 96ff.

Ælfsige (**Ælsi**) –1075–1087 Occ. 1075 (Wilkins, I, 364, with Wulfwold 'Chertsey', and with W. in *Ctl. Bath*, I, p. 37); 1077 (Thorpe, p. 617); d. 1087 (Florence, II, 19–20). Also occ. in several manumissions in Kemble, no. 1351. Cf. *AS Writs*, p. 580; *AS Chts.*, p. 488.

The abbey was acquired by John de Villula, bp. Wells, in 1088, and converted into a Cathedral Priory (R. A. L. Smith, *Coll. Papers*, pp. 76ff.; *Eccl. Docts.*, p. 21).

PRIORS

John Occ. 1106 × 9 (Anselm, *Epp.*, ed. Schmitt, no. 450 (IV, 397–8)); 4 Apr. 1122 (*Ctl. Bath*, I, no. 54).

Benedict Occ. 1136 × 59[2] (*Ctl. Bath*, II, no. 273); 24 June 1151 (*Reg. St Osmund*, I, p. 269); n.d.[3] (*Ctl. Bath*, I, no. 75).

---

[1] In Lives of St Dunstan by Osbern, Eadmer and William of Malmesbury he is called abb. Bath in 984; but in the Life by Adelard he is just abb. (*Mem. Dunstan*, pp. 116, 217, 312, 61).

[2] Eustace and Martin archds. (Bath dioc.); cf. Robinson (1921), pp. 74–6.

[3] The dating clause attached in *Ctl. Bath* belongs to the previous document; it is evidently from a papal bull, and the dislocation is clear in the MS.

Peter Occ. 13 Dec. 1157 (*Ctl. Gloucester*, II, p. 106); 4 Nov. 1159 (*HMC Wells*, I, 27); 1162 × 6[1] (ib., I, 18–19); 1168 × 75 (Lambeth MS 1212, f. 41r–v).

Hugh Occ. 1174 × *c.* 1189[2] (*Ctl. Bath*, II, no. 42, pp. 11–12; cf. p. 9).

Master[3] Walter –1198 Prev. subpr. Hyde; d. at Wherwell 1198, buried at Bath 31 May (*Ann. Winchester*, p. 68). Occ. 1186 × 9 (*c.* 1189,[4] *HMC Wells*, I, 28); –1191 (*Ctl. Bath*, II, p. 90, no. 452); 1190[5] × 1 (*CDF*, no. 764); 1191 (Devizes, pp. 56–7); 1199 + (*Berkeley Chts.*, p. 35). Retired to Witham for a time *c.* 1190 (*MO*, p. 384; cf. *Ch. Witham*, p. 506, ed. Wilmart, p. 232).

Robert of Bath –1223 Occ. *c.* 1198 (*Ctl. Bath*, II, p. 7, no. 22); 1204 (*Rot. Chart.*, p. 136b; *Ctl. Bath*, II, no. 63); 1198 × 1205 (*Ctl. Bruton*, no. 183); 18 Mar. 1214 (?1215: *HMC Wells*, I, 480); 10 May 1223 (*Ctl. Bath*, II, p. 24, no. 115). El. abb. Glastonbury 1223 (*Ad. Dom.*, II, 478).

BATTLE (Sussex), St Martin (and Holy Trinity and St Mary)[6] f. 1067
List in *VCH Sussex*, II, 55 from *Ch. Battle*. Ann. in BM Cott. MS Nero D. ii, ff. 240v–241, printed *Ch. Battle*, pp. 183–4.

Robert Blanchard App. *c.* 1067 and drowned same year (*Ch. Battle*, p. 9).

Gausbert *c.* 1076–1095 M. of Marmoutier, app. *c.* 1076 (ib., pp. 9, 25); d. 27 July 1095 (ib., pp. 42–3) after *c.* 20 years. (For the years, cf. ib., pp. 41, 44, 183.)

Henry 1096–1102 M. of Bec, pr. of Christ Church, Canterbury (*Vita Herluini* in *Gilbert Crispin*, p. 103; *Ch. Battle*, p. 43); el. 11 June 1096 (*Ch. Battle*, p. 44; cf. p. 183); d. 18 June 1102 (ib., p. 47, cf. p. 183; BM Arundel MS 68, f. 195).

Abbey vacant 1102–7, cf. *Ch. Battle*, pp. 47–51. Geoffrey, m. Saint-Calais, *custos*; d. 16 May 1107.

Ralph 1107–1124 M. of Bec, m. and pr. of Caen, pr. of Rochester; el. 1 Aug. 1107 (*Ch. Battle*, pp. 51–2; *Vita Lanfranci*, iv, 10; *PL*, CL, 38); occ. –1108 (*Text. Roff.*, f. 198); d. 29 Sept. 1124, abb. 17 years 20 days, aged 84 (*Ch. Battle*, p. 59). For the years, cf. *Ch. Battle*, p. 183.

Warner 1125–1138 M. of Canterbury, el. *c.* 8 Mar.; enthroned Friday, 24 Apr. 1125 (*Ch. Battle*, pp. 60–1); res. Dec. 1138 (ib., pp. 64–5, cf. p. 183); or dep. (*JW*, p. 53); retired to Lewes Pr. in 14th year (*Ch. Battle*, pp. 64–5, 183); d. 23 Sept. (BM Cott. MS Nero C. ix, f. 12; Arundel MS 68, f. 224).

Walter de Lucy 1139–1171 M. of Lonlé, brother of Richard de Lucy, el. 8 Jan. 1139 (*Ch. Battle*, p. 65; cf. p. 183);[7] d. 21 June 1171 (*Ch. Battle*, p. 138: in 33rd year; cf. p. 183). Occ. 1154 × 5 (BM Cott. MS Tib. B. v, f. 88r–v).

1171–5 abbey in the king's hand (*PR 17 Henry II*, p. 130 – *21 Henry II*, p. 84). Still vacant 1–8 July 1175 (*Gesta Hen. II*, I, 91–3; Diceto, I, 401); cf. *Ch. Battle*, pp. 138–56.

Odo 1175–1200 Pr. Canterbury, el. 10 July 1175 (*Ch. Battle*, pp. 155–6, cf. pp. 145, 183; *Ann. Tewkesbury*, p. 51); d. 1200 (*Ch. Battle*, p. 184; *Ann. Winchester*, p. 73); 20 Jan. (*Epp. Cant.*, p. 557; BM Cott. MS Nero C. ix, f. 4; etc.); 21 Jan. in BM Cott. MS Vitell. C. xii, f. 116v. *DNB*.

John de Duvra (?Dover) 1200– El. 1 May 1200 (*Ch. Battle*, p. 184; *Ann. Winchester*, p. 73); occ. 1203 (*CRR*, II, p. 178); 1204 (*Sussex F.*, no. 102).

---

[1] Richard archd. Poitiers (for refs. to his career, see *GFL*, p. 539).
[2] Richard dean Wells (Robinson (1921), p. 65). [3] *Ch. Witham*, p. 506 (ed. Wilmart, p. 232).
[4] See Bradenstoke.
[5] Gilbert archd. Totnes (cf. Morey, p. 125). [6] Cf. *Ch. Battle*, p. 23.
[7] Richard of Hexham, p. 175, and John of Hexham, p. 299, have an abb. 'Adam' el. and bl., according to John by the legate, in the Council of Westminster of Dec. 1138 in which Warner was dep. (cf. *JW, loc. cit.*). Presumably the name is a slip; but it may well be that the preliminary discussion of the election took place in Dec. Cf. *Councils and Synods*, I (forthcoming).

[BATTLE]

Richard 1215–1235 M. of Battle, el. 1215 (Gervase, II, 109); royal assent 22 Jan. 1215 (*Rot. Lit. Pat.*, p. 126b); occ. 23 Mar. 1219 (*Devon F.*, no. 75); 18 May 1232 (*Kent F.*, p. 118); d. 1235 (*Ann. Tewkesbury*, p. 99).

BEDFORD (Beds), St Paul[1] f. –971; collegiate –1066

Thurcytel kinsman of Oscytel abp. York: occ. as abb. 971 (*ASC* B, C); later expelled (*Lib. El.*, p. 105): 971 × 96 – but it seems likely from the context that this is soon after 971, and this must be so if he was the same as the re-founder of Crowland, q.v. (which is almost certain, since he also is recorded to have been related to Oscytel). Presumably the Th. who occ. 968, 969, 970 (*Mon.*, II, 323–4; Birch, nos. 1230, 1266).

BIRKENHEAD (Ches), St Mary and St James f. *c.* 1150

List in Stewart-Brown, *Birkenhead Priory*, pp. 84–5.

Robert Occ. ?*c. 1190 × 1200* (Stewart-Brown, pp. 71–2; cf. *VCH Lancs*, v, 186n., 238n.); 1206+ (*Ctl. Whalley*, III, pp. 828–9, dated by Stewart-Brown, p. 85).

Ralph Occ. *c. 1200* (NRA, MS of Eric Barker Esq., of Worthing, no. 2).

Oliver Occ. temp. John (Stewart-Brown in *Cheshire Sheaf*, 1923, p. 61); *c.* 1216 (Stewart-Brown, p. 85).

BRADWELL (Bucks), St Mary f. ? –1136 (see below)

List in *VCH Bucks*, I, 351.

William ?–1136–1164 See Walden and Luffield where he was also pr. Pr. Bradwell before Walden, according to Ch. Walden ('susceperat'). D. 12 Dec. 1164.

Nigel Occ. –1184 (*Luffield Chts.*, I, no. 38; cf. no. 35).

Richard Occ. ? *c. 1200* (*Ctl. Dunstable*, no. 236, cf. p. 300); 12 Nov. 1201 (*Bucks F.*, p. 21).

John Occ. 12 × 25 Nov. 1218 (ib., p. 39); 3 × 24 June 1219 (ib., p. 39); 1219 (*Reg. Wells*, II, p. 48).

The next recorded pr., Richard, res. 1237 (*Reg. Grosseteste*, p. 344; cf. *Luffield Chts.*, I, no. 35).

BUCKFAST, *see under* Cistercian Houses.

BURTON (Staffs), St Mary and St Modwenna f. 1004 (so *Ann. Burton*, p. 183)

List in *VCH Staffs*, III, 213 (U. C. Hannam and M. S. Greenslade). Most of the following dates come from the 14th cent. annals of Burton and these contain some definite errors, and in the mid-late 12th cent. seem to run a year late; but were evidently based on sound information. There are some pieces of useful evidence in the generally unreliable 15th cent. annals in *Mon.*, III, 47–8.[2]

Wulfgeat ?1004–1026 Dates as *Ann. Burton*, pp. 183–4; 15th-cent. ann. calls him a m. Winchester, gives the same years, and makes him die after 22 years of office, on Thursday, 20 Apr. 1026, 10 Cnut (20 Apr. was a Wednesday (Thursday in 1027)). Occ. 1004, 1008, ?1012 (Kemble, no. 710; Aberystwyth, Nat. Lib. Wales, Peniarth MS 390, pp. 363–4, 366).

Brihtric I ?1027–1050 Dates as *Ann. Burton*, pp. 184–5; confirmed by 15th cent. ann. which calls him m. Winchester, gives him 24 years, and makes him die on Saturday, 20 Apr. 1050. 20 Apr. was a Friday; and cf. Wulfgeat. It is possible that B. I is a confusion in

---

[1] Professor Whitelock notes that it is not certain that St Paul's represents the early abbey. For a possible later reference, see *The Will of Æthelgifu*, ed. Whitelock (Roxburghe Club, 1968), p. 31.

[2] These commonly give the day of the week, month and year of death, but they often fail to fit the calendar (see below, and *GFL*, pp. 532, 537).

the *Ann.* for B. II, whom they omit; or he may just possibly be the B. who occ. ?1018, ?1019 (Kemble, nos. 728–9).

Leofric ?1051–1066 Also abb. Peterborough, q.v. and other houses: he d. 31 Oct. or 1 Nov. 1066 (15th cent. ann. say '13 Jan.'). *Ann. Burton*, p. 185, confirmed by the 15th cent. ann. make him abb. 1051–85 (the latter calls him m. Winchcombe; there seems no other evidence of this).

Brihtric II 1066/7–?1085 Previously abb. Malmesbury, q.v. Leofric's obit date in the annals may well belong to B.

Geoffrey de Mala Terra 1085–1094 M. Winchester; expelled in 1094 (15th-cent. ann.; *Ann.*). Dates as *Ann.*, p. 185.

Nigel 1094–1114 M. and sacrist Winchester; d. 3 May (*ASC* H; 2 May in 15th-cent. ann. calling it a Saturday, correct for 1114). Occ. 1111 + [1] (*Ctl. Burton*, p. 30). Dates as *Ann.*, pp. 185–6.

Geoffrey 1114–1150 Previous pr. Winchester, q.v. Dates as *Ann.*, p. 186; 1114 confirmed by *ASC* H, which gives his app. *c.* 14 Sept., and fits evidence that 1132 was in his 19th year (*Ctl. Burton*, p. 32, MS f. 38); occ. 1116 (ib., f. 39). Res. 1150; d. 1151 (*Ann.*, p. 186).

Robert 1150–1159 ?M. Winchester (15th-cent. ann.). Dep. and expelled in 1159 (dates as *Ann.*, pp. 186–7); restored 1176.

Bernard 1160–1174? Previously m. and pr. Gloucester, abb. Cerne (q.v.). *Ann.* gives 1160–75 (p. 187); Gregory of Caerwent (v. Gloucester: BM Cott. Vesp. A. v, f. 199 v) 1160–73; 15th-cent. ann. give his obit as Tuesday, 29 Jan. – which would fit 1174. On the whole, the *Ann.* seem to be running a year late. See *GFL*, pp. 76–9, 507–9, 531–2. Occ. 1166 (*Ctl. Burton*, p. 38).

Robert 1176 See above: restored 1176, d. 1177, according to *Ann.*, p. 187; but obit 17 Nov. (Friday, 15th-cent. ann., but this fits neither year,[2] though it would fit 1178) and his successor was el. *c.* 1 July 1177, so Robert presumably d. 1176.

Roger Malebranche 1177–1182 Prev. pr. Great Malvern, q.v. El. *c.* 1 July 1177 (*Gesta Hen. II*, I, 180; *Ann.*, p. 187, gives 1178; *Ann.* and 15th-cent. ann. give 1182 'Sunday', 6 May – which was Ascension Day). See *GFL*, p. 537. It is possible that 1182 and 1187 (below) are still a year late.

Richard 1182–1187 Prev. pr. Rochester, q.v. Dates as *Ann.*, pp. 187–8; occ. 1185 (*Ctl. Burton*, p. 15 = *Mon.*, III, 42). Obit Friday, 19 Apr. (15th-cent. ann.: impossible, except for 1185).

Nicholas 1187–1197 Prev. pr. Abingdon (*Ann.*; cf. *Ctl. Burton*, p. 53, MS, f. 59; *Ann. Chester*, p. 34, s.a. 1186). Dates as *Ann.*, pp. 188–94; obit 'Thursday' 13 Dec. (impossible).

William Melburne 1200–1213 M. Reading (15th-cent. ann.); *Ann.* p. 203 gives 1 Feb. 1200 ('venit'); *Ann. Waverley*, p. 273, gives 1213 for his death; 15th-cent. ann. gives Thursday, 25 July 1210 – but the day is correct for 1213. Occ. *c.* 30 Nov. 1203 (*Ctl. Athelney*, no. 197); 24 × 31 May 1204 (*Derbys F.* (1885), p. 203).

Stephen Pr. Winchester cathedral, el. –25 Jan. 1214 (see Winchester).

Roger 1214–1216 A Norman m., pr. Sherborne, el. 1214 (*Walt. Cov.*, II, 216; *Ann.*, p. 224); death as *Ann.*; 15th-cent. ann. gives Monday, 14 Sept. (impossible).

BURY ST EDMUNDS (Suffolk), St Edmund f. 1020

List in *VCH Suffolk*, II, 72; basis in ann. etc. in *UGQ*, pp. 97–155 (Ann. 1 = *Mem. Bury*, II, 1ff.); *Mon.*, III, 155f. (Ann. 2); *Mem. Bury*, III, 1ff. (Ch. Bury); *Mem. Bury*, I, 353ff. (insertions in MS of Florence, Bodl. 297).

---

[1] Richard abb. S. Pierre-sur-Dives, + 1111 (*GC*, XI, 732).

[2] In *GFL*, p. 537, it is stated that 17 Nov. was a Friday in 1176: it was actually a Wednesday.

[BURY ST EDMUNDS]

Ufi 1020–1044 Prev. pr. St Benet's Hulme (*Ctl. Hulme*, I, p. 35; cf. *Mon.*, III, 135; *AS Writs*, p. 576). Dates as Ann. 2; 1020–41 in Oxenedes, pp. 430–1; Ann. 1.

Leofstan 1044–1065 Prev. m. Hulme and Bury, probably dean Bury: occ. 1043/4 (*AS Wills*, p. 82, cf. p. 196; *AS Chts.*, no. 97). App. 1044 (Ann. 2; Oxenedes, p. 431; Ann. 1); d. 15 July 1065 (*Mem. Bury*, I, 344, Ann. 1; *Mon.* III, 155 gives 1 Aug.). Prob. the L. who occ. 1048 (Aberystwyth, Nat. Lib. Wales, Peniarth MS 390, p. 368); possibly one of the abbs. L. in a spurious cht. dated 1062 (Kemble, no. 813); cf. St Albans. On him cf. *AS Writs*, p. 566; *WMGP*, p. 156; Douglas, *Bury*, p. lxi, n. 5.

Baldwin 1065–1097/8 Born at Chartres, m. St-Denis, King Edward's physician, pr. of Leberaw (Germany) and 'pr.' Deerhurst[1] (q.v.), abb. 32 years, 5 months (*UGQ*, pp. 129, 244–5 and n.; *Mem. Bury*, I, 56; *WMGP*, p. 156). Dates as Ann. 2; *ASC* E, s.a. 1098, but d. during Christmas festival, and obit is given as 29 Dec. 1097 by Florence, II, 41[2] and Ann. 2 (1 Jan.: *Mem. Bury*, III, 4). Occ. in spurious chts. dated 28 Dec. 1065 (Kemble, nos. 824–5); also 1072, 1075, etc. (Bishop and Chaplais, facing pl. xxix; Wilkins, I, 364). *DNB*.

Robert I 1100–1102 Son of Hugh, earl of Chester; m. St-Évroult, app. or intruded 1100; dep. 1102, at Council of London (+29 Sept.) (*Mem. Bury*, I, 353, 355; Ann. 1, pp. 130–1; Ann. 2; cf. Eadmer, p. 142); on his intrusion see Anselm, *Epp.* 266ff. (cf. *Epp.* 251–2).

Robert II 1102–1107 Pr. Westminster, el. 1102 (*Mem. Bury*, III, 5; Ann. 1, p. 131 – abb. 4 years; Ann. 2). Bl. by St Anselm 15 Aug. 1107 (Eadmer, p. 188; cf. *Mem. Bury*, I, 355); d. Monday, 16 Sept. 1107 (*Mem. Bury*, I, 356; Ann. 2; cf. *ASC* E; Florence, II, 57).

Alebold of Jerusalem 1114–1119 M. Bec (*ASC* H; Eadmer, p. 226, cf. p. 205); pr. S. Nicaise, Meulan (Ann. 1, p. 131; abb. just over 4 years); el. 16 Aug., bl. 1 Nov. 1114 (*ASC* H; Eadmer, p. 226; 1115 in *Mem. Bury*, I, 356, III, 5; Ann. 2). D. 1 Mar. 1119 (*Mem. Bury*, I, 356; Ann. 2; cf. *Mem. Bury*, III, 5; Orderic, IV, 429; 1118 in Ann. Thorney, BM Cott. MS Nero C. vii, f. 81v).

Anselm 1121–1138, 1138–1148 Nephew of St Anselm, m. of Chiusi, abb. S. Saba, Rome; legate to England 1115–19; see account of him by R. W. Southern in *Med. and Renaissance Studies*, IV, 190ff., esp. refs. on pp. 191 n. 1, 199–200; *Letters of Osbert of Clare*, pp. 192ff. (as legate, cf. Tillmann, pp. 24–5). El. 1121; el. bp. London 1138, but soon returned and restored to Bury; d. 3 Jan. 1148 (*Mem. Bury*, III, 5; Ann. 2 – 28 years; cf. Ann. 1, p. 131 – 26 years; for 1138, Diceto, I, 250, 252). Occ. 1123 (*ASC* E).

Ording 1138, 1148–1156 M. and cellarer Bury (Douglas, *Bury*, p. 109, cf. 115); pr. Bury, el. 1138; expelled when Anselm returned; restored 1148, d. 4 Feb. 1156 (see above; *Mem. Bury*, III, 5–6; Ann. 1, p. 133; Ann. 2 – 9 years). The restoration took place –16 Apr. 1148 (*Reg.*, III, no. 760).

Hugh I 1157–1180 Pr. Westminster, el. 1157 (*Mem. Bury*, III, 6–24 years; Ann. 1, p. 133, s.a. 1156; Ann. 2); bl. 1157 (Gervase, I, 163); d. 14 or 15 Nov. 1180 (Jocelin Brak., p. 7;[3] Ann. 2; cf. Ann. 1, p. 135; Florence, II, 155; *Ann. Tewkesbury*, p. 52. Cf. also *PR 27 Henry II*, p. 93: *c.* 6 weeks between Michaelmas and abb.'s death).

The abb. vacant 2 years 3 months (Ann. 2).

Samson of Tottington 1182–1211 Subpr. Bury, el. and confirmed 28 Feb., installed 21 Mar. 1182 (Jocelin Brak., pp. 23, etc.; *Mem. Bury*, III, 7; Ann. 1, p. 135 – 30 years

---

[1] For his grant of Deerhurst, see *Reg.* I, no. 26; *AS Writs*, p. 293.
[2] The better MSS of Florence apparently give the date as a Tuesday, which would fit 29 Dec. 1097.
[3] On the morrow of St Bricius, whose feast was celebrated on 13 Nov. at Bury (F. Wormald, *Eng. Kalendars before 1100*, p. 250); 15 Nov. in Ann. 2; BM Cott. MS Nero C. ix, f. 15v.

less 2 months; Ann. 2 – 30 years). D. 30 Dec. 1211 (*Mem. Bury*, III, 9; Ann. 1, p. 150, d. 6th day of Christmas; Ann. 2; *Epp. Cant.*, p. 561; BM Cott. MS Nero C. ix, f. 18v; etc.; 28 Dec. in BM Add. MS 29, 436, f. 44). On him see Jocelin Brak., *passim*; *Kalendar of Abb. Samson*, ed. R. H. C. Davis.

Hugh of Northwold 1213–1229 M. Bury, el. 7 Aug. 1213; bl. 1215 after confirmation by judges-delegate on 11 Mar. (*Mem. Bury*, II, 33, etc.; III, 9–11; Gervase, II, 109; Ann. 2); res. 1229, bp. Ely (*Mem. Bury*, III, 26, Ann. 2); el. –3 Feb., consec. 10 June 1229; d. 6 Aug. 1254. Benefactor of Cambridge University (M. B. Hackett, *The Original Statutes of Cambridge University* (Cambridge, 1970), pp. 38–9).

CANTERBURY, CHRIST CHURCH CATHEDRAL PRIORY (Holy Trinity) f. 997

D.G. Lists in Le Neve, new ed., II, 8–12 (D. Greenway); *VCH Kent*, II, 119–20, from Searle (1902), pp. 155–6. Obits in BM Cott. MS Nero C. ix, ff. 3–18v (obit 1); BM Arundel MS 68, ff. 12–52v (obit 2); Lambeth MS 20, ff. 157–248v (a copy of obit 2, so not cited here). Also a fragment of an obituary in BM Cott. MS Claud. C. vi, ff. 171–2 (obit 3).

(DEANS, PRIORS)

Æthelnoth –1020 Abp. Canterbury 1020–38 (see *ASC* D, E, s.a. 1020; E, s.a. 1038; cf. *DNB* (Ethelnoth); *AS Writs*, p. 554; Searle (1902), p. 155).

Godric Occ. 1023, 1045×7, 1044×8, 1052×70 (?1054) (*AS*, II, 145; *AS Chts.* nos. 101, 103, 116). D. 8 July (obit 2, f. 33v).

The following also occ. in obits: Agelwinus, 27 July (obit 2, f. 36); Alfricus, 11 July (obit 2, f. 34); Ælfwine (Alfwinus) 12 Dec. (obit 1, f. 21v; obit 2, f. 51); Kynsige (Kynsinus) 23 Nov. (obit 1, f. 21).

Henry *c.* 1074–1096 M. Bec and Christ Church, later abb. Battle ('Vita Herluini', Robinson (1911), p. 103; *Ch. Battle*, pp. 43–4; Orderic, ed. Chibnall, II, 192; Eadmer, p. 219). For the date of his appointment, see Anselm, *Ep.* 58, and Southern, *St Anselm*, p. 269n.; suggesting *c.* 1076; Dr Helen Clover in *La Normandie Bénédictine* (Lille, 1967), pp. 437–8, suggests an earlier date: her reconstruction would point to 1074×5. For Henry's el. to Battle, *Ch. Battle*, pp. 43–4, and see Battle.

Ernulf *c.* 1096–1107 M. Beauvais (S.-Simphorien, Ivo, *Ep.* 78; S.-Lucien, *WMGP*, pp. 137–8);[1] then m. Christ Church (Eadmer, p. 219); res. 1107 to be abb. Peterborough (q.v., cf. Eadmer, *HN*, p. 197; *Ann. Winchester*, p. 42); bp. Rochester 1114–24.

Priory still vacant 30 June 1108 (Eadmer, *HN*, pp. 196–7).

Conrad 1108/9–1126 M. Christ Church (and sacrist, Oxenedes, p. 294), succeeded before Anselm's death on 21 Apr. 1109 (Eadmer, p. 219); occ. 1108×9 (*Ctl. St Gregory, Canterbury*, no. 2). Res. 1126 to be abb. St Benet's Hulme (q.v.); this is confirmed by the long obit (obit 2, ff. 16v–17; cf. obit 3).

Pr. Theodoric who seems to occ. *c.* 1120×2 (*Anc. Chts.*, no. 9) must be an error; perhaps a confusion with the monk Thidiricus (Anselm, *Epp.* 334, 379).

Geoffrey *c.* 1126–1128 Res. 1128 'petente David rege' to be abb. Dunfermline (Florence, II, 90 = *JW*, p. 28; cf. *Reg. Reg. Scot.*, I, no. 8). Occ. 1126×8 (*Text. Roff.*, ff. 179v–80).

Elmer –1137 Occ. prob. 4 May 1130 (Gervase, I, 96; cf. *Letters of Osbert of Clare*, pp. 208–9). D. 11 May 1137 (Gervase, I, 100; day in obit 2, f. 27; 16 May in BM Cott. MS Vitell. C. xii, f. 129v). His letters were printed in Herbert Losinga, *Epp.*, ed. R. Anstruther (Caxton Soc., 1846).

Jeremiah 1137–*c.* 1143 M. Christ Church, el. 1137 (Gervase, I, 97, 100); dep. in or about

---

[1] On the whole, Ivo of Chartres seems more likely to be right, and William of Malmesbury could easily have substituted the older and more famous S.-Lucien for S.-Simphorien.

[CANTERBURY, CHRIST CHURCH CATHEDRAL PRIORY]

1143; reinstated but soon after res. and retired to become a m. St Augustine's (Gervase, I, 126–7; cf. Saltman, p. 58).

Walter Durdent *c.* 1143–1149 Occ. 1 Sept. 1143 (Saltman, pp. 447–9, no. 222); res. 1149 to be bp. Chester-Coventry (consec. 2 Oct.) (see Gervase, I, 141); d. 7 Dec. 1159.

Walter (Parvus) de Meri, Moyri 1149–1152/3 Chapl. of Abp. Theobald and m. of Christ Church, app. 1149 (Gervase, I, 141; cf. Saltman, p. 215; occ. as chapl. ib., nos. 146, 164–5 – 'de Moyri' etc.; 'de Meri', as pr., in *PUE*, I, no. 58). Dep. 1152 × 3 by Abp. Theobald (Gervase, I, 145–6; *JS Epp.*, I, no. 1 and nn. after imprisonment: see *JS* loc. cit. n. for possibility that he was dep. 1154; Saltman, pp. 59–61, and Le Neve give evidence for 1152). D. ?7 Jan. or 6 Feb. (obit 1, ff. 3, 5; obit 2, ff. 12v, 15v – prob. the former: see below).

Wibert 1152/3–1167 Subpr. of Christ Church (Gervase, I, 48, 146); occ. as m. 1146 (Saltman, pp. 537–8); as subpr. 1148, 1152; as subpr. acting pr. 1152,–1153 (Urry, pp. 391–4); app. pr. 1152 × 3 (Gervase, loc. cit.: see above) or 1154 (*JS* loc. cit. n.); occ. as pr. 28 Mar. 1155 (Saltman, pp. 535–6). D. 27 Sept. 1167 (Gervase, I, 205; cf. obit 2, f. 43; etc.).

Odo 1167/8–1175 Prev. subpr. (*MB Epp.*, 27; cf. no. 366). App. or el. during Becket's exile: el. presumably + 16 May 1168 (*MB Epp.* 412); prob. – Nov. 1169, but not recognised by Becket (ib., no. 502). (For the storm this caused, see *MB Epp.*, 351, 412, etc.; for chronology see *JS Epp.*, II, forthcoming.) Occ. 1173 (Diceto, I, 369). Res. 1175 to be abb. Battle (q.v.; Gervase, I, 256; *Ch. Battle*, pp. 148–60; Diceto, I, 403).

Benedict 1175–1177 M. Christ Church and chancellor of Abp. Richard (Gervase, I, 256); res. 29 May 1177 as el. to be abb. Peterborough (*Gesta Henrici II*, I, 166; Gervase, I, 262). Occ. 1177 (Urry, pp. 405–6).

Herlewin 1177–1179 M. Christ Church, chapl. of Abp. Richard; el. 1177 (Gervase, I, 263); res. 6 Aug. 1179 (ib., p. 293 – but see below); d. 9 May at Rome (obit 2, f. 26v). Occ. (H.) ?1177, ?27 Aug. 1179 (Urry, pp. 409–11).

Master Alan 1179–1186 M. Christ Church; English by origin but prev. canon of Benevento; el. 6 Aug. 1179 (Gervase, I, 293); res. ?May 1186 to be abb. Tewkesbury (q.v.; ib., p. 335; *Ann. Waverley*, p. 244; *Ann. Tewkesbury*, pp. 53–4, s.a. 1187); d. 1201.

Honorius 1186–1188 M. and cellarer Christ Church, el. 13 July 1186 (Gervase, I, 336); d. 21 Oct. 1188 at Velletri, and was buried in the Lateran cloister (ib., p. 429; for the day, see obit 1, f. 14 (at Rome), obit 2, f. 46; obit 3; *Epp. Cant.*, p. 561 – this makes him die in Lateran, buried at chapter house door).

Roger Norreis 1189, 6 Oct.–30 Nov. Prev. cellarer; imposed on community by Archbp. Baldwin; removed the same year and made abb. Evesham (*Ch. Evesham*, pp. 102–3; Gervase, I, 460, 481; see Evesham).

Osbert of Bristol 1191 M. Christ Church, el. 18 Feb. 1191 (Gervase, I, 484; cf. *Gesta Henrici II*, II, 142 for his name); expelled 10 May 1191 (ibid.; Gervase, I, 495).

Geoffrey 1191–1213 Subpr. Christ Church; el. 10 May 1191 (Gervase, I, 496); occ. 1 July 1191 (*PUE*, II, no. 263); (G.) 28 Jan. 1195 (*CDF*, no. 141); 25 Nov. 1204 (*Kent F.*, p. 36); 17 May 1205 (Cheney, *Inn. III*, no. 626); d. abroad 15 June 1213 (Gervase, II, 108; cf. obit 2, f. 31 – 'Eltho' (?)).

Walter 1213–1222 El. 1213 (Gervase, II, 108; cf. Le Neve); d. 1222 (ib., p. 112), 6 Feb. (or 7 Jan.: obit 1, ff. 3, 5; obit 2, ff. 12v, 15v; cf. Walter de Meri, above). Occ. 1216 (Cheney, *Inn. III*, no. 1174).

CANTERBURY (Kent), St Augustine (St Peter and St Paul and St Augustine) f. 598 × 605 (Monastic life may have subsisted throughout the 9th and 10th cents.)

List in *VCH Kent*, II, 132. Basis in Thorne (T) and Elmham's *Chronologia* (E) (14th–15th cent.); 13th-cent. list (names only) in BM Cott. MS Julius D. ii, f. 2 v. Obits in BM Cott. MS Vitell. C. xii.

?Eadhelm ?942–951/2 E, pp. 20–1, has Sigeric 942–55 (perhaps by confusion with Sigeric II below); T, pp. 1778–9, makes Ælfric abb. 942–71; Eadhelm is not in the list. But an Eadelm abb. St Augustine's occ. in a will of 942 × 58 (*AS Chts.*, no. 32), and it seems likely that he is to be identified with the E. who occ. 949, 951 (Birch, nos. 880, 890; cf. Hart (1966), pp. 155–6); and was killed by the men of Thetford in or before 952 (*ASC* D; Florence, I, 135)[1]—or possibly with the bp. Selsey, –963–979 × 80.

Ælfric ?955–971 E, p. 21; T, as above. An Æ. signs frequently from 958 × 9, 959 to 970 (Birch, nos. 1030, 1045–6, etc., 1257, 1266, 1268–9); also later; but see Glastonbury, Malmesbury, St Albans.

Æthelnoth 971–980 So T, pp. 1779–80; E, pp. 21–2 (Elfnothus in list).

Sigeric (Siric) ?980–?985 T, p. 1780, gives 980–8, and makes him first bp. Winchester, then abp. Canterbury: E, pp. 22–3, gives 980–8 and makes him bp. Ramsbury. He was in fact bp. Ramsbury 985–90, abp. 990–4, and had previously been a m. Glastonbury (*WMAG*, p. 92). T may imply that he remained abb. until his translation to the archbishopric. Presumably the S. who occ. 980, etc., to 985 (Kemble, nos. 624, etc., 648, 1283), but possibly also the S. who occ. 975 (Birch, no. 1315).

Wulfric I ?985–1006 990–1006 in T, pp. 1780–1, 989–1006, in E, p. 23; see above. Occ. 993, 997 and presumably the W. who occ. 25 July 997, 1002, 1004, 1005 (Kemble, nos. 684, 698; *OS Facs.*, III, no. 35; Kemble, nos. 707, 1297, 710, 714). D. 9 Oct. (obit; Feltoe, *Three Canterbury Kalendars*, p. 26).

Ælfmaer 1006–1023 × 7 1006–22 in T, pp. 1781–2 (but '1017' on p. 1783), E, pp. 23–4. Bp. Sherborne: T, pp. 1782–3; E, p. 24; *WMGP*, p. 628 (marginale in one MS); but his dates are very uncertain. Searle makes him die in 1023, but this is doubtful: see p. 15 on the problem of the bps. Brihtwine. Æ.'s successor as bp. first occ. 1031 (Kemble, no. 744). For his dates as abb. see *AS Chts.*, p. 410; cf. *AS Writs*, p. 548. Presumably the Æ. who occ. 1011, 1016 × 20, 1018, ?1022, 1023 (*ASC* C, D, E; *AS Chts.*, no. 77, cf. no. 75; *OS Facs.*, III, no. 39; Kemble, no. 734; *AS Chts.*, no. 82); and see Tavistock. Prob. a m. Old Minster, Winchester (*LVH*, p. 27). On him see Goscelin, *Hist. translationis S. Augustini, Acta Sanctorum, Maii*, VI, 428. D. 6 Apr. (obit); 5 Apr. (Feltoe, *Three Canterbury Kalendars*, p. 14).

Ælfstan 1023 × 7–1045/6 Prev. pr., abb. 1022–47 in T, pp. 1782–3 ('1017', see above), 1784, E, pp. 24–6. But see above; from *ASC* E his death may be dated 5 July 1046 (s.a. 1044), and it may be deduced that he had res. in the previous year (s.a. 1043) because of infirmity (he fell ill 4 years before his d. according to Goscelin (see below), p. 429). He occ. 1027, 1030 (T, p. 1783), and is presumably the Æ. who occ. ?1032, 1035, etc., 1044, 1045 (*AS Chts.*, no. 86; *OS Facs.*, III, no. 42; Kemble, nos. 774, 776: +22 Apr. 1045; his signature in the spurious no. 779 of 1 Aug. 1045 is doubtful). Cf. *AS Chts.*, pp. 420, 437; *AS Writs*, p. 550; Goscelin, *Miracula* and *Hist. translationis S. Augustini* in *Acta Sanctorum, Maii*, VI, 402–3, 429 (cf. also Æthelstan, Abingdon, Ramsey).

Wulfric II 1045–1061 Bl. 26 Dec. 1045, d. 18 Apr. 1061 (*ASC* E, s.a. 1043, 1061; 18 Apr. also in BM Cott. MS Nero C. ix, f. 10; 16 Apr. in Feltoe, *Three Canterbury Kalendars*, p. 14; *ASC* D gives 19 Mar. Goscelin, *ut sup.*, pp. 429–30, gives Tuesday after Easter, i.e. 17 Apr. in 1061). 1047–59 in T, pp. 1784–5; E, pp. 26–7. Occ. 1049 (*ASC* E s.a. 1046). Cf. Goscelin, loc. cit., and cf. Ely.

Æthelsige 1061–?1067 M. St Swithun, Winchester; bl. 26 May 1061 (*ASC* E), presumably

---

[1] A curious incident, and it is difficult to understand, as Professor Whitelock has pointed out to us, why the event is recorded only in D and why the abb. of St Augustine's should be at Thetford, unless on a royal mission.

[CANTERBURY]

the Æ. who occ. 1061 × 5, and the 'Ælfsie' who occ. 1066 (*AS Chts.*, no. 117; Kemble, no. 897). T, pp. 1785–7, gives dates 1059–67 (?), and says he fled to Denmark (he may have been sent: see H. Thurston, *Month*, CIV (July–Dec., 1904), pp. 1–15). He was abb. Ramsey 1080–7, q.v., E, p. 28 also gives 1059, but puts his res. ('fugit') under 1070, the year of Scotland's app. – perhaps rightly. Cf. Goscelin, *ut sup.*, p. 430.

Scotland (Scollandus) 1070–1087 M. Mont-S.-Michel (Orderic, ed. Chibnall, II, 248); dates as T, pp. 1787–92, cf. E, pp. 28–9. D. 9 Sept. (obit; Feltoe, *Three Canterbury Kalendars*, p. 24; BM Cott. MS Nero C. ix, f. 11v; 3 Sept. 1087 in E, pp. 29, 344; T, p. 1792). Occ. 1075 (Wilkins, I, 364; see p. 23).

Guy (Wido) 1087–1093 M. St Augustine's, el. 1087 (E, p. 346); 1087 × 8 (18 Lanfranc: *Acta Lanfranci*, p. 290): dates 1087–91, T, pp. 1793–4; 1087–99, E, pp. 29–30. D. 1093 (Florence, II, 31), 9 Aug. (obit –?10 Aug.; 9 in Feltoe, *Three Canterbury Kalendars*, p. 22; BM Arundel MS 68, f. 37v). Occ. 27 Jan. 1091 (*Reg.*, I, no. 315).

Hugh de Flori (?Fleury) –1126 M. Bec, not prev. in orders (Eadmer, p. 188); ex-knight, novice at St Augustine's, related to William II, according to T, pp. 1794–5. Dates 1099–1124 in T, and E (pp. 30–2) – clearly wrong. Bl. by Anselm 27 Feb. 1108 (Eadmer, p. 190; cf. Gervase, II, 376; E, p. 30 alleges he was bl. by Maurice, bp. London);[1] d. 1126 (Florence, II, 85 = *JW*, p. 23 and n.; 1124, T, p. 1798; E, p. 32), 29 Mar.[2] (BM Arundel MS 68, f. 22v); 24 Apr. (T). For his name (E, T) see also *Reg.*, III, no. 152.

Hugh of Trottiscliffe[3] 1126–1151 M. Rochester; dates as T, pp. 1798–1810/11; E, pp. 32, 35. Bl. 12 June 1127 (Florence, II, 88 = *JW*, p. 25; cf. Gervase, II, 381; 1128 in T); d. 1151 (Gervase, I, 147; Ann. Dover, BM Cott. MS Julius D. v, f. 24), 25 June (T) or 26 June (Feltoe, *Three Canterbury Kalendars*, p. 18; BM Arundel MS 68, f. 32). Occ. 8 Sept. 1131 (*Sarum Chts.*, pp. 6–7).

Silvester 1151–1161 Pr. St Augustine's, el. 1151 (T, p. 1811; E, p. 35; Gervase, I, 147; JS *HP*, ed. Chibnall, p. 86); bl. by Abp. Theobald, after dispute, on 28 Aug. 1152 (T, pp. 1813–14; cf. Gervase, loc. cit., II, 385); made profession to Theobald 1157 (Gervase, I, 163–5); d. 1161 (T, p. 1815; E, p. 35), 10 Aug. (obit; Feltoe, *Three Canterbury Kalendars*, p. 22; 13 August, in T).

Clarembald 1163–1173 Prev. pr. Montacute (q.v.) and Thetford (St Mary, q.v.). Intruded 1163 (Gervase, I, 173; cf. Diceto, I, 308); dep. 1173 (Diceto, I, 354; cf. Gervase, I, 256; T, pp. 1817–19; E, pp. 35–7 – 1163–76). D. 18 Mar. (obit).

Vacant 1173–5 (for 1–8 July 1175, *Gesta Henrici II*, I, 91–3; Diceto, I, 401; cf. *PR 21 Henry II*, p. 221 for vacancy and el. in 1175).

Roger[4] 1175–1213 M. Christ Church, Canterbury (Diceto, I, 428–9); el. 1175 (see above; Gervase, I, 256); occ. as abb.-elect 1177 (Urry, pp. 405–6); bl. by pope 28 Jan. 1179 (Diceto, I, 428–9). Occ. 1180 (*Reg. Rochester*, p. 178); 8 Mar. 1182 (Lambeth MS 1212, f. 68r–v); from 19 Oct. 1197 to 15 June 1208 (*Kent F.*, pp. 8–46 *passim*). D. 1213 (Ann. Southwark – Merton, BM Cott. MS Faust. A. viii, f. 139; dates 1176/9–1212 in E, pp. 37–41; cf. T, pp. 1819–64), 21 Oct. (obit; BM Cott. MS Nero C. ix, f. 14; 20 Oct. E, T; 22 Oct. ('R.'), BM Arundel MS 155, f. 6v).

Master Alexander 1213–1220 M. St Augustine's; bl. by pope (T, pp. 1864–71, with dates 1212–20; so also E, p. 41. *Ann. Dunstable*, p. 41 gives el. abb. 1213, but without naming

---

[1] 3 id. May=Sunday after Ascension (T), which is correct for 1100.
[2] Struck with paralysis on Passion Sunday=28 Mar. 1126, *JW*, p. 23n.
[3] For the name see E, p. 32; T, p. 1798; this unusual place-name is in Kent, and *JW*, p. 25 says that he came from the diocese of Rochester.
[4] Called 'Lurdingden' in E, p. 37.

him). Occ. 27 Jan. 1219 (*Kent F.*, p. 62). D. 1220 (E, T), 4 Oct. (ibid.; Feltoe, *Three Canterbury Kalendars*, p. 26).

His successor, Hugh III, was el. Aug. 1220 (T, p. 1873 gives 24 Aug.; E, p. 41, 26 Aug.).

CANWELL (Staffs), St Giles (*Bk of Seals*, no. 52) f. –1148
List in *VCH Staffs*, III, 216 (A. Saltman).

William   Occ. 12 April 1148 (JL 9236 = *Mon.*, IV, 106).

Denis   Occ. mid 12th cent. (*SHC*, III, 189; also *SHC*, 1939, pp. 182ff.).

H.   Occ ?*c.* 1209 (?1200 × 8: *Ctl. Oseney*, V, pp. 96–8 = *SHC*, XVII, 248–50; cf. Cheney, *Inn. III*, no. 1158); +1209 (*Mon.*, IV, 112; cf. Cheney, *Inn. III*, no. 846, for date). Possibly the Hugh of very uncertain date of *SHC*, XVII, 242, 251.

CERNE (Dorset), St Peter and St Ethelwold f. –987
List in *VCH Dorset*, II, 57.

VCH gives Ælfric the homilist as first abb.; but all that we really know is that he was m. of Winchester and sent 'to take charge of the teaching' at Cerne on its foundation, and remained there till he became abb. Eynsham in 1005: Whitelock, *EHD*, I, 849f.; Knowles, *MO*, pp. 61–2; cf. Ælfric's *Homilies*, ed. B. Thorpe, I (London, 1844), pp. 2–3. On the other hand, it is not impossible that he was abb. Cerne. Two Ælfrics occ. in Kemble, no. 712 (990 (× 1)), but were possibly the abbs. of Malmesbury and St Albans.[1] For Æ. see Eynsham.

Leofsuna   Occ. 1012 (*AS Chts.*, no. 74, cf. pp. 392–4).

Edward   Occ. 1075 (Wilkins, I, 364; cf. p. 23).

William   Occ. 1093 × 8, ?1095 (*Mon.*, III, 546).

Hamo   –1102 Dep., before he was bl., for simony at Council of Westminster, +29 Sept. 1102 (Eadmer, p. 142; *WMGP*, p. 119).

William Scotus   1114–1144/5 M. of Caen, app. early 1114 (*ASC* H, s.a.); occ. 1121 (*Mon.*, VI, 21); 1123 (*Reg.*, II, no. 1391); dep. 1144 × 5 (*GFL*, p. 507, and refs. for this *cause célèbre*). Called William 'de Luscel'' (?Loucelles near Caen; cf. Loyd, p. 55) in a case of 1219 (*CRR*, VIII, p. 20; refers to temp. Henry I or II). Cf. *GFL*, pp. 531–2.

Master Bernard   1145–1148 Pr. of Gloucester, app. 1145 by legate (*GFL*, no. 53); res. and retired to Gloucester (*GFL*, p. 509); abb. Burton 1160–74 (or 1175: see Burton). See *GFL*, p. 532.

William Scotus   *c.* 1148–*c.* 1158 Reinstated 1148(?), d. *c.* 1158 (*GFL*, p. 532; see below). The letters of Gilbert Foliot (esp. no. 51) show that William returned to Cerne in 1145–6; whether he was ever formally reinstated is not clear, but his supporters had made the abb. untenable for Bernard by 1148, and Bernard's withdrawal presumably left William in possession of the field. ?D. 28 Jan. (Mont-S.-Michel obit, *HF*, XXIII, 576).

Robert of St Pancras   1158– M. Mont-S.-Michel, el. 1158 (Torigny, p. 198); occ. 1166 (*Red Book*, I, 212). Presumably the abb. Robert commemorated under 23 Aug. in obit Mont-S.-Michel (*HF*, XXIII, 579).

Roger   Occ. as (?) former abb. 13 Jan. 1206 (*Rot. Chart.*, p. 163b).

Denis   –1219/20 Occ. 1204 × 5 (*Ped. Fin.*, II, p. 94); 1206 (*Rot. Lit. Pat.*, p. 64b); 1216 × 20 (*Ctl. Loders*, pp. 62–4: see Axmouth); 1208 × 9 (*PR 11 John*, p. 101). Res. shortly before 12 Feb. 1220 (*CPR*, *1216–25*, p. 228). See note in *HMC Middleton*, p. 52 (W. H. Stevenson).

LVD, 1st edn., p. 137 notes an Abb. Guy (?), perhaps late 12th cent. This may be an error for William.

---

[1] *Mon.*, II, 623 and Hutchins, *Hist. Dorset*, IV (3rd edn., 1870), 22, give Ælfric Puttoc in 1023 (when he became abp. of York), but without reference. This is probably due to confusion with the homilist.

CHERTSEY (Surrey), St Peter   ref. –964
Lists in *Ctl. Chertsey*, II, pp. ix ff. (C. A. F. Meekings); *VCH Surrey*, II, 63. Obits in Bodl. MS Lat. Liturg. e. 6, ff. 4–8 (obit).

Ordbriht   964–?988/9 App. 964 (*ASC* A); very likely to be identified with the O. who was bp. Selsey 988/9–1009 (Earle and Plummer, II, 158; cf. *AS Writs*, pp. 568–9); and with O. abb. who occ. 964, 966, etc., 987, 988 (*Ctl. Muchelney*, no. 3; Birch, nos. 1143, 1175–6,[1] 1189–90, etc.; Kemble, nos. 657, 663–5). Possibly the O. who had been m. Glastonbury and Abingdon under Ethelwold (*Ch. Abingdon*, II, 258). (The name is not common.)

Lyfing, al. Ælfstan, Æthelstan (cf. *ASC* D, s.a. 1019; Florence, I, 166 and n.)   ?c. 989–999 Occ. 997 (Kemble, no. 698); 995×9 (*AS Wills*, p. 44); prob. the L. who occ. 993 (Lifinc (f)ont'?), 998 (Kemble, nos. 684, 700); prob. the L. who was bp. Wells 999–1013, abp. Canterbury 1013–20 (cf. *AS Wills*, p. 150; J. A. Robinson (1918), p. 50).

?Wulfsige   The unidentified W. who occ. 1042, 1043, 1045 (Kemble, nos. 762, 767, 777–8) is so identified in a late 11th-cent. copy of the spurious *AS Chts.*, no. 85 (cf. p. 418). But in Kemble, no. 778, Wulfsige and Siward both subscribe.

?Siward   An Abb. S. occ. 1042×4, 1045 (Kemble, nos. 769,[2] 776, 778); 1045×7 (*AS Chts.*, no. 101) and became bp. Rochester in 1058 (d. 1075) (*ASC* D, E, F): he has been identified as abb. Chertsey (*Ann. Waverley*, p. 187n. – the editor's note; no reference given). Cf. Abingdon.

Wulfwold   ?1058–1084: also abb. Bath. Cf. *Ctl. Chertsey*, II, p. ix; *AS Writs*, p. 580; P. Grierson in *Rev. Bénédictine*, LII (1940), 97–8. D. 19 April 1084 (*ASC* E; cf. Grierson, p. 98n.; *Ann. Winchester*, p. 34). Occ. ?1062 (Kemble, no. 812); 1072 (Bishop and Chaplais, facing pl. xxix); 1075 (Wilkins, I, 364; see p. 23) and in spurious chts. dated 1044, 1055 (Kemble, nos. 771, 801 – but W. om. in Kemble's text of the latter; see BM Cott. MS Vesp. B. xxiv, ff. 70v–1); presumably the W. who occ. 1061 (Kemble, no. 810).

Odo   *c.* 1084–1092 Res. 1092 (*Ann. Winchester*, p. 34; cf. below). Occ. 27 Jan. 1091 (*Reg.* I, no. 315).

(Ranulf Flambard occupied the abbey, 1092–1100: *Ann. Winchester*, p. 37; cf. p. 40.)

Odo   was restored 1100 (ibid., p. 40); occ. 3 Sept. 1101 (*Reg.*, II, nos. 544, 548).

Hugh   1107–1128 M. of Winchester, el. 1107 (*Ann. Winchester*, p. 42); d. 20 (obit) or 22 July 1128 (Florence, II, 90 = *JW*, p. 29 and n.; cf. *PR 31 Henry I*, p. 140, which shows vacancy in 1128–9, but not later).

William   1129– El. 1129 (see above); occ. –1133 (*Reg.*, II, nos. 1768, 1817, 1818). D. ?29 Dec. (BM Add. MS 29,436, f. 44).

(William of St Helen, m. of Abingdon, app. by Stephen, removed by the pope at instance of Bp. Henry of Winchester (*Ch. Abingdon*, II, 291–2).)

Hugh   *c.* 1149–1163 Illegitimate son of Count Theobald IV of Blois, and nephew of King Stephen; m. Tiron, abb. St Benet's Hulme, el. 1148×9 (Torigny, pp. 218–19, cf. *Ctl. Hulme*, II, pp. 194–5;[3] cf. *Reg.*, III, no. 169). Occ. 16 Feb. 1150 (*PUE*, I, no. 46); –1152 (*Reg.*, III, no. 170). Res. abb. of Lagny-sur-Marne, 1163 (Torigny, pp. 218–19).

Aimar   *c.* 1163–1183 Occ. (A.) 1166 (*Red Bk.*, I, 198); 18 Feb. 1176 (*PUE*, I, no. 137); res. early 1183 (*PR 29 Henry II*, p. 18, cf. 85).
Abbey vacant for half a year in 1183 (ib., p. 18).

Bertram   *c.* 1183–*c.* 1197 Pr. St Faith, Horsham (occ. 1182: see Horsham); occ. 1×6 Dec. 1187 (BM Harl. MS 391, ff. 88v–9); 18 Nov. 1188, 7 Dec. 1194 (*Ctl. Chertsey*, I, pp. 116–

---

[1] But in the original of Birch, no. 1176 (Sawyer, no. 738) – *BM Facs.*, III, no. 27 – Ordbriht's title *abbas* is erased and he is at the head of the *duces*.
[2] Two sign Kemble, no. 769: presumably one was abb. Abingdon (q.v.) who became a bp. in 1044.
[3] *GFL*, no. 75 strongly suggests that he was abb. Hulme still in Apr.–May 1148.

17, 122, nos. 124–5, 134). Bertram d. 20 Aug. (obit) and was succeeded in 1197; but Martin was app. in B.'s lifetime (*Ann. Winchester*, p. 65).

Master Martin 1197–1206 El. 1197 (*Ann. Winchester*, p. 65); occ. 8 Sept. 1197 (*Ctl. Chertsey*, I, p. 107); 1203 (Cheney, *Inn. III*, no. 1183); d. 2 Mar. (obit) 1206 (between Jan. and 16 Apr. 1206, *CRR*, IV, pp. 64, 119; cf. *Ann. Worcester*, p. 394).

Vacant 1206–10; cf. *Rot. Lit. Pat.*, pp. 68, 70 – royal presentations to livings, cited by Meekings; the vacancy ended *c.* 25 Apr. 1210 (*PR 10 John*, pp. 94–5).

Adam 1210–1223 See above; vacant by 4 Apr. 1223 (*CPR, 1216–25*, pp. 369–70). D. 4 Apr. (obit).

CHESTER (Ches), St Werburgh f. 1092 × 3 (*Ctl. Chester*, I, p. xxiii; R. W. Southern in *Med. and Renaissance Studies*, III (1954), 87–8).

List in *Ctl. Chester*, I, pp. iff. (J. Tait). Basis in *Ann. Chester* and obits (ed. M. V. Taylor in *Liber Luciani*, pp. 85–102, with notes on abbots and variants from other MSS of *Ann.*).

Richard of Bec 1092/3–1117 1st abb. (obits); m. of Bec; app. 1093 (or 1092, cf. *Ann. Chester*, p. 16, s.a. 1093; Tait, p. xxiii; cf. Eadmer, p. 27 and ff.); d. 15/16 Apr. 1117 (obits, p. 94: 15 Apr. in earliest MS, Bodl. Tanner 169, f. 3v. 1116 in *Ann. Chester*, p. 18, but see Tait, p. in.).

William 1121–1140 2nd abb. (obits); el. 1121 (*Ann. Chester*, p. 18, cf. Tait, p. xxvi); d. 5 Oct. (obits, p. 100); 1140 (*Ann. Chester*, pp. xx, 20).

Ralph 1141–1157 3rd abb. (obits); el. 22 Jan. 1141 (*Ann. Chester*, pp. xx, 20); d. 16 Nov. (obits, p. 101) 1157 (*Ann. Chester*, pp. xx, 22). Occ. *c.* 1155[1] (*Ctl. Trentham*, p. 301).

Robert I, son of Nigel 1157–1175 Bl. 6 Dec. 1157 (*Ann. Chester*, p. 22); d. 31 Jan. (obits, p. 91) 1175 (*Ann. Chester*, pp. xx, 26).

Robert II 1175–1184 5th abb. (obits); el. 3 Feb. 1175 (*Ann. Chester*, pp. xx, 26); d. 27 or 31 Aug. or 1 Sept. 1184 (obits, p. 99; 2 kal. Sept. 1184, *Ann.*, pp. xx, 30).

Abbey vacant for half year 1184–5; custody then given to bp.-el. Hugh de Nonant (*PR 31 Henry II*, p. 142).

Robert III of Hastings 1186–1194 For his name, *Ctl. Chester*, II, no. 667. 6th abb. (obits); m. of Christ Church, Canterbury; el. May, bl. 13 July 1186 (Gervase, I, 335–6); *Ann. Chester*, pp. xx (1186), 34 (s.a. 1185); res. 1194 (*Ann. Chester*, pp. xx, 44, 127). Occ. 30 Mar. 1188 (*PUE*, II, no. 252). D. 29 June or 25 Sept. (obits, pp. 96, 100; 25 Sept. in Canterbury obits, BM Cott. MS Nero C. ix, f. 12v; etc.).

Geoffrey 1194–*c.* 1208 El. 1194 (ibid.); d. 7 May (obits, pp. 94–5) ?1208 (see obits, loc. cit.).

Hugh Grylle 1208–1226 M. of Spalding (BM Harl. MS 2071, f. 16(2)); el. 1208 (*Ann. Chester*, p. 48; cf. p. xx: installed 30 Mar. 1214 after Interdict), d. 22 July 1226 (*Ann. Chester*, pp. xx, 54, 127). Occ. (H.) 1209, 1215 × 16 (*Ctl. Chester*, I, nos. 60, 307).

CHOLSEY (Berks) f. 990– (see below); suppressed, and endowment later incorporated in Reading Abbey.[2]

Germanus Alleged by *Ch. Ramsey*, pp. 110–11, to be the same G. who had been abb. Winchcombe, and to have become abb. Cholsey in 992. If so his career as abb. ran from *c.* 972–1019+ and was of a length only paralleled by the 11th-cent. abbs. of Cluny; and Miss Robertson noted (*AS Chts.*, p. 374) that a G. signed as abb. *Ramsey* in 993 (Kemble, no. 684). A G. also signs as abb. 'Fleury' in ?995 (*Mon.*, VI, 1443–6). There must, however, be some confusion in any case, and 992 seems too late for the app. of G. abb. Cholsey. He is presumably to be identified with the G. who occ. 989 × 90 (*AS Chts.*,

---

[1] Refers to a cht. of Henry II, given at Northampton (i.e. not before 1155); William abb. Radmore (Stoneleigh).

[2] *WMGP*, p. 193. For a full study of this, see B. R. Kemp, 'The Foundation of Reading Abbey'.

[CHOLSEY]

no. 63; cf. p. 374), 993 (see above: called Ramsey in error?), 997, 1002, 1005, etc., 1012, 1013, ?1019 (Kemble, nos. 698, 1297, 714, etc., 1307–8, 729). See Winchcombe for a possible reference in 995.

COLCHESTER (Essex), St John the Baptist f. 1096 × 7

List in *VCH Essex*, II, 101. Basis in 16th cent. list in BM Cott. MS Nero D. viii, ff. 345–6 (whence all the surnames) and Ann. in *UGQ*, pp. 158ff.

Hugh of York 1102–1115 M. of York (cf. Ann. Rochester, below), pr. then abb. Colchester; res. and returned to York (*UGQ*, pp. 161–2; cf. list). For 1102, see Ann. Rochester (BM Cott. MS Vesp. A. xxii, f. 28). Occ. 1107 + [1] (*Reg.*, II, no. 1114).

Gilbert de Lungrill' (?) 1117–1140 M. of Bec.; app. 1117, d. Aug. 1140 (*UGQ*, pp. 162–3); abb. 25 years, list.[2] Occ. Dec. 1138 (*Reg.*, III, no. 928, of dubious authenticity).

William de Scuri 1140–1142 M. of Colchester; app. 1140, d. 1142 (*UGQ*, p. 163); abb. 4 years, list.

Hugh de Haya 1142–1158 M. of Colchester; app. 1142, d. 1158 (*UGQ*, p. 163); abb. 17 years (list). Occ. 1145 (Gibbs, no. 154).

Gilbert de Wicham 1158–1168 M. of Colchester; app. 1158, d. 1168 (*UGQ*, p. 163); abb. 18 years, list. Occ. 1158 × 62 (*Ctl. Colchester*, II, p. 546).

Walter de Walensis (*sic*, list) 1168–1184 M. of Colchester; app. 1168, d. 1184 (*UGQ*, pp. 163–4), 15 Aug. (BM Arundel MS 68, f. 38); abb. 17 years, list. Occ *c.* 1175 × 9 (*GFL*, no. 464).

Osbert 1185– M. of Colchester, pr. Snape; app. 1185 (*UGQ*, p. 164); abb. '17 years', list *sic*, evidently by confusion with Walter. If list is correct in regnal years of Adam, Osbert presumably d. *c.* 1194 × 5. Occ. 1190 (*Acta Chichester*, no. 140): 1185 × 92 (*Ctl. Colchester*, II, p. 567); *c.* 1189 × 98 (Gibbs, no. 96).

Adam de Campes *c.* 1194/5–1237/8 Abb. 44 years, list: licence to el. his successor, William de Wanda, granted 22 Feb. 1238 (*CPR, 1232–47*, p. 211: cf. list). Occ. 23 Jan. 1197[3] (*FF.*, PRS xx, no. 74); 1205 × 6 (*Essex F.*, p. 35); 11 Jan. 1221 (*Ctl. Colchester*, II, pp. 532ff.); 1227 (ib., pp. 545f.); 1237 (Gibbs, nos. 97–101).

COVENTRY (Warws), St Mary, St Peter, St Osburga and All Saints f. 1043 (*AS Writs*, pp. 463–4, citing lost Ch. of Geoffrey pr. Coventry, on which see p. 41 n. 1); Cathedral Priory 1102.

List in *VCH Warws*, II, 58.

ABBOTS

Leofwine I *c.* 1043–1053 Bp. Lichfield 1053 (*ASC* C; Florence, I, 211; *AS Writs*, p. 567; cf. pp. 463–4 on his app.). Occ. ?1047 (Kemble, no. 785).

Leofric *c.* 1053–1066 Also abb. Peterborough, q.v., etc. D. 1 Nov. 1066.

Leofwine II occ. 1075 (Wilkins, I, 364, see p. 23 – 'Leuuinus'. *VCH* cites BM Add. Cht. II, 205, but this is spurious: see Bishop and Chaplais, p. xxi.)

PRIORS

German Occ. 18 Apr. 1139 (*PUE*, II, no. 18).

Laurence –1179 Occ. 4 May 1144 (*Reg. Lichfield*, no. 455; cf. *PUE*, II, no. 18, n. *h*); 26 Jan. 1149 (Saltman, p. 546); 1159 (*Mon.*, III, 455–6); 1176[4] (Morey, p. 139). D. 29 Jan.

---

[1] Henry I at Winchester, temp. Ranulf the Chancellor.

[2] Perhaps ignoring the vacancy (see p. 8); but the figures are not reliable and the reckoning seems to have been inclusive.

[3] Richard occ. 1196 × 7 (*Suffolk F.* (Rye), p. 2) is evidently an error for Adam.

[4] Confirmed by the Pope, Feb. 1177 (*PUE*, I, no. 141).

1179 (Dugdale, *Warws*, I, 164, citing the lost Ch. of Geoffrey, pr. Coventry):[1] 29 Jan. also in BM Cott. MS Vitell. C. xii, f. 117v.

?**Nicholas** Occ. ?*c.* 1179 in William of Canterbury's *Miracula S. Thomae* (*MB*, I, 343; cf. p. 115 n. 3), where Nicholas is referred to as 'venerandae memoriae'. One would expect the incident to belong to the early-mid 1170s, and it is probable that there is a mistake of some kind.

Moses 1183–1191/8 Chaplain of Archbp. Richard, el. pr. the day before Geoffrey Pucelle was el. bp. Coventry, i.e. Jan. 1183 (*Mon.*, VI, 1242; Gervase, I, 306; BM Cott. Roll xiii, 26). Occ. 1183 × 4 (Lambeth MS 1131, pp. 23–4). Expelled, with whole community, by Bp. Hugh Nonant in 1191, who substituted secular canons;[2] occ. as formerly pr. in 13 and 21 Dec. 1194 (*Rot. Cur. Reg.*, I, 3, 66–7); 1195 × 6 (*CDF*, no. 143); the monks were restored 18 Jan. 1198 (Diceto, II, 159); but Moses d. the same year, at Rome (Canterbury obit, below), prob. 16 July 1198 (Dugdale, loc. cit., from lost Ch. Geoffrey, pr. Coventry; for the day cf. Canterbury obit, *Epp. Cant.*, p. 558; BM Arundel MS 68, f. 34v).

Master Joybert, Josbert (Jocabertus)[3] 1198–1216 Prev. m. La Charité, pr. Much Wenlock (q.v.), el. 1198 (*Ann. Winchester*, p. 67; *Ann. Tewkesbury*, p. 56; *Ann. Worcester*, p. 389); d. 14 June 1216 (Dugdale, loc. cit., from lost Ch. Geoffrey pr. Coventry). Occ. 1205 × 6 (*Leics F.*, PRO transcripts); 1215 × 16 (*Ches. Chts.*, pp. 23–4). Retained Wenlock with Coventry; also pr. Daventry and Bermondsey, according to Wendover in *MPCM*, II, 445–6; cf. *MPHA*, II, 67.

The next pr., Geoffrey, was el. 1216; royal assent 7 July 1216[4] (*Rot. Lit. Pat.*, p. 190).

CROWLAND (Lincs), St Bartholomew and St Guthlac ref. +971 (see below)

List in *VCH Lincs*, II, 117; basis in Orderic, II, 281ff. 15th cent. list from BM Cott. MS Vesp. B. xi, ff. 80–1, in Gough, Appendix, pp. 138ff.[5]

Thurcytel Noted as clerk of London, kinsman of Abp. Oscytel of York, and first abb. of re-founded abb. in Orderic's survey of Crowland's history (II, 281–2); presumably, therefore, the same as the T. kinsman of Oscytel who had been abb. of Bedford in 971 and was later expelled (see Bedford). Cf. D. Whitelock in *Saga Book of the Viking Soc.*, XII, iii (1941), 174–5. D. 12 July (Orderic, II, 283).

Ægelric I nephew of T. succeeded according to Orderic (II, 283).

Ægelric II also related to T., next in Orderic, II, 283. Cf. Athelney.

Osketel (Oscytel) next in Orderic, II, 283–4. Perhaps the O. who occ. 1012 and in a probably spurious cht. with a witness list possibly of 1022 × 3 (Kemble nos. 719, 735). D. 21 Oct. (Orderic, II, 284).

---

[1] This lost Ch., presumably written by the Pr. Geoffrey who was el. 1216 (see below), seems only to be known from Dugdale's references, from which other citations (e.g. *AS*, I, 463) probably derive. Cf. J. C. Lancaster, *BIHR*, XXVII (1954), 115n.

[2] Devizes, pp. 13, 69, 71: the scheme was first planned in 1190 (cf. *PR 2 Richard I*, p. 43), executed in 1191. Cf. Cheney, *Inn. III*, no. 28 (mandate to restore M(oses) on 3 June 1198); Joc. Brakelond, pp. 94–5.

[3] 'John' in *Warws F.*, no. 134 (13 Aug. 1202).

[4] But el. 17 July according to Dugdale, loc. cit.

[5] References only noted when it adds to Orderic; another copy of this list is in Leland, *Itinerary*, ed. L. T. Smith, II, 126ff.

The evidence of the Pseudo-Ingulf is ignored: the latest study of his account of Crowland's early history is in Orderic, ed. Chibnall, II, introd. It is certain that Pseudo-Ingulf had access to a genuine list of abbs., and possibly to genuine tradition of the abbs.' terms of office; but if so, he misunderstood or garbled these beyond any possibility of recognition. His continuator (cited occasionally from Fulman) can be helpful. Thurkytel, Oskytel, 'Ulskytelus', Godric, 'Algericus', Ingulf and Wulfgeat are listed in *Roul. Morts*, p. 200 (1113).

[CROWLAND]

Godric next in Orderic; d. 19 Jan. (II, 284).

Brihtmær next in Orderic, II, 284; d. 7 Apr. Prob. the B. who occ. ?1018, 1019, 1023, etc., 1031, 1053 × 5 (Kemble, no. 728 (and *OS Facs.*, II, Exeter 10); *EHD*, I, 553ff.; *AS Chts.*, no. 82 and Kemble, no. 739; ib., no. 744; *OS Facs.*, II, Exeter 11; *AS Chts.*, no. 115, cf. p. 468). See Evesham, Winchester, New Minster.

Wulfgeat Abb. Peakirk, united abbs. with Edward the Confessor's consent, ruled Crowland 'longo tempore' and d. 7 July, acc. to Orderic (II, 284–5). Cf. *AS Chts.*, p. 468; *AS Writs*, pp. 577–8. Occ. in spurious cht. dated 1051 (Kemble, no. 795; cf. no. 794). Cf. Appendix I.

Leofric According to the Peterborough chronicles Leofric of Peterborough (q.v.) was abb. Crowland along with four other abbeys. He may have exercised sway there for a short time, or this may mean no more than that he was given the deciding vote in appointing the abb. of a neighbouring abb. by the Confessor (cf. Thorney).

Wulfketel *c.* 1061/2–1085/6 M. Peterborough, app. by Abb. Leofric and King Edward (Orderic, II, 285). Orderic and the list agree that he was abb. 24 years; *DB*, I, 377r–v seems to confirm that he was abb. –1066. He was dep. at the Christmas court at Gloucester in 1085 (i.e. Dec. 1085 or early Jan. 1086: *Acta Lanfranci*, *ASC*, ed. Earle and Plummer, I, 290; for the date cf. *ASC* E).

Ingulf 1085/6–1109 M. St-Wandrille; abb. 24 years; d. 16 Nov. (Orderic, ed. Chibnall, II, 344–7).

Geoffrey d'Orleans 1109–*c.* 1124 Born at Orleans, m. and pr. St-Évroult, app. 1109, abb. 15 years, d. 5 June (Orderic, ed. Chibnall, II, 346–51; cf. ed. Le Prévost, III, 382; IV, 428).

Waltheof *c.* 1126–1138 Son of Gospatric, earl of Dunbar (cf. Orderic, ed. Chibnall, II, 350–1; ed. Le Prévost, IV, 428–9); cf. also *GASA*, I, 69. M. Crowland, abb. 12 years (list). Occ. 1127 (Haddan and Stubbs, II, i, 215; cf. Nicholl, *Thurstan*, p. 102), 1128 (Lawrie, nos. 75–6). Dep. by the legate Alberic Dec. 1138 at the legatine council of Westminster (*JW*, p. 53; Ric. Hexham, p. 175 – not named; cf. list). D. 2 kal. . . (month missing: list).

Godfrey 1138/9–1143 Pr. St Albans (list), el. Dec. 1138 or soon after, bl. by the legate (Ric. Hexham, p. 175; cf. *GASA*, I, 120–1); abb. 4 years, d. 6 Apr. (list: cf. below).[1]

Edward 1143–1173 M. and pr. Ramsey; abb. 30 years; d. 19 Jan. (list), for year, see below. Abbey vacant from 1172 × 3 (*PR 19 Henry II*, p. 201); still vacant 1–8 July 1175 (*Gesta Henrici II*, I, 91–3; Diceto, I, 401).

Robert 1175–1190 M. Reading, pr. Leominster, abb. 15 years; d. 17 Mar. or 24 Mar. 1190 (list;[2] Fulman, I, 456: 1190 not quite clear in this ch., but confirmed by ch. Barnwell, *Walt. Cov.*, I, p. xli n.). Occ. 1176 (*CDF*, no. 650; BM Cott. MS Claud. A. viii, ff. 121v–122).[3] Occ. (not named) 3 Sept. 1189 (*Gesta Hen. II*, II, 79).

Henry de Longchamp 1190–1236 Brother of William de Longchamp, bp. Ely; m. Evesham; el. 1190 (Fulman, I, 456; date confirmed by *Walt. Cov.*, I, p. xli; *Ch. Peterborough*, p. 3; other details by list); abb. 46 years (list). See below. Occ. 15 Nov. 1208 (*Lincs F.*, PRS LXVII, no. 273); 1234 × 5 (*Cambs F.*, p. 20).

Royal assent to el. of Abb. Walter of Weston, 28 Sept. 1236 (*CPR, 1232–47*, p. 159; cf. p. 161).

---

[1] For what it is worth, 1143 is given as the date of Godfrey's d. and Edward's accession in the *Ch. Ang. Peterborough* (ed. Giles), p. 92.

[2] 9 k. Apr. in MS, Vigil Easter in Fulman; 15 k. Apr. in Gough.

[3] Both dated '1175', but in the council held by Cardinal Hugh Pierleoni, i.e. 14 × 19 Mar. 1176 (*Handbook*, p. 550).

DURHAM, St Cuthbert Cathedral Priory f. 28 May 1083 (*Sim. Dur.*, I, 122; for the community's previous history, see Jarrow)

D.G. Lists in *VCH Durham*, II, 102f.; Le Neve, II, 32–6 (D. E. Greenway); 15th-cent. lists in Durham 'Cart. II', *ad init.* (list 1, unreliable – printed version in *Sim. Dur.*, I, pp. xlviii–l); Reg., II, f. 350v (list 2) and BM Cott. MS Vesp. A. vi, f. 62v (list 3);[1] 15th-cent. ch. in BM Cott. MS Claudius D. iv (ch.). Obits from Durham Cathedral MS B. IV. 24, ff. 1ff. (obit 1);[2] *LV Durham*, 1st ed. pp. 139ff., 149–50 (obit 2); BM Harl. MS 1804, ff. 13ff. (obit 3), and 4664, ff. 126–7v (obit 4). On obits 3 and 4 see Wormald, *Kalendars after 1100*, I, 162–3 – the obits are 15th cent., and 3 may be later, but is the more careful.

Aldwin 1083–1087 Dates as *Sim. Dur.*, I, 122–7, cf. 171; d. 10, 11 or 12 Apr. (10th ibid., obit 4; 11th, obits 1–3; 12th, ch., f. 46v; 12th-cent. note in Durham Cath. MS B. II. 35, p. 277; list 1); 1087 also in Florence, II, 60; cf. list.

Turgot 1087–1109 Citizen of Lincoln, visited Norway, became m. Durham on his return 1083×7 (*Sim. Dur.*, II, 202–4; cf. I, 127); pr. 1087 (ibid.; ch., f. 46v); nominated bp. St Andrews 1106/7, consec. 1 Aug. 1109, d. 1115 (*Sim. Dur.*, II, 204; *Ch. Melrose*, p. 31; cf. *WMGP*, pp. 273–4). D. 31 Aug. (obit 1). Author of *Vita S. Margarete* (in *Sim. Dur.*, ed. Hinde, I, 234ff.). *DNB.*

Algar 1109–?1138 Prev. m. Durham, occ. Sept. 1104 (*Reginald Dun.*, p. 84); pr. after Turgot's consec., according to ch., f. 67v (cf. Le Neve). Occ. 15 May 1123, 18 Jan. 1126 (*PUE*, I, nos. 5, 11); 20 Mar. 1132 (*Feodarium Dun.*, p. 56n.). D. 18, 19 or 20 Mar. (commemorated with Laurence and Absalom, 18 Mar., obits 1, 2, 4; also 19, obit 1; also 20, obit 2); 1137 in lists 1 and 2, *c.* 1138, in ch., f. 73.

Roger ?1138–1149 Prev. subpr. (occ. 1127: Offler, p. 97); dates *c.* 1138 (also list 2)–*c.* 1149 in ch., ff. 73, 79; d. 1148 in list 1, 1149 in list 2. Occ. 1137×?1140 (Offler, no. 24a); 6 Dec. 1142, 24 Mar. 1146 (*PUE*, II, nos. 29, 51); *c.* 1148 (Offler, no. 38); 1148 (*Misc. D. M. Stenton*, p. 206). Cf. Godric of Finchale, pp. 94f., 150, 357f.

Laurence *c.* 1149–1154 Prev. subpr. (occ. 14 Nov. 1147: Offler, no. 36); *c.* 1149–54 in list 1, 1149–54 in list 2; d. Feb.×May 1154 (*Scriptores Tres*, p. 6); d. 16 or 18 Mar. (16 Mar., obits 1, 2; 18 Mar. – with Algar and Absalom – obits, 1, 2, 3). Evidently d. Mar. 1154. Occ. *c.* 1149 (Offler, no. 39); 16 Jan. 1154 (*PUE*, II, no. 82). Cf. G. V. Scammell in *Archaeol. Aeliana*, 4th Series, XXXIII (1955), 61–2.

Absalom 1154–1158 El. 1154 (list; ch., f. 81v). D. *c.* 1158 (list 1); 1158, list 2; *c.* 1158, list 1; 18 Mar. (obits 1, 2, 3). Occ. 1155×6 (*Feodarium Dun.*, p. 121n.); 3 Feb. 1157 (*PUE*, II, no. 94). Cf. Scammell, loc. cit.

Thomas ?1161/2–1163 El. Dec. 1161×Dec. 1162, according to list 1; succeeded Absalom (i.e. presumably *c.* 1158) according to ch., f. 82v; *Scriptores Tres*, p. 8; el. 1158, res. 1162, list 2; occ. 15 Oct. 1162 (*PUE*, II, no. 107). D. 25 Apr. (obits 1, 2, 3; ?also 11 Apr. in 1, 2), and so 1163 rather than 1162 (list 1 has 1163 corrected to 1162). Cf. Scammell, loc. cit.

German 1163–1189 El. 1162 according to lists 1, 2; ch., f. 83; but see above, and 1170 in his 8th year (*Scriptores Tres*, p. 9); occ. 29 May 1163 (*PUE*, II, no. 111) so presumably el. Apr.–May[3] 1163. Last occ. 26 July 1188×9 (*Mem. St Giles, Durham*, Surtees Soc., XCV (1896), p. 204). D. 31 July 1189 (Durham, Misc. Cht. 5828/14, m. 2v; for day, cf. obits 2, 3; for year list 2). Cf. Scammell, loc. cit.

Bertram 1189–1212/13 El. 1189 (list 2), *c.* 1189 (Ch.); d. 1212 (*Scriptores Tres*, p. 27; lists 1 and 2); 8 Feb. (obits 2, 3, 4), so possibly d. 1213. Occ. Mar. 1195 (Scammell, *Hugh du*

---

[1] These lists mostly add errors to list 1, and are only cited when the information corrects or improves it.
[2] Obits, 1, 2 both contain two sets; hence the divergences noted below.
[3] It would normally have been very remarkable for the papal curia to issue a bull addressed to a new pr. within a month of his election, but at this time the pope was at Paris, Chartres and Tours, so that news could travel much faster than to Rome.

[DURHAM]

Puiset, pp. 260–1); 15 Sept. 1202 (*Northumberland and Durham F.*, no. 24); pr. not named
c. 13 Jan. 1209 (Cheney, *Inn. III*, no. 831).

William (of Durham) 1212/13–1218 El. 1212/13 (*Scriptores Tres*, p. 27; said to be a native
of Durham; list 1 gives –1208, list 2 1212–14); occ. c. 1213 (*Rot. Chart.*, p. 208a–b);
20 Feb. 1214, c. June 1215 (ib., p. 207b); d. 14 May 1218 (*Ch. Melrose*, p. 70; cf. obits
2, 3; '1214' in list 1).

ELY (Cambs), St Peter and St Etheldreda   ref. 970 (*Lib. El.*, p. 74n.); pr. from 1109
D.G. Lists in *Lib. El.*, pp. 410ff. (abbs. only: E. O. Blake); Le Neve, new ed. (prs. only,
D. Greenway); *VCH Cambs*, II, 209 (prs. only; D. M. B. Ellis and L. F. Salzman). Lists
and dates in late ch., on which see *Lib. El.*, pp. xxv–xxvii, 410;[1] some also in *Lib. El.* itself.
Obits in Cambridge, Trinity Coll. MS O. 2. 1, ff. K1ff.[2] (obit 1); BM Cott. MS Vesp. A.
vi, f. 130v (obit 2); list, Trinity MS O. 2. 1, f. K14 (names only, Brihtnoth to Richard, including Geoffrey 'procurator').

ABBOTS

Brihtnoth   970–996 × 9 First abb., from foundation (*Lib. El.*, p. 74n.); occ. 991 (*Ch. Ramsey*,
pp. 93, 95–6); 993 (Kemble, no. 684); presumably the B. who occ. from 970 (Birch,
nos. 1257, 1269) to ?995 (*Mon.*, VI, 1443–6); 996 (Kemble, no. 1292; cf. *EHD*, I, 531–4).
Ch. makes him d. 981. Prev. pr. Winchester, q.v. (so *Lib. El.*, p. 74). See *Lib. El.*, p. 411.
D. 5 May (obit, f. K5v, noted as 1st abb.).

Ælfsige   996 × 9–1012 × 16 (or 1019) Occ. 999 (Kemble, no. 703), and must be one of the
two Æs. who occ. 1002, 1005 (Kemble, no. 707; *Ctl. Eynsham*, I, 19–28); 1007, 1008, 1012
(Kemble, nos. 1303–5,[3] 719); presumably to be identified with some of the occs. of Æ.
in this period, but cf. Æthelsige of New Minster, Winchester and Ælfsige of Peterborough. *Ch.* makes him d. 1019; *Lib. El.* in reign of Ethelred (p. 149).

Leofwine   1019–1022? Dep. and reinstated and d., prob. 1023. *Ch.* gives him three years
from 1019; in 1022 he was driven from Ely and cleared himself before the pope of the
charges against him (*ASC* E); in the same year Leofric occ. (*Lib. El.*, pp. 150–1). *Lib. El.*
(pp. 150–1) makes Leofwine die soon after being reinstated and it may be that this is
correct: that Leofric had been app., that Leofwine was restored, and Leofric himself
restored after Leofwine's death. See *Lib. El.*, pp. 411–12, where this and other evidence
is fully discussed. In Kemble, nos. 734–5 (?1022, 1022 × 3), Abbs. Leofwine and Leofric
occ. together; a Leofwine also occ. 1020, 1021 × 3 (Kemble, nos. 1316, 736 – 'Leowine');
in *Lib. El.*, p. 411, it is suggested that L. 'need not have been the abbot of Ely'. See
Appendix I.

Leofric   ?1022/3–1029 See above; occ. ?1022, 1022 × 3 (Kemble, nos. 734–5); d. 1029,
29 June (obit 1, f. K6v; the year, by calculation from *Ch.*: 15 years before 1044; cf.
Lib. El., p. 411). Occ. ?1019 in Kemble, no. 729; but see p. 233.

Leofsige   1029–?1044 *Ch.* gives 15 years; d. 1044; cf. below. D. 5 Nov. (obit 1, f. K11v:
'Leofsinus'). Presumably the L. who occ. in and between 1042, 1044, 1045 (Kemble,
nos. 763, 774, 778; cf. no. 769; *AS Chts.*, no. 97; *AS Wills*, p. 82, cf. p. 196). In *AS
Writs*, p. 566, it was argued that L. d. 1055. One, perhaps two, abbs. L., unidentified,

---

[1] References below to '*Ch.*' are to this *Chronicon*, whose evidence is indicated in *Lib. El.*, loc. cit., where
MSS and editions are also noted. Additional chronicle evidence is also discussed in *Lib. El.*, p. 410.

[2] On which see B. Dickins in *Leeds Studies in English*, VI (1937), 14–24. An Abb. Ægfridus (not
identified – but see St Albans, pp. 65–6) occ. under 28 Oct., f. K1ov.

[3] Kemble, no. 1304 = *Crawford Chts.*, no. 11, which has 3 Æs. He may be one of the two also in
Kemble, no. 715 ('1006', ? for 1002).

occ. 1053 × 5 (*AS Chts.*, no. 115): see Thorney. But the only evidence to associate either with Ely is a spurious writ (*AS Writs*, no. 62). On all this, see *Lib. El.*, p. 412.

Wulfric ?1044 × 5–?1066 *Ch.* gives 1044 + 22 years; *Lib. El.*, p. 164, gives 1045, and calls him a relative of Edward the Confessor. For other evidence, *Lib. El.*, p. 412. Presumably the W. who occ. 1048, 1061 and in spurious cht. of '1065' (Aberystwyth, Nat. Lib. Wales, Peniarth MS 390, p. 368; Kemble, nos. 810, 817). Obit 19 Aug. (calendar, f. K8v); for year, see below. Cf. Canterbury, St Augustine; Winchester, New Minster.

Thurstan ?1066–1072/3 M. Ely, app. by Harold, according to *Lib. El.*, p. 169 (and *Ch.*), after a vacancy in which Archbishop Stigand had held the abbey. But if Wulfric was abb. 22 years from 1044, he d. 1066, and the space between 19 Aug. 1066 and Harold's death allows very little room for Stigand's invasion and Thurstan's appointment. *Ch.* makes T. d. in 1071 in his 5th year, *Lib. El.* in 1076 in his 11th (p. 195). Both are wrong: *Lib. El.*, p. 197 gives the vacancy after Theodwine's death as almost (or about) 7 years; it probably ended in 1082, and this may lead us to suspect that 1076 was the date of Theodwine's death, not Thurstan's (for another explanation of '1076', see *Lib. El.*, pp. 412, 430). In any case, Thurstan occ. May 1072; Theodwine 1075 (Bishop and Chaplais, facing plate xxix; Wilkins, I, 364). Thurstan d. 7 July (obit 1, f. K7v), perhaps in 1072 (as suggested in *Lib. El.*, p. 412), but if Theodwine was abb. 2½ years, 1073 seems more likely for the latter's accession.

Theodwine ?1073–1075/6 See above; *Lib. El.*, pp. 412–13. M. Jumièges (*Lib. El.*, pp. 195–6). D. 4 Dec. or 13 Jan. (obit 2, f. 130v; obit 1, f. K1v), i.e. probably end of 1075 or opening of 1076.

Vacant 1075/6–1082, when abb. administered by m. Godfrey, later abb. Malmesbury (q.v.).

Simeon 1082–1093 Brother of Walkelin bp. of Winchester, pr. Winchester (q.v.) (*Lib. El.*, p. 200). *Ann. Winchester*, p. 33, gives his accession as 1082; *Lib. El.*, p. 221 makes him d. 1093, after 14 years' rule (13, *Ch.*). See *Lib. El.*, p. 413, where 1081 is proposed as an alternative, to fit *Ch.*; but even this does not fit the abbatial years in *Lib. El.*, and *Ann. Winchester* seems the soundest evidence, though not very secure (see under Winchester). It should be noted that the *Lib. El.* here gives a pattern of two seven-year vacancies separated by a 14-year abbacy which may indicate rationalisation. Simeon d. 21 Nov. (obit 1, f. K11v).

Richard 1100–1102; ?1103–1107 Son of Richard de Bienfaite (see pedigree in Round, *Feudal England*, facing p. 473); m. Bec. app. 1100 (*Ch.*; cf. *Lib. El.*, pp. 224–5; Orderic, III, 344, IV, 93); dep. at Council of Westminster, +29 Sept. 1102, but resumed his abbacy, though not recognised by pope and archbishop till May 1107 (Eadmer, pp. 142, 178–9, 185; Florence, II, 51; *Lib. El.*, pp. 226ff.; cf. Diceto, I, 234. The chronology of his restoration is obscure; see discussion in *Lib. El.*, p. 413). He d. 1107 (Florence, II, 57; *ASC* E) on 16 June (obit 1, f. K6v).

PRIORS

Vincent Occ. 1109 × *c.* 1128 (*Lib. El.*, pp. 279, 346).

Henry Occ. *c.* 1129 × 30[1] (CUL Add. MS 3020, f. 166v). Res. –5 Jan. 1134, prob. in 1133 (*Lib. El.*, pp. 288–9, cf. 289 n. 1).

William 1133/4–1135/7 M. Ely; app. May 1133 × 5 Jan. 1134; dep. Nov. 1135 × Nov. 1137 (*Lib. El.*, pp. 295–6, 288). But W. pr. occ. 1140 × 2 (*Ch. Ramsey*, p. 307). D. 29 Jan. (obit 1, f. K1v).

Thembert, Theinbert Occ. 1144 and 1145, –1151 (*Lib. El.*, pp. 335, 337, cf. pp. 340, 386; Ely Dioc. Recs. (CUL), Lib. M, MS G. 3. 28, pp. 150–1).

---

[1] About the date of the dedication of Thorney abb. (cf. Rochester).

[ELY]

Alexander Prev. m. Ely; occ. Feb. 1151 × June 1152, Apr. 1154, +*c.* 1158[1] (*Lib. El.*, pp. 316, 351–2, 364; Ely Dioc. Recs. (CUL), Lib. R, MS G. 3. 27, ff. 213v–214).

Solomon –1176 Prev. precentor, prob. (*Lib. El.*, p. 351, and n.). Occ 1163 (according to Bentham, *Ely*, I, 216, citing lost ctl.); –May 1169 (Miller, *Ely*, p. 286); 1174+ (*Mon.*, III, 613); abb. Thorney 1176 (q.v.).

(B.[2] or G. occ. 1183 (*Reg. Pinchbeck*, pp. 423–4) is an error for G(eoffrey) bp. Ely: CUL MSS Ee. iii. 60, f. 184; Mm. iv. 19, ff. 121–2, 169r–v, etc.).

Richard Occ. 2 Dec. 1189 (BM Cott. MS Tib. B. ii, f. 254); 1174 × 89 (*Ch. Ramsey*, p. 294). Prob. prev. subpr. and perhaps wrote parts of *Lib. El.* (op. cit., pp. xlviiff.).

Robert de Longchamp –1197 Brother of William de Longchamp, bp. Ely and royal chancellor, res. 1197 to be abb. St Mary, York (Diceto, II, 151–2; and see York). Possibly the chancellor's brother who was m. Caen, intruded unsuccessfully into Westminster in 1191 (Devizes, pp. 39, 54). Occ. 3 June 1194 (Lib. M *ut sup.*, p. 318). Abb. St Mary's, York 1197: el. 17 Mar.; bl. 23 Mar., installed 2 Apr. (Diceto, II, 151–2).

John de Strateshete 1197/8– El. late Feb. 1197/8 (Bentham, I, 217, citing lost ff. 39–40 of BM Add. MS 9822); occ. 1198 (ibid.); 28 June 1200 (*Rot. Chart.*, p. 73b). For his name cf. *AS*, I, 684: 'Stratfeld' or 'Straget'.

Hugh Occ. ?May 1199 × May 1200 (presumably an error: Bentham, *Ely*, I, 217, citing lost *ctl.*); early 1203 (*CRR*, II, p. 140); May 1207 (Lib. M, p. 597); May 1207 × May 1208 (*Cambs F.*, p. 7).

Roger de Bergham M. Ely (*CRR*, II, p. 140). Occ. –Feb. 1215 (BM Cott. MS Tib. C. ix, f. 152r–v); (R.) 1215 × 19, 1220 × 5, 1225 × 8 (Lib. M, pp. 167 *bis*, 170, 407; p. 170 gives his name in full). Bentham, I, 217, makes him die early in 1229, citing lost ff. 39–40 of BM Add. MS 9822.

Vacant 6 Mar. 1229 (*CR, 1227–31*, p. 235).

EVESHAM (Worcs), St Mary and St Ecgwin ref. *c.* 970; ms. expelled *c.* 975; ref. 995 × 7 (*Ch. Evesham*, pp. 78ff.; see below).

List in *VCH Worcs*, II, 126, based on *Ch. Evesham* (here *Ch.*), esp. pp. 78ff.: 14th cent anns. (1) in Harl. MS 3763, ff. 169ff., printed *Penwortham Docts.*, pp. 84ff., and (2) in Harl. MS 229, ff. 17vff., printed in *Mon.*, II, 36ff. Obits in BM Cott. MS Vitell. E. xii, ff. 20–38 (damaged; checked by copy in Lansd. MS 427, ff. 1–19).

Osweard *c.* 970–*c.* 975 Expelled (*Ch.*, p. 78). Occ. in spurious cht. dated 966 (Birch, no. 1179); dates 960–*c.* 975 in Ann. 2; prob. the O. who occ., in genuine chts., in 970, 974 (Birch, nos. 1257, 1269, 1303–4).

Secularised *c.* 975 but eventually passed into the hands of Bishop 'Agelsius', presumably Æthelsige of Sherborne, res. or d. 990 × 2; then Bishop 'Æthelstanus', presumably Ælfstan of Rochester (d. 995) or of London (d. 995 × 6). After Æ.'s death Ealdwulf, bishop of Worcester, established Ælfric and Ælfgar as abbs. (*Ch.*, p. 80).

Ælfric App. +995; occ. 997 (Kemble, no. 698). D. 25 Nov. (obit).

Ælfgar App. by Bishop Ealdwulf, who d. (bishop and archbishop of York) in 1002 (see above). Prob. the Æ. who occ. 1002 (Kemble, nos. 707, 1295). D. 17 Aug. (obit).

Brihtmær (Brithmar) Occ. next in *Ch.*, pp. 80–1. Cf. Crowland, Winchester, New Minster. D. 25 Nov. (obit).

Æthelwine Occ. next ('Ægelwin') in *Ch.*, p. 81: bp. Wells 1013–24 (Florence, I, 237; *WMGP*, p. 194; J. A. Robinson (1918), pp. 50, 52, 68). ?Occ. ?1012 (Kemble, no. 1307), see Athelney.

---

[1] Richard FitzNeal, king's treasurer.

[2] B., occ. 1133 × 69 in *Hundred Rolls*, II, 358, is prob. also an error: see Gray, *St Radegund*, p. 3n.

Ælfweard *c.* 1014–1044 M. Ramsey, related to Cnut, but app. by Ethelred II on his return after Swein's death (*Ch.* pp. 81, 83), i.e. 1014 (so Ann. 2); but the *Ch.* (p. 82) seems to place the battle of Ashingdon 'eodem anno', so its chronology seems not very precise. Æ. became bishop of London in 1035, but retained the abbey (*Ch.*, pp. 83, 85); he d. 25 July 1044 (*ASC* D; Florence, I, 199 – 'feria quarta'; 27 July in Ann. 2, obit; cf. *AS Wills*, p. 191). On him see *DNB*; *AS Chts.*, pp. 396–7. Presumably the Æ. who occ. 1014 × 16, –1023, ?1022, etc., 1033 (*AS Chts.*, nos. 76, 81; Kemble, nos. 734, 751). Cf. Æthelweard, Glastonbury, Malmesbury.

Mannig 1044–1058 M. Evesham, el. 1044, bl. 10 Aug. (*ASC* D; Florence, I, 199 – 'feria sexta': also called *Wlmarus*; *Ch.*, p. 86). Paralysed and res. 1058 (Æthelwig abb. 7 years before Edward the Confessor's death, *Ch.*, p. 88).[1] D. *c.* Epiphany, 6 Jan. 1066 (*Ch.*, p. 88; 6 Jan. in obit; but *Ch.* says that it was the same day as the king, i.e. 4 or 5 Jan.). M. was a notable craftsman, esp. in metal: see *Ch.*, p. 86; Knowles, *MO*, pp. 536–7. The name is very rare, and he may be confidently identified in the M. who occ. from 1045 to 1053 × 5, *c.* 1053 (Kemble, nos. 777, etc.; *AS Chts.*, no. 115; *BM Facs.*, IV, no. 32).[2]

Æthelwig 1058–1077 El. 1058, bl. 23 Apr. (Darlington, art. cit., below; *Ch.*, p. 88); d. 16 Feb. 1077 (*Ch.*; and Ann. 2; obit and BM Cott. MS Nero C. ix, f. 5v; 17 Feb. in Rud, p. 215; cf. *Ann. Winchester*, p. 32). Occ. 1058, 1061 × 5, etc., 1075, 1077 (Earle, pp. 247–8; *AS Chts.*, no. 117; Wilkins, I, 364 (see p. 23; 'Eluinus'); Thorpe, p. 617). On him see R. R. Darlington in *EHR*, XLVIII (1933), 1ff., 177ff.

Walter 1077–1104 M. Caen (*WMGP*, p. 137 – Cérisy, *Ch.*, p. 96). App. 3rd month after Æthelwig's death (*Ch.*, p. 96); d. 1104 (Florence, II, 53), 20 Jan., obit; d. 20 Jan. '1086', abb. 8 years (Ann. 1, 2). Occ. 1081 (*Reg.*, I, no. 135, of doubtful authenticity); 27 Jan. 1091 (*Reg.*, I, no. 315); 3 Sept. 1101 (*Reg.*, II, no. 544).

Robert Prev. m. Jumièges (*Ch.*, p. 96). Date wrongly given as 1096 in Ann. 1, 2.

Maurice –1130 M. Evesham; d. 1130 (Ann. 1, 2 – '32' years, d. 1122, but see below. Cf. *Ch.*, p. 98).

The abbey was in the king's hand for a short time in 1130 (*PR 31 Henry I*, p. 109).

Reginald Foliot 1130–1149 Uncle of Gilbert, abb. Gloucester etc. Prev. m. Gloucester, abb. 1130–49, d. 25 Aug. (Ann. 1, 2; cf. *Ch.*, pp. 98f.; *Ann. Winchcombe*, pp. 126, 129; Gregory of Caerwent, BM Cott. MS. Vesp. A. v, ff. 198–9; obit). Bl. 27 Jan. 1130 (*JW*, p. 29). Chts. dated 1130 and 1131 in his first year in BM Cott. MS Vesp. B. xxiv, ff. 27, 31. Cf. *GF*, p. 36; *GFL*, p. 533.

William de Andeville 1149–1159 M. Christ Church, Canterbury (*Ann. Winchester*, p. 56); pr. Dover (q.v.; cf. Saltman, p. 542); dates, Ann. 1, 2; cf. *Ch.*, pp. 99f.; Gervase, I, 141; *Ann. Winchester*, p. 56; *Ann. Tewkesbury*, p. 47. D. 4 Jan. (obit; Ann. 2). See *GFL*, p. 533, and on his el. no. 89; 3 Jan. in BM Arundel MS 68, f. 12.

Roger 1159–1160 M. St Augustine's, Canterbury, abb. 1159–60, d. 4 Jan. (Ann. 2; cf. *Ch.*, p. 100; 4 Jan.[3] confirmed by obit; d. 1159, *Ann. Winchester*, p. 56). See *GFL*, p. 533. On his el., see *JS Epp.*, I, no. 109.

Adam 1161–1189 M. La Charité, pr. Bermondsey (q.v.; cf. *Ch.*, p. 100; m. Cluny in Ann. 2); abb. 16 Apr. 1161–1189 (1161, *Ann. Bermondsey*, p. 441; 1161–91, Ann. 1, 2: see below; cf. *Ch.*, pp. 100–2); d. 12 Nov. (obit). For his el., see *GFL*, no. 134; on him see *GFL*, p. 533. Occ. 4 July 1161 (*Mon.*, V, 181).

[1] *Ch.*, loc. cit., says that Æ. was bl. on St George's Day in Easter Week: this seems decisive for 1058 as against 1059; and Æ. occ. in 1058 – Earle, pp. 247–8. See R. R. Darlington in *EHR*, XLVIII (1933), 3 n. 2.

[2] A 'Godric' abb. E. signs in ?1047 (Kemble, no. 785): this is clearly a mistake. Mannig occ. in a spurious cht. of ?1043 (Kemble, no. 916).

[3] So Ann. 2 and obit – the same day as Abb. William. But another Abb. Roger had 19 July as his obit, and another William 3 Aug.

[EVESHAM]

Roger Norreis 1190–1213 M. and pr. Christ Church, Canterbury (q.v.; Gervase, I, 380–2, 460ff., 481; on him see *Ch.*, pp. 102ff.); bl. +13 Jan. 1190 (Gervase, I, 484); dep. 22 Nov. 1213 (ib., pp. 250, 253; cf. Ann. 1, 2; *Ann. Tewkesbury*, p. 61; *Ann. Worcester*, p. 402). Ann. 1, 2, date Adam's d. 1191; but it was shown in *MO*, p. 331n., that this was too late – the move of Roger Norreis had evidently been accomplished before Abp. Baldwin left England on 6 Mar. 1190 (cf. Stubbs in *Epp. Cant.*, pp. lxxvff.; *MO*, pp. 330ff.). Occ. in papal bull of 25 Jan. 1191 (*PUE*, I, no. 269). See Penwortham.

Randulf 1214–1229 M. Evesham, pr. Worcester (q.v.), el. 22 Jan. 1214 (*Ch.*, p. 255; cf. p. 266 – 1215 in 2nd year; royal assent to el. 24 Jan. 1214 (*Rot. Lit. Claus.*, I, p. 162); cf. *Ann. Worcester*, p. 403). D. 17 Dec. 1229 (*Ch.*, p. 263 and n.; Ann. 1, 2; obit). Occ. 15 Sept. 1221 (BM Add. MS 4934, f. 160).

EXETER (Devon), St Peter (?) f. 968 (Florence, I, 141): suppressed 1050 and converted into secular Cathedral. Probably two houses at first, one of monks, one of nuns: *WMGP*, p. 201; cf. *AS Chts.*, p. 344. But it is not certain that the house of nuns was at Exeter. See p. 211.

ABBOTS

Sideman 968–?973 App. 968 (Florence, I, 141). Presumably the S. who occ. 969, 972, ?972, and in spurious chts. dated 969 (Birch, nos. 1145, 1230, (?) 1282,[1] 1284, cf. 1302, 1145; also nos. 1228, 1264). The name is rare, so he is very prob. to be identified with the S. who was bp. Crediton 973–7.

Leofric It seems clear from *AS Chts.*, no. 47, that there was an abb. Exeter of this name; and he is presumably to be identified with one of the two abbs. Leofric who occ. 983 to 990, 990 (× 1) (Kemble, nos. 636, 655, 657, 664–5, 673, 712; cf. *Liber de Hyda*, pp. 231–6. See Muchelney, St Albans).[2] Possibly the L. who occ. 974, 980, 982 (Birch, no. 1303; Kemble, nos. 624, 632–3, 1278; Birch nos. 1228 = 1264,[3] dated 969, are spurious).

Brihthelm occ. with title Exeter 993, 997 (Kemble, nos. 684, 698); and may be the B. who occ. 994, 995, 996 (Kemble, nos. 686–7, 692, 1292; cf. *AS Wills*, pp. 44, 150); ?995 (*Mon.*, VI, 1443–6); but see Malmesbury.

Æthelwold occ. ?1019 (Kemble, no. 729); perhaps to be identified with the Æ. who occ. ?1018, ?1019, 1024 (Kemble, nos. 728 (and *OS Facs.*, II, Exeter 10), 730, 741).

EYNSHAM (Oxon), St Mary (etc.) f. 1005; refounded –1086 and again in 1091 (at Stow, Lincs); 1094 × 5 (returned to Eynsham).
Lists in *VCH Oxon*, II, 67; *Ctl. Eynsham*, I, pp. xiii–xxi (H. E. Salter).

Ælfric Ælfric the homilist was first abb. Eynsham; for his previous career see Cerne. He was m. and mass-priest +987 (see excellent survey of Ælfric by P. Clemoes, 'Aelfric', in *Continuations and Beginnings: Studies in Old English Literature*, ed. E. G. Stanley (London, 1966), pp. 176–209, esp. p. 179; see also Whitelock (1955), p. 849). His date of d. is quite uncertain; +1006, and his last work was written *c.* 1010 (see D. Whitelock in *Modern Languages Review*, XXXVIII (1943), 122–6). Prob. one of the Æs. who occ. 1005 (Kemble, no. 714). Cf. Athelney.

Remigius, bp. of Lincoln kept the abbey in his hand until Jan. × Sept. 1091[4] when he appointed

---

[1] The reading in BM Cott. MS Aug. ii. 6 is doubtful.
[2] *AS Chts.*, no. 47, relates to land in Stoke Canon (probably) which is to be the abbot's, and after him to go to the Minster. We presume that later occs. (1002 +) of two Ls. refer to Muchelney and St Albans.
[3] = *Crawford Chts.*, no. 6; see Appendix III.   [4] 4 William II, 24 Bp. Remigius.

Columbanus 1091– See *Ctl. Eynsham*, I, pp. 32–5, 48, nos. 5–6, 26 for his app.; William II confirmed the app. after Remigius' death. Occ. 1093+, prob. 1094; 1094+ (ib., I, nos. 6, 26 and n.).

Nigel –1128 D. 9 May 1128 (*JW*, p. 29n.). Prob. occ. 1116×18: see Luffield.

Walter I and II *Ctl. Eynsham*, II, no. 658 (–1151), refers to a 'Walteri abbatis secundi', so it seems that two men of the name spanned the period 1129–1139×50.[1] The first was app. 1128×9 and prev. pr. St Albans; he occ. 2 Aug. 1129 (*GASA*, I, 85). A Walter occ. 1 Dec. 1136 (*Antiq. Journ.*, XIV (1934), pl. 1 (H. C. Andrews)); 1136×8 (BM Egerton MS 3031, f. 16); Dec. 1138 (*Reg.*, III, no. 928, forged; but soon after the supposed date); *c.* Jan. 1139 (H. E. Salter, *EHR*, XXXIV (1919), 383).

William Occ. –1151 (H. E. Salter in *EHR*, XXXIV (1919), 384); prob. 1149×50 (*Oxford Chts.*, no. 60).

Godfrey 1150×1–1195 Prob. pr. Eynsham (cf. H. E. Salter, in *EHR*, XXXIV (1919), 384). D. 1195 in his 44th year; app. *temp.* Stephen (*Magna Vita S. Hugonis*, iv, 8, II, p. 39; cf. p. 41 and *Visio*, c. 27, in *Ctl. Eynsham*, II, pp. 330ff. Two and a half year's vacancy after his death. This enforces 1195 not 1196 as the date of d.). Occ. *Ctl. Eynsham*, II, no. 703 and, as 'Gumf.', *Ctl. Dunstable*, no. 165; (G.) 1173×82 (*Ctl. Eynsham*, I, no. 58).

The abbey was vacant two and a half years, evidently 1195–7 (see above and below).

Robert 1197–1208 Subpr. Canterbury cathedral (see obit below); pr. Dover (q.v.); el. 1197, bl. 11 Nov. (Gervase, I, 543–4; cf. *Magna Vita*, II, pp. 42, 47). Occ. 1197 (*Oxford F.*, p. 4); 4 Feb. 1199 (*FF.*, PRS XXIV, no. 290); 30 Sept. 1200 (*Ctl. Eynsham*, II, p. 238); (R.) 1203 (*CDF*, no. 146); 1 July 1205 (*CRR*, IV, p. 39). D. 1208 (*Ann. Dunstable*, p. 31), probably 8 Sept. (obit in BM Cott. MS Nero C. ix, f. 11).

The abbey was still vacant in June 1213 (cf. *Walt. Cov.*, II, 213), owing to the interdict.

Adam 1213/14–1228 Subpr. and possibly pr. Eynsham (see *Mag. Vita*, I, pp. viiiff.). Occ. 1 July 1214 (*Ctl. Eynsham*, I, no. 230); 1219 (*Oxford F.*, p. 57); 1225 (ib., p. 74); dep. 1228 by Hugh, bp. of Lincoln and became m. Crowland (*Ann. Tewkesbury*, p. 70;[2] *Walt. Cov.*, I, p. xli). Author of the *Magna Vita* of St Hugh (see *Magna Vita*, loc. cit.).

FAVERSHAM (Kent), St Saviour f. 1148[3]

List in *VCH Kent*, II, 141.

Clarembald 1148–1177 (prob.) First abb., chosen by Stephen, formerly pr. Bermondsey (Saltman, p. 82; cf. note under Bermondsey); bl. by Abp. Theobald 11 Nov. 1148 (Gervase, I, 138, s.a. 1147; cf. ib., II, 385 and below n. 3; profession ed. C. E. Woodruff, *Arch. Cant.*, XXXVII (1925), pp. 64–5). D. 4 April (BM Cott. MS Nero C. ix f. 9), presumably in 1177 (see below). Occ. 1148×50 (Saltman, p. 283, no. 57); 1150×2 (ib., pp. 379–80, no. 155); 1163×4[4] (*CDF*, no. 1336); 1174×5 (Thorne, p. 1818).

In 1177–8 the abbey was in the king's hands for 20 weeks (*PR 24 Henry II*, p. 124).

---

[1] Godfrey, Nigel and one Walter are mentioned in 1214 as former abbs. (*CRR*, VII, p. 52).

[2] Giving date 1 June 1228; but he occ. 10 June 1228 (*Reg. Wells*, II, p. 145), and possibly Nov.; probably succeeded by Dec. 1228 (cf. *Ctl. Eynsham*, I, pp. xx, 237–8 and n.).

[3] Gervase, I, 138, dates the first abb.'s bl. 11 Nov. 1147, but he clearly intended to date the event to 1148, for it is in a context of events belonging to that year (1148 in *Ann. Bermondsey*, p. 438; but see p. 114; and also perhaps by implication in John of Salisbury, *HP*, ed. Chibnall, p. 89, since he normally omits events earlier than 1148). It is strange that the event should have taken place in a year when archbp. and king were at loggerheads; but the conclusion leading to Clarembald's blessing may have been part of the reconciliation *c.* Oct. (cf. *GFL*, pp. 115, 505).

[4] Contemporary with no. 1335: Henry II at Rochester, while Becket was archbp. but not in exile: prob. Mar. 1163.

[FAVERSHAM]

Guerric 1178–1188(?) Formerly pr. Bermondsey; el. 1178[1] (Gervase, I, 277); bl. by Abp. Richard (ib., II, 398);[2] d. 23 Aug. (*Epp. Cant.*, p. 559; BM Cott. MS Vitell. C. xii, f. 137 v), presumably in 1188, or just possibly 1189 (see below).

Ailgar 1189– El. 15 Sept. 1189, at Pipewell (Gervase, I, 458); bl. by Abp. Baldwin (ib., II, 405). Occ. 28 Jan. 1195 (*CDF*, no. 141); 1198 × 1205 (*Ctl. Canterbury, St Gregory*, no. 9); 4 Oct. 1202 (*Kent F.*, p. 25); 1203 (*CRR*, II, p. 141); 16 April 1206 (*Kent F.*, p. 38).

Nicholas 1215–1234 Cellarer of Faversham, el. 1215 (Gervase, II, 109; *Rot. Lit. Pat.*, p. 127b); occ. –1216 (*Ctl. Chichester*, p. 75, no. 278); res. 1234, –9 Dec. (*CPR, 1232–47*, p. 85).

GLASTONBURY (Soms), St Mary   ref. 940 (Stenton, *Anglo-Saxon England*, p. 440) Lists in J. A. Robinson (1921), pp. 40–3 (10th–11th cents.); *VCH Soms*, II, 98; basis in a 10th-cent. list and *WMAG* (in *Ad. Dom.*) on which see Robinson, op. cit., chap. 1. WM's dates before 1000 are ignored.

St Dunstan 940–957+ For 940 see above; cf. *WMAG*, p. 72; 942 in Florence, I, 133; 943, *ASC* A; bp. Worcester 957, bp. London, 959; abp. Canterbury 960–88 – but 'we do not know at what precise date he ceased to be abbot of Glastonbury' (Robinson, op. cit., p. 42); cf. *Mem. Dunstan*, pp. 25ff., and *passim*. Occ. 949, etc., 956 (Birch, nos. 880, 883; 924, 941 = 949). In exile 956–7 (Florence, I, 136–7; *ASC* A).

?Ælfric occ. next in 10th-cent. list, but all the occs. from 958/9 to the late 960s could refer to the abb. St Augustine's, Canterbury, q.v. Cf. also Malmesbury, St Albans. The list and WM ignore Ælfstan, and it is possible that Ælfric is a slip for Ælfstan.

WMAG, p. 76, inserts Elsius 'pseudo-abbas', when Dunstan was in exile in 956; this is clearly based on Birch, no. 933, in which 'uidelicet abbati Glastingensi' is probably an interpolation: see Watkin in *Ctl. Glastonbury*, III, p. ccxvi. Elsius was apparently a layman.

Ælfstan 964–970 The Ælfstan who was bp. Ramsbury 970–81 had been m. Abingdon, and abb. of some house unnamed, according to the *Vita Ethelwoldi* (*Ch. Abingdon*, II, 259:[3] cf. *WMGP*, p. 181). He is not named in either Glastonbury list: but see above – Ælfric may well be a slip for Ælfstan. He is identified as Abb. G. in Florence, I, 141, s.a. 970 (occ.), and in spurious chts. dated 966 (Birch, nos. 1178–9), and there is no obvious alternative. If the identification is correct, he was prob. the Æ. who occ. from 964 to 968 (Birch, nos. 1143, 1135 – dated 28 Dec. 964 but at least partly spurious – etc., 1216–17; *AS Chts.*, no. 45). According to *LVH*, p. 23, he was also m. Old Minster, Winchester; this was ref. 964, and if correct Æ. must have moved on to G. the same year. Cf. *AS Chts.*, p. 341.

Sigar (Sigegar) c. 970–975(?) M. Old Minster, Winchester (*LVH*, p. 23), abb. between 'Ælfric' and Ælfweard (10th cent. list); bp. Wells 975–97 (*WMAG*, pp. 93f.; Florence, I, 147–8 – a house not named, but the only Abb. S. known – cf. J. A. Robinson (1921), pp. 41–2; id. (1918), p. 48 and n.). Prob. the S. who occ. 974, 975 (Birch, nos. 1303, 1312, 1315). Occ. ?965, ?979+ (*WMAG*, pp. 85, 87, 101).

---

[1] He occ. in a cht. dated 15 May 1177 in *Reg. Rochester*, pp. 410–11 = BM Cott. MS Domit. A. x, ff. 204–5 = Royal 5. A. iv, ff. 197–8 (where he is called Gregory). Its evidence must, however, be discounted. It refers to Alvred, pr. Rochester 1182/3 (or +)–1186; and Benedict the archbp.'s chancellor who was pr. of Canterbury Cathedral from 1175 (and abb. Peterborough from 18 May 1177).

[2] Also in profession list printed in Somner, I, App. XLI, p. 51, which is not, however, reliable: it correctly gives Clarembald making profession to Theobald; but gives Ailgar, Peter (?for Nicholas), Peter, making profession to Boniface.

[3] 'deinde episcopus Uintoniensis ecclesiae', evidently for 'Uiltoniensis', i.e. Ramsbury.

Ælfweard   *c.* 975–?1009+ *WMAG*, p. 87, omits Æ. and apps. his successor *c.* 1000; his 10th-cent. dates are, however, ingenious guesses (Robinson (1921), chap. II), and Æ. is the last name in the 10th-cent. list, and thus well authenticated. Occ. 993, 997, and prob. the Æ. who occ. 985, 988, etc., 1008, 1009 (Kemble, nos. 684, 698; 650, 665, etc., 1305, 1306). Cf. Æthelweard I, Malmesbury.

Brihtred (Beorhtred)   occ. next (*c.* 1000) in *WMAG*, pp. 87, 101 (16 years) and may be the B. who occ. 1013, 1014 (Kemble, nos. 1308–9).

Brihtwig   Prob. –1019–1024 Bp. Wells 1024–33 (*WMAG*, p. 94; J. A. Robinson (1918), pp. 5off.; *AS Chts.*, p. 411). Prob. the B. who occ. ?1018, ?1019, etc., ?1022, 1023 (*OS Facs.*, II, Exeter 10; Kemble, nos. 730, etc., 734, 739; *AS Chts.*, no. 82); an Abb. Brihtwig, unidentified, occ. in 1024 × 32 with the bp. Wells and an Abb. Æthelweard (Kemble, no. 1324).

Æthelweard (Aegelweard)   *c.* 1024–1053 Succeeded B., d. 1053, 9 Nov. (*WMAG*, p. 89: 26 years from 1027; *ASC* C, D, s.a. 1053; Florence, I, 211; for the day, see BM Cott. MS Vitell. C. xii, f. 148v). An Æ. occ. frequently from 1023, 1024, ?1026 to 1050, ?1052 (?for 1050) but the first occ. is too early for the abb. G., and some of the references may be to the abb. Malmesbury, q.v. (*c.* 1033/4–*c.* 1043/4) (Kemble, nos. 739, 741, 743, etc., 791–3, 796). Cf. also Ælfweard, Evesham.

Æthelnoth   1053–1077/8 M. Glastonbury; el. 1053 (*ASC* D; *WMAG*, p. 90; Florence, I, 211). Occ. 1067, 1072, 1075 (Florence, II, 1; Bishop and Chaplais, facing pl. xxix; Wilkins, I, 364; see p. 23: Elnoldus); dep. in Lanfranc's Council of London between Aug. 1077 and Aug. 1078 (*Acta Lanfranci* in *ASC*, ed. Earle and Plummer, I, 289), retired to Canterbury Cathedral Pr. (*Mem. Dunstan*, p. 420; cf. *ASC*, ed. cit., II, 316). Possibly the Æ. who occ. ?1059, 1061, etc., 1066 (*OS Facs.*, II, Exeter 14; Kemble, no. 811; *AS Writs*, no. 71), but the earlier references may be to Ælfnoth of New Minster, Winchester, q.v. Cf. *AS Writs*, pp. 553–4.

Thurstan   *c.* 1077/8–1096+ M. Caen; sent back to Caen after the famous riot in the abbey in 1083, but not formally dep.; restored by William II though he is said not to have resided (*ASC* E, s.a. 1083; Florence, II, 16–17; *WMGP*, p. 197; *WMGR*, II, 329; *WMAG*, pp. 110ff. (1082); Orderic, II (ed. Chibnall), 270–1 and n.; cf. *Ann. Winchester*, p. 33). See *MO*, pp. 114–15. Occ. in royal chts. etc. 1086, 1089, 1089 × 91, 27 Jan. 1091, 1093, 1094, 1096 (*Reg.*, I, nos. 220, 310, 326, 315, 338, 349, 378). D. 11 Mar. (BM Cott. MS Vitell. C. xii, f. 122).

Herluin   1100–1118 M. Caen (Orderic, IV, 94); abb. from 1100 for 19 years (list in *WMAG*, p. 104; 1101, p. 114; 1100 in Orderic). D. 24 Oct. 1118 (for the day, BM Cott. MS Vitell. C. xii, f. 147; for the year, ann. in BM Cott. MS Nero C. vii, f. 81v; *Ann. Winchester*, p. 45 (1116)). Occ. (H.) 1100 × 2, 1102 × 3, 1103 × 6, 1107 (*Reg.*, II, nos. 622, 573, 800, 825).

Seffrid Pelochin   1120/1–1125 Brother of Ralph d'Escures, archbp. Canterbury (and son of Seffrid and Guimordis d'Escures); m. Séez; abb. 1120 (for 6 years, *WMAG*, p. 120); 1121 (*Ann. Winchester*, p. 46); bp. Chichester, 1125–45 (H. Mayr-Harting, *The Bishops of Chichester, 1075–1207*, pp. 4ff.; cf. *JW*, p. 18; *WMAG*, p. 120). Occ. 1123 (*Reg.*, II, no. 1391).

Henry of Blois   1126–1171 Son of Stephen, count of Blois and Chartres, and Adela, daughter of King William I; nephew of Henry I; brother of Stephen; m. Cluny; ?pr. Montacute (q.v.); abb. 1126, bp. Winchester nominated 4 Oct., consec. 17 Nov. 1129, but retained abbey till his death, 8 Aug. 1171 (on him see *Ad. Dom.*, II, 304ff.; *JW*, p. 29; cf. Orderic, IV, 189; Voss, *passim*; *MO*, pp. 286ff.; Knowles, *EC*, pp. 34ff.). Occ. 1126 × 9 (*Reg.*, II, nos. 1590, 1599a).

The abbey was vacant 1½ years, 1171–3 (*PR 19 Henry II*, p. 197).

[GLASTONBURY]

Robert 1173–1180 Pr. Winchester (*Ad. Dom.*, II, 331); el. 1173 (*Ann. Winchcombe*, p. 134; *Ann. Winchester*, p. 61; Torigny, p. 257; *Ad. Dom.*, II, 331). D. 28 Apr. 1180 (1180, *Ann. Waverley*, p. 242; *Ann. Tewkesbury*, p. 52; cf. *Ad. Dom.*, II, 332: 28 Apr. after 7 years). 28 Apr. also in BM Cott. MSS Vitell. C. xii, f. 126v; Nero C. ix, f. 10v; etc.

The abbey was vacant 1180–9 (1180–1 – 1½ years – *PR 27 Henry II*, p. 15, cf. pp. 5, 160; cf., for 1182–7, *PR 33 Henry II*, pp. 27–8; 1188–9; *PR 1 Richard I*, p. 147).

Henry de Soilli 1189–1193 Pr. Bermondsey (q.v.; cf. *Gesta Hen. II*, II, 85 – not named); el. 15 Sept. 1189 at Pipewell (Gervase, I, 458); bp. Worcester, 1193–5 (el. 4 Dec., consec. 12 Dec. 1193) – see *Ann. Waverley*, p. 249. Cf. *Ad. Dom.*, II, 341, 358, etc.

Savaric Fitzgeldewin, bishop of Bath 1193–1205 Bishop Savaric took Glastonbury for his cathedral and called himself bishop of Bath and Glastonbury. See *Ad. Dom.*, II, 352ff.; J. A. Robinson (1921), pp. 68ff., 142ff.; *MO*, pp. 328–9.

Master William Pica m. Glastonbury, was el. by the monks in 1198, but el. quashed in 1200, and William d. at Rome before the case could be finally settled, in 1200 (*Ad. Dom.*, II, 377–99; cf. Cheney, *Inn. III*, nos. 159, 245–6, 256).

Jocelin of Wells bishop of Bath, 1206 (el. ?3 Feb.; temporalities restored 3 May; consec. 28 May)–1242, retained the title of Bath and Glastonbury from his succession until his death on 19 Nov. 1242; but in 1218–19 a compromise was reached (*Ctl. Glastonbury*, I, pp. xlff., 73ff.), and William of St Vigor el. abbot (*Ad. Dom.*, II, 466–76).

GLOUCESTER, St Peter ref. ?1022 (1022 in Ch. Gloucester: see below. Cf. D. Whitelock in *Wulfstan, Sermo Lupi*, 3rd edn. (1963), p. 12 and n.).

List in *VCH Glos*, II, 61; partial list in *GFL*, p. 534; based largely on Ch. Gloucester, in *Ctl. Gloucester*, I, for which see *Celt and Saxon*, pp. 26off.; cf. *GF*, p. 36 n. 1.

Eadric 1022–1058 Dates as *Ctl. Gloucester*, I, p. 8 (37 years); occ. *c.* 1022 in doubtful cht., Kemble, no. 1317.[1] Cf. Malmesbury.

Wulfstan[2] 1058–1072 M. Worcester. Dates as *Ctl. Gloucester*, I, pp. 8–9 (and BM Cott. MS Vesp. A. v, f. 195v; cf. Florence, I, 217); this places 1072 in his 14th year, and also the 17th of Edward the Confessor, which could be correct for 1058. Greg. Caerwent makes him d. 9 Feb. 1072 (BM Cott. MS Vesp. A. v, f. 195v). Presumably the W. who occ. 1062 × 6 (Kemble, no. 823; cf. nos. 964, 813, prob. spurious). He d. on pilgrimage to Jerusalem (for the year, see also *Ann. Tewkesbury*, p. 43).

Serlo 1072–1104 Prev. can. Avranches, then m. Mont-S.-Michel; for career and dates, *Ctl. Gloucester*, I, pp. 10–13 (d. 1104, 33rd year); cf. *Ch. Evesham*, p. 90; Florence, II, 53 gives obit 4 Mar. 1104, Thursday, 3 Mar. in *Ctl.*, and 3 Mar. in Greg. Caerwent (BM Cott. MS Vesp. A. v, f. 196v) and Cambridge, Trinity Coll. MS O. 9. 25, f. 157, 4 Mar. in Bodl. MS Rawl. Lit. f. 1, f. 5; 24 Feb. in obit S. Benigne, Dijon (Montfaucon, *Bibliotheca*, II, p. 1161). Occ. 1075, 1077, etc., 3 Sept. 1101 (Wilkins, I, 364; Thorpe, p. 615; cf. *Celt and Saxon*, pp. 263, 266ff.; *Reg.*, II, no. 544). On him cf. *WMGP*, p. 293; *GF*, pp. 82–3.

Peter 1107–1113 Prev. pr. el. 5 Aug. 1107, d. 17 July 1113 (*ASC* H; *Ctl. Gloucester*, I, pp. 13–14; Gregory, ff. 196v–7, who, however, dates his death 1114; for 1113, *Ctl.* (7th year 'et semis'); *Ann. Winchester*, p. 44 — cf. p. 42 for accession).

William Godemon 1113–1130 Prev. m. and pr. Gloucester (pr. in Gregory); app. 5 Oct. 1113 (*ASC* H; *Ctl.*, I, p. 14; Gregory, f. 197, s.a. 1114; cf. *Ann. Winchester*, p. 44); res. 1130; d. 1131, 3 Feb. (*Ctl.*, I, pp. 14–15, but gives 13 July 1131 as d. – so *JW*,

---

[1] The same cht. has 'Anna' abb. St Oswald. But there is no evidence that St Oswald's, Gloucester was an abb. at this date (it was probably a house of secular canons). See Aua in Appendix I.

[2] 'Wilstanus' in *Ctl. Gloucester*, I, pp. 8–9; but 'Wulstanus' in Florence, I, 217, and Greg. Caerwent, BM Cott. MS Vesp. A. v, f. 195v.

pp. 30–1 and 31n.; Gregory, f. 198, giving day as here; for the years also *Ann. Winch-combe*, p. 126. *Ctl.* has evidently confused the events of 1130 and 1131, since it says he *died* in the 17th year 'et semis' of his rule).

Walter de Lacy 1130–1139 M. Gloucester; bl. Sunday, 3 Aug. 1130; d. *c.* 6 × 7 Feb. 1139: d. early Feb.; buried 8 Feb. (*Ctl.*, I, pp. 15–17; Gregory, f. 198; Florence, II, 92 (= *JW*, p. 31), 114; d. *c.* 2 Feb.; *Ann. Worcester*, p. 378).[1]

Gilbert Foliot 1139–1148 Prev. m. Cluny, pr. Cluny and Abbeville; bl. 11 June 1139 (*GFL*, pp. 65, 294; *Ctl.*, I, pp. 17–18 (promoted in 10th year); Florence, II, 114–15). Bp. Hereford, app. or el. +16 Apr., consec. 5 Sept. 1148; bp. London 1163–87. See *GF*, *GFL*, *passim*: esp. *GF*, ch. v and pp. 96ff.; *GFL*, Epp. 1–78, 284–8.

Hamelin 1148–1179 Prev. subpr.; el. 26 Sept. 1148, bl. 5 Dec. 1148, d. 10 Mar. 1179 – d. in his 31st year (*Ann. Winchcombe*, pp. 129, 137; *Ctl.*, I, pp. 19, 22: after 31 years; cf. Gregory, f. 199r–v; *GFL*, p. 534).

Thomas Carbonel 1179–1205 Prev. pr. St Guthlac's, Hereford, enthroned 17 Sept. 1179, d. 21 July 1205 (*Ctl.*, I, pp. 22–3 – in his 26th year; Gregory, f. 199v; *Ann. Winchcombe*, p. 137; cf. *GFL*, p. 534).

Henry Blont 1205–1224 Prev. pr., bl. 29 Sept.[2] 1205; installed Oct. 1 or 2; d. 23 Aug. 1224 (*Ctl.*, I, pp. 23 (29 Sept., 1 Oct.; 23 Aug.), 26 (19th year); Gregory, f. 200r–v (13 Oct., 2 Oct., 23 Aug.)). Occ. 30 Apr. 1214 (Cheney, *Inn. III*, no. 964).

HORTON (Dorset) f. ?10th cent. as abb. of nuns; ref. *c.* 1050 (1033 × 61) as abb. of monks (H. P. R. Finberg in *EHR*, LVIII (1943), 195); 1122 × 39 (as pr. subject to Sherborne). See p. 213.

List in *VCH Dorset*, II, 73 (from 1286).

ABBOT

Osirich Occ. 1075 (Wilkins, I, 364: see p. 23).

HUMBERSTON (Lincs), St Mary and St Peter f. *c.* 1160

List in *VCH Lincs*, II, 134.

John Occ. temp. Henry II (pal.: *DC*, no. 476).

Simon Occ. 20 Apr. 1203 (*Lincs F.*, PRS LXVII, no. 170); 19 Oct. 1224 (*Lincs F.*, I, p. 168). The next recorded abb., William of Kirkwold, pr. of Humberston, was el. abb. 1226 (*Reg. Wells*, III , p. 151).

LUFFIELD (Bucks and Northants), St Mary f. 1116 × 18[3]

Lists in *VCH Bucks*, I, 349; *VCH Northants*, II, 97.

Mauger First pr. app. 1116 × 18, or ?1124, by Abb. Nigel of Eynsham (*Reg.*, II, no. 1198 = CXVIII; *CRR*, VII, p. 52; *Luffield Chts.*, I, nos. 4, 1); also occ. 1119+ (*Mon.*, IV, 346).

William –1164 App. by Abb. Walter of Eynsham, –1148 (*CRR*, VII, p. 52); occ. 1148[4] (*Ctl. Eynsham*, I, no. 115); 13 Feb. 1152 (*PUE*, I, no. 51); d. 12 Dec. 1164 (see Walden). Also pr. Walden, q.v.

Master Reginald 1164– Also pr. Walden, q.v. He was pr. Walden 1166–90, abb. 1190–1203/4, when he d. Evidently he res. Luffield at a fairly early stage.

Ralph Occ. 10 June 1174 (*Luffield Chts.*, I, no. 7).

---

[1] Florence, II, 114 seems to be abbreviating a Gloucester source better rendered in the *Ctl.*

[2] So *Ctl.*: 13 Oct. in Gregory (13 kal.: 13 id.); but both place the bl. before installation. Occ. 1211 (*Ctl. Lanthony* (Irish), pp. 75–8).

[3] *Luffield Chts.*, I, no. 1n., argues for 1124: but the monastic founder, Mauger, occ. 1116 × 18.

[4] When the see of Lincoln was vacant: the ed. suggests 1166+, but William d. 1164.

[LUFFIELD]

Peter App. 1164×95 by Abb. Godfrey of Eynsham (*CRR*, VII, p. 52).

John App. +1174 by Abb. Godfrey (*CRR*, VII, p. 52); occ. *c.* 1180×4 (*Luffield Chts.* I, no. 40).

William II App. –1195 by Abb. Godfrey (*CRR*, VII, p. 52); occ. 1203×4 (N'hants F., PRO transcripts); 1203[1]×4 (*Luffield Chts.*, I, no. 40).

Roger –1231 Occ. 1 July 1214 (*Ctl. Eynsham*, I, no. 230) and also in 1214 in a suit in which five earlier prs. are named (*CRR*, VII, p. 52); 1220×1 (*Luffield Chts.* I, no. 196); d. 1231 (*CPR, 1225–32*, p. 432: lic. to el. his successor 30 April 1231).

MALMESBURY (Wilts), St Mary and St Aldhelm   f. *c.* 965 (cf. J. A. Robinson (1923), p. 116)

List in *VCH Wilts*, III, 230 (Dom A. Watkin), largely based on *WMGP*, pp. 404ff., esp. p. 411. Medieval list to late 12th cent. from Hearne transcript in *Ch. Edward I and II*, II, pp. cxviii–cxix (list).

Ælfric I prob. *c.* 965–977 App. by King Edgar before 974 (*WMGP*, p. 404 = Birch, no. 1301; cf. *Ctl. Ramsey*, II, p. 59); became bp. Crediton 977 (*WMGP*, p. 406; cf. Florence, I, 145). Cf. Canterbury, St Augustine, Glastonbury, St Albans; and below.

Æthelweard I Succeeded Ælfric (*WMGP*, pp. 410–11), and may be identified in some of the signatures of an Æ. between 980 and 985 (Kemble, nos. 624, etc., 1283), and prob. with one of the two Æ.s who sign in 982 (Kemble, nos. 632–3: a second Æ. occ. in MS 2 of the latter). Cf. Ælfweard, Glastonbury.

Cyneweard Succeeded Æ., according to *WMGP*, p. 411. Cf. Milton.

Ælfric II Occ. 993, 997 (Kemble, nos. 684, 698). WM identified Ælfric I of Malmesbury with Ælfric the homilist. He seems to have confused the two Æ.s (he omits the second), and it is possible, though very unlikely,[2] that Ælfric II was in fact the homilist; among the numerous Æs. of this era, confusion was easy. Æ. II was prob. one of the Æs. who occ. 990(×1) (Kemble, no. 712) and the Æ. who occ. ?995 (*Mon.*, VI, 1443–6); 25 July 997 (*OS Facs.*, III, no. 35); 1002 (Kemble, no. 707). For Ælfric occ. 994 (Kemble, no. 686), read Ælsie (see p. 232 n. 3).

Brihthelm Succeeded Cyneweard according to *WMGP*, p. 411. Cf. Exeter.

Brihtwold I Occ. next in *WMGP*, p. 411; and was prob. the B. who occ. 1004, 1005 (Kemble, nos. 710, 714, etc.) and one of the two Bs. of Kemble, no. 1303, of 1007; and possibly the B. who occ. later – to 1012; but see below, and Winchester, New Minster.

Eadric (Edericus) Occ. next in *WMGP*, p. 411, and was probably the E. of Kemble, no. 719, of 1012, and possibly of no. 736, 1021×3 – but cf. Gloucester.

Wulfsine occ. next in *WMGP*, p. 411; occ. *c.* 1023×4 (*VCH Wilts*, III, 214, 230); d. *c.* 1033×4 (see below).[3]

Æthelweard II was abb. 10 years (*WMGP*, p. 411), i.e. *c.* 1033/4–*c.* 1043/4 (see below); but may be one of the two Æs. of Kemble, no. 746, of 1032. See Glastonbury (and cf. Ælfweard, Evesham).

Ælfwine was abb. 1½ years (*WMGP*, p. 411), i.e. *c.* 1043/4–*c.* 1045/6. See below; and cf. Ramsey, Winchester, New Minster.

[1] William of Blois archd. Bucks (presumably app. archd. by William of Blois bp. Lincoln, 1203–6; he was bp. Worcester 1218–36).

[2] The chronology of his writings makes it almost impossible, as Professor Whitelock has pointed out to us. He was writing at Cerne in 991–2, and some works later than this do not call him abb.

[3] These dates depend on calculation back from 1052–3, which is not a firm base, but cannot be far wrong: we follow Dom Aelred Watkin in making these calculations, and in covering them with a caution.

Brihtwold II was abb. 7 years (*WMGP*, pp. 411–12), i.e. *c.* 1045/6–1052/3 (see below; cf. *VCH Wilts*, III, 214, 230).

Herman bishop of Ramsbury tried to take over Malmesbury after his death, but was frustrated by Earls Godwin and Harold, i.e. probably between G.'s return in Sept. 1052 and death in Apr. 1053; certainly before Herman's withdrawal from the country in 1055. *WMGP*, pp. 182–3, 420; cf. Florence, I, 214; and for the dates, *VCH Wilts*, III, 230.

Brihtric *c.* 1052/3–1066/7 For his accession, see above; he was removed by William I and made abb. Burton soon after the Conquest (*WMGP*, p. 420); Burton was vacant by the death of Leofric of Peterborough, q.v. on 31 Oct. or 1 Nov. 1066. B.'s translation presumably took place in late 1066 or early 1067. He occ. in two spurious chts. of 1061 × 2 and ?1065 (Kemble, nos. 964, 817). *WMGP*, p. 420, says he was abbot seven years; but an accession as late as 1059 does not fit the evidence of Herman's attempted invasion.

Turold 1066/7–1070 M. Fécamp; became abb. Peterborough 1070 (q.v.; *WMGP*, p. 240; for his appointment to Malmesbury 'vivente Britrico', cf. BM Cott. MS Vitell. A. x, f. 159).

Warin 1070–*c.* 1091 M. Lire (*WMGP*, p. 421; BM Cott. MS Vitell. A. x, f. 159); d. +1087 (BM Cott. MS Vitell. A. x, f. 159; cf. *WMGP*, p. 431, 15 day vacancy after his d.; *VCH*, loc. cit.). Occ. 1075 (Wilkins, I, 364); 1084 (Bodl. MS Wood Empt. 5, ff. 55–6).

Godfrey M. of Ely and Jumièges; proctor of Ely abb. in the vacancy from 1075/6–1082 (*Lib. El.*, pp. 196–200; cf. p. 413, and see Ely). The *Lib. El.* translates him immediately from Ely to Malmesbury in 1081/2, but in the light of Vitell. A. x, f. 159r–v and list a date +1087 (temp. William II) seems clear, but not later than Jan. 1091. Occ. 27 Jan. 1091 (*Reg.* I, no. 315). *WMGP*, p. 431, and list makes him a m. Jumièges; this may account for the interval 1082–1087 × 91.

Eadwulf 1106–1118 Dates as *Ann. Winchester*, pp. 42, 45 (dep.). Formerly sacrist of Winchester; cf. Anselm, *Ep.* 384.

Roger, bishop of Salisbury, held the abbey from *c.* 1118 to his death on 11 Dec. 1139 (cf. *Ctl. Malmesbury*, I, p. 335; *WMHN*, p. 38; list).

John 1140 El. prob. Jan. 1140 (a few days after Christmas, at Reading); d. 19 Aug. 1140 (Florence, II, 122 = *JW*, p. 59; *WMHN*, p. 40).

Peter Moraunt 1141–*c.* 1158/9 Native of Bourges (Leland, *Collectanea*, II, 235 (2nd ed.), III (1770), 272); m. Cluny (BM Cott. MS Vitell. A. x, f. 160; list); (?)pr. La Charité, superior (?abb.) of St-Urban, near Joinville (Florence, II, 129; but cf. Peter the Venerable, *Epp.*, ed. Constable, II, p. 298); app. Apr. 1141 (*WMGR*, II, 573); occ. 1153 × 4; (R.) *c.* Dec. 1153 (*Reg.*, III, nos. 837, 875); d. 1160 (?1159), 5 Feb. (list). But a writ of ?Apr. 1158 may suggest that the abb. was vacant then (*Ctl. Malmesbury*, I, 334–5; cf. Eyton, *Itinerary*, p. 36). On him see *VCH*, loc. cit.; *GFL*, pp. 74–5; *WMGP*, pp. 192–3, and for his name, *Ctl. Malmesbury*, II, p. 222, list, etc.

Gregory ?1159–1168 See above. M. Lire. D. 22 Feb. (*HF*, XXIII, 471) 1168 (*PR 15 Henry II*, p. 22). Occ. Mar. 1163 (*GASA*, I, 157).

Robert 1171/2–*c.* 1180 'de Veneys', physician to King Henry (list); m. Malmesbury; for dates, *PR 18 Henry II*, p. 128; see below. Occ. Aug. 1175 (*Gesta Hen. II*, I, 99); 31 Mar. 1177 (*Ctl. Malmesbury*, I, p. 433). After a long delay he was bl. by bp. Llandaff +1174 (see *Sarum Chts.*, pp. 41–2; Haddan and Stubbs, *Councils*, I, 385–6, dated 1177, but without any clear grounds; cf. *GFL*, p. 526, no. (11)).

Osbert Foliot 1180–1182 Pr. Gloucester, el. 1180 (*Ann. Winchcombe*, p. 137; cf. Greg. Caerwent, BM Cott. MS Vesp. A. v, f. 200 – the annotator of one MS of Ann. Winchcombe has converted this into the el. of Robert Foliot on the death of Osbert, evidently by a spoonerism). D. 1181, 17 Mar. Greg. Caerwent, loc. cit.; 1182 (*Ann. Tewkesbury*, p. 52, *Ann. Worcester*, p. 385; cf. *PR 28 Henry II*, p. 88).

Master Nicholas of St Albans (list) 1183–1187 M. St Albans, pr. Wallingford, el. 1183

[MALMESBURY]

(*Ann. Waverley*, p. 243; *Ann. Tewkesbury*, p. 53, cf. *Gir. Camb.*, VIII, 195; Jocelin Brak., p. 22); dep. or res. 1187 (*PR 33 Henry II*, p. 182); d. 1205 (*Ann. Tewkesbury*, p. 57).

Robert of Melun 1189/90–1205 Sub-pr. Winchester Cathedral[1] (*Ann. Winchester*, p. 63, s.a. 1187); el. 1189/90 (*PR 2 Richard I*, pp. 120, 123); d. 1205 (see n. 1; cf. *PR 10 John*, p. 201). Occ. 1200 (Cheney, *Inn. III*, no. 278 = *CRR*, I, p. 426); 1201 (ibid.). Royal 'clericus' and justice (*Ctl. Malmesbury*, I, p. 337; cf. *VCH*, loc. cit.). *Ann. Dunstable*, p. 3 makes an unnamed abb. d. 1208.

Walter Loring 1208–1222 M. Malmesbury; m. 30 years, abb. '19' years (*Ctl. Malmesbury*, I, p. 251); el. 1208 (*PR 10 John*, p. 195); d. 1222 (*Ann. Dunstable*, p. 77 – without name); –28 Oct. (cf. *CPR*, *1216–25*, p. 349).

MILTON (Dorset), St Mary, St Michael, St Samson and St Branwalader[2] f. 964

List in *VCH Dorset*, II, 62.

Cyneweard 964–974 App. 964 (*ASC* A; Florence, I, 140); presumably to be identified with the C. who occ. 964, 966, etc., 972, 972 × 3, 974 (Birch, nos. 1135, 1176, etc., 1282 (see pp. 230–1), 1283–4, 1304–5); bp. Wells. 974–5 (occ. 974, Birch, no. 1303; *AS Chts.*, p. 342, suggests 973, citing Florence, I, 143; J. A. Robinson (1918), p. 47 and n., suggests 974). Cf. Malmesbury.

Ælfhun Occ. 993 (Kemble, no. 684); probably to be identified with the Æ. who occ. 975 ('Ælfhim'), 982, 989 × 90, 990 (× 1), 992 × 5, 995 + (Birch, no. 1315; Kemble, nos. 633 (and 1278); *AS Chts.*, no. 63 (see note on p. 375); Kemble, nos. 712, 1289; *AS Chts.*, no. 69); possibly to be identified with the bp. London, 1002 × 4–?1013.

Eadred,[3] Edward, Ælfric before 1113 – ?11th cent.; but Ælfric may be an error for Ægelric, below (see also Pershore) (*Roul. Morts*, p. 190).

Aldwin (Elduinus) Occ. 1075 (Wilkins, I, 364; see p. 23; occ. in *Roul. Morts*, p. 190).

Ægelric –1102 Dep. 1102 (Eadmer, p. 142; *WMGP*, p. 119).

Bp. Roger of Salisbury (1102/7–39) was custodian for five years – ?1102–7 – and then:

R. was established by Bp. Roger and Henry I (*Red Book*, I, 210).

A. Occ. 1166 (ib.).

In 1184–5 the abbey was in the king's hand for half a year (*PR 31 Henry II*, p. 203).

Eustace 1198–*c.* 1222 Sacrist of Milton; el. 1198 (*Ann. Winchester*, p. 69). Occ. 1206 (*Rot. Cht.*, p. 163); *c.* 16 June 1219 (*Dorset F.*, p. 21); 1216 × 20 (*Ctl. Loders*, pp. 62–4).

Royal assent to the el. of the next recorded abb., William de Stokes, 10 Nov. 1222 (*Rot. Lit. Claus.*, I, 520; cf. *CPR 1216–25*, p. 351).[4]

MUCHELNEY (Soms), St Peter ref. *c.* 959

List in *VCH Soms*, II, 107; *Ctl. Muchelney*, pp. 18–19.

Ælfwold Occ. 964 (*Ctl. Muchelney*, no. 3), and so presumably to be identified with the Æ. who occ. 958 × 9, 963, and possibly 980, 982 (but see Winchcombe) (Birch, nos. 1030, cf. 1045–7, 1120, 1124; Kemble, nos. 624, 633; cf. also *AS Wills*, p. 150).

Leofric Occ. 989 × 90, 993, 997 (*AS Chts.*, no. 63 – 989 × 90, but written 993 – Kemble, nos. 684, 698). Prob. to be identified with some of the references to L. between 980 and 1005 (Kemble, nos. 624 (but see above), etc., 714; two Leofrics in 983, Kemble, no. 636, etc., to 1005, Kemble, no. 714), perhaps including L. 'also called Ethelnoth' ?995 (*Mon.*, VI, 1443–6). See *AS Chts.*, p. 374. See also Exeter, St Albans.

---

[1] So also Ann. Winchcombe in BM Cott. MS Faust. B. i, ff. 21 v, 23 v, which gives dates 1187–1205 (d.).
[2] All occ. in *AS Chts.*, no. 23 (933 × 4).
[3] He may be the Eadred who occ. 1004 (Kemble, no. 710), Edred, Edward, Alfric in the *Roul. Morts*.
[4] The reference to 'Richard' former abb. in 1228 (*CRR*, XIII, no. 1046) seems to be an error.

Liuuard (Leuuardus = Leofweard) Occ. 1066 (Exon DB in *DB*, IV, 173); 1068 (*Reg.*, I, no. 23); 1075 (Wilkins, I, 364; see p. 23).

— –1102 Dep. +29 Sept. 1102, at Council of London (Eadmer, p. 142; Florence, II, 51; cf. *Handbook*, p. 549). None of the sources for the council names him; it is possible, but unlikely, that Liuuard was still alive.

Ealdwulf (Ealdolf) 1114– Prev. m. Muchelney, app. 14 Sept. 1114 (*ASC* H); occ. n.d., *Ctl. Muchelney*, no. 126.

Alan Occ. 4 Nov. 1159 (*HMC Wells*, I, 27).

?Hugh I Occ. –1166 (with Bp. Robert, i.e. –1166, unless there is a scribal error: *Ctl. Athelney*, no. 133).

Abbey vacant, in king's hand, 'a morte abbatis', 1172–3: *PR 18 Henry II*, p. 78; *19 Henry II*, p. 197; still vacant 1–8 July 1175: *Gesta Hen. II*, I, 91–3; Diceto, I, 401.

Hugh ?II Occ. 1175 (*Gesta Hen. II*, I, 401); 1177 (BM Egerton MS 3031, f. 48r–v); *c.* 1184×90[1] (BM Egerton MS 3316, f. 50v).

Robert Prev. pr. St Guthlac's, Hereford, intruded and ejected 1191 (Devizes, pp. 40, 55).

Osbert Occ. as abb. elect 1193×8 (Forde Abb., Ctl. Forde, p. 289).[2] D. 5 Sept. (BM Cott. MS Nero C. ix, f. 11).

Richard I Occ. 1193×1205[3] (*HMC Wells*, I, 367); 17 Oct. 1198 (*Ctl. Bath*, II, no. 18); 1 Dec. 1201 (*Ctl. Muchelney*, no. 12); 1200×5 (*CDF*, no. 770); 1218×19 (*Soms F.*, p. 35); 1228 (*CRR*, XIII, no. 1030).

The next abb., Richard II, was el. 1235 (*CPR, 1232–47*, p. 105).

NORWICH (Norfolk), Holy Trinity, Cathedral Priory f. 1096×1101 (B. Dodwell in *TRHS*, 5th Series, VII (1957), 11)

D.G. Lists in Le Neve, new ed., II, 58–61 (D. E. Greenway); *VCH Norfolk*, II, 327. Obits in BM Harl. MS 3950, ff. 3ff.; also Norwich Cath., Sacrist's Book and *Norwich Customary* (only referred to for obits not in Harl. 3950).

Ingulph[4] Occ. *c.* 1110×19, 1121+ (B. Dodwell in *Misc. D. M. Stenton*, pp. 160–1, 148n.); 1121×31 (*Mon.*, III, 330–1); +1136 (Bodl. MS Top. Suff. d. 15, f. 38r–v; see Le Neve). D. 16 Jan. (obit).

William de Turba –1146 Prev. m. and precentor Norwich (occ. as m. 1121×35, *Misc. D. M. Stenton*, pp. 158–9, cf. 148n.; as precentor, Bodl. Top. Suff. MS as above). Occ. as pr. –1145 (BM Cott. MS App. xxi, f. 36v). El. and consec. bp. Norwich 1146 (possibly early 1147, Le Neve), d. 1174 (Saltman, pp. 102–3; *Reg. Norwich*, pp. 70, 76, 82; *GFL*, p. 537). On him see Knowles, *Episcopal Colleagues*, pp. 31–3.

Elias *c.* 1146–1150 Occ. 1146×53 (*Ctl. Hulme*, I, no. 84); Mar. 1150 (*St William of Norwich*, p. 116); d. 22 Oct. 1150 (ib., p. 166; cf. obit; *Customary of Norwich*, p. 10). Bart. Cotton (p. 67) makes him d. in 1146, which seems impossible.

Richard de Ferrariis 1150– For name, *St William of Norwich*, p. 142; prob. subpr. (ib., p. 130); el. –Christmas 1150 (ib., p. 173). Occ. –1 Mar. 1155, 15 Mar. 1157 (*PUE*, II, nos. 85, 95). Bart. Cotton (p. 71) makes him d. 1158, d. 16 May (obit).

John Occ. –1168 (*Ctl. Hulme*, I, no. 94); *c.* 1168 (John of Salisbury, ed. Giles, *Ep.* 267);

---

[1] Richard of Coutances archd. (or archd. of Coutances); Master Alexander not yet dean of Wells (see J. A. Robinson (1921), pp. 67, 87–8).

[2] Ex inf. Dr C. Holdsworth. He occ. with Abp. Hubert Walter, i.e. 1193+; and was presumably earlier than Richard I, and so –1198. It is possible that this was another unsuccessful election following Robert's ejection; or else Osbert's abbacy was short.

[3] With Savaric, bp. of Bath and Glastonbury; see p. 52.

[4] Occ. in cht. apparently of 1106×7 (Roger Bigot d. 1107; *CP*, IX, 578); but it cannot be genuine as it stands (*Mon.*, III, 330, no. II; cf. Le Neve).

[NORWICH]

1161×74 (*HMC Var. Coll.*, VII, 171). Possibly the m. John who occ. –1168, with Pr. Richard (BM Harl. MS 2110, f. 124). D. 6 Apr. (Sacrist's Book, p. 3v).

Ranulf Occ. 1161×74 (*Reg. Norwich*, p. 80: 'Ralph'; PRO C115 A1 K2/6683, sec. xiii, no. 13). D. 29 May (obit), 28 May (Sacrist's Book, p. 4). Possibly before John.

?Elric –1172 'Elricus' d. 11 June (obit); and an otherwise unidentified 'H'ericus' d. 1172 (Ann. Horsham, Cambridge, Trinity Coll. MS R. 14. 9, f. 9v: see Horsham).[1]

Tancred 1172–1175 Dates as Ann. Horsham, f. 9v; occ. n.d. (1146×74: BM Harl. MS 2110, f. 124v; also *HMC Var. Coll.*, VII, 242–3). D. 15 June (obit).

Gerard 1175– El. 1175 (Ann. Horsham, f. 9v). Said to have d. 1201 (Bart. Cotton, p. 92), but occ. 6 July and 1 Aug. 1202 (*Norfolk F.*, PRS LXV, no. 353; *Suffolk F.*, PRS LXX, no. 332); d. 17 Dec. (obit). Also n.d. (*DC*, no. 207); 1199 (*Ctl. Wardon*, no. 224); 1199×1200 (Cheney, *Inn. III*, no. 250).

William of Walsham App. 1201 (but see above), d. 1217, according to Bart. Cotton, pp. 92, 109. Occ. 10 Feb. 1205 (*Norfolk F.*, PRS LXX, no. 68); 3 Nov. 1211 (Norwich D. and C. Cht. 4067); 1212 (*CRR*, VI, pp. 194, 212 (3 Feb.)). Prob. d. 23 Feb. (obit).

The next pr., Master Ranulf of Wareham, was el. bp. Chichester –17 Dec. 1217, consec. 7 Jan. 1218 (dates as *Handbook*); said to have been pr. Norwich by *Ann. Dunstable*, p. 52 (not named); *Ann. Tewkesbury*, p. 63, *Ann. Worcester*, p. 410 etc.; also bp.'s official (*CPR, 1216–25*, p. 130; Cheney, *Inn. III*, no. 1029; *Rot. Lit. Pat.*, pp. 166b, 171b). Odd as the combination of m., pr. and official in one may seem, it appears to be confirmed by the evidence that Master Ranulf of Wareham, m. of Norwich, was also an administrator who could take charge of the see when vacant on the king's behalf (ib., pp. 123b–4, 152 *bis*). See Le Neve.

PERSHORE (Worcs), St Mary ref. *c.* 970 (see below)

List in *VCH Worcs*, II, 136. *Ann.* (of little importance) in Leland, *Coll.* (1st edn.), 283ff., (2nd edn.), 240ff. = *Mon.*, II, 415.

Foldbriht *c.* 970–988 Presumably the F. who occ. 970, 972 (Birch, nos. 1257, 1269, 1282 (see pp. 230–1), 1284; also in the spurious no. 1264, dated 969, and in no. 1309 of 970×2); d. 988 (revived by St Oswald, then d.: *Hist. York*, II, 21; dated 988 by *Ann. Worcester*, p. 369).

Brihteah –1033 Bp. Worcester 1033–8; nephew of Abp. Wulfstan I of York (Florence, I, 189; cf. *Lib. El.*, p. 156); ?m. Worcester (Atkins, p. 17). Occ. in spurious cht. dated 1032 (Kemble, no. 748); presumably the B. who occ. in *AS Chts.*, no. 76 (not long after 1012).[2]

Ælfric Occ. ?1046×50 (Kemble, no. 939); 1046×56 (*AS Chts.*, no. 112); and may be identified with the Æ. who occ. ?1033, 1035, etc., 1045, 1051×3 (Kemble, nos. 1318, 1322, 777–8, 807, etc.). See Milton.

Edmund –1058–1085 D. 15 June 1085 (Florence, II, 18; *Ann. Winchcombe*, p. 118; Atkins, p. 30); prob. to be identified with the E. who occ. 1058 (Earle, pp. 247–8). Occ. 1075 (Wilkins, I, 364); 1077 (Thorpe, p. 615); and in three dubious or spurious chts., Kemble, nos. 964 (could be based on a document of 1061×2), 813 (?1062), 825 ('28 Dec. 1065').

Thurstan 1085–1087 M. Gloucester; dates as Florence, II, 18, 20; app. also in *Ann. Winchcombe*, p. 118.

---

[1] The ann. contain notices of priors whose house(s) are not named. The first is evidently Horsham; Tancred and Gerard undoubtedly belong to Norwich; and so presumably 'H'ericus' was a pr. Norwich also. The ann. were printed in extract by M. R. James in his *Catalogue of MSS...*, II, 292; James read 'Henricus' and om. Gerard.

[2] Not –1012, because of Æthelstan bp. Hereford. Since it is the marriage agreement of the sister of Wulfstan, bp. from 996, the marriage is not likely to have taken place much after 1012.

Hugh   D. before 1113 (*Roul. Morts*, p. 313; 'Orate pro Eadmundo, Turstino, Hugone abbatibus') and so prob. between Thurstan and Guy.

Guy   –1102–1136/7 Dep. for simony 1102, +29 Sept., in Council of Westminster (Florence, II, 51; Eadmer, p. 142; *WMGP*, p. 119). Evidently reinstated, since an abb. of the same name occ. 1113×22 (*Ctl. Winchcombe*, I, pp. 212–13); 1125 (*JW*, p. 19); and d. 5 Aug. 1136 or 1137 (Florence, II, 98 = *JW*, p. 41 (1136); *Ann. Tewkesbury*, p. 46 (1137)).

William   1138– M. of Eye, el. 1138 (Florence, II, 113 = *JW*, p. 52; *Ann. Tewkesbury*, p. 46).

Thomas   Occ. 1143×5 (*Ctl. Worcester*, p. 230); suspended and reinstated between 1145 and 1150 (Saltman, no. 311).[1] Occ. 1145×53 (*Ctl. Gloucester*, II, p. 110); 1151×5 (Hemming, I, 291).

Reginald   –1155–1174 Occ. prob. *c.* 29 Sept. 1155[2] (*CDF*, no. 225 = Delisle-Berger, I, pp. 99–100); 15 Dec. 1157 (*Ctl. Gloucester*, II, p. 106); 1166 (*Red Book*, I, 302). D. 1174 (*Ann. Tewkesbury*, p. 51); 1175 (*Ann.*, with Simon succ.).

Simon   1175–1198 El. 1175 (*Ann. Tewkesbury*, p. 51; *Ann.*); occ. 4 Nov. 1178 (*Ctl. Worcester*, p. 89); d. 12 May 1198 (*Ann. Winchester*, p. 67;[3] *Ann. Tewkesbury*, p. 56; Ann. St Davids, BM Cott. MS Domit. A. i, f. 150).

Master Anselm   1198–1203 M. Reading; el. 1198 (*Ann. Tewkesbury*, p. 56; *Ann. Winchester*, p. 69); d. 1203 (*Ann. Tewkesbury*, p. 57; *Ann. Worcester*, p. 392).

Gervase   1204–1234 El. and bl. 1204 (*Ann. Tewkesbury*, p. 57; *Ann. Worcester*, p. 392; *Ann.*); occ. 1228 (*CRR*, XIII, no. 648); d. 1234 (*Ann. Tewkesbury*, p. 93; *Ann.*).

PETERBOROUGH (Northants), St Peter   ref. *c.* 966

List from 1155 in *Ctl. Peterborough*, p. 224; also list in *VCH Northants*, II, 93. Names to 1155 based on *ASC* E and Candidus; first three noted by Goscelin in *Mir. S. Ivonis*, *Ch. Ramsey*, p. lxi. Basis for later abbs. in early 13th cent. Ann. in Lambeth MS 1106, ff. 116–120v;[4] *Ch. Peterborough* (13th cent.) and fuller chs. in Sparke (13th–14th cents.). The obits used here are: 1, London, Soc. of Antiquaries, MS 59; 2, Bodl. Barlow MS 22; 3, Lambeth MS 198a (cf. *Ctl. Peterborough*, p. 224).[5]

Ealdwulf   *c.* 966–992 Bp. of Worcester, 992–1002; abp. York, 995–1002 (*ASC* E, s.a. 963, 992; C, s.a. 992; Florence, I, 149; cf. *Vita Ethelwoldi*, *Ch. Abingdon*, II, 262; Candidus, pp. 29–47). 972–92 in Ann. Occ. 991 (*Ch. Ramsey*, pp. 93, 95–6). Prob. the E. who occ. 982, 989×90, 990 (×1) (Kemble, no. 633; *AS Chts.*, no. 63; Kemble, no. 712; cf. *AS Chts.*, no. 40).

Coenwulf   992–1006 ?M. Old Minster, Winchester; bp. Winchester, 1006 (cf. *ASC* E, s.a. 963, 992, 1006; Florence, I, 149, 158; Candidus, pp. 47–8). Occ. 993, 997, and prob. the C. who occ. 996, 999, etc., 1005 (Kemble, nos. 684, 698; 696, 703; etc.; 714, 1301).

Ælfsige   1006/7–1042 Abb. '50 years', d. 13 Jan. (obit 1) 1042 (*ASC* E, s.a. 963 (12th cent. insertion), 1041 (for 1042); cf. Candidus, pp. 48–65). Accompanied Ælfgifu/

---

[1] Theobald, abp. and primate, not legate: i.e. prob. 1145×50 or 1159×60; but Reginald was abb. well before 1159 (cf. *GFL*, p. 506).

[2] 1155 or, just possibly, 1157×8; witnessed by Thomas the chancellor at Winchester *in concilio*, and Thomas and Henry II were not together in England while T. was chancellor after 1158. Prob. from the council of Michaelmas 1155: cf. Eyton, *Itinerary*, pp. 12–13.

[3] An election of an abb. is noted by Gervase, I, 458, as 15 Sept. 1189, with several others. This is clearly an error.

[4] Inaccurate in early years, and so mostly ignored. Evidently from its contents it is a Peterborough abb. ann., whose original hand ceases in 1220; later additions attach it to Peterborough, Ramsey abb. and possibly Huntingdon pr. (cf. N. R. Ker, *Med. Libraries of Great Britain*, 2nd ed., London, 1964, p. 103).

[5] The first consists of 13th/14th cent. additions to the Psalter of Robert of Lindsey of *c.* 1220; the other two are of the 14th cent. (cf. *Ctl. Peterborough*, p. 224).

[PETERBOROUGH]

Emma to Normandy in 1014 (*ASC* C, D, E). He is presumably one of the three Æ.s who occ. in 1007 in *Crawford Chts.*, no. 11 (Kemble, no. 1304), and may be the Æ. who occ. 1012, etc., ?1022, 1016×23 (Kemble, nos. 719, 734; *AS Chts.*, no. 81); but from 1019 he cannot be distinguished from Æ. abb. St Benet of Hulme, q.v.

Earnwig 1041–1052 M. Peterborough; res., d. 8 years later (*ASC* E, s.a. 1041 (for 1042), 1052; cf. Candidus, p. 65; d. 26 May, obit 1). Presumably the E. who occ. 1044×51, 1048 (Kemble, no. 797; Aberystwyth, Nat. Lib. Wales, MS Peniarth 390, p. 368).

Leofric 1052–1066 Nephew of Earl Leofric of Mercia; m. Peterborough; granted by King Edward and Queen Edith abbeys of Burton, Coventry, Crowland and Thorney (q.v.) (Candidus, pp. 65–76, esp. pp. 66–7; *ASC* E, s.a. 1052, 1066). D. 1066, 31 Oct. or 1 Nov. (*ASC* E; Candidus, p. 75; 1 Nov. also in obit 1). Occ. 1053 × 5, etc., and in spurious chts. dated 1065 (*AS Chts.*, no. 115; Kemble, nos. 824–5). Cf. *AS Writs*, p. 565; R. R. Darlington, in *EHR*, LI (1936), 403 n. 1.

Brand 1066–1069 Pr. Peterborough; acknowledged Edgar Ætheling as king in 1066, but reconciled to William. D. 1069, 27 or 29 Nov. (*ASC* E, s.a. 1066, 1069; Candidus, pp. 76–7; 27 Nov. also in obit 1). Later tradition made Hereward the Wake his nephew (Freeman, *NC*, IV, 806, 809).

Turold 1070–1098 M. of Fécamp, abb. Malmesbury (q.v.). Dates as *ASC* E; cf. *UGQ*, p. 13; d. 5, 7 or 10 April (obits 1, 3). On him see *MO*, p. 114; Candidus, pp. 77–86 (abb. 28 years).

Godric ?1101–1102 Brother of Brand; prev. archbp. el. of Dol. Dep. by St Anselm in 1102 (Candidus, pp. 86–7) – abb. one year; cf. *WMGP*, p. 119. But accession in 1098 in ann. in Candidus, p. 138.

Matthew Ridel 1102–1103 Brother of Geoffrey Ridel (Candidus, p. 87); m. of Mont-S.-Michel (Orderic, IV, 429). Dates as *ASC* E, s.a. 1103: enthroned 21 Oct. 1102; d. at Gloucester 21 Oct. 1103 (*ASC* E; Candidus, pp. 87–8; 1103, *UGQ*, p. 13; 20 Oct., obit 1; 21 Oct. obit 2; 22 Oct., obit 3).

Ernulf 1107–1114 Pr. of Christ Church, Canterbury (q.v.); el. 1107 (*ASC* E; *UGQ*, p. 13). El. Bp. Rochester 1114, el. confirmed 15 Sept. 1114, 'invested' by archbp. 28 Sept.; enthroned 10 Oct. (*ASC* E; Eadmer, p. 225). On him see Candidus, pp. 90ff., 96–7.

John 1114–1125 M. of Séez (Eadmer, p. 226; Candidus, p. 96). D. 14 Nov. 1125 (14 Oct., *ASC* E; 14 Nov., obit 1; 7 Nov., obit 2; 11 years abb., d. 1125, Candidus, p. 99). Occ. 28 Sept. 1116, 1120 (Peterborough D. and C. MS 1, ff. cxii v–cxiii, cxviii r–v).

Henry of Poitou 1127–1132 Related to Henry I and the duke of Aquitaine, prob. secular clerk and bp. elect of Soissons, then m. Cluny; pr. Souvigny; pr. Cluny; abb. S. Jean-d'Angely[1] (Orderic, IV, 430; with dates, *ASC* E; Candidus, pp. 100ff.). For the troubles of his abbacy see ib., pp. 102–3: dep. by Henry I, retired to Angely.

Martin of Bec 1132–1155 Prev. m. Bec and pr. St Neots (q.v.). Received at Peterborough 29 June 1132; dates as Candidus, pp. 103–24; cf. *ASC* E, s.a. 1132 (1133–55 in ann. in Candidus, pp. 138–9). D. 2 Jan. 1155 (Candidus, p. 124: after 20 years, 6 months, 8 days – *sic*; 2 Jan. also in obit 1; 3 Jan., obit 3). Occ. 1133 (Peterborough D. and C. MS 1, f. cxiii r–v).

William of Waterville 1155–1175 M. Peterborough (Candidus, pp. 124ff.; for dates, see *Ch. Peterborough*, pp. 2, 4). Dep. 1175: 27 Sept. (Gervase, I, 256) or 30 Oct. (Diceto, I, 402). Dates 1155–75 (Ann.). His obit was kept 30 Nov. (obit 3), but the year of d. is unknown. Occ. 1156 × 7 (Saltman, p. 246, no. 16).

The abbey was vacant 1175–7 (*PR 23 Henry II*, p. 104).

[1] These adventures have been checked so far as the evidence allows in a remarkable piece of detective work by Miss Cecily Clark in *EHR*, LXXXIV (1969), 548–60.

Benedict 1177–1193 Pr. Christ Church, Canterbury (q.v.); el. 29 May (*Gesta Hen. II*, I, 166; years also in Ann.; cf. *Gesta*, pp. 11 ff. etc.; *UGQ*, p. 13); d. 25 Sept. (obit 3) or 29 Sept. (Sparke, III, 103; obit 1; BM Cott. MS Nero C. ix, f. 12 v; etc.) 1193 (so Sparke; 1194 in *Ch. Peterborough*, p. 5).

Andrew *c.* 1193–1199 M. and pr. Peterborough (Sparke, *Ch. Peterborough*, *ut sup.*). D. 20 (obit 1) or 21 Feb. (obit 3) 1199 (Sparke, III, 104; *Ch. Peterborough*, p. 5; *Ann. Winchester*, p. 71).

Akarius (Acharius) 1200–1210 Pr. St Albans[1] (Sparke, III, 104 and n.; R. Vaughan, in *EHR*, LXXIII (1958), 71). El. Mar. 1200 (*Ann. Winchester*, p. 73, etc.). D. 12 (obit 3), 14 (Sparke, III, 107; Cambridge, Trinity Coll. MS O. 9. 25, f. 157) or 15 Mar. (obit 1) 1210 (Sparke, III, 107; *Ch. Peterborough*, p. 6; *Walt. Cov.*, II, 201; etc.).

Robert of Lindsey 1214–1222 M. and sacrist Peterborough; el. 11 June 1214 (Ann.; Sparke, III, 107; *Ch.*, p. 7, cf. *Rot. Lit. Pat.*, p. 109. D. 25 Oct. 1222 (Sparke, III, 114; obit 1; BM Cott. MS Nero C. ix, f. 14 v; cf. *CPR, 1216–25*, p. 351; etc.). Dates 1214–22 in Ann. See *Ctl. Peterborough*, p. 224.

RAMSEY (Hunts), St Benedict f. 969 (*Ch. Ramsey*, p. 40)
> List in *VCH Hunts*, I, 384; basis in *Ch. Ramsey* (henceforth *Ch.*); dates in 14th-cent. Ann., ed. in *Ch.*, pp. 339 ff., mostly reliable.

St Oswald 969–992 Remained abb. till his death (29 Feb. 992); Ramsey under charge of prs. (deans) Germanus, 969–*c.* 970 (see below; cf. *Ch.*, p. 42), then abb. Winchcombe, q.v. (and see p. 97); Eadnoth Senior, 970–92 (*Ch.*, pp. 40–2, 110; Ann.).

?Germanus see Cholsey.

Eadnoth 993–1006 M. Worcester, Ramsey; bp. Dorchester, 1006–16 (*Ch.*, pp. 110, 115; *Hist. York*, I, 423, 430). Ann. gives dates 993–1008 as abb. – '16 years' (p. 339). Prob. the E. who occ. 1001, 1002, 1005, 1007 (Kemble, nos. 705, 1297, 714, 1301, 1303–4).

Wulfsige 1006–1016 M. Ramsey; d. at battle of Ashingdon, 18 Oct. 1016 (*Ch.*, pp. 116–18; for the date cf. B. Dickins in *Leeds Studies in English*, VI, 20–1). Ann., p. 339, gives dates 1008–16. Cf. *Lib. El.*, p. 422 for a discussion of the story that he refused hospitality to Ealdorman Brihtnoth on his way to Maldon in 991 – it is attributed to Wulfsige both in *Lib. El.* and in *Ch. Ramsey* (p. 116).

Wythman 1016–1020 A German, deserted monastery and res. (*Ch.*, pp. 121–5). Dates as Ann., p. 340.

Æthelstan 1020–1043 Son of Ærnketel and Wulfrun; m. Ramsey, el. while Wythman on pilgrimage, and W. res. on his return (*Ch.*, pp. 66–7, 124–5). Murdered 28 or 30 Sept. 1043 (1020–43, d. 28 Sept., Ann., p. 340; cf. Ann. Thorney, BM Cott. MS Nero C. vii, f. 80 v; *Ch.*, pp. 155–6, says that he was attacked during Vespers on Michaelmas Day and died early the following morning – possibly it means first Vespers, i.e. on the 28th). Prob. the Æ. who occ. 1022 × 3, ?1022, 1042 (Kemble, nos. 735, 734, 763). Cf. *AS Writs*, p. 554; cf. also Abingdon (and Ælfstan, Canterbury, St Augustine).

Ælfwine 1043–1079/80 Son of priest Eadbriht (of Essex: *UGQ*, p. 205). Pr. Ramsey (*Ch.*, pp. 127, 156), el. 1043 (date in Ann., p. 340; cf. *Ch.*, pp. 156–7: between accession of Edward the Confessor and res. Ælfweard bp. London i.e. 1042 × 4). Abb. 38 years (*Ch.*, p. 156: 26, Ann., p. 340). D. 1080 (Ann., p. 340) or 1081 (Ann. Thorney, BM Cott. MS Nero C. vii, f. 81); but cf. *AS Writs*, pp. 551–2. Occ. at the Council of Rheims in 1049, 1072, 1075, *c.* 1080 (*ASC* E, s.a. 1046; cf. *Acta Sanctorum, Maii*, VI, 429; Bishop and Chaplais, facing pl. xxix; Wilkins, I, 364 (Aluuinus): see p. 23; *Mem. Bury*, I, 65; cf. *UGQ*, p. 205 and n. 13). Prob. sometimes the Æ. who occ. 1043, 1044, etc., 1050,

----

[1] Possibly also pr. Tynemouth, q.v.

[RAMSEY]

?1059, and in spurious chts. dated 1062, 1065 (Kemble, nos. 767, 774, 791; *OS Facs.*, II, Exeter 14; Kemble, nos. 813, 824); but cf. Malmesbury, Winchester, New Minster.

Ælfsige (Ælsi) 1080–1087 Abb. St Augustine's, Canterbury, el. 1080 (*Ch. Ramsey*, p. 177; for date, Ann., p. 340: 1080, 8 years); d. 1087 (*Mon.*, II, 580). On him see R. W. Southern in *Med. and Renaissance Studies*, IV (London, 1958), pp. 194ff.

Herbert Losinga 1087–1090/1 Pr. Fécamp (*WMGP*, p. 151); el. 1087 (Ann., p. 340); el. and consec. bp. Thetford (later Norwich) 1090 × 1 (*Ann. Winchester*, pp. 36–7, s.a. 1091; cf. *WMGP*, p. 151); d. 1119. Abb. 4 years (Ann., p. 340) or 3 years (*Reg. Norwich*, p. 22); signs as bp. 27 Jan. 1091 (*Reg.*, I, no. 315), and he was prob. consec. on 6 Jan. 1091 (see B. Dodwell in *TRHS*, 5th Series, VII (1957), 4), and so el. 1090. Occ. as abb. 17 June 1088 (*Ctl. Ramsey*, I, pp. 120–1). On him see Dodwell, art. cit.; *Epistolae*, ed. R. Anstruther (Brussels, 1846); E. M. Goulburn and H. Symonds, *Life, Letters and Sermons of Bishop Herbert de Losinga* (2 vols., Oxford and London, 1878).

Aldwin (Ealdwin) 1091–1102 Dates and dep. in Council of London, Ann., pp. 340–1, cf. 347; cf. Eadmer, p. 142 (1092 in Ann. Thorney, BM Cott. MS Nero C. vii, f. 81; Ann. Peterborough, Lambeth MS 1106, f. 118, which gives his dep. s.a. 1108 (?1109)). Occ. 3 Sept. 1101 (*Reg.*, II, no. 544). Restored 1107; occ. 1109, d. 1112 (4 years and occ. 1109, Ann., p. 341; 1107, Eadmer, p. 188).

Bernard of St Albans 1102–1107 5 years, Ann., p. 341. M. St Albans, ib. D. 14 Jan. (Cambridge, Trinity Coll. MS O. 9. 25, f. 156).

Aldwin 1107–1112 (see above).

Vacant for one and a half years (Ann., p. 341).

Reginald 1113/14–1131 M. Caen, app. *c.* Christmas 1113 (*ASC* H; cf. Ann., p. 341, s.a. 1114). D. 20 May 1131 (Florence, II, 92 = *JW*, p. 31n. – 20 May; cf. also *Mon.*, II, 566. After Easter 1131, Torigny, p. 119). Occ. 1115 × 16 (*Lib. El.*, p. 267).

Walter 1133–1160 El. 1133; d. 4 July 1160 (1133, 27 years: Ann., p. 341; d. 4 July, p. 336; 1159, Ann. Peterborough, Lambeth MS 1106, f. 119, 1161 in *Ch. Peterborough*, p. 3; see below). Dep. 1143.

Daniel was abb. for 18 days (*Ch. Ramsey*, p. 329); then Walter reinstated. Walter occ. 1145 (Saltman, p. 450). Walter and Daniel may have been ms. Ramsey, who occ. 1127 (CUL, Add. MS 3020, f. 145v).

Vacant in king's hands, 1160–1 (*PR 7 Henry II*, p. 11).

William Anglicus 1161–1177 (1178) M. Cluny, pr. S.-Martin-des-Champs. Abb. 16 years (Ann., p. 341). El. abb. Cluny 1177, but did not leave Ramsey until 1178; d. Jan. 1180 (*GFL*, p. 468n.; *Ch. Ramsey*, p. 341; Torigny, pp. 210, 287–9; *HF*, XII, 316, 447; Diceto, I, 424; *Ann. Winchester*, p. 61; cf. *PR 26 Henry II*, p. 38).

Vacant 1179–80 (ibid.); vacant two years (Ann., p. 341).

Robert Trianel 1180–1200 Pr. St Andrew, Northampton, el. 1180 (*Ann. Waverley*, p. 241; Ann., p. 341: el. 1180, d. after being abb. 20 years; cf. *PR ut sup.*); occ. 26 Nov. 1198 (BM Cott. MS Vesp. E. ii, f. 51).

Eudo 1200–1201/2 Pr. Peterborough; el. 1200, Ann., p. 342; el. 1200, d. 1201 (Lambeth MS 1106, f. 119v); d. 5 Apr. (London, Soc. of Antiquaries MS 59, f. 27v); *Ch. Peterborough*, p. 5 (1200–1). Occ. 1200 (*Hunts F.*, p. 2).

Robert of Reading 1202–1206 El. 1202 (Ann., p. 342; *Ch. Peterborough*, p. 5); res. 1206, royal assent 3 Apr. (*Rot. Lit. Pat.*, pp. 61, 64b); dep., according to *Ch. Peterborough*, p. 6, s.a. 1206; year before 1207, Ann., p. 342; 1208, *Ann. Dunstable*, p. 31, with other misdated events). D. at Reading, where he had presumably been a m. (Ann., p. 342). Occ. 15 Sept. 1202 (*Norfolk F.*, PRS LXV, no. 460); 6 Oct. 1205 (BM Cott. MS Vesp. E. ii, f. 52v).

Vacant 1206–14 (from *c.* 24 June 1206, *PR 9 John*, p. 110; cf. *PR 10 John*, p. 189; but no account in later PRs. 7 years, ending 1214, Ann., p. 342).

Richard 1214–1216 Prev. abb. Selby, el. Ramsey 1214 (see Selby). D. 1216 (after 2 years, Ann., p. 342; see below); occ. 9 Jan. 1215 (*Ctl. Glastonbury*, I, no. 141).

The next abb., Hugh Foliot, was abb. 1216–31 (Ann., p. 342; *Rot. Lit. Pat.*, p. 187 – royal assent 14 June; *CPR, 1225–32*, p. 441; etc.).

READING (Berks), St Mary and St John the Evangelist f. 1121 (but not fully established, with abb., until 1123)

Lists in *VCH Berks*, II, 72–3; B. R. Kemp, 'The Foundation of Reading Abbey' (unpubl. Ph.D. thesis). Basis in *UGQ*, pp. 10–11 (Ann. 1); *EHR*, XXXVII (1922), 400–1 (Ann. 2, ed. C. W. Previté-Orton). Calendar with obits in BM Cott. MS Vesp. E. v, ff. 11ff. (obit).

Hugh of Amiens 1123–1130 M. of Cluny; pr. Limoges *c.* 1115–20; pr. Lewes 1120–3 (see Lewes); app. abb. Reading 1123 (Ann. 1);[1] abp. Rouen 1130 (Ann. 1;[1] Torigny, p. 117); consec. 14 Sept. D. 10 Nov. 1164 (10 Nov. in obit; cf. *HF*, XXIII, 369). *DNB*.

Ansger (Anker, Ancher) 1130–1135 Prev. pr. Lewes *c.* 1126–30 (q.v.). Dates as Ann. 1 (for 1130 cf. *JW*, p. 30, not named). D. 27 Jan. (Ann. 1; obit).

Edward 1136–*c.* 1154 El. 1136 (Ann. 1); occ. 1141 × 2 (*Reg.*, III, no. 709); 1145 (Saltman, p. 450); (E.) *c.* 1147 × 8 (*GFL*, no. 73); *c.* 1150 × 4 (ib., no. 334). Cf. *GFL*, p. 538.

Master Reginald 1154–1158 Clerk to King Stephen, m. Grestain (see Walden), m., pr. Reading; abb. 1154–8; res., later pr. and abb. Walden 1166–1203/4 (q.v.; see *GFL*, pp. 477 and n., 538; for dates, *Flor. Hist.*, II, 72, 75; Ann. 2). Occ. (R.) 1154 (BM Egerton MS 3031, f. 26); 13 Dec. 1157 (*Ctl. Gloucester*, II, p. 106). Cf. *Reg.*, III, pp. xi, xiv.

Roger 1158–1165 Dates as Ann. 2; cf. *Ann. Winchester*, p. 58, s.a. 1164; *Flor. Hist.*, II, 75. D. 20 Jan. (obit). Occ. 1164 (PRO E315/53/223). Cf. *GFL*, p. 538.

William the Templar 1165–1173 Abp. Bordeaux, consec. 25 Feb. 1173, d. (?)15 Sept. 1187 (dates as abb., Ann. 2; cf. *Flor. Hist.*, II, 84; *HF*, XII, 443). On him see *GFL*, p. 538 and index; Delisle-Berger, Introd., p. 474; *GC*, II, 818–19.

Joseph 1173–1186 Prev. pr. Reading (cf. *MB*, I, 418); el. 1173, res. 1186, d. 8 Feb. 1190 (Ann. 2; for the day, cf. obit). Occ. 1173 × 4 (BM Egerton MS 3031, f. 56v).

Hugh 1186–1199 Pr. Lewes; el. 1186 (Ann. 2; *Ann. Waverley*, p. 244); abb. Cluny 1199 (*Ann. Waverley*, pp. 251–2; *Ann. Winchester*, p. 73). D. 29 Aug. 1207 (*GC*, IV, 1144; cf. for the day, obit). Occ. 1189 (BM Stowe MS 925, ff. 34v–35v).

Elias 1200–1212 M. Reading, el. 1200 ('can.' Reading, Ann. 2; cf. *Ann. Worcester*, p. 390, s.a. 1199); d. 20 (Trokelowe, ed. Hearne, p. 389) or 21 July (obit) 1212 (*Ann. Dunstable*, pp. 38–9; *Ann. Waverley*, p. 273; 1213, *Ann. Tewkesbury*, p. 61). Occ. 12 Nov. × 2 Dec. 1201 (*Bucks F.*, p. 21); Oct. 1202 (Cheney, *Inn. III*, no. 352); 26 Feb., 23 Mar. 1207 (ib., nos. 739, 744).

Simon the Chamberlain 1213–1226 El. 1213 (*Ann. Dunstable*, p. 40); d. 13 Feb. 1226 (obit; Ann. 2; cf. *Ann. Dunstable*, p. 100; *Ann. Worcester*, p. 419; 14 Feb. in Trokelowe, ed. Hearne, p. 385).

The next abb., Adam, pr. Leominster, el. 1226 (Ann. 2).

ROCHESTER (Kent), St Andrew ref. 1080

D.G. List in Le Neve, revised edn., II, 78–80 (D. Greenway); *VCH Kent*, II, 125.

?Arnulf D. –1113 (*Roul. Morts*, p. 203).

Ralph –1107 M. of Caen; came to England with Lanfranc; res. 1107 to be abb. Battle (el. 1 Aug.: *Ch. Battle*, pp. 51–2; cf. Orderic, ed. Chibnall, II, 192).

---

[1] Confirmed by ann. (?Wenlock) in Cambridge, Corpus Christi Coll., MS 111, f. 9.

[ROCHESTER]

Ordoin[1] (Ordwynus) Occ. –Mar. 1108, 1114×24 (*Textus Roffensis*, f. 198; cf. ff. 193r–v, 196v–197); +1125 (*Reg. Rochester*, p. 8). Possibly m. Canterbury (see Le Neve).

?Thomas Occ. 1126×36, prob. 1129×30[2] (CUL Add. MS 3020, ff. 166v–7).

Brian Occ. 1144×8 (*Reg. Rochester*, p. 10); 1 Sept. 1145 (Saltman, pp. 447–9, no. 222; cf. n. 1); 25 Feb. 1146 (*JL* 8870, *AS*, I, 344; BM Cott. MS Nero D. ii, ff. 113v–114). D. 5 Dec. (ib., Nero C. ix, f. 17).

Reginald Occ. 8 Mar. 1155 (*PUE*, II, no. 88); (R.) 1160 (*Reg. Master David*, no. 68 = Liverani, p. 753: 'Frater R. sancti A. de R. presbiter' ('sancti Asaph', Liverani)).

?William of Borstal Formerly cellarer, occ. as pr. n.d., before Silvester (*Reg. Rochester*, p. 121).

Silvester Occ. (S.) 15 May 1177 (*Reg. Rochester*, pp. 410–11); 8 Apr. 1180 (*PUE*, II, no. 197).

Richard –1182/3 Occ. +Nov. 1181 (*Reg. Rochester*, p. 168); 1 May 1182 (*Kent F.*, p. 1); +Dec. 1182[3] (*Reg. Rochester*, p. 481). Res. '1182' to be abb. Burton (q.v.; *Ann. Burton*, p. 187), presumably for 1183.

Alvred –1186 Res. 1186 to be abb. Abingdon (q.v.).

?Osbert of Sheppey Noted by Wharton, *AS*, I, 393, as prev. sacrist: occ. n.d. (*Reg. Rochester*, p. 121); prob. = O. pr. occ. 1189×90 (BM Cott. MS Domit. A. x, ff. 165–6).

Ralph de Ros Prev. sacrist Rochester (*AS*, I, 393). Occ. 1193 (*Reg. Hamonis Hethe*, I, p. 5); 4 Oct. 1202 (*Kent F.*, p. 24); Jan. 1203 (*CRR*, II, p. 160); –18 May 1208 (*Rot. Cht.*, p. 179).

Elias Prob. prev. sacrist (occ. Jan. 1203, *CRR*, II, p.160). Occ. 1 Nov. 1214 (Rochester, D. and C., T. 193/1); (H. for Helias) +1215 (Bodl. MS Rawl. B. 461, f. 57).

The next pr., William, occ. 6 Oct. 1218 (*Kent F.*, p. 57); Apr. 1222 (ib., p. 75).

ST ALBANS (Herts), St Alban ref. *c.* 970 (cf. *Hist. York*, I, 427)[4]

List in *VCH Herts*, IV, 414ff., cf. pp. 369ff. Basis in *GASA* and writings of Matthew Paris; 14th-cent. list in Oxford, Magdalen Coll. MS 53 (deposited in Bodl.), p. 1 (which seems to be based on *GASA*, and is of no independent value).[5] Obits in BM Cott. MS Julius D. vii, ff. 35v–41 (obit) and Belvoir martyrology (Cambridge, Trinity Coll. MS O. 9. 25: Belvoir obit; see Belvoir for printed ed.).

---

[1] Ordoin occ. in a cht. of Bp. Gundulf (d. 1108) dated in various forms 1089 and 1091, and on this account has been supposed to have been twice pr. But the cht. (in all forms) notes the consent of King Henry (+1100) and Abp. Anselm (1093–1109) and is witnessed by Ralph abb. of Séez (1089–1108, but in England *c.* 1103/4–8: cf. Orderic, III, 308–9, IV, 192); and in one form (*Reg.*, II, no. 845) by Ralph abb. Battle (1107+). It is probably a forgery, and the dates must be wrong. The forms are printed in: *Mon.*, I, 175 from BM Cott. Cht. viii, 10 (dated 1089); Saltman, no. 222, Cheney, *English Bishops' Chanceries*, p. 151 (abbreviated; cf. p. 94n. for a discussion of its authenticity), from Canterbury Cathedral Cht. Ant. R. 50, inspex. of 1277 (dated 1091); also in *Reg. Rochester*, pp. 6–7, 87–8; abstr. in *Reg. Hamonis Hethe*, I, 433 and *Reg.*, II, no. 845 (no date, but assigned by eds. to 1107). Dr Martin Brett has made a special study of this document, and we gratefully acknowledge his help: we hope he will publish shortly a full statement of the case for forgery.

[2] Abp. William as legate; dedication of Thorney abb. (see MS cit., f. 6).

[3] Waleran bp. Rochester: he was el. Oct. 1182, and it is just possible that this document belongs to his period as bp. el., Oct. × Dec. 1182.

[4] After the Easter Council, which may have been that at which the *Regularis Concordia* was promulgated, i.e. *c.* 970 (cf. *Reg. Concordia*, ed. T. Symons, NMT, pp. xxiiff.). Of the St Albans sources we have normally only cited *GASA*, composed by Matthew Paris, but based in fair measure on a twelfth-century source, the roll of Adam the Cellarer: for this, and the history of the texts of *GASA*, see Vaughan, *Matthew Paris*, pp. 182ff. We have only cited Wendover or Paris's chs. when they give material not in *GASA* (Wendover is cited from *MPCM*, II).

[5] With dates of d. etc. +1066, only noted when different from *GASA*.

Ælfric *c.* 969–?990 First abb. of re-foundation (*GASA*, I, 23–4; cf. list); *GASA* makes him die as abb. (see Leofric below), but Eadmer tells us he was the Æ. who became bp. Ramsbury in 990 and abp. Canterbury 995–1005 (*Hist. York*, II, 22; cf. *AS Wills*, pp. 160–1; *GASA*, I, 30n. shows some knowledge at St Albans that Ælfric became abp.). But he occ. 991 in *Ch. Ramsey*, p. 93. *WMGP*, p. 32, makes Ælfric abb. Abingdon; but there seems no place for him in the Abingdon list.[1] In his will (*AS Wills*, no. 18) he shows an interest in Canterbury cathedral and in Cholsey, but chiefly in St Albans and Abingdon, to the former of which he left his books; and this might lead one to suppose that he had been a m. of Abingdon and abb. St Albans.[2] Florence, I, 152, however, says he had been a m. Glastonbury, although one MS makes him (?also) a m. Abingdon (I, 158n.). He was possibly the Æ. who occ. 972, etc., 975 (Birch, nos. 1282, 1284, etc., 1312–13, 1315–16) and one of the two of 990(×1) (Kemble, no. 712). Cf. Canterbury, St Augustine's, Cerne, Glastonbury, Malmesbury.

Leofric ?*c.* 990– Brother of Abp. Ælfric, occ. 997, 1007 (Kemble, nos. 698, 1304); called 'Abb.' in Æ.'s will (1002×5; see *AS Wills*, no. 18); possibly the L. who occ. ?995, 996, etc., 1003, and prob. one of the two Ls. of 1002 and 1005 (*Mon.*, VI, 1443–6; Kemble, nos. 1292, 1299, 1295, 714 – see Muchelney). *GASA*, I, 28–31, makes him son of the earl of Kent and later abp. Canterbury; the latter is due (as Vaughan shows, *Matthew Paris*, p. 199) to an exchange between Ælfric's and Leofric's names in Matthew Paris's copy of *GASA*.[3] *GASA* also places him after Eadmar, and so makes the next two entries very doubtful. Obit 20 Apr. (Belvoir obit, f. 157v).

?Ealdred placed between Ælfric and Eadmar in *GASA*, I, 24–5.

?Eadmar placed between Ealdred and Leofric (*sic*: see above) in *GASA*, I, 25–8. Possibly the Eadmær who occ. 1012 (Kemble, no. 719).

?Ælfric II placed between Leofric and Leofstan by *GASA*, I, 31–8 and made to die as abb. This may be entirely due to confusion with Ælfric I (see note 3); but see below, under Ecgfrith. The list runs Eadmær, Ælfric (II), Leofric (II – called brothers), Leofstan, Frederick...

?Leofstan *GASA*, I, 38–41, places him (also called 'Plumstan' on p. 38n.) between Ælfric II and Frederick; makes him die *c.* 1066 and yet be succeeded in or *c.* 1064 (see below).[4] He or the abb. Bury may be the L. who occ. 1061 (Kemble, no. 810): 2 Leofstans occ. in a spurious cht. dated 1062 (Kemble, no. 813).

?Ecgfrith The *Liber Eliensis* (pp. 176–7) tells a story of how Abp. Stigand went to Ely (presumably early in 1070: cf. ib. pp. 425–6) to deposit his treasures there, and summoned Ecgfrith, whom he had made abb. St Albans,[5] to bring his treasures and the

---

[1] Searle, copying Birch, makes Ælfric abb. Abingdon occ. in 993, from Kemble, no. 684. This is a mistake: Wulfgar is abb. Abingdon in Kemble, no. 684, Ælfric of Malmesbury.

[2] The next abb., Leofric, was apparently Ælfric's brother: this might confirm the attribution, or alternatively explain the abp.'s interest in St Albans. Æ. also left money to the people of Wilts, which suggests the identification with the bp. Ramsbury.

[3] *GASA* makes Ælfric II Leofric's brother, which implies a confused memory that he had been abp., and attributes the grant of Kingsbury to him (cf. *AS Wills*, no. 18). All these points belong to Ælfric I; and the rest of *GASA*'s account relates to the relics of St Alban, a probably fictitious story, on which see below.

[4] *VCH Herts*, IV, 372, 414, adds Abp. Stigand in 1066. There is evidence (ibid., p. 372n.) that he had some grip on the estates, and this was no doubt connected with the authority of the later abps. over St Albans. But there is no evidence that Stigand was even titular abb. there. The *Lib. El.*, p. 168, notes St Albans among the abbs. over which he had control; but at the others – Glastonbury, St Augustine's, Canterbury and Ely (cf. ibid., p. 412) – there is reason to suppose that he was not abb.; at Winchester (also listed) he was, of course, bp. and so in a sense titular abb.

[5] Freeman, *NC*, IV, 399n. cites confirmatory evidence from *GASA*, Eadmer, Gervase and the *Ann. Worcester* of a special relationship between the abps. of Canterbury and the abbey: the other evidence

[ST ALBANS]

relics of St Alban to Ely. Stigand was then deposed, and Paul made abb. of St Albans, and so Ecgfrith stayed at Ely and the relics of St Alban were solemnly enshrined there. This story reflects a controversy between Ely and St Albans as to who possessed the genuine relics of St Alban, and this has led, not unnaturally, to great confusion in the sources. The *GASA* makes no mention of Ecgfrith, but divides his activities into two: Ælfric II (above) is made to trick the monks of Ely by sending false relics; Frederick (below) is made to retire to Ely after a spirited rebellion against the Conqueror. Everything it says about Frederick seems to be legend except his name,[1] and in so far as the legend can be related to history, it clearly refers to the period *c.* 1070–1, and not later, although we know Frederick was abb. in 1072 and 1075. The Ely and St Albans accounts confirm one another in making the last OE abb. retire to Ely at the time of the rebellion; but as they also confirm one another in making Paul immediately succeed as abbot, and both contain legendary elements, it is doubtful how seriously their evidence should be taken, even when they agree. They are in a sense independent, but evidently the fruit of controversy, and so may well have affected each other; and this is confirmed by another version of the Ely story (evidently based on a common, 12th cent., source), which calls the abbot Ælfric.[2] At first sight this seems to fit the *GASA* evidence; yet there is other good evidence that an Abb. Ecgfrith, not an abb. of Ely, was remembered there.[3] It is clear that St Albans retained a very hazy knowledge of its abbots before Paul, and that, if the Ely story is anywhere near correct, there were strong positive reasons for forgetting Ecgfrith. On the whole it seems probable that the last OE abbot of St Albans was called Ecgfrith, and that he retired to Ely *c.* 1070.

Frederick Occ. 27 May 1072 (Bishop and Chaplais, facing pl. xxix), 1075 (Wilkins, I, 364 – 'Verolamii'; see p. 23). On his name and origin, see below, n. 1.

Paul 1077–1093 M. of Caen, nephew of Abp. Lanfranc; el. 1077 (*GASA*, I, 51; cf. Eadmer, p. 15); d. 11 Nov. 1093 (after 16 years 4 months: *GASA*, I, 64; Florence, II, 31; 11 Nov. also in Belvoir obit, f. 164v; cf. BM Royal MS 2. B. vi, f. 7). Occ. 27 Jan. 1091 (*Reg.*, I, no. 315). *DNB*.

Abbey vacant, in king's hand, 1093–7 (*GASA*, I, 65).

Richard d'Aubigny[4] 1097–1119 M. of Lessay (*GASA*, I, 66); d. 16 May (Belvoir obit, f. 158v; BM Cott. MS Vitell. C. xii, f. 129v) or 15 May 1119 (after 21 years: *GASA*, I, 72).[5]

relates to Lanfranc and Anselm, but Stigand is a likely person to have started so curious a link, and it looks as if the Ely tradition had access to sound information on this point. There are valuable discussions of the problem in *Lib. El.*, pp. xxxvii–viii and Vaughan, *Matthew Paris*, pp. 198–204.

[1] Cf. Freeman, *NC*, IV, 802–4. The legendary elements include the fanciful account of his origin – that he was an Old Saxon with Danish connections, related to Cnut. The name Frederick was rare outside Germany. There are a few scattered references for Frithuric in Searle's *Onomasticon* from the 7th–10th cents., so an OE origin is not impossible. The only other Frederick known in England in this period, however, was brother or brother-in-law of William de Warenne – more probably the latter, and so a Fleming (see Clay, in *EYC*, VIII, pp. 44–5). It is therefore probable that the abbot of St Albans who flourished in the 1070s was a representative of the invaders. The *GASA* as we have it is basically the work of Matthew Paris. A thirteenth-century writer of the age of the Emperor Frederick II would naturally assume that Frederick was a German name, and the whole account of his origin may be fantasy; but it is not impossible that some genuine tradition lies behind it.

[2] See *Lib. El.*, pp. xxxvii–viii for a discussion of this; the variant version is in John of Tynemouth's *Nova Legenda Anglie* (ed. C. Horstmann, Oxford, 1901), p. 36; an alternative reading is *Alfridus*.

[3] In an Ely calendar which records the death of an abb. Ægfridus (no house named) under 28 Oct. (see *Lib. El.*, p. xxxviii).   [4] *MPHA*, I, 98, 228; cf. Loyd, *BHRS*, XIX (1937), 105–6.

[5] 21 years should bring us to 1118, and this conforms with the indication in *GASA*; but 1119 agrees with the epact, and is confirmed by Ann. Thorney, BM Cott. MS Nero C. vii, f. 223. D. 17 May (obit).

Geoffrey de Gorron[1] 1119–1146 From noble family of Normandy and Maine, born in Maine, pr. St Albans; el. 1119 (*GASA*, I, 72–3; *Ann. Winchester*, pp. 45–6); occ. 1125 (*ASC* E); 1138 × 9 (*Reg.*, III, no. 819); 1145 (Saltman, no. 223n.); d. 25 Feb. 1146 (*GASA*, I, 96; 1145, *Ann. Winchester*, p. 53; his obit is confirmed by Belvoir obit, f. 156v).

Ralph Gubion 1146–1151 Englishman, m. St Albans, formerly chaplain of bp. of Lincoln; el. 8 May 1146 (*GASA*, I, 106; for date *MPCM*, II, 178). Retired 1150, finally res. 1151 (*MPCM*, II, 184, 187; 4th or 5th year: *GASA*, I, 108); d. 6 July 1151 (*GASA*, I, 110; Belvoir obit, f. 160v).

Robert de Gorron 1151–1166 A Norman, nephew of Abb. Geoffrey; m., sacrist and pr. St Albans; made *procurator* in 1150; el. 1150, bl. 19 May 1151 (*GASA*, I, 110–11; for dates, *MPCM*, II, 187; *Ann. Winchester*, p. 54, gives it under 1150 with d. of Ralph); d. 1166, 23 Oct. (a Sunday, after 15 years, 4 months and a few days: *GASA*, I, 182; 26 Oct. in *LV Durham*, 1st edn., p. 146, 28 Oct. in Wendover, I, 41 = *MPCM*, II, 234 – after 14 years; 29 Oct. in obit, Belvoir obit, f. 163v; BM Cott. MS Nero C. ix, f. 14v).

Simon 1167–1183 An Englishman, pr. of St Albans; el. *c.* 21 May[2] 1167 (*GASA*, I, 183–4; *MPCM*, II, 239; *Ann. Worcester*, p. 382. Succession given with Robert's death as 1166 in *Ann. Winchester*, p. 59). D. 12 July (Belvoir obit, f. 160) 1183 (after *c.* 15 years: *GASA*, I, 194; *Ann. Waverley*, p. 243; *Ann. Winchester*, p. 60, has 1170 in error; list, 1184).

Master Warin of Cambridge 1183–1195 Pr. St Albans (cf. *Ann. Waverley*, p. 243), and formerly studied at Salerno; el. 1183 (*GASA*, I, 194; cf. p. 217 – el. *c.* Aug.?); d. 29 Apr. 1195 (after 11 years, 8 months, 8 days: *GASA*, I, 217; cf. Diceto, II, 124n.; for the day, cf. Belvoir obit, f. 157v; BM Cott. MS Nero C. ix, f. 10v; *Epp. Cant.*, p. 558; 1196, list).

John de Cella 1195–1214 Pr. Wallingford, q.v. (cf. *Ann. Waverley*, p. 250); born near Studham (Beds); student at Paris (*GASA*, I, 217); el. 20 July 1195 (*MPCM*, II, 411; *Ann. Waverley*, p. 250; for the day, Diceto, II, 124n.); installed 30 July 1195 (ibid.). D. 17 July 1214 (in his 19th year: *GASA*, I, 249–50; confirmed by Ann. Merton, Corpus Christi College, Cambridge, MS 59, f. 171v. 17 July also by Belvoir obit, f. 160; cf. *Ann. Dunstable*, p. 41; 1215, list).

William of Trumpington 1214–1235 M. St Albans; el. 20 Nov. 1214; bl. 30 Nov. (*GASA*, I, 253);[3] d. 24 Feb. 1235 (*GASA*, I, 300; 24 Feb. also Belvoir obit, f. 156v; 23 Feb., obit).

ST BENET OF HULME (Norfolk), St Benedict ref. 1019

Lists in *Ctl. Hulme*, II, pp. 191–8 (J. R. West); *VCH Norfolk*, II, 336; based on 14th-cent. list in *Ctl.*, I, p. 172; Oxenedes's Ch.; 15th cent. list and extracts from calendar etc. in Worcestre (ed. Harvey), pp. 230ff., cf. pp. 222ff.

Ælfsige 1019–1046 D. 23 Oct. (*Ctl. Hulme*, II, p. 191, from Worcestre, ed. Harvey, pp. 230, 232 for year). Cf. Peterborough: possibly occ. –1023; presumably the Æ. who occ. 1042 × 4 (Kemble, no. 769); 1043 × 4 (*AS Chts.*, no. 97); 1044 (Kemble, no. 774). Cf. Æthelsige of Abingdon.

Thurstan *c.* 1046–1064 2nd abb. (epitaph in Worcestre, p. 224); called 'of Ludham' in Worcestre, p. 232. D. 7 Oct. (Worcestre, pp. 224, 230; dates, pp. 224, 232).

Ælfwold 1064–1089 D. 14 Nov. (Worcestre, pp. 230, 232; Oxenedes, pp. 38, 293; cf. *Ctl. Hulme*, I, p. 172; II, p. 192; Stenton in *EHR*, XXXVII (1922), 233).

Ralph I ?1089–1101 App. s.a. 1089 (Oxenedes, p. 38). D. 6 Oct. 1101 (Oxenedes, p. 293; year also in Worcestre, p. 232). Dr West suggests that he was not strictly abb., but a m.

---

[1] Cf. *St Albans Psalter*, p. 143.

[2] Sunday after Ascension (21 May), but called 20 May, *GASA*, I, 183; Diceto (I, 330n.: but 22 May) and Wendover (following Diceto) make it Ascension Day (18 May). Diceto dates the bl. the same day.

[3] St Edmund, king and martyr (20 Nov.): cf. *MPCM*, II, 583 – a Thursday; bl. St Andrew's day, 1st Sunday in Advent. These details are correct for 1214. El. 1213/14, d. 1235, in *Ann. Dunstable*, pp. 42, 141.

[ST BENET OF HULME]

in charge of temporalities, and cf. the monk Ranulf in *Ctl. Hulme*, I, no. 3; the names, however, were normally distinct, and the identification is not certain: Ralph was clearly commemorated as an abb.

Richer 1101–1125 Dates as Oxenedes, pp. 293–4, 432 (cf. Worcestre, p. 232; *Ctl. Hulme*, I, p. 172); obit 19 Jan. (Oxenedes, p. 294; Worcestre, p. 230).[1]

Conrad 1126–1127 Prev. m., sacrist and pr. Christ Church, Canterbury (q.v.); abb. 18 weeks, d. 16, 17, or 18 Feb. (16 Feb., Oxenedes, p. 294; 17 Feb., Worcestre, p. 230; BM Cott. MS Nero C. ix, f. 6; 18 Feb., BM Cott. MS Claud. C. vi, f. 171; BM Arundel MS 68, ff. 16v–17; *Ctl. Hulme*, I, p. 172).

William Basset 1127–1134 Prev. m. S. Évroult (Orderic, III, 382–3, called Bassus); dates as Oxenedes, p. 294; for his death, *Ctl. Hulme*, I, p. 172; Worcestre, p. 232 gives 1133. Obit. ibid., p. 230, 31 Mar.

Anselm *c.* 1134–1140 Called pr. Dover by Worcestre (p. 232) – but this seems to be an error; d. 1140 (ibid.; Oxenedes, p. 432; *Ctl. Hulme*, I, p. 172); obit 9 Dec. (BM Cott. MS Nero C. ix, f. 17v; Worcestre, p. 232). Occ. *Ctl. Hulme*, I, pp. 75ff.

Daniel *c.* 1141– –1146 Prev. m. Hulme (Oxenedes, p. 295, cf. Worcestre, p. 232); twice abb. (cf. *Ctl. Hulme*, I, p. 171); occ. prob. 1141 × 6 (ib., I, no. 161; cf. ed.'s notes); 7 June 1143 (*Reg.*, III, no. 655). Dep. –1146 (see below).

Hugh –1146–*c.* 1150 Nephew of King Stephen[2] (illegitimate son of Count Theobald); m. Tiron, abb. Hulme, abb. Chertsey from 1147 × 9, later of Lagny-sur-Marne (see Chertsey; Torigny, pp. 218–19; cf. Worcestre, p. 232; Oxenedes, pp. 294–5). Occ. –1146 (*Ctl. Hulme*, I, p. 142); 10 May 1147 (*PUE*, I, no. 36); 1147 × 50 (*Ctl. Hulme*, I, no. 68).

Daniel (restored) *c.* 1150–1153 Occ. ?*1150* (*Ctl. Hulme*, I, no. 84); (D.) 12 Jan. 1152 (*PUE*, I, no. 49). D. 8 or 9 Nov. 1153 (Oxenedes, p. 295, cf. p. 432; Worcestre, p. 230, cf. p. 232; *Ctl. Hulme*, I, p. 172). Worcestre, p. 232, gives him a son named Henry, companion of Thomas Becket and later abb. Ramsey: this seems to be fiction, deriving from Hulme tradition.

William II *c.* 1154–1168 Possibly pr. (cf. *Ctl. Hulme*, I, nos. 84, 141); occ. 1153 × 4, 25 Feb. 1155, etc. (*Ctl. Hulme*, I, nos. 53, 152 = *Reg.*, III, nos. 403–4; *PUE*, I, no. 59). D. 8 or 21 Feb. 1168 (Oxenedes, p. 295, cf. p. 433; Worcestre, pp. 230, 232). For the year see also *Ctl. Hulme*, I, p. 172. Called Geoffrey s.a. 1157, in *Ch. Battle*, p. 87.

Vacant 1168–75; *PR 14 Henry II*, p. 33 to *PR 21 Henry II*, p. 125: this implies el. at Woodstock *c.* late June, i.e. *c.* 1–8 July (Eyton, *Itinerary*, p. 192; cf. *Gesta Hen. II*, I, 91–3 (1 July); Diceto, I, 401 (8 July)).

Thomas 1175–1186 Prob. el. *c.* 1–8 July 1175 (see above; s.a. 1168, Oxenedes, p. 433); d. 11 Sept. 1186 (Oxenedes, p. 296, cf. p. 433; Worcestre, pp. 230, 232 – on p. 230 the year is given as 1176; *Ctl. Hulme*, I, p. 172). Occ. 21 July 1183 (*PUE*, I, no. 214).

Ralph 1187–1210 Prev. m. Cluny, pr. Ramsey (Oxenedes, p. 296; Worcestre, p. 223; *Ch. Ramsey*, p. 341); date of app. 1186 in *Ch. Ramsey* and Oxenedes, but *PR 33 Henry II*, p. 23, accounts for ¾ year before election: i.e. he was el. *c.* 24 June 1187. D. 4 Feb. 1210 (Oxenedes, pp. 296, 434; Worcestre, pp. 230, 232; *Walt. Cov.*, II, 201; *Ctl. Hulme*, I, p. 172).

John le Chamiel 1214 M. Bury (cf. *Mem. Bury*, II, 34), d. as abb.-el., according to Worcestre, p. 232, 31 Dec. 1213; Oxenedes, p. 296, gives 1214. 31 Dec. is confirmed by BM Cott. MS Vitell. C. xii, f. 155. His el. was no doubt delayed by the interdict, and will have taken place in 1214 (cf. Tillmann, pp. 101ff.), perhaps among the many abbatial els.

---

[1] *Reg.*, II, no. 549, carries his *signum*, and is very similar to no. 548, dated 3 Sept. 1101. Richer's signature makes it probable that no. 549, if genuine, was issued a month or two later; it cannot be later than 1102, when the abb. Ramsey who also signs was dep.

[2] Cf. *Reg.*, III, no. 402; etc.; cf. Chertsey.

of Oct.–Nov. 1214 (ibid., p. 103) which would explain why he was still unblessed at his death.

Reginald *c*. 1215–1229 M. Hulme (Oxenedes, p. 296); d. 24 May 1229 (Worcestre, pp. 230, 232; Oxenedes, pp. 297, 435). Occ. 6 Feb. 1219 (BM Cott. MS Galba E. ii, f. 87); 3 May 1229 (ib., f. 88).

SANDWELL (Staffs), St Mary Magdalene f. *c*. 1180
List in *VCH Staffs*, III, 219 (A. Saltman).
Reginald Presented *temp*. John and referred to as former pr. in 1224 (*CRR*, XI, no. 1572).
John Occ. 1218 (*Bucks F.*, p. 37); 1195 × 1222 (*Mon.*, IV, 107).

SELBY (Yorks, W.), St Mary and St Germanus f. 1069 × 70 from Auxerre (*EYC*, I, pp. 359–63)
List in *VCH Yorks*, III, 99; *Hist. Selby* in *Ctl. Selby*, I, [1ff.], gives narrative to Abb. German.
Benedict 1069/70–1096/7 Sacrist, St Germanus, Auxerre; first abb. Selby (*Hist. Selby*, pp. 6, 12, etc.; *Roul. Morts*, p. 195); res. 1096/7, retiring to Rochester (*Hist. Selby*, p. 21: after 27 years, 4 William I to 10 William II).
Hugh *c*. 1096/7[1]–*c*. 1122 Pr. Selby; res. *c*. 1122, d. *c*. 1124 (*Hist. Selby*, pp. 22, 24–5; abb. 26 years; 10 William II to 23 Henry I, d. after 2 years). Occ. (H.) 1101 × 8, 1109 + (*Ctl. Selby*, II, nos. 875–6); 20 Aug. 1110 (BM Cott. MS Julius A. x, f. 19 – not 1103, as f. 13).
Herbert *c*. 1122–1125 M. St Albans; res. to legate John of Crema at York (i.e. mid 1125),[2] retired to St Albans (*Hist. Selby*, pp. 26–7: 'scarcely four years').
Durand *c*. 1125–1134/5 M. St Mary's, York; compelled to res. by Abp. Thurstan and retired to Cluny, later made pr. in England (possibly Montacute, q.v.) (*Hist. Selby*, pp. 27–8: 9 years, to last of Henry I).
A vacancy of 2 years: *Hist. Selby*, p. 31; abbey vacant in spring 1136, cf. papal letter of 22 Apr., *Hist. York*, III, 66.
Walter 1137–1143 Pr. Pontefract; d. 28 Feb. (*Hist. Selby*, pp. 31–2, 6 years; cf. Clay, *YAJ*, XXXVIII (1955), 456 – on Pontefract). Occ. 1137 × 40 (*EYC*, III, no. 1470).
Elias Paynel 1143–1152, 1153–4 Pr. Holy Trinity, York (*Hist. Selby*, p. 33); res. after 9 years at command of Abp. Henry Murdac, but returned *c*. 18 months later (ibid., pp. 44–5, says 3 months before Murdac's death (14 Oct. 1153), i.e. *c*. July 1153); his return lasted for *c*. 6 months and he was dep. by Abp. Theobald in synod. *GASA*, I, 120 says that the pope deposed him after an appeal by the abb. of St Albans. Very likely Theobald was acting on a papal mandate. Occ. prob. 1143 (*Lancs PR*, p. 281).
German 1152, 1154–1160 M. St Albans, pr. Tynemouth (*GASA*, I, 120; *Hist. Selby*, p. 44; cf. *Ctl. Whitby*, I, p. 9); app. 1152, restored 1154 (see above); abb. 7 years; d. 23 Nov. (*Hist. Selby*, pp. 45–6), presumably 1160 (1161 is too late: see below; 1159 is possible, if the *Hist.* was reckoning from 1152, but this would necessitate a long vacancy).
Gilbert de Vere *c*. 1161–1183 Brother of Guy de Vere (*Ctl. Selby*, II, no. 1221; cf. no. 1190); a date in 1167 fell in his 7th year and a date in 1174 in his 14th (*Hist. Selby*, pp. 50, 54); these and the evidence about his predecessor make 1161 the probable year of his accession. *PR 31 Henry II*, p. 79 – *PR 34 Henry II*, p. 1, show a vacancy running from *c*. Michaelmas 1183 to later than Michaelmas 1188 (in fact 1189; see below).
Roger of London 1189–1195 Pr. Selby, app. at Pipewell, 16 Sept. 1189, bl. 6 Dec. 1189; d. Jan. 1195 (*Gesta Hen. II*, II, 85, 100; Howden, III, 283).
Richard 1195–1214 Pr. Selby, app. 1195 (Howden, II, 283); res. abb. Ramsey in 1214

---

[1] But the *Hist.* (p. 22) refers to his promotion 'archiepiscopi Gerardi approbatione'; Gerard was abp. 1100–8.   [2] Cf. Tillmann, *Legaten*, p. 28.

[SELBY]

(*Walt. Cov.*, II, 216; *Ann. Worcester*, p. 403 (no name); *Ad. Dom.*, II, 449 (before 9 Jan. 1215)). Occ. 1199 × 1203 (Bodl. MS Top. Yorks c. 72, f. 47a).

Alexander 1214–1221 Pr. Selby; royal assent to el. 14 Dec. 1214 (*Rot. Lit. Pat.*, p. 125); res. 1221 (*Walt. Cov.*, II, 250): no name, but Alexander occ. 1219 (*Ctl. Selby*, II, p. 59); lic. to el. successor 21 June 1221 (*CPR, 1216–25*, p. 293).

SHERBORNE (Dorset), St Mary f. *c.* 993 (cathedral pr.); 1075 × 8 (priory); 1122 (abbey) List in *VCH Dorset*, II, 68–9.

PRIORS (DEANS)

Ægelward (Agelwardus) Occ. 1045 × 58 (Goscelin, *Life of St Wulsin*, ed. C. H. Talbot, *Revue Bénédictine*, LXIX (1959), 82; cf. p. 72).

Wulfric Occ. 1058 × 78 (ib., p. 73).

Ælfric (Alfricus) Occ. 1078 × 99 (ib., p. 84).

Thurstan –1122 Pr. Sherborne, bl. as abb. in 1122 when Sherborne and Horton were combined and Sherborne raised to an abbey (BM Cott. MS Faust. A. ii, f. 26v). Occ. as pr. 1107[1] × 15 (*Welsh Epis. Acts*, I, 237).

ABBOTS

Thurstan 1122– Bl. 1122 (see above). Occ. 1123 (*Reg.*, II, no. 1391); 30 Jan. 1126 (*PUE*, III, no. 13); 1122 × 39 (J. Fowler in *Soms. and Dors. N. and Q.*, XXIII (1942), 319–20).

Robert D. *c.* 1142 × 5 (see below).

Peter Prev. m. and pr. Monkton Farleigh, forced on Sherborne in irregular el. organised by Jocelin bp. and Azo dean of Salisbury, according to a letter of Eugenius III of 1145 (ib., p. 320: see below).[2] Peter occ. 1145 (*PUE*, II, no. 45; cf. Saltman, p. 450, no. 223). It seems likely that he was removed in 1145 × 6, when a new el. took place.

Henry 1146– On 4 Feb. 1146 the pope ordered the bp. of Salisbury not to interfere with an el. at Sherborne: by 13 Nov. 1146 Henry was abb. (*PUE*, III, nos. 50, 65); also occ. n.d. (*Reg. St Osmund*, I, pp. 249–50).

Clement[3] Occ. Sept. 1155 (*CDF*, no. 225; *Chts. Newington Longeville*, p. 7); 1155 × 65[4] (*Reg. St Osmund*, I, p. 235); 1175[5] × 84 (Gloucester Cathedral Lib. Reg. A, f. 160r–v). For his tomb see A. W. Clapham, *English Romanesque Architecture after the Conquest* (Oxford, 1934), p. 157 and pl. 43.

The abbey was in the king's hands in 1189 (*PR 1 Richard I*, p. 6).

William of Stoke 1189–1211 M. of Worcester (*Ann. Worcester*, p. 386); el. at Pipewell 15 Sept. 1189 (Gervase, I, 458); occ. 6 June 1191 (*Sarum Chts.*, p. 48); 1201 × 2, 1204 × 5 (*Ped. Fin.*, II, 77, 93); d. 3 Apr. 1211 (*Ann. Worcester*, p. 400; cf. Ann. Winchcombe, BM Cott. MS Faust. B. i, f. 24v, where he is called William de Theok' – ?Tewkesbury).

Philip Occ. 1211 × 17 (*Reg. St Osmund*, I, p. 265); *c.* 13 Oct. 1217 (*Dorset F.*, p. 19); 2 Feb. 1225 (ib., p. 27).

The next abb., Henry, pr. of Sherborne, el. 1227 (*CPR, 1225–32*, p. 132).

---

[1] Since Roger bp. of Salisbury is dedicating a cemetery, this was evidently after his consec. in 1107.

[2] Presumably some time before 4 Feb. 1146.

[3] Abbs. E. and G. occ. in two chts. of Henry II printed in *Mon.*, I, 340. Eyton, *Itinerary*, pp. 84–5 dates them as prob. 1165. They were confirmed by Edward II on 17 Aug. 1326 (*CChR*, III, p. 493). Eyton suggests that both E. and G. may be errors for C(lement).

[4] Henry dean of Salisbury (see *GFL*, p. 530; cf. p. 533).

[5] Azo archd. Salisbury (he succeeded Jordan, dean from *c.* 1175: cf. *VCH Wilts*, III, 207; cf. *Ctl. Bayeux*, I, pp. 119–20, 155–6).

SHREWSBURY (Salop), St Peter and St Paul f. *c.* 1083 × 7 (?1087)[1]

Lists in *VCH Salop* (forthcoming, by M. Chibnall) and *Ctl. Shrewsbury* (forthcoming, by U. Rees).[2]

Fulchered *c.* 1087–1119 First abb., m. of Séez, app. ?*c.* 1087[1]; occ. 1100 (Orderic, II, 421; IV, 85); –1108 (*Reg.*, II, no. 765); +1108 (Eyton, *Salop*, IV, 85; cf. VII, 220). D. 15 Mar. 1119 (*JW*, p. 28 n.; cf. *VCH Salop*, loc. cit.).

Godfrey *c.* 1119–1128 Second abb., m. Séez (Orderic, II, 421; IV, 430). Occ. 1121 (*Reg.*, II, no. 1297). D. 21–2 Mar. 1128 (xi[3] Kal. Mar., feria 4, *JW*, p. 28; but 22 Mar. was a Thursday in 1128).

Herbert 1128–1138 Third abb., m. Shrewsbury (Florence, II, 90 = *JW*, p. 29; cf. Orderic, IV, 430); bl. by Abp. William (Gervase, II, 381); dep. *c.* 17 Dec. 1138 (*JW*, p. 53).

Ranulf Occ. 1138 × 41, 1144[4] × 8 (Eyton, *Salop*, VII, 353; V, 170 = *Lancs PR*, pp. 282–3); and as Robert's predecessor in Saltman, p. 473, no. 249.

Robert –1168 Occ. 1150 × 9 (Saltman, p. 473, no. 249). D. 1168 (*Ann. Tewkesbury*, p. 50).

Adam –1175 Occ. 1168 × 73 (*Ctl. Salop*, no. 343); 1171 × 4 (*MB*, I, 211). Dep. 1175 (*Ann. Tewkesbury*, p. 51).

The abbey was vacant on 8 July 1175 (Diceto, I, 401).

Ralph 1175– M. Christ Church, Canterbury, el. 1175 (Gervase, I, 256; *Ann. Tewkesbury*, p. 51); occ. 1186 × 7, 1186 × 90 (Eyton, *Salop*, V, 42; IV, 154n.).

?William Occ. 1186 × 92 (Eyton, *Salop*, I, 98).

Hugh de Lacy –1190–1220/1 Occ. 23 Oct. 1190 (*Ctl. Salop*, p. 352); 22 Nov. 1192 (Eyton, *Salop*, VI, 329); 6 Feb. 1196 (*Lancs. F.*, p. 2 = PRS, XVII, no. 113); 7 May 1197 (PRS, XX, no. 151); 1210 × 11 (Salop F., PRO transcripts); 12 Nov. 1219 (Salop F., *Trans. Salop Arch. Soc.*, VI (1906), 168). Abb. unnamed dep. – July 1221 (*Rolls of Justices in Eyre*, Selden Soc., LIX, pp. 462, 503–4: see below); and an abb. unnamed occ. Nov. 1220 (*CRR*, IX, p. 311). The abb. was vacant on 6 July 1221 (*CPR*, *1216–25*, p. 296).

The next abb. Walter, pr. Leominster, was el. 1221: royal assent 23 July (*CPR*, *1216–25*, p. 297); his successor el. 1223 (ib., p. 382).

TAVISTOCK (Devon), St Mary and St Rumon f. 975 × 80 (destroyed 997, but re-established. See Finberg (1951), pp. 1ff.)

H.P.R.F. List by H. P. R. Finberg in *Devon and Cornwall Notes and Queries*, XXII (1943), 159ff.; partly based on *Ann. Tavistock*, in Newburgh, ed. Hearne, III, 709–10, checked by Finberg with Bodl. MS Digby 81, ff. 67ff.

— 1st abb. (*Mon.*, II, 494; Finberg, p. 160).

Ælfmær –994–?1009 Occ. 994 (*Mon.*, II, 495; cf. Finberg, loc. cit.); possibly the Æ. who occ. 1004, 1005, 1007, 1008 (Kemble, nos. 710, 714, 1304–5) – but see Canterbury, St Augustine; and very likely to be identified with the bp. Selsey, 1009–*c.* 1032; if so, he seems to have been a m. Glastonbury (*WMAG* in *Ad. Dom.*, I, 94; cf. Finberg, pp. 160–1).

---

[1] Orderic, II, 420–1 says that the abbey was founded in 1083; but he seems to be describing a prolonged process of building, and specifically says of Fulchered: 'Primus abbas...Guillelmo Rufo regnante...fuit' – also that the first two abbots, Fulchered and Godfrey (cf. *Reg.*, II, no. 1297 = cxxxix), reigned 'fere xl annis'. The famous foundation cht., of dubious authenticity but no doubt representing early tradition, dates the foundation 1087 (*Mon.*, III, 521).

[2] We are much indebted both to Mrs Chibnall and to Mrs Rees for our references to this, and to the latter for kind permission to refer to her list and to include some references to her edition. (Most of our references to the Ctl. are to the MS or older printed versions; this full edition to be published by the National Library of Wales will be most welcome.)

[3] ix Kal. Mar. in Florence, II, 90. Godfrey occ. in a cht. dated –1115 by Eyton (*Salop*, III, 232–3); but the relevant set of witnesses need not be so early.

[4] Godfrey, archd. Worcester (*GFL*, pp. 73, 540).

[TAVISTOCK]

Lyfing *c.* 1009–1027 Prob. also m. Glastonbury (*WMAG* loc. cit.; or of Winchester, *WMGP*, p. 200; cf. Finberg, p. 160); presumably the L. who occ. 1024 (Kemble, no. 741); accompanied Cnut to Rome in 1027, made bp. Worcester same year (Freeman, *NC*, I, (3rd edn., Oxford, 1877), pp. 751ff.; cf. Florence, I, 193; Finberg, p. 160); d. 1046.

Ealdred *c.* 1027–*c.* 1043 M. Winchester, succeeded Lyfing as bp. Worcester (Florence, I, 199–200; cf. *WMGP*, p. 251). Lyfing died in 1046, but Ealdred occ. as bp. ?1043, ?1044, 1044, 1046 (Kemble, nos. 916, 772; *OS Facs.*, II, Exeter 12, Kemble no. 784, cf. 912 (cited Finberg, p. 161n.), 939; see pp. 233–4), and may have been Lyfing's coadjutor in his last years, possibly because Lyfing held the see of Crediton as well as Worcester (Finberg, p. 161). Bp. Worcester 1046–62; bp. Hereford and Worcester, 1056–60; abp. York and bp. Worcester, 1061–2; abp. York alone, 1062–9.

Sihtric *c.* 1043–1082 Presumably the S. who occ. 1045×6 (*AS Chts.*, no. 105); 1049 (Kemble, no. 787 – Sihtric in MS); 1050 (Barlow (1963), pp. 154–5); 1068 (*Reg.*, I, no. 22 (?spurious), cited Finberg, p. 162); and in a spurious cht. dated 1062 (Kemble, no. 813). On the tradition that he joined Hereward the Wake at Ely, see Finberg, p. 162, who dismisses the story. *WMGP*, p. 204, tells us, however, that he became a pirate. D. 6 Apr. 1082 (*Ann.*, p. 709).

Geoffrey *c.* 1082–*c.* 1088 Occ. 1086 (*Exon DB* in *DB*, III, 165, f. 179); d. 1088 according to *Ann.*

Wimund –1096–1102 Occ. 1096 (*Mon.*, II, 497); dep. at Council of Westminster, +29 Sept. 1102 (Eadmer, p. 142; cf. *Handbook*, p. 549).

Osbert –1131 Administered house from 1102 (Finberg, p. 161 and n.); Finberg suggests he succeeded formally in or about 1107; occ. Sept. 1114, 1123 (*Reg.*, II, nos. 1068, 1391); d. 2 July 1131 (*Ann.*: cf. Finberg, p. 162).

Robert of Plympton *c.* 1131–1145 Occ. 1136 (*Reg.*, III, no. 284); (R.) 18 Oct. 1143 (Oliver, p. 45); d. 21 Jan. 1145 (*Ann.*: possibly for 1146, Finberg).

?Roger (possibly a mistake for Robert: see below) occ. 1146 (Original Cht., Cambridge, King's Coll., Muniments, 2. W/2).

Robert Postel ?1146–1154 Possibly administered abb. before el.; d. 14 Mar. 1154 (?for 1155). (*Ann.*; cf. Finberg, p. 174): perhaps he should be 'Roger', but 'Robert' occ. twice in *Ann.*

Walter *c.* 1154–*c.* 1168 M. Winchester; succ. ?1154 (*Ann.*); occ. –1160, –1161 (Saltman, nos. 259–60; cf. Finberg, p. 174); +1160, 1166 (*Mon.*, II, 500; *Red Book*, I, 250); according to *Ann.*, d. 10 Oct. 1174, but the year at least is prob. a confusion with his successor. Walter became the subject of an Exchequer 'joke' and is named in *PRs* regularly to 1178, and once in 1187 (cf. Finberg, pp. 174–5; last in *PR 30 Henry II*, p. 146).

Godfrey *c.* 1168–*c.* 1173 Full name occ. only in cht. of 29 Sept. 1169 (Morey, p. 147: 'Gottfridus' = *CDF*, no. 900 ('Goffridus'), from the Ctl. of Loders, now destroyed), and it is possible that Walter survived till 1173, when *PR 19 Henry II*, p. 201 records an abb.'s death, without naming him. Abb. 'G.' occ. n.d., 1171 (Finberg, p. 175 and n.).

Baldwin 1174–1184 App. before Michaelmas 1174 (*PR 20 Henry II*, p. 93, but not named; 1174–83, d. 8 Aug. in *Ann.*, but see Finberg, p. 175 and n.). For occs. see Finberg, p. 175. Presumably d. 1184, since abb. fell vacant in the third quarter of year (see below).

Abb. vacant 1184–1186 (*PR 31 Henry II*, p. 204; *32 Henry II*, p. 204: till *c.* Easter 1186 (1183–5, *Ann.*)).

Herbert 1186–1200 Occ. 1186×91 (Finberg, p. 186 and n.); 29 May 1193 (*Mon.*, II, 498); also in cht., presumably spurious, of –1184 (*Mon.*, II, 498; cf. Finberg, p. 186). D. 23 Nov. 1200, *Ann.*

Andrew *c.* 1200–1202 D. 23 Nov. 1202, *Ann.* (but repetition of Herbert's obit seems unlikely).

Jordan *c.* 1203–1219/20 For occs. see Finberg, p. 186; d. late 1219 or early 1220 (*CRR*, VIII, p. 327; 1220, *Ann.*).

TEWKESBURY (Glos), St Mary ref. *c.* 980 (dependent on Cranborne); independent 1102

List in *VCH Glos*, II, 65 (Rose Graham). Basis in *Ann. Tewkesbury* and history in *Mon.*, II, 59; obit 1 in calendar in BM Royal MS 8. C. vii, ff. 6–8v; obit 2 in calendar in CUL MS Gg. iii. 21, ff. 5–9v.

Gerald of Avranches 1102–1109 Clerk of Hugh, earl of Chester; m. of Winchester Cathedral (Orderic, III, 4f., 13–16; cf. *Ann. Winchester*, pp. 34, 43); abb. Cranborne –1086–1102 (q.v.); transferred abbey to Tewkesbury in 1102 (*Ann. Tewkesbury*, p. 44). Retired to Winchester in 1109 (*Ann. Winchester*, p. 43); d. 21 Nov. (obits 1 and 2) 1109 or 1110 (1109, *Ann. Winchcombe*, p. 123, *Ann. Tewkesbury*, p. 44; Orderic, loc. cit.).

Robert I 1109/10–1123 Chaplain of Robert FitzHamon; succeeded 1110, according to *Ann. Tewkesbury*, p. 44; *Ann. Winchester*, p. 45; d. 8 Dec. 1123 (Florence, II, 78 = *JW*, p. 18; *Ann. Tewkesbury*, p. 45, s.a. 1124; cf. obit 2).

Benedict 1124–1137 Pr. Tewkesbury, el. 1124; bl. 23 May 1125 (Florence, II, 80 = *JW*, p. 19; *Ann. Tewkesbury*, p. 45); d. 8 or 15 Mar. 1137 (obit 1 gives 8 Mar.; obit 2, 15 Mar.; so also Florence, II, 98 = *JW*, p. 41 and n. 1, cf. *Ann. Tewkesbury*, p. 46).

Roger 1137–1161 Succeeded 1137 (*Ann. Tewkesbury*, p. 46); occ. 1137 (PRO C115 A1 K2/6683 sec. i, no. 2); 1141 (*WMHN*, p. 51); 13 Dec. 1157 (*Ctl. Gloucester*, II, p. 106); d. 1 or 3 June (obits 1, 2) 1161 (*Ann. Tewkesbury*, p. 49 – 'Robert'); cf. *GFL*, p. 539.

Fromund 1162–1178 El. 1162, and bl. at Worcester 1162 (*Ann. Tewkesbury*, p. 49; cf. *Ann. Worcester*, p. 380; *GFL*, nos. 135–7); d. 18 May (obits 1, 2) 1178 (*Ann. Winchcombe*, p. 136; *Ann. Winchester*, p. 61).

Robert II 1182–1183 El. 1182 and bl. at Worcester (*Ann. Tewkesbury*, pp. 52–3; cf. *Ann. Worcester*, p. 385); d. 1183 (*Ann. Tewkesbury*, p. 53); prob. 20 Nov. or 24 Dec. (obit 2).

The abbey was held for three years – i.e. 1183–6 – by the bp. of St Davids (*Gir. Camb.* I, 321–2).

Master Alan 1186–1202 Magister (*Ctl. Winchcombe*, II, p. 301); prev. pr. of Christ Church Canterbury (Diceto, II, 24; *Ann. Waverley*, p. 244); el. 1186 (Gervase, I, 335; *Ann. Tewkesbury*, pp. 53–4, s.a. 1187); occ. 27 Oct. 1201 (*Earldom of Hereford Chts.*, no. 67); d. 6 or 7 May 1202 (*Epp. Cant.*, p. 572; BM Arundel MS 68, f. 26v; etc. – 6 May; obits 1, 2 – 7 May; *Ann. Tewkesbury*, p. 56; *Ann. Worcester*, p. 391, gives 1201).

Walter 1203–1214 Sacrist of Tewkesbury, el. 1203 (*Ann. Tewkesbury*, p. 56; *Ann. Worcester*, p. 392); occ. ?Jan × Aug. 1203 (Cheney, *Inn. III*, no. 505); 1204 (*Rot. Lit. Pat.*, p. 44b); d. 7 May 1214 (obits 1, 2; *Ann. Tewkesbury*, p. 61; cf. *Ann. Winchcombe*, BM Cott. MS Faust. B. i, f. 25).

Hugh 1214–1215 Pr. Tewkesbury, el. 1214; bl. by bp. of Hereford (*Ann. Worcester*, p. 403); d. 9 June 1215 (obits 1, 2; *Ann. Tewkesbury*, p. 61).

Bernard 1215 M. Tewkesbury, el. 1215 (*Ann. Worcester*, p. 404); 'electus sed postea cassatus' (*Ann. Tewkesbury*, p. 61).

Peter of Worcester 1216–1232 M. of Tewkesbury; royal assent to el. 26 May 1216 (*Rot. Lit. Pat.*, p. 184); bl. 8 Sept. 1216 (*Ann. Worcester*, p. 405; cf. *Ann. Tewkesbury*, p. 62). Occ. 15 May 1219 (*Devon F.*, no. 86); 1226 (*CPR, 1225–32*, p. 26); 22 June 1228 (*Devon F.*, no. 166). D. 30 Mar. 1232 (obits 1, 2; *Ann. Worcester*, p. 424).

THORNEY (Cambs), St Mary, Holy Trinity and St Botolph f. 973 (or possibly 972: CUL Add. MS 3020, ff. 6, 167v; cf. BM Add. MS 40,000, f. 11 – 973)

List in *VCH Cambs*, II, 217, cf. p. 211 (D. M. B. Ellis and L. F. Salzman) basis in CUL Add. MSS 3020–1, ff. 6ff. (Ann. I, giving usually accession only) and 414vff. (Ann. II,

[THORNEY]

Gesta abbatum), both 14th cent.; BM Cott. MS Nero C. vii, ff. 81ff. (Ann. III, 12th cent. with additions; printed *Mon.*, II, 611, but not accurately, and so cited from MS). Also 12th-cent. list in BM Add. MS 40,000, f. 10, on which see D. Whitelock in *Saga-Book of Viking Soc.*, XII, ii (1937-8), 131; 14th cent. MS cit. f. 11.[1]

?St Æthelwold ?973-984 The founder is said in Ann. II (f. 415v) to have held the abb. himself till his death in 984; in his *Vita* (*Ch. Abingdon*, II, 262) to have established Godeman as abb. The second is the better authority and it is on the whole unlikely that Æ. was regarded as abb.; but the *Vita* may only mean that G. was designated as his successor, or acted as coadjutor for a time; and if G. was abb. from the foundation, he seems to have been in office for forty years, which is possible, but not very probable.

Godeman App. by Æthelwold (see above), previously m. Old Minster, Winchester (*LVH*, p. 24; Ann. II, f. 415v; m. Winchester, chaplain to Æthelwold). Occ. 991 (*Ch. Ramsey*, pp. 93, 95-6); 993 (Kemble, no. 684) and prob. the G. who occ. 990 (× 1), etc., ?1012, 1013 (Kemble, nos. 712, 1307-8).

Leofsige -1016 Prev. pr. Thorney; bp. Worcester 1016-33 (Ann. II, f. 415v; Florence, I, 180; 1017 in Ann. III, f. 80v). See below.

Leofsine M. Thorney, next in Ann. II, f. 415v; Ann. III, f. 80v (s.a. 1017). Possibly the Leofsige who occ. 1016 × 23, 1021 × 3 (*AS Chts.*, no. 81; Kemble, no. 736); or the Leofwine of 1020-1022 × 3 (see Appendix I, Ely).

Oswig -1049 M. Thorney, d. '1048', Ann. II, f. 415v; 1049, *ASC* C, D (D, s.a. 1050), Ann. III, f. 80v; Florence, I, 203. Occ. 1048 and in spurious cht. dated 1032 (Aberystwyth, Nat. Lib. Wales, Peniarth MS 390, p. 368; Kemble, no. 748).

Leofwine m. Thorney, next in Ann. II, f. 415v. Just possibly one of the Abb. Leofsiges of *AS Chts.*, no. 115 (1053 × 5: cf. Ely). But he occ. as 'Leofwinus' abb. Thorney in the doubtful Kemble, no. 795, dated 1051. Cf. Coventry.

Leofric abb. Peterborough, held Thorney as one of his five abbs.: see Peterborough; but see also Crowland – it is possible that he appointed an abb. to Thorney rather than exercising direct sway there himself, as seems to have been the case at Crowland. He is omitted from lists and from Ann. II, which notes, however, that neither of the next two abbs. was bl. (f. 416). Siward may have acted for L. at Thorney. L. d. 1066.

(Siward a Dane, unbl. (Ann. II, f. 416). Cf. *AS Writs*, p. 572: 14th-cent. list in BM Add. MS 40,000, f. 11, gives him *c.* 10 years.)

(Fulcard or Folcard *c.* 1068-1084/5 Orderic, IV, 281 describes him as a m. St Bertin who acted as abb. (*abbatis vices supplevit*) for 16 years unbl. and then res. owing to a difference with the bp. Lincoln; Ann. II (f. 416) describes him as a Fleming *viceabbas* who was dep. by Lanfranc in a council at Gloucester in 1084. There is, however, no other evidence of a council at Gloucester in that year, and it seems likely that F. was dep. at the Christmas council of 1085, i.e. at the turn of 1085-6: cf. Crowland. Author of lives of St Botolph, St John of Beverley, and possibly of Edward the Confessor (see Barlow's ed. of *V. Ædwardi*, pp. liff.).)

Gunter of Le Mans 1085-1112 Royal chaplain, archd. Salisbury; m. S. Wandrille and Battle; 'prepositus' of Battle; app. 1085 (Orderic, IV, 282; Lot, *St-Wandrille*, no. 36, pp. 81-2; *Ch. Battle*, pp. 31-2; Ann. I, f. 6; Ann. II, f. 414v; Ann. III, f. 81 – not 1082 as *Mon.*); bl. 22 Feb. 1086 (Oxford, St John's Coll. MS 17, f. 29); abb. 26 or 27 years (Orderic, IV, 282; Ann. II); d. 18 July (ibid.) 1112 (Ann. II, Ann. III, f. 81v – in a contemporary hand; cf. *Mon.*, II, 611). Occ. 23 Oct. 1111 (possibly 1110: Oxford, St John's Coll. MS 17, f. 29v).

---

[1] The 12th-cent. list has Godeman, Leofwin (*sic*), Leofsine, Oswig, Gunter, Fulcard; the 14th-cent. G., Leofwin, Leofsine, Siward, Fulcard...

Robert de Prunelai 1113/14–1151 Son of Hamo de Prunelai (later m. S.-Évroult); prev.
m. S.-Évroult and pr. Noyon, 1107–13 (Orderic, IV, 280–3; cf. for dates Ann. II, f. 415v;
Ann. III, ff. 81v–82; Orderic, IV, 278). App. c. Christmas 1113 (*ASC* H; cf. Ann. I, f. 6;
Ann. II, f. 415v; Ann. III, f. 81v). Abb. 37 years; d. 1151 (Ann. II; 1151 also in Ann. III,
f. 82). Occ. 1115×16 (Orderic, III, 126); 1127 (CUL Add. MS 3020, f. 145r–v).

Gilbert 1151–1154 M. Thorney (a Gilbert m. occ. 1127, CUL Add. MS 3020, f. 145v);
dates as Ann. III, f. 82; Ann. I, f. 6v: app. 1151; abb. 3 years; d. 1154, Ann. II, f. 420v.

Walter I 1154–1158 M. Thorney; abb. 4 years (Ann. I, f. 6v (1154); Ann. II, ff. 420v–421v
(4th year = 1158; Ann. III, f. 82)).

Herbert 1158–1162 M. St Nicholas, Angers; abb. 5 years, or d. in 5th year, 1162 (Ann. II,
f. 421v; Ann. I, f. 6v, gives 1158; Ann. III, f. 82, 1158–62).

Walter II 1163–1169 M. and pr. (Ann. in *Ch. Ramsey*, p. 341) Ramsey (Ann. II, Ann. III);
el. 1162, Ann. II, f. 421v; Ann. III, f. 82; 1163 Ann. I, f. 6v, confirmed by *Ch. Ramsey*,
p. 341. Abb. 7 years, Ann. II; d. 1169, Ann. I; ?17 July 1169, Ann. III, f. 82.

Vacant 1169–1176 (*PR 16 Henry II*, p. 95; *22 Henry II*, p. 76; for 7 years, Ann. II, f. 421v;
cf. Diceto, I, 401; *Gesta Hen. II*, I, 91–3).

Solomon 1176–1193 Prev. pr. Ely (q.v.). El. 1176 (So Ann. I, f. 6v, Ann. III, f. 82, confirmed by *PR 22 Henry II*, p. 76; but *Gesta Hen. II*, I, 173, has 1175 (c. Pentecost), and
Ann. II, f. 421v, has '1172', 23 Henry II = Dec. 1176×7 – bl. by bp. Ely). Abb. 17 years
(? corr. to 16, Ann. II, f. 421v); but d. 1193, 5 Richard I (1193×4), in 16th year, f. 424;
1193 also in Ann. III, f. 82v; d. 24 Oct. (Ely obit, BM Cott. MS Vesp. A. vi, f. 130v).

Robert II 1193–1195 M. Gloucester; bl. 1193 by bp. Ely; dep. 4 July 1195 (Ann. II,
f. 424r–v (printed *PUE*, III, p. 57; dep. 3rd year); Ann. III, f. 82v; cf. Gervase, I, 530;
1193–4 in Ann. I, f. 6v). D. 1198 (Ann. III, f. 82v).

Vacant 1195–8: for 3 years (Ann. II, ending '3rd year' 1198), starting in 1195 (Ann. I).

Ralph Simplex 1198–1216 M. Crowland, pr. Freiston, el. 1198 (Ann. I, f. 6v; Ann. II,
f. 424; Ann. III, f. 82v; Ch. Barnwell, *Walt. Cov.*, I, p. xli). Bl. 1199×1200 (Ann. II).
Abb. 18 years, d. 1215 = 18 John (i.e. 1216) in Ann. II, ff. 424, 427v; 1216 in Ann. III,
f. 82v; *Walt. Cov.*, II, 234.

The next abb., Robert, held office 1217–37 (Dec. '1216', a year after Ralph's death, to 1237,
according to Ann. II, ff. 427, 437v; years also (1217–37) in Ann. III, ff. 82v–83; cf. Ann. I,
f. 7). Royal assent to el. 17 Dec. 1217 (*CPR, 1216–25*, p. 132); vacant Aug. 1237 (*CPR,
1232–47*, p. 193).

WALDEN (Essex), St Mary and St James f. ?1136 (priory);[1] 1 Aug. 1190 (abbey)
List in *VCH Essex*, II, 114; basis in *Ch. Walden*.[2]

PRIORS

William ?1136–1164 M. of Luffield, pr. Bradwell (*Ch. Walden, Essex Rev.*, XLV, 79). Occ.
25 Apr. 1148 (*PUE*, I, no. 43). D. 12 Dec. 1164. Also pr. Luffield, Bradwell (q.v.: *Ch.
Walden*, XLV, 149; cf. p. 79 and *passim*).

Vacant 1 year, 1 month, 2 days, according to *Ch. Walden*, XLV, 149.

Master Reginald 1166–1190 (as pr.) Prev. m. Grestain (Ch. Walden, BM MSS Cott. Vesp.

---

[1] *Ch. Walden* gives 1136 (so MSS and epitome) and by Geoffrey de Mandeville and Rose his wife – but
makes an early stage in the process be performed with the consent of Bps. Robert of London (1141–
50), Nigel of Ely (1133–69) and William of Norwich (1146–74). It is possible that one should amend
to 1141 (mcxxxvi read for mcxxxxi), but also that the foundation was a prolonged affair, conceived
in 1136 and executed in the 1140s – though hardly later than Geoffrey's fall in 1144.

[2] Usually cited by *Essex Review*, XLV–XLVII (see List of Printed Books); but the references have been
checked by the MSS (both 16th–17th-cent. transcripts: BM MSS Cott. Vesp. E. vi, Arundel 29)
and, where possible, by the 15th-cent. epitome in BM Cott. MS Titus D. xx.

[WALDEN]

E. vi, f. 32 v, Arundel 29, f. 4 v); abb. Reading (q.v.); app. pr. *c.* Jan. 1166; for his career as pr. and abb. see *Ch. Walden*, XLV, 149–51, XLVI, 164–5, 220; and for the chronological difficulties, *GFL*, p. 477n. Occ. *c.* 1174 × 80 (*GFL*, no. 443); (R.) *c.* 1181 × 3 (ib., no. 446). Also pr. Luffield q.v. (*Ch. Walden*, XLV, 151).

ABBOTS

Master Reginald 1190–1203/4 (as abb.) 1st abb., promoted 1 Aug. 1190 (*Ch. Walden*, XLVI, 164–5). Occ. Jan. 1191 (*PUE*,ˈI, no. 268). D. 5 Feb. 1203 × 4 (*Ch. Walden*, XLVI, 220; 3 Feb. in BM Cott. MS Vesp. E. vi, f. 12; 1200 in Titus D. xx, f. 80v).

Robert –1210 2nd abb.; d. 1210 (BM Cott. MS Titus D. xx, f. 81: but in the same year as Geoffrey FitzPeter, who d. 1213). Occ. 24 Apr. 1206+ (j.d.: BM Add. MS 46,353, f. 294v).

Roger –1222 3rd abb.; d. 1222 (BM Cott. MS Titus D. xx, f. 83v). Occ. 1214 × 15 (*Essex F.*, p. 47); and as 'Robert' 1221 (*Ctl. Colchester*, II, pp. 534–5); also 'Robert' in BM Harl. MS 3697, f. 211r–v (1220), but Roger later in the same cht.

WESTMINSTER, St Peter ref. *c.* 959 (*AS Writs*, p. 579; cf. p. 548, and for earlier history, pp. 580–1)

Lists in Flete, pp. 139ff. (J. Armitage Robinson); *VCH London*, I, 454–5. Unreliable base in Flete's ch., corrected by Robinson, loc. cit.

St Wulfsige 958–993/7 A Londoner (*Vita* – see below, p. 73). First abb., according to Flete, from 958 to his death; became bp. after 25 years or in his 25th year (*Vita*, pp. 77, 79). First occ. 966 (Birch, no. 1178); bp. Sherborne ?992–1001/2; he held both offices together for a time (occ. 993, Kemble, no. 684),[1] but in fact seems to have res. the abb. by 997 (Kemble, no. 698; cf. *AS Writs*, p. 579). On him, see Goscelin's *Vita*, ed. C. H. Talbot in *Rev. Bénédictine*, LXIX (1959), 68ff., esp. 75–6. He d. 1001 or 1002: prob. 1002 if 8 Jan. is correct for obit – so Flete; *Vita*, p. 79 seems to confirm (3rd day of Epiphany, but calls it 8 id. Jan., prob. by a slip). Presumably the W. who occ. 966, etc., 990 (× 1) (Birch, no. 1178; Kemble, no. 712).

Ælfwig –997–*c.* 1020(?) Flete (pp. 80–1) gives Æ. 20 years, making him d. on 19 Mar.; and Wulfnoth 30 years, making him d. on 19 Oct., *c.* 7 Edward the Confessor – which would have been 19 Oct. 1049. These regnal years are probably little more than guesses. Æ. occ. 997, 1002 (Kemble, no. 698; cf. *AS Writs*, pp. 548, 579; Robinson (1911), pp. 167–8), and was presumably the Æ. who occ. ?995, 1005, 1012, 1018, and possibly 1024 (*Mon.*, VI, 1443–6; Kemble, nos. 714, 719; *OS Facs.*, III, no. 39; Kemble, no. 741): see Bath.

Wulfnoth *c.* 1020(?)–1049 See above. D. 1049 (*ASC* C, D; Florence, I, 203); 19 Oct. according to Flete (pp. 81–2). Presumably the W. who occ. 1023, 1035, 1045 × 7, 1046 (*AS Chts.*, nos. 82, 101; *OS Facs.*, III, no. 42; Matthew, pp. 143–5).

Eadwine *c.* 1049– M. Westminster and first abb. of the new foundation by Edward the Confessor. Flete makes him die 12 June 1068; Armitage Robinson (Flete, p. 140) suggests he lived till *c.* 1071, but the chts. he cites are all spurious (see *AS Writs*, p. 560). Presumably the E. who occ. 1061 (Kemble, no. 810).

Geoffrey Occ. *c.* 27 May 1072 (Bishop and Chaplais, facing pl. xxix); dep. in or after his 4th year according to Flete (pp. 84–5).

Vitalis 1076–1085(?) Abb. Bernay (prev. m. Fécamp) app. 1076 (*ASC* E). Occ. 1080 (*Ctl. Rouen, Ste Trinité*, no. 89, p. 466); + 1081 (Flete, p. 141). For date of death, see Robinson in Flete, pp. 141–2. D. 19 June (Belvoir martyrology, Cambridge, Trinity Coll. MS O. 9. 25, f. 160).

---

[1] Ælfwig also signs at the foot of this document; either he is a later addition, or he was already acting as Wulfsige's coadjutor.

Gilbert Crispin (?)1085–1117/18 Prev. m. Bec. (on him see Robinson in Flete, pp. 141–2 and *Gilbert Crispin*). Occ. 29 Jan. 1091, +1116 (*Reg.*, I, no. 315; II, no. 1180). D. 6 Dec. (Flete) 1117 (*ASC* E; *Ann. Winchester*, p. 45); or 1118 (Ann. Thorney, BM Cott. MS Nero C. vii, f. 81v, in a contemporary hand).

Herbert 1121–*c.* 1136 M. and almoner of Westminster, el. 1121 (Eadmer, p. 291; cf. *JW*, p. 16; Flete, p. 142). Occ. 1121 (*Reg.*, II, no. 1301). He d. 3 Sept. (Flete, p. 88), 1136×8 (see below; cf. discussion in Flete, p. 142).

Gervase 1138–*c.* 1157 Son of King Stephen (John of Hexham in *Sim. Dur.*, II, 330; Lees, *Templars*, p. 215); presumably app. by his father, not before Dec. 1135; bl. by legate Alberic 17 Dec. 1138 (*JW*, p. 53). Occ. 1138×9 (*Reg.*, III, no. 819); 1156×7 (Saltman, pp. 245–6, no. 16). He was still abb. 1 June 1157 (Westminster Abbey, Domesday Ctl., ff. 3v–5v; the bull cited by Robinson in Flete, p. 143n., is dated at the Lateran, 8 kal. Jun., so cannot be earlier than 1157); Laurence had succeeded by 1159, probably by Aug. 1158 (so Robinson, loc. cit.). Gervase was removed by Henry II (John of Hexham, loc. cit.). Cf. P. Chaplais, in *Misc. D. M. Stenton*, pp. 90ff.; Richardson and Sayles, *Governance*, pp. 413ff.; *GFL*, p. 539.

Master Laurence *c.* 1158–1173 Prev. m. St Albans (see *Vita Ailredi*, p. xlviii n.). D. 10 Apr. (Cambridge, Trinity Coll. MS O. 9. 95, f. 157v) or 11 Apr. (Flete) 1173 (*PR 19 Henry II*, pp. 155, 184; cf. p. 201). The vacancy lasted till 1175 (*PR 21 Henry II*, p. 79; *Gesta Hen. II*, I, 91–3 and Diceto, I, 401, show the abbey was still vacant on 1–8 July 1175).

Walter 1175–1190 Prev. pr. St Swithun's, Winchester (q.v.; Devizes, p. 25). Prob. el. 1175, bl. 1176 (Diceto, I, 401, 404; cf. Torigny, p. 268 – unnamed). Occ. 2 Feb. 1190 (Westminster Abbey, Domesday Ctl., f. 648r–v). D. 27 Sept. 1190 (Devizes, p. 25; cf. Flete, p. 96 ('1191'), 144).

William de Longchamp tried to intrude his brother, Henry de Longchamp, m. Caen, but unsuccessfully (Diceto, II, 100; Devizes, p. 39).

William Postard 1191–1200 Prev. pr. Westminster (Flete; Diceto, II, 100; cf. Devizes, p. 54). El. 9 Oct. 1191, bl. 13 Oct. (Diceto, II, 100–1 and n.). D. 4 May (Flete) 1200 (vacant 1200, Diceto, II, 172). Occ. 13 Jan. 1192 (*PUE*, I, no. 301).

Ralph Arundel 1200–1214 Pr. Hurley; el. 30 Nov. 1200, bl. 17 Dec. (Diceto, II, 172; 1201, Flete, p. 99). Occ. Oct. 1202 (Cheney, *Inn. III*, no. 352). Dep. by order of papal legate, 23 Jan. 1214 (Flete, p. 100, following *Flor. Hist.*, II, 147; cf. Flete, p. 144; *MPCM*, II, 576). D. 12 Aug. (Flete, p. 100); 1223 (*Ann. Dunstable*, p. 85).

William du Hommet 1214–1222 A Norman; m. Caen; pr. Frampton (q.v.). El. 4 May 1214 (Sunday); bl. Sunday 25 May (Flete, p. 101, from *Flor. Hist.*, II, 147f.). Occ. 15 May 1214 (Westminster Abbey, Domesday Ctl., f. 473v). D. 20 Apr. 1222 (Flete, p. 102). Occ. (W.) 9 Jan. 1215 (*Ctl. Glastonbury*, I, no. 141).

WHITBY (Yorks N.), St Peter and St Hilda ref. as pr. –1077; formal organisation 1078; soon moved to Lastingham; from 1086 to *c.* 1091×2 at Hackness to escape pirates. For this, and the dates of the first four prs., see A. H. Thompson in *YAJ*, XXVII (1923–4), 388–405 (analysing *Sim. Dur.*, I, 111; II, 201–2; *Ch. St Mary's York*; and cf. Abb. Stephen's narrative, *Mon.*, III, 544–6; *Ctl. Whitby*, I, pp. 1–7 and pp. xxxviiif.). Became an abb. –1109.
C.T.C. List in *VCH Yorks*, III, 104.

PRIORS OF WHITBY AND HACKNESS

Reinfrid First pr. ?–*c.* 1078, res.

Stephen *c.* 1078–*c.* 1080 Res. abb. St Mary's York.

Reinfrid *c.* 1080– D. prob. –1092, possibly –1086 (cf. A. H. Thompson, art. cit., pp. 399–401).

[WHITBY]

Serlo de Percy Prob. –1092– Brother of William de Percy (see *EYC*, XI, no. 1; *Ctl. Whitby*, I, 2). Occ. 1091 × 1109 (*EYC*, I, no. 384);[1] *c.* 1091 × 96 (ib., XI, no. 1); 1091 × 5 (ib. II, no. 863); 1108 × 9 (*Ctl. Whitby*, I, no. 261).

ABBOTS OF WHITBY

William Nephew of William de Percy (*Ctl. Whitby*, I, p. 2), occ. 1109 (*Ctl. Whitby*, I, no. 382); *c.* 1109 × 14, –1125 (*EYC*, II, nos. 859, 874; for the date of no. 859, see *EYC*, XI, no. 4).

Nicholas Occ. 9 Dec. 1125 (*Ctl. Whitby*, I, no. 148) – for date cf. *JL* 7,230; *c.* 1130 × 9 (*EYC*, II, no. 873); d. 1139 according to *VCH* citing Charlton, *Hist. Whitby*, p. 96.

Benedict –?1148 Occ. 1143 (J. Hex. in *Sim. Dur.*, II, 315); 1143[2] (*Lancs PR*, p. 281); 1145 × 8 (*EYC*, I, no. 149); res. ?1148 (*Ctl. Whitby*, I, p. 9).

Richard I 1148–1175(?6) Pr. Peterborough, app. May–June 1148; tenure 26 years 7 months 15 days; d. 1 Jan. 1175 (*Ctl. Whitby*, I, 1175, cf. 10n.; *LV Durham* (1st edn.), p. 140;[3] but see below). Occ. 1148 × 53 (*Ctl. Bridlington*, p. 429).

Richard II of Cornwall 1177– M. of S. Nicholas, Angers, pr. Monks Kirby (q.v.; the former in *Ctl.*, the latter in *Gesta*: Monks Kirby was a dep. of S. Nicholas); el. 29 May 1177 (*Gesta Hen. II*, I, 166; but installed 29 June 1176 according to *Ctl. Whitby*, I, p. 10).
The abb. was vacant 1181–2(?3), from *c.* Whitsun 1181 (*PR 27 Hen. II*, p. 50; *28 Hen. II*, p. 62 – 1182–3).

Peter –*c.* 1211 Occ. *c.* 1190 × 1211 (*EYC*, I, no. 565); (P.) 1196 (*Ctl. Bridlington*, pp. 77–8); 1198 × 1200 (Cheney, *Inn. III*, no. 277); 22 Aug. 1202 (*Yorks F., John*, p. 48); 1202 × 12 (*Ctl. Whitby*, I, no. 54). Res. (ib., I, p. 41n.). D. 23 Sept. (BM Cott. MS Vitell. C. xii, f. 142v).
The abbey was vacant on 18 Aug. 1212 and 16 Jan. 1214 (*Rot. Lit. Pat.*, pp. 94, 108), and again on 31 May 1223, when custody was granted to the pr., Roger; Roger was soon after el. abb. and his el. received royal assent on 18 June 1223 (*CPR 1216–25*, pp. 374–5). Thus we may suppose that Abb. John, occ. 1219 × 23 (*Ctl. Whitby*, I, no. 39; cf. nos. 42, 94 etc.) fills the gap 1214–23. This confirms the statement of Charlton, *Hist. Whitby*, pp. 158, 169, that John of Evesham was appointed abb. by the papal legate in 1214, and died in 1222 (prob. rightly 1223); but he gave no reference, and no source has been found. Thus the list concludes:

John (?of Evesham) prob. 1214–1223.

WINCHCOMBE (Glos), St Mary (formerly St Peter) and St Kenelm ref. *c.* 970 (see below; dedicated 972, BM Cott. MS Tib. E. iv, f. 17v)
Lists in *VCH Glos*, II, 72 (Rose Graham); *Ctl. Winchcombe*, II, pp. xviff. Basis in Ann. Winchcombe, BM Cott. MS Tib. E. iv (also Faust. B. i) ed. (from 1049) by R. R. Darlington in *Misc. D. M. Stenton*, pp. 111ff.

Germanus *c.* 970–975 M. Fleury, pr. Westbury-on-Trym and Ramsey, first abb. Winchcombe (cf. Ramsey for date); expelled and returned to Fleury, later to Ramsey 975 (*Ch. Ramsey*, pp. 29, 42, 73; cf. *WMGP*, p. 294; *AS Chts.*, p. 374). Presumably the G. who occ. 972 (Birch, no. 1282, cf. 1284); see Cholsey. One 'Germanus Floriacensis abbas' (?G. in retirement) occ. ?995 (*Mon.*, VI, 1443–6). His accession is dated 966 by a later hand in BM Cott. MS Tib. E. iv, f. 17v.

?Ælfwold Kemble, no. 684, dated 993, has Ælfwold abb. 'Wind''; Winchcombe seems the only likely identification (*via* 'Wincl'). If this is correct, he is presumably to be identified

---

[1] Prob. –1100 because of the reference to King William.
[2] William abp. York; Henry bp. Winchester papal legate.　　　[3] Cf. Rud, p. 215.

with the Æ. who occ. 980, 982 (but see Muchelney), 990(×1) (Kemble, nos. 624, 633, 712); 995×9 (*AS Wills*, no. 16 (2)); 996, 1001, 1002 (Kemble, nos. 696, 705, 707; cf. *AS Wills*, p. 150).

Godwine –1042–1053 Occ. 1042 (*AS Chts.*, no. 94). D. (*c.* Nov.) s.a. 1053 in *ASC* C, D; Florence, I, 211. Presumably the G. who occ. 1041×2, 1044×51 (Kemble, nos. 764, 797); 1044 (*OS Facs.*, II, Exeter 12); 1045, ?1047 (Kemble, nos. 777, 785).

Ealdred bp. Worcester held abb. in his hands until Godric's app. (Florence, I, 211; *ASC* D).

Godric 1054–1066 Son of Godeman, royal chaplain (Florence, I, 211; cf. Barlow (1963), p. 157); app. 1054, Florence, I, 212; removed by William I in 1066 (*Ann. Winchcombe*, p. 117; cf. *Ch. Evesham*, p. 90: in Abb. Æthelwig's custody for *c.* 3 years). Occ. 1058 (Earle, pp. 247–8); 1062×6 (Kemble, no. 823). Retired to Evesham (Thorpe, p. 617).

Galandus, Galannus 1066–1075 *Ann.*, pp. 117–18, gives 1066–74, but all the entries under 1074 seem to belong to 1075, and G. occ. in the Council of 1075 (Wilkins, I, 364: i.e. +25 Dec. 1074; cf. Brooke in *Studia Gratiana*, XII (1967), 46n., 59). *Ann.* makes him m. 'Cert''(?) – perhaps Chertsey, but more probably Cérisy, since G. was evidently a nominee of the Conqueror brought in very soon after his accession.

Ralph 1077–1093 Dates as *Ann.*, pp. 118–20. Occ. 1077 (Thorpe, p. 617).

Girmund 1095–1122 M. of Gloucester; dates as *Ann.*, pp. 120 and n., 125 – d. 10 June 1122. Occ. 1113×14 (*Ch. Abingdon*, II, 104–5).

Godfrey 1122–1137 Pr. Winchcombe (*Ann.*, p. 125); d. 6 Mar. 1137 (1138, *Ann.*, p. 128, but the annals for 1137–9 belong in fair measure to 1136–8, and Florence, II, 98n. = *JW*, p. 42, gives 1137). Occ. 24 May 1125 (*JW*, p. 19).

Robert 1138–1152 M. Cluny, said to be related to King Stephen (Florence, II, 105 = *JW*, p. 48: bl. 22 May; *Ann.*, p. 128, gives 1139, but see above). D. 15 Jan. 1151 (*Ann.*, p. 130, s.a. 1151, but following the burning of the abb. on 28 Oct. 1151).

William 1152–?1157 M. Christ Church, Canterbury; *Ann.*, p. 130; date of d. is not given.

Gervase 1157–1171 M. Winchcombe; dates as *Ann.*, pp. 130, 134. Occ. 13 Dec. 1157 (*Ctl. Gloucester*, II, pp. 105–7).

Henry 1171–1181 Pr. Gloucester; dates as *Ann.*, pp. 134, 137; Greg. Caerwent (BM Cott. MS Vesp. A. v, ff. 199v–200): d. 8 Nov.; cf. *Ctl. Winchcombe*, I, pp. 45, 68; *Ann. Waverley*, p. 242; *Ann. Tewkesbury*, p. 52.

Crispin 1181–1182 Pr. Winchcombe (*Ann.*, p. 137, s.a. 1181; *Ann. Tewkesbury*, p. 52); bl. 7 June 1181 (*Ann. Worcester*, p. 384); abb. scarcely a year (*Ctl. Winchcombe*, I, p. 68); succession and d. in *Ann. Tewkesbury*, p. 52; *Ann. Worcester*, pp. 384–5; d. also in Ann. Winchcombe, BM Cott. MS Faust. B. i, f. 21. Occ. 1181 (*Ctl. Winchcombe*, I, p. 45).

Ralph 1183–1194/5 Succession in *Ann. Tewkesbury*, p. 53; Ann. Winchcombe, loc. cit. s.a. 1182, called 'Robert'; *Ctl. Winchcombe*, I, p. 44, gives him ten years from 31 Henry II (i.e. succ. + 19 Dec. 1183); occ. 1193/4 (+12 Dec. 1193: ib., I, p. 93); his successor was app. 1196; and so Ralph presumably died in 1194 or 1195.

Master Robert of Hasleton 1196–1221 Dates as Greg. Caerwent, f. 200r–v: d. 8 June (cf. *Ctl. Winchcombe*, I, p. 44). For d. 1221, cf. *CPR 1216–25*, p. 296: consent to successor's el. on 8 July; *Ann. Worcester*, p. 414.

WINCHESTER CATHEDRAL (Hants), St Swithun   ref. 964

D.G. List in Le Neve, new edn., II, 88–91 (D. Greenway); *VCH Hants*, II, 114.[1]

Brihtnoth ?964–970 Became abb. Ely, q.v. (*Lib. El.*, p. 74).

[1] By J. C. Cox, who includes a Pr. Brithwold, *c.* 1006, said to have become bp. Winchester. No such person seems to have existed. Coenwulf, abb. Peterborough, became bp. in 1005 and he may have been a m. Winchester.
On *Ann. Winchester*, see J. T. Appleby, in *BIHR*, XXXVI (1963), 70ff.

[WINCHESTER CATHEDRAL]

Ælfric Puttoc –1023 Became abp. York (Florence, I, 184, says that he had been provost of Winchester; it is just possible that he was the Æ., provost of New Minster, noted in *LVH*, p. 32; if so it is odd that the *LVH* failed to note his promotion). Cf. *DNB*.

?Wluuinus Occ. BM Add. MS 29,436, f. 73 v, in a context possibly suggesting a mid-11th-cent. date.

?Wulfsige *AS*, I, 324 cites 'Chron. breve Winton. vetus' for Wlfsigius, 1065.

Simeon –1081/2 Brother of Bp. Walkelin and pr. Winchester (*Lib. El.*, p. 200); M. S. Ouen, Rouen, *Ann. Winchester*, p. 33, which gives 1082. Abb. Ely, q.v., from 1081/2.

Godfrey 1082–1107 Born at Cambrai, m. Winchester, d. 1107 (*Ann. Winchester*, pp. 33, 43, s.a. 1082, 1107). Occ. 1102×6 (*Reg.*, II, no. 803); 1107 (*Ctl. Winchester*, no. 9).

Geoffrey I 1107–1111 M. Winchester; dep. by Bp. William (*Ann. Winchester*, p. 43). Abb. Burton, 1114–50 (q.v.). Occ. 1110 (*Reg.*, II, no. 948).

Geoffrey II 1111–1126 M. and ?granarer, d. 1126 ('hordarius', *Ann. Winchester*, pp. 43, 48, s.a. 1111, 1126).

Ingulph *c.* 1126–1130 Res. abb. Abingdon in 1130; bl. 8 June (*JW*, p. 30 and n.; see Abingdon: Vincent abb. Abingdon d. 1130 and Robert was pr. before Michaelmas: *PR 3 Henry I*, p. 38. On him see *Ch. Abingdon*, II, 173). For a possible occ. *c.* 1124, see Le Neve.

Robert Occ. 1130 (see above). Commonly stated to be the m. Lewes who became bp. Bath in 1136, but there seems no contemporary evidence of this (see R. H. C. Davis in *EHR*, LXXVII (1962), 224, n. 1).

Geoffrey III Occ. 1139×53, 1142×7, ?1144×8 (*Ctl. Winchester*, nos. 5, 10, pp. 4, 6; *GFL*, no. 30 and n.).

William –1165 D. –19 July 1165 (*Ctl. Winchester*, no. 75, p. 35).

Robert –1173 Occ. 19 July 1165 (*Ctl. Winchester*, p. 35); 6 Aug. 1171 (*Reg. Pontissara*, II, p. 629); 15 Feb. 1172 (*PUE*, II, no. 125); res. abb. Glastonbury 1173 (q.v.: for the date, *Ann. Winchester*, p. 61; *Ann. Winchcombe*, p. 134; cf. *Ad. Dom.*, II, 331; Torigny, p. 257).

Walter *c.* 1173–1175 Res. abb. Westminster *c.* July 1175 (q.v.: Flete, p. 144; cf. p. 95; Diceto, I, 401, implying el. *c.* July 1175; p. 404 – bl. 1176). But occ. as pr. +7 Nov. 1176 (Westminster Abb. Domesday Ctl., f. 571).

John –1187 Occ. 10 Apr. 1185 (Eyton, *Itinerary*, p. 263); d. 1187 (*Ann. Winchester*, p. 63).

Master[1] Robert son of Henry 1187–1191 Dates as *Ann. Winchester*, p. 63; res. 1191 to be Carthusian at Witham (cf. Devizes, pp. 1–2, 26).

Stephen –1214 Prob. de Lucy: see Le Neve. Occ. j.d. +19 Mar. 1199 (*Reg. St Osmund*, I, 354; cf. Cheney, *Inn. III*, no. 88); Oct. 1201 (*CRR*, II, p. 37). Res. abb. Burton: royal assent (S.) 23 Jan. 1214 (*Rot. Lit. Pat.*, pp. 108b–9; cf. *Rot. Lit. Claus.*, I, 161b).

The next pr., Walter, occ. 1216 (Cheney, *Inn. III*, no. 1174), and d. 1239 (*Ann. Waverley*, p. 323).

WINCHESTER (Hants), New Minster, later Hyde Abbey, St Peter and St Grimbald,[2] ref. 964 (*ASC* A; Florence, I, 140); 1110 (to Hyde)

Lists in *VCH Hants*, II, 121; *LVH*, pp. xxviff. (Birch); 11th-cent. list in *LVH*, p. 31, with 14th-cent. note inserted; calendar and ann. of 11th cent. printed ibid., pp. 269ff., 276. Ann. (2) is 15th cent. ann. not of much worth in BM Harl. MS 1761, ff. 14ff.

Æthelgar 964–?988 M. Glastonbury and Abingdon, app. by St Æthelwold (*ASC* A; Florence, I, 140); bp. Selsey, consec. 2 May 980, abp. Canterbury *c.* Sept. 988–90,

---

[1] *Ch. Witham*, p. 506 (ed. Wilmart, p. 232).

[2] See *LVH*, p. viii, for the range of dedications (though Birch's notes do not sufficiently distinguish the documents on which his list is based); variously ascribed to the Holy Trinity, the Saviour, St Mary and St Peter in 10th–11th cents.

d. 13 Feb. (*WMGP*, p. 32; *Vita S. Ethelwoldi, Ch. Abingdon*, II, 260–1; *ASC* C, s.a. 980, 988, E, s.a. 988; Florence, I, 146, 148). *LVH*, p. xxviii and the documents there cited seem to show that he held his abb. after his promotion, until at least 988, when his successor prob. first occ. Æ. prob. occ. as abb. in doubtful cht. of 964, and frequently from 964, 965 to 975, 979 (Birch, nos. 1135, 1169, etc., 1313, 1316; Kemble, no. 621). Cf. *LVH*, pp. xxviff.; *AS Writs*, p. 553; *DNB* (Ethelgar). A 14th-cent. insertion in *LVH* (p. 31) makes him abb. for 13 years from 965 (965–77 in ann. (2)).

Ælfsige ?988(988–)–1007 See above: he is presumably the Æ. who occ. 988, 990, etc., 995+, 996 (Kemble, nos. 663, 673; *AS Chts.*, no. 70; Kemble, no. 696), and one of the three in *Crawford Chts.*, no. 11 of 1007 (= Kemble, no. 1304); he occ. with title 993, 997 (Kemble, nos. 684, 698). The 14th-cent. note in *LVH*, p. 31, gives him 17 years but makes his predecessor d. in 997: 11th-cent. calendar and ann. make him d. 1007 (*LVH*, p. 276). Accession 978(?) in Ann. (2). See Ely, Peterborough.

Brihtwold, Byrhtwold 1007–1012 Æ., d. 1007, B. d. 1012, 17 Mar. (calendar and ann. *LVH*, pp. 272, 276). 3rd abb.: *LVH*, p. 31. Presumably one of the two Bs. who occ. 1007 (Kemble, no. 1303;[1] otherwise a B. occ. from 1004, 1005 to ?1012 (Kemble, nos. 710, 714, etc., 1307). The first and second references are probably to Malmesbury; the later references may be to the abb. New Minster (occ. 995 in Ann. (2)).

Brihtmær 4th abb. (*LVH*, p. 31) and probably the B. who occ. 1012, 1013, 1014, 1015; he d. 8 kal. (Jan.) = 25 Dec. (Kemble, nos. 719, 1308–9; *AS Wills*, p. 62; BM Add. MS 29,436, f. 44). See Crowland, Evesham. (Acc. 1008, in Ann (2).)

Æthelnoth, apparently next abb. in *LVH*, p. 31; ?the Ælfnoth who occ. ?1019 and the Æthelnoth of ?1026 (Kemble, nos. 730, 743). D. 2 Nov. (*LVH*, p. 272). Cf. Appendix I. (Acc. 1021 in ann. (2).)

Ælfwine 1031/2–1057 Son of Æthelnoth and Wulfwynn; d. 1057, 24 Nov. (*LVH*, pp. 270, 273, 276; cf. p. 33). Occ. 1044, 1047+, ?*c.* 1053 (*OS Facs.*, II, Exeter 12; *AS Chts.*, nos. 101, 107, 114) and prob. the Æ. who occ. 1032, 1033, etc., 1048 and possibly 1053 × 5 (Kemble, nos. 746, 751; Aberystwyth, Nat. Lib. Wales, Peniarth MS 390, p. 368; *AS Chts.*, no. 115); but cf. Ramsey, Malmesbury. Thus he was prob. abb. by 1032, but not in 1031, when *LVH* first written (Ker, *Catalogue of MSS containing Anglo-Saxon*, pp. 338–40). Cf. *AS Writs*, p. 551 (acc. 1035 in Ann. (2)).

Ælfnoth ?1057–*c.* 1063 M. New Minster (*LVH*, p. 34). Date of acc. as Ann. (2). Possibly the Æ. who occ. 1061 (Kemble, no. 810; cf. no. 815, dated 1065: evidently spurious, but with a possible witness list for a date *c.* 1062 or a little earlier). D. 9 Dec. (*LVH*, p. 273). Cf. Glastonbury.

Ælfwig (Ælfwy) ?1063–1066, d. 14 Oct. M. New Minster: *LVH*, p. 35, where a slightly later hand has added 'abbas...occisus in Bello' ('occiditur' in Ann. (2): occ. ibid. 1063). This much seems well authenticated, but the later tradition that made him Harold's uncle and Godwin's brother is confused and doubtful. This was accepted by Freeman, *NC*, II, 644–5, III, 731, from *Mon.*, II, 437; for the details, cf. Round in *VCH Hants*, I, 417–19. As Freeman saw, it is curious that a brother of Godwin, and an oblate ('puer', *LVH*, p. 35) should have had to wait till 1063 for promotion; and his attempt to identify him with Ælfwine is impossible, in the light of the evidence of the mid-11th-cent. calendar as to Ælfwine's family and death. It is indeed possible, though hardly likely, that Ælfwy is wholly legendary, and the *LVH* additions foisted on an obscure monk of the name.

Wulfric ?1069–1072 M. New Minster, *LVH*, p. 35. Acc. 1069 after 2-year vacancy Ann. (2). Dep. *c.* 8 April 1072 (*Acta Lanfranci*, in *ASC*, ed. Earle and Plummer, I, 288; for the date, cf. Bishop and Chaplais, facing pl. xxix). Cf. also *Ann. Winchester*, p. 30. Cf. Ely.

[1] Possibly also of Kemble, no. 1304 = *Crawford Chts.*, no. 11; but see above, under Ælfsige.

[WINCHESTER]

Riwallon (Rualo, Riuualonus) 1072–1088 App. 1072 (*Ann. Winchester*, p. 30: 1078 in Ann. (2)). Occ. *c.* 27 May 1072 (Bishop and Chaplais, facing pl. xxix); 1075 (Wilkins, I, 364; see p. 23). *Ann. Winchester*, p. 36, gives d. of 'Ralph' in 1088; the date may well be right, ?d. 17 Jan. (a Riwallon abb., with no abbey named, occ. in St Augustine's Canterbury obit, BM Cott. MS Vitell. C. xii, f. 116).

Abbey committed to Ranulf Flambard, 1088 (*Ann. Winchester*, p. 36).

Robert Losinga –1098 Father of Herbert Losinga, bp. Norwich (*WMGR*, II, 385; cf. *LVH*, p. 36). App. 1091 according to Ann. (2), but occ. 27 Jan. 1091 in *Reg.*, I, no. 315. D. 1098 (Florence, II, 41). Robert follows Riwallon in *Roul. Morts*, p. 186; and cf. *LVH*, p. 37. Occ. 1090 (*Mon.*, II, 266).

Hugh 1100– M. Winchester, St Swithun's, el. 1100 (*Ann. Winchester*, p. 40).

HYDE

Geoffrey I –1110(?1106)–1124 El. 1106 in Ann. (2); moved abb. to Hyde in 1110 (*Ann. Winchester*, p. 43; cf. *LVH*, pp. xxxvii, 38); occ. 29 May 1110, 13 Sept. 1114, 1123 (*Reg.*, II, nos. 947, 1070, 1391). D. 1124 (Florence, II, 78 = *JW*, p. 18).

Osbert 1125–(?)1135 App. 1125[1] (*Reg.*, II, no. 1425): dates 1124–35, when he d. Ann. (2). Abb. vacant, according to Ann. (2), for 6 years and more, under the control of Bishop Henry of Blois (cf. *LVH*, p. xlvii).

Hugh ?1142–?1149 1142–9, dep. in Ann. (2), perhaps, the Hugh de 'Lens' (?Lewes) of *Ann. Winchester*, p. 54 – occ. 1149; abb. a short time and professed no ms. (*LVH*, p. 41).

If Ann. (2) reliable abb. vacant for two years.

Selida, Salidus ?1151–1171 Succeeded 1151 according to Ann. (2); d. 1171 (ibid.; Ann. Merton, Corpus Christi Coll. Cambridge MS 59, f. 164v). Occ. –1171 (Voss, pp. 161–2); 6 Jan. 1171 (*Ctl. Winchester*, no. 3). Cf. *LVH*, p. 41.

Abbey vacant 5 years (*PR 17 Henry II*, p. 42 to *PR 21 Henry II*, p. 199 – half and part of a quarter year before el.); still vacant on 1–8 July 1175, when pr. and some ms. summoned for el. (*Gesta Hen. II*, I, 91–3; Diceto, I, 401).

Thomas 1175–1180 Pr. Montacute (q.v.), el. 1175, ?July (*Ann. Winchester*, p. 61; see above; Ann. (2) give 1177). Res. 1180[2] (*Ann. Winchester*, p. 62). Cf. *LVH*, p. 42.

John 'Suthil' *c.* 1180–1222 Succeeded 1181 according to Ann. (2); d. 1222 (*Ann. Winchester*, p. 84; *Ann. Waverley*, p. 296 – 'Suthil'). Occ. 1185 (*Ann. Winchester*, p. 62); 1189 (*Epp. Cant.*, p. 545); etc.

The abb. was vacant on 1 June 1222; royal assent to el. of Abb. Walter de Aystun on 7 July 1222 (*CPR, 1216–25*, pp. 333, 335).

WORCESTER CATHEDRAL, St Mary   ref. 964 or 969 (969 in Florence, I, 141; Robinson (1919), pp. 33ff. dated it *c.* 974×7; but cf. *AS Chts.*, pp. 360–1 (for 969); E. John in *Journ. of Eccl. History*, IX (1958), 159ff., and *Rev. Bénédictine*, LXXII (1963), 73–87 (for 964).)

D.G. List in *VCH Worcs*, II, 111: for period +1062, see *Ctl. Worcester*, pp. lviff. (R. R. Darlington); Le Neve, new edn., II, 102–4 (D. E. Greenway). Basis in Florence; cf. Sir Ivor Atkins in *Antiquaries Journal*, XX (1940), 1–38, 203–29; for obits, see pp. 29–30, 32 – from *Leofric Collectar*, II, ed. E. S. Dewick and W. H. Frere, pp. 601–2. Corpus Christi Coll. Cambridge MS 391, p. 12, gives an Ædwi dean under 6 Oct.

---

[1] The presence of both abps. suggests Oct. 1125 (*Reg.*, II, no. 1427n.; Hugh the Chanter, pp. 121ff.; *ASC* E s.a. 1125; Tillmann, p. 30). The abb. Battle and bp. Chichester forbid a date in 1124; 1126 is possible (cf. Hugh the Chanter, p. 128), but seems too late.

[2] *LVH*, p. xxxviii n. 4 has a ref. from an ann. Hyde, of which an extract survives in BM Add. 4797, f. 16, giving the date 1181 for Thomas's and John's succession.

DEANS AND PRIORS (primus monachus, primus, presbyter, sacerdos, prepositus, decanus, prior)

Wynsige ?969–*c.* 985 M. Ramsey, moved to Worcester 969 (Florence, I, 141); occ. ?969, ?974, 977, 975 × 8 (Birch, no. 1243; cf. *AS Chts.*, pp. 360–1; OE note to Birch, no. 1298 – but cf. Robinson loc. cit., *AS Chts.*, nos. 55–8, and p. 369). Cf. Atkins, pp. 9ff., 30; ?obit 20 May (not called pr.).

Æthelstan occ. 983 × 5, 987, etc., 990, 991 (*AS Chts.*, no. 61; cf. p. 321; Kemble, nos. 660–1; *AS Chts.*, nos. 64–5, 67; Kemble, nos. 677–8). Cf. Atkins, pp. 10ff.: prev. sacrist.

Ægelsige (Ethelsinus) I and II are noted with obits on 7 July and 4 Dec. Æ. II d. *c.* 1016 (Hemming, I, 276–7). One or other occ. 996, ?early 11th cent. (Kemble, no. 695 – cf. Atkins, p. 12, N. R. Ker in *Powicke Studies*, p. 75 – 'Ægelsie').

?Godwine occ. as first *sacerdos* in 1016 (Kemble, no. 724: taken to be pr. in Atkins, p. 14, but see pp. 15ff. for cases in which the leading *sacerdotes* Godwin and Eadric do not consistently witness first and so were very likely not prs.).

Ægelwine occ. 1051 × 3, *c.* 1053 (Kemble, no. 807; Atkins, p. 25 = *BM Facs.*, IV, no. 32); cf. Atkins, pp. 22ff. Obit, 26 Apr. Perhaps the Æthelwine dean who occ. 1044 × 51 (Kemble, no. 797).

St Wulfstan –1057–1062 M. and pr. Worcester; app. bp. *c.* Easter 1062, formally el. 29 Aug., consec. 8 Sept. 1062 (*WMVW*, pp. 8–9, 11, 18–19; Florence, II, 218–21; cf. Darlington in *WMVW*, p. xxvi and nn.). *WMVW* places an incident of 1054 within Wulfstan's priorate (pp. 15–16), but too much weight should perhaps not be laid on this. W. occ. –1057 (Atkins, p. 27; Hemming, II, 403–5); 1058 ('sacerdos': Earle, pp. 247–8): cf. Atkins, pp. 26ff.

Ælfstan *c.* 1062–1077 + Brother of Wulfstan (Hemming, II, 407); occ. + 1066 (*Ctl. Worcester*, no. 2); 1077 (Thorpe, p. 615),[1] etc.

Thomas –1080–1113 Succeeded Ælfstan (Hemming, II, 407). Occ. (T.) –1080 (*Ctl. Worcester*, no. 304);[2] 21 May 1089 (Hemming, II, pp. 418–20); 1092 (*Ctl. Worcester*, no. 52); 1109 × 13 (*Reg.*, II, no. 940);[3] d. 1113, 4 Oct. (Florence, II, 66; for the year cf. *Ann. Winchcombe*, p. 123; *Ann. Worcester*, p. 375).

Nicholas *c.* 1113–1124 Prev. m. Worcester and pupil of Bp. Wulfstan (*WMGP*, p. 287); occ. 15 Aug. 1116 (Atkins, p. 225); d. 24 June 1124 (Florence, II, 78 = *JW*, p. 18, correcting the day to *feria tertia*).

Warin *c.* 1124–*c.*1142 Occ. –1133[4] (*Reg.*, II, no. 1045); 1140 (*Mon.*, IV, 175, but see Alcester); 1140 × 1 (see Oxford, St Frideswide, p. 180n. 4).

Ralph of Bath 1142–1143 Name and date in one MS of *Ann. Winchcombe* (ed. Darlington, p. 129nn.).

David 1143–1145 Succeeded 1143, dep. 1145 (*Ann. Winchcombe*, p. 129nn.; *Ann. Tewkes-bury*, p. 46; cf. *GFL*, no. 47 and n. and p. 540; Saltman, p. 86). Occ. 28 Dec. 1143 (*Ctl. Gloucester*, I, p. lxxvi).

Osbert 1145–1146 Dates as *Ann. Winchcombe*, p. 129nn. (1145 confirmed by *Ann. Tewkes-bury*, p. 46; cf. *GFL*, p. 540 where the '*c.*' before the 1146 can be omitted).

Ralph of Bedford 1146–1189 Accession and name, *Ann. Winchcombe*, p. 129n.; 26 Jan. 1148/9 fell in his third year, so he succeeded after 26 Jan. 1146 (*Ctl. Worcester*, no. 73;

---

[1] Dated by Ralph abb. Winchcombe and Æthelwig abb. Evesham.

[2] With Ælfwine ('Alwinum') abb. Ramsey, q.v.

[3] Cf. note ad loc. and p. xvi; Henry I was first in England in 1109 after Roger d'Abitot succeeded as sheriff of Worcs. The editors suggest 1110 as the date, but the writ may belong to 1112 × 13 in the vacancy of the see.

[4] Dated by eds. of *Reg.* (with hesitation) 1114 × 18; but the 'pro salute' clause is not cogent evidence (see *EYC*, IV, pp. xxviiff.). The writ is dated at Worcester, which Henry I cannot have visited later than 1133.

[WORCESTER CATHEDRAL]

cf. note ad loc.; *GFL*, p. 540). Occ. –1148 (Worcester D. and C. cht. B167); 26 Jan. 1149 (Saltman, no. 299 – and as above); (R.) 15 May 1181 (*Ctl. Eynsham*, I, no. 162); for length of tenure cf. Diceto, II, 42. D. 23 July 1189 (*Ann. Worcester*, p. 386; *Ctl. Worcester*, no. 340).

Master Senatus 1189–1196 Prev. m., precentor, and chamberlain (*Ctl. Worcester*, p. lviii and n.). Dates as *Ann. Worcester*; res. 20 Nov. 1196, d. 1207 (pp. 388, 395). On him see R. W. Hunt in *TRHS*, 4th Series, XIX (1936), 29–30.

Peter 1196–1203 Prev. m. Worcester, dep. 24 Dec. 1203 (*Ann. Worcester*, pp. 388, 392). D. 1204 (ibid.).

Randulf 1203–1214 Prev. m. Evesham (*Ch. Evesham*, pp. 255–6); dates, 24 Dec. 1203–14 as *Ann. Worcester*, pp. 392, 402–3; el. bp. Worcester 1213, abb. Evesham 1214 (q.v.).

Silvester 1214/15–1216 M. Worcester, el. 21 Jan. 1214 or 1215 (*Ann. Worcester*, pp. 403–4; cf. Darlington in *Ctl. Worcester*, p. lix). El. bp. Worcester 3 Apr., consec. 3 July 1216; d. 16 July 1218 (cf. *Ann. Worcester*, p. 407).

YORK, St Mary Offshoot of the same community as Whitby; f. at Lastingham *c.* 1078; moved to York –1086 (A. H. Thompson in *YAJ*, XXVII (1924), 388–95; *Domesday Book*, I, 305, ref. to 'abbas Eboracensis').

List in *VCH Yorks*, III, 111; names Stephen-Clement in *Sim. Dur.*, II, 201. List (1) of names and dates in *Ch. St Mary's York*, pp. 1–2 (= *Mon.*, III, 569), some demonstrably false; list (2) in *Anonimalle Chronicle*, pp. xlviif.

Stephen *c.* 1080–1112(?) First abb. and founder (foundation narrative, *Mon.*, III, 544–6); tenure 24 years, d. 1112 according to *Ch.*; 24 years, list (2); obit 9 Aug. (*Ch.*, p. 113). Occ. ?1091[1] (Offler, pp. 48ff.), 1089×93 (*EYC*, IV, no. 2); 1108+ (*Ctl. Selby*, I, no. 492).

Richard 1113/14–1118 M. York, app. *c.* Christmas 1113 (*ASCH*, s.a. 1114). D. 1118 (not named, but clearly Richard, Ann. Thorney, BM Cott. MS Nero C. vii, f. 81v); d. 1131 acc. to *Ch.*, but see below; obit 31 Dec., *Ch.*, p. 111. Less than one year, list (2).

Geoffrey *c.* 1119–*c.* 1138 On him see Clay in *EYC*, IV, no. 105n. Occ. prob. 1122 (*Hist. Selby*, p. [24]); 31 Jan. 1123 (Hugh Chantor, p. 109); +1132 (*Ctl. Whitby*, I, no. 198). 29 years, list (2). Obit 17 or 18 July (*Ch.*, pp. 1, 111).

Savaric (Severinus) 1138–1161(?) App. 1138 (*JW*, p. 48, without name); d. 3 Apr. 1161 *Ch.*, p. 1, or 4 Apr., *Ch.*, p. 112. 23 years, list (2).

Clement *c.* 1161–1184 Occ. Mar. 1163 (*GASA*, I, 157); 1174×5, 1175×6 (Mowbray, nos. 110, 119 = *Ctl. Fountains*, I, 204ff., 145); d. 1184 (Howden, II, 288; *Ch.*); obit 18 Aug. (*Ch.*, pp. 1, 113). 14 years (*sic*), list (2).

Vacant 1184–6 (*PR 31 Henry II*, pp. 77–8; *32 Henry II*, pp. 84–5).

Robert I de Harpham *c.* 1186–1195 See above: *Ch.* gives accession s.a. 1184. Dep. 13 June 1195 (Howden, III, 294); obit 19 Apr. (*Ch.*, pp. 1, 112; '1189', *Ch.*, p. 1). Occ. 1186 (Durham D. and C. 1. 1. Arch. 8). 5 years (*sic*), list (2).

Robert II de Longchamp 1197–1239 Brother of William de Longchamp; pr. Ely; el. 17 March, bl. 23 March (by Abp. Hubert Walter), enthroned 2 Apr. 1197 (Diceto, II, 151–2; for the year, also Howden, IV, 17; Florence, II, 162; cf. *Ctl. Guisborough*, II, no. 672). Occ. in fines 27 Jan. 1200–15 Oct. 1233 (*Yorks F., John*, p. 2; *1232–46*, p. 7). D. 11 Jan. 1239 (*Ch.*, p. 2, obit also p. 111; tenure 43 years, p. 2; 43 years, also list (2)).

---

[1] Offler, pp. 50–1, points out that although the charter is undoubtedly spurious the lay witness list is consistent; it may well be based on a genuine list of *c.* 14 Nov. 1091.

THE BENEDICTINE HOUSES: DEPENDENCIES

Some small houses and cells, founded before 1216, yield no names, and have therefore not been included. The existence of a prior is no guarantee that there was anything like a regular conventual establishment (see pp. 1, 20).

ALKBOROUGH (Lincs), St John the Baptist (Spalding) f. 1052
Hugh Occ. 25 Nov. 1203 (*CRR*, III, p. 82); 27 Jan. 1205 (*Lincs F.*, PRS LXVII, no. 195).

ALVECOTE (Warws), St Blaise (Great Malvern) f. 1159.
  List in *VCH Warws*, II, 62.
Thomas Occ. 1161 × 77 (*HMC Middleton*, p. 8).

BELVOIR (Lincs), St Mary (St Albans) f. 1076 × 88
  List in *VCH Lincs*, II, 126. Obits in Cambridge Trinity Coll. MS O. 9. 25, printed in Nichols, *Leics*, II, i, App. pp. 25ff.; here cited from MS.
Brientius Occ. prob. *temp.* Stephen (*HMC Rutland*, IV, 98–9 and n. 8; cf. *Reg.*, III, no. 85).
German Occ. 1145 (Gibbs, no. 154).
Lemmaer Occ. *?mid-12th cent.* (*HMC Rutland*, IV, 130).[1]
Simon Occ. *c.* 1174 × 7,[2] 1183 × 95 (*HMC Rutland*, IV, 113, 146); *temp. Henry II* (pal.: *DC*, no. 413); d. 4 Feb. (obit, f. 156v).
  ohn Occ. *c.* 1174 × 78[3] (*HMC Rutland*, IV, 160); 1182+ (Madox, *Form.*, no. 251; Nichols, *Leics*, II, i, App. pp. 4–5); 1183 × 95 (*HMC Rutland*, IV, 143). ?D. 25 Mar. (obit, f. 157).
?Eustace Occ. 1195 × 1214 or mid-13th cent. (*HMC Rutland*, IV, 146; cf. p. 164).
Master Ralph Simplex Preceded Roger of Wendover (*GASA*, I, 270); possibly d. as monastic archd. 13 Oct. 1217 (*MPCM*, VI, 270).
Roger of Wendover The historian; occ. 6 Oct. 1224 (*HMC Rutland*, IV, 143). Dep. by Abb. William ?1231 × 5 (*GASA*, I, 270, 274, cf. 273). D. 6 May 1236 (*MPCM*, VI, 274; commemorated on 6 May in obit, f. 158v).
The next pr., Martin of 'Bodekesham' (*GASA*, I, 274), occ. –1235 (*Ctl. Bushmead*, no. 296; cf. no. 297), and d. 3 Jan. 1249 (*MPCM*, VI, 278).

BINHAM (Norfolk), St Mary (St Albans) f. –1093
  List in *VCH Norfolk*, II, 345.[4]
Robert Occ. 1121 × 35 (*Misc. D. M. Stenton*, p. 159; cf. p. 149n.).

[1] 'Rodbertus nepos Lemmaer prioris' (sic).
[2] Bull of Alexander III, Anagni, 9 Feb.: i.e. 1160, 1161, 1174, 1176 or 1178; but the pope was not recognised in England in Feb. 1160 (see now M. G. Cheney in *EHR*, LXXXIV (1969), 474–97; but see p. 479 for known papal letters of Jan. 1160). 1161 is possible.
[3] Referred to in a document confirmed by Abp. Richard (+1174), with Peter of Blois, not archd., as witness (probably –1177; see p. 11 n. 1).
[4] The first name in the *VCH* list, Osgod, comes from Blomefield, *Norfolk*, IX, 210, who had it from *Mon.*, III, 346 (cf. p. 342); but this Osgod was *presbiter*, not *prior*.

[BINHAM]
Enisand Occ. 1133 × 46, prob. 1143[1] (*Mon.*, III, 348).
Geoffrey Occ. 1167 × 83 (BM Cott. MS Claud. D. xiii, f. 165r–v).
Peter Occ. 12 Mar. 1190 (ib., f. 25); (P.) n.d. (ib., f. 164v).
Ralph Gubiun Occ. 29 Jan. 1199 (*Norfolk F.*, PRS LXV, no. 213); n.d., 1195 × 9 (Ralph Gubiun: BM Cott. MS Claud. D. xiii, ff. 126v, 132).
Thomas (Th.) Occ. (Th.) 26 Nov. 1199 (ib., ff. 125v–126); (Th.) 1 July 1200, 7 Mar. 1201 (ib., ff. 131v–132, 23v); 27 Jan. 1205 (*Norfolk F.*, PRS LXX, no. 67); +22 Mar. 1206 (j.d.: see Wymondham); dep. 1207 × 13 by abb. St Albans (*GASA*, I, 226, cf. p. 228: during the Interdict).
Richard (see below) Occ. 3 May 1215 (*Norfolk F.*, PRS LXX, no. 279); 1220 × 1 (*Cambs F.*, p. 11).
Richard le Rus, Richard de Kancia and Miles are referred to as former prs. in 1249 × 50 in PRO Ass. Roll (J1) 560, m. 53 (52). The next recorded pr., William de Gedding, d. 17 Apr. 1227 (*MPCM*, VI, 292).

BRECON, St John the Evangelist (Battle) f. ?*c.* 1110[2]
Walter 1st pr., m. Battle (*Ch. Battle*, p. 35).
?William Occ. 1131 × 7 (BM Harl. MS 6976, f. 14v) – possibly a mistake for Walter.
Ralph Occ. 1148 × 54(?) (*GFL*, no. 290); 1139 × 57 (*Mon.*, III, 26–7); 1165 (*Earldom of Hereford Chts.*, p. 50; for date, cf. pp. 9–10).
John Occ. 1203 (*Gir. Camb.*, III, 308; cf. IV, 36); 1203 × 5 (Gloucester Cathedral Reg. A, ff. 110–11); 8 Nov. 1221 (Eyton, *Salop*, III, 26).

BRISTOL (Glos), St James (Tewkesbury) f. *c.* 1137
List in *VCH Glos*, II, 74.
Picot Occ. 1164 × 79 (*Glam. Chts.*, V, p. 1683).
W. Occ. 1186 × 1202 (ib., II, no. 256); 2 April 1207 (*Reg. Lichfield*, no. 291).
The next recorded pr., Jordan, d. 1231 (*Ann. Tewkesbury*, p. 80).

BROMFIELD (Salop), St Mary (Gloucester) f. –1115; 1155 (dependent on Gloucester) M.C. List in *VCH Salop* forthcoming (M. Chibnall). For dedication cf. Eyton, *Salop*, V, 210ff.; A. L. Moir, *Bromfield Priory* (Chester, 1947).
Osbert Occ. *c.* 1115[3] (Eyton, *Salop*, III, 232–3); 1132 (Oxford, Balliol MS 271, f. 88); 1129 × 47 (*Mon.*, VI, 231–2).
Robert of Haseley 1155– App. 1155; M. of Gloucester; first pr. of dep. (*GFL*, pp. 364, 368).
Robert Occ. 1193 × 4 (*PR 6 Richard I*, p. 144); possibly the same as above.
Elias Occ. 1203, 1208 (Eyton, *Salop*, V, 218; cf. p. 213).
Henry Foliot –1228 M. Gloucester, el. abb. Gloucester 1228: royal assent, 26 May (*CPR*, *1225–32*, p. 189).

CARDIFF (Glamorgan), St Mary (Tewkesbury) f. –1106
List in *South Wales and Mon. Rec. Soc.*, II (1960), 151n. (W. Rees).

---

[1] Walter, *quondam* abb. Ramsey – he was dep. for a time in 1143. But the phrase may possibly have been used of an extant official.
[2] So *KH*, p. 52. The *Ch. Battle*, p. 35, describes its foundation under the first abb. Battle (d. 1095); but it was clearly a process of some duration, so that *c.* 1110 may not be too late. Cf. Lloyd, II, 436–7.
[3] Cyprian archd. Colchester; Reinelm bp. Hereford. A Hugh 'canon' of Bromfield occ. 1131 × 48 (*Ctl. Worcester*, no. 54); he may have been Osbert's successor, since any real community can hardly have existed –1155.

Robert of Westbury   Occ. 1148 × 83 (*Glam. Chts.*, I, pp. 128–9).

Eustace   Occ. 1193 × 1218 (*Glam. Chts.*, VI, p. 2335).

CARDIGAN, St Mary (Gloucester, Chertsey)   f. *c.* 1110 × 15 (dependent on Gloucester); 1165+ (dependent on Chertsey)

?Osbert   Occ. 1139 × 48 as pr. of one of Gloucester's Welsh deps., possibly Cardigan (*GFL*, no. 10 and n.). He may possibly have been pr. Ewenny.

CRANBORNE (Dorset), St Mary (Tewkesbury)   f. *? c.* 980 (abbey); 1102 (cell of Tewkesbury)

List in *VCH Dorset*, II, 71.

Gerald   M. of Winchester, occ. 1086 (*Ann. Winchester*, p. 34); in 1102 transferred the abbey to Tewkesbury (*Ann. Tewkesbury*, p. 44).

The next recorded pr., Adam of Preston, d. 1262 (*Ann. Tewkesbury*, p. 169).

DEEPING (Lincs), St James (Thorney)   f. 1139

List in *VCH Lincs*, II, 129.

Jocelyn or Jollan   Occ. ?1154 × 69[1] (BM Harl. MS 3658, f. 17v).

The next recorded pr., Richard of Stamford, occ. 1216 × 37 (CUL Add. MS 3021, f. 462v) and was el. abb. of Thorney 1237 (*CPR, 1232–47*, pp. 194, 204).

DENNY (Cambs) (Ely), St James and St Leonard   f. *c.* 1160 (Ben.); –1169 (Templars) (*Lib. El.*, pp. 387ff., cf. 387n.).

Reginald   occ. 1133 × 69, prob. *c.* 1160 (not called pr.: ibid.).

DOVER (Kent), St Martin (Christ Church, Canterbury)   f. 1131 (Augustinian pr.); 1136 (Benedictine)

Lists[2] in *VCH Kent*, II, 136; C. R. Haines, *Dover Priory*, pp. 183ff.; Ann. (not very reliable) in BM Cott. MS Julius D. v, ff. 14ff., partly printed in *Mon.*, IV, 536, partly in Saltman, pp. 542–3; list from this in Wharton, Lambeth MS 585, p. 217; 14th cent. list in *Lit. Cant.*, III, 376.

William de Longueville   1136–1137 Sacrist of Christ Church, app. 1136 but sent back to Canterbury in 1137 (Gervase, I, 99).

Ascelin[3]   1139–1142 Sacrist of Christ Church, app. 1139 (Gervase, I, 109); res. 1142 to be bp. Rochester (Ann.; Saltman in *EHR*, LXVI (1951), 74; cf. *AS*, I, 343). D. 23 × 24 Jan. 1148. Reckoned first pr. in Ann.

William de Andeville   1142–1149 2nd pr. (Ann.); sacrist of Christ Church, app. 1142 (Gervase, I, 141; Ann. f. 23v = Saltman, p. 542 (1143)); occ. 1142 × 8 (*Ctl. Canterbury, St Gregory,* no. 5); res. to be abb. Evesham 1149 (q.v.; Gervase, I, 141; *GFL*, p. 533). D. 1159.

Hugh of Caen   1149–1157 Sacrist Christ Church (Gervase, I, 141); occ. m. Christ Church, Saltman, p. 310 (but m. Dover according to Ann.). 3rd pr. app. 1149 succeeded by Richard in 1157 (Ann., f. 24 = Saltman, p. 542); d. 9 Feb. (BM MSS Cott. Nero C. ix, f. 5v; Arundel 68, f. 15v); occ. (Hu.) 17 Feb. 1156, 9 Jan. 1157+ (*PUE*, II, nos. 91, 103); so presumably d. Feb. 1157.

---

[1] With W. abb. Thorney, i.e. 1154 × 8, 1162 × 9 (see Thorney) or 1261 × 93 (Abb. William of Yaxley).

[2] Miss Melanie Barber is preparing an edition of the ctl. (Lambeth MS 241), and with it a list with fuller references than is possible here: we gratefully acknowledge her help meanwhile. Lambeth MS 20, f. 197 has an obit of Pr. Robert (not definitely identifiable).

[3] Called Anselm in Ann., f. 23 (Saltman, p. 542), and given dates 1140–2 (1143 Saltman: the MS is rubbed, but the reading seems to be 1142). Cf. St Benet of Hulme.

[DOVER]

Richard 1157–1174 Chapl. of Abp. Theobald (?occ. Saltman, p. 310),[1] presumably m. Christ Church, app. 1157 (Ann., f. 24 = Saltman, p. 542); occ. 1160 (ib., p. 543); el. Abp. Canterbury 3 June 1173 (cf. Gervase, I, 244; Ann., f. 24; *GFL*, p. 292 and n., cf. pp. 293ff.); consec. 7 Apr. 1174, d. 16 Feb. 1184.

Master Warin 1174–1180 5th pr. (Ann., f. 24 s.a. 1180); cellarer of Christ Church, app. 1174 (Gervase, I, 251); occ. 1177 × 81[2] (Canterbury Cathedral Reg. E, f. 61v); d. 21 Sept. 1180 (BM MSS Cott. Nero C. ix, f. 12; Arundel 68, f. 42v; Gervase, I, 295; Ann., f. 24).

John 1180–1186/7 6th pr. (Ann.); cellarer of Christ Church, app. 1180 (Gervase, I, 295); occ. 1181 (PRO E164/29, f. 20r–v); 11 May 1182 (*PUE*, II, no. 220); d. 15 Feb. (BM Arundel MS 68, f. 16v) 1186 – so Ann., f. 24v, but perhaps for 1187.[3]

William 1187–1188 7th pr., app. 1187, d. 1188 (Ann., f. 25); prev. m. Christ Church, app. *c.* 17 May 1187 (Gervase, I, 365). A William pr. Dover d. 5 July and others on 10 July and 12 Oct. (BM Arundel MS 68, ff. 32v, 33v, 45).

Osbert 1189–1193 M. Dover, 8th pr., on 5 years, 1189–93 (Ann., f. 25); d. 31 Dec. (BM MSS Cott. Nero C. ix, f. 18v; Arundel 68, f. 52v) – presumably 31 Dec. 1193. Occ. 1193 (Lambeth MS 241, f. 225v).

Robert *c.* 1194–1197 Subpr. Canterbury Cathedral (see Eynsham); 9th pr. Dover, 1193 (*sic*)–1196 (*sic*), res. abb. Eynsham: Ann., f. 25; Gervase, I, 543–4 (and cf. Eynsham) establishes 1197. Occ. 1193 × 5[4] (Lambeth MS 241, f. 59v).

Felix de Rosa 1197–1212 For his name, see list in *Lit. Cant.*, III, 376; cellarer of Christ Church, then sacrist (Gervase, I, 544); 10th pr. 1196–1212 (Ann., f. 25r–v); d. 19 July (BM Arundel MS 68, f. 35v). Occ. 23 July 1197 (*PUE*, II, no. 291); 20 Jan. 1201 × 2 (*Kent F.*, p. 22); 1211 × 12 (Lambeth MS 241, f. 119).

Reginald of Sheppey 1212–1228/9 Prev. m. Christ Church (*Lit. Cant.*, III, 376, also giving his name); 11th pr. 1212–28 (Ann., ff. 25v, 28v) – but d. under end of ann. for 1228, and as he d. 1 Feb. (BM Arundel MS 68, f. 15) this may be meant to indicate 1229. Occ. 1 Nov. 1223 (*Kent F.*, p. 80).

DUNSTER (Soms), ?St George[5] (Bath) f. 1090+

List in *VCH Soms*, II, 82.

Hugh Occ. 8 Nov. 1186 (*Ctl. Buckland*, no. 11).

?Martin Occ. ?late 12th cent. (ib., no. 338); n.d. (*Glam. Chts.*, I, p. 77). But his date seems very uncertain, and *VCH* has Martin occ. 1274.

EARLS COLNE (Essex), St Andrew, St Mary and St John the Evangelist (Abingdon) f. –1107

List in *VCH Essex*, II, 104.

Mainard Occ. 1141 × 53[6] (*Ctl. Colne*, no. 58).

Hugh Occ. –Jan. 1174 (*Mon.*, IV, 101); (H.) *c.* 1181 × 3 (*GFL*, no. 365).

Ansketil, Anchetil Occ. 1185 × 6 (*Ch. Abingdon*, II, 243).

R. Occ. 1184 × 94 (Eyton, *Salop*, VII, 366n.). Probably = Reginald, occ. late 12th cent. (*Ctl. Colne*, nos. 73, 103).

Osbert Occ. prob. 1204 × 14[7] (*Ctl. Colne*, no. 36).

---

[1] But there were several monks called Richard in Theobald's entourage: see Saltman, p. 215.

[2] William archd. Gloucester (*GF*, p. 284); Richard abp. and legate.

[3] It is, however, the first entry in a long annal.

[4] Abp. Hubert Walter, not legate, i.e. 1193 × 5.

[5] Cf. *VCH Soms*, II, 81.

[6] Earl Gilbert FitzRichard (Hertford).

[7] If Earl Aubrey = the 2nd earl of Oxford.

William Occ. 1204×21 (*Ch. Abingdon*, II, 294–5); Jan. 1209, *c.* Easter 1224 (*Essex F.*, pp. 43, 67).

The next recorded pr., Richard, occ. 2 Nov. 1227 (*Essex F.*, p. 77).

EWENNY (Ogmore) (Glam), St Michael (Gloucester) f. 1141

List in Birch, *Hist. Margam*, p. 338.[1]

Robert 1141–1144 D. 14 Oct. 1144 (Greg. Caerwent, BM Cott. MS Vesp. A. v, f. 199).

John Occ. early 1145 (*GFL*, no. 43).

?Osbert see Cardigan.

The order of the next three prs. is quite uncertain.

Roger Occ. 1148×66,[2] 1148×83 (*Glam. Chts.*, I, pp. 131–2, 129).

?Ralph Occ. 1148×83 (*JNLW*, III, 133 (ed. J. Conway Davies): but of doubtful authenticity; see *GFL*, p. 108n.).

Bertram Occ. 1148×83 (*Glam. Chts.*, I, p. 133; also in cht. of ?same date, but doubtful authenticity, *JNLW*, III, 129; cf. *GFL*, loc. cit.).

Maurice Occ. 2nd half 12th cent.[3] (*Hist. Margam*, p. 31).

J. Occ. prob. 1194×1203 (*Glam. Chts.*, II, p. 196).

David Occ. 1205×24 (*Glam. Chts.*, II, p. 440).

EXETER (Devon), St Nicholas (Battle) f. 1087

List in Oliver, p. 114; 15th-cent. list in BM Cott. MS Vitell. D. ix, f. 23; *Ctl.*, ibid., abstr. in *CTG*, I, 60–5, 184–9, 250–4, 374–88 from which charter numbers are given here. The 15th-cent. list starts Cono, Benedict, Ralph, Alfred, Osbert.

Benedict Occ. 1138×60 (BM Cott. MS Vitell. D. ix, f. 72v = *Ctl.*, no. 167, p. 189).

Alvred Occ. n.d. (*Ctl.*, no. 109, p. 186).

Osbert Occ. 1160×7[4] (*Ctl.*, f. 72v = no. 168, p. 189).

After Osbert, the list continues: Geoffrey, Maurice, John, Theobald, Peter, Roger... Of these John seems to be misplaced, and there is no other evidence of Theobald.

Geoffrey Occ. n.d. (*Ctl.*, no. 198, p. 252).

Maurice Occ. 1180×90 or 1203×10[5] (ib., no. 182, p. 250).

Peter Occ. 1212 (*Ctl.*, ff. 48v–49v = nos. 77–8,[6] p. 184); 23 Mar. 1219 (*Devon F.*, no. 75); 1221×2 (*Ctl.*, no. 39, p. 63).

John Occ. 1227 (*Ctl.*, no. 158, p. 188).

Roger Occ. prob. 1224×30[7] (*Ctl.*, no. 333, p. 381).

FINCHALE (Durham), St Mary and St Godric (Durham) f. (cell 1170) 1196

List in *VCH Durham*, II, 105 from Raine, *Finchale*, p. xxv.

Thomas App. 1196, sacrist of Durham (Geoffrey of Coldingham in *Scriptores Tres*, p. 18).

John 2nd. pr.; occ. *c.* 1205(1197)×1211 (*EYC*, XII, no. 236).

The next recorded pr., Ralph, occ. 1234×44[8] (Raine, *Finchale*, no. 26).

---

[1] Adam and Peter are given without dates, and a second John (? = J.) temp. Conan abb. Margam (occ. −1166 − +1194); outside limits 1155×1203.

[2] Robert, son of William, earl of Gloucester (*Ann. Margam*, p. 16).

[3] With Conan, abb. Margam.

[4] Hugh de Ralegh, sheriff of Devon.

[5] William Brewer, sheriff of Devon.

[6] In no. 77 the pr. is called both Peter and Nicholas in the MS: the second name is clearly a scribe's slip, based on the priory's dedication.

[7] Hilary Blund, mayor of Exeter (see Miss R. C. Easterling, in *Trans. Devon Assoc.* LXX (1938), 471–2).

[8] Thomas pr. Durham (see Le Neve, II, 35).

FREISTON (Lincs), St James (Crowland) f. 1114+
List in *VCH Lincs*, II, 129.
John Occ. –1172 (*DC*, no. 157).
Roger Occ. *c.* 1160 × 92[1] (?*1185* × 9) (*Genealogist*, New Series, XVII (1901), 33).
Ralph[2] Simplex –1198 Prev. m. Crowland; res. 1198 to be abb. Thorney, q.v. Occ. 1190 × 7 ('simplex': Lincs Arch. Office, 3 Anc. 2/1, f. 15 v); n.d. (Norman Moore, I, 178–9).
Nicholas –1228 Occ. 18 Nov. 1208 (*Lincs F.*, PRS, LXVII, no. 286); res. 1228 to be abb. Eynsham (*Ann. Dunstable*, p. 109; Ch. Barnwell in *Walt. Cov.*, I, p. xlin.); d. 9 Feb. 1242 (*Ann. Tewkesbury*, p. 126).

GOATHLAND (Yorks N.) (Whitby)
A hermitage under a priest called **Osmund**, which was absorbed by Whitby 1109 × 14 (*Mon.*, IV, 544–5; *EYC*, I, no. 398; cf. *Reg.*, II, nos. 926–7 and n. – ?1109).

GREAT MALVERN (Worcs), St Mary and St Michael (Westminster) f. 1085 (*Ann. Worcester*, p. 373); dependent on Westminster soon after (J. A. Robinson (1911), pp. 33 f.).
List in *VCH Worcs*, II, 142.
Aldwin First pr., established by St Wulfstan (*WMVW*, p. 26; cf. pp. xli–xlii; *WMGP*, pp. 285–6). Supposed to have started preparations –1056 (cf. ibid. and *Mon.*, III, 440, from Reg. Godfrey Giffard – document of 1268), but he was apparently still alive +1125 (*temp.* Bp. Simon of Worcester, *Ctl. Worcester*, no. 300), and this span seems very improbable.
Walcher –1125 Occ. 23 May 1125 (*JW*, p. 20): d. 1 Oct. 1125 (1135, J. Nott, *Some of the Antiquities of 'Moche Malverne'* (Malvern, 1885), p. 28; but see R. W. Southern, *Medieval Humanism*, p. 166n.). A Lotharingian, astrologer and mathematician, living in England by 1091 (see Haskins, *Studies in Medieval Science* (2nd edn.), pp. 113–17; W. Thomas, *Descriptio ecclesiae Maj. Malverne*, p. 35 (d. 1125), in *Antiqu. Prioratus Majoris Malverne* (London, 1725)). D. 1140 according to *MPCM*, II, 174.
Richard Occ. *c.* 1125 (*Ctl. Worcester*, no. 300, with Aldwin); 1144 × 8, –1150 (*GFL*, no. 28, cf. p. 537; the name is confirmed by *Ctl. Worcester*, no. 300).
Roger Malebranche –1159–1177 Occ. 1159, *c.* 1158 × 69 (*Mon.*, III, 455; Nott, *op. cit.*, pp. 40–1); became abb. Burton in 1177 (*Gesta Hen. II*, I, 180; *c.* 1 July; and see Burton; *GFL*, p. 537).
Walter *c.* 1177–*c.* 1216 Presumably succeeded Roger, though not instituted formally until 1191 after a dispute with the bp. of Worcester (W. Thomas, *op. cit., Chart. Orig.*, pp. 96–7; *GFL*, no. 239 and n.). Occ. –1190 (Westminster Abb., Domesday Ctl., f. 648v); 1193 (Thomas, Appendix, p. 97); prob. 1194 (*Ctl. Worcester*, p. 160); 1204 (Westminster Abb. Domesday Ctl., ff. 574v–576); prob. the W. who was deprived before 1224 (*Acta Stephani Langton*, pp. 16off.: cf. *GFL*, no. 239n.).
The next pr., Thomas, was app. 1216 × 18 (*Reg. G. Giffard*, II, p. 178). And see Little Malvern.

HATFIELD PEVEREL (Essex), St Mary (St Albans) f. 1100+
List in *VCH Essex*, II, 106.
Matthew Occ. 6 June 1197 (*FF*, PRS XX, no. 166);[3] 13 Oct. 1206 (*CRR*, IV, p. 225).
The next recorded pr., Alexander de Burgo, was dep. in 1230 by the abb. of St Albans (*GASA*, I, 274).

[1] Baldric de Sigillo, archd. Leicester (*GFL*, p. 164n.).
[2] Adolphus (from [R]adulfus) in *Walt. Cov.*, I, p. xii.
[3] Hatfield *Peverel*.

HEREFORD, St Guthlac and St Peter (Gloucester) f. *c.* 1100 × 1 in St Peter's Hereford;[1] amalgamated with St Guthlac's and moved outside the city, 1143

John   Pr. of St Peter's, occ. 1131 × 6 (BM Harl. MS 6976, f. 14 v).

Warin   Occ. 1143 × 8 (*GFL*, no. 21).

Ernulf   Occ.1148 × *c.*1150 (Oxford, Balliol Coll. MS 271, ff. 50 v–51); 1148 × 55 (*GFL*, no. 333).

Robert   Occ. 1159 × 60 (*GFL*, no. 325).

Osbert   Occ. 1168, 2 Oct. 1172 (Oxford, Balliol MS 271, ff. 16, 107 v–8).

Thomas Carbonel   –1179 Occ. *c.* 1158[2] × 79 (Eyton, *Salop*, I, 75–6); res. 1179 to be abb. of Gloucester, q.v.

William   Occ. 1179 × 89[3] (*Ctl. Brecon, Arch. Cambr.*, 4th Series, XIV, 228–9); 1184 (*GFL*, no. 379); (W.) 19 Mar. 1185 (Oxford, Balliol Coll. MS 271, f. 89 v); 1186 × 91 (ib., ff. 49 v–50).

Robert   –1191 Res. 1191 to be abb. Muchelney, but ejected the same year (see Muchelney).

John   Occ. 1186 × 98 (Oxford, Balliol Coll. MS 271, f. 90 v).

Henry   Occ. *c.* 1186 × *c.* 1200[4] (–1205); *c.* 1203 × 5; (H.) 1203 × 21; 1205 + (Oxford, Balliol Coll. MS 271, ff. 55, cf. 49 v, 108 v; 69; 102; 63 v); (H.) 30 Apr. 1214 (Cheney, *Inn. III*, no. 964); *quondam*, –18 Nov. 1215 (Balliol MS 271, f. 50).

S.   Occ. ?1220.[5]

Jocelin   Occ. 1205 × 24; 1231 × 4[6] (Balliol MS 271, ff. 49 v, 55); (J.) 13 Aug. 1232 (*CPR 1225–32*, p. 523).

HERTFORD, St Mary (St Albans) f. –1093
   List in *VCH Herts*, IV, 421.

Ralph   Mid-twelfth cent.[7] (BM Lansd. MS 863, ff. 158 r–v).

Nigel   Occ. (N.) *c.* 1179[8] (*HMC Var. Coll.*, VII, 33–4); 2nd half 12th cent. (BM Lansd. MS. 863, f. 159; see also BM Add. Cht. 15,470).

William   Occ. 1195 × 7[9] (BM Harl. MS 391, f. 98 r–v).

William de Sandruge   ? inst. 1213 in place of the pr. of Hertford who died in that year (*Ann. Dunstable*, p. 41); d. 6 July 1222 (*MPCM*, VI, 270).

HOXNE (Suffolk), St Edmund (Norwich Cath. Priory) f. 1130
   List in *VCH Suffolk*, II, 77, from the list in Blomefield, *Norfolk*, III, 609–10. He evidently took the names from the cartulary, then in the possession of T. Martin of Palgrave, but now lost (see ib., p. 607; Davis, no. 496), and he was unable to determine the order or the dates of the first five priors given.

---

[1] Cf. *GF*, p. 84n., *GFL*, p. 55, where it is wrongly stated that the pr. first became conventual in 1143. Chts. of Hugh de Lacy in Balliol MS 271, ff. 51 v, 93 v, seem to establish that it was conventual at or soon after the original gift of St Peter's church in Hereford, which is dated 1100 in *Ctl. Gloucester*, I, p. 326; 1101 in ib., I, 84. Cf. also *Mon.*, VI, 130.

[2] G(eoffrey) dean Hereford (*GF*, p. 267).

[3] Master Peter de 'Lehe' not yet archd. Worcester.

[4] Richard, dean of Hereford (Z. N. and C. N. L. Brooke in *CHJ*, VIII, iii (1946), 182).

[5] Ctl. Shrewsbury, Nat. Lib. Wales MS 7851D, pp. 323–4, dated 1228: but a judge-delegate decision on a mandate of Honorius III of 26 Nov. 1219, with no indication that the pope is dead or of any delay. Perhaps the original was dated 1220, 8 kal., non. or id....

[6] Ralph dean of Hereford (see p. 178 n. 3; bp. Hereford 1234).

[7] Lansdowne MS 863, ff. 157 v ff., has a series of charters by the Limésy family, Ralph the founder (occ. 1086, 1113 × 16); his son, Alan, grandson Gerard and great-grandsons John and Alan II (Loyd, p. 54, *Reg.*, II, no. 1150). Pr. Ralph occ. with Alan I and Gerard; Prior Nigel with John.

[8] 1168 × 79 – Baldwin abb. Forde; Roger bp. Worcester: siege of Empress in Oxford (1142) said to be 'fere' 40 years earlier.

[9] Abp. Hubert legate (and John abb. St Albans).

[HOXNE]
Hervey
Richard of Hoxne
Roger
William of Acle
John de Shamelisford
The next on Blomefield's list is given the date 1411; the last two above are designated 'Sir', presumably for 'dominus', which may suggest a 13th-cent., or even 14th-cent., date.

HURLEY (Berks), St Mary (Westminster) f. –1087
Lists in *VCH Berks*, II, 76; Wethered (1909), p. 11. Wethered (1898), pp. 89–225, calendars Hurley documents in Westminster Abbey Munts.

Aeiricus (*sic*) Occ. prob. –1140[1] (Westminster Abbey Munts. 3551, calendared in Wethered (1898), no. 7).

William Occ. *c.* 1158 × 73 (Westminster Abbey Munts. 2280, 2270; Wethered (1898), nos. 16–25).

?John de Rocella Occ. 1166 × 89[2] in Westminster Abbey Munts. 2222, Wethered (1898), no. 18; but in 2203, 3746, 3763 (nos. 22, 20, 21: 1169 × 89) John de Roch', Rochel', Rochell' is witness, without title, among layfolk; and it seems probable that John de Rocella and the pr. were two separate witnesses in 2222.

Ralph of Arundel –1200 El. abb. Westminster 30 Nov. 1200 (Diceto, II, 172; cf. *Ann. Winchester*, p. 73). Occ. 1189 × 1200 (BM Egerton MS 3031, ff. 71 v–2); n.d. (Westminster Abbey Munts., 2265, 2238, 2154; Wethered (1898), nos. 27–9).

William Occ. (W.) –1205 (Canterbury D. and C. Eastry Correspondence, Group III, no. 25); 1213 × 14,[3] 1221 × 2 (Westminster Abbey Munts., 3779, 2185; Wethered (1898) nos. 45, 50).

Richard –1236 El. abb. Evesham 25 Sept. 1236 (*Flor. Hist.*, II, 217; cf. *CPR, 1232–47*, p. 166;[4] *Ch. Evesham*, p. 278; *MPCM*, III, 379). Occ. 1222 × 36[5] (Westminster Abbey Munts. 2251; Wethered (1898), no 51); 1223[6] × 35 (*Mon.*, I, 311).

JARROW, St Paul, and **MONKWEARMOUTH**, St Peter (Durham) f. (JARROW) 681; 1073/4 (pr.); 1083 (cell of Durham); (MONKWEARMOUTH) 674; *c.* 1075 (pr.); 1083 (cell of Durham)
List in *VCH Durham*, II, 85.

Aldwin 1073/4–1083 Prev. pr. Winchcombe, pr. of Jarrow 1073/4, of Monkwearmouth *c.* 1075; res., 1st pr. Durham (*Sim. Dur.*, I, 108–10, 113, 122–3; see Durham. *Sim. Dur.*, I, 122 shows that 1083 was in his 10th year; I, 127 that 1087 was in his 14th; I, 113 that the f. took place in bp. Walcher's 3rd year). D. 12 Apr. 1087.

Elfwi Pr. for a short time *c.* 1075 when Aldwin was at Melrose (*Sim. Dur.*, I, 111).

KILPECK (Hereford) (Gloucester) f. 1134
Philip Occ. 1172 × 9 (Oxford, Balliol MS 271, f. 107).

---

[1] Geoffrey de Mandeville not called earl.
[2] William earl of Essex.
[3] Nicholas of Tusculum, legate.
[4] But on p. 159 (royal assent, 4 Oct.) he is called pr. Carlisle; this was evidently a slip.
[5] Richard abb. Westminster: Flete, p. 139.
[6] William dean of Lincoln (his predecessor d. 1223; *Walt. Cov.*, II, 252; *Reg. Lincoln*, VIII, p. xxiii).

KING'S LYNN (Norfolk), St Margaret (Norwich Cathedral) f. *c.* 1100
  List in *VCH Norfolk*, II, 329.
Robert Occ. 1178 × 9[1] (BM Harl. MS 2110, f. 81 r–v).
William Occ. 21 July 1182 (ib., f. 81).

LAMANNA (Cornwall), St Michael (Glastonbury) f. –1114; in 1239 Glastonbury had licence to dispose of it (see Oliver, p. 70; *KH*, p. 69)
Elias Occ. prob. early 13th cent. (see Oliver, p. 70, from *Ad. Dom.*, II, Auct., pp. 599–600, from Cambridge, Trinity Coll. MS R. 5. 33, f. 105 v – an entry in a 14th-cent. hand; cf. M. R. James, *Catalogue of Western MSS, Trinity Coll. Cambridge*, II, Cambridge, 1901, p. 201. But presumably –1239, and the form of the charter suggests a date not earlier than *c.* 1200; for the donor see Oliver, p. 70, also probably implying an early 13th-cent. date).

LEOMINSTER (Hereford), St Peter and St Paul (Reading) f. *c.* 666; 1139: Ann. Reading, *UGQ*, p. 11; cf. B. Kemp, in *EHR*, LXXXIII (1968), 505ff.
  List ibid., esp. pp. 507, 513.

PRIOR, DECANUS (cf. Kemp, art. cit.)
Joseph 1139– (Ann. Reading, *UGQ*, p. 11; cf. Kemp, art. cit., p. 513).
Edmund Occ. 1144 × 8 (Eyton, *Salop*, V, 170 = *Lancs PR*, p. 283).
Robert –1175 Abb. Crowland, q.v.
Gervase Occ. 1186 × 98 (BM Egerton MS 3031, f. 57; cf. BM Cott. MS Domit. A. iii, f. 111).
Philip Occ. 5 Apr. 1202, 1200 + [2] (BM Cott. MS Domit. A. iii, ff. 110 v–11, 107 v–8).
Walter[3] –1221 El. abb. Shrewsbury 1221 (*CPR, 1216–25*, p. 297); d. 1223 (*CPR, 1216–25*, p. 382).

LEONARD STANLEY (Glos), St Leonard (Gloucester) f. 1121 × 30 (Aug.); 1146 (Ben.)
  List in *VCH Glos*, II, 73.
Sabriht[4] Occ. 1149 × 50, prob. 1150 (*Ctl. Gloucester*, I, p. 113; Saltman, pp. 476–7, no. 254; cf. *GFL*, p. 125 and n.).
Alexander occ. 1177 (BM Egerton MS 3031, f. 48 r–v).
William of Cirencester Occ. ?Jan. × Aug. 1203 (Cheney, *Inn. III*, no. 505); late 12th or early 13th cent.[5] (Hereford Cath. Arch., no. 1894).
The next recorded pr., Peter, occ. ?*c.* 1230 (Gloucester Cath. Lib., Seals and Documents, V, 1).

LINCOLN, St Mary Magdalene (St Mary, York) f. ?*c.* 1135
  List in *VCH Lincs*, II, 127.
?Robert de Rothewelle 1st pr. (Leland, *Coll.* (2nd edn.), I, 25).
Hugh Occ. prob. 1210 (*Reg. Lincoln*, VIII, no. 2304; cf. editor's note).

---

[1] See Castle Acre.
[2] With W. archd. Hereford (Z. N. and C. N. L. Brooke, *CHJ*, VIII, i (1944), 16).
[3] A dispute about Leominster's relation to Reading settled in 1217 × 18 (probably 1218, since confirmed by the Pope in 1219; Kemp, p. 508 and n.) may indicate an approximate date for Walter's accession.
[4] 'Tabrithus', Hist. Gloucester (15th-cent. MSS); 'Sabrihthi' in the corresponding entry in Gregory of Caerwent's *Chronicle* (BM Cott. MS Vesp. A. v, f. 199; 16th-cent transcript of 13th-cent. chronicle); 'Sabrietus' in Saltman, from Dugdale.
[5] With Henry pr. Hereford.

LINDISFARNE (Holy Island) (N'humberland), St Peter (Durham) f. 635; 1083
S.   Occ. 17 July 1202 (j.d.: *Ctl. Lanercost*, xiii, 26; cf. Cheney, *Inn. III*, no. 291 and n.).

LITTLE MALVERN (Worcs), St Giles (Worcester) f. 1171
   List in *VCH Worcs*, II, 147.
Jocelin 1171– First pr., app. 1171 (*Ann. Worcester*, p. 382; cf. *Ctl. Worcester*, p. li).
Edred Second pr. (locc. cit.).
William Norman Occ. (W.) 1200×12 (*CDF*, no. 281); el. pr. Worcester 1222 (*Ann. Worcester*, pp. 415–16); d. 1224. Presumably pr. *Little* Malvern because of connexion with Worcester, though the documents do not make the distinction, and *VCH* attributes him to *Great* Malvern.

LYNN, *see* **KING'S LYNN**

LYTHAM (Lancs), St Cuthbert (Durham) f. +1191[1]
   List in *VCH Lancs*, II, 110 (J. Tait).
Tait opens his list with William, occ. 1205×6, John and Elias of doubtful date, and Roger, occ. 1217×49. But the documents cited all appear to be of the late 13th or early 14th cent.: Durham, D. and C. muniments, 2. 4. Ebor. 41 (for William) is a document of 1325 referring to events of *c.* 1265×6: 3. 2. 4. Ebor. 45 (for Roger of Tynemouth) is +1320 (cf. Cart. III, ii, f. 143).
   There is a document of 1191×7[2] in *Glam. Chts.*, I, pp. 206–7, no. 200, to which W. pr. 'Lithun' was witness. Since the parties and witnesses of this cht. all relate to Glamorgan and Worcs, Lytham seems an unlikely identification. But it is not possible to produce a convincing alternative (Llanthony is hardly possible since its pr. was Geoffrey and the cht. printed from an original), and the abb. of Evesham, who also witnesses, was involved in the foundation of Lytham (presumably because of the Evesham interest in Lancs, represented by Penwortham pr.).
   The earliest firm date seems to be Clement, occ. 1233 (*Ann. Durham*, pp. 119–20).

MALVERN, *see* **GREAT MALVERN, LITTLE MALVERN**

PENWORTHAM (Lancs), St Mary (Evesham) f. –1122(?)
   List in *VCH Lancs*, II, 106 (J. Tait).
?Henry Occ. –1164 (*Lancs PR*, p. 375; for date cf. p. 376; Penwortham not named, but presumably either pr. of this house or a layman).
William of Winchcombe Occ. late 12th cent. (ib., p. 411).
Robert of Appleton Occ. *c.* 1200 (Hulton, *Pr. Penwortham*, p. xl, dated *1194×1207* by Tait).
Master Adam Sortes 1207–1213 Pr. 1207–13 (*Ch. Evesham*, p. 224; dep. or res. 1213, cf. p. 231; cf. Hulton, *Pr. Penwortham*, p. 89; for date see below).
Roger Norreis 1213–1214, 1218–1223 Prev. abb. of Evesham (*Ch. Evesham*, pp. 251–2; Hulton, p. 89); app. 27 Nov. 1213, held office for 5 months, then dep. Restored by the legate Pandulph about five years later, and held office for 6 years; d. 19 July (*Ch. Evesham*, pp. 251, 253 and n.; cf. Hulton, p. 89). Cf. Evesham.
John Occ. early 13th cent. (*Ctl. Burscough*, no. 141).

[1] Durham, D. and C. Muniments, 2.2.4. Ebor. 57–61, of the late 12th cent. relate to the first gifts of Lytham; but in the copy of them in 2.2.4. Ebor. 63, is also a copy of a document of R(oger) abb. Evesham (1191 +), referring to the foundation of a pr. as a matter still of intention. Dr D. Greenway has kindly inspected the Lytham chts. at Durham for us and this entry is based on her findings.
[2] R. abb. Evesham; P(eter) archd. Worcester.

PILTON (Devon), St Mary (Malmesbury) f. 12th cent.
> List in Oliver, p. 244. Difficult to distinguish from the Hospital of St Margaret, annexed to it.

Ralph Occ. 1183 × 7 (*Ctl. Malmesbury*, II, p. 32); 1194 × 1206 (*Archaeologia*, XII (1796), 211 (B. Incledon)).

The next recorded pr., John, occ. 30 June 1228 (*Devon F.*, no. 240).

REDBOURN (Herts), St Amphibalus (St Albans) f. +1178
> List in *VCH Herts*, IV, 418.

Martin Occ. 17 Dec. 1215 (*Ctl. Dunstable*, no. 391).

Gilbert de Sisseverne Occ. 1218 × 35 (*GASA*, I, 289).

RICHMOND (Yorks N), St Martin (York, St Mary) f. 1100 × 37
> List in *VCH Yorks*, III, 112.

?John de Popilton First pr. (Leland, *Coll.* (2nd edn.), I, 25).

Herbert Occ. *c.* 1151 (*EYC*, V, no. 169).

RUMBURGH (Suffolk), St Michael (Hulme, York) f. 1047 × 64 (dependent on St Benet Hulme); 1135 (dependent on St Mary, York)
> List in *VCH Suffolk*, II, 78.

(Blakere, m. Hulme, established at Rumburgh 1047 × 64 (*Ctl. Hulme*, I, p. 89, no. 159).)

?Humphrey de Wouchum 1st pr. as dependancy of York (Leland, *Coll.* (2nd edn.), I, 25).

John of Acaster 1199/1200– App. 1199/1200 (*Mon.*, III, 613).

Henry Occ. 1199 × 1206 (BM Harl. Cht. 44.1.24; cf. Cheney, *Inn. III*, no. 593); (H.) 5 Sept. 1221[1] (Chelmsford, Essex Rec. Office, MS D/DBy Q19, f. 36).

The next recorded pr., Odo, occ. 1228 (*CRR*, XIII, no. 844).

ST BEES (Cumb) (St Mary, York) f. +1120
> Lists in *VCH Cumb*, II, 183; *Ctl. St Bees*, pp. 602ff.

Robert 1st pr. (Leland, *Coll.* (2nd edn.), I, 25); occ. mid-12th cent.: prob. –1159[2] (*Ctl. St Bees*, pp. 43–4).

Richard Occ. ?–1179[3] (ib., p. 550).

William Occ. 1152 × 87[4] (ib., p. 489).

Deodatus Occ. 1178 × 84 (ib., pp. 136–8; for dates see ed.'s note).

Robert Occ. 23 Sept. 1202 (*Ctl. St Bees*, p. 544 = *Ped. Fin.*, II, p. 5).

J. Occ. (J.) 1207 (*Ctl. St Bees*, p. 430).

Daniel Occ. 2 Feb. 1211 (ib., p. 435).

Ralph Occ. early 13th cent. (?*c.* 1220: ib., pp. 303–4).

ST IVES (Hunts) (Ramsey) f. *c.* 1017
> List in *VCH Hunts*, I, 389.

William Occ. 1143 (*Ch. Ramsey*, p. 329); 1185 (*Ctl. Ramsey*, II, p. 162); 1185 × 87 (*Mon.*, II, 632).

R. Occ. 1198 × 1200 (Cheney, *Inn. III*, no. 248).

---

[1] Monday before the Nativity of St Mary, 2nd year after the Translation of St Thomas the Martyr (?1222).

[2] With Osbert archd. (Richmond: *JS Epp.*, I, pp. 261–2).

[3] William, count of Aumale; but it is not certain that he was alive.

[4] Godred (II) king of Man.

[ST IVES]

Richard Scot –1221 Possibly the same; named in full as former pr. in document of 1251 (*Ctl. Ramsey*, I, p. 286; cf. p. 285). El. abb. Selby 1221: royal assent 21 June (*CPR, 1216–25*, p. 300).

SANDTOFT (Lincs) (St Mary's, York) f. 1147 × 86

Thomas Plunkett was first pr. of Henes (or Haines) and Sandtoft (Lincs), according to the notes in Leland, *Coll.* (2nd edn.), I, 25. Neither was more than a tiny cell, and he may well have been simply the monk in charge of this group of properties (cf. *KH*, pp. 67, 76).

SCILLY (Trescaw) (Cornwall), St Nicholas (Tavistock) f. –1114 (see below)

List in Oliver, p. 73.

Turoldus Occ. *c.* 13 Sept. 1114 (*Reg.*, II, no. 1068).

The next recorded pr., Alan de Cornwall, el. abb. of Tavistock 8 June 1233 (*CPR, 1232–47*, p. 18).

SNAPE (Suffolk), St Mary (Colchester) f. 1155

W. Occ. 26 May 1163 (*Mon.*, IV, 558).

Osbert –1185 Prev. m. Colchester, pr. Snape to 1185, abb. Colchester (*UGQ*, p. 164).

Egelwy Occ. prob. 1199 × 1206 (BM Harl. Cht. 44. I. 24; cf. 43. I. 18 (E.) and Cheney, *Inn. III*, no. 593).

STAMFORD (St Leonard) (Lincs), St Leonard (Durham) f. +1083

List in *VCH Lincs*, II, 128.

Thorald Occ. 1143 × 73 ('de S. Leonarno', *HMC Rutland*, IV, 161).

Matthew Occ. j.d. +26 Oct. 1218 (CUL, Add. MS 3020, f. 229r–v: 'Stamford' – so possibly not this house; see nuns).

The next recorded pr., Walter, was presented by pr. of Durham in 1222 (*Reg. Wells*, III, p. 121).

STANLEY, *see* LEONARD STANLEY

TYNEMOUTH (Northumberland) St Mary and St Oswin (St Albans) f. (An early monastery was destroyed by the Danes in 875; a dependency of Durham was formed for a short time *c.* 1083–5) –1089 (cf. *GASA*, I, 56–7)

List in *Hist. of Northumberland*, VIII, 122–3; several are named in the *Miracula S. Oswini*, BM Cott. MS Julius A. x, ff. 10ff. (printed *Misc. Biographica*, ed. J. Raine, Surtees Soc., 1838; here cited from MS).

German –1152 M. St Albans, pr. Tynemouth; res. 1152 to be abb. Selby (see Selby; cf. *GASA*, I, 120); d. 1160. Occ. 1135 × 52 (*Miracula*, f. 26); 1143 × 52 (*EYC*, II, no. 649); 1148 (*Ctl. Whitby*, I, p. 9).

Ruelendus Occ. presumably 1152 × 66 (*Miracula*, ff. 27vff. – between German and Geoffrey; cf. extracts from ibid. in Leland, *Coll.* (1st edn.), III, 180, (2nd edn.), IV, 115).

Geoffrey Occ. 1152 × 66 (*Miracula*, f. 30v).

?Gilbert D. temp. Henry II.[1]

Akarius M. and pr. of Tynemouth, succeeded temp. Henry II (*Mon.* III, 317; see n. 1); occ. (A.) j.d. + 10 May 1197 (*Ctl. Guisborough*, II, p. 50); n.d. (*Miracula*, f. 42v). Possibly = Akarius, abb. Peterborough, 1200–10, who had been pr. St Albans.

Walter Occ. 1201 (*CRR*, I, 439).[2]

[1] In Placita de Quo Waranto of 1293, cited *Mon.*, III, 317, succeeded by pr. Akarius.
[2] In *Northumberland Pleas*, nos. 129, 137, Prs. 'John' and Walter occ. in 1210; but the date is 1201, and John's name is not apparently in the MS (= *CRR*, I, pp. 414, 439).

Ralph Gubion (for his name, see *GASA*, I, 271–3). Occ. 20 Nov. 1208, 3 Feb. 1212 (*Northumberland and Durham F.*, nos. 40, 50); res. *c.* 1216[1] (*GASA*, I, 272–3).
The next pr., C., occ. +28 Jan. 1224 (j.d.: *Ctl. Newminster*, p. 214); pr. Richard 1225 × 6 (*CRR*, XII, no. 2043). A pr. Henry d. 17 Apr. in Belvoir martyrology (Cambridge, Trinity Coll. MS O. 9. 25, f. 157v), but he may be of 13th or 14th cent.

WALLINGFORD (Berks), Holy Trinity (St Albans)   f. *c.* 1087 × 9
   List in *VCH Berks*, II, 79.
Hubert   Occ. 1112 × 13 (*Ch. Abingdon*, II, 114).
Clement   Occ. 1149 (*Ctl. Oseney*, IV, p. 28).
Master Nicholas of St Albans (or of Wallingford)   Prev. m. Malmesbury; res. 1183 to be abb. Malmesbury (q.v.); occ. 1171 × 3[2] (*Ctl. Oseney*, IV, pp. 112–13).
Walter   Occ. 1183 × *c.* 1190[3] (BM Egerton MS 3031, ff. 39v–40); (W.) 1190 × 1 (*Ctl. Oseney*, V, p. 43).
John de Cella   –1195 Res. 1195 to be abb. St Albans (*GASA*, I, 217; Gervase, I, 529).
Simon   Occ. Jan. 1204 (*Oxford F.*, p. 25).
Richard   Occ. May 1210 (ib., p. 43).
The next recorded pr., Thomas, occ. May 1224 (ib., p. 68). A pr. Rualend occ. 13th cent., but in a cht. confirmed in 1284 (*Cal. Bodl. Chts.*, p. 11).

WESTBURY-ON-TRYM (Glos), St Mary (Worcester)   f. *c.* 963 × 4 (priory); *c.* 1093 (cht. of 8 Sept. 1093, Hemming, pp. 421–4)
Germanus   *c.* 963 × 4 – *c.* 969 × 70: see Winchcombe.
Colman   Occ. *c.* 1093 (*WMVW*, p. 52; cf. pp. xxxix–xl); not named in Hemming, loc. cit., but evidently the pr. of the re-foundation.
The cell was disbanded by Bp. Samson (1096–1112) and Colman returned to Worcester (*WMGP*, p. 290).

WETHERAL (Cumberland), Holy Trinity, St Mary and St Constantine (St Mary, York) f. *c.* 1106
   Lists in *VCH Cumb*, II, 188; *Ctl. Wetheral*, ed. J. E. Prescott, pp. 504ff.
?Richard de Reme   First pr. (Leland, *Coll.* (2nd edn.), I, 25).
Ralph   Occ. early 12th cent. (*Ctl. Wetheral*, no. 72; cf. note *ad loc.* – ? *c. 1130*).
Rainald   Occ. –1159 (*EYC*, III, no. 1668; cf. no. 1669n).
William   Occ. 1178 × 84 (*Ctl. St Bees*, pp. 136–8: see ed.'s note).
Thomas   Occ. 1203 × 14 (*Ctl. Holm Cultram*, no. 16).
Suffred (*sic*)   Occ. (S.) 1219 × 23 (*Ctl. Lanercost*, viii, pp. 474, 521); (Suffred) *Ctl. Whitby*, I, no. 39).
The next recorded pr. William Rundel, occ. (W.) 2 Oct. 1225 (*Ctl. Wetheral*, no. 225); (William) 1229 (*CRR*, XIII, no. 1508).

WYMONDHAM (Norfolk), St Mary (St Albans)   f. 1107
   List in *VCH Norfolk*, II, 342–3; early 14th cent. list in Oxford, Magdalen Coll. MS 53 (deposited in Bodl.), p. 4.[4]

---

[1] During the visitation of Abb. William (i.e. 1214+), but 'tempore guerre' (i.e. *c.* 1215 × 16 or a little later): *GASA*, I, 270ff.
[2] Dated by John of Salisbury (see *JS Epp.*, II, introd., forthcoming).
[3] Azo archd. Salisbury took the cross *c.* 1190 and died on crusade (*CRR*, PRS, XIV, p. 113).
[4] Giving the first twelve prs. as Nigel, Alexius, Galyenus, Ralph de Nuers, Nicholas, Donatus, Raymond, Ralph of Dunstable, Alexander, Ralph of Whitby, Thomas medicus, William of St Albans...

[WYMONDHAM]

Nigel Occ. 1121[1] × 31 (*Mon.*, III, 330–1 = BM Cott. MS Titus C. viii, ff. 70v–71).

?Succeeded by Alexius and Galyenus (list).

Ralph de Nuers M. of St Albans, occ. *c.* 1162 × 3[2] (*GASA*, I, 166ff.); 1156 × 80 (Douglas, *Bury*, no. 192, p. 166).

?Succeeded by Nicholas and Donatus (list).

Raymond (Regimundus, Reimundus) Occ. 1187 (BM Cott. MS Titus C. viii, f. 64r–v); n.d. (ib., f. 56v).

R. j.d. + 22 Mar. 1206 (Norwich D. and C. Muniments, no. 839 = Reg. I, ff. 141v–142; cf. Cheney, *Inn. III*, no. 696n.).

Ralph of Dunstable (list) Occ. 1195 × 1214 (Norwich, Reg. I, ff. 67v–68): he may be the same as R. above or Ralph below.

Alexander of Langley Occ. 1215; soon recalled to St Albans (*GASA*, I, 260).

Ralph of Whitby (list) *c.* 1215–1217 Pr. Whitby; replaced Alexander *c.* 1215; dep. 1217 and returned to Whitby (*GASA*, I, 274); followed by Thomas medicus in list, but he succeeded William de Fécamp (*GASA*, I, 275) and d. 1248 (*MPCM*, VI, 278).

William de Fécamp App. *c.* 1218,[3] but pr. only briefly (*GASA*, I, 274–5).

---

[1] Queen Adela.

[2] *Temp*. Robert abb. St Albans (1151 × 66): reference to Thomas Becket seems to enforce the date given above.

[3] Shortly before the earl of Arundel went on Crusade in 1218 (cf. *CP*, I, 236–7).

THE BENEDICTINE HOUSES:
ALIEN PRIORIES

Numerous small houses and cells, founded before 1216, yield no names, and have therefore not been included.

ABERGAVENNY (Monmouth), St Mary (S. Vincent du Mans) f. 1087 × 1100
Durand   Occ. *temp.* Henry II[1] (*Mon.*, IV, 616).
Henry –1193   Consec. bp. of Llandaff 12 Dec. 1193 (cf. *Lib. Landav.*, pp. 303, 312).

ANDOVER (Hants), St Mary (S. Florent, Saumur) f. –1087
   List in *VCH Hants*, II, 221 (from 1264).
John   Occ. early 13th cent., perhaps *temp.* Henry III (pal.: Winchester Coll. Muniments, no. 2126).
Nicholas Hermita   Occ. 1st half 13th cent., prob. *temp.* Henry III (ib., nos. 2125, 2131); 19 Dec. 1234 (*CChR*, I, p. 189).

ANDWELL (Mapledurwell) (Hants), St Mary (Tiron) f. *temp.* Henry I
   List in *VCH Hants*, II, 225.
Hugh   Occ. 1130 × 50 (*c.* 1135 × 45)[2] (Winchester Coll. Muniments, nos. 2794, 2798); 1143[3] (Oxford, Balliol MS 271, f. 96r–v). Ex-pr. in Saltman, p. 236, 1150 × 4.[4]
Walter Britellus   Occ. *c.* 1145 × 50[5] (Winchester Coll. Muniments, no. 2792).
Froger   Occ. 1154 × 89, prob. –1172[6] (*Oxford Chts.*, no. 21).
Gervase   Occ. 1213 + [7] (*HMC, 4th Rep.*, App. p. 455); 1210 × 11 (PRO E40/241; *Cat. Anc. Deeds*, I, 26); early 13th cent. (*Ctl. Lewes*, III, pp. 25–6).
Nicholas   Occ. 1266/7, 1277 and freq. *temp.* Henry III, Edward I (Winchester Coll. Muniments, nos. 2818, 2834, etc.).

APPULDURCOMBE (Isle of Wight), St Mary (Montebourg) f. *c.* 1100
   List in *VCH Hants*, II, 232.
Richard   Occ. early 13th cent. (BM Add. Cht. 15,694). Cf. St Cross.

---

[1] H(ugh) de Beauchamp, lord of Abergavenny (d. 1187).
[2] Grants by Roger de Port (see *GFL*, p. 538; on the Ports and St Johns see J. H. Round in *Genealogist*, New Series, XVI (1900), 1–13; XVIII (1902), 137–9).
[3] Henry bp. Winchester and legate (1139–43) confirms (in effect) the refoundation of St Guthlac's Hereford (1143).
[4] The references to charters of Stephen and the Empress seem to indicate that this was granted before the accession of Henry II.
[5] A grant by Sybil d'Aubigny, wife of Roger de Port, presumably soon after her husband's retirement to Andwell *c.* 1145 or a little later (*GFL*, p. 538).
[6] *Temp.* Henry II and Adam de Port, presumably (but not certainly) the Adam who was exiled in 1172. The name is given as Roger in NRA, Oxford, Queen's College, I, Chts. of Sherborne Priory, no. 87.
[7] William of St John, son of Adam de Port.

ARUNDEL (Sussex), St Nicholas (from 1177) (Séez) f. 1102
List in *VCH Sussex*, II, 120 (L. F. Salzman).
Gratian 1102– M. of Séez, app. 1102 (14th cent. account in M. A. Tierney, *History...of Arundel*, pp. 747–51, esp. p. 748).
William Occ. 20 June 1199 (*Rot. Cur. Reg.*, I, 405).
?Walter Occ. 18 Nov. 1200 (*Sussex F.*, no. 48). Possibly a slip for William.
William Occ. *c.* 1210 × 35 (PRO E326/3905; see Lancaster). Possibly the same William as above.
The next recorded pr., Warner, occ. April 1239 (*Ctl. Sele*, no. 30).

ASTLEY (Worcs), St Peter (S. Taurin, Evreux) f. –1086
List in *VCH Worcs*, II, 182.
Gilbert Occ. 26 Jan. 1149 (Saltman, p. 546 = *Ctl. Worcester*, p. 43); 1151 × 5 (Hemming, ed. Hearne, I, 291).
W. Occ. 1193 × 1205 (*HMC, Var. Coll.*, I, 239).

AXMOUTH (Devon) (Montebourg) f. *temp.* Henry II
Richard of Cherbourg Occ. 1193 × 5; 1195 × 8[1] (*HMC, Var. Coll.*, IV, 57), also pr. Loders (*Ctl. Loders*, pp. 77–8).
Baldwin Occ. 1193 × 1205 (*HMC, Wells*, I, 50 = II, 551); presumably also pr. Loders, q.v.
R. Occ. 1216 × 20[2] (*Ctl. Loders*, pp. 62–4).

BLYTH (Notts), St Mary (Ste Trinité-du-Mont, Rouen) f. 1088[3]
List in *VCH Notts*, II, 88.[4]
R. de Pauliaco Occ. 24 July 1188 (BM Harl. MS 3759, f. 100 = Raine, *Hist. of Blyth*, p. 50); (R.) *c.* 1188 × 91 (*Chts. Newington Longville*, no. 36); (R.) 1198 × 1216 (Cheney, *Inn. III*, no. 1148).
The next recorded pr., Gilbert, occ. 1224 (BM Harl. MS 3759, f. 99 = Raine, p. 36); but a pr. Ascelin occ. n.d., prob. early 13th cent. (Harl. MS, f. 94 v; Nichols, *Leics*, III, ii, 808).

BOXGROVE (Sussex), St Mary and St Blaise (Lessay) f. 1105 +
Lists in *VCH Sussex*, II, 59 (L. F. Salzman); *Ctl. Boxgrove*, ed. L. Fleming, pp. xlii–xliii.[5]
Ralph Occ. *c.* 1155 × 64 (*Ctl. Boxgrove*, no. 58 = *Acta Chichester*, no. 20); 1167 (*Ctl. Boxgrove*, no. 343); Oct. 1174 (ib., no. 159); 15 Jan. 1179/80 (ib., no. 61 = *Ctl. Bruton*, no. 339 = *Acta Chichester*, no. 60); (R.) 1180 + (*Ctl. Boxgrove*, no. 24).
Nicholas Occ. (N.) *c.* 1180 × *c.* 1189[6] (*Ctl. Boxgrove*, nos. 10, 11); (N.) 1200 (*ib.*, no. 349); (N.) 1204 (ib., no. 346).

---

[1] With Archbp. Hubert before he was legate and as legate. The R. cited *HMC*, loc. cit., n. from Oliver, Add. Supplement, p. 28, may have been Baldwin's successor, below.

[2] The next document shows that he was acting as j.d. of Pope Honorius III, i.e. 1216 + ; Denis abb. Cerne res. 1219 × 20.

[3] So BM Harl. MS 3759, f. 100 v, but with reference to King William and Queen Matilda, which might suggest a date –1087.

[4] Includes 'William Wastell' n.d., but apparently *c.* 1200; presumably = Pr. William I (occ. 1231, BM Harl. MS 3759, f. 83 v), but possibly William II, William Burdon (occ. 1282, 1298, ib., ff. 8, 134 v).

[5] In *Ctl. Boxgrove*, p. xlii, n. 5, the editor makes important corrections to the list given in *VCH Sussex*, II, 59, and shows (p. 13 n.) that 'Prior' in 'Odingar Prior' is a surname and does not refer to a pr. of Boxgrove, as had been supposed.

[6] Before the death of William of St John (cf. *Ctl.*, p. xxxiv and pedigree facing).

Geoffrey (G.) instituted pr. 1180 × 1204 (*Acta Chichester*, no. 115; cf. *Ctl.*, p. xliv); (G.) 1207 (*Ctl.*, no. 351; cf. no. 162); (G.) 1198 × 1213 (Cheney, *Inn. III*, no. 944).

Robert Occ. 1215 (*Ctl.* no. 350); 1216 (ib., no. 98).

Ansketil Occ. ?*c. 1216–22* (ib., no. 99); (A.) 1225 (ib., no. 352); 1233 (*Bucks F.*, p. 63); Apr. 1239 (*Ctl. Sele*, no. 25); 1252 (*Ctl. Boxgrove*, no. 277).

The next pr., Walter of Shoreham, occ. 1253 (ib., no. 182).

BURWELL (Lincs) (La Grande-Sauve, Bordeaux) f. –1110
  List in *VCH Lincs*, II, 239.

Gilbert Occ. 1160 × 89 (*CDF*, no. 1243); n.d. (*Reg. Lincoln*, V, no. 1688).

Bernard Occ. late 12th cent. (pal.: late Henry II, *DC*, no. 409 = BM Harl. Cht. 44. B. 38).

CARISBROOKE (Isle of Wight), St Mary (Lire) f. *c.* 1156
  List in *VCH Hants*, II, 231.

Gilbert Occ. late 12th cent. (pal.: BM Harl. Cht. 112. C. 12).

John Occ. late 12th cent. (PRO E326/2836).

Hilary Occ. –1197[1] (NRA, Oxford, Queen's Coll., II, God's House Munts., no. 945).

R. Occ. –1197[1] (ib., no. 955).

CHEPSTOW ('Striguil' etc.) (Monmouth), St Mary (Cormeilles) f. –1071
Odo Occ. 1138 × 48[2] (*Mon.*, IV, 596–7).

Robert Occ. 1195 (BM Add. MS 18,461, ff. 8v–10).

CLARE, *see* **STOKE BY CLARE**

COGGES (Oxon), St Mary (Fécamp) f. 1103
  List in *VCH Oxon*, II, 162 (H. E. Salter).

Sampson Occ. 2nd half of 12th cent. (*Ctl. Eynsham*, I, no. 131); prob. 1168 × 94 (*Ctl. Thame*, II, p. 104, see ed.'s note).

Michael Occ. 7 Nov. 1195 (*FF.*, PRS, XVII, 68); +1 June 1197 (*CDF*, no. 144: papal mandate); 1205 (*Rot. de Finibus*, p. 319). Occ. as m. Fécamp and proctor of ms. Fécamp, 8 April 1195, +21 Nov. 1202 (*CDF*, nos. 142, 146).

The next recorded pr., Roger, occ. *c.*1221 (*Ctl. Oseney*, IV, no. 144).

COVENHAM (Lincs), St Mary and St John (St-Calais) f. *c.* 1082
  List in *VCH Lincs*, II, 238 (from 1238).

Reginald Occ. *mid Henry II*[3] (pal.: *Gilbertine Chts.*, p. 107); late 12th cent. (*Reg. Lincoln*, V, no. 1621).

The next recorded pr., Geoffrey, res. –1238 (*Reg. Grosseteste*, p. 16).

COWICK (Devon), St Andrew (Bec) f. –1144
  List in Oliver, pp. 153–4.

---

[1] Shortly before (or during) the foundation of God's House, Southampton, which was confirmed by Richard I (apparently with the property with which these documents are concerned) on 1 Sept. 1197 (ib., I, no. 310). Approximately contemporary is also no. 956, +1194 (William de Reviers, earl of Devon): *c.* 1197 is a likely date for all these charters.

[2] Evidently during the earldom of Gilbert earl of Pembroke.

[3] With Thomas, pr. North Ormsby.

[COWICK]

Walter Occ. 1186×91 (Oliver, p. 153).

Henry Occ. 20 May 1219 (*Devon F.*, no. 78).

William App. 1218×21[1] by the legate Pandulph (Oliver, p. 154 from the ctl. of St John's, Exeter).

DEERHURST (Glos) (St Mary and (?) St Denis (St-Denis) ref. ?–*c*. 970; destroyed *c*. 975; ref. –1059 as dependency of St-Denis

List in *VCH Glos*, II, 105 (Rose Graham).

?ABBOTS

(?St Ælfheah   The only evidence for the existence of Deerhurst *c*. 970 is that his *Vita* by Osbern (cf. Hardy, *Cat.*, I, 620), William of Malmesbury (*GP*, p. 169) and Florence (I, 147) state that Ælfheah first became a monk there, and later a recluse at Bath. It is not clear that this means that there was a community at Deerhurst, and there is no evidence that Æ. was abb.).

PRIORS

Baldwin M. St-Denis; became abb. Bury in 1065 (q.v.). *Reg.*, I, no. 26 (Bishop and Chaplais, pl. xxviii: 1069) states that King Edward had given him the church before he became abb.

Roderick (Rodericus, Redericus, Riericus) Occ. 1144[2]×8 (PRO C115 A1 K2/6683, sec. i, no. 98); also n.d. (*Mon.*, II, p. 83); and doubtless = the m. St Denis who occ. prob. 1145×1148 (*GFL*, no. 66 and n.).

Andrew Occ. Oct. 1209 (*Oxon F.*, p. 43).

The next recorded pr., William, occ. 1 July 1235 (ib., p. 97). An H. pr. occ. n.d. (PRO C115 A1 K2/6683, sec. v, no. 35: in MS of *c*. 1350).

EYE (Suffolk), St Peter (Bernai)   f. *c*. 1080

V.B. List in *VCH Suffolk*, II, 75. Obits in BM Egerton MS 3140, ff. 64ff.; Ctl. = Chelmsford, Essex Rec. Office, MS D/DBy Q 19.

?Robert Occ. (not called pr.) 1106×13 (*Reg.*, II, no. 933; cf. no. 932n.). Hubert is called first pr., but is unlikely to have been appointed as early as *c*. 1080; Robert may have been a monk in charge, Hubert first effective pr.

Hubert Occ. 1106×18 (Ctl., ff. 23v–24); 1113×25,[3] (H.) 1125×35 (Stenton, *Feudalism*, p. 265); 1121×38 (Ctl., f. 49). D. 24 Feb. (obit: called 'primus prior').

Gauselinus, Gaulenus (?Jocelin) Occ. *c*. Dec. 1137×Mar. 1138 (*Reg.*, III, no. 288); 1135×43[4] (*Reg. Norwich*, p. 58); (Zolinus) 1143 (*Lib. El.*, p. 324). D. 12 Aug. (obit).

Osbert Succeeded Gauselinus (Ctl., f. 132), and occ. 10 May 1155 (Ctl., f. 32r–v = *PUE*, III, no. 99); 1162×3 (Ctl., f. 132); 22 Jan. 1168[5] (Ctl., ff. 32v–34 = *PUE*, III, no. 154); 1175+ (Ctl., f. 19r–v). D. 30 Aug. (obit).

Walkelin Occ. prob. 1185×1200[6] (Ctl., ff. 39r–v, 70v).

---

[1]   Cf. *Councils and Synods*, II, i, 51–2.   [2]   Godfrey archd. Worcester (*GFL*, nos. 33–4 and n.).

[3]   Stephen, count of Mortain, lord of the honour of Eye (ex inf. Mrs Vivien Brown (= V.B.)).

[4]   Walkelin archd. Suffolk; William son of Humphrey, archd. Sudbury, had prob. been succeeded by 1143 (cf. *JS Epp.*, I, p. 82n). 'J.' occ. 1135×54 (*Reg.*, III, no. 291).

[5]   8 Alexander III (1166×7), but all the other elements point to 1168, which is enforced by the place, Benevento.

[6]   Prob. Bp. John of Oxford, not John de Gray (V.B.); Geoffrey archd. (Norwich diocese; Suffolk); Walkelin presumably preceded Richard, but a date 1211×13 (W. pr. Butley) is not impossible. R. abb. Leiston fits the earlier date; he is not known to fit later.

?Walter Occ. 1175 × 1200 (Ctl., f. 71 v); 1189[1] × 95 (*Ctl. Colchester*, II, p. 514). Possibly errors for Walkelin.

Richard Occ. 9 Aug. 1202 (Cheney, *Inn. III*, no. 431 and n.); 27 Oct. 1202 (*Pleas before the king or his Justices*, II, no. 1152). Presumably the pr., unnamed, who was dep. –27 Jan. 1203 (*CRR*, II, p. 160).

Roger de Mungumbray Name in obit, 6 Sept.; occ. 1203 (*Reg. Pinchbeck*, I, pp. 421–2 = Ctl., f. 139); 22 Nov. 1206 (CUL Add. MS 4220, f. 103r–v; cf. Great Bricett); 8 May 1211 (*Suffolk F.*, PRS LXX, no. 545); 30 Sept. 1228 (Ctl., f. 50; cf. *Suffolk F.* (Rye), p. 29).[2] He was paralysed by June 1230 and another pr. substituted (*CRR*, XIV, no. 228).
According to the obituary, Pr. 'Ricardus Jacob' d. 14 June 1237 (conceivably = Pr. Richard, dep. 1202 × 3). An unplaced Girolimus d. 19 Apr. (obit), Goodwynus 9 Apr. (obit).

FRAMPTON (Dorset) (St-Étienne, Caen) f. –1077
List in *VCH Dorset*, II, 116.

William du Hommet M. Caen; el. abb. Westminster 4 May 1214 (*Flor. Hist.*, II, 147f.; Flete, p. 101; cf. *Walt. Cov.*, II, 216).

Roger Occ. 1193+ or 1214+ (*Ctl. Montacute*, no. 49).

GOLDCLIFF (Monmouth) (Bec) f. 1113
William Occ. –1191 (*Glam. Chts.*, VI, pp. 2274–5); res. Oct. 1219 to be bp. of Llandaff (*Ann. Margam*, p. 64; cf. *Lib. Landav.*, pp. 303, 312; Ann. Dore, BM Egerton MS 3088, f. 133).

The next recorded pr., Henry, occ. 1248 × 9 (*Soms F.*, I, p. 148).

GROVEBURY (Leighton Buzzard, La Grove) (Beds) (Fontevrault) f. 1164+
List in *VCH Beds*, I, 404 (from 1258).

Vitalis Occ. 26 May 1196 (*Beds F.*, no. 8). Cf. Nuneaton.

The next recorded pr., William, occ. 1230 (*CRR*, XIV, no. 645).

HAMBLE (Hants), St Andrew (Tiron) f. –1128
List in *VCH Hants*, II, 223.

Geoffrey Occ. n.d., ?12th cent. (*CDF*, no. 1015).

Walter Occ. 24 June 1194 (Winchester Coll. Muniments, no. 10,631).

HATFIELD REGIS (Broad Oak) (Essex), St Mary and St Melaine (St Melaine, Rennes) f. *c.* 1135
List in *VCH Essex*, II, 110. Evidence in chts. in *HMC 7th Rep.*, pp. 579–80, now BM Add. Chts. 28,323–28,398 *passim* – most have to be cited from MS for critical purposes. Easily confused with Hatfield Peverel.

William Occ. 1143 (BM Add. Cht. 28,323 = *HMC*, pp. 588–9); 1163 × 80 (*c.* 1179) (*GFL*, no. 376). Cf. *Bk. Seals*, no. 354 and n. (evidently referring to this Hatfield).

Richard Occ. late 12th cent. (pal.: BM Add. Cht. 28,353 = *HMC*, p. 579).

Hervey Occ. –1214[3] (ib., 28,354; cf. 28,360, 28,362, 28,364 and *HMC*, pp. 579–80).

Eudo Occ. early 13th cent. (pal.: BM Add. Cht. 28,396).

Roger Occ. prob. 1214 × 21[4] (*HMC*, p. 579); (R.) 1229 (*CPR*, *1225–32*, p. 268).

The next recorded pr., Stephen, occ. 1231 (*Cambs F.*, p. 15).

---

[1] John, count of Mortain, lord of honour.
[2] The next entry in Rye gives Pr. William, but this must be an error.
[3] Aubrey de Vere, earl of Oxford.
[4] Robert de Vere, earl of Oxford (presumably the third earl).

HINCKLEY (Leics), St Mary (Lire)   f. –1173(?)
　　List in *VCH Leics*, II, 52 (R. A. McKinley).

Richard de Capella   Admitted as administrator 1224 × 5 (*Reg. Wells*, II, p. 300); occ. as
　　pr. 1226 (*Ctl. Tutbury*, nos. 266, 267); 1227 (PRO, E40/5785); 1230 (*CRR*, XIV, no. 589);
　　res. 1230 × 1 (*Reg. Wells*, II, pp. 315–16).

HORSHAM ST FAITH (Horsford) (Norfolk), St Mary and St Faith (Conches)   f. 1105
(Ann., f. 9 – see below)
　　List in *VCH Norfolk*, II, 348. Some dates in ann. in Cambridge, Trinity Coll. MS R. 14. 9
　　(884), ff. 9, 9v (ed. in M. R. James, *Catalogue*, II, 292).[1]

Savernius (Severinus)   1134–1147 Dates in ann., f. 9. Occ. 1135 × 43 (*Reg. Norwich*, p. 58;
　　cf. Eye); 1139 + (Ctl. Coxford, Norfolk and Norwich Rec. Office, Dioc. Recs., SUN/8,
　　f. 57v).

Isarnus(?)   1147– Ann., f. 9; but the name may well be corrupt.

Bertrand (Bertram)   –*c*. 1183 Occ. 26 May 1163 (*Mon.*, III, 637 = BM Cott. MS Aug. ii,
　　136); –Jan. 1174 (*HMC Lothian*, p. 12); (B.) 29 July 1175 (MS ut supra, ff. 57v–8,
　　correcting *Norfolk Archaeol.*, XVII (1910), 294); 1182 (Jocelin of Brakelond, ed. H. E.
　　Butler, p. 22); res. abb. Chertsey *c*. 1183 (q.v.; cf. ibid.).

Deodatus   Occ. 8 Nov. 1196, 1 Apr. 1197 (*FF*, PRS XX, nos. 29, 105); 19 Apr. 1209
　　(*Norfolk F.*, PRS LXX, no. 188).

Eustorgius (Austorgius)   Occ. early 13th cent. (pal.: BM Add. Cht. 15,185); 1227 × 8
　　(*Norfolk F.* (*Rye*), p. 42); doubtless the same as 'Austorgius', occ. in a cht. in *HMC
　　Lothian*, p. 10, there dated '*c*. 1120 × 30?'.

HORSLEY (Glos) (Troarn)   f. *temp*. William I. Given to Bruton Priory in 1260
　　List in *VCH Glos*, II, 93 (R. Graham: from 1269).

Gilbert   Occ. 1214 (*CRR*, VII, p. 161).

Stephen, prob. the first Augustinian pr., occ. 1262 (*Ctl. Bruton*, no. 316).

KIRBY, *see* **MONKS KIRBY .**

LANCASTER, St Mary (Séez)   f. 1094
　　List in *VCH Lancs*, II, 172 (J. Tait).

John   Occ. 1141 +[2] (*Lancs PR*, p. 276).

Nicholas   Occ. 1154 × 95 (*CDF*, no. 671 = Scammell, *Hugh du Puiset*, p. 252); 1186 × 92
　　(*EYC*, VII, no. 32).

William   Occ. 1188 × 98 (?*c*. 1193: *Lancaster Hist.*, I, p. 112; cf. p. 111); 23 Nov. 1202,
　　11 July 1204 (*Lancs F.*, pp. 151, 23).

John de Alench' (presumably **Alençon**)   Occ. *c*. 1210 × 35[3] (PRO E326/3905 = *Cat. Anc.
　　D.*, III, 271); (John Redufo) early 13th cent. (*Ctl. Cockersand*, III, i, p. 922).

The pr. was taken into the sheriff's hands, so presumably vacant, –2 Nov. 1230 (*CR,
1227–31*, p. 460; cf. *Lancaster Hist.*, I, pp. 150–1). The next recorded pr., Geoffrey, occ. 12
Nov. 1241 (*Lancaster Hist.*, I, p. 32 = *Lancs F.*, p. 82).

---

[1] These annals show particular interest in Horsham and in Norwich cathedral priory; and they contain
two groups of priors, with no house named. It would seem a natural assumption that both groups
belonged to the same house; yet this seems to be impossible. The first fits Horsham, but not Norwich,
and is used here; the second fits Norwich, but not Horsham, since it covers the years 1172–5, when
Bertrand was pr. Horsham. See Norwich.

[2] Jordan, probably chancellor of the king of Scots for a short time from 1141 (*Handbook*, p. 173; *Reg.
Reg. Scottorum*, I, pp. 111–12).

[3] William abb. Séez (*GC*, XI, 721–2).

LAPLEY (Staffs), (S.-Rémi, Rheims) f. 1061
  List in *VCH Staffs*, III, 343 (J. L. Kirby).
Godric and Fulk occ. ms. S. Rémi, and presumably in charge of Lapley, in chts. of Henry I of 1107 × 23; since Godric had defended title to Lapley itself it is possible he was the earlier and established or reestablished the pr. there (*Reg.*, II, nos. 1054, 1412).
P. was dep. by Peter, abb. S. Rémi, 1162 × 81, and succeeded by Absalom[1] (Peter of Celle, *Ep.* 152, *PL*, CCII, 596; for Peter's dates, see *JS Epp.*, I, pp. ix–xn.).
Absalom. *See above.*
Inganus Also occ. 1162 × 81 (Peter of Celle, *Ep.* 154, coll. 597–8); evidently after Absalom, since he occ. 1206 × 7 (*PR 9 John*, p. 9).

LEWISHAM (Kent) (St Peter, Ghent) f. 918; 1044
  List in *VCH Kent*, II, 238.
Siger (Sigo) Occ. *c.* 1193;[2] 1185 × 1214 (*Reg. Rochester*, pp. 470, 648).
The next recorded pr., Arnold, occ. 14 Feb. 1229 (*CChR*, I, 91).

LLANGENNITH (Glamorgan), ?St Keneder[3] (S. Taurin, Evreux) f. –1123
William Gabriel Occ. early 13th cent. (pal.: *Glam. Chts.*, II, p. 501, no. 497 = BM Harl. Cht. 75. C. 28).

LLANGUA (Llangwyfan) (Monmouth) (Lire) f. –1183
Hilary of Llangiwen (?Llangwyfan) Occ. 26 Aug. 1196 (*FF*, PRS XVII, no. 220).

LODERS (Dorset), St Mary Magdalene (Montebourg) f. *c.* 1107
  List in *VCH Dorset*, II, 118.
Richard of Cherbourg Pr. Loders and Axmouth: see Axmouth. Evidently preceded Baldwin.
Baldwin Presumably also pr. Axmouth, q.v. Occ. 1205 (*Rot. de Finibus*, p. 313).
R. ?also pr. Axmouth, q.v. Occ. prob. 1205 +[4] (*Sarum Chts.*, p. 80).

MINTING (Lincs), St Andrew (S. Benoît-sur-Loire, Fleury) f. *c.* 1129
  List in *VCH Lincs*, II, 239–40.
Raymond Occ. *c.* 29 June 1213 (BM Cott. MS Vesp. E. xviii, f. 164r–v).
The next recorded pr., John, m. of Fleury, app. 1239 (*Reg. Grosseteste*, p. 27).

MODBURY (Devon), St George (S. Pierre-sur-Dives) f. *c.* 1140
  List in Oliver, p. 298; the following list is based on notes by H. N. Blakiston and his transcripts in PRO from Eton College Muniments.
H. *dictus Anglicus* App. by H(amo) abb. S. Pierre, *c.* 1140 × 8[5] (Blakiston transcripts, no. XXXII/29).
William Occ. 1138 × 60 (*Ctl. Buckfast* in *Reg. Grandisson*, III, pp. 1572–3).
Laurence Occ. late 12th – early 13th cent. (Blakiston transcripts, no. VIII).
Ralph Occ. 1207 × 27, app. by S. abb. S. Pierre (ib., no. XXXII/30).
Gervase and Durand occ. in no. XXXII/1 and 17, n.d., but the latter perhaps late 12th cent.

---

[1] Cf. *JS Epp.* (ed. Giles), no. 322, referring to Absalom as in England (evidently at Lapley) in ?1171.
[2] Miss Anne Oakley, to whose help with this list we are much indebted, has pointed out to us that this is an early grant by the founder to Strood Hospital, f. 1193, which shares most of its witnesses with the f. chts. of the Hospital.
[3] See *CDF*, no. 316.
[4] R. abb. Montebourg presumably followed William, for whom *GC*, XI, 927 gives the date –1185–1205 +.
[5] For abbs. S.-Pierre-sur-Dives, see *GC*, XI, 732.

MONK SHERBORNE[1] (Pamber) (Hants), St Mary and St Fromund (Cérisy-la-Forêt) f. *c.* 1120 × 30

List in *VCH Hants*, II, 228–9.

Robert Occ. 1158 × 9[2] (*Ctl. Montacute*, no. 109).

Roger Occ. *c.* 1170 +[3] (ib., no. 110); *c.* 1170[3] × 77 (*Ctl. Sandford*, II, 194–5); (R.) *c.* 1200 or shortly + (NRA, Oxford, Queen's Coll., I, no. 262).

William Occ. 1213 + ; early 13th cent. (*HMC, 4th Rep.*, pp. 455, 453–4); 1225 (*CRR*, XII, no. 1428).

James Occ. early 13th cent. (NRA Oxford, Queen's Coll., I, no. 22).

MONKS KIRBY (Warws), St Mary, St Nicholas and St Denis (S. Nicholas, Angers)   f. 1077

List in *VCH Warws*, II, 131.

Richard of Cornwall –1176/7 Occ. (full name) *c.* 1160 × 77 (BM Harl. Cht. 53. G. 55 = Mowbray, no. 192, q.v. for date); *c.* 1160[4] × 77 (BM Cott. Cht. xi, 10; PRO E326/8649). El. abb. Whitby 29 May 1177 (?1176: see Whitby).

Baldwin Occ. 1177 × 90 (Mowbray, no. 87); rel. of Abp. Baldwin, 1188 × 90 (*Ch. Evesham*, p. 334). Possibly Baldwin m. who occ. in Mowbray, no. 192.

?Orricus 'Orrico pr. de Circhebi' witnessed a cht. in a Warws setting between 1138 and 1186 (*temp.* Roger de Mowbray, before his departure on 3rd Crusade: *Genealogist*, New Series, XVI, 153; cf. Mowbray, p. xxxii; *CP*, IX, 371). The name may be corrupt – perhaps for Richard.

A.[5] Occ. 1183 × 4 (*CDF*, no. 817, presumably contemporary with no. 818, dated by Bernard abb. Cîteaux – not Clairvaux).

Ralph Occ. 30 Sept. × 6 Oct. 1200 (*Bucks F.*, p. 19).

The next recorded pr., John, occ. 1226 (*Ctl. Tutbury*, nos. 266–7);[6] 1229 (*Reg. Wells*, III, pp. 183, 185); 1230 (*CRR*, XIV, no. 589).

MONMOUTH, St Mary and S. Florent (S. Florent, Saumur) f. –1086

Geoffrey Parvus (*Mon.*, IV, 597) Occ. 1131 × 44 (*CDF*, no. 1141); 1138 × 48 (*Mon.*, IV, 596–7; see Chepstow); 1138 +[7] (*CDF*, no. 1139).

Robert Occ. 1148 × 55 (*GFL*, nos. 332–3); *c.* 1151 × 7 (*CDF*, no. 1146; cf. no. 1147); (R.) +1163 (*GFL*, no. 152); n.d. (mid or late 12th cent., *Glam. Chts.*, II, pp. 421–2).

Robert de Cormeilles (Cormeliis) Peter's predecessor, but not certainly later than Geoffrey and Robert (Bodl. Rawl. MS B. 461, f. 7).

Peter Occ. (Peter and P.) 1160 × 80 (*Mon.*, IV, 597).[8]

The next recorded pr., Florence, occ. 1230 × 40 (*Mon.*, IV, 597–8).

[1] Easily confused with Sherborne (Dorset). But the NRA and *HMC* references are from the Monk Sherborne muniments, and William is specifically called pr. *Monk's* Sherborne; and the reference to Robert and the first two to Roger are from chts. of the Port family, founders of Monk Sherborne.

[2] Robert of Inglesham archd. Surrey: Ralph was archd. in 1158 (*Ctl. Winchester*, p. 198); Thurstan sheriff (of Hants). But see Le Neve, II, 94.

[3] Adam de Port son of John de Port (J. H. Round in *Genealogist*, New Series, XVI, 6ff.).

[4] Baldric archd. Leicester (see *GFL*, pp. 163–4 and n.).

[5] A. priore de 'Thir' (*sic*), witnesses an English decision relating to S. Serge, Angers.

[6] Identified by ed. as pr. of Kirby Bellars, but this was not f. till 1359. Pr. John was certainly pr. of a house dependent on S. Nicholas, Angers, and in all these cases the identification, though not certain, is highly probable.

[7] Not earlier than *Mon.*, IV, 596–7, because of Rose wife of Baderon of Monmouth.

[8] In two chts., one (no. IV), temp. Hugh de Lacy and Rose his wife: i.e. +1160, but before her death –1180 (Wightman, *The Lacy Family*, pp. 189ff.; and second chart facing p. 260). Thus Peter must be later than Robert. The other cht. (no. VII) was later than no. VI, in which pr. Geoffrey occ.; P. occ. temp. Henry II, according to the 18th-cent. transcriber of Bodl. MS Rawl. B. 461.

OGBOURNE ST GEORGE (Wilts) (Bec) f. –1147
List in *VCH Wilts*, III, 396 (M. Chibnall).
Ranulf Occ. 1206 (*PR, 8 John*, p. 40).
The next recorded pr., Ralph, occ. April 1228 (*CRR*, XIII, no. 424); and was succeeded by William before Michaelmas (ib., no. 799).

OTTERTON (Devon), St Michael (Mont-S.-Michel) f. *temp.* William I
List in Oliver, p. 248.
Richard Occ. 1164 (*EYC*, IV, no. 72); 1169^1 × 84 (*CTG*, I, 65, no. 62).
William Occ. 1184 (*EYC*, V, no. 316 = *Ctl. St Michael's Mount*, no. 56).
Nicholas Occ. 1191 × 1212, perhaps after 1201 (*Ctl. St Michael's Mount*, no. 8); 24 April 1205 (*Devon F.*, no. 54); 1212 (BM Cott. MS Vitell. D. ix, ff. 48 v–49 v).
William de Kernet –1220 El. abb. of Tavistock 1220; royal assent 20 Feb. 1220 (*CPR, 1216–25*, p. 229); abb. 1220–4 (Finberg in *Devon and Cornwall Notes and Queries*, XXII, (1942–3), 186–7, q.v. for his name and family).

PEMBROKE, St Nicholas (Séez) f. *c.* 1098
William de Cuchi Occ. 1179 × 98^2 (*Gir. Camb.*, I, 325).
Fulk Occ. Oct. 1203 (ib., III, 318; cf. H. E. Butler, *Autobiography of Gir. Camb.*, pp. 341–2 for date).
Philip Occ. 1203 × 14 (*Gir. Camb.*, III, 353; cf. *Welsh Episcopal Acts*, I, p. 337, dated 1205 × 10); without name but prob. the same, *c.* 1211 (*Gir. Camb.*, *Speculum Duorum*, pt. ii, *ep.* 6 – ex inf. M. Richter; MS Vat. Regin. 470, ff. 88 v, 96).

RUISLIP (Middlesex) (Bec) f. *c.* 1087
List in *VCH Middlesex*, I, 204 (M. Chibnall). For the prior's function, see M. Morgan (Mrs Chibnall), *English Lands of the Abbey of Bec* (Oxford, 1946), pp. 23–4.
Richard de Coleliva M. of Bec (Gibbs, no. 165); occ. 1179 × 87^3 (ib.); 1176 × 88 (*Bec Documents*, p. 8); probably also 1196 × 8^4 (Newcourt, *Repertorium*, II, 230–1n.; cf. *VCH Middlesex*, I, 204n.).
The next recorded pr., William, occ. July 1224 (*Oxon F.*, p. 72).

ST CROSS (Isle of Wight) (Tiron) f. +1132
Walter Occ. 1202 × 3 (*Hants F.*, PRO transcripts); early 13th cent. (pal.: BM Add. Cht. 15,694). Cf. Appuldurcombe.

ST DOGMELLS (St Dogmaels) (Pembroke) (Tiron) f. *c.* 1115 (priory); 1120 (abbey)
Fulchard First abb. (*Mon.*, IV, 130).
Walter Occ. 1198 (*Gir. Camb.*, I, 95); (W.) 1202 (*Rot. Lit. Pat.*, p. 9^5); 15 Apr. 1203, when his el. as bp. of St Davids was quashed (Cheney, *Inn. III*, no. 468; occ. as el. 1199 × 1203, *Bk. Seals*, no. 362).

---

[1] Robert archd. Totnes (see Morey, p. 121).
[2] Probably early in the dispute between Giraldus Cambrensis and Bishop Peter of St Davids, which seems to have broken out between 1179 and 1183 (H. E. Butler, *Autobiography of Gir. Camb.*, pp. 69, 75–7, 361), but may have lasted a number of years (ib., pp. 75–6). The bishop d. in 1198.
[3] Osbert abb. Bec (*Ch. Bec*, p. 24).
[4] Richard m. Ruislip occ. 'custos rerum' of the ms. of Bec. Dated by Alard archd. London and Richard bp. London.
[5] *Mon.*, IV, 503, in which Abb. Andrew occ., is dated by eds. '*c.* 1200'; it appears to us to be undatable, though probably not later than the 13th cent.

ST MICHAEL'S MOUNT (Cornwall) (Mont-S.-Michel) f. –1050 (cell); *c.* 1087×91 (priory)

> Lists in *Ctl. St Michael's Mount* (P. L. Hull), p. 63; Taylor, *St Michael's Mount*, pp. 52–71 (later prs. only).

Richard de Wenilia Occ. 1187 (*Ctl. St Michael's Mount*, no. 38).

William de Argentein Occ. *c.* 1201 × 12 or a little earlier (ib., no. 66).

William de Walchin Mentioned 1215 as former pr. (ib., no. 68).

Ralph de Kankale Occ. *c.* 1209×14 (ib., nos. 12, 13).

John Mentioned 1226 as former pr. (ib., no. 16).

ST NEOTS (Hunts) (Bec) f. *c.* 974 (dependent on Ely); *c.* 1081×2 (as cell of Bec)

> List in *VCH Hunts*, I, 388.

Martin of Bec –1132 Occ. 21 Sept. 1127 (CUL, Add. MS 3020, f. 145r–v); res. 1132 to be abb. Peterborough, q.v.

Walter Occ. 1145×8[1] (*Ctl. Canterbury, St Gregory*, no. 14 = Saltman, pp. 285–6, no. 59); 1148×66 (BM Cott. MS Faust. A. iv, f. 39)[2].

Herbert Occ. 1152×8 (*Reg. Lincoln*, II, no. 322); 1159, 1173 (BM Cott. MS Faust. A. iv, ff. 89v, 38r–v); 1189×95[3] (*Ctl. Eynsham*, I, pp. 44–5). Presumably the H. m. Bec who was a candidate for the abbacy of Bury in 1182 (Jocelin of Brakelond, p. 22).

Geoffrey Occ. 4 or 18 July 1199 (BM Cott. Faust. A. iv, ff. 50v–51); 1198×1205, prob. 1198×9 (Cheney, *BHRS*, XXXII, p. 19); *c.* 20 Oct. 1202 (*Beds F.*, no. 78); 7 June 1204 (BM Cott. MS Faust. A. iv, f. 89r–v); 1203+ (*Ctl. Newnham*, no. 92).

William Occ. 1 July 1206 (*Suffolk F.*, PRS LXX, no. 462); *c.* 15 July 1209 (BM Cott. Faust. A. iv, ff. 49–50).

Roger –1225 Occ. *c.* 15 July 1219 (ib., f. 50); 1223 × 4 (*Hunts F.*, p. 9); n.d. (*Ctl. Newnham*, no. 145); d. 1225 (*Ann. Dunstable*, p. 94, not named).

SELE (Beeding) (Sussex), St Peter (S. Florent, Saumur) f. –1126 (*Oxford Chts.*, no. 3 and note)[4]

> List in *VCH Sussex*, II, 62 (L. F. Salzman), from W. D. Macray, *Notes from the Muniments of Magdalen College, Oxford* (Oxford and London, 1882), p. 8.

Robert Occ. 1126×39 (*Oxford Chts.*, no. 3; see note to no. 5); Jan. 1144 (ib., no. 4); 1135×53 (ib., no. 6).

Daniel Occ. 1153 (*Oxford Chts.*, no. 9: 'Robertus multis annis...prior et Daniel...eius successor'); d. –1169 (*Acta Chichester*, no. 47).

Thomas Occ. +1153 (*Oxford Chts.*, no. 11); 1153×69 (*Acta Chichester*, no. 47).

Warin[5] Occ. 1174×84 (*Ctl. Sele*, no. 21).

Laurence[5] Occ. 1181 (Lees, *Templars*, p. 230).

Peter Occ. ('proctor') *c.* 1187×*c.* 1197 (*Acta Chichester*, no. 134; cf. *Ctl. Sele*, no. 55).

The next recorded pr., Walter, occ. 1232 (*Ctl. Sele*, no. 39).

SHERBORNE, *see* MONK SHERBORNE

---

[1] Abp. Theobald, primate, not legate (see *GFL*, p. 506); Walter archd. Canterbury.

[2] Ctl. St Neots, abstracted in G. C. Gorham, *History...Eynesbury and St Neots*, II (London, 1824), pp. 288–317 and Supplement, pp. v–lxvi (also abstracting BM Stowe MS 941). References here are to the MS, since Gorham's abstract is inadequate for our purpose.

[3] Hamo dean Lincoln; Roger of Rolleston not yet archd. Leicester (see pp. 170 n. 1, 182 n. 7).

[4] This cht. was dated ?1096 by Round (*CDF*, no. 1119); hence the date –1096 sometimes given for the foundation of the priory.

[5] Warin and Laurence are each known from one reference only to 'Guar" and 'Laur": it is possible that one pr. lurks under the two names, owing to a rubricator's error.

SPALDING (Lincs), St Mary (S. Nicholas, Angers) f. 1052 (dependent on Crowland); 1074 (dependent on S. Nicholas, Angers)

List in *VCH Lincs*, II, 123–4. In the Ctl., BM Add. MS 35,296, ff. 39, 421, are two attempts at a list of the early priors, mainly derived from documents in the ctl.[1] Obits in Cambridge, Gonville and Caius College, MS 314/376, pp. 1ff., all apparently later.[2]

Herbert Occ. *c.* 1150×2 (PRO C115 A1 K2/6683, sec. x, no. 58; cf. Saltman, pp. 367–8, no. 145); 1148×55 (BM Harl. MS 742, f. 270r–v); 1152+ (*Reg. Lincoln*, I, no. 133).

Garinus Occ. 1162×84 (*Ctl. Dunstable*, no. 157).

Reginald Occ. *c.* 25 July 1176 (BM Add. MS 35,296, f. 300v).

Geoffrey Occ. late 12th cent. (prob. 1176×89;[3] ib., f. 337); (G.) *c.* 25 July 1182 (ib., f. 300v).

Nicholas I Occ. 1189; dep. *c.* 1191 (*Hist. Crowland*, pp. 453, 457); also occ. 1186×93 (Peterborough D. and C. MS 5, f. 68 = MS 1, f. 195r–v).

Jollanus (Jocelin, Goslenus) Occ. *c.* 1 July 1194 (*Hist. Crowland*, p. 459); 24 Nov. 1194 (*Rot. Cur. Reg.*, I, p. 74); 8 Sept. 1195 (*Lincs F.*, I, p. 4); 20 May 1196 (*FF.*, PRS XVII, no. 153); (J.) 17 Oct. 1198 (BM Add. MS 35,296, f. 337v).

Nicholas II Occ. 1202 (*Lincs Ass. Roll*, LRS XXII, no. 910); 22 June 1203 (*Lincs F.*, PRS LXVII, no. 175); 27 June 1204 (ib., no. 187).

Ralph –1229 Occ. 3 Nov. 1224 (*Lincs F.*, I, p. 173); 1229 (*CRR*, XIII, no. 1806); d. 1229 (*Reg. Wells*, III, p. 182).

The next pr., Simon de Hautbourg, m. Spalding was el. 1229 (ib., p. 183).

SPORLE (Norfolk), St Mary (S. Florent, Saumur) f. –1123

List in *VCH Norfolk*, II, 464.

John Occ. early *temp*. Henry II[4] (BM Harl. MS 2110, f. 46v).

?G. Occ. *c.* 1187×*c.* 1197 (*Ctl. Sele*, no. 55).[5]

STOGURSEY (Soms), St Andrew (Lonlay) f. 1100×7

Lists in *VCH Soms*, II, 171;[6] *Stogursey Chts.* p. xxviii (T. D. Tremlett and N. Blakiston).

---

[1] The list on f. 39 is intended to distinguish the properly elected perpetual priors starting with Simon, from the priors 'datiui' who preceded, who are then listed retrospectively: Nicholas, temp. John, Ralph, temp. John (but citing the fine of 1224), 'Johannes Hyspanus' temp. Richard I; Jollanus, temp. Richard I; Reginald occ. 1176; Garinus occ. 1182; Geoffrey; Herbert. The list on f. 421 gives the order Herbert, Reginald, Geoffrey, Simon. For 'Johannes Hyspanus' and 'Garinus' f. 39 gives references which are evidently to documents on ff. 337v and 300v, where the priors are I. and G., i.e. probably Jollanus and Geoffrey. It is possible that the author of the ctl. had access to other evidence of the existence of prs. of these names – in the case of Garinus, very probable – but no other trace has been found of John.

[2] The earliest seems to be Simon, d. 14 Mar. (p. 3); all but one (William pr., 25 Jan., p. 1) are printed in M. R. James, *Descriptive Catalogue of the Manuscripts in the Library of Gonville and Caius College*, I (Cambridge, 1907), p. 359. The same MS (15th cent.) has biographical etc. notes on pr. Simon and his successors, pp. 31ff.

[3] If he is correctly placed; i.e. if he is rightly identified with the G. who occ. 1182. In any case this document also has Richard (d'Ameri) precentor of 'St Mary' – presumably Lincoln Cathedral – and archdeacon of the West Riding, i.e. Stow: he gives outside limits of 1160×92, but it is unlikely he held both offices in the late 1180s (*GFL*, p. 246n.), so that it is virtually certain that Geoffrey preceded Nicholas I, less certain that he succeeded Reginald.

[4] Ref. to Henry II suggests not long after his accession, 'pro anima Henrici regis (sc. Henry I) qui me nutriuit et pro domino meo Henrico rege nepote illius'.

[5] Of approximately the same date as *Ctl. Sele*, no. 20 = *Acta Chichester*, no. 132.

[6] Including Gerin d'Alençon, 1175; but he was a layman (cf. *Stogursey Chts.*, nos. 12, 34). Some of the Stogursey Chts. were printed, less accurately, in *HMC 9th Rep.*, App., pp. 353–5 (where 'Goll'' in no. 34 is printed 'Walter', p. 354a).

[STOGURSEY]

Richard de Alesscunh (?Alençon) Occ. mid–late 12th cent. (*Stogursey Chts.*, no. 2); *temp.* Henry II (*Ctl. St Mark's, Bristol*, no. 237).

Geoffrey Occ. –1171 (*Stogursey Chts.*, no. 6). Possibly before Richard. Also occ. as 'Coll'',[1] –1174 (ib., no. 51 (11)); 'Goll'', 1175 (ib., no. 12); 'Goll'', n.d. (ib., no. 34).

G. App. *c.* 1220 × 42 (*HMC Wells*, I, 367; cf. *GC*, XIV, 494).

STOKE BY CLARE (Suffolk), St John the Baptist (Bec) f. 1090 (at Clare); 1124 (at Stoke)

List in *VCH Suffolk*, II, 155.

G. Occ. –1145 (BM Cott. MS App. xxi, ff. 35ff.).

Robert Occ. 1147; 1141 × 53[2] (ib., ff. 46r–v, 19).

Nicholas Occ. 30 June 1174 (ib., ff. 72ff.); *c.* 1179 × 80 (*GFL*, no. 457).

Hugh of St Edmund 1197– BM Cott. MS App. xxi, f. 114, has cht. dated his 2nd year = 1 John; since he occ. 31 Dec. 1197 (*FF.*, PRS, XXIII, no. 108), he must have succeeded in 1197. Also occ. Sept. × Oct. 1202 (*Essex F.*, p. 25; BM Cott. MS App. xxi, ff. 17v–18); *c.* 28 Jan. 1203 (ib., f. 18).

Richard Occ. April 1205 (ib., f. 17v; *Essex F.*, p. 34); 1221; 10 July 1225 (BM Cott. MS App. xxi, ff. 146, 50r–v); *c.* Easter 1229 (*CRR*, XIII, no. 2110); 31 May 1229 (*CPR, 1225–32*, p. 290).

The next recorded pr., John, occ. 27 Oct. 1234,[3] *c.* 14 April 1247 (BM Cott. MS App. xxi, ff. 17, 16r–v). A Pr. Geoffrey occ. ?early 13th cent., ib., f. 31: he is referred to as in the past, and could be pr. G. of –1145, or before Hugh of St Edmund.

SWAVESEY (Cambs), St Andrew (S. Serge, Angers) f. –1086

List in *VCH Cambs*, II, 318 (D. M. B. Ellis and L. F. Salzman), from W. M. Palmer and C. Parsons, 'Swavesey Priory', pp. 34ff.

Theobald Occ. as ex-pr. with Reginald.

Reginald Occ. 1155 × 66 (Ctl. Crowland, Spalding, Gentlemen's Society, f. 242r–v, cited from transcript in Lincs Archives Office); perhaps also the R. who is referred to as former pr. in cht. of 1200 cited below.

Benedict Occ. 1198 × 9 (*Cambs F.*, p. 2); (B.) 1200 (BM Add. MS 5849, f. 23; cf. Cheney, *Inn. III*, no. 248).

The next recorded pr., John, occ. 1231 (*CRR*, XIV, no. 1936).

TICKFORD (Newport Pagnell) (Bucks), St Mary (Marmoutier) f. *c.* 1100

List in *VCH Bucks*, I, 364.

Robert de Bohun Occ. (Newport) 1187 (*Mon.*, V, 204); 1184 × 97[4] (*Ctl. Oseney*, V, pp. 144–5), 1193 × 9 (Peterborough D. and C. MS I, f. cxciiiir–v).

Bernard Occ. 18 Nov. 1199 (*Bucks F.*, p. 16); early 1200 (ib., p. 18).

Hugh Occ. 1214 (*CRR*, VII, p. 51); res. 1220 (*Reg. Wells*, II, pp. 51–2).

TOTNES (Devon), St Mary (S. Serge, Angers) f. *c.* 1088

List in Oliver, p. 239.

Aymerius Occ. 1138 × 60 (*Reg. Grandisson*, III, pp. 1572–3).

---

[1] 'Coll'' would suggest the rare name Colinus, Colin; but the forms 'Goll'' point to some spelling of Geoffrey – ?Gollefridus. It is quite possible that we have conflated two distinct priors.

[2] Gilbert FitzRichard de Clare, earl of Hertford.

[3] Dated Friday before Sts Simon and Jude 18 Henry III: 19 Henry III began on 28 Oct. 1234, so it is possible that the date was 21 Oct. 1233.

[4] Robert of Burnham, archd. Bucks (*GFL*, p. 156n).

Rivallonus Occ. mid 12th cent. (–1169: Oliver, pp. 39–40, no. viii).
A pr. Richard occ. 12th/13th cent. (*CTG*, I, 61, no. 20).[1]

TUTBURY (Staffs), St Mary (S. Pierre-sur-Dives) f. 1080+
  List in *VCH Staffs*, III, 339 (A. Saltman).
The names of the first three prs. are given in an Okeover cht. (*SHC*, New Series, VII, 128),
prob. –1148. The donor of the cht. is Pr. William and he speaks of prs. Herbert, Ralph and
William. Perhaps, as has been assumed, there were two Williams: but the context rather
suggests that only one is referred to.[2] Professor Saltman reckons that there were four Williams
aud two Richards in the 12th cent.; this seems unnecessary, though not impossible.
Herbert
Ralph
William Occ. 1125 (*Ctl. Tutbury*, no. 88); 1139[3] × 55 (ib., no. 70).
Richard Occ. 1153 × 5 (*Mon.*, VI, 163 = Eyton, *Salop*, VIII, 216–17); 1155[4] × 59 (*Ctl.
  Burton*, p. 16); 1177+ (*Bk. Seals*, no. 144).
Fulk Occ. 1161 × 82 (*Ctl. Tutbury*, nos. 58, 142, 167; *Ctl. Burton*, no. 4).
William de Esnes (for name, *Ctl. Thame*, I, p. 78); occ. 1175[5] × 82, prob. +1177 (*Ctl.
  Tutbury*, no. 11); j.d. +1191 × 7[6] (*Ctl. Tutbury*, no. 262); c. 24 June 1199 (ib., no. 23);
  1203 (*Northants Assize Roll*, NRS, V, no. 643).
?H. Occ. early 13th cent. (*Ctl. Dunstable*, no. 687).
Bartholomew Occ. (B.) j.d. +28 July 1210 (*HMC Rutland*, IV, 33–4; cf. Cheney, *Inn. III*,
  no. 873); (B.) 1215 × 16 (*Ches. Chts.*, p. 23); 1217 × 22 (*Burton Chts.*, nos. 72–3; for his
  name, also *Derbys Chts.*, nos. 1544, 2575, etc.).
The next recorded pr., Nicholas, occ. 19 Apr. × 17 May 1226 (*Derbys F.* (1886), p. 17).

TYWARDREATH (Cornwall), St Andrew (S. Serge, Angers) f. c. 1088
  List in Oliver, p. 34; on pp. 36–7 he lists obits from a 14th cent. psalter; those of the prs.,
  however, are cited on p. 34.
Osbert Occ. mid-twelfth century; prob. 1156 × 60[7] (Oliver, pp. 39–40, 40–41).
Baldwin Occ. 1169 (*Mon.*, IV, 657 = Oliver, p. 38).
Hamelin Referred to as former pr. in a cht. of late 12th or early 13th century (before
  6 May 1235: *Mon.*, IV, 656 = Oliver, pp. 37–8). D. 1 Apr. (obit).
Andrew Occ. late 12th or early 13th cent.[8] (Oliver, p. 42).
?Theobald Occ. n.d. (Oliver, p. 40. Oliver seems to treat this as 13th cent., or even possibly
  12th, on p. 34).
Oliver notes obits of prs. James (22 Mar.), Roger (12 Oct.) and John Loenter (6 Apr.), of
uncertain date.

WARE (Herts), St Mary (S. Evroult) f. –1081
  List in *VCH Herts*, IV, 457.

---

[1] The other 'priors' in this document were parish priests (cf. the MS, BM Cott. Vitell. D. ix, f. 31).
  N.d. – c. 1168 in *CTG* – but the MS is first half of the 13th cent. (+1227).
[2] Esp. the association with Robert de Ferrers (not called earl, so prob., but not certainly, –1138).
[3] Robert junior earl of 'Nottingham' (cf. *Handbook*, p. 442: presumably Derby).
[4] Helias archd. Staffs: Ralph was still archd. 11 Jan. 1155 (*SHC*, II, pp. 233ff.).
[5] Alan archd. Staffs: +1175 (*PUE*, II, no. 146).   [6] If 'N.' is correct for pr. Notley, –1194.
[7] Robert, bp. Exeter (1138–55 or 1155–60); 'Auco' archd. Cornwall, presumably for 'Aluredo'
  (c. 1150–6) rather than William de Auco (d. 1150, which is too early); William treasurer of Exeter
  (said to have d. 1154, but this is probably due to a misreading of the Exeter Martyrology); John
  precentor of Exeter, who succeeded Robert after 1156 (*HMC Wells*, I, 20).
[8] Witnessed by Robert of Cardinam, in whose cht. Hamelin occ., and who was grandson of Robert
  son of William of the mid-twelfth century (Oliver, pp. 39–40).

[WARE]

?Richard   Occ. 1174 as general proctor of S. Evroult for England[1] and may have acted as pr. (*CDF*, no. 645).

Hubert   Occ. 1190 × 1212; 1203 × 6 (*Bk. Seals*, no. 5 and n., correcting *CDF*, no. 648).

R.   Occ. prob. 1209 × 23 (*Reg. Lincoln*, III, no. 870).

A.   Occ. 1219 (*Reg. Wells*, I, p. 49).

The next recorded pr., William, occ. 1221 × 2 (*Warws F.*, no. 326).

WAREHAM (Dorset), St Mary (Lire)   f. *temp.* Henry I
List in *VCH Dorset*, II, 122.

H.   Occ. 1191 × 1204 (*DC*, no. 323).[2]

Robert   Occ. 1191 × 7[3] (*CDF*, no. 1089; prob. = Bodl. Dugdale MS 12, p. 266).

W.   Occ. 15 Oct. 1216 (*Rot. Lit. Pat.*, p. 199).

WARMINGTON (Warws) (Préaux)   f. –1123
Ralph   Occ. 1206 × 7 (*Warws F.*, no. 157).

WATH (Yorks N.) (Mont-S.-Michel)   f. –1196 (see below; also *EYC*, V, p. 46 and n.).
Hamo   Occ. 1196 (*Ctl. St Michael's Mount*, no. 57).

Richard   Occ. *c.* 1200 (*EYC*, V, no. 141); early 13th cent. (*Ctl. Fountains*, II, p. 500).

WEEDON LOIS (Weedon Pinkney) (Northants), St Mary (S. Lucien, Beauvais)   f. –1123
List in *VCH Northants*, II, 185.

Odo   Occ. prob. late 12th cent.[4] (BM Harl. MS 4714, f. 246v).

Adam[5]   Occ. prob. late 12th cent. (ib., f. 247v).

Philip   Occ. prob. early 13th cent. (ib., f. 247).

Nicholas   Occ. 30 Dec. 1228; 25 Feb. 1232 (*Reg. Wells*, II, pp. 230, 247); and see n. 4.

WILMINGTON (Sussex) (Grestain)   f. –1086
List in *VCH Sussex*, II, 123 (L. F. Salzman; from 1243).

R.   Occ. ?1197 × 1204[6] (*Ctl. Chichester*, pp. 88–9, no. 331).

The next recorded pr., John, occ. 1242 × 3 (*Sussex F.*, no. 416).

WILSFORD (Lincs) (Bec)   f. 1135 × 54
List in *VCH Lincs*, II, 240.

Roger   Occ. 6 July 1202 (*Lincs F.*, PRS LXVII, no. 79).

The next recorded pr., Adam de Subiria, was presented 1226 (*Reg. Wells*, III, p. 151).

---

[1] Roger of Le Sap, later abb. S. Evroult (1091–1123) held a similar position –1091 (Orderic, III, 31; cf. III, 381–2, IV, 433, 437).

[2] Dated by Robert IV, earl of Leicester. It is stated in *DC*, no. 323 that the extension of War' is uncertain. Wareham is prob. correct as the cellarer of Lire is also a witness and the cht. is by a member of the Beaumont family who were the founders of Wareham.

[3] Hawise, countess of Gloucester d. 24 Apr. 1197 (*CP*, V, 688).

[4] Most of the documents cited here (ff. 246ff.) can only be dated by the family of the founder of the pr., Gilo of Pinkney (de Picquigny). His son, Robert, was contemporary with Robert, bp. Lincoln (ibid.: presumably 1148 × 66); his grandson, Gilbert, was contemporary with pr. Odo. To this cht. a monk called Adam was witness, and he may be the Adam 'prir'' who witnesses another cht. of Gilbert. Pr. Philip was contemporary with Gilbert's son, Henry, and Pr. Nicholas occ. 1232, in the time of Henry's son, Robert (f. 248); see above. On the origin of the family, see Loyd, p. 78.

[5] See n. 4.

[6] When Robert, abbot of Grestain, seems to have visited Chichester (*Ctl. Chichester*, nos. 194, 277. R. abbot of Grestain witnesses no. 331. But R. could be Rodulf or Robert, which gives a possible range of date of 1186 × 97 or 1197 × 1233, according to *GC*, XI, 843).

WOOTTON WAWEN (Warws), St Peter (Conches) f. 1086+

List in *VCH Warws*, II, 135–6, from Dugdale, *Warwickshire*, II, 816. Ctl. = Ctl. Wootton Wawen in Evreux, Archives Dép. Eure, II. F. 2463.

Ralph Occ. ?late 12th cent. (Ctl., ff. 12 v–13 v: preceded Gerard).

Gerard Occ. ?early 13th cent. (Ctl., ff. 12 v–13 v).[1]

Reginald Occ. 22 Sept. 1221 (*Warws F.*, no. 294 = Ctl., ff. 4 v–5; on f. 4 v he is called Roger, but f. 5 and the foot of the fine give Reginald).

Prs. called Roger and Richard of St John occ. n.d. ?13th cent. (Ctl. ff. 3 v, 5 v–6). Dugdale and *VCH* listed also Robert (temp. Stephen), Grimbald, Ernulph (temp. Henry II), Roger de Bretoil, Roger de Conches, and (after Ralph, temp. John) Taurinus (temp. Henry III). We have found no evidence for any of these.

YORK, Holy Trinity (Marmoutier) f. 1089

C.T.C. List in *VCH Yorks*, III, 390.

Seward Dead by 1113 (*Roul. Morts*, p. 194).

Hicmarus (or Hemarus) Occ. 1109 × 14 (*EYC*, II, no. 729; *CDF*, no. 1233).

(**Martin**, referred to by Stapleton, *Holy Trinity Priory*, York. Arch. Inst., 1848, p. 28, seems based on a misunderstanding of *Roul. Morts*, p. 331, where 'donno Martino' not called prior, occ. We have found no early evidence for Robert, cited as occ. 1130 by Stapleton, loc. cit.; cf. Solloway, *Alien Benedictines of York* (Leeds, 1910), pp. 62–3.)

Elias Paynel Res. 1143, abb. Selby. Younger son of Ralph Paynel (*Ctl. Selby*, I, p. [33]).

Gilbert Occ. 1143 × 53 (*EYC*, I, no. 450).

Philip Occ. *c.* 1150 × 4 (*EYC*, VI, no. 50); 1164 × 75 (ib., no. 82); 1175+ (ib., I, no. 506); Mar. 1176 (*Ctl. Fountains*, I, pp. 206–7; cf. pp. 209, 211).

Bernard Occ. 1175 × 86 (*EYC*, VI, no. 29).

Robert Occ. ?1175 × *c.* 1185 (*EYC*, XI, no. 203 – cf. ed.'s note); *c.* 1180 × 6 (ib., VIII, no. 138); 1191 × 1212 (ib., II, no. 1122); 18 May 1206 (ib., I, no. 555); 2 Nov. 1208 (*Yorks F., John*, p. 134). He also occ. in *EYC*, I, no. 296, dated *1180 × 90*, but the document is probably later and cannot be precisely dated.

?T. Occ. ?early 13th cent. (*EYC*, I, no. 208n.).

William Occ. (W.) 9 Sept. 1216 (*Rot. Lit. Pat.*, p. 196b); 9 Oct. 1220 (*Ctl. St Bees*, no. 104); also occ. 29 Oct. 1223 (*Yorks F., 1218–31*, p. 54).[2]

[1] Temp. Robert de Stafford; for whom cf. ff. 1 r–v, 23 v – there were two of the name, the father of the mid-late 12th, the son of the early 13th cent.

[2] A Ranulf occ. 1218+ (*EYC*, I, no. 558, dated by Farrer *c. 1190 × 1206*; but it is a charter to Healaugh Park priory (*Ctl.*, pp. 82–3) and so prob. 1218+, and Ranulf later than William).

THE CLUNIAC HOUSES

Of the houses founded before 1216, no names have been found in this period for Church Preen, Clifford, Great Witchingham, Horkesley, Kersal, Malpas, St Carrok, St Clears, St Helen's, Wangford.

BARNSTAPLE (Devon), St Mary Magdalene (St Martin-des-Champs) f. *c.* 1107
  List in Oliver, p. 196.
Richard Occ. 1157 (Cambridge, King's Coll. Muniments 2. W/6 = *Mon.*, v, 106 = Oliver, p. 194, where 'Bardeneia' is a misreading for Bard' = Barnstaple); 14 Aug. 1159 (Cambridge, King's Coll. Muniments 2. W/7).
Norman Occ. 1159 × 60 (*CDF*, no. 1272); 1157 × *c.* 1179[1] (*Mon.*, v, 198).
Martin de Bovele Possibly before Norman. Mentioned as former pr. in 1206 (*CRR*, IV, p. 198).
The next recorded pr., Richard, occ. early 1227 (Prynne, *Records*, III, 74).

BASFORD, *see* **NOTTINGHAM**

BERMONDSEY (Surrey), St Saviour (La Charité) f. 1089 (see below)
  Lists in Rose Graham, *English Ecclesiastical Studies*, pp. 121ff.; *VCH Surrey*, II, 75 (the latter from *Ann. Bermondsey*). Miss Graham, pp. 93ff., showed how unreliable in general the annals are; but it has been suggested above, p. 6, that the case is (paradoxically) somewhat better for the twelfth than for later centuries; and they have been used here, though with caution. Dates which fit into the pattern of other evidence may be accepted, since in this period the compiler followed a good source for most of his information about the priors; but he shows here as elsewhere his tendency to introduce names out of context and to multiply brief priorates; and we may be reasonably sure that the multiplication of Peter, Adam and Henry de Soilli is an example of this mode of error.
Petreus 1089–1118/19 App. 1089 (*Ann. Bermondsey*, p. 427; the date of f., 22 July 1089, is confirmed by Ann. Montacute, BM Cott. MS Tib. A. x, f. 163; Ann. Southwark, BM Cott. MS Faust. A. viii, f. 131 v; *Flor. Hist.*, II, 21; *MPCM*, II, 29). D. 10 June 1119 (*Ann. Bermondsey*, p. 433; *Flor. Hist.*, II, 47); 1118 in Ann. Montacute, f. 163 v.
Herebrannus (Herebrandus) 1118/19–1120. 1119–20 according to *Ann. Bermondsey*, p. 433; succeeded 1118, Ann. Montacute, f. 163 v. The *Ann. Bermondsey* here insert Peter, 1120; he is presumably a ghost.
Walter 1120–1134 Dates as *Ann.*, pp. 433–5; d. 1134 confirmed by Ann. Montacute, f. 163 v and Ann. Southwark, f. 133 v.
Clarembald 1134–1148 Succ. 1134 (*Ann. Bermondsey* confirmed by Ann. Montacute and Southwark). Occ. 1145 (Saltman, p. 450). Res. to be first abb. Faversham, 1148 (Gervase, I, 138; *HMC 5th Rept.*, p. 442a–b).[2] Gervase dates the blessing of C. as abb. Faversham 11 Nov. 1147; *Ann. Bermondsey*, p. 438 dates his res. 1148, correctly; see under Faversham.

---

[1] William de Braose I (grandson of Judhael) *floruit c.* 1150–79; cf. *DNB*, VI, 229.
[2] Cf. Saltman, p. 82; *Letters of Peter the Venerable*, ed. G. Constable, II, 297 and n. The letter of B. pr. La Charité, consenting to C.'s departure, is the only evidence of B.'s existence, and his priorate must be fitted in *c.* 1146–*c.* 1148.

Robert de Belesme 1148–1155 El. 1148; res. 1155 (*Ann. Bermondsey*, p. 438). Occ. Nov. × Dec. 1153, Apr. × Oct. 1154 (*Reg.*, III, nos. 272, 866). A Reading ctl. calls him 'Robertus de Belemia' (BM Egerton MS 3031, f. 44; cf. *Reg.*, III, no. 682n.); a document from the lost ctl. Bermondsey preserved in transcripts has 'Bellismo' (BM Cott. MS Claud. A. viii, f. 121r–v) or 'Belesme' (BM Harl. MS 4757, f. 10r–v) (1148 × 53).[1]

Roger de Laigle 1156–1157 App. 16 Apr. 1156; res. 18 Feb. 1157 on el. as abb. St-Ouen, Rouen (*Ann. Bermondsey*, pp. 439–40). There is no independent evidence that he was pr. Bermondsey, but Roger, formerly m. Cluny was abb. St-Ouen 1157–1167/8 (*GC*, XI, 145–6; Torigny, p. 193), so the dates fit perfectly.

Adam 1157–1161 M. La Charité, later abb. Evesham, 1161–91 (see *Ch. Evesham*, p. 100; *GFL*, pp. 177–8, cf. p. 533). App. pr. 6 June 1157; res. on el. as abb. Evesham 16 April 1161 (*Ann. Bermondsey*, pp. 440–1).

Ann. Bermondsey here insert, pp. 441–2, Geoffrey, 1161–3, Peter, 1163–6, for whom there is no other evidence.

Reginald d'Etampes (?)1166–1167 App. and res. *Ann. Bermondsey*, p. 442. Occ. (Reginald) 1163 × 73[2] (Lees, *Templars*, pp. 164f.); (Reginald d'Etampes, quondam pr. – which confirms that he res.) as ex-pr. 1171 + – in a letter to the pr. Canterbury about a miracle of St Thomas Becket (*MB*, I, 410).[3]

Roger II 1167–1175 Dates as *Ann. Bermondsey*, pp. 442–4; res. 1175, abb. Abingdon (ibid.; Torigny, p. 268; *Ann. Winchester*, p. 61 (not named); cf. below). See Abingdon, where it is shown that he became abb. Aug. × Dec. 1175; *Newington Longeville Chts.*, no. 70, shows that he was pr. –1173, abb. +1173/4.

Ann. Bermondsey, p. 444, inserts Robert 'de Bethleem', who seems to be the same as Robert de Belesme above. *CDF*, no. 644 offers a Robert about this time but the original (Arch. Orne, H. 937) reads 'Ro.', i.e. probably 'Rogero'. The document ref. to by R. Graham, loc. cit., was probably that discussed below, n. 1. It seems that the *Ann.* have misplaced Robert.

Guerric 1176–1178 El. 1176, res. 1178 to be abb. Faversham (*Ann. Bermondsey*, p. 444); the latter is confirmed by Gervase, I, 277, and for the date see Faversham.

Bertram 1178–1184(?) Dates as *Ann. Bermondsey*, pp. 444–5; the former seems confirmed (see above) and the latter cannot be far wrong, since he occ. +29 Sept. 1183 (BM Harl. MS 4757, f. 12); also occ. 23 Apr. 1182 (Westminster Abbey, Domesday Ctl., f. 479).

Constantine (?)1184–1186(?) Dates as *Ann. Bermondsey*, pp. 445–6. Occ. ?1178 × 89 (R. Graham, loc. cit., but the document she cites contains no ref. to him).

Henry de Soilli (?)1186–1189 *Ann. Bermondsey*, p. 446, gives H. de S. succ. 1186 (for his name cf. BM Cott. Faust. A. iii, f. 246); then d. and succ. by Adam and Henry; on p. 447, s.a. 1189, pr. Henry becomes abb. Glastonbury at Michaelmas (15 Sept. or a little + in Gervase, I, 458). Henry de Soilli, pr. of Bermondsey, undoubtedly became abb. Glastonbury (q.v.) in Sept. 1189; and it seems clear that the interpolation of Adam and duplication of Henry in 1186 is due to the annalist's confusion. The double entry perhaps confirms that his source(s) gave 1186 for Henry's accession, and the year cannot

---

[1] In the ctl. Bermondsey this document was adjacent to another dated '1175' (for 1176): it refers to Hugo Pierleoni as legate dealing with the same dispute. This seems to have confused a Bermondsey historian at some period, so that Robert de 'Bethleem' appears in the *Ann.*, p. 444, under 1175–6. The annalist calls the pr. of 1148–55 'Blesensis', a name which might gain some colour from the fact that he was app. under, perhaps by, King Stephen, and was one of the very few monastic prs. to witness Stephen's charters. But the evidence cited above leaves little doubt that he was usually called 'de Bellême' or by some closely similar name.

[2] Geoffrey archd. Canterbury (1173 if Henry is correctly styled 'Dei gratia').

[3] The letter is in William of Canterbury's *Miracula*, begun in 1172, but not completed for many years; on the other hand the letters incorporated in it could have been written at any time after the martyrdom. Cf. E. Walberg, *La tradition hagiographique de S. Thomas Becket* (Paris, 1929), pp. 62ff.

[BERMONDSEY]
 be far wrong. Occ. as pr. (H. in both cases) 26 Sept. 1188, 5 Dec. 1188 (Bodl. Dodsworth MS 90, f. 24; BM Cott. MS Claud. A. viii, ff. 115v–16); (Henry) 12 Aug. 1189 (*Epp. Cant.*, p. 545); also BM Cott. MS Faust. A. iii, f. 246r–v (–1189).

Richard 1189–1201(?) Dates as *Ann. Bermondsey*, pp. 447, 449 (called Norman, Northam respectively in the two entries); succ. 6 Dec. 1189. Occ. 1189×90 (1 Richard I, BM Harl. MS 4757, f. 12); 1189×96 (Gibbs, no. 268); (R.) 1191×1201 (j.d. of Celestine III, 1191×8: Norwich, Sacrist's Book, f. 30r–v); 1194 (R.) (*HMC 7th Rept.*, p. 589).

The *Ann. Bermondsey* (pp. 449ff.) here plunge into wild confusion. In the following list, the dates and names in italics seem to bear some relation to reality.

Hugh, 1201–10; Richard, 1210–21 (*pr. Wenlock*); *Hugh, 1221*; Geoffrey, 1221–2; Odilo, 1222; *Hugh, 1222*; Odilo, 1222–3; Haymo, 1223; *Hugh, 1223–5*; Gilbert, 1225–6; *Hugh, 1226*; William, 1226–7; Josbert, 1227–9; Bernard, 1229; Haymo, 1229–31; *Hugh, 1231–4*; *Peter, 1234–40*; *Humbert*, or Ingelbert or Gilbert, 1240–5; Roger, 1245–7; *Imbert (Humbert)*, 1247–53…All these may be genuine names misplaced, especially Josbert (see below) and Haymo (1252–61). But it is clear that after 1201 or 1210 the ann. take leave of actual events and cannot be used as evidence.

Hugh Occ. 1202×3 (*Surrey F.*, p. 5); ?pr. 1201–10 (see above, below).

Master Josbert, Joybert Pr. Coventry, 1198–1216 (when he d.), is said by Roger of Wendover (in *MPCM*, II, 445–6, s.a. 1198) to have been also pr. Bermondsey, Daventry and Wenlock (q.v.). The story sounds incredible, but his rare name occ. as pr. of all these houses except Daventry. The three Cluniac houses were all dependent on La Charité – her only daughter houses, apart from Northampton, still acknowledging any relationship at this date. It is therefore intelligible that he should have oversight of this group of houses;[1] and if the date of Hugh's death in the ann. is correct, it is possible that he took over Bermondsey in the difficult circumstances of the interdict in 1210. It is also possible that Hugh remained as nominal pr. under his direction, and that Hugh of 1202×3 is identical with the next pr. But this hardly seems likely; and Josbert occ. as pr. in two chts., n.d. (*HMC Var. Coll.*, VII, 30; BM Add. MS 47,677, f. 366v).

Hugh Occ. 16 Oct. 1219 (*Soms F.*, p. 39); 1222×3, 1225×6, 1231×2, 9 Feb. 1235 (*Surrey F.*, pp. 12, 13, 18; *Essex F.*, no. 371); etc.

Peter Occ. 1 July 1236, 12 Nov. 1236 (*Soms F.* pp. 84, 101).

Guichard 1238– Royal consent to app. 10 June 1238 (*CPR, 1232–47*, p. 223). Occ. n.d. (G.) (*Chartes de Cluny*, VI, 294–5).

Imbert (Humbert) Prob. also pr. Wenlock, q.v. 1238–*c.* 1252. Occ. *c.* 29 Sept. 1239 (BM Harl. MS 4757, f. 5); 1241×2,…1249×50 (*Surrey F.*, pp. 26,…33). Haymo succ. in 1252 (*CR, 1251–3*, p. 148).

BROMHOLM (Norfolk), St Andrew (Castle Acre) f. April 1113 (dependent on Castle Acre); 1195 (dependent on Cluny)
 List in *VCH Norfolk*, II, 363.

Adam Occ. 1170×82 (CUL, MS Mm. ii. 20, f. 35v); n.d. (ib., f. 26v).

?Wlricus Occ. 12th or 13th cent. (ib., ff. 43v–44).

W. Occ. 28 Jan. 1226 (ib., f. 10r–v).

The next recorded pr.,[2] Vincent, occ. Mar. 1239 (*Cluny Chts.*, II, p. 202); 20 Apr. 1245 (CUL, MS Mm. ii. 20, ff. 2v–3).[3]

---

[1] And apparently placed at Coventry to reconstruct the community after Bp. Hugh Nonant's death.
[2] Blomefield, XI, 26 has Philip, occ. 1210, but without reference.
[3] Evidently the source of Blomefield's statement (ibid.) that Vincent occ. temp. Henry I (*sic*, for III).

CASTLE ACRE (Norfolk), St Mary (Lewes) f. 1089
 List in *VCH Norfolk*, II, 358; 15th cent. list, names only,[1] in Ctl., BM Harl. MS 2110, f. 144v.
Lambert Occ. 1101 × 7 (*Mon.*, III, 342).
Hugh Occ. 1121 × 31 (*Mon.*, III, 330–1).
Angwus (*?sic*) Occ. 1121 × 45 (BM Harl. MS 2110, f. 123v). ? = Magnus, list.
William Occ. *temp.* William de Warenne III (?), 1138 × 48 (ib., f. 4); 1146 × *c.* 1169 (CUL, MS Mm. ii. 20, f. 12v).
?Henry Occ. 1170[2] (*Ctl. Lewes, Norfolk*, no. 120); 1146 × 74, prob. late (BM Harl. MS 2110, ff. 124v–5).[3]
Jordan Occ. 1146 × 74 (ib., f. 124; *Ctl. Lewes, Norfolk*, no. 61); 1178 × 9[4] (BM Harl. MS 2110, f. 81r–v).
Maino Occ. 1170 × 82 (CUL, MS Mm. ii. 20, f. 35v).
Henry Occ. 21 July 1182 (Harl. MS 2110, f. 81).
Odo Occ. 1171 × 92[5] (ib., f. 128).
Hugh Occ. 12 May 1191 (ib., f. 114).
Lambert (? of Kempston: so list) Occ. 1191 × 1200 (BM Harl. MS 2110, ff. 126v–7); 1200 (*CRR*, I, p. 220); 6 July 1202 (*Norfolk F.*, PRS LXV, no. 290).
Philip (? of Mortimer) Occ. Oct. 1202 (*Pleas before the King or his Justices*, II, no. 1084); 20 Jan. 1203 (*Norfolk F.*, PRS LXX, no. 18); 18 Jan. 1209 (ib., no. 134).
Robert (? de Bozoun: so list – ? d'Alençon). Occ. 6 Oct. 1220 (BM Harl. MS 2110, f. 115); *c.* Easter 1224 (*Essex F.*, p. 67); 1228 (*CRR*, XIII, no. 834); 1230 (*CRR*, XIII, no. 2642).

DAVENTRY (Northants) (St Mary and) St Augustine (La Charité) f. *c.* 1090 (at Preston Capes); 1107 × 8 (at Daventry)
 List in *VCH Northants*, II, 113.
Osbert Prev. m. Bromholm, almoner of Wenlock (Osbert de Clare, *Ep.* 33, p. 116; cf. p. 219); occ. 1135 × 6 ('in anno decessionis Henrici regis': BM Cott. MS Claud. D. xii, f. 82v; cf. f. 83r–v); *c.* 1142 (*c.* 6 Stephen, because 9 Stephen 3 years later: i.e. 26 Dec. 1141 × 25 Dec. 1142: *Mon.*, V, 179).
Herbert Occ. 12 Jan. 1146 (*Mon.*, V, 182); 1143 × 70 (BM Cott. MS Claud. D. xii, f. 142v; cf. ff. 87, 121v).
Joybert, Josbert Pr. Daventry –1198; also pr. Bermondsey, Coventry, Wenlock q.v. (see *MPCM*, II, 67).
?William de Bonay ? Occ. *c.* 1200[6] (BM Cott. MS Claud. D. xii, f. 57v).
Benedict Occ. 1202 (*Northants Ass. Roll*, no. 535); 1203 (*CRR*, II, p. 160; III, p. 17); 9 Oct. 1204 (BM Cott. Claud. D. xii, f. 104v). See p. 228.
Alelm Occ. 1206 (*CRR*, IV, p. 225); 15 Apr. 1208 (BM Cott. MS Claud. D. xii, f. 110); 1 Jan. × 2 July 1215 (BM Stowe MS 937, f. 147; Cheney, *Inn. III*, no. 1008n.).
VCH cites BM Cott. MS Claud. D. xii, f. 172 for various other early prs. without dates. This is a 16th–17th-cent. index of prs. who occ. in the MS. Of these names Ralph (f. 72v) could be 12th or 13th cent.; Reyner (ff. 33, 148v) is called 'dompnus' on f. 121v, which perhaps

---

[1] Hugh, Magnus, Lambert de Kempston, Jordan, Philip, Robert Bozoun, Henry (inserted), Ralph de Wesenham...
[2] *c.* Michaelmas after the Inquest of Sheriffs. [3] With William archd. Norwich.
[4] Michaelmas after the summons by Pope Alexander to the Roman Council – i.e. III Lateran; the summons went in Sept. 1178, the Council was held in March 1179.
[5] With S(teingrin) archd. (Norwich).
[6] Jordan of London 'olim seruiens' of pr. William de Bonay (or Bouay), occ. 1217 (loc. cit.).

[DAVENTRY]
rather suggests a 13th-cent. date; James was prob. first half 13th cent. (ff. 49, 70v–71, 82r–v, 91v, and on 107 with Robert archd. Northampton, who occ. 1206, 1218: *Ctl. Oseney*, IV, p. 22; *Reg. Lincoln*, II, no. 586); Nicholas was somewhat later (occ. 1242, f. 103v); and Richard and Samson we cannot trace either in index or text.

DERBY, St James (Bermondsey)   f. –1140
   List in *VCH Derbys*, II, 46.
Richard   Occ. *early Henry II* (*pal.*: *DC*, no. 419).
Arnold   Occ. *temp.* Henry III (PRO Ass. Roll 167, m. 29d).
Frumond   Occ. *temp.* Henry III (ib.).

DUDLEY (Worcs), St James (Much Wenlock)   f. 1149 × 60
   List in *VCH Worcs*, II, 161.
Osbert   Occ. 1176 × 92 (Erdeswick, *Survey of Staffs*, p. 341; *Mon.*, v, 83).
Everard   Occ. 16 June 1182 (*Bk. Seals*, no. 59 = *Mon.*, v, 83).
William Frond   Occ. 1190 × 1203 (*SHC*, III, 217); (William) 1198 × 9 (*Ped. Fin.*, I, p. 107).

EXETER (Devon), St James (St Martin-des-Champs)   f. 1141
   List in Oliver, p. 192.
Richard   1st pr., occ. 1146 (Oliver, pp. 194–5).
Alvred   Occ. 1157 (ib., p. 194 = *Mon.*, v, 106).
Reginald   Occ. 29 Sept. 1169 (Morey, p. 147 = *CDF*, no. 900).
Anger (or Auger)[1]   Occ. 1177[2] × 84, 1186 × 9[3] (Cambridge, King's Coll. Muniments, 2. W/15–18, 11).
The next recorded pr., John, occ. 1232 (*Devon F.*, no. 257).

FARLEIGH, *see* **MONKTON FARLEIGH**

HOLME EAST (Dorset), St Mary[4] (Montacute)   f. *c.* 1107
   List in *VCH Dorset*, II, 82.
Gilbert   M. of Holme and prob. 1st pr. (*Ctl. Montacute*, no. 118).
Ralph of Ilchester   Occ. *c.* 1159 (ib., no. 130: see Montacute).
Adam   Occ. *c.* 1170 × 1213[5] (ib., no. 110); 16 Oct. 1195 (ib., no. 127); 1191 × 1212 (BM Add. Cht. 74, 470); 1217 × 18 (*Dorset F.*, I, p. 19).

HORTON, *see* **MONKS HORTON**

KERSWELL (Devon) (Montacute)   f. 1119 × 29
   List in Oliver, p. 312.
Nicholas   Occ. 1 July 1201 × 2 (*Devon F.*, no. 38).
The next recorded pr., Richard, occ. 1 Aug. 1228 (*Devon F.*, no. 172; *CRR*, XIII, no. 1172).

LENTON (Notts), Holy Trinity (Cluny)   f. 1102 × 8
   List in *VCH Notts*, II, 100.
Humphrey   Occ. ? mid-late 12th cent. (Nichols, *Leics*, II, i. 419; with Richard Bussel; cf. Thoroton, ed. Throsby, I, 3. But Nichols dates it *temp.* Henry I).
Thomas   –*c.* 1163 Res. *c.* 1163 (*GFL*, no. 147 and n.).

---

[1] No doubt Augustine, occ. n.d., Oliver, p. 195, is an error for Anger or Auger.
[2] Walter, archd. Cornwall (Morey, pp. 122, 127).
[3] William, archd. Totnes (Morey, pp. 125, 127).   [4] *Ctl. Montacute*, no. 120.
[5] *Temp.* Adam son of John de Port (see Round in *Genealogist*, New Series, XVI, 6).

Robert de Broi *c.* 1163– App. *c.* 1163 (ib.).

Philip Occ. *c.* 24 March 1176 (*Ctl. Rievaulx*, no. 132).

Alexander Occ. (A.) 1154 × 81 (*CRR*, v, p. 141); 1189 × 96 (*Nottingham Borough Records*, I, 8).

Peter –1214 Occ. 1199 × 1200 (Northants F., PRO transcripts); 1200 (*CRR*, I, p. 327); 18 July 1207 (*Beds F.*, no. 161); 2 Dec. 1212 (*Cart. Antiq.*, PRS LV, no. 227). Res. 1214, to be abb. of Bardney (q.v.).

R. Occ. 1213 × 14 (*HMC Middleton*, pp. 55–6).

Roger Occ. 1230 (*CRR*, XIII, no. 2324); 13 Jan. × 3 Feb. 1231 (*Derbys F.* (1886), p. 28).

LEWES (Sussex), St Pancras (Cluny) f. 1077 (see below; the foundation cht. is of *c.* 1078 × 82: *EYC*, VIII, no. 2).

List in *VCH Sussex*, II, 69 (L. F. Salzman); an account of prs. in B. M. Crook, 'General History of Lewes Priory in the Twelfth and Thirteenth Centuries', *Sussex Arch. Coll.*, LXXXI (1940), 68–96, esp. pp. 71–7, based on ann., ed. Liebermann in *EHR*, XVII (1902), 86ff. (ref. to as Ann.) and on Ann. Montacute, based on, or incorporating Lewes material, in BM Cott. MS Tib. A. x, printed in *Sussex Arch. Coll.*, II (1849), 23ff. (ed. W. H. Blaauw).

Lanzo 1077–1107 M. of Cluny (*WMGR*, II, 513); 'uenit in Angliam', 1077 (Ann. Montacute; cf. Ann. Southwark, BM Cott. MS Faust. A. viii, f. 131v; *Ann. Bermondsey*, p. 425); 1078, Ann. D. 1 April 1107 (Ann.; Ann. Montacute; *WMGR*, II, 513ff.; *WMGP*, p. 207; cf. Bodl. Douce MS 296, f. 2v). Cf. Crook, art. cit., pp. 71–2, 75–6; *MO*, pp. 151–2.

Eustace of Beauvais 1107–1120 M. Lewes (*Mon.*, v, 152). App. 1107; *UGQ*, p. 93; d. 1120, ibid., p. 94, Ann. 1.

Hugh of Amiens 1120–1123 M. Cluny; pr. Limoges *c.* 1115–20; app. pr. Lewes 1120 (*Letters of Osbert of Clare*, pp. 183–4; Ann.; *UGQ*, p. 94).[1] Occ. 1121 (*Ancient Chts.*, nos. 7, 8). Res. 1123, abb. Reading (Ann. Reading, *UGQ*, p. 10; Corpus Christi Coll., Cambridge, MS 111, f. 9); consec. abp. Rouen 14 Sept. 1130; d. 10 Nov. 1164. Cf. Crook, p. 76.

Ralph *c.* 1123–1126 D. 1126 (Ann.).

Ansger (Anker, Ancher) *c.* 1126–1130 Res. 1130 to be abb. Reading (Florence, II, 92 = *JW*, p. 30; cf. *UGQ*, p. 10). Cf. Crook, p. 76. D. 1135 (Ann.).

Hugh of St Margaret –1143 D. 1143 (Ann.).

Aimarus Occ. 1145 (Saltman, p. 450); also 1145, as Ademarus, Osbert de Clare, *Ep.* 32 (cf. *GFL*, pp. 505–6).

William I –1159 Occ. 1147 (*Acta Chichester*, pp. 106–7n.); 1147 × 8 (*Ctl. Lewes*, I, p. 25); 14 Nov. 1148 (*Ctl. Chichester*, no. 299n.); 1153 × 4 (*Reg.*, III, no. 569); 1154 × 9 (*CRR*, XIII, no. 1799); d. 1159 (Ann.). Cf. Crook, p. 76.

William II Occ. 1170 × 1 (*Ctl. Lewes*, II, p. 85). Cf. Crook, pp. 76–7.

Osbert Occ. 1174 × 8 (*Ctl. Lewes*, I, p. 127); n.d. (O.) (PRO E40/2389; *Cat. Anc. Deeds*, II, 73 = *Ctl. Lewes*, III, *Wilts etc.*, no. 91). Cf. Crook, p. 77; V. H. Galbraith in *EHR*, LXIX (1954), 296 and n.: possibly identical with Osbert *dean*, m. Lewes.

Hugh III –1186 Occ. 1179 × 86 (*Anc. Chts.*, no. 48); 1181 × 2 (*Acta Chichester*, no. 119); res. 1186 to be abb. of Reading; later abb. Cluny (see Reading; cf. *Ann. Waverley*, p. 244).

William III Occ. ?1188 (*Epp. Cant.*, p. 243); 1190 × 1 (*PUE*, I, no. 273); 29 Oct. 1194 (*FF.*, PRS, XVII, no. 18 = *Sussex F.*, no. 2); 25 April 1196 (*PUE*, I, no. 330; II, no. 276). Cf. Crook, p. 77.[2]

---

[1] Occ. in *Ctl. Lewes*, I, pp. 145, 135, dated '*c.* 1110', '*c.* 1115': these must belong to the period 1120 × 3; the former is calendared in *Reg.*, II, no. 1360 and its authenticity queried.

[2] He is referred to in a case of 1213 × 14 (*CRR*, VII, p. 156 = *Abb. Placitorum*, p. 89) as occ. in the time of Bishop Seffrid of Chichester (1180–1204); this has led to his being referred to as occ. 1213 × 14.

[LEWES]

Master Alexander 1201– App. 10 June 1201 (*Cluny Chts.*, I, p. 98); 1201 × 4 (*Acta Chichester*, p. 177). Cf. Crook, p. 77.

Humbert Occ. 1202 × 3 (*Sussex F.*, no. 60); (Umbert) 24 June 1207 (*Ctl. Lewes, Norfolk*, p. 67, no. 213); May 1209 (*Norfolk F.*, PRS LXX, no. 225). Cf. Crook, p. 77.

Stephen Occ. 25 May 1218 (*Sussex F.*, no. 140; *Ctl. Lewes*, II, p. 75n.). Presumably the pr. who res. 1220 (*CRR*, IX, p. 69 = *Bracton's Note Book*, III, 355). Cf. Crook, p. 77.

The next recorded pr., Hugh, occ. 1224 × 5 (*Sussex F.*, no. 189).

MENDHAM (Suffolk), St Mary (Castle Acre) f. –1155
List in *VCH Suffolk*, II, 87.

John of Lindsey Occ. *c.* 1200 × 3 (*Mon.*, V, 59); (J.) j.d. + 3 Apr. 1219 (Chelmsford, Essex Rec. Office, MS D/DBy Q 19, f. 36); a letter in the *Gentleman's Mag.*, LXXVIII, pt. ii (1808), 969, gives John occ. 1206, but cites no evidence. The next recorded pr., John, possibly the same, occ. ?1239 (Blomefield, *Norfolk*, V, 376, citing a court roll).

MONK BRETTON (Yorks W.) (Lunda; cf. *Mon.*, V, 136–9) St Mary Magdalene (Pontefract) f. *c.* 1153 × 4 (see Pontefract; cf. *Letters of Peter the Venerable*, ed. G. Constable, II, 297). C.T.C.; Lists in Walker, *Monk Bretton Priory*, p. 60; *VCH Yorks*, III, 94.

Adam Pr. of Pontefract, first pr. of Monk Bretton (*EYC*, III, nos. 1670, 1665; cf. *Ctl. Pontefract*, I, no. 46; *Ctl. Monk Bretton*, p. 13); certainly in office by 1159 (see under Pontefract).

William Occ. *c.* 1185 × 1211 (*EYC*, III, no. 1819).[1]

The next recorded pr., Adam, occ. 12 Nov. 1226 (*Yorks F.*, *1218–31*, p. 77).

MONKS HORTON (Kent), St Mary and St John the Evangelist (Lewes) f. 1142
List in *VCH Kent*, II, 152.

William Occ. 1144 (*Arch. Cant.*, X, 272 (J. R. Scott)). D. 30 Oct. (BM Cott. MS Nero C. ix, f. 14v).

S. Occ. 1191 × 1207 (*Reg. Rochester*, p. 343; cf. Cheney, *Inn. III*, no. 749).

Adam Occ. 1218 × 19 (*Suffolk F.* (Rye), p. 18); 13 Oct. 1227 (*Kent F.*, pp. 97–8).

MONKTON FARLEIGH (Wilts), St Mary Magdalene (Lewes) f. 1120 × 3
List in *VCH Wilts*, III, 268 (H. F. Chettle and J. L. Kirby).

Peter –*c.* 1142 × 5, abb. Sherborne (q.v.).

John Occ. 1174 (PRO, C115 A1 K2/6683, sec. viii, no. 10); *c.* 1174 × 81 (*Earldom of Hereford Chts.*, p. 58).

Stephen Occ. 23 Aug. 1184 (*CPL*, V, 409, misdated 1194).[2]

Walter Parvus Dep. 21 Apr. 1191[3] (PRO, DL 27/3).

Mainer[4] M. and chamberlain of Lewes, el. 21 Apr. 1191 (ib.). Occ. 6 Oct. 1204 (*Wilts F.*, p. 9); Oct. 1218 (*Ctl. Lewes, Wilts etc.*, p. 13).

The next recorded pr., Henry, occ. *c.* 27 June 1227 (*Wilts F.*, p. 18).

---

[1] For date see *ib.* p. 318 (William de Neville d. 1210–11); cf. also no. 1715 – but an earlier date is possible. W. of Monk Bretton and Reiner of Pontefract were proctors, not priors, in the document in *Ctl. Monk Bretton*, p. 224, See p. 124; and Cheney, *Inn. III*, nos. 329, 403; which show a dispute as to the el. of the pr. of Monk Bretton in 1198 × 1201 and April 1202.

[2] Given at Verona, so 1184 is probable; 1185 is just possible, but 1194 is a less likely corruption from 1185 than 1184.

[3] In the presence of William Longchamp, bp. Ely, chancellor and legate in fact as well as name, at Cambridge on 21 April – i.e. 1191; cf. Round, *Commune of London*, p. 214; Tillmann, pp. 86–7.

[4] Variously given as 'Maurus' or 'Main': Mainer is the most probable form.

MONTACUTE (Soms), St Peter (and St Paul) (Cluny) f. ?1078 (so Ann., f. 162v)[1]
Lists in *VCH Soms*, II, 114–15; *Ctl. Montacute*, pp. lxviii–lxxv; 14th-cent. Ann. and list in BM Cott. MS Tib. A. x, ff. 145–76, 181 (list printed in *Mon.*, v, 164).[2]

?Walter ?1078–1087 D. of (?) Tiernus, 1st pr. Montacute, s.a. 1087 in Ann., f. 163; Walter first pr. in list.

Ranulf –1112 Ranulf pr. occ. 1112, Ann., f. 163; though not specified, this is almost certainly meant to refer to his death. Leland has an account of the origin of the pr. which makes its first pr. 'Reginaldus cancellarius'.[3] This seems to be based on a confusion between *Ranulf* the chancellor who was a benefactor of Montacute (*Reg.*, II, no. 1399) and *Ranulf* the physician of Henry I, who became a m. of Montacute in the period ?1107 × 22 (*Reg.*, II, no. 1307; cf. p. ix). But none of the documents is above suspicion. R. pr. occ. –1120 (*Ctl. Montacute*, no. 47).

Henry of Blois –1126 According to Ann. in *Red Book*, II, 752, he was pr. between being m. Cluny and abb. Glastonbury (1126, see Glastonbury; bp. Winchester 1129–71). This is not unlikely in itself as a step in the career of a Cluniac; but it is surprising to find so eminent a man in so small a house, and even more surprising to find no other evidence of it. If the tradition enshrined in Leland (n. 3) is true, Henry may have been designed for first abb. of a larger foundation.

Arnold –1139 D. 5 Nov. 1139 (Ann., f. 163v); occ. (E.) 1136, (Ernald) n.d. (*Ctl. Montacute*, nos. 48, 155). His house is not named, as with the next two; but coincidence of names, and the context, make clear that it is Montacute.

---

[1] The date usually given, *c.* 1102, seems to depend on the narrative in Leland cited in n. 3, and this, however correct it may have been, only establishes a date before 1106. It does, however, agree with the Ann. in calling William count of Mortain (1090–1106, when he forfeited) the founder; and at first sight this may suggest that the Ann. has placed the f. some years too early. But since the Ann. makes the first pr. d. 1087 and the founder d. 1088, its belief in a f. date –1090 was evidently circumstantial, although the fact that it makes Count William d. 1088 – evidently an error for Count Robert, d. 1090 – shows that no great reliance can be placed on it. Yet the other Cluniac dates about this period are mostly right (including f. Lewes s.a. 1077), though other dates are sometimes misplaced (thus Domesday Book is s.a. 1083).

On the whole, the most likely solution seems to be that Montacute was f. in or about 1078, by Count *Robert*; but that the f. cht. (*Ctl. Montacute*, no. 1) was issued by Count William, so that later tradition confused father and son; and the forfeiture of Count William led in any case to a confused period in Montacute's history (see n. 3), which makes it unlikely that precise traditions of the first founder would survive.

[2] 'Galterus (primus-*etc.*), Pontius, Guigonus, Ranulfus, Almerus, Arnaldus, Durandus, Uill'mus, Iocelinus, Thomas qui postea abbas de la Hide, Hugo, Uigo, Ricardus, Pontius, Petrus, Symon, Symon, Daniel, Durannus, Marcus fisicus bonus sacerdos...' – clearly this involves much repetition and confusion.

[3] 'This Counte of Moreton began a priory of blake monkes, a 3 or 4 in numbre, under the rootes of Montegue hille, enduing it with 3 fair lordeshippes, Montegue and Titenhul joyning to it. The 3 was Criche a 10 miles from Montegue west by south west. The Counte of Moreton toke part with Robert Curthose agayn King Henry the first, and after that was toke, put in prisone and his landes attaintid at which tyme the 3 lordeshipes gyven to Montegue priory were taken away and then were the monkes compellid to begge for a certein season. At the laste King Henry the first had pyty of them and offerid them their owne landes again and more so that they wold leave that place and go to Lamporte wher at that tyme he entendid to have made a notable monasterie. But the monkes entretid hym that they might kepe theyr old house and apon that he restorid them their 3 lordeshipes, translating his mynde of building an abbay from Lamporte to Readyng. Then cam one Reginaldus Cancellarius, so namid by likelihood of his office, a man of great fam about King Henry the first, and he felle to relligion and was prior of Montegue, and enlargid it with buildings and possessions.' Leland, *Itinerary*, ed. Toulmin-Smith, I, pt. ii, 158. *Reginald* 'Cancellarius' is otherwise unknown, unless he was the Reginald the chaplain of William I (see *Reg.*, I, p. xx), or the chaplain of Stephen who became abb. Reading, 1154–8, and later of Walden (q.v.), but the identification given above is more likely.

[MONTACUTE]

?Durand See p. 121 n. 2 and Selby – 'Durandus' followed Arnaldus in list, and Durandus, ex-abb. Selby, was a Cluniac pr. in England some years after 1134 (see Selby). Prob. occ. n.d., but ?early–mid-12th cent. (*Ctl. Montacute*, nos. 141–2).

Nicholas –1152 A native of Troyes, nephew of Hatto bp. Troyes (1123–45), d. 1152 (or possibly succeeded – the ann. does not specify, but the name occ. in a run of obits: Ann., f. 164).

Clarembald 1155–*c*. 1158 Norman by birth, later pr. Thetford (St Mary), and abb. St Augustine's, Canterbury (Ann., f. 164; see Thetford, Canterbury, St Augustine). Occ. (Clarembertus) *c*. 1155 × 64 (*Reg. Beauchamp*, p. 57).[1]

William 1158(1159?)– 'Willelmus prior uoluminis huius ordinator et compositor, natione Pictauensis, de Vico Angelico' (Ann., f. 164 – s.a. 1158, ?1159, because followed by papal schism); occ. 4 Nov. 1159 (*HMC Wells*, I, 27); n.d. (*Ctl. Montacute*, no. 130).

Thomas –1175 Occ. 29 Sept. 1169 (*CDF*, no. 900; Morey, p. 147); res. 1175 to be abb. Hyde, Winchester (q.v.).

G. Occ. 1175 × 82[2] (*Ctl. Montacute*, no. 38).

Oliver Occ. 1175 × 86 (PRO E40/217; *Cat. Anc. Deeds*, I, p. 23).

Jocelin Occ. 3 Oct. 1187 (*Ctl. Montacute*, no. 58); 1190 (Devizes, p. 18).[3]

Durand Occ. 1197 × 1205 (*HMC Wells*, I, 57); ejected 21 Dec. 1207 (*Rot. Lit. Pat.*, p. 78); restored 1217 but again ejected in 1220 (BM Cott. MS Tib. A. x, f. 167, partly quoted *Mon.*, v, 163 and n.).

The next recorded pr., Mark, succeeded 1221 (BM Cott. MS Tib. A. x, f. 167); occ. 1231 (*Soms F.*, p. 74).

Pontius pr., who occ. second in list (p. 121 n. 2), d. 30 Apr. (BM Cott. MS Nero C. ix, f. 10v).

MUCH WENLOCK (Salop), St Milburga (La Charité-sur-Loire) f. 1080 × 1

M.C. List in Eyton, *Salop*, III, 249–50; *VCH Salop* (forthcoming: M. Chibnall).

?Peter Occ. 1120(?) (Eyton, *Salop*, IV, 134 from Davis, no. 1009; but the entry seems to have been corrupt and possibly misdated. The reference may well be to Peter de Leia).

Reginald Occ. –1138 (*Ctl. Shrewsbury*, ed. Rees, no. 334); 1131 × 48 (Eyton, *Salop*, I, 207); 1144 × 5 (*PUE*, III, no. 361);[4] 10 Apr. 1148 and 1148+ (*AS*, II, 296, 318); 1151 × 7 (*Ctl. Oseney*, V, p. 31).

?Wynebald Occ. ?1155 × 60[5] (Eyton, *Salop*, X, 322): possibly a corruption for Humbald.

Humbald Occ. ?–1155 (BM Harl. MS 2188, f. 123; see Haughmond); ?1155 × 60 (see note 5: Eyton, *Salop*, IV, 42–3; cf. III, 249); 1169 (*Ch. Melrose*, f. 19(20) v, p. 38); 1171 × 5 (*MB*, I, 338); (H.) 1175+ (*Ctl. Rydeware*, p. 269).

Peter de Leia –1176 Res. 1176, bp. St Davids: consec. 7 Nov. (Gervase, I, 260; Diceto, I, 415; *Ann. Tewkesbury*, p. 51; *Ann. Cambriae*, p. 55 (s.a. 1177); cf. *Gir. Camb.*, I, 44). Occ. n.d. (Eyton, *Salop*, II, 5).

John Occ. 23 Oct. 1190 (*Ctl. Shrewsbury*, ed. Rees, p. 352); n.d. (Erdeswick, *Survey of Staffs*, p. 341).

Robert Occ. 1176 × 98 (Eyton, *Salop*, II, 280n.; G. Morris in *Trans. Salop Arch. Soc.*, XI (1888), 331); 22 Nov. 1192 (Sunday = St Cecilia's day: Eyton, *Salop*, VI, 329).

---

[1] Robert archd., Ivo dean Wells (J. A. Robinson (1921), pp. 75ff., esp. 76, 64).

[2] Robert de Beauchamp sheriff for the second time.

[3] Devizes tells the story of a fellow-m. who received letters of appointment from the abb. Cluny to supplant Jocelin but died before he could execute them.

[4] Attributed by the ed. to Pope Lucius III (1181–5, following Eyton); but the prior's name seems to establish that it belongs to Lucius II.

[5] Attributed by Eyton to the period between William FitzAlan's restoration and his death. Neither terminus seems certain, since William's son bore the same name, and the precise situation before William's restoration is quite unclear. Cf. Eyton, *Salop*, I, 250ff.; VII, 236ff.

Henry   Occ. before or after Robert (Eyton, *Salop*, III, 294); if his death really occ. *c.* 1196, as was said in 1226 (*CRR*, XII, no. 2641) – *c.* 30 years earlier – he prob. succeeded Robert and d. *c.* 1196 × 8.

Master Josbert, Joybert   Pr. Daventry, Much Wenlock: made pr. Coventry in 1198, pr. Bermondsey ?1210–?1216. See under Coventry and Bermondsey. He was apparently pr. Much Wenlock by 1198 (Wendover in *MPCM*, II, 445–6); occ. –1203 (Eyton, *Salop*, V, 112; cf. IV, 375); ?Jan. × Mar. 1202 (*Gir. Camb.*, III, 212 = Cheney, *Inn. III*, no. 401). The prs. Coventry and Wenlock were apparently treated as separate on 15 July 1215 (*Rot. Lit. Pat.*, p. 149), but this may be a chancery convention or misunderstanding, and there is no other evidence that he surrendered his office before his death on 14 June 1216 (see Coventry). 'Sebertus' mentioned in 1231 as former pr. (*CRR*, XIV, no. 1174) may be a slip for Josbert, more prob. for Robert as in Bracton's text.

The next pr., Imbert or Humbert, occ. from 12 Nov. 1221 to 22 Aug. 1260 (Eyton, *Salop*, III, 340, 250 but the latter without ref.); perhaps also pr. Bermondsey 1238/9–*c.* 1252 (see Bermondsey). Josbert is called his predecessor in *CRR*, XIII, no. 159 (1227).

NEWTON LONGVILLE (Bucks), St Faith (Longueville, Ste Foi)   f. –1102
Lists in *VCH Bucks*, I, 396; *Newington Longeville Chts.*, pp. xlvi–xlvii.

William   Occ. 1185 × 90 (proctor)[1] (ib., no. 55); (W.) 1188 × 91 (proctor) (ib., no. 36).
Roger   Occ. 1200 × 5 (proctor) (ib., no. 38); (R.) probably 1198 × 1205[2] (prior) (ib., no. 37); (R.) 1199 (proctor) (ib., no. 46).
William   Occ. 1199 × 1216[3] (proctor) (ib., no. 47).

The next recorded head, Richard de Wadden, occ. 1225 (proctor) (ib., no. 80).

NORMAN'S BURROW (Reinham) (Norfolk), St Mary and St John the Evangelist
(Castle Acre)   f. *c.* 1160 (Augustinian); *c.* 1200 (Cluniac, dependent on Castle Acre).
List in *VCH Norfolk*, II, 359.

?Roger[4]   Occ. n.d. ?late 12th cent. (BM Harl. MS 2110, f. 82v; cf. *Mon.*, V, 69).
Simon   Occ. 1228 (*CRR*, XIII, no. 611); 26 July 1228 (BM Harl. MS 2110, f. 115).

NORTHAMPTON, St Andrew (La Charité)   f. 1093 × 1100
List in *VCH Northants*, II, 108–9.

Arnulf   Occ. –1153[5] (*Northants Chts.*, p. 144).
Samson   Occ. 1145 × 53 (*PUE*, I, no. 55).
Robert Trianel   Occ. ?1176 (*CDF*, no. 534: dated '1186'); res. 1180 to be abb. Ramsey (q.v.; *Ann. Waverley*, p. 241).
Henry   Occ. 1183 × 4[6] (Stenton, *Feudalism*, pp. 276–7).[7]
Walter   Occ. 15 July 1199 (*Rot. Cur. Reg.*, II, 449); 1200 (BM Harl. MS 6952, ff. 99v–100); 20 Apr. 1203 (*Beds F.*, no. 122); (W.) ?1205 × 7 (–1216: *Ctl. Cirencester*, II, no. 699; cf. Cheney, *Inn. III*, no. 1160; see Sulby); 1207 × 8 (Northants F., PRO transcripts).

The next pr., Ralph, occ. 1 Aug. 1224 (*CPR, 1216–25*, p. 477).

[1] With Abp. Baldwin, primate, not legate. It is stated on p. xlvi that the prior of Newton and the proctor of Longueville were usually the same man. In the early period the title of proctor was the more common.
[2] Abp. Hubert Walter, not legate (but 1193 × 5 is possible).
[3] Richard, archd. Colchester.
[4] Possibly = Roger 'de Reynham', d. 28 Mar.; Norwich calendar, BM Harl. MS 3950, f. 4.
[5] C. the f. of Delapré abb. (q.v.) – ?*c.* 1145. The Thomas who occ. in Peter the Venerable's *Letters* (ed. Constable, no. 45) was not pr.   [6] Ralph Morin, sheriff Northants.
[7] A pr. Henry occ. in a record of Edward II's time, which dates him 12 John, but temp. Walkelin abb. St James, Northampton (1180 × 1206). It seems likely that the second indication is more reliable than the first, and that the same pr. is meant (BM Cott. MS Vesp. E. xvii, f. 80; cf. f. 82).

NOTTINGHAM, BASFORD (Lenton) f. –*c.* 1200 (see below, and *KH*, p. 102)[1]

Philip Occ. *c.* 1200 (pal., confirmed by witnesses: *HMC Middleton*, pp. 40–1 = Notting-ham Univ. Lib., Manuscript Dept., Middleton Collections, Mid. 1).

PONTEFRACT (Yorks W.), St John the Evangelist (La Charité-sur-Loire) f. *c.* 1090
C.T.C. Lists in *YAJ*, xxxviii (1955), 456 ff. (Sir Charles Clay) and *VCH Yorks*, iii, 186.

Walter –1122–1137 Occ. –1122 (*c.* 1121) in cht. not certainly genuine (*EYC*, iii, no. 1468; cf. Clay, art. cit., pp. 456–7); res. abb. Selby (q.v.).

Martin Occ. 1137 × *c.* 1141 (*EYC*, iii, no. 1490; for date see Clay, p. 457).

Reginald Occ. 1137 × 40 (*EYC*, iii, no. 1470; one version gives the name as 'Roger'). Possibly pr. before Martin.

Herbert Occ. *c.* 1144 (*DC*, no. 452, dated by Clay, pp. 457–8).

Adam –1146–1154 × 9 Occ. (A.) 1143 × 6 (*EYC*, iii, no. 1476, dated by Clay, p. 458). Res. to be first pr. of Monk Bretton in or soon after 1154, certainly –1159 (Monk Bretton was founded *c.* 1153 × 4, but Adam is ref. to as pr. of Pontefract still in a confirmation by Abp. Roger, i.e. not earlier than 10 Oct. 1154: *EYC*, iii, no. 1670). He was pr. of Monk Bretton by 1159 (ib., no. 1665). For all this, see Clay, pp. 458–9.

Bertram Occ. –1164, *c. 1160 × 80, –1177* (*EYC*, iii, nos. 1478, 1323, 1626).

Henry Occ. –1184 (ibid., no. 1549, dated by Clay, p. 459n., before 1185, which means he preceded Pr. Hugh).

Hugh Occ. summer 1184 (*EYC*, iii, no. 1779); –1185 (ibid., no. 1761); 1191 × 8 (*Ctl. Pontefract*, i, no. 65); 15 Jan. and probably 23 Dec. 1195 (Howden, iii, 312–16, with-out name, but cf. p. 278. The last ref. is a papal mandate. Clay, pp. 459–60).

Walter Occ. *c.* 22 Sept. 1201, prob. dep. by 9 June 1202 (*Ctl. Pontefract*, i, p. xxvi, dated by Clay, p. 469); in May 1201 (on the pr.'s complaint), and again on 9 June 1202 the pope issued a mandate to inquire into a dispute about the institution and removal of a pr. of Pontefract (Cheney, *Inn. III*, nos. 321, 425; cf. Clay, pp. 460–1 – it is just possible that this refers to Walter's predecessor).

Fulk Occ. –1211 (Clay, p. 461; his place in the list is reasonably certain).[2]

Walter Occ. 21 Jan. 1219 (*Yorks F., 1218–31*, p. 11).
The next name, Hugh, occ. 8 June 1225 (ib., p. 60 and n.).

PRITTLEWELL (Essex), St Mary (Lewes) f. –1121
List in *VCH Essex*, ii, 140.

Reginald Occ. 2nd half 12th cent. (Norman Moore, i, 190).

William Occ. 1190 × 1200[3] (Gibbs, no. 172); *c.* Easter 1203 (*Essex F.*, no. 80); *c.* 22 Apr. 1235 (?the same) (*Essex F.*, no. 400).
The next recorded pr., Simon of Walthon, m. of Lewes, was app. 1241 (*CPR, 1232–47*, p. 251).

STANSGATE (Essex), St Mary Magdalene (Lewes) f. 1112 × 21
List in *VCH Essex*, ii, 142.

Alexander Occ. 1176, 1176 × 84 (*Ctl. Clerkenwell*, nos. 32, 33).

Gilbert Occ. 1196 × 1237[4] (*Ctl. Colchester*, i, pp. 555–7).

Nicholas Occ. 1228 (*CRR*, xiii, no. 679).

[1] We are indebted for help with this to Mrs M. E. Welch, Keeper of Manuscripts, Nottingham Univ. Lib., who kindly drew our attention to other evidence of the existence of a small cell here.

[2] See p. 120 n. 1. Reiner (see Clay, p. 461) was proctor, not prior; cf. Clay in *YAJ*, xlii (1967), 740; Cheney, *Inn. III*, no. 403 (pp. 329–30); cf. no. 321.

[3] Richard, archd. Colchester; Ralph de Diceto dean St Paul's.

[4] Adam abb. Colchester. Prob. late: with Ralph, pr. Bicknacre.

THETFORD (Norfolk), St Mary (Cluny) f. 1103×4 (dependent on Lewes); 1114 (dependent on Cluny)

List in *VCH Norfolk*, II, 368. The prs. of this house are easily confused with those of the other houses at Thetford.

Malgod 1103/4–1106 First pr. app. 110(3×)4 (1104, 234 years +d. St Edmund (870), 37 +1066); dep. after about 3 years (*Mon.*, v, 151–2).

Stephen 1106– App. 1106 (*Ann. Bermondsey*, p. 430, which makes him first pr.; see *Mon.*, v, 152 and above). Occ. ?1106×7 (see Norwich, p. 57 and n. 4); 1121+ (*Mon.*, III, 330–1).

Constantius Occ. n.d., but prob. mid 12th cent. with Gilbert, pr. Holy Sepulchre, Thetford (Bodl. MS Gough, Norfolk 18, f. 19v).

Clarembald *c.* 1158–1163 Prev. pr. Montacute (q.v.); from 1163 abb. St Augustine's, Canterbury (q.v.).

?Christian Occ. 1167×79 (*Chts. Luffield*, I, no. 28); he may be pr. Holy Sepulchre.

Philip Occ. 1175×86 (*Ctl. Hulme*, I, no. 232); but also possibly of Holy Sepulchre.

Martin Occ. ?*c.* 1185[1] (Bodl. MS Tanner 425, f. 44); (M.) 27 Mar., 27 Oct. 1189 (*Ctl. Oseney*, v, pp. 110, 114); 6 Nov. 1194 (*Rot. Cur. Reg.*, I, p. 23 – pr. 'Tieford'); 8 Apr. 1197 (BM Harl. MS 391, f. 108r–v; cf. f. 108v); 1193×8 (Lambeth MS 1212, f. 107v).

Vincent Occ. 1 July 1201 (*Essex F.*, p. 22); 1 Aug. 1202 (*Norfolk F.*, PRS LXVII, no. 445); 1206 (*CRR*, IV, p. 81); early 13th cent.[2] (*Ctl. Colchester*, II, pp. 554–5; *HMC Rutland*, IV, 160).

?W. Occ. –1216 (*Ctl. Cockersand*, II, i, pp. 466–7 = *Mon.*, v, 150); but possibly another priory, or just possibly = Vincent.

The next recorded pr., Richard, occ. 1223×4 (*Suffolk F.* (Rye), p. 23); ?early Henry III (?pal.: *Berkeley Chts.*, no. 198).

WENLOCK, *see* MUCH WENLOCK

[1] *Temp.* Theobald of Valognes, founder of Hickling pr.
[2] With Adam abb. Colchester (limits 1196 × 1238).

THE CISTERCIAN HOUSES

All dedications were to St Mary except where stated. For the following houses, founded before 1216, we have found no names: Conway (Aberconway), Medmenham, Wyresdale.

ABBEY-CWMHIR (Cwmhir) (Radnor) (Whitland) f. 22 July 1143 (at Tyfaenor); 1 Aug. 1176 (at Cwmhir)
Meurig –1184 D. 1184 (*Brut: Peniarth*, p. 72; *Red Book*, p. 169; *RS*, p. 233).
Canaucus Occ. late 12th cent. and early 13th (*Gir. Camb.*, I, 241).
Rind Occ. *c.* 1201 (*Mon.*, V, 637).

ABBEY DORE (Hereford) (Morimond) f. 26 April 1147
Adam[1] Occ. 1186 × 9 (Shrewsbury Borough Lib., Ctl. Haughmond, f. 206); 1198 (cf. *Gir. Camb.*, I, 104); 1204 × 5 (Hereford F., PRO transcripts).
Adam II Occ. (A.) 2 Oct. 1214 (PRO C115 A1 K2/6683, sec. viii, nos. 77–81, esp. 80); 28 July 1216 (*Rot. Lit. Pat.*, p. 191); 1217 (*Gir. Camb.*, IV, 206). On him see Russell, *Dict.*, p. 4.

BASINGWERK (Flint) (Savigny) f. 11 July 1131
Gilbert Occ. 1155 (*CDF*, no. 819; see Revesby). *DNB*.
Matthew Occ. *c.* 1180 (*Eccl. Docs.*, pp. 52–3: see Neath).
Robert Occ. 22 Nov. 1192 (Eyton, *Salop*, VI, 329).
The next abb. known, Simon, occ. 22 Sept. 1226 (*Derbys F.* (1886), p. 17).

BEAULIEU (Hants), St Mary Magdalene (Cîteaux) f. –2 Nov. 1203 (at Faringdon); 13 June 1204 (at Beaulieu)
List in *VCH Hants*, II, 146.
Hugh 1203–1219 Occ. (H.) 25 Aug. 1206, 2 Jan. 1214, 8 Jan. 1215 (*Rot. Lit. Pat.*, pp. 67, 107, 126b). In 1218–19 he became bp. Carlisle: el. –1 Aug., temporalities restored 25 Aug. 1218; consec. 24 Feb. 1219 (*CPR*, *1216–25*, p. 164; cf. *Ann. Waverley*, p. 291; *Ann. Worcester*, p. 410). D. 1223. According to *Ann. Waverley*, p. 291, he had previously been dep. as abbot.

BIDDLESDEN (Bucks) (Garendon) f. 10 July 1147
List in *VCH Bucks*, I, 367–8.
Alexander Occ. 1143 × 51 (*Oxford Chts.*, no. 51): this cht. could be later (–1168), but if so there were two abbs. Richard.
Richard Occ. ?1148 (*Ctl. Eynsham*, I, no. 114; see Luffield); 1148 × 51[2] (BM Cott. MS Vesp. E. xvii, f. 291 v); 1148 × 61 (prob. 1148 × 50 or 1159 × 61; Saltman, p. 249, no. 21). D. 1192 (*Ann. Waverley*, p. 248).
William Wibert –1198 Occ. 1193 × 8 (*HMC Wells*, I, 9); 1196 (*CRR*, PRS LXIX, p. 86); dep. 1198 (*Gir. Camb.*, I, 95; *Ann. Waverley*, p. 251). On him, see *Gir. Camb.*, I, 203ff., IV, 156ff. and index, VIII, 340.

---

[1] For the two Adams see *Gir. Camb.*, IV, 203, 206, 220. 1186 × 9 fixed by William bp. and Jordan dean of Hereford (*CHJ*, VIII, 8).　　[2] Robert Foliot, not yet archd. Oxford (*GFL*, p. 537).

Adam of Bath 1198– For his name see BM Harl. MS 4714, f. 33. Cellarer of Bruern, el. 1198 (*Ann. Waverley*, p. 251); occ. 1198 × 1203 (Cheney, *Inn. III*, no. 482); n.d. (*c. 1210*) *Ctl. Oseney*, II, p. 443); *c.* 23 June 1210 or before (BM Add. MS 29, 436, f. 31 v).

Maurice Occ. n.d. (*c.* 1210 × 26) (*Ctl. Oseney*, V, p. 288); ('Ahamricus') *c.* 12 Apr. 1220 (BM Harl. MS 4714, f. 26 v); 1 June 1225 (BM Cott. MS Vesp. E. xix, f. 9 v); 9 Sept. 1226 (*Lincs F.*, I, p. 214).

BINDON (Dorset) (Forde) f. 22 or 27 Sept. 1172
  List in *VCH Dorset*, II, 86.

William[1] Occ. (W.)1180 (–10 Aug.: Forde Abbey, *Ctl. Forde*, p. 470); (W.) 1186 × 90: *c.* 1186 × 7 (*HMC Wells*, I, 40). ?Res. (see n. 1).

John of Forde –1191 Pr. of Forde (*Vita Wulfrici*, p. 7; ib., Introd. pp. x ff.); res. 1191 to be abb. of Forde (*Ann. Margam*, p. 21).

Henry –1212 Occ. 1191 × 7[2] (*CDF*, no. 1089); n.d. (BM Add. Cht. 74,470); res. 1212 to be bp. of Emly, Ireland (*Ann. Waverley*, p. 267); d. 1227.

The next recorded abb., Ralph, occ. (R.) 1213 × 14[3] (BM Cott. Roll xiii. 26); 19 Mar. 1227 (*Dorset F.*, p. 30).

BORDESLEY (Worcs) (Garendon) f. 22 Nov. 1138
  List in *VCH Worcs*, II, 154.

Hamo I 1138–*c.* 1155(?) *Ctl. Stoneleigh*, pp. 15, 149, seems to show that there were two Hamos, and suggests that the second was abb. by *c.* 1153. But Delisle-Berger, I, nos. XLVII, LI, indicate a vacancy *c.* 1155 × 8. Cf. *GFL*, p. 531. Occ. 1139 × 48 (ib. no. 7); Hamo (I or II) also occ. 1149+, prob. 1151 × 7 (*Ctl. Worcester*, p. 69); 1164 × 79 (PRO E164/22, ff. 22–3); 1166+ (*Ctl. Trentham*, p. 316; cf. *GFL*, p. 531).

Hamo II *c.* 1155(?)–1166+ See above.

William –1188 Occ. 1180 × 4 (PRO E164/22, f. 23). Res. 1188 in visitation (*Ann. Waverley*, p. 245).

Richard 1188–1199 Sub-pr. Bordesley, el. 1188 (*Ann. Waverley*, p. 245). Occ. 1199 (Glos F., PRO transcripts). Res. 1199 (*Ann. Waverley*, p. 252).

William of Stoneleigh (?Pershore) 1199–1204 M. and abb. of Stoneleigh, q.v. *Ctl. Stoneleigh*, p. 251, indicates *c.* 1196 for his transfer to Bordesley, but this seems impossible: see above, and *Ann. Waverley*, p. 252, which places his el. in 1199. Ibid. calls him William of Stoneleigh; *Ctl. Stoneleigh* calls him William of Pershore. It is possible that we have two different men: more probable that he was known as 'of Pershore' at Stoneleigh, but as 'of Stoneleigh' elsewhere. Occ. *c.* Easter 1203 (*Warws F.*, no. 85). D. 1204 (*Ann. Waverley*, p. 256).

William Occ. ?1206 (Cheney, *Inn. III*, no. 732 and n.); (W.) n.d. (*Cal. Bodl. Chts.*, p. 685).

Philip[4] Occ. 7 June 1218 (*Ann. Worcester*, p. 409).

The next abb., Richard, occ. *c.* 20 Oct. 1222 (*Warws F.*, no. 325); and was presumably the abb. unnamed, who d. 1223 (*Ann. Waverley*, p. 298).

---

[1] A William 'quondam abb. de Binetona' occ. as author of some legends of Our Lady in Aberdeen Univ. MS 137, f. 132 (cf. also Cambridge, Sidney Sussex Coll. MS 95, f. 136). The relevant sections of the latter refer to John *abb.* of Forde and so were partly at least written +1191. Either William was writing as ex-abb., or he really belongs after John. The former seems more likely. (Ex. inf. C. J. Holdsworth.)

[2] See Wareham. [3] *Temp.* Nicholas, papal legate.

[4] It is just possible that the name is wrong, by confusion with abb. Philip who occ. 3 Nov. 1237 (*Warws. F.*, no. 553) to 6 Oct. 1247 (*Soms F.*, p. 130).

BOXLEY (Kent) (Clairvaux) f. 23 Oct. 1143 or 1146

List in *VCH Kent*, II, 155; basis in profession list, ed. C. E. Woodruff, in *Arch. Cant.*, XXXVII (1925), 54ff.; cf. Somner, I, app. xli, p. 51.

Lambert Bl. by Abp. Theobald *c.* 1143 (Saltman, p. 549; cf. p. 82, which gives 1146 – but see *KH*, p. 116; cf. also Gervase, II, 385). Occ. 1143 × 7 (*Reg.*, III, nos. 198–9).

Thomas M. Fontenay; bl. in Canterbury Cathedral 2 Mar. 1153 (profession: Woodruff, p. 56; 2 May 1152 in Gervase, I, 151; cf. II, 385).

Walter Bl. by Abp. Thomas, i.e. 1162 × 4 (profession: Woodruff, p. 56; attributed to Theobald, Gervase, II, 385).

John Bl. by Abp. Richard, 1174 × 84 (Gervase, II, 398; cf. Woodruff, p. 56); occ. 1178 × 88 (*Ctl. Oseney*, VI, p. 171).

Denis Bl. by Abp. Baldwin, 1184 × 90 (Gervase, II, 405; cf. Woodruff, p. 57).

William Occ. 29 June 1191 (Kent Archives Office DRc/T389/1).

Robert –1214 Occ. +1191 (*HMC De L'Isle and Dudley*, I, 42); (R.) 12 May 1196 (*FF.*, PRS, XVII, no. 142); 22 Apr. 1197 (*FF.*, PRS, XX, no. 114); (R.) 1193 × 8 (Lambeth MS 1212, f. 107v); (R.) 28 May 1208 (*Glam. Chts.*, III, p. 330); 6 Oct. 1212 (*Kent F.*, p. 51); d. 1214 (*Ann. Waverley*, p. 282).

John ?1216–1236 Said to have been pr. Robertsbridge, el. 1216 (*VCH*; but with a wrong reference). Occ. 20 Jan. 1219 (*Kent F.*, p. 61); res. 1236 to be abb. Cîteaux (*Ann. Waverley*, p. 316).

BRUERN (Oxon) (Waverley) f. 10 July 1147

List in *VCH Oxon*, II, 81 (H. E. Salter).

David Occ. 25 July 1163 (Bodl. Dodsworth MS 76, f. 18).

Richard –1176 D. 17 Jan. 1176 at Merton (*Ann. Waverley*, p. 240).

Christopher 1176–1187 Pr. of Bruern, el. Jan. 1176 (*Ann. Waverley*, p. 240); res. 1187 to be abb. of Waverley (ib., p. 244).

Geoffrey Occ. 15 Jan. 1195 (Madox, *Form.*, p. 218); 1198 × 1201 (Cheney, *Inn. III*, no. 361).

Jocelin Occ. (J.) 1203 (*CDF*, no. 147); 1206, 1207 (Glos F., PRO transcripts, II); 1200 × 18 (*Ctl. Oseney*, V, p. 96; cf. Cheney, *Inn. III*, no. 1158); n.d. (*Ctl. Sandford*, II, pp. 273–4; E. Marshall, *Hist. of Woodstock*, pp. 34–5).

W. Occ. j.d. + 11 Dec. 1214 (*Ctl. Oseney*, IV, pp. 206–7; cf. Cheney, *Inn. III*, no. 983). The next abb., Richard, was app. 1218 (*Ann. Waverley*, p. 291).

BUCKFAST (Devon) (Savigny) f. 1018 suppressed ?–1100 (Benedictine); 27 Apr. 1136 (Cistercian).

Lists in Oliver, p. 371; Dom John Stephan, *Buckfast Abbey* (revised edn. 1962), p. 33.

Ælfwine (Alwin) Occ. 1045 × 6 (*AS Chts.*, no. 105); *c.* 1066 in Exon. Domesday (*VCH Devon*, I, p. 432).

Eustace Occ. 18 Oct. 1143 (*HMC, Var. Coll.*, IV, 45).

William Occ. (W.) 1180 (Forde Abbey, Ctl. Forde, p. 470: –10 Aug.); (W.) 1186 × 91 (*HMC, Var. Coll.*, IV, 55); 1188 + [1] (*CDF*, no. 1274); *c.* 1199 (Dublin, Trinity MS. E. 5. 15, f. 56v).

Nicholas Abb. of Stanley; el. 1205 (*Wm. Newb.*, II, 508).

The next recorded abb., Michael, occ. 1223 (*Ctl. Buckfast*, nos. xx, lxix = *Reg. Grandisson*, III, pp. 1579, 1598).

---

[1] J.-d. of Pope Clement III (el. Dec. 1187).

BUILDWAS (Salop), St Mary and St Chad (Savigny) f. 8 Aug. 1135
  List in Eyton, *Salop*, VI, 332ff.; *VCH Salop* (M. Chibnall), forthcoming.
Ingenulf 1135–1155 First abb. (Eyton, *Salop*, VI, 321); occ. 1139×47[1] (ib., VI, 321–2); 1155[2] (*Reg. Lichfield*, no. 301; *SHC*, III, 183).
Ranulf[3] 1155–1187 Occ. 1155 (Eyton, *Salop*, VIII, 216–17); 26 Nov. 1156 (*Eccles. Docts.*, pp. 51–2); 1174×6, prob. 1175 (*Mon.*, V, 363)[4]; 1186×7 (Eyton, *Salop*, V, 62). D. 1187 on his way to the General Chapter (*Ann. Waverley*, p. 244).
?H. Occ. 1189×92 (*Eccles. Docts.*, p. 54). Possibly = Huctred below.
?William Occ. 1198×1208 (Eyton, *Salop*, VIII, 191 = *Ctl. Wombridge* in *Trans. Salop Arch. Soc.*, IX (1886), 317–18). 'Will'o' is undoubtedly the reading of the MS (BM Egerton MS 3712, f. 8v); but it may be a mistake for 'Vh'o' or the like; i.e. Huctred.
H. Occ. –1203 (CUL MS Dd. iii. 87(20), f. 24v); 1204 (Cheney, *Inn. III*, no. 525 and n. = *CRR*, V, p. 80).
Eustace Occ. 1206 (*Pleas before the King or his Justices*, III, no. 1870).
Huctred Occ. *c.* 1210 (Eyton, *Salop*, VII, 244); (H.) 1216×22 (ib., X, 336).
The next recorded abb., Stephen, occ. 28 Oct. 1227 (Eyton, *Salop*, II, 39).

BYLAND (Hood) (Yorks N.) (Savigny) f. (Calder, Cumberland) 10 Jan. 1135; (Hood) 1138; (Old Byland) Sept. 1142 (cf. Clay (1952), p. 10); (Stocking) 1147; (Byland) 30 Oct. 1177 C.T.C. Lists in Clay (1952), pp. 9ff.; *VCH Yorks*, III, 133. The dates of the first three are based on *Mon.*, V, 349–54, as corrected by Clay.
Gerald 1135–1142 M. Furness; d. 24 Feb. 1142 (not 1143: see Clay (1952), pp. 9–10).
Roger 1142–1196 M. Furness, sub-cellarer Calder, novice-master Hood. Occ. *c.* 1147 (Mowbray no. 198 = BM Egerton 2823, f. 83v); 1149 (*Mon.*, V, 570–1); 12 Jan. 1167 (*Vita Ailredi*, pp. 59–60, 62); 6 Apr. 1184 (*Ctl. Fountains*, I, 215); 1189 (*HMC Rutland*, IV, 75). Res. 1196; d. *c.* 1199.
Philip 1196–1197/8 Prev. abb. Lannoy ('Briostel', dioc. Beauvais, cf. Clay (1952), pp. 11–12n.).
Hamo Bl. 11 Oct. 1198 (Howden, IV, 77). Occ. Jan. 1200 (*Yorks F., John*, p. 2).
Hugh Occ. 1203 (*EYC*, II, no. 686n.); –1203 (*EYC*, II, no. 1054); (H.) 1204+ (*Ctl. Fountains*, II, p. 650; for dates see Clay (1952), p. 12).
Herbert Occ. 25 Nov. 1209 (*Yorks F., John*, p. 160); (H.) 1209×11 (*Ctl. Furness*, II, ii, p. 343).
Walter Occ. 1209×12 (*Yorks Deeds*, II, no. 144); *c.* 13 May 1212 (*Ctl. Fountains*, II, p. 626). Succeeded by R(obert) by *c.* 1219 (*Ctl. Sallay*, I, nos. 61–2).

CALDER II (Cumberland) (Furness) f. 1142×3 (for Calder I see Byland)
  List in *VCH Cumberland*, II, 177.
Hardred (Hardreus) 1142×3– M. of Furness; 1st abb. (*Mon.*, V, 350); occ. n.d. in *1160×80* (*Ctl. Furness*, II, iii, p. 793).
Walter Occ. *c.* 1161×84 (*Ctl. St Bees*, pp. 438–40, no. 440; cf. no. 441).
P. Occ. 1198×1202 (BM Cott. MS Nero D. iii, ff. 22v–23; cf. Cheney, *Inn. III*, no. 360 for date). Possibly the abb. dep. by General Chapter in 1200 (Canivez, I, 259).
David Occ. 1198×1208 (*Ctl. Furness*, II, iii, p. 775); 1208 (ib., I, ii, p. 440).

---

[1] Roger bp. Chester–Coventry went on crusade in 1147; d. 1148. Ingenulf is called 'Engen'' in BM Harl. MS 3650, f. 35 (–1148); 'Hengen'' in *SHC*, III, 183.
[2] Helias, archd. Staffs, was still archd., 11 Jan. 1155 (*SHC*, II, 233ff.); see below.
[3] Occ., evidently by error, as 'Robert' in 1182 (Eyton, *Salop*, VI, 328).
[4] Henry II 'Dei gratia', at Feckenham (+1174); Earl Richard of Pembroke (d. 1176). Prob. 1175; cf. Eyton, *Itinerary*, p. 196.

[CALDER II]
John 1211– Occ. 1210 × 21 (ib., II, iii, p. 712); n.d. (*Ctl. Furness*, II, ii, p. 57). Presumably the abb., unnamed, bl. 13 Dec. (*Ch. Melrose*, p. 55, f. 29).
G. Occ. 1214+ (*Ctl. St Bees*, no. 288, pp. 300–1).
The next recorded abb., Jolan, occ. from 1241 (*VCH* cites fines from 1241 to 1246).

CLEEVE (Soms) (Revesby) f. 25 June 1198
List in *VCH Soms*, II, 118.
Ralph 1198– First abb. occ. 1199 (*Bec Documents*, pp. 4–5, 12–13; cf. *Mon.*, V, 734).
William Occ. 1219 (*Soms F.*, I, no. 22).

COGGESHALL (Essex) (Savigny) f. 3 Aug. 1140
List in *VCH Essex*, II, 128.
William Occ. 1148 × 50[1] (*Ctl. Colne*, p. 57).
Simon de Toni 1167–1168 Second abb., m. of Melrose (*Ralph Cogg.*, p. 16; cf. *Ch. Melrose*, f. 21, p. 39); returned to Melrose 1168 (*Ralph Cogg.*, p. 16); 23 Jan. 1172 consecrated bp. of Moray (ibid., p. 17). According to the *Ch. Melrose* (f. 21, p. 39) he was el. bp. 1171. D. 17 Sept. 1184.
Odo 1169–1176 Third abb., el. 1169, d. 1176 (*Ralph Cogg.*, pp. 16, 18).
Peter 1176–1194 Fourth abb., m. of Vaudey, brother of Master Stephen, chancellor of Lincoln, el. 1176 (*Ralph Cogg.*, p. 18); occ. (P.) 1183 × 4[2] (*Ctl. Furness*, II, iii, 715); (P.) 1190 (*Acta Chichester*, no. 140); d. 1194 (*Ralph Cogg.*, p. 65).
Thomas 1194–1207 Fifth abb., m. of Coggeshall (*Ralph Cogg.*, p. 65); d. 1207 (ibid., p. 162).
Ralph 1207–1218 Sixth abb., m. of Coggeshall, el. 1207 (ibid., p. 162); res. 1218 after eleven years and two months on account of ill-health (ibid., p. 187).
Benedict of Stratford 1218–1223 Seventh abb., prev. abb. of Stratford Langthorne, el. 1218 and d. 1223 (*Ralph Cogg.*, pp. 187, 192).

COMBE (Warws) (Waverley) f. 10 July 1150
List in *VCH Warws*, II, 75.
Henry Occ. 1157 × 63[3] (*DC*, no. 58 = BM Harl. Cht. 52. G. 20).
Martin –1177 D. 11 May 1177 (*Ann. Waverley*, p. 241).[4]
Ralph 1177–1180 Cellarer of Combe, el. 1177; d. 1180 (ib., pp. 241, 242).
Erminfred 1180–1183 M. of Combe, el. 1180 (ib., p. 242); dep. 1183 (ib., p. 243).
William I 1183–1192 Pr. of Woburn, el. 1183 (ib., p. 243); occ. (W.) 1189 × 92 (*Eccles. Docts.*, p. 54); d. 1192 (*Ann. Waverley*, p. 248).
William II[5] Occ. 20 Jan. 1200 (BM Cott. MS Vitell. A. i, f. 58v); 1205 (*CRR*, III, p. 342); 1208 × 9 (*Warws F.*, no. 188); early 13th cent. (*Berkeley Chts.*, p. 45).
Michael –1234 Occ. (M.) 1217+ (*Ctl. Tutbury*, no. 264); 1223 × 4 (*Warws F.*, no. 342); 1227 (*CPR, 1225–1232*, p. 165); res. 1234 (*Ann. Waverley*, p. 315).

COMBERMERE (Ches), St Mary and St Michael (Savigny) f. 3 Nov. 1133
William 1133– First abb. occ. 1146 (*Mon.*, V, 628; *Ches. Chts.*, p. 1ff., q.v. for the date).
Geoffrey Occ. 1153 × 5, ?c. 1155 (Eyton, *Salop*, VIII, 216–17; cf. Buildwas).
Walter Occ. *c.* 1162 × 7[6] (*Glam. Chts.*, I, p. 153).

---

[1] At the dedication of Colne pr., said to be in 1148 – but we have not found the evidence for this date.
[2] B. abb. Cîteaux: see *GC*, IV, 989.   [3] Walter sheriff (of Lincs).
[4] Calling Martin first abb. Henry occ. in an original cht., so the *Ann.* is likely to be mistaken – but an error in the name of one or other is possible.
[5] Walter occ. 8 July 1200 (*SHC*, III, 170); presumably an error for William.
[6] Jollanus abb. Savigny (*HF*, XIV, 519; cf. XII, 781).

John   Occ. 1172×81,[1] 1172×87 (*Ctl. Whalley*, I, 14–15, II, 532–3).

Thomas   was apparently dep. *c.* April 1201 (*CRR*, I, p. 454, II, p. 9); but either he or another of the same name[2] was abb. again by 1203×4 (T.: Cheney, *Inn. III*, no. 542); also occ. (T.) 1215×23 (*Ctl. Dieulacres*, p. 311); (Thomas) 29 Aug. 1228 (*CPR, 1225–32*, p. 223). The next abb., Robert, occ. +1228, *?1230×2* (*SHC*, 1911, p. 423; cf. Dieulacres).

CROXDEN (Staffs) (Aunay-sur-Odon)   f. 1176 (at Cotton); 19 May 1178 (at Croxden)
List in *VCH Staffs*, III, 230 (A. P. Duggan and M. W. Greenslade); Ann. and list in BM Cott. MS Faust. B. vi.

Thomas of Woodstock   1178–1229 1st abb., el. 28 May 1178, abb. 51½ years, d. 4(?) Dec. 1229 (Ann., ff. 72–73v; list, f. 92); occ. 27 Apr. 1208 (*Lincs F.*, PRS LXVII, no. 235); 1229 (*CRR*, XIII, no. 1557).

CWMHIR, *see* **ABBEY CWMHIR**

CYMMER (Merioneth) (Abbey-Cwmhir)   f. 1198×9
Esau   occ. 1209 (*Mon.*, V, 459).

DIEULACRES (Staffs), St Mary and St Benedict (Combermere)   f. 12 May 1158 (at Poulton); 1 May 1214 (at Dieulacres)
List in *VCH Staffs*, III, 234 (A. P. Duggan and M. W. Greenslade).

Ralph   Occ. 1191×1211[3] (*Ctl. Whalley*, I, p. 11).

Richard   First abb. Dieulacres; occ. 1214 and + (*CRR, 1339–41*, pp. 204–5; *SHC*, 1913, p. 73).

Robert[4]   Occ. 1216×19(?)[5] (BM Harl. MS 3868, f. 7); 3 Nov. 1228 (*Lancs F.*, p. 55); 1228 (*CRR*, XIII, no. 825).

DORE, *see* **ABBEY DORE**

DUNKESWELL (Devon) (Forde)   f. 16 Nov. 1201
List in Oliver, p. 394.

Gregory   Occ. 1202 (*Ann. Margam*, p. 26); n.d. (Forde Abbey, Ctl. Forde, p. 213).

William   Occ. 1201×19 (*Ctl. Canonsleigh*, no. 62).

John   Occ. 19 Mar. 1219 (*Dorset F.*, p. 24).[6]
The next recorded abb., Richard, occ. 25 July 1228 (*Devon F.*, no. 152).

FLAXLEY (Dene) (Glos) (Bordesley)   f. 30 Sept. 1151
List in *VCH Glos*, II, 96 (Rose Graham), from *Ctl. Flaxley*, pp. 85–6.

Waleran   –1188 Dep. in 1188 in visitation (*Ann. Waverley*, p. 245).

Alan   1188– M. of Bordesley, el. 1188 (ib., cf. *Ctl. Flaxley*, nos. 31, 44 etc.).

Richard   Occ. *?c.* 1200: in *Ctl. Flaxley*, no. 44, A(lan) occ. as recent predecessor of Richard – not necessarily immediate predecessor (both temp. Roger de Bosco); n.d.[7] (ib., nos. 40–3, 48–9 etc.).

---

[1] Between the f. of Stanlow abbey and death of Hugh earl of Chester; prob. not 1174–7 when Earl Hugh was in disgrace.
[2] Unless the *CRR* mislead and Thomas's predecessor was dep. in 1201.
[3] Roger de Lacy: see *Ches Chts.*, p. 19.
[4] R. occ. 1214×26 (*Berkeley Chts.*, no. 150): ?Richard or Robert.
[5] Ralph of Maidstone not treasurer of Lichfield (*Reg. Lichfield*, no. 358); but he occ. without title in 1221 (ib., no. 306); by 1222 he was archd. Chester (*Ctl. Whalley*, I, pp. 43–4).
[6] An abb. of Dunkeswell, prob. John, d. 1223 (*Ann. Waverley*, p. 298).
[7] The MS (now lost) was 13th cent.

[FLAXLEY]

Roger Occ. 1209×10 (Glos F., PRO transcripts, II); (R.) 2 Oct. 1214 (PRO C115/A 1, K2/6683, sec. viii, no. 80).

The next recorded abb., Osmund, occ. Easter 1229 (*CRR*, XIII, no. 1707).

FORDE (Dorset, formerly Devon) (Waverley) f. 3 May 1136 (at Brightley); 1141 (at Forde)

List in Oliver, pp. 339–40.

Richard 1136– 1st abb., m. of Waverley, d. –1141 at Brightley (Oliver, p. 342 = *Mon.*, v, 378).

Robert of Penington 2nd abb.; m. of Waverley, el. –1141 (ib.); occ. 1155 (*CDF*, no. 819: see Revesby); 1168 (BM Harl. MS 6974, f. 30, citing lost Ctl. Plympton: see Davis, no. 780).

Baldwin –1180 Archd. Totnes *c.* 1161–1169/70 (last occ. 29 Sept. 1169), then m. of Forde (Morey, pp. 120–1, 127). Occ. 1169×75 (*Glam. Chts.*, 1, p. 146); 28 July 1177 (*Morey*, p. 141); (B.) 15 Jan. 1179/80 (*Ctl. Boxgrove*, no. 61); res. 1180 to be bp. of Worcester (*Ann. Waverley*, p. 241); 1184 el. archbp. of Canterbury, d. 1190.

Robert 1180–1190 Occ. 1180×4 (*Reg. St Osmund*, 1, p. 224); (R.) +1186 (*HMC Wells*, 1, 40); d. 1190 (*Ann. Margam*, p. 21; ?at Acre, *Gesta Henrici II*, 11, 147).

John of Forde 1191–1214 Prev. abb. of Bindon (*Ann. Margam*, p. 21); occ. 1195, 1195×8 (*HMC Var. Coll.*, IV, 57); 1200 (*Ped. Fin.*, 11, p. 76); 1209×10 (ib., p. 98); d. 21 Apr. 1214 (*Ann. Waverley*, p. 281). On him see C. J. Holdsworth, in *TRHS*, 5th series, XI (1961), 118ff.; *Vita Wulfrici*.

Roger 1214–1236 Sub-pr. of Forde, app. 1214 (*Ann. Waverley*, p. 282); occ. 1 June 1228 (*Devon F.*, no. 151); 1235 (*Soms F.*, 1, p. 97); res. 1236 (*Ann. Waverley*, p. 316).

FOUNTAINS (Yorks W.) f. 27 Dec. 1132

C.T.C. Lists in *VCH Yorks*, III, 137–8; Clay (1952), pp. 13ff.; early history in *Mem. Fountains*, I, *passim*;[1] ch. of the abbots, ib., pp. 130–55 – 15th cent., but 'carefully compiled', giving regnal periods, ignoring vacancies, and noting months and days according to the lunar calendar: Clay (1952), pp. 13–15. These calculations are noted by Clay and precisely checked, and so not repeated here.

Richard 1132–1139 Pr. of St Mary's, York, el. confirmed 27 Dec. 1132 (*Mem. Fountains*, I, 130); d. at Rome 30 Apr. 1139 (ib., I, 72, 130).

Richard II –1141–1143 Pr. Fountains, formerly sacrist, St Mary's, York. Occ. 16 Sept. 1141 (ib., 11, 63); d. Clairvaux 12 Oct. 1143 (ib., 1, 130). As the Ch. of the abbots ignores vacancies, the date of his and of some other els. cannot be calculated.

Henry Murdac 1143–1153 Master at York; m. Clairvaux, abb. Vauclair, el. +Oct. 1143; prob. 1144 (ib., 1, 84, cf. Clay (1952), p. 16n.); occ. 29 Jan. 1146 (*EYC*, 1, no. 79); el. abp. York, July, consec. 7 Dec. 1147; d. 14 Oct. 1153 (*Mem. Fountains*, 1, 102–3 and n.; cf. Knowles, *Historian and Character*, pp. 87ff.). From 1147–53 his successors at Fountains were suffragan abbs. under him. The next two abbs. are not numbered in the list. *DNB*.

Maurice 1148 M. and abb. Rievaulx (1145–7); app. by Abp. Henry on a visit to Fountains (i.e. early 1148?). Res. within three months and returned to Rievaulx (ib., 1, 104, 131; cf. Clay (1952), p. 17).

Thorald 1148–1150 M. of Rievaulx. Res. ?1150 (*Mem. Fountains*, 1, 105); occ. 28 Feb. 1150 (*Mon.*, v, 420); abb. Trois Fontaines (Champagne) *c.* 1151.

---

[1] On the sources for the early history of Fountains, see D. Nicholl, *Thurstan archbishop of York* (York, 1964), chap. VI and pp. 251ff.; D. Bethell, in *Journ. Eccl. Hist.*, XVII (1966), 11ff.; L. G. D. Baker in *Northern History*, IV (1969), 29–43; *Analecta Cisterciensia*, XXV (1969), 14–41.

Richard III *c.* **1150–1170** Described as 4th abb.; native of York; precentor of Clairvaux; abb. Vauclair; suffragan abb. of Fountains until death of Abp. Henry 14 Oct. 1153 (*Mem. Fountains*, I, 108, 131). D. 31 May 1170 (ib., I, 132, 154; cf. Clay (1952), p. 18n.).

Robert 1170–1180 Described as 5th abb.; prev. abb. Pipewell. D. Woburn 9 Jan. 1180 (*Mem. Fountains*, I, 115, 132).

William *c.* **1180–1190** Described as 6th abb.; prev. Aug. can. of Guisborough; abb. of Newminster (Northumberland) *c.* 1159–*c.* 1180; d. 6 Nov. 1190 (*Mem. Fountains*, I, 115–16, 132).

Ralph Haget 1190/1–1203 Described as 7th abb. Son of Bertram Haget (see Clay (1952), p. 19n.); m. of Fountains; abb. of Kirkstall; d. 4 June 1203 (ib., I, 117, 122, 133).

John of York 1203–1211 Described as 8th abb.; prev. cellarer of Fountains; abb. of Louth Park (*Mem. Fountains*, I, 125, 128, 133). Occ. 1203 (*EYC*, II, no. 686n.; for date, cf. Clay, p. 12); Jan. 1210 (*Yorks F., John*, p. 162). D. 14 June 1211 (*Mem. Fountains*, I, 133).

John II 1211–1219/20 Bl. at Melrose 13 Dec. 1211 (*Ch. Melrose*, p. 55).[1] El. bp. of Ely –21 Jan., consec. 8 Mar. 1220 (*Mem. Fountains*, I, 171; cf. *CPR, 1216–25*, p. 224; Ann. Southwark–Merton, BM Cott. MS Faust. A. viii, f. 142).[2] D. 6 May 1225 (*Mem. Fountains*, I, 134).

FURNESS (Lancs) (Savigny) f. 4 July 1124 (Tulketh); 1127 (Furness)
Lists in *VCH Lancs*, II, 130 (F. M. Powicke); *Ctl. Furness*, I, iii, pp. xxvff.; cf. II, iii, pp. xi, 836; based on medieval list in *Ctl.* I, i, pp. 8–10. This list is very misleading, and for the most part is ignored here.[3]

Ewan of Avranches 1124–*c.* 1138 First abb.; m. Savigny (*Ctl.* I, i, pp. 8, 21, cf. 121). Res. abb. Savigny ('Euanus Anglicus') after d. abb. Geoffrey 8 July 1138 (1138: Torigny, ed. Delisle, II, 189, cf. 161; cf. for Geoffrey's death Sauvage in *An. Bollandiana*, I, 408 (1139); Ch. Savigny in *HF*, XII, 781 (1138)). The list distinguishes two men, Ewan and Eudo de Surdevalle, and 'Eudo' occ. *c.* 1139 (–1139: *Ctl.*, II, iii, pp. 708–9); Eudo is clearly a different name from Ewan, but the confusion of the list suggests that two men

---

[1] *Ch. Melrose* gives no name, but it is almost certain that it must refer to John II.

[2] For the date, cf. Clay, pp. 20–1.

[3] The list is in two parts: first a general list of abbs., which seems to be reasonably accurate from *c.* 1220 or a little later to the early 15th cent.; then a list of those who had been abb. for more than ten years, and so qualified for entries 'in mortuario suo'. The full list down to mid-13th cent. may be summarised thus (retaining original spelling):

Eudo de Sourdevalle, Michaelis de Lancastre, Petrus de Eboraco (abb. when submission of Savigny to Clairvaux took place), Ricardus de Baiocis (m. Savigny), Johannes de Cawncefeld, Walterus de Millum, Joslenus de Pennyngton, Conanus de Bardoule, Willelmus Niger (formerly abb. Swineshead), Girardus Bristaldun, Michael de Dalton, Ricardus de Sancto Quintino, Radulphus de Fletham (formerly abb. Swineshead), Johannes de Newby, Stephanus de Ulverstona, Nicholas de Meaux (canon of Warter, m. Meaux, bp. Sodor), Robertus de Dentona (formerly abb. Swineshead), Laurencius de Acclome...

The short list, of longer-lived abbs., contains only Ewan, John de Cawncefeld, William Niger, Ralph de Fletham, Robert de Dentona.

It is clear that there is a sound tradition behind some of this, but also that none of the details can be relied on unless supported by other evidence. No other Cistercian house had so many short-lived abbots, and it sits on the surface of the list that there are too many abbs. here – and probably too many ex-abbs. of Swineshead. Other evidence crowds some of them out and it is highly probable that John of Cawncefeld was really the mid-13th-cent. abbot's seneschal of that name (cf. *Ctl. Furness*, II, iii, pp. 744, 756). In our list some of the information has been used with caution, some of the surnames noted; but no attempt has been made to fit in abbs. only recorded in the list. How the confusion arose – by misunderstanding of some annalistic material, probably, and of calendars or the 'Mortuarium', almost certainly – is matter for intriguing speculation.

[FURNESS]

> have been made out of one. Ewan occ. as 'Yvo' in *Ch. Man*,[1] p. 62, s.a. 1134, but following events of 1135; also occ. *Ctl.*, I, ii, pp. 456, 482; II, iii, pp. 780–1.

Peter (? of York) –*c.* 1150 Occ. 1147; res. *c.* 1150 (*Ctl.*, I, i, pp. 8–9; II, iii, pp. 730–3; cf. Delisle in *Journ. Brit. Arch. Ass.*, VI (1851), 420–2; Auvry, III, 9ff.; *VCH Lancs*, II, 115); later (–1161) abb. Quarr; q.v.

Richard (? of Bayeux) M. Savigny, el. *c.* 1150, abb. a short time (*Ctl.* ,I, i, p. 9; cf. Auvry, *VCH*, loc. cit.).

John Occ. 1152 (*Ctl. Furness*, I, iii, pp. 591–5); 1155 (*CDF*, no. 819; cf. Revesby); 1158 (*Lancs PR*, p. 308). 'De Cauncefeld' in list, *Ctl.* I, i, 9; see p. 133 n. 1. Cf. Auvry, loc. cit.

?Walter Occ. ?16 Aug. 1175: according to *Ctl. Furness*, I, i, p. 9, the bull in ib., I, iii, 537–9 = *PUE*, I, no. 122, whose protocol is now lost, was addressed to Abb. Walter of Millom.

Jocelin (? of Pennington) Occ. 1181 × 5 (*PUE*, I, no. 223); n.d. (*Dep. Keeper's Repts.*, XXXVI (1875), 167). Just possibly the J. who was abb. Savigny 1164–79 and occ. as ex–abb. in *Eccl. Docts.*, p. 53 (*c.* 1180: see Neath).

Michael (? of Dalton) Occ. 1194 × 8 (*PUE*, I, no. 346).

Ralph (? de Fletham) M. Furness, prev. abb. Swineshead (*Ctl.*, I, i, p. 19: cf. Swineshead). Occ. (R.) 1194 × 1205 (*Lancs PR*, p. 339; *Ctl. Cockersand*, III, ii, p. 1039); (R.) 1198 × 1202 (BM Cott. MS Nero D. iii, ff. 22v–23; cf. Cheney, *Inn. III*, no. 360); 29 Sept. and 25 Dec. 1209; 1209 × 11 (*Ctl. Furness*, II, ii, pp. 577, 343). D. at Mellefont 1210 × 11 (*Ch. Man*, p. 80, s.a. 1189).[2]

Nicholas 1211–*c.* 1219 Prev. can. Warter, m. Meaux (cf. *Ch. Meaux*, I, 380); occ. 1211 (*Ctl. Furness*, II, ii, pp. 576–7) and so the abb. unnamed who was bl. 13 Dec. 1211 (*Ch. Melrose*, f. 29, p. 55); occ. (N.) 1211 × 14 (*Ctl. Guisborough*, II, p. 319). Bp. Isles –9 Nov. 1219 to 1224 × 5 (res.) (cf. *Ctl. Furness*, II, iii, p. 712; J. Dowden, *The Bishops of Scotland* (Glasgow, 1912), pp. 274–5). N. abb. Furness occ. with N. bp. Isles in PRO DL 27/111.

?William Prev. abb. Swineshead, then abb. Furness, acc. to *Ctl.*, I, i, p. 9; and a William abb. S. occ. 1200–9+; also a William *quondam* abb. Furness ?'1200–16' (*Ctl.*, II, ii, p. 477). But this may be the later William, who occ. 18 Nov. 1246 (*Ctl.*, II, ii, p. 434)·

Gerard Occ. *c.* 1219 × 5[3] (*Ctl. Sallay*, II, no. 417); n.d. (PRO, DL 25/449); ? = G. n.d. (*Ctl. Furness*, I, i, p. 246; *Ctl. Sallay*, I, no. 372).

Robert Occ. frequently from (R.) 24 Jan. 1225 (?1226) (BM Egerton MS 2823, f. 78r–v = *Ctl. Fountains*, I, p. 217); (Robert) 1 Jan. 1230 (?1231) (*Ctl. Furness*, I, ii, pp. 441–2), etc. to (R.) 14 May 1235 (*Ctl. Furness*, I, i, 253–4). According to *Ctl.* I, i, p. 9, Robert de Dentona, prev. abb. Swineshead.

GARENDON (Leics) (Waverley) f. 28 Oct. 1133

> List in *VCH Leics*, II, 7 (R. A. McKinley).

Robert Occ. ?1139 × 48[4] (*Reg. Lincoln*, II, no. 324); 1144 × 5 (*PUE*, I, no. 31).

Godfrey Occ. (G.) *c.* 1146 (Mowbray, no. 155); 1147 (*Reg. Lincoln*, III, no. 921); 1155 (*CDF*, no. 819).

---

[1] The *Ch. Man* is a 13th-cent. compilation evidently taken from diverse sources not adequately digested: thus of the two entries referring to abbs. Furness the first seems slightly, the second much out of context. But both are probably based on good tradition, as the close links between Furness and Man would lead us to expect (the entries have been checked against the MS, BM Cott. MS Julius A. vii).

[2] 'Rodolfus.' The date is impossible: it seems likely that the entry has slipped from 1210, the only year in the 1210s with an annal in *Ch. Man* before 1217.

[3] The editor's date (1227) is too late, since Robert de Percy witnesses as rector of Gargrave (i.e. –Jan. 1226: see Sir Charles Clay and N. K. M. Gurney, *Fasti Parochiales*, IV, Yorks Arch. Soc., Rec. Series, CXXXIII, pp. 45–6). We are much indebted to Sir Charles Clay for help on Abb. Gerard.

[4] Abbot of 'Geuedona'; with Gervase, abb. of Louth Park and Roger d'Ameri not yet precentor of Lincoln (*GFL*, pp. 117–18n.).

?Robert[1] Occ. *c.* 1153 (*Ctl. Trentham*, p. 300).

Thurstan –1189 Occ. 1155×65 (Nichols, *Leics*, III, 805–6); 1155×9, prob. 1158×9[2] (*CDF*, no. 1062); *c.* 1173×4 (*EYC*, IV, no. 92); d. 1189 (*Ann. Waverley*, p. 246).

William 1189–1195 Pr. of Garendon, el. 1189 (ib.); res. 1195 (ib., p. 250); occ. 1193×5 (see Ralph, pr. Breedon).

Reginald 1195– Abb. of Merevale, el. 1195 (ib., p. 250); occ. n.d. (*Berkeley Chts.*, no. 444); (R.)? 1198×1203 (Cheney, *Inn. III*, no. 665); 1202×3 (Leics F., PRO transcripts, v).

Adam –1219 Res. 1219 to be abb. of Waverley (*Ann. Waverley*, p. 292).

HOLM CULTRAM (Abbey Town) (Cumberland) (Melrose) f. 30 Dec. 1150
List in *VCH Cumberland*, II, 172.

Everard 1150–1192 First abb., can. of Kirkham, m. of Melrose (*Ch. Melrose*, f. 19, p. 35); d. 1192 (ib., f. 25v, p. 48).

Gregory 1192– Sub-cellarer of Holm, el. 1192 (*Ch. Melrose*, loc. cit.).

William de Courcy –1215 Occ. 1203×14 (*Ctl. Holm Cultram*, no. 23); (W.) *c.* 1210 (*Ctl. Guisborough*, II, p. 319); res. 16 Nov. 1215 to be abb. of Melrose (*Ch. Melrose*, f. 32, p. 61), 31 Aug. 1216 became abb. of Rievaulx (*Ch. Melrose*, f. 33, p. 63); d. 1 Feb. 1223 or 1224 (see Rievaulx).

Adam of Kendal 1215–1223 Occ. (A.) 1215×23 (*Ctl. Holm Cultram*, no. 23a); res. 1223 (*Ch. Melrose*, f. 39v, p. 76).

JERVAULX (Wensleydale) (Yorks N.) (Byland from Fors) f. (Fors, Yorks N.) 1143;[3]
10 Mar. 1150 (as abb.); (Jervaulx) 1156
C.T.C. Lists in Clay (1952), pp. 21ff.; *VCH Yorks*, III, 142.

John of Kinstan 1149/50–*c.* 1185 M. Furness, Byland (i.e. Calder and Hood: *Mon.*, v, 349, 571). First abb. Jervaulx (grave slab: W. H. St John Hope in *YAJ*, XXI, 319). Occ. 1155 (*CDF*, no. 819: see Revesby); 1179+ (*c.* 1180: *Eccl. Docts.*, pp. 53–4; see Neath); as former abb. in 1190 (Canivez, I, 131).

Y. Occ. *c.* 1185 (*Ctl. St Bees*, nos. 86–7; cf. no. 82n.; Clay (1952), p. 22).

William Third abb. (grave slab: *YAJ*, XXI, 319); occ. 1198 (*Ctl. Fountains*, I, p. 216); 7 Nov. 1208 (*Yorks F., John*, p. 141); 1209×11 (*Ctl. Furness*, II, ii, p. 343).

Thomas Occ. 1 July 1218 (*Yorks F., 1218–31*, p. 2); 1219×23 (*Ctl. Fountains*, I, p. 200). Succeeded by Eustace (5th abb.) before May 1224 (*Yorks F., 1218–31*, p. 56; cf. *YAJ*, XXI, 319).

KINGSWOOD (Glos, formerly Wilts) (Tintern) f. 7 Sept. 1139 (at Kingswood); *c.*
1149/50 (at Hazelton); *c.* 1150×4 (at Tetbury); Kingswood II, *c.* 1164 or 1166×*c.* 1170 (at Kingswood). (On all this, see *GFL*, pp. 510ff.).
List in *VCH Glos*, II, 101 (R. Graham).

Thomas 1139– First abb., prev. pr. of Tintern (*GFL*, pp. 105–6).

Payne (Pagan) Occ. 1157×61 as abb. Tetbury (*Mon.*, v, 426; cf. *GFL*, p. 512).

Hugh –1180 Dep. 1180 (*Ann. Waverley*, p. 242; *Mon.*, v, 426).

William 1180–1181 Cellarer of Forde (*Ann. Waverley*, p. 242); dep. 1181 (ib.); 1184 became abb. of Thame (*Ann. Waverley*, p. 243).

Eudo 1181–1188 Pr. Waverley (*Ann. Waverley*, p. 242); res. to be abb. of Tintern, 1188 (ib., p. 245).

William II 1188– Prev. pr. Kingswood, el. 1188 (ib., p. 245); occ. 1190×1220 (*Berkeley*

---

[1] Abbot 'G...' and so it is far from certain that he was abb. Garendon, but if the reading is correct a likely alternative is not easy to find. He occ. with William abb. Radmore and Ranulf earl of Chester.
[2] Cf. Clay, *Fasti*, p. xiii n.
[3] A small settlement of brother Peter and some ms. from Savigny (*Mon.*, v, 568).

[KINGSWOOD]

Chts., no. 36; cf. *CP*, II, 126); 1198 × 1210, 1206, 1206 × 7 (Cheney, *Inn. III*, nos. 874–5, 732 and n., 736); 19 Oct. 1210 (Gloucester Cathedral, Reg. A, f. 97 v).

The next recorded abb., John, occ. 22 July 1241 (*Berkeley Chts.*, no. 273).

KIRKSTALL (Yorks W.) (Fountains) f. (Barnoldswick) 19 May 1147; (Kirkstall) 19 May 1152 (cf. Clay (1952), p. 24)

C.T.C. Lists in Clay (1952), pp. 23ff.; *VCH Yorks*, III, 145. Basis in *Fundacio, Miscellanea*, Thoresby Soc., IV, pp. 173ff.

Alexander 1147–1182 M. and pr. of Fountains (*Fundacio*, pp. 174ff.; cf. *Mem. Fountains*, I, 90–3); d. 1182 (abb. 35 years, *Fundacio*, pp. 174, 181). Occ. 1155 (*CDF*, no. 819; cf. Revesby); 1167 × 74 (*Ctl. Fountains*, II, 740; cf. Clay (1952), p. 39n.).

Ralph Haget 1182–1190/1 Res. abb. Fountains 1190 or 1191 (abb. 9 years: *Fundacio*, pp. 181–3); d. 4 June 1203.

Lambert 1190/1–1192/3 M. of Fountains and Kirkstall (*Fundacio*, pp. 183–4); d. 1192 or 1193 (in 3rd year: *Fundacio*, p. 185).

Turgisius 1192/3–1201/2 M. of Fountains; res. and returned there after 9 years as abb. (*Fundacio*, pp. 185–6). Occ. 30 July 1195 (*Ctl. Guisborough*, II, no. 673); 1199 × 1203 (ib., no. 1164).

Elias 1202/3–*c.* 1204 M. of Roche (*Fundacio*, p. 186); succeeded 1202 or 1203; occ. 28 Feb. 1204 (*Yorks F., John*, p. 88).

Ralph of Newcastle *c.* 1204–1231/3 M. of Fountains (*Mem. Fountains*, I, 123); occ. (R.) +9 Dec. 1204 (*EYC*, III, no. 1560); Oct. 1209 (*Yorks F., John*, p. 157); 22 Sept. 1230 (*Reg. Greenfield*, II, p. 209); d. 6 Apr. 1231/3 (*Fundacio*, p. 187; cf. Clay (1952), p. 27).

KIRKSTEAD (Lincs) (Fountains) f. 2 Feb. 1139; (to Kirkstead II) 1187

List in *VCH Lincs*, II, 137–8.

Robert of Southwell[1] 1139– M. of St Mary's, York, then Fountains; 1st abb. Kirkstead (*Mem. Fountains*, I, 68; *Ch. York*, p. 1; *Ch. Meaux*, I, 74).

Walter Almoner of St Mary's, York, then m. of Fountains (*Ch. Meaux*, I, 74; *Ch. York*, p. 1); occ. 1147 (*Reg. Lincoln*, III, no. 921); 1148 × 50 (Lees, *Templars*, pp. 243–4); Aug. 1161 (ib., p. 246); 1164 (*Ctl. Rievaulx*, no. 246); 1174 (Bodl. MS Laud Misc. 642, f. 130 v).

Ralph Occ. 1174 × *c.* 1178 (Lincs Arch. Office, 3 Anc. 2/1, f. 10 v); n.d. (*DC*, no. 171).

Richard Occ. –1185[2] (Lincs Arch. Office, 5 Anc. 1/1/3 = *HMC 13th Rept.*, VI, 204); 1 May 1191 (*Lincs F.*, PRS LXVII, p. xxxvii); 22 Oct., 27 Nov. 1197 (*FF.*, PRS XXIII, nos. 61, 102); (R.) 1199 (*Rot. Cur. Reg.*, II, 28); (R.) 1198 × 1201 (Cheney, *Inn. III*, no. 363).

?H. Occ. Jan. × Mar. 1201 (Foreville, *S. Gilbert*, pp. 24–5).

Thomas Occ. 1202 (*Lincs Ass. Roll*, LRS XXII, no. 11); 20 June 1202, (T.) 27 Aug. 1206 (*Lincs F.*, PRS LXVII, nos. 32, 217).

William Occ. 18 Nov. 1208, 26 Nov. 1210 (*Lincs F.*, PRS LXVII, nos. 283, 316).

The next recorded abb., Henry, occ. *c.* 27 Jan. 1225, 30 Sept. 1231 (BM Cott. MS Vesp. E. xviii, f. 208 r–v).

LLANTARNAM (Caerleon) (Monmouth) (Strata Florida) f. 22 July 1179

Walter Occ. 1193 × 1218 (*Glam. Chts.*, VI, p. 2335).

LOUTH PARK (Lincs) (Fountains) f. 1137 (at Haverholme); 2 Feb. 1139 (at Louth Park)

List in *VCH Lincs*, II, 140–1.

---

[1] 'Siuella' in *Mem. Fountains*, I, 68; 'Stuteuyll' presumably by error, in *Ch. York*, p. 1.

[2] Simon de Crevequer (D. M. Stenton in *Lincs Assize Roll*, pp. lxxxff.; ex inf. D. Smith).

Gervase 1139– 1st abb.; prev. sub-pr. St Mary's, York, m. Fountains (*Mem. Fountains*, I, 68, cf. pp. 13, 26n.; *Ch. Meaux*, I, 74; Nicholl, *Thurstan*, pp. 159, 176, 240); res. before his death (see testament, ed. C. H. Talbot in *Analecta Sacri Ordinis Cisterciensis*, VII (1951), pp. 32ff.). Occ. 1147 (*Reg. Lincoln*, III, no. 921); mid-12th cent. (*Gilbertine Chts.*, pp. 104–5).

Ralph of Norway M. St Mary, York (and so presumably of Fountains: *Ch. St Mary's, York*, p. 1). Occ. 22 Jan. 1155 (Lees, *Templars*, pp. 241–2); 1155 (*CDF*, no. 819; see Revesby); 1163 (*DC*, no. 186); 1164 (*Ctl. Rievaulx*, no. 246); 1174 (Bodl. MS Laud Misc. 642, f. 130v); 1176×7[1] (*EYC*, II, no. 774).

John –1203 M. and cellarer Fountains (*Mem. Fountains*, I, pp. 125, 133). Occ. (J.) 1183×4 (*Ctl. Furness*, II, iii, p. 715; see Vaudey); 14 Oct.[2] 1197 (*FF*, PRS XXIII, no. 49); 3 Oct. 1202 (*Lincs F.*, PRS LXVII, no. 164); res. 1203 to be abb. Fountains (*Ann. Waverley*, p. 255).

Warin Occ. (W.) 1203×5 (*HMC Var. Coll.*, I, 236ff.); 1203×11 (*Reg. Lincoln*, V, no. 1614); 3 Nov. 1205 (*Lincs F.*, PRS LXVII, no. 203); 2 Aug. 1207 (ib., no. 228); 1213 (Bodl. MS Laud Misc. 625, f. 130v); 6 Sept. 1226 (*Lincs F.*, I, p. 215).

The next abb., Richard of Durham, m. Kirkstead, was el. 1227 (*Ch. Louth Park*, p. 12); occ. 1228 (*CPR, 1225–32*, p. 209).

MARGAM (Glam) (Clairvaux)   f. 21 Nov. 1147

Lists in *Arch. Camb.*, 3rd series, XIII, 313–14 (G. T. Clark); Birch, *Hist. Margam Abbey*, p. 375.[3]

William of Clairvaux 1147–1153 First abb. (*Ann. Margam*, p. 14; for name, see *Glam. Chts.*, I, p. 126); occ. 10 Mar. 1148 (just possibly for 1149; *Mon.*, V, 427; cf. *GFL*, p. 512n.); 12 Aug. 1150 (*CDF*, no. 816); 'discessit' 1153 (*Ann. Margam*, p. 14).

Andrew –1155 Second abb., d. 31 Dec. 1155 (*Ann. Margam*, p. 15).

Conan *c*. 1156–1193+ Occ. –1166,[4] 1169×75 (*Glam. Chts.*, I, pp. 147–8, 146); 1181×3 (*Ctl. Cirencester*, II, no. 421); 1188 (*Gir. Camb.*, VI, 67); 1193 (ib., I, 206: cf. p. 203, and for date, H. G. Richardson in *EHR*, LXXIV (1959), 201–2).

Roger Occ. 1193×1203 (*Arch. Camb.*, 3rd series, XIV, p. 33; cf. p. 52 (G. T. Clark)).

Gilbert –1213 M. Kirkstead (*Ann. Margam*, p. 32); occ. 20 Nov. 1203 (Cheney, *Inn. III*, no. 518); res. 17 June 1213, in visitation, and d. at Kirkstead 12 May 1214 (*Ann. Margam*, p. 32).

John of Goldcliff 1213–1236×7 El. 17 June 1213 (*Ann. Margam*, p. 32); occ. 1213×16 (*Ctl. St Mark's, Bristol*, no. 89); (J.) 1228 (*Glam. Chts.*, II, pp. 457ff.); 11×17 June 1234 (ib., II, pp. 490–1); d. Nov. 1236 or 24 Aug. 1237 (*Ann. Tewkesbury*, p. 101; Ann. in Domesday Breviate, PRO, E164/1, p. 33 = *Glam. Chts.*, III, p. 859 = *Welsh Episcopal Acts*, II, p. 714).

MEAUX (Yorks E.) (Fountains)   f. 1 Jan. 1151

C.T.C. Lists in Clay (1952), pp. 28ff.; *VCH Yorks*, III, 149. Based on *Ch. Meaux* and abbatial list (printed ib., I, 47–9).

---

[1] Henry II 'Dei gratia' (i.e. +1173), with Geoffrey provost of Beverley (d. 1177), chancellor of the young king (+1176: Diceto, I, 406; cf. Clay in *YAJ*, XXXVI, 411 (1947)).

[2] If this is the right translation of St Edward.

[3] Also *CTG*, VI, 188–9, which includes John '1170' and Conrad '1215', both evidently in error, since the early chts. in the Talbot collection (cited ibid.) are printed in *Glam. Chts.* and none supports these dates. (In II, p. 243, John's name is added by the ed., and in *Penrice and Margam MSS*, I, p. 11, nos. 26–7 are chts. re-dated 1213×34 and *c*. 1216 in *Glam. Chts.* II, pp. 471, 355).

[4] See Whitland.

[MEAUX]

Adam 1151–1160 M. Whitby, St Mary's, York, Fountains. First abb. Meaux. Res. 1160 (in 10th year); d. 1180 (*Ch. Meaux*, I, 73–4, 76, 107, 178n.). Occ. 13 June 1151, 23 Nov. 1156 (*EYC*, III, nos. 1383, 1388).

Philip 1160–1182 M. Kirkstead, abb. Hovedö (Norway), pr. Kirkstead. Abb. 22 years. D. 1182 (*Ch. Meaux*, I, 159, 178). Occ. 18 Dec. 1172, 22 June 1177 (*EYC*, III, nos. 1391–2).

Thomas 1182–1197 Pr. Meaux (18 years). Res. 1197 (in 15th year); d. 1202 (*Ch. Meaux*, I, 217, 234).

Alexander 1197–1210 M. Forde (Devon). Res. 1210 (in 14th year); d. 1212 (*Ch. Meaux*, I, 328–9). Occ. 1198 (*Gir. Camb.*, I, 94, 103); 1208 (*Yorks F., John*, p. 148).

Hugh 1210–1220 Pr. Meaux (over 5 years). El. 6 Dec. 1210. Res. 1220 (in 10th year); d. 1222 (*Ch. Meaux*, I, 353, 380). Occ. 1212 × 14 (*Bk. Seals*, no. 444); June 1219 (*Yorks F., 1218–31*, p. 33).

MEREVALE (Warws) (Bordesley) f. 10 Oct. 1148

List in *VCH Warws*, II, 78.

?Reginald Occ. –1159 (*Ctl. Burton*, p. 50).[1]

?H. Occ. prob. 1159 × 90 (*Ctl. Darley*, II, p. 576n.: see ed.'s note).

William –1192 Occ. *c.* 1171 × 81 (*Mon.*, IV, 221; see Breedon); d. 1192 (*Ann. Waverley*, p. 248).

Reginald *c.* 1192–1195 Res. 1195 to be abb. of Garendon (ib., p. 250).

Henry 1195– Sub-pr. of Merevale, el. 1195 (ibid.); occ. 1210 × 11 (*Warws F.*, no. 202).

John Occ. 1216 × 22 (*Burton Chts.*, nos. 72, 73).

The next recorded abb., William, occ. *c.* 1226 (*Ctl. Darley*, I, p. 179).

NEATH (Glam) (Savigny) f. 25 Oct. 1130

List in W. de G. Birch, *History of Neath Abbey*, pp. 51, 167; idem, *Hist. of Margam Abbey*, p. 333.

Richard 1130–1145 First abb.; d. 1145 (*Ann. Margam*, p. 14).

Ralph Occ. 12 Aug. 1150 (*CDF*, no. 816); 1169 × 75 (*Glam. Chts.*, I, p. 146).

Walter Occ. 1169 × 79 (BM Cott. MS Faust. A. iv, f. 6v); 1178 × 9[2] (*Eccles. Docts.*, pp. 52–3); 1191 (*Mon.*, II, 68); 1194 (*Gir. Camb.*, I, 206; cf. Lloyd, II, 579ff.); 1196 + (*Glam. Chts.*, I, no. 214, pp. 219–20).

Abraham Occ. (A.) 1201 (*Glam. Chts.*, II, p. 263); n.d. (*Gir. Camb.* IV, 131).

Clement –1218 D. 1218 (*Ann. Margam*, p. 33). Prob. prev. pr. (*Glam. Chts.*, II, p. 263).

NEWMINSTER (Northumberland) (Fountains) f. 5 Jan. 1138 (? for 1139)

Lists in *Ctl. Newminster*, pp. xiif.; *Arch. Aeliana*, 3rd Series, XII (1915), 206ff. (A. M. Oliver).

St Robert 1138/9–1159 First abb. (see *Vita*, ed. P. Grosjean, in *Ann. Boll.*, LVI (1938), 343–60, esp. pp. 345, 354–5); m. Whitby and Fountains (cf. *Sim. Dur.*, II, 300; *Mem. Fountains*, I, 60); d. 6 or 7 June 1159 (*Vita*, pp. 354–5 and 354n.; cf. p. 341). Occ. 1155 (*CDF*, no. 819; see Revesby). *DNB.*

William *c.* 1159–*c.* 1180 Can. Guisborough, m. Newminster; res. *c.* 1180 (+9 Jan. 1180) to be abb. Fountains, q.v.

Geoffrey Occ. (G.) 1185 (*PUE*, III, no. 475); late 12th cent. (*Ctl. Sallay*, I, no. 101); n.d. (*EYC*, II, no. 717); res. –1195 (cf. *Ctl. Newminster*, p. 120).

---

[1] William, earl of Ferrers (Derby), succ. 1159; Walter, bp. of Coventry d. 7 Dec. 1159 – unless Walter is misnamed and the document belongs to the 1190s.

[2] William (de Tolosa) abb. Savigny: Baluze, *Misc.*, II, 312; *c.* 20 years + 1157 and so not William de Dobra.

William Occ. 1189×95 (Durham, D. and C., 4. 1. Pont. 5); Mar. 1195 (Scammell, *Hugh du Puiset*, p. 260); (W.) j.d. +10 May 1197 (*Ctl. Guisborough*, II, p. 50); *c.* 1212 (–1213) (*Ctl. Sallay*, II, no. 644).

H. Occ. 1 June 1218 (*Ctl. Rievaulx*, p. 223).

Robert Occ. 20 Apr. 1220 (*Northumberland and Durham F.*, no. 59); j.d. 1224+ (*Ctl. Newminster*, p. 215).

PIPEWELL (Northants) (Newminster) f. 13 Sept. 1143

List in *VCH Northants*, II, 121; early 14th-cent. list (?*c.* 1320×2) in BM Cott. MS Otho B. xiv, f. 197 = *Mon.*, V, 433n.[1]

Geoffrey First abb. (list).

Robert Second abb. (list); occ. *c. 1160* (pal.: *DC*, no. 341); (Ro.) 1155×67 (BM Cott. MS Vitell. D. xviii, ff. 12v–13); res. 1170 to be abb. Fountains, q.v. (*Mem. Fountains*, I, 114–15).

Roger Occ. 11 Sept. 1193 (BM Stowe MS 937, f. 122); 25 Oct. 1197 (*FF.*, PRS XXIII, no. 72).

William Occ. 14 Nov. 1199 (BM Stowe MS 937, f. 118); 16 Nov. 1201 (*SHC*, IV, p. 260); 14 July 1205 (or 7 July if St Margaret = St M. of Scotland: BM Stowe MS 937, f. 121).

Robert (?of Pattishall)[2] Occ. 1209×10 (BM Cott. MS Calig. A. xiii, f. 145v); *c.* 13 Oct. 1211 (BM Stowe MS 937, ff. 23, 120v); ?1214×15 (Cheney, *Inn. III*, no. 1008); 1230 (*CPR, 1225–32*, p. 354); 17 Sept. 1235 (BM Stowe MS 937, f. 26 = Cott. Calig. A. xii, ff. 26v–27).

QUARR (Isle of Wight) (Savigny) f. 27 April 1132

List in *VCH Hants*, II, 139; MS list supplied by Dom S. F. Hockey of Quarr Abbey; see now Hockey, *Quarr Abbey*, pp. 259–60, 294–6.

Gervase Occ. –1147[3] (Madox, *Form.*, no. 497; BM Egerton MS 3667, f. 69v); 1141[4]×50 (Winchester Coll. Muniments, no. 17213); 1129×50 (Voss, p. 175).

William Occ. 12 Aug. 1150 (*CDF*, no. 816). Possibly the unnamed abb. who occ. 1146–7 (?1147–8) in *Mon.*, V, 569–71.

Peter El. *c.* 1150 or + (see Furness, of which he was prev. abb.; cf. *Ctl. Furness*, I, p. 9); occ. 1161 (BM Cott. MS Tib. D. vi, pt. i, f. 106); *c.* 1162×78,[5] possibly 1176+ (Gibbs, no. 169 = *Ctl. Clerkenwell*, no. 282).

Simon Occ. late 12th cent. (*Bk. Seals*, no. 214); (S.) 1189 (PRO E 326/8901).

William Occ. 1192 (*Mon.*, V, 426; cf. *GFL*, p. 510 and n.).

Walter Occ. ?1194+ (*Ctl. Sandford*, II, no. 294 with William, pr. of Quarr, prob. the next abb.); –1197 (NRA, Oxford, Queen's College, II, God's House, no. 945; cf. no. 310); 26 Jan. 1199 (*Devon F.*, no. 29).

William –1205 Res. 1205 (*Wm. Newb.*, II, 508).

H. Occ. 1206 (*Ctl. Canonsleigh*, no. 181).

John Occ. 24 Apr. 1219 (PRO CP 25 (1)/203/File 4, 30).

The next abb., Henry, occ. 29 Apr. 1228 (Madox, p. 374); 22 June 1228 (*Devon F.*, no. 228). An Abb. Philip also occ. early 13th cent. (PRO E 326/8887).

[1] Geoffrey, Robert, William 'quondam', Roger 'quondam', Robert, Roger 'quondam', William 'quondam', Robert 'de Pateshulle', William 'de Kynton' quondam',...William de Kynton' occ. as cellarer 1235 (BM Cott. MS Calig. A. xii, f. 27) and as abb. (W.) 1242 (BM Stowe MS 937, ff. 89v–90), 1247 (BM Cott. MS Calig. A. xiii, f. 67r–v. There seem clearly to be too many Rogers and Williams in the list, and it is possible that the five names above comprise the full list before William de Kynton'.   [2] See n. 1.

[3] 'Heldearius', i.e. Hildierius, abb. Lire, d. 1147 (Torigny, ed. Delisle, II, 155).

[4] Baldwin, earl of Devon.   [5] Jocelin abb. Savigny: see Baluze, *Misc.*, II, 311–12.

REVESBY (St Laurence) (Lincs), St Mary and St Laurence (Rievaulx)   f. 9 Aug. 1143
(cf. *Vita Ailredi*, p. xlv and n., 23ff., 27ff.)

List in *VCH Lincs*, II, 142.

St Ailred   1143–1147 M. and novice master of Rievaulx (*Vita Ailredi*, ut supra); res. 1147 to be abb. of Rievaulx, q.v.

?John   Occ. ?1149 (*Ctl. Bridlington*, p. 423); but possibly an error.

Walo (Gualo)   Occ. 1147 × 9 (*Rufford Chts.*, no. 748); 28 Feb. 1150 (*Mon.*, V, 420; see Rufford); (G.) 1147 × 53,[1] 22 Jan. 1155 (Lees, *Templars*, pp. 262, 241–2); (G.) 1152 × 5 (*Reg. Lincoln*, I, no. 133); (Galo) 1148 × 55 (*Ctl. Bridlington*, p. 351).

Philip   Occ. 1155 (*CDF*, no. 819);[2] 1155 × 60[3] (*Gilbertine Chts.*, p. 3); 1164 (*Ctl. Rievaulx*, no. 246); ?d. 1166 (*Ch. Ang. Pet.*, p. 99; cf. *Vita Ailredi*, pp. lxixf.).

Hugh   Occ. 1 Apr. 1172 (*Mon.*, V, 455); 1174 (Bodl. Laud MS Misc. 642, f. 130v); 1191 (BM Cott. MS Vesp. E. xviii, f. 147); 24 Nov. 1200 (*Lincs F.*, PRS XLVII, no. 16); 13 July 1202 (ib., no. 149); 1203 × 6 (*Reg. Lincoln*, I, no. 216; cf. no. 218).

Ralph   Occ. *early 13th cent.* (pal.: *DC*, no. 524); 20 Oct. 1208 (*Lincs F.*, PRS XLVII, no. 250).

Elias   1217– Abb. Rievaulx (q.v.), el. Dec. 1217 (*Ch. Melrose*, pp. 59, 68). Occ. 1230 (*CR*, *1227–1231*, p. 390); 8 or 20 July 1231 (*Lincs F.*, I, p. 229).

RIEVAULX (Yorks N.) (Clairvaux)   f. 5 Mar. 1132

C.T.C. Lists in *VCH Yorks*, III, 152; Clay (1952), pp. 31ff.

St William   1132–1145 M. of Clairvaux; d. 2 Aug. 1145 (*Ch. Melrose*, p. 34; C. Peers in *Arch. Journal*, LXXXVI (1929), 20–8). See Knowles, *MO*, pp. 228–30.

Maurice   1145–1147 Subpr. of Durham, succ. 1145, res. not later than Nov. 1147 (*Ch. Melrose*, p. 34); abb. Fountains for about three months in *c.* 1147–8 (*Mem. Fountains*, I, 104, 131), returned to Rievaulx (cf. Clay, p. 17, and n.). Prob. d. +1167 (Clay, p. 32 and n.).

St Ailred   1147–1167 Born 1110; m. and novice master Rievaulx; first abb. Revesby 1143–7; el. to Rievaulx before 30 Nov. 1147; d. 12 Jan. 1167 (*Vita Ailredi*, passim, esp. p. 62; Powicke's introd. to op. cit., esp. pp. xc–xciv; *MO*, pp. 240–5, 257–66. D. 11 Jan., Durham obit, Rud, p. 215).

Silvanus   1167–1188 Abb. Dundrennan (*Ch. Melrose*, p. 37); res. 1188, d. 9 Oct. 1189 (*Ch. Melrose*, pp. 46–7).

Ernald   1189–1199 Sixth abb. Melrose, el. 2 Mar. 1189 (*Ch. Melrose*, p. 47); res. 1199 (ib., pp. 49, 50); occ. 1189 (*CDF*, no. 1026; cf. Clay, p. 34n.); 1198 (Knowles, *MO*, p. 666).

William de Punchard[on]   1199–1203 El. 1199 (*Ch. Melrose*, p. 50); occ. 23 Jan. 1201 (*Yorks F., John*, p. 7); +4 June 1203 (*EYC*, II, no. 686n.); d. late 1203 (*Ch. Melrose*, p. 52; *Ann. Waverley*, p. 255; cf. Clay, p. 35).

Geoffrey   1204– M. of Rievaulx (*Ann. Waverley*, p. 255); el. abb. 1204 (*Ch. Melrose*, p. 52).

Warin   –1211 Occ. 11 Nov. 1208 (*Yorks F., John*, p. 143); d. 1211 (*Ch. Melrose*, p. 55).

Elias   1211–1215 Cellarer Rievaulx, succeeded Warin in 1211 (*Ch. Melrose*, p. 55); res. 1215 (ib., p. 59); el. abb. Revesby, Dec. 1217 (*Ch. Melrose*, pp. 59, 68).

Henry   1215–1216 Abb. Wardon (Beds) succeeded Elias 8 Apr. 1215 (*Ch. Melrose*, p. 59); d. at Rufford 1216 (ib., p. 63).

William III   1216–1223/4 Abb. of Holm Cultram; abb. of Melrose, el. 16 Nov. 1215; el. abb. Rievaulx 31 Aug. 1216 (*Ch. Melrose*, pp. 61, 63); d. 1 Feb. 1223 or 1224 (*Ch. Melrose*, p. 76, under 1223; *Ann. Waverley*, p. 299, under 1224).

---

[1] G. de Gant as earl (1147 + : *CP*, VII, 672–3); B. pr. Bridlington.
[2] Not –1155 (see above); and cf. Clay (1952), p. 33.
[3] Humphrey subdean of Lincoln d. 1160 (*Reg. Lincoln*, VII, p. 203 and n.).

ROBERTSBRIDGE (Salehurst) (Sussex) (Boxley), f. 29 Mar. 1176 (at Salehurst); ?*c.* 1250 (at Robertsbridge)

List in *VCH Sussex*, II, 73–4 (L. F. Salzman).

Denis Occ. 1183 × 4[1] (*HMC De L'Isle and Dudley*, I, 40).

William Occ. (W.) 1194 (*HMC De L'Isle and Dudley*, I, 43–4); 1195 (*Robertsbridge Chts.*, nos. 24–5); (W.) 1203+ (*Ctl. Lewes, Norfolk*, p. 33; cf. Cheney, *Inn. III*, no. 500); 1215 × 17 (*Ctl. Chichester*, p. 92); 1218 × 19 (*Sussex F.*, no. 162); 1222 (*Robertsbridge Chts.*, no. 285).

Nicholas Occ. 19 June 1222 (*Kent F.*, p. 76).

ROCHE (Yorks W.) (Newminster) f. 30 July 1147

C.T.C. Lists in Clay (1952), pp. 37ff.; *VCH Yorks*, III, 155. Based on medieval list from a MS formerly in St Mary's Tower, York (*Mon.*, V, 505).

Durand 1147–*c.* 1159 Presumably m. Newminster; first abb., in office 12 years (list). Occ. –1153 (*EYC*, I, no. 145).

Denis *c.* 1159–*c.* 1171 Abb. 12 years (list).

Roger of Tickhill *c.* 1171–*c.* 1179 Abb. 8 years (list); occ. *c.* 24 Mar. 1176 (*Ctl. Rievaulx*, no. 132).

Hugh of Wadworth *c.* 1179–*c.* 1184 Abb. 5 years (list).

Osmund *c.* 1184–*c.* 1213 Cellarer of Fountains; abb. 29 years ('39', list: see Clay (1952), p. 37). Occ. 1183 × 4 (*Ctl. Furness*, II, iii, p. 715); 7 Apr. 1186 (*Mon.*, V, 505); 12 Nov. 1208 (*Yorks F., John*, p. 146); *c.* 1212 (*Ctl. Sallay*, II, no. 644).

Reginald *c.* 1213–*c.* 1228 ?M. Roche (Clay (1952), p. 38n.); abb. 15 years (list); occ. Jan. 1223 (*Lincs F.*, I, 165); +16 Oct. 1224 (*Ctl. Sallay*, I, no. 219); succeeded by Richard in or about 1228 (–8 Sept. 1229: *CPR, 1225–32*, p. 305).

RUFFORD (Notts) (Rievaulx) f. 13 July 1146

C.J.H. List in *VCH Notts*, II, 104; and by Dr C. J. Holdsworth in *Chts. of Rufford Abbey* (Thoroton Soc., forthcoming).

Gamel Occ. 28 Feb. 1150 (*Mon.*, V, 420); (G.) 1149 × 55 (*Ctl. Bridlington*, p. 423; cf. p. 351). Cf. epitaph in Laurence of Durham (Surtees Soc., LXX, p. 77, and ed. J. H. Mozley, *Medium Aevum*, XI (1942), 1–45, esp. 1–4, 33).

Elias Occ. 1155 (*CDF*, no. 819; see Revesby); (?) 8 Nov. 1156 (*PUE*, I, no. 62); 20 Nov. 1160 (ib., no. 80); ?1160 × ?1176 (*EYC*, II, no. 1174 = *Bk. Seals*, no. 88).

Matthew Occ. *c.* 1174 (*EYC*, XII, no. 112); 1161 × *c.* 1176, 1161 × 81 (*Rufford Chts.*, nos. 202, 690); 1189 × 1201 (*EYC*, III, no. 1411; for date cf. XII, no. 112n.).

William Occ. 1189 × 95 (Durham D. and C., 3. 1. Pont. 4. 19; 4. 1. Pont. 5); 1194 × 9 (Dublin, Trinity Coll. MS E. 5. 15, f. 56v = *Mon.*, VI, ii, 924–5); Mar. 1195 (Scammell, pp. 258, 260, 262); 1196 × 1202 (*Revesby Chts.*, ed. E. Stanhope, p. 20).

Ernisius –1203 Occ. *c.* 3 Feb. 1202 (*Pleas before King or his Justices*, III, Selden Soc., p. 58, no. 583); 24 July 1202 (*Rufford Chts.*, nos. 432–3); d. 1203 (*Ch. Melrose*, f. 27, p. 51).

?William Occ. 1204 × 5 (Notts F., PRO transcripts): possibly a reference to the former abb.

Walter Occ. *c.* 13 Oct. 1211 (*EYC*, XII, p. 137 = *Rufford Chts.*, no. 307); 25 July 1215 (*Rot. Lit. Pat.*, p. 150b). Ill in 1217 and so possibly d. *c.* 1217 (Canivez, I, 469).

The next recorded abb., Robert, occ. 13 Nov. 1219 (*Reg. Lincoln*, VIII, p. 113n.).

SALLAY or SAWLEY (Yorks W.) (Newminster) f. 6 Jan. 1147 (*EYC*, XI, p. 27)

C.T.C. Lists in Clay (1952), pp. 39ff.; *Ctl. Sallay*, II, 191–2; *VCH Yorks*, III, 157–8.

Benedict 1147–1154+ (*EYC*, XI, no. 12 = *Ctl. I*, 1; ib., I, nos. 52n., 49). M. of Newminster.

---

[1] B. abb. Cîteaux (*GC*, IV, 989).

[SALLAY or SAWLEY]

Gilbert Occ. 18 Dec. 1172 (*PUE*, III, no. 192); 1167 × 74 (*Ctl. Fountains*, II, p. 740).

Geoffrey –1181–*c.* 1198 Occ. –1181 (*Ctl.* II, no. 576); 1186 (*EYC*, VI, no. 148). Res. between 1189 and 1198 (*Ctl. Newminster*, p. 120).

Adam 1198– Bl. 11 Oct. 1198 (Howden, IV, 77; for other refs. see Clay (1952), p. 40).

R. Occ. +2 Nov. 1209 (j.d.: *Ctl. Kirkstall*, p. 254; cf. Cheney, *Inn. III*, no. 856 and n.).

William Occ. 1209 × 11 (*Ctl. Furness*, II, ii, p. 343); j.d. +18 Dec. 1218 (*Ctl. Kirkstall*, pp. 252–3). Succeeded by Richard and Stephen –Christmas 1224 (*Ctl. Sallay*, II, nos. 534n., 598).

SAWTRY (Hunts) (Wardon) f. 3 July 1147

List in *VCH Hunts*, I, 392.

Roger 1147– First abb., occ. 9 Sept. 1147 (*PUE*, I, no. 42).

Hugh Occ. 1152 × 4 (*Ctl. Colchester*, II, pp. 527–8); n.d., mid-12th cent. (BM Harl. Chts., 83. B. 2; 83. B. 12); 8 Sept. 1164 (*PUE*, I, no. 102).

Payne Occ. 1164 × 7 (*Anc. Chts.*, PRS x, no. 37); 1173 (BM Cott. Faust. A. iv, f. 38r–v = Gorham, p. 53); 3 June 1176 (*PUE*, I, no. 139); 1174 × 9[1] (*Reg. Lincoln*, III, no. 803).

Alexander Occ. 15 March 1185 (*PUE*, I, no. 231); 25 Feb. 1195 (ib., no. 321); 1201 × 2 (*Cambs F.*, p. 4); d. 1204 (*Ch. Melrose*, f. 27v, p. 52).

Ralph Occ. (R.) 1210 (CUL Add. MS 3021, f. 322); 1213 × 14[2] (Peterborough, D. and C., MS 1, f. xcvi = MS 5, f. 66v); 1217 × 18 (*Hunts F.*, p. 5).

The next recorded abb., Alard, occ. 27 May 1228 (BM Cott. MS Tib. C. ix, f. 153r–v).

SIBTON (Suffolk) (Wardon) f. 22 Feb. 1150

List in *VCH Suffolk*, II, 90–1.

Hugh Occ. 1 Nov. 1150 (*PUE*, III, no. 77); 20 Nov. 1160 (ib., I, no. 81).

Ralph Occ. 1195 (BM Harl. MS 2110, f. 64v); (R.) 1199 × 1206 (BM Harl. Cht. 44. I. 24).

Laurence Occ. 1199 × 1206 (BM Harl. Cht. 43. I. 18); 1205 × 6 (ib., 44. I. 25; cf. Cheney, *Inn. III*, no. 593). For his name see BM Cott. MS Vesp. E. xiv, ff. 53v–4.

Alexander Occ. 1212 (*CRR*, VI, p. 241).

The next recorded abb., Constantine, occ. 1228 × 9 (*Suffolk F.* (Rye), p. 30). Abbs. Walter, John and S. occ. n.d. in Bodl. Rawl. MS B. 421, ff. 40v, 19r–v, 21.

STANLEY (Drownfont) (Wilts) (Quarr) f. 1151 (at Loxwell); 1154 (at Stanley)

List in *VCH Wilts*, III, 274 (H. F. Chettle and J. L. Kirby).

Nicholas Occ. 1180 (BM Add. MS 47,677, ff. 128v–129); Easter term 1201 (*CRR*, I, p. 426); 1203 × 4 (*Wilts F.*, p. 8); dep. 1204 (*Wm. Newb.*, II, 508); res. 1205 to be abb. of Buckfast (ib.).

(The 'H.' who occ. June × July 1198 (*Epp. Cant.*, p. 423), is presumably a slip for 'N.')

Thomas of Calstone 1205– Pr. of Stanley, el. abb. 1205 (*Wm. Newb.*, II, 508); occ. *c.* 13 Oct. 1212 (*Wilts F.*, I, p. 11); 1217 + (*Ctl. Chertsey*, I, no. 74).

The next recorded abb. R(alph) occ. 7 Oct. 1221 (*Sarum Chts.*, p. 114) and as Ralph ex-abb. 28 Mar. 1224 (*Rot. Lit. Claus.*, I, 590). Stephen had succeeded by 25 Nov. 1223 (*CRR*, XI, no. 1248).

STANLOW or STANLAW (Ches) (later Whalley, Lancs) (Combermere) f. (Stanlow) 11 Nov. 1172; (moved to Whalley) 4 Apr. 1296

List in *VCH Lancs*, II, 139 (J. Tait); transcript of medieval list in BM Cott. MS Titus F. iii, f. 261r–v – to 1355.

---

[1] R(ichard) abb. Mortemer (*HF*, XII, 782–3).   [2] Nicholas, bp. Tusculum, legate.

?**Robert** Occ. 1172 × 8[1] (*Ctl. Whalley*, I, no. 13, pp. 13–14; cf. *Ches Chts.* p. 6, where it is shown that Robert is the reading of the original cht.).

Ralph[2] –1209 Occ. –1189 (*Ches. Chts.*, p. 16, and facsimile facing); said on the medieval list to be first abb., and to have d. 24 Aug. 1209. Occ. 14 Nov. 1202 (Cheney, *Inn. III*, no. 443 – where for 'Robert' read 'Ralph'; so BM Egerton MS 3126, f. 91); (R.) 1209 (*Ctl. Whalley*, II, pp. 534ff.).

Osbert was placed between Ralph and Charles in the list; d. 1 May (ibid.). ?Occ. (O.) ?1198 × 1203[3] (Cheney, *Inn. III*, no. 668): the dates do not fit, but no satisfactory solution presents itself.

W. occ. 1209 × 11 (*Ctl. Furness*, II, ii, p. 343: not in list).

The next name on the list, Charles, occ. 3 Jan. 1226 (*CPR, 1225–32*, p. 71; cf. *Ctl. Whalley*, I, p. 89); d. 3 Jan., list. As K., 1224 × 31 (PRO DL 25/273; see Norton).

STONELEIGH (Warws) (Bordesley) f. ?1133 (hermitage); ?c. 1153 (Cist. at Radmore); 1155 (Stoneleigh); see *Ctl. Stoneleigh*, pp. xiv–xv, 10–12, 15, 249.
List in *VCH Warws*, II, 81; 14th cent. Acta Abbatum in *Ctl. Stoneleigh*, pp. 251–4.

William c. 1153–1159 First abb.; occ. c. June, c. June–July 1153 (Radmore), 1155 (Stoneleigh); d. 13 Dec. 1159 (*Ctl. Stoneleigh*, pp. 12–13, 15–16 – cf. *Reg.*, III, nos. 841n., 459); cf. *Ctl.*, pp. lviii–lix, 251: abb. '19 years' perhaps by confusion with Roger; cf. also, for occ., *Ctl. Trentham*, p. 301; etc. He was presumably the William abb. 'Stanle' who occ. in Ctl. Kenilworth, BM Add. MS 47,677, f. 128r–v.

Roger c. 1160–1178 Prev. m. Bordesley and Stoneleigh, D. 5 Feb. 1178; abb. 19 years (*Ctl. Stoneleigh*, p. 251).

Nicholas c. 1178–1188 D. 29 Aug. 1188; abb. 10 years (ibid.).

Henry 1188–1189 D. 11 Sept. 1189; abb. '2' years (ibid.; cf. *Ann. Waverley*, pp. 246–7).

William of Pershore c. 1189–1199 M. and cellarer Bordesley; abb. 7 years; res. 1199 to be abb. Bordesley (ibid.; cf. *Ann. Waverley*, p. 247). Occ. (William) 1194 (*Ctl. Cirencester*, II, nos. 700, 703). See Bordesley: the evidence seems to establish the date 1199, though the Stoneleigh list presupposes c. 1196.

William of Campden 1199–c. 1204 M. of Bordesley and Stoneleigh. El. 23 July (?: St Apollinaris) [1199]; abb. 8 years (list: see above); and ruled until c. 1204 – see below.

William de Tysto c. 1204–1217 D. 23 July 1217 after 12 years as abb. (ibid.); occ. 12 May 1204;[4] 1208 × 9–c. Michaelmas 1208 (ibid., p. 21; *Warws F.*, no. 187); +1209 (*Mon.*, IV, 112; for date cf. Cheney, *Inn. III*, no. 846).

STRATA FLORIDA (Cardigan) (Whitland) f. 1 June 1164; +1184 (re-built after fire)
List in S. W. Williams, *The Cistercian Abbey of Strata Florida* (London, 1889), Appendix, p. cxii.

David –1185 D. 1185 (*Brut: Red Book*, p. 169; *Peniarth*, p. 73).

Seisillus[5] Occ. 1188 (*Gir. Camb.*, VI, 119).

Deniawal Occ. c. 1201 (*Mon.*, V, 637).

Cedifor –1225 D. 1225 (*Brut: Red Book*, p. 227; *Peniarth*, p. 100).

---

[1] Between the foundation of Stanlow abb. and *Ctl.* nos. I, XIV.

[2] Ranulf according to Aberystwyth Nat. Lib. Wales, MS 7851D, p. 288 (–1203); but 'Radulfo' in the original cht. cited above.

[3] So Cheney, showing it to be well before 10 May 1206; j.d. with Geoffrey abb. Chester, 1194–1208.

[4] Unless this is a mistake for 1205; see *Ctl.*, p. 22 and n.

[5] S. W. Williams, Appendix, p. cxii gives 'Sissilus...witnesses Mailgwn's charter, 1198'; but no such witness appears in the charter as printed on p. xiv, nor in BM Harl. MS 6068, f. 11.

STRATA MARCELLA (Trallwng = Welshpool; Pool) (Montgomery) (Whitland) f. 22 July 1170; 1172 (?) (second site)
> List in *Montgomeryshire Coll.*, VI, 336 (M. C. Jones).

Enoch (Enatus) Presumably first abb., abandoned habit well before 1188 (*Gir. Camb.*, VI, 59), but called abb. Whitland[1] (q.v.), ib., II, 248; an abb. in Powys, *Gir. Camb.*, IV, 168, 172.

Ithel Occ. 1176 (J. Conway Davies, in *Mont. Coll.*, LI (1949), 164–5). D. 1187 according to the *Brut* (*Peniarth*, p. 73; *Red Book*, p. 171). But the year seems too late (see below).

Griffith (Gruffud) Occ. 18 April 1183, 9 May 1185, 13 May 1198 (*Mont. Coll.*, LI, 165–8). D. 1196 according to *Brut* (*Peniarth*, p. 76; *Red Book*, p. 177); but presumably this is too early.

Philip Occ. *c.* 1201 (*Mon.*, V, 637); 4 March 1201 (*Mont. Coll.*, LI, 172). Probably = pr. Philip who occ. 1183, 1198 (*Mont. Coll.*, LI, 165, 168).

David Occ. 1215 (*Mont. Coll.*, LI, 185).

The next recorded abb., G., occ. 15 July 1227 (M. C. Jones in *Mont. Coll.*, IV, 320–2).

STRATFORD LANGTHORNE (Ham) (Essex), St Mary and All Saints (Savigny) f. 25 July 1135
> List in *VCH Essex*, II, 133.

Henry Occ. 1169(× 70) (*MB Epp.* 526).

?Ernald[2] Occ. prob. 1176 × 81 (*Ctl. Clerkenwell*, no. 228).

William Occ. (W.) 1186 × 91 (*HMC Var. Coll.*, IV, 55); 20 July 1192 (*Ctl. Oxford, St Frideswide*, II, p. 156); 1195 × 7 (BM Harl. MS 391, f. 98r–v; cf. *CDF*, nos. 1368, 1366: *c.* 1195).

Benedict *c.* 1197–1218 El. *c.* 1197 (*Ralph Cogg.*, p. 187); occ. (B.) 14 June 1197 (*Ctl. Godstow*, I, pp. 229–30 = Westminster Abb. Domesday Ctl., ff. 378v–9); 5 July 1198 (Cheney, *Inn. III*, no. 149); 25 Jan. 1199 (*FF.*, PRS XXIV, no. 249); 1203 (*CRR*, II, p. 283); 1208 (*Lancs PR*, p. 362); res. 1218, after 19 years as abb. Stratford to be abb. Coggeshall (*Ralph Cogg.*, p. 187).

The next abb., Richard, occ. *c.* Trinity, 1218 (*Essex F.*, p. 49).

SWINESHEAD (Holland) (Lincs) (Furness) f. 1 Feb. 1135
> List in *VCH Lincs*, II, 146.

John Occ. 1146 × 53, prob. 1150 (*EYC*, V, no. 308).

Gilbert –1172 M. Clairvaux (C. Heinriquez, *Menologium Cistertiense*, Antwerp, 1630, p. 172). Occ. 1155 (*CDF*, no. 819; see Revesby); *c.* 1154 × 5 (*EYC*, IV, no. 28); prob. 1167 (*Reg. Lincoln*, IV, no. 1293). D. 1172 at L'Arivour ('quondam' – perhaps having res.: Ch. Clairvaux, *PL*, CLXXXV, col. 1248). Commemorated on 25 May (*Menologium*, loc. cit.). Author of *Sermons on the Canticle*, etc. (cf. Ch. Clairvaux, ut sup.; ed. in *PL*, CLXXXIV, coll. 11–298). *DNB*.

Ralph Occ. 1167 × 86[3] (*CDF*, no. 853); (R.) 1183 × 4 (*Ctl. Furness*, II, iii, p. 715; see Vaudey). Res. to be abb. Furness (q.v.).

William Occ. 28 June 1202, 20 Nov. 1208 (*Lincs F.*, PRS LXVII, nos. 48, 288); 1209 × 12 (*Ctl. Furness*, II, ii, p. 343); res. to be abb. Furness (q.v.).

The next abb. known was either Robert Denton, if it is correct that he was abb. Swineshead before he became abb. Furness, or Geoffrey, occ. *c.* 6 May 1240 (*Lincs F.*, I, ii, p. 306).

---

[1] 'Albalanda'; Strata Marcella was called 'Alba Domus' in its f. cht. (*Mont. Coll.*, IV (1871), 16).

[2] 'Ernaldus' in the document in *Ctl. Clerkenwell*, 'Reginaldus' in the heading: the latter may be due to confusion with a later abb. – see ed.'s note. The cht. seems certainly –Jan. 1182; prob. +1176.

[3] A grant by Alexander brother of H. chancellor of Lincoln: H(amo) d. –1186 (*Ctl. Gloucester*, II, p. 156) – but it is not certain that he was alive.

THAME (Oxon) (Waverley) f. 22 July 1137 (at Otley); *c.* 1140 (at Thame)

Lists in *VCH Oxon*, II, 85 (H. E. Salter) and (medieval) *Ctl. Thame*, II, p. 201.

Everard 1138– App. 1138 (*Ctl. Thame*, II, p. 201); occ. 11 Mar. 1141 (*PUE*, III, no. 36); 5 Feb. 1146 (*Ctl. Thame*, II, p. 143); 1147 (*Ctl. Oseney*, IV, p. 87).

Serlo 1148–1184 2nd abb., el. 1148 (*Ctl. Thame*, II, p. 201);*occ. –Feb. 1152 (ib., I, pp. 41–2; cf. p. 45); 1154 × 64 (ib., I, p. 91); 15 May 1179 (*PUE*, III, no. 269); res. 1184 (*Ann. Waverley*, p. 243).

William of Forde 1184– 3rd abb., formerly cellarer of Forde, abb. of Kingswood, but dep. 1181 (*Ann. Waverley*, p. 242); app. abb. Thame 1184 (ib., p. 243; *Ctl. Thame*, II, p. 201, no. 242); occ. (W.) 1191 (*Ctl. Oxford, St Frideswide*, II, p. 332); (W.) 1197 (*CDF*, no. 145); *c.* 9 May 1204 (*Ctl. Thame*, I, no. 196).

Simon 1205–1224 4th abb., formerly pr. of Bruern, el. 1205 (*Ctl. Thame*, II, p. 201); occ. 1210 × 11 (*Ctl. St Frideswide*, II, p. 246; cf. Cheney, *Inn. III*, no. 871); 26 Aug. 1211 (*Ctl. Thame*, II, p. 125); 7 Dec. 1218 (*Oxford F.*, p. 59); 2 Feb. 1224 (ib., p. 72); d. 1224 (? for 1225; see below. *Ann. Waverley*, p. 300).

Laurence, 5th abb., m. of Thame, app. 1224 on death of Simon (ib.); app. 1225 (*Ctl. Thame*, II, p. 201).

TILTY (Essex) (Wardon) f. 22 Sept. 1153

List in *VCH Essex*, II, 136.

Auger Occ. 1168 × 81 (*Ctl. Colchester*, II, p. 528: 'Thiretei'); n.d.[1] (BM Cott. MS Nero E. vi, f. 331).

Simon –1214 Occ. prob. 1181 (*HMC Rutland*, IV, 6);[2] 16 Mar. 1188 (Ann. Dunmow, BM Cott. MS Cleop. C. iii, f. 291); 1195 × 8 (BM Harl. MS 391, f. 98r–v: see Stratford); 1199 (*Ctl. Wardon*, no. 224); *c.* Michaelmas 1205, *c.* Michaelmas 1207 (*Essex F.*, pp. 36, 42); d. 1214 (*Ralph Cogg.*, p. 169, where he is stated to have been the fourth abb.).

Walter Occ. 1219 × 20, *c.* Jan. 1230 (*Essex F.*, pp. 56, 86).

An abb., Robert, occ. n.d. in Ctl. Tilty (Chelmsford, Essex R.O. T/B3, from f. 108, etc.).

TINTERN (Monmouthshire) (L'Aumône) f. 9 May 1131

William Occ. *c.* 1139, d. –1148 (*GFL*, no. 72).

Henry Occ. –1153; res. 1154 × 61 to be abb. Waverley (*Vita Wulfrici*, pp. xxxvii, 68ff.; *JS Epp.*, I, 263; *GFL*, p. 513).[3]

William II –1188 Occ. (W.) –1169 (PRO C115 A1/K2/6683 sec. iv, no. 106; cf. *Acta Chichester*, no. 37); res. 1188 in visitation (*Ann. Waverley*, p. 245).

Eudo 1188– Formerly pr. Waverley; abb. Kingswood *c.* 1180–1188 (*Ann. Waverley*, p. 245); occ. (E.) (*Mon.*, V, 425–6; cf. *GFL*, pp. 510ff.).

VALLE CRUCIS (Denbigh) (Strata Marcella) f. 28 Jan. 1201

List in G. Vernon Price, *Valle Crucis Abbey* (Liverpool, 1952), pp. 41–2.

?Philip ?Occ. *c.* 1201 (*Mon.*, V, 637, from Cht. Roll 23 Edward I, PRO C 53/81, m. 3: 'Phill' abbate de Polaiphill. abbate de Vale Crucis'. This must be corrupt; 'Polai' would be a natural form for Strata Marcella, and 'phill' is either the name of the abb. Valle Crucis or a scribal aberration, possibly due to the name of the abb. of Strata Marcella).

David Occ. 15 Jan. 1206 (?1207) (M. C. Jones in *Mont. Coll.*, IV (1871), 305–6).

[1] With Henry of Northampton, fl. –1178–92 (*GF*, pp. 282–3).

[2] Cf. adjacent cht., dated *c.* Easter 1181. An abb. R. (scribal error for S(imon)) occ. 1190 (*Acta Chichester*, no. 140).

[3] But the Canterbury Cathedral charter said to show Henry still abbot of Tintern on 17 July 1157 cannot be found and may have been due to confusion with the decision of the papal judges-delegate of that date, printed in *GFL*, no. 293 (from Canterbury Cathedral archives).

[VALLE CRUCIS]

John Occ. –1215 (Eyton, *Salop*, x, 347–8 (and *Mont. Coll.*, IV, 315): he is a witness to a cht. of –1215 in an inspeximus in Shrewsbury Borough Library, Ctl. Haughmond, f. 158, inspeximus of 1213 × 15 of the cht. of Abp. Stephen Langton. The name was om. in the 18th cent. transcript of the Ctl. in BM Add. MS 33,354, f. 67v; hence also *Acta S. Langton*, no. 35).

VAUDEY (Lincs) (Fountains) f. 23 May 1147 (at Bytham); +1149 (at Vaudey)
   List in *VCH Lincs*, II, 144–5.[1]

Warin 1147– 1st abb., from 1147 (*Mem. Fountains*, I, 93). Occ. 28 Feb. 1150 (*Mon.*, v, 420); 1148 × 66 (*Gilbertine Chts.*, p. 4).

J. Occ. 1156 × 63 (*Rufford Chts.*, no. 733).

Acius Occ. (A.) 1155 × 66 (*DC*, no. 218n.); 1164 (*Ctl. Rievaulx*, no. 246); *c.* 1170 × 84 (*Rufford Chts.*, no. 751).

Simon Occ. 1183 × 4[2] (*Ctl. Furness*, II, iii, p. 715); (S.) –1186 (Bodl. Queen's Coll. Muniments (Monk Sherborne), nos. 284–5); (S.) 1184+ (Poynton in *Genealogist*, New Series, XV, 161); 1175 × 90 (Peterborough D. and C. MS 5, ff. 79v–80).

Richard Occ. 1200 (*CRR*, I, p. 274); 13 Oct. 1204 (*Lincs F.*, PRS LXVII, no. 190).

William Occ. (W.) ?1214 × 15 (Cheney, *Inn. III*, no. 1008); j.d. +26 Oct. 1218 (CUL Add. MS 3020, f. 229r–v); 1219 (BM Lansd. MS 207C, f. 206); 1219 +[3] (*Mon.*, VI, 693).

The next abb., Nicholas, occ. 29 Sept. 1227 (*CPR, 1225–32*, p. 165); 1229; 1230 (*CRR*, XIII, nos. 1362, 2569); during his time William and John 'quondam' abbs. witness a charter (Lincolnshire Arch. Office, 2 Anc. 1/1/10).

WARDON (de Sartis) (Beds) (Rievaulx) f. 8 Dec. 1136
   Lists in *VCH Beds*, I, 365; *Ctl. Wardon*, pp. 357–8.

Simon 1st abb., occ. 1136 × 43 (*Ctl. Wardon*, no. 12); 1147 × 53[4] (*Chicksands Chts.*, p. 104); 1151 (PRO C 115/A1 K2/6683, sec. x, no. 4).

Hugh Occ. 1173 (*Ctl. Wardon*, p. 357: cf. BM Cott. MS Faust. A. iv, f. 38r–v – Wednesday, 18 Aug.); 1174 × 81 (*EYC*, IV, no. 95); (H.) 1174 × 9 (*Reg. Lincoln*, III, no. 803: cf. Sawtry).

Payne –1198(9) Occ. (P.) 1185 × 95, prob. early (*CDF*, no. 817); (P.) 1186 (Gorham, II, p. lxxiv); 1192 (*BHRS*, XXXII, pp. 4–5, 13–14); 6 Dec. 1196 (*FF*, PRS, XX, no. 64). Res. 1198 or early 1199 (see C. R. Cheney in *BHRS*, XXXII (1952), pp. 14, 15, 19: P., and P. *quondam*).

Warin I Occ. 1199 (*Ctl. Wardon*, no. 143); ?1198 × 9 (Cheney, *Inn. III*, no. 176); (W.) 1199 × 1200 (*Ctl. Cirencester*, II, no. 715).

Roger I Occ. 13 Oct. 1200 (*Beds F.*, no. 67).

Warin II Occ. 1205 (*Ctl. Wardon*, no. 113; *CRR*, III, p. 278). The dates suggest that he = Warin abb. of Rievaulx from 1205 × 8 (Rievaulx was the mother house), as was suggested in *Ctl. Wardon*, pp. 357–8.

Laurence Occ. (L.) 28 May 1208 (*Glam. Chts.*, II, p. 330); 8 June 1208 (*BHRS*, XII (1928), p. 77); 1212 × 13 (Fines, Unknown Counties, PRO transcripts).

Henry –1215 El. abb. Rievaulx 8 Apr. 1215 (*Ch. Melrose*, f. 31, p. 59).

---

[1] 'Silvanus' abb. Vaudey occ. in *NRA, Ancaster*, for what is now Lincolnshire Archive Office 2 Anc. 1/1/7. Dr David Smith, to whom we are much indebted for help with this list, has kindly inspected the charter and says that the name of the house is now mainly illegible, but we agree with him that Rievaulx is the likely identification.

[2] B(ernard) abb. Cîteaux (cf. *GC*, IV, 989).   [3] Adam abb. Melrose (*Ch. Melrose*, p. 71).

[4] Henry Murdac, archbp. York took effective possession of his see in 1151 (JS, *HP*, ed. M. Chibnall, p. 83 and n.): the dates should therefore probably be 1151 × 3.

Roger II 1215–1223/4 M. of Wardon, master of conversi, el. abb. 29 Apr. 1215 (ib.); occ. 1217×18 (BM Cott. MS Faust. C. i, f. 20v);[1] 25 June 1219 (*Beds F.*, no. 227); 1221 ('Robertus': *Ctl. Colchester*, II, p. 534); el. abb. Rievaulx 1223/4, res. 1239 (Clay (1952), p. 36, citing *Ch. Melrose*, pp. 76, 86).

WAVERLEY (Surrey) (L'Aumône) f. 24 Nov. 1128
List in *VCH Surrey*, II, 88 from *Ann. Waverley*.

John 1128 First abb., d. 1128 at Midhurst while returning from Chapter (*Ann. Waverley* p. 221).

Gilbert 1128– El. 1128 (ibid.); occ. 1137 (*Ctl. Thame*, I, p. 65); 28 May 1147 (*PUE*, I, no. 37); 1151×7 (*EYC*, XI, no. 290).

Henry –1182 3rd abb. (Gilbert's successor), formerly abb. of Tintern (*Vita Wulfrici*, pp. 68ff.); still at Tintern +1154; occ. –1161 (*JS Epp.*, I, p. 263; cf. *GFL*, pp. 511–13); 25 July 1177 (Morey, pp. 140–1 = *Acta Chichester*, no. 69); 1180 (Forde Abbey, Ctl Forde, p. 470); d. 1182 (*Ann. Waverley*, p. 242).

Henry of Chichester 1182–1187 M. of Waverley, el. 1182 (ib., p. 242); res. 1187 (ib., p. 244).

Christopher 1187–1196 Formerly abb. of Bruern; 'amotus...a villicacione sua' 1196 (ib., p. 250).

John II 1196–1201 M. and Guestmaster of Waverley, el. 1196 (ib., p. 250); occ. 1196×7 (*Surrey F.*, p. 2); 1 July 1199 (*Ped. Fin.*, I, p. 107); d. 16 Sept. 1201 at Marton (*Ann. Waverley*, p. 253).

John III 1201–1216 Cellarer of Waverley, el. 1201 (ib., p. 253); occ. 1201 at founding of Dunkeswell (*Ann. Margam*, p. 26); 1202×3 (*Surrey F.*, p. 5); 1210 fled house for fear of King John (*Ann. Waverley*, p. 265); 7 May 1214 (*Wilts F.*, I, p. 11); d. 3 Aug. 1216 (*Ann. Waverley*, p. 286).

WHITLAND (Albalanda, Alba Terra, Ty Gwynn)[2] (Carmarthen) (Clairvaux) f. 16 Sept. 1140 (at Trefgarn); *c.* 1151 (at Whitland)

Morfran –1147 Slain 1147 (*Brut: Red Book*, p. 127; *Peniarth*, p. 56).

Conan (Cynam, Kananus) –1176 Occ. –1166[3] (*Glam. Chts.*, I, p. 148; cf. VI, p. 2273); d. 1176 (*Brut: Red Book*, p. 167; *Peniarth*, p. 71; cf. *Gir. Camb.*, VI, 59: 'Kanano').

Richard (Rhyddirch) –1184 Occ. 1176+ (*Arch. Camb.*, 4th ser., XIV, p. 137); d. 1184 (*Brut: Red Book*, p. 169; *Peniarth*, p. 72).

John Occ. 1188 (*Gir. Camb.*, VI, 119).

Peter –1202 Occ. 1198 (*Gir. Camb.*, I, 95); *c.* 1201 (*Mon.*, V, p. 637); dep. Nov.–Dec. 1202 (*Gir. Camb.*, III, 240).[4]

Martin (Cadugan of Llandyfai) –1215 Named in *Brut: Red Book*, p. 205; *Peniarth*, p. 91; res. 1215 to be bishop of Bangor (bp. 1215–1235×6) (*Ann. Worcester*, p. 404; *Ann. Tewkesbury*, p. 61; Ann. Southwark–Merton, BM Cott. MS Faust. A. viii, f. 140r–v; *Rot. Lit. Pat.*, p. 132b).

WOBURN (Beds) (Fountains) f. 28 May 1145
List in *VCH Beds*, I, 370.[5]

---

[1] Roger: but misspelt Robert in the translation, *Ctl. Huntingdon*, p. 268.
[2] See Strata Marcella, called 'Alba Domus' in its f. cht., hence the confusion which led Enoch abb. Strata Marcella to be attributed by *Gir. Camb.* (II, 248) to Whitland.
[3] Robert son of William, earl Gloucester (see p. 89 n. 2).
[4] Not named, but his identity is clear from the context (for the date cf. H. E. Butler, *Autobiography of Giraldus Cambrensis*, pp. 264–6; cf. index s.v. Whitland).
[5] Includes William, occ. 1180, and Nicholas, 1208, from Browne Willis's notes cited by Cole, BM Add. MS 5827, f. 176v, without references.

[WOBURN]

Alan 1145– 1st abb., m. of Fountains, app. 1145 (*Mon.*, v, 301; *Mem. Fountains*, I, 88).

Peter –1204 Occ. 1183×95 (BM Cott. MS Julius D. iii, ff. 123v–124); (P.) 26 May 1196 (*FF*, PRS XVII, no. 166); (P.) 1203 (*Ctl. Dunstable*, no. 169); dep. 1204 (*Wm. Newb.*, II, 508); d. 1204 at Vaucluse ('Vacell'') (*Ch. Melrose*, p. 52, f. 27v).

Richard –1234 Occ. j.d. +19 Dec. 1208 (BM Lansdowne MS 375, ff. 131v–132; cf. Cheney, *Inn. III*, no. 808); 23 June 1219 (*Beds F.*, no. 230); 1228 (*Ann. Dunstable*, p. 108); dep. 1234 (ib., p. 140).

THE CARTHUSIAN MONKS

WITHAM (Soms), St Mary   f. 1178×9

List in *VCH Soms*, II, 128. Basis in *MVH* of St Hugh, and *Ch. Witham*, ed. E. M. Thompson, *BJRL*, XVI (1932), 482–506, and A. Wilmart, *Analecta Praemonstratensia*, IX (1933), 215–32 – p. nos. in brackets. The *MVH*, ii, 1 (1, pp. 46–7, cf. p. xxv) describes the first two prs. without naming them: the first soon res., the second d.; St Hugh was the third from *c.* 1180.

Narbert   *c.* 1178–*c.* 1179 For his name see Le Couteulx, *Ann.*, II, 456 (cf. E. M. Thompson (1930), p. 51).

Hamo   *c.* 1179–*c.* 1180   Named in cht. of *c.* 1180[1] (*Ctl. Bruton*, no. 138), and so presumably the second pr. who d. *c.* 1180.

St Hugh of Avalon   *c.* 1180–1186 For him as pr. see *MVH*, bk. ii (1, 47ff.); E. M. Thompson (1930), pp. 54–5; *MO*, pp. 381ff.; *Gir. Camb.*, VII, 92–3. Res. when el. bp. of Lincoln, May 1186 (consec. 21 Sept.) but retained authority over Witham (*Ch. Witham*, pp. 505–6 (231)); d. 1200. Occ. 1181[2] (*MVH*, ii, 6, 1, 64–8; cf. p. xxv).

Albert de Portes   *c.* 1186– M. of Portes and Witham; dep. by St Hugh (*Ch. Witham*, pp. 505–6 (231)). Occ. 1191 (*Ch. Witham*, p. 506).[3]

Bovo   –*c.* 1200 M. Chartreuse (*MVH*, ii, 3, 1, 54); ?res. *c.* 1200 (Le Couteulx, *Ann.*, II, 280);[4] cf. E. M. Thompson (1930), pp. 70, 74.

Robert I   *c.* 1201– Can. and procurator Witham, made pr. +1200 (*MVH*, v, 16, II, 195; cf. *Ch. Witham*, p. 502n.);[5] occ. 1205 (*Ch. Witham*, pp. 501ff. (224ff.)).

Robert II de Caveford (Keyford in Frome: see n. 5)   Occ. Palm Sunday 1210×13[6] (*Ch. Witham*, p. 504 (229)); (R.) *c.* 1212 (*Mag. Vit.*, i, prol., 1, 1); and see above. For his name *Ch. Witham*, p. 504 (229) and n.

The next recorded pr., Giles, occ. 1226 (*CPR, 1225–32*, pp. 79, 292).

[1] With Walter pr. Buckland, a house dissolved *c.* 1180 (certainly well before 1186) so that Hamo must have preceded Hugh.

[2] Date confirmed by J. Lally ,'The Court and Household of King Henry II' (University of Liverpool, Ph.D. Thesis, 1969), p. 277; cf. *PR 28 Henry II*, pp. 108–9, 115.

[3] He was pr. when Robert pr. Winchester and Walter pr. Bath came to Witham: Robert came in 1191, Walter –1191 (Devizes, pp. 26–7).

[4] Le Couteulx identified him with Bovo 'Sacerdos et Monachus' d. 2 Dec., 'in antiquo Calendario Cartusiae' and suggested that he was therefore no longer pr. when he died, and that he res. *c.* 1200 and d. *c.* 1201. All this seems to be conjecture.

[5] Miss Thompson gives evidence to suggest he came from La Chartreuse, and so was presumably distinct from Robert II, who came from near Witham, and who may be called 'of Keyford' to distinguish him from Robert I. But it is not certain that there were two Roberts.

[6] When Adam of Dryburgh d. on Palm Sunday during the interdict, after 24 years at Witham. He arrived +1186 (*Ch. Witham*, p. 485 (221)) and so d. 1210×13.

THE AUGUSTINIAN CANONS

For the following houses founded or prob. founded before 1216, no names have been found in this period: Alnesbourn, Anglesey, Baxterwood, Beddgelert, Bentley, Berden, Bradley (Leics), Breadsall, Bromehill, Carham, Dodford, Fineshade, Haverfordwest, Ipplepen, Letheringham, Marsh Barton, Mottisfont, North Creake, North Ferriby, Nottingham, Holy Sepulchre, Patrixbourne, Peterstone, Pynham, Ratlinghope, Sandleford, Sheringham, Shulbred, Skewkirk, Stamford, St Sepulchre, Stonely, Thelsford, Tiptree, Tregony, Weybourne, Woodspring (Dodlinch), Wormegay.

For Baswich, see under Stafford. Some small cells, groups attached to convents of nuns etc., communities of doubtful origin and hospitals have been omitted.

ARBURY (Warws.), St Mary f. 1154+
List in *VCH Warws*, II, 91.
William Occ. 1157 × 66 (*EYC*, II, nos. 1109, 1111 = *Bk. Seals*, nos. 515, 517).
Adam Occ. 13 Aug. 1202 (*Warws F.*, no. 139); ?1203[1] (PRO, Le Neve's Indexes, XXIV, 5). The next recorded pr. Albinus, occ. 1227 × 8[2] (PRO E40/5785; *Cat. Anc. Deeds*, III, p. 223).

BARLINCH (Soms), St Nicholas f. 1174 × 91 (?c. 1180: see below)
List in *VCH Soms*, II, 134.
Master Walter Occ. +1180 (*Ctl. Buckland*, no. 34); c. 1184 × c. 1188[3] (ib., no. 181; *HMC Wells*, I, 38). ? = Master W. pr. Buckland.
?Geoffrey Occ. late 12th cent; +1180 (*Ctl. Buckland*, no. 140: ref. to Henry II, alive or recently dead).
Elias Occ. 1191 × 1225, prob. c. 1200 (*Ctl. Canonsleigh*, no. 151).
The next recorded pr., John, occ. 1225 × 6 (*Rot. Lit. Claus.*, II, p. 112); 3 Feb. 1242/3 (*Soms F.*, p. 120).

BARNWELL (Cambs), St Giles and St Andrew f. ?c. 1092 (at Cambridge); 1112 (at Barnwell) (*Ch Barnwell*, p. 46)
Lists in *VCH Cambs*, II, 248–9 (D. M. B. Ellis and L. F. Salzman); *Ch. Barnwell*, pp. xv–xviii (J. W. Clark) based on dates and length of tenure noted in *Ch.*, but sometimes difficult to interpret precisely.
Geoffrey of Huntingdon 1092–c. 1112 Can. of Huntingdon; pr. for 20 years; d. after move to Barnwell (*Ch. Barnwell*, pp. 39, 64).
Gerard c. 1112–c. 1143 × 7 El. c. 1112 (ib., pp. 46, 64); occ. 1133 × 6 (CUL, Add. MS 3020, f. 168). His d. is noted in *Ch. Barnwell*, p. 65, but the date has to be deduced from his successors' careers.
Richard Norel c. 1143 × 7–c. 1145 × 9 Res. within two years (ib., p. 65).
Hugh Domesman c. 1145 × 9–c. 1165 × 9 Son of Osbert Domesman; can. Barnwell; d. in 20th year of his priorate (ib., p. 65).
Robert Joel c. 1165 × 9–1198 × 1202 Res. after 33 years – app. and res. on Thursday in

---

[1] Possibly based on the same fine as above.   [2] See Nuneaton.
[3] Ralph (of Lechlade) archd. Bath (1184/5–c. 1188), Richard of Coutances archd. (c. 1184–c. 1190: J. A. Robinson (1921), pp. 87–9).

Easter week (ib., p. 67); occ. Nov. 1180 (Gray, *St Radegund*, p. 91); 1198 × 9 (*Cambs F.*, p. 2).

William of Devon   1198 × 1202–1213 Occ. 1202 × 3 (*Ped. Fin.*, I, p. 305); 8 June 1203 (*CRR*, II, p. 251); 24 Apr. 1206+ (j.d.: BM Add. MS 46,353, f. 294v); d. Saturday, 25 May 1213 (*Ch. Barnwell*, p. 67).

William of Bedford   1213–1214 Sacrist of Barnwell, el. Wednesday, 23 Oct. 1213 (*Ch. Barnwell*, p. 68); *Ch.* says he died 'post paucos dies', but the contemporary Barnwell Ch. in Walter of Coventry, II, 218n., gives his death as Friday, 28 Nov. 1214.

Richard de Burgo   *c.* 1215 'Cito sublatus est de medio' (*Ch. Barnwell*, p. 68).

Laurence of Stansfield   *c.* 1215–*c.* 1252 Can. and pr.'s chaplain; d. in 38th year – and his successor, Henry of Eye, d. in 3rd year as pr., when the see of Ely was vacant, i.e. 6 Aug. 1254 × *c.* 29 Sept. 1254 (el.) or 15 Aug. 1255 (consec. of Bp. William of Kilkenny) (*Ch. Barnwell*, pp. 69–70). Occ. 1219 × 20 (*Cambs F.*, p. 10); 1227 (*Ctl. Colchester*, II, pp. 545–6); 30 Sept. 1229 (*CPR, 1225–32*, p. 309); 1231 × 2 (*Suffolk F.* (Rye), p. 32).[1]

BASWICH, *see* STAFFORD

BECKFORD (Glos) (Ste Barbe-en-Auge)   f. 1128 × 35

List in *VCH Glos*, II, 102 (R. Graham) (1298+); on its early history see *Ch. Ste Barbe*, *passim*, esp. pp. 33–4, 40–5, 49–52.

Master Daniel   –1153 Res. 1153, el. pr. Ste Barbe (*Ch. Ste Barbe*, pp. 49–52); d. *c.* 1183, after *c.* 30 years as pr. Ste Barbe (ibid., p. 57).

A pr., unnamed, occ. 1208 (*Rot. Lit. Claus.*, I, p. 113).

The next recorded pr., Sampson, occ. 2 June 1225 (*Lincs F.*, I, p. 175).

BICESTER (Oxon), St Edburga and St Mary   f. 1182 × 5

List in *VCH Oxon*, II, 95 (H. E. Salter).

John   Occ. 1182 × 4[2] (W. Kennett, *Par. Antiq.*, I, Oxford, 1818, pp. 186–7).

Robert   Occ. late 12th–early 13th cent. (PRO E315/49/277); early 13th cent. (BM Add. Cht. 10,594); j.d. +25 Apr. 1212; +3 Mar. 1217 (*Ctl. Oxford, St Frideswide*, II, pp. 50–1, 267; cf. Cheney, *Inn. III*, no. 899; *Ctl. Oseney*, IV, p. 433); 1224 (*Bucks F.*, p. 51).

The next recorded pr., William, occ. 1227 (*Oxford F.*, p. 78).

BICKNACRE (Woodham Ferrers) (Essex) St John the Baptist   f. 1175

List in *VCH Essex*, II, 145.

Thomas   Occ. as pr. of Woodham (*Ctl. Colchester*, II, p. 450. A generation earlier than Robert and Ralph).

?Robert   Occ. as pr. of Woodham (ib., II, p. 453, about the same time as Ralph).

Fulk   Mentioned 1232 as former pr. (*CRR*, XIV, no. 2066).

Ralph   Occ. early 1230 (*Essex F.*, I, p. 87): licence to el. his successor, 1237 (*CPR, 1232–47*, p. 177).

BLACKMORE (Essex), St Laurence   f. 1152 × 62

List in *VCH Essex*, II, 147.[3]

Richard   Occ. *c.* June 1203 (*Essex F.*, p. 33).

The next recorded pr., William, occ. 1232 (*CRR*, XIV, no. 2343A).

---

[1] Asegod or Osegod (*CRR*, XI, no. 707) occ. 1223, was not pr. of Barnwell, but a grantee of land.
[2] Robert of Wheatfield, sheriff of Oxon.
[3] Including Roger, occ. 1199 × 1216, citing PRO Ass. Roll 23, m. 5; but the reference cannot be found.

BLYTHBURGH (Suffolk), St Mary, (St Osyth) f. –1135
List in *VCH Suffolk*, II, 94, mostly from the *Ctl.*, BM Add. MS 40,725 (late 14th cent.), which gives a number of prs. very difficult to date.
Elias Occ. 1195 (BM Harl. MS 2110, f. 64v); n.d. (BM Add. MS 40,725, f. 60v).
W. Occ. 1198 × 1216 (Cheney, *BIHR*, XLIV (1971), 101, no. 1204); possibly = Guy.
Guy (Guido) Occ. 7 Nov. 1218 (Chelmsford, Essex Rec. Off., MS D/DBy Q 19, ff. 43–4); also n.d. (BM Add. MS 40,725, ff. 30–1), and possibly as 'Wyth'' (f. 60), but on f. 59 a pr. Guy occ. in 18 Edward (I?).
The following names occ. n.d. in the Ctl.: Nicholas (f. 8v, prob. –1290); Osbert (ff. 39v, 46); Richard (f. 30); Roger (f. 29); Thomas (possibly mid-13th cent., ff. 8v, 36, 46); William (ff. 39v–40).

BODMIN (Cornwall), St Petroc f. *c.* 1124[1]
List in Oliver, p. 16.
Reginald –1149 D. 1149 (Ann. Plympton, *UGQ*, p. 30).
William Occ. 1155 × 7[2] (*HMC, Var. Coll.*, IV, 47; cf. Oliver, p. 40).
Roger Occ. *c.* Jan. and 19 June 1177 (*Gesta Hen. II*, I, 179). Cf. *Antiquity*, XXII (1939), 403–15 (G. H. Doble).
A Hugh m. ?of Westminster, pr. of St Petroc, d. 30 Dec., according to the Winchester calendar in BM Add. MS 29,436, f. 44.

BOLTON (Yorks W.), St Mary f. (Embsay, St Mary and St Cuthbert) 1120 × 1; (Bolton) 1154 × 5
C.T.C. Lists in *EYC*, VII, pp. 293–6 (Sir Charles Clay), and *VCH Yorks*, III, 199.

EMBSAY
Reginald 1120 × 1 Prob. can. of Huntingdon and first pr.; occ. *c.* 1120 or later (–1135 and 1135 × 40 (*EYC*, VII, nos. 2 and n., 8, cf. p. 293).
Robert Occ. 1146 × 53, 1155 × *c.* 1164 (ib., nos. 14, 24; still called pr. of Embsay, though the cht. must be after the move to Bolton).

BOLTON
Geoffrey Occ. *c.* 1170 × 90 (*EYC*, VII, no. 86; it is not wholly certain that Geoffrey preceded Walter).
Walter Occ. 1186 (*EYC*, VI, no. 148); 1178 × 87 (ib., VII, no. 29); *c.* 1170 × *c.* 1195 (ib., VII, no. 171); –*c.* 1195 (ib., I, no. 253).
There is a ref. to William pr., *c.* 1185, *Ctl. St Bees*, no. 86; for the date cf. Clay, p. 294 and n. 'William' may be an error for 'Walter'.
Henry Occ. *c.* 1190 × 5 (*EYC*, III, nos. 1868, 1866n., dated Clay, p. 294 and n.).
John Occ. –1203 (*EYC*, VII, no. 65); 24 Jan. 1206 (*Yorks F., John*, p. 97); *c.* 1218 × 20 (*EYC*, VII, no. 102); 19 Feb. 1219 (*Yorks F., 1218–31*, p. 27).
The next recorded pr., Robert, occ. 2 Feb. 1222 × 3 (*Ctl. Fountains*, II, p. 464); also in *Ctl. Furness*, II, ii, pp. 420–1, 1200 × 20.

BOURNE (Lincs), St Peter (Arrouaisian) f. 1138
List in *VCH Lincs*, II, 178.

---

[1] Or perhaps about the time Algar became bp. Coutances, ?1132 (cf. C. Henderson, *Essays in Cornish History*, Oxford, 1935, pp. 220–1).
[2] *Temp.* Robert II, bp. Exeter; Alfred archd. Cornwall (res. 1155 × 7: Morey, pp. 118–19).

ABBOTS

William Occ. 1143 × 73 (*HMC Rutland*, IV, 161); (W.) n.d.[1] (*CDF*, no. 1452).

David Possibly earlier than William, occ. 1147 × 55 (BM Cott. MS Vesp. E. xx, f. 91v); n.d. *?c.* 1160 (*Reg. Lincoln*, II, no. 347); 1163 (*DC*, no. 186); 25 July 1163 (Bodl. MS Dodsworth 76, f. 18).

Henry Occ. 1202 (*Northants Assize Roll*, no. 611); (H.) ?1198 × 1212 (Cheney, *Inn. III*, no. 1093).

Baldwin Occ. 15 Apr. 1212 (*Lincs F.*, PRS LXVII, no. 328); 3 Nov. 1222 (*Lincs F.*, I, p. 166). The next recorded abb., Everard Cutt, occ. 25 Nov. 1225 (ib., p. 177); d. 14 Sept (BM Cott. MS Calig. A. viii, f. 20v).

BRADENSTOKE (Clack) (Wilts), St Mary f. *c.* 1139 (Cirencester until 1184 × 9)
   List in *VCH Wilts*, III, 288 (D. Styles).

Adam –1177 Res. to be abb. Cirencester (Ann. Winchcombe, BM Cott. MS Faust. B. i, f. 20).

William –1183 Occ. 15 Dec. 1182 (*PUE*, I, no. 209). D. 1183 (Faust. B. i, 21).

Matthew 1184– El. 1184 (confirmed in *PUE*, I, no. 221, cf. no. 220 – of 13, 19 May); occ. *c.* 1189+ (+1186)[2] (*HMC Wells*, I, 28).

Henry –1200 Occ. j.d. + 16 Feb. 1197 (*Ctl. Bruton*, nos. 283–4); (H.) 1198 × 1200 (*HMC Wells*, I, 526; cf. Cheney, *Inn. III*, no. 810). This last reference could be to a pr. H. after William. D. 1200 (Ann. Winchcombe, BM Cott. MS Faust. B. i, f. 23).

William Occ. 1203 (*c.* 15 Nov.: BM Stowe MS 925, f. 168 = BM Cott. MS Vitell. A. xi, f. 20); 1205 (*Rot. Cht.*, p. 155b).

The pr. was probably vacant in 1208 when it was committed to the keeping of the earl of Shrewsbury (*Rot. Lit. Claus.*, I, 109b).

Simon Occ. (S.) 9 July 1215 (*Rot. Cht.*, p. 212b); 13 Nov. 1221, 1222 (*c.* 20 Oct.: BM Stowe MS 925, f. 168r–v); *c.* 4 May 1224 (*Wilts F.*, p. 13); 1229 (*CRR*, XIII, no. 1814); 29 Aug. 1232 (BM Stowe MS 925, f. 123).

?William Occ. 27 May 1237 (*Oxford F.*, p. 133).

Simon Occ. 1 July 1238 (*Yorks F., 1232–46*, p. 51); *c.* 30 June 1241 (*Wilts F.*, p. 35).

Followed by William again, occ. from 1246 (*Wilts F.*, p. 36). The alternation of Simon and William seems improbable; four[3] different prs. of the same name, William, in 60 years seems even more so. It is likely that the William of 1237 is an error. Prs. named Geoffrey and Hugh occ. n.d. in BM Stowe MS 925, ff. 75r–v, 58r–v.

BREAMORE (Hants), St Michael f. 1128 × 33
   List in *VCH Hants*, II, 172.

Robert Occ. 1139 × 43[4] (Madox, *Form.*, p. 39); 1142+, prob. *c.* 1146 (*Sarum Chts.*, pp. 16–17; cf. *Reg. St Osmund*, I, 249–50, *temp.* Henry, abb. Sherborne who was el. 1146. The case prob. came up soon after his el.).

Gardinus Occ. 1170 × 3 (BM Cott. MS Tib. D. vi, pt. i, ff. 57v–58; cf. f. 58); 1186 × 91 (*CTG*, I, 62 = BM Cott. MS Vitell. D. ix, f. 32); (G.) *c. 1188* (late 12th cent.: *Ctl. Sandford*, II, no. 292); (G.) *c.* 1180 × 9[5] (Madox, *Form.*, pp. 22–3 = 368–9).

Ralph Occ. 22 July 1202 (*Wilts F.*, p. 8).

The next recorded pr., Simon, occ. 1241 (ib., p. 32).

---

[1] With Baldwin Wac (Wake), probably late 12th or early 13th cent. (*Henry of Pytchley's Book of Fees*, ed. W. T. Mellows, Northants Rec. Soc., pp. 80–4 notes).

[2] Alexander, dean of Wells succeeded *c.* 1189 (predecessor j.d. +21 Aug. 1186, and occ. 8 Nov. 1186: J. A. Robinson (1921), p. 65).

[3] Five, if the pr. Bradenstoke in *CRR*, IX, p. 173, of 1220, is meant to carry the name William son of Robert which precedes his title; but they were probably two separate people.

[4] Henry of Blois, bp. Winchester and papal legate.

[5] Evidently in the court of Henry II, with Ranulf Glanville and Godfrey de Lucy as chief witnesses.

BREEDON (Leics) St Mary and St Herdulf (Nostell) f. –1122

List in *VCH Leics*, II, 9 (R. A. McKinley).

Elias Occ. 1154[1] × 9 (*Derbys. Chts.*, nos. 531, 1939).

Thomas Occ. *late 12th cent.* (pal.: *DC*, no. 418).

William Occ. j.d. *c.* 1174 × *c.* 1181[2] (*Mon.*, IV, 221–2; *JL*, no. 13, 528).

Ralph Occ. 1193 × 5 (Nichols, *Leics*, III, 865–6; cf. *VCH Leics*, II, 9n.).

The next recorded pr., Gervase, formerly sub-pr. of Nostell, acc. April 1223 (*Reg. Wells*, II, p. 290).

BRICETT, *see* **GREAT BRICETT**

BRIDLINGTON (Yorks E.), St Mary f. –1114

C.T.C. List in *VCH Yorks*, III, 204.[3]

Wicheman or Guikeman Occ. 1119 × 24 (*Ctl. Bridlington*, p. 435 = *PUE*, III, no. 11); –1125 (*EYC*, II, no. 874).

Bernard Occ. 1141 × 3 (*EYC*, I, nos. 152–3); 1147 × 53 (*Ctl. Whitby*, I, no. 296; cf. *EYC*, II, no. 878); Dec. 1148+ (*Mon.*, VI, 319).

Roger Occ. 1149 × 53 (*HMC Rutland*, IV, 75 – original cht.).

Robert the Scribe Occ. *c.* 1147 × 56[4] (*CChR*, IV, p. 235); *c.* 1150 × 60, presumably d. or res. –1159 (see below). On him see B. Smalley in *Recherches de Théologie ancienne et médiévale*, VII (1935), 248ff., esp. 250–1; cf. also VIII (1936), 34, IX (1937), 367, 372ff.; W. Ullmann in *YAJ*, XXXVII (1948–51), 466.

Gregory Occ. 1154 × 9[5] (*EYC*, II, no. 674); 24 Mar. 1176 (ib., IX, nos. 159–60); (G.) 26 Nov. 1181+ (*Ctl. Guisborough*, II, no. 719; cf. *YAJ* ut sup., pp. 466, 469n.). Perhaps can. Bridlington: cf. *HMC Rutland*, IV, 75.

Hugh Occ. *1185 × 95* (*EYC*, I, no. 369); 1189 (*Ctl. Bridlington*, pp. 420–1); (H.) 1189 × 95 (BM Harl. MS 391, f. 102; see Wellow); 15 Feb. 1198 or 1199 (*Ctl.*, p. 346n.); 1198 × 1200 (Cheney, *Inn. III*, no. 277). (References to H. pr. occ. in the 1190s: *Ctl. Bridlington*, pp. 78–9 and +1198, *Reg. Gray*, p. 5on.; but the last could be to (H)elias.)

Elias Occ. 2 May 1200 (*Yorks F., John*, p. 4); 20 Aug. 1202 (ib., p. 43); (H.) 27 Apr. 1205 (Cheney, *Inn. III*, no. 619); 1210 (*Ch. Meaux*, I, 354).

He had been succeeded by Hubert by 22 Dec. 1226 (*Yorks F., 1218–31*, p. 99). H(elias) or H(ubert) occ. *c.* 1213 × 14 (BM Cott. MS Nero D. iii, f. 55).

BRINKBURN (Northumberland), St Peter and St Paul (Pentney) f. –1135 (dependent on Pentney); *c.* 1188 (independent)

List in *Hist. Northumberland*, VII, 465.

Ralph 1st pr.: prev. m. of St Mary de Insula[6] (*Ctl. Brinkburn*, p. 1).

Nicholas Occ. 1143 × 52 (*EYC*, I, no. 566); 1153 (*Sim. Dur.*, II, 329).

Geoffrey Occ. 1185 × 7 (*PUE*, I, no. 237 and n.).

Ralph Occ. 18 Mar. 1186 × 7 (*PUE*, I, no. 241); (R.) 1185 × 95 (*Ctl. Brinkburn*, p. 181).

The next recorded pr., Alan, occ. 1231 (*CPR, 1225–32*, p. 447).

---

[1] See Repton.

[2] Occ. in j.d. decision on mandate from Alexander III (not 'bone memorie'), dated 19 Nov., Tusculani, i.e. 1170 × 2, 1178, or 1180.

[3] In *VCH Yorks*, III, 204 Adebold appears as second pr.; the ultimate authority for this is a cht. printed in *EYC*, III, no. 1367, where the editor notes that Adebold (Adelulf) was in fact pr. of Nostell.

[4] Gilbert de Gant, earl of Lincoln.

[5] John, son of Letold, not yet archd. (Clay, *YAJ*, XXXVI (1944–7), 418).

[6] 'Pentney priory, or possibly some previous community from which Pentney developed' (Dickinson, *Origins of the Austin Canons*, p. 125n.).

BRISTOL (Glos), St Augustine, Victorine f. ?1148[1]

List in *VCH Glos*, II, 79 (R. Graham), based on 'Abb. Newland's Roll' (16th cent. Ch. and list, ed. in *BGAS*, XIV (1889–90), 124–7).[2]

ABBOTS

Richard of Warwick ?1148–1176/7 Can. St-Victor, Paris and (briefly) of Shobdon (Wigmore; ch. Wigmore in Wright, *Ludlow*, p. 111; cf. Wigmore). Abb. from ?1148 or shortly after (see n. 2); occ. 1154 (*Berkeley Chts.*, no. 6); (R.) 1169 × 75 (*Glam. Chts.*, I, p. 146); 18 Oct. 1175 (BM Egerton MS 3031, ff. 47v–48); 8 April 1176 (*Luffield Chts.*, I, no. 31). ?D. 4 Sept. 1176 (see note 2).

William de Saltmarsh 1176/7–1186 Occ. 16 Mar. 1177 (PRO C115 A1 K2/6683, Ctl. Lanthony, sec. xvii, no. 6: William 'Scotro' – *sic*); el. bp. Llandaff 3 Dec. 1184 (*Gesta Hen. II*, I, 320); consec. 10 Aug. 1186.

John 1186/7–1216 Abb. 29 years; d. 12 Feb. 1216 (Roll). Occ. 1186 × 91 (*Berkeley Chts.*, no. 23); *c.* 1190 × 1205[3] (*Sarum Chts.*, p. 58); 24 Sept. × 14 Oct. 1207 (*Bucks F.*, p. 32); 1208 (*CRR*, V, p. 230); 1209 × 10 (Divers Counties F., PRO transcripts).

Joseph 1216 Pr. St Augustine's; royal assent to el. 6 April 1216 (*Rot. Lit. Pat.*, p. 174b). D. 17 Sept. 1216, after 31 weeks (Roll) – i.e. from John's death (cf. Fountains).

BROOKE (Rutland), St Mary (Kenilworth) f. –1153

List in *VCH Rutland*, I, 160.

Ralph Occ. 1180 (*Mon.*, VI, 234). R. occ. ?1199 (1198 × 1200; Cheney, *Inn. III*, no. 814). The next recorded pr., Richard de Ludintone, can. of Kenilworth, was presented 30 May 1222 (*Reg. Wells*, II, p. 110).

BRUTON (Soms), St Mary f. 1127 × 35

List in *VCH Soms*, II, 138; *Ctl. Bruton*, p. xxxiff.

William Occ. *c.* 1159 × *c.* 1164[4] (*HMC Wells*, I, p. 53); 4 Nov. 1159 (ib., I, p. 27 = *CDF*, no. 496); 1163 × 6 (*HMC Wells*, I, p. 19).

Philip Occ. 1169 × 75 (*Glam. Chts.*, I, p. 146); 1174 × 84 (*HMC Wells*, I, 53).

---

[1] See below.

[2] This is a 16th-cent. *Historia abbatum*, and clearly not reliable. Its account of the origin of the abbey (pp. 124–5) has several errors, though these can be in a measure controlled by the 15th-cent. version in the Ctl. (Berkeley Castle Muniments, Bodl. microfilm, f. 8r–v). Both place the foundation in 1140, the dedication in 1146 – by R. bp. of Worcester, B. bp. of Exeter and N. of Llandaff ('Robert', 'Boniface' and Nicholas in the *Historia*) – and the induction of the first group of canons in 1148 (temp. Stephen, Ctl.), but performed by Alfred, bp. of Worcester. The dedication may reasonably be attributed to 1164 × 79 and the times of bps. Roger, Bartholomew and Nicholas; what Bp. Alfred (1158–60) did is beyond conjecture, but the canons must have been installed before his consecration. The Roll says that he inducted 6 canons from Wigmore on 11 Apr., Easter Day, 1148. Easter fell on 11 Apr. indeed in 1148; none the less, the date is probably too early. The better founded Wigmore ch. says that Richard of Warwick, can. of St Victor, came to Shobdon (the community which later settled at Wigmore) in August, shortly after Robert de Bethune's death (i.e. +16 Apr. 1148), and lived there a short time only. It also says that he was later abb. Bristol, but does not say that he went to Bristol immediately on his departure. Since the young Duke Henry (= Henry II) could say in 1153 that he had helped 'the Church of St Augustine of Bristol *de canonicis regularibus...initio iuventutis mee*' (*Reg.*, III, no. 126) an effective foundation much later than 1148 seems out of the question.
 Abb. Newland's Roll omits Abb. William de Saltmarsh altogether and gives Richard 38 years, 1148–4 Sept. 1186. It may be conjectured that 4 Sept. was Richard's obit day; 1186 was the year when William left to be bp. The Roll's account of the Abbs. John and Joseph, however, seems sound. 'Robert' occ. 1161 × 72, presumably in error for Richard (*PL*, CXCVI, col. 1386, dated by Ernisius abb. S.-Victor; cf. *GFL*, p. 181).

[3] Robert archd. Taunton (J. A. Robinson (1921), pp. 89–90).

[4] Robert archdeacon (Wells) and Ivo dean Wells (cf. J. A. Robinson (1921), pp. 61–2, 79ff.).

[BRUTON]

Robert Occ. 1184 (ib., p. 56).

Gilbert Occ. *c.* 6 June 1199[1] (*Ad. Dom.*, II, 384); 1197[2] × 1205 (*HMC Wells*, I, 57); (G.) 1200 (*CDF*, no. 514); 28 May 1208 (*Ctl. Bruton*, no. 174).

Ralph ?early 13th cent. (*Ctl. Bruton*, no. 81).

Richard Occ. 25 Mar. 1222 (*Ctl.*, no. 425); 1231 × 2 (*Ctl.*, no. 131).

BUCKENHAM (Norfolk), St James (perhaps also St Mary and All Saints: *Mon.*, VI, 419) f. *c.* 1146
  List in *VCH Norfolk*, II, 378.

William Occ. 1216 (Blomefield, *Norfolk*, I, 387); (W.) 15 May 1220 (Norwich D. and C., no. 1686).

BUCKLAND (Soms), St Mary and St Nicholas f. *c.* 1166; dissolved *c.* 1180[3] and soon after given to the Hospitallers to found a convent of nuns (q.v.; cf. *Ctl. Buckland*, nos. 3–5)

Master Walter Occ. 1174 × *c.* 1180 (BM Egerton MS 2104A, ff. 116v–117v); also *HMC Wells*, I, 432;[4] *Stogursey Chts.*, p. 48); 1180 (Heales, App., pp. xix–xx); *c.* 1180 (+1178; *Ctl. Bruton*, no. 138 – see Witham). Res. (cf. *Ctl. Buckland*, nos. 3–5); possibly the Walter ex-canon Buckland transferred to Barlinch, *Ctl. Buckland*, no. 4, and the 'Master' Walter later pr. Barlinch, q.v.; but he was not the only Walter can. Buckland, and the identification rests solely on the title 'master'.

BURSCOUGH (Lancs), St Nicholas f. *c.* 1190
  Lists in *VCH Lancs*, II, 151 (J. Tait);[5] *Ctl. Burscough*, pp. 17–18 (A. N. Webb).

Henry Occ. 1189 × 99 (*Ctl. Burscough*, pp. 229–30).

Geoffrey Occ. before Pr. Benedict (*Ctl.*, no. 19).

Benedict Occ. 1229, 14 May 1235 (*Ctl.*, nos. 16, 14).

BUSHMEAD (Beds), St Mary f. *c.* 1195; became regular –1215 (*Ctl. Bushmead*, pp. xv–xvi)
  Lists in *VCH Beds*, I, 386–7; *Ctl. Bushmead*, pp. xv–xvii, 2 (G. H. Fowler and J. Godber); late 14th-cent. list ib., p. 1.

(William Chaplain of Colmworth, Rector of Bushmead, occ. 31 Dec. 1198 (ib., no. 1).)

Joseph[6] of Coppingford –1215–*c.* 1233 Occ. 30 Aug. 1215 (*Ctl. Bushmead*, no. 13); 1227 (*Beds Eyre*, p. 101); 3 Nov. 1231 (*Ctl. Bushmead*, no. 193; *Beds F.*, no. 330). Chaplain of Coppingford hermitage (*Ctl. Bushmead*, no. 238; cf. *Ctl. Bushmead*, pp. xvif.).

His successor, John de Wildeboef, was el. 1233 (*Reg. Wells*, III, 31; cf. *Ctl. Bushmead*, p. xvii).

BUTLEY (Suffolk), St Mary f. 22 Feb. 1171 (*UGQ*, p. 163)
  List in *VCH Suffolk*, II, 98.

---

[1] Cf. J. A. Robinson (1921), p. 69. Gilbert occurs twice in the list in *Ctl. Bruton*, p. xxxi; the first with references to *HMC Wells* (i.e. the first Wells *Rep.* = *10th Rep.*, III (1885), p. 170; but this = *HMC Wells*, I, 57 – see above). [2] See Taunton.

[3] Not before 1180 (see below). The transfer to the Hospitallers was formally confirmed in a series of documents ranging from 8 Nov. 1186 (the bp. of Bath), prob. *c.* Jan. 1187 (king and archbishop; cf. Eyton, *Itinerary*, p. 276), to 6 June 1187 (the pope – just possibly 1186): *Ctl. Buckland*, nos. 7–11. But some time had elapsed since the res. of Walter and the dispersal of the canons to Barlinch and elsewhere, which is described in *Ctl. Buckland*, nos. 3–6.

[4] Richard (of Guildford) archd. Taunton (Bath) indicates a date in any case earlier than *c.* 1184 (J. A. Robinson (1921), pp. 87, 90).

[5] Tait included William, occ. ?–1199, early 13th cent. The references are probably to the Pr. William who occ. +1229.

[6] 'John' in *Beds Eyre*, no. 98 of 1227; but no. 101 gives Joseph – John is clearly a scribe's slip.

Gilbert 1171–1192 Can. and precentor of Blythburgh (*Ann. Colchester, UGQ*, p. 165); occ. 1184 (Chelmsford, Essex Rec. Office, D/DBy Q 19, f. 45r–v); 1185 × 92 (*Ctl. Colchester*, II, p. 567); (G.) 9 Oct. 1189 (Colvin, p. 350); res. 1192 (*Ann. Colchester*, p. 165).

William de Boytone 1192– App. 24 June 1192 (*Ann. Colchester, UGQ*, p. 165); occ. 1195 (BM Harl. MS 2110, f. 64v); 16 Oct. 1198 (*FF*, PRS XXIV, no. 11); 1209 × 10 (*Norfolk F.*, PRS LXX, no. 248).

Robert Occ. 1212 × 13 (*Suffolk F.*, PRS LXX, no. 556).

Adam Occ. 6 Oct. 1219 (*Lincs F.*, I, p. 119); (A.) 1227 × 30 (Norwich D. and C., no. 4194); 3 Feb. 1235 (*Essex F.*, p. 103); 1236 × 7 (*Suffolk F.* (Rye), p. 39).

CALDWELL (Beds), St John the Baptist and St John the Evangelist f. *c.* 1154
List in *VCH Beds*, I, 384.

Osbert Occ. 1178 (*Ctl. Newnham*, no. 139); (O.) *c.* 1180 (*HMC Var. Coll.*, VII, 377); (O.) 1186 (Gorham, *Hist. of St Neots*, II, p. lxxiv; cf. p. xl); 18 Oct. 1188 (*Ctl. Harrold*, p. 57).

Hugh Occ. (H.) ?1198 × 9 (Cheney, *Inn. III*, no. 176); 8 July 1200 (*Beds F.*, no. 65);[1] *c.* 1200 × 3 (*Bk. Seals*, no. 375).

Alexander 1212–1229 Sub-pr. of Dunstable, el. 28 Oct. 1212 (*Ann. Dunstable*, p. 39); occ. 1216 × 18 (*Ctl. Newnham*, no. 443); 1227 (*Beds F.*, no. 295); d. 1229 (*Ann. Dunstable*, p. 115).

CALKE (Derbys), *see* **REPTON**

CALWICH (Staffs) (Kenilworth) f. –1148; cell of Kenilworth –1169
List in *VCH Staffs*, III, 239 (J. C. Dickinson).

?Florence Occ. 18 Oct. 1130 × 2 as pr. 'Wich' (*Bk. Seals*, no. 130).

Henry Occ. *c.* 1197 × 1210 (F. Taylor, in *BJRL*, XXXIII (1950–1), 155, cited *VCH*, loc. cit.).

CANONS ASHBY (Northants), St Mary f. 1147 × 51
List in *VCH Northants*, II, 132.

?William Occ. n.d. ?mid-12th cent. (BM Egerton MS 3033, f. 2: followed by cht. of mid-12th cent.: see Gresley).

Alexander Occ. (A.) *c.* 1181 × 5 (see Dorchester); 1186 × 95 (BM Cott. MS Tib. E. v, f. 52v); 1197 × 1205 (*Mon.*, v, 192–3; cf. Northampton, St Andrew); 1198 × 1201 (Cheney, *Inn. III*, no. 361). On his scholarly work, see Russell, *Dict.*, pp. 12–13; R. W. Hunt in *TRHS*, 4th Series, XIX (1936), 20, 28–9.

Hugh Occ. 1213 × 14, 20 Jan. 1215 (BM Egerton MS 3033, ff. 117v, 98v).
The next recorded pr., Osbert, res. –14 Feb. 1226 (*Reg. Wells*, II, p. 217).

CANONSLEIGH (Devon), St Mary and St John the Evangelist f. *c.* 1161
List in *Ctl. Canonsleigh*, p. 116, q.v. for dates of chts. cited.

Aibrich ?Can. of Plympton, occ. *c.* 1161 (*Ctl. Montacute*, no. 138).

Richard[2] Occ. *c.* 1177 × 96 (*Ctl. St Nicholas, Exeter*, no. 134 in *CTG*, I, 187).[3]

Jordan Occ. –1196 (*Ctl. St Nicholas, Exeter*, no. 135);[3] *c.* 6 June 1199 (*Ad. Dom.*, II, 384–6).

---

[1] In the same fine in *Ped. Fin.*, I, p. 27, Hugh is printed as Henry.

[2] A Pr. Richard also occ. in *Ctl. Canonsleigh*, no. 153, which is just possibly before 1196, but is more probably 1200 × 19; he may thus be identical with R. occ. 1206.

[3] The MS, BM Cott. MS Vitell. D. ix, f. 63r–v, shows that both chts. were issued by William de Clavile II, whose father founded Canonsleigh, and who d. before 9 May 1196 when his widow appears in a fine (*FF*, PRS XVII, no. 136).

[CANONSLEIGH]
R. (?Richard II)   Occ. 1206 (*Ctl. Canonsleigh*, no. 181).
The next recorded pr., Roger, occ. 1238 (*Ctl. Canonsleigh*, no. 142).

CANTERBURY (Kent), St Gregory   f. –1086 (hospital); *c.* 1123 (priory)
  Lists in *VCH Kent*, II, 159; *Ctl. St Gregory, Canterbury*, ed. A. M. Woodcock, pp. 172–3.
Alvred   Occ. 1126×36 (*Text. Roff.*, f. 203); 1139×40 (Saltman, no. 161, pp. 384–5);
  1142×8 (*Ctl. St Gregory*, nos. 5, 6); 10 Dec. 1146 (ib., no. 25); 1148 (Canterbury Cathedral, Cart. Ant. M. 20, cited Woodcock, loc. cit.).
Richard   Occ. (Rikeward) 29 Jan. 1170 (*Ctl.*, no. 143); 1182×4 (*Reg. Roff.*, pp. 169–70);
  13 July 1185 (*Ctl.*, no. 27); 1186×7 (ib., no. 24). Abb. Cirencester 1187–1213 (q.v.).
Dunstan   Occ. 1187 (Gervase, I, 365); 23 Nov. 1198 (*FF.*, PRS XXIV, no. 152); +1198 (*Ctl.*, no. 8).
Robert of Oseney   1213–*c.* 1215 El. 1213; res. 'post aliquot annos' to be m. of Clairvaux (*Ann. Dunstable*, p. 41; cf. *Ctl.*, p. 172).
Peter   Occ. (P.) –1216 (ib., no. 45); *c.* 1222 (ib., no. 170); 1223 (*Kent F.*, p. 78).
The next recorded pr., Thomas, occ. July 1227 (*Ctl.*, p. 168).

CARLISLE (Cumberland), St Mary (Arrouaisian)   f. 1122[1] (priory); 1133 (Cath. Priory).
  D.G. Lists in *VCH Cumberland*, II, 150; Le Neve, new ed. forthcoming (D. Greenway).
Walter   Occ. 1133×57; *c.* 1165×9 (*Ctl. Wetheral*, no. 281, p. 421); 1150[×1] (*Ctl. Holm Cultram*, p. 92); *c.* 1151 (*EYC*, V, no. 169); 1154×81 (*Ctl. Whitby*, I, p. 39); 1169 (*Ctl. Lanercost*, viii, 5); *c.* 1175 (*Ctl. Wetheral*, no. 38).
John   Occ. prob. 1185×9 (*Ctl. Holm Cultram*, no. 50; cf. nos. 49a–e, 50a); 20 Apr. 1194 (*Cartae Antiquae* (1938), no. 195); 23 Apr. 1197 (*FF.*, PRS XX, no. 128); March 1201 (Cheney, *Inn. III*, nos. 306–9); ?1203×13 (ibid., no. 945); 6 May 1204 (*Ped. Fin.*, II, p. 8). A pr., unnamed, occ. 26×31 May 1214 (*Rot. Lit. Pat.*, pp. 138b, 142b).
The priory was vacant 26 June 1214 (*Rot. Lit. Claus.*, I, 207b).
Henry de Mareis   1214– ?Can. Merton, el. –25 Aug. 1214 (*Rot. Lit. Claus.*, I, 211b); occ. Nov. 1214 (*Ch. Lanercost*, p. 14); (H.) *c.* 1203×14 (*HMC 10th Rep.*, IV, 322).
Prob. vacant Apr. 1217 (Rymer, *Foedera*, I, 147; cf. Le Neve).
Bartholomew   –1231 Prob. appointed 1218 (*CChR, 1257–1300*, pp. 363–4). Occ. (B.) 1219×23 (*Ctl. Wetheral*, no. 20 – as Bartholomew prob. 1219×23, no. 29);[2] 1229 (*CRR*, XIII, no. 1508); d. 1231(×2) (*Ch. Lanercost*, p. 41).

CARMARTHEN, St John the Evangelist and St Theulac
Pr. John Edrich, occ. *Ctl. Carmarthen*, p. 7, has been attributed to the 13th cent.; he was in fact of the late 13th cent. (cf. *Litt. Wallie*, ed. J. G. Edwards, Cardiff, 1940, p. 183), and no known pr. falls within the period of this book.

CARTMEL (Lancs), St Mary   f. 1189×94
  List in *VCH Lancs*, II, 148 (J. Tait).
Daniel[3]   Occ. (D.) 1194×1205 (*Lancs PR*, p. 339 = *Ctl. Furness*, II, iii, p. 735); (D.) 1198× 1202 (BM Cott. MS Nero D. iii, f. 22 v; cf. Cheney, *Inn. III*, no. 360).
William   Occ. (W.) 1201×13[4] (*Lancs PR*, p. 365); (W.) 1205×6 (*Lancaster Hist.*, II, 385–6); 20 Jan. 1208 (*Lancs F.*, p. 39); 14 Aug. 1214 (*Ctl. Furness*, II, ii, p. 312).
The next recorded pr., Absalom, occ. 6 July 1221 (ib. II, ii, p. 321).

---

[1] Or possibly 1102: see Le Neve.
[2] It is not certain that Bp. Hugh (1219–23) was still alive in no. 29.
[3] For the name, Tait seems to cite County Placita (Chancery) Lancs, no. 26, but the reference cannot be traced.   [4] Master H(onorius) effective archd. Richmond (Clay, *Fasti*, p. 46).

CHACOMBE (Northants), St Peter and St Paul f. *temp*. Henry II
   List in *VCH Northants*, II, 134 (from 1241).
Walter Occ. late 12th cent. (PRO E315/49/83); (W.) prob. 1191 × 3 (Madox, *Form.*,
   p. xiv; PRO E326/8776; see Launde).
The next recorded pr., Thomas, occ. 1226 × 7 (*Warws F.*, no. 384).

CHARLEY (Leics) f. –1190
   List in *VCH Leics*, II, 24 (R. A. McKinley).
William Occ. 1207 × 19[1] (Nichols, *Leics*, III, 120); *temp*. Henry III (pal.: *HMC Hastings*,
   I, 12).
The next recorded pr., Simon, res. 1264 (*Reg. Gravesend*, p. 143).

CHIRBURY (Salop), St Michael f. *c.* 1190 (at Snead); *c.* 1195 (at Chirbury). On Chirbury, cf. Eyton, *Salop*, XI, 58ff.
   M.C. List in *VCH* Salop (forthcoming).
Richard –1217 Res. 1217 to be abb. of Wellow (Grimsby): royal assent 10 Aug. (*CPR*,
   1216–25, p. 83).

CHRISTCHURCH (Twynham) (Hants), Holy Trinity f. –1066 (secular canons);
c. 1150[2] (Augustinian)
   List in *VCH Hants*, II, 160.
Reginald Occ. 14 Apr. 1152 (*PUE*, I, no. 52).
?Julian Occ. 1161 (*HMC Rutland*, IV, 60).[3]
Reginald Occ. 10 July 1169 (*PUE*, I, no. 111); 1170 × 3 (BM Cott. MS Tib. D. vi, pt. i,
   ff. 57v–58).
Peter Occ. 1203 × 4 (Hants F., PRO Transcripts); d. or res. –1221 (*CRR*, X, p. 222).
Roger Occ. *temp. John* –?early 13th cent. (?pal.: *Berkeley Chts.*, no. 96); *c.* 1216[4] (PRO
   E326/8494); 13 × 21 Jan. 1225 (*Dorset F.*, p. 27); 21 May 1227 (*Wilts F.*, p. 17).
The next recorded pr., Richard, occ. *c.* 13 Feb. 1232 (ib., p. 21).

CHURCH GRESLEY (Derbys), St Mary and St George f. ?*temp*. Stephen
   List in *VCH Derbys*, II, 57; *SHC*, New Series, I (1898), 175ff. (F. Madan).[5]
Reginald Occ. 1151 × 7 (BM Harl. MS 3650, f. 18r–v); n.d. (BM Egerton MS 3033, f. 2v).
Walter Occ. prob. *c.* 1210 × 40[6] (BM Add. MS 6671, f. 15v).

CIRENCESTER (Glos), St Mary f. –839 (College); 1131 (abbey)
   Lists in *VCH Glos*, II, 83–4 (R. Graham); *Ctl. Cirencester*, I, pp. xliiif. (C. D. Ross).
ABBOTS
Serlo 1131– Can. and prob. dean of Salisbury (see K. Edwards in *VCH Wilts*, III, 207, citing
   Leland, *Itin.* (ed. Toulmin Smith), I, 265); app. and bl. 1131 (Florence, II, 92 = *JW*,
   p. 31).[7] Occ. 1133 (*Reg.*, II, no. 1782); 21 Dec. 1136 (*Ctl. Cirencester*, I, no. 145); in papal

[1] Saher de Quincy, earl of Winchester.
[2] Although the f. cht. or its confirmation (*Reg.*, III, no. 903) is spurious, the date (1150) presumably
   represents early tradition and cannot be far wrong.
[3] The date has been kindly checked for us on the original cht. in Belvoir Castle by Dr L. A. Parker.
[4] The reference to King John may suggest he was dead, but not long dead (for the case, see *CRR*, VI,
   pp. 118, 120 (1211); VII, p. 290 (1214)).
[5] We have ignored Cox's list in *VCH* and followed Madan's which was carefully compiled from the
   same sources, and is fully documented.
[6] Dated by Geoffrey de Gresley, see Madan, ut supra, pp. 35ff., 176.
[7] S.a. 1130, but apparently referring to 1131 – between the bl. of Walter abb. Gloucester and consec.
   of Robert, bp. Hereford.

[CIRENCESTER]

  bull of 11 Feb. 1147 (ib., no. 148 = *PUE*, III, no. 61). D. 30 Jan. (Leland, op. cit., I, 265–6), i.e. 1147[1] × 9.

Andrew –1176 Occ. 1149 (*Reg.*, III, no. 455); 1155 × 66 (*Ctl. Cirencester*, II, no. 615); 1168 × 75 (Lambeth MS 1212, f. 41r–v). D. 27 Dec. 1176 (*Gesta Hen. II*, I, 136; *Ann. Tewkesbury*, p. 51; cf. *GFL*, p. 532).

Adam 1177–1183 Pr. Bradenstoke, app. 1177 (Ann. Winchcombe, BM Cott. MS Faust. B. i, f. 20; cf. *Ann. Tewkesbury*, p. 52); occ. 5 May 1178 (*PUE*, III, no. 248); d. 1183 (BM Cott. MS Faust. B. i, f. 21).

Robert[2] 1183–1186 App. 1183, d. 1186 (BM Cott. MS Faust. B. i, f. 21); occ. 1183 × 6 (*Ctl. Cirencester*, II, no. 708).

The abbey was vacant for 3 terms, Michaelmas–Easter 1186–7 (*PR 33 Henry II*, pp. 26–7).

Richard 1187–1213 Pr. St Gregory, Canterbury (q.v.), app. 1187 (see above; BM Cott. MS Faust. B. i, f. 21v). Occ. 1189 (BM Stowe MS 925, ff. 34v–35); j.d. +16 Feb. 1197 (*Ctl. Bruton*, nos. 283–4); *c.* 14 Oct. 1203 (*Bucks F.*, p. 27). Presumably the unnamed abb. who d. 1213 (*Ann. Waverley*, p. 273); and possibly the abb. who d. 1 July (BM Lansd. MS 427, f. 11).

Master Alexander Nequam 1213–1216 Licence to el. 24 July 1213 (*Rot. Lit. Claus.*, I, 146b); return of temporalities, 1 Aug. 1213 (*Ctl. Cirencester*, I, no. 86). Occ. 21 July 1215 (ib., no. 88). D. 31 Mar. 1217 (for the day Floyer and Hamilton, p. 92; for the year *Ann. Worcester*, p. 409, and see below). On him see Russell, *Dict.*, pp. 14–17.

Walter of Gloucester 1216–1230 Cellarer of Cirencester; royal assent to el. 27 Apr. 1217 (*Rot. Lit. Claus.*, I, 307b). D. –5 Dec. 1230 (*CPR 1225–32*, p. 418). Occ. 21 Oct. 1219 (*Ctl. Cirencester*, I, no. 193); 5 Mar. 1225 (ib., I, no. 196).

COCKERHAM (Lancs), St Michael f. 1207 × 8

  List in *VCH Lancs*, II, 153 (J. Tait).

A. Occ. 1208 (*Lancs PR*, p. 365).

The next recorded pr., Henry, occ. *c.* 1250 (*Lancaster Hist.*, II, 431); cf. Tait's notes in *VCH*.

COLCHESTER (St Botolph) (Essex), St Julian and St Botolph f. *c.* 1093 (secular); *c.* 1100 × 6 (Augustinian)

  List in *VCH Essex*, II, 150.

Ainulf 1st pr. occ. 1108 (*Wm. Newb.*, ed. Hearne, III, 694, 696 f.); 1116 (*Mon.*, VI, 106).

John Occ. 1140 × 3 (*Reg.*, III, no. 210); 1145 (Gibbs, no. 154).

William Occ. 1153 × 95 (*Ctl. Rievaulx*, no. 49).

Godfrey Occ. 11 June 1180 (*GFL*, no. 374).

Henry Occ. 1205 (*Essex F.*, p. 35); 1206 (*Ctl. Colchester*, II, pp. 541–2); 1207+ (ib., II, pp. 557–8).

The next recorded pr., Robert, occ. 11 Jan. 1221 (ib., p. 534).

COLD NORTON (Oxon), St John the Evangelist and St Giles f. 1148 × 58

  List in *VCH Oxon*, II, 97 (H. E. Salter).

Master Samuel Occ. (late 12th or) early 13th cent. (PRO E315/49/277); (S.) j.d. +25 Apr. 1212 (*Ctl. Oxford, St Frideswide*, II, p. 50; Cheney, *Inn. III*, no. 899); (S.) 1200 × 18 (*Ctl. Oseney*, V, pp. 96–8 = Cheney, *Inn. III*, no. 1158).

The next recorded pr., Roger, occ. 1229 (*CRR*, XIII, no. 1717).

[1] 1147 is possible since his death would not have been known in the papal Curia by 11 Feb.
[2] No evidence has been found for the existence of Robert I, app. and d. 1183, in the older lists.

COMBWELL (Kent), St Mary Magdalene   f. *temp.* Henry II (abbey); *c.* 1216 × 20 (priory)
List in *VCH Kent*, II, 161.

ABBOTS

Hurso   First abb., occ. prob. *temp.* Henry II ('Charters of Combwell Pr.', *Arch.Cant.*, V, 197).

Andrew   Occ. 1178 × 88 (*Ctl. Oseney*, VI, p. 171); n.d. (*CChR*, II, 298).

John   Bl. 1184 × 90 by Abp. Baldwin (Gervase, II, 405); occ. +1 Oct. 1194 (*HMC De L'Isle and Dudley*, I, 45); n.d. (*Robertsbridge Chts.*, no. 32).

William   Occ. (W.) +17 Feb. 1205 (BM Egerton Cht. 382: cf. Cheney, *Inn. III*, no. 601); 1210 (*CRR*, VI, p. 94); res. *temp.* Abp. Stephen Langton, prob. 1216 × 19 (*Arch. Cant.*, V, 214; cf. *Acta Stephani Langton*, no. 44 and n.).

Henry   Succeeded William *c.* 1216 × 19 (*Arch. Cant.*, V, 212–13; cf. *Acta, ut supra*).

PRIORS

Henry   Former abb., became first pr. (ib.); occ. 21 Sept. 1227 (*Kent F.*, p. 85); 1230 (*CRR*, XIII, no. 2546); 1236 (*Kent F.*, p. 126).

CONISHEAD (Lancs), St Mary   f. –1181
List in *VCH Lancs*, II, 143 (J. Tait).

R.   Occ. 1194 × 1205 (*Lancs PR*, p. 339 = *Ctl. Furness*, II, iii, p. 735).

T.   Occ. 1194 × 1205 (*Ctl. Cockersand*, III, ii, 1038–9); 1201 × 13 (*Lancs PR*, p. 365); 1208 (*Lancs PR*, p. 362 = *Ctl. Furness*, I, ii, p. 438); 14 Aug. 1214 (*Ctl. Furness*, II, ii, pp. 312–13).

The next recorded pr., Augustine, occ. 6 July 1221 (ib., II, ii, p. 321; also, n.d., *Ctl. St Bees*, pp. 300–1).

COXFORD (Norfolk), St Mary   f. *c.* 1140 (at Rudham); *c.* 1216 (at Coxford)
Lists in *VCH Norfolk*, II, 380; *Ctl. Coxford*,[1] ed. H. W. Saunders, *Norfolk Archaeology*, XVII (1910), pp. 284ff., esp. 346–54.

Matthew   1st pr. (*Ctl.* pp. 288–9, 332), occ. 4 Apr. 1144 (*Ctl.*, pp. 288–9 = MS, f. 3; cf. p. 346); d. –8 May 1171 (*Ctl.*, p. 338).

Ralph   Occ. (R.) 29 July 1175 (ib., p. 294, corrected by MS, ff. 57v–8); 10 Sept. 1177 (ib., p. 295; for date see MS, f. 3).

Herbert   Occ. 29 Sept. 1198 (MS, f. 12; *Norfolk F.*, PRS LXV, no. 93); 11 May 1203 (*Norfolk F.*, PRS LXX, no. 27); 7 Dec. 1207 (BM Add. MS 47,784, f. 73v); 15 Apr. 1212 (*Norfolk F.*, PRS LXX, no. 265: *Ctl. MS*, f. 15v, cf. f. 16r–v).

Reyner   Occ. early 13th cent. (*Ctl.*, pp. 305–6, 337–8, 346).

?Robert   Occ. 1209 × 34[2] (*Ctl.*, p. 346).

William   Occ. 6 Oct. 1223, June 1230 (*Ctl.*, MS, ff. 52, 51v); *c.* 27 Jan. 1233 (BM Add. MS 47,784, f. 30).

The next recorded pr., Adam, occ. 14 Jan. 1235 (ibid.).

DARLEY (Derby) (Derbys), St Mary (formerly St Helen)   f. 1137 (at Derby) (St Helen); *c.* 1146 (at Darley) (St Mary of the Derwent); cf. *Ctl. Darley*, I, pp. ii, iii
Lists in *VCH Derbys*, II, 53; *Ctl. Darley*, I, p. lxxx (R. R. Darlington).

ABBOTS

Albinus   First abb. (Dale Ch. – see Dale – p. 9); occ. 1151 (*Burton Chts.*, no. 13); *c.* 1153[3] (ib., no. 14); 1175 (*Ctl. Darley*, II, p. 539); 1176 (*Ctl. Oseney*, V, p. 71).

---

[1] The printed calendar is very inadequate: we owe the references to the MS (Norfolk and Norwich Rec. Office, SUN/8) to Dr Greenway.

[2] With Robert pr. Castle Acre; but his existence is not established.

[3] Ranulf, earl of Chester (d. 16 Dec. 1153) and William, abb. 'Radmore' (see Stoneleigh).

[DARLEY]

?William Occ. *c.* 1190 (*Ctl. Darley*, I, pp. 174–5).

Walter –1210 Occ. 1187 × 97 (*Burton Chts.*, no. 37); 1189 × 97[1] (*Reg. Lincoln*, III, no. 922); 1200 × 10 (*Burton Chts.*, no. 45); 1210 (*Ctl. Darley*, II, p. 414).

Henry of Repton –1214–1223 Occ. as abb. elect in j.d. decision +28 July 1210 (ibid.; cf. Cheney, *Inn. III*, no. 873); put in possession 21 Dec. 1214 (*Rot. Lit. Pat.*, p. 125). Occ. 1216 × 22 (*Burton Chts.*, no. 72); (H.) 1222 (*Ctl. Tutbury*, no. 14); 22 Sept. 1226 (*Derbys F.* (1886), p. 18); *c.* 1227 (*Glapwell Chts.*, ed. R. R. Darlington, nos. 19–20); d. –20 Aug. 1233 (*CPR, 1232–47*, p. 24).

DODNASH (Suffolk), St Mary f. *c.* 1188

List in *VCH Suffolk*, II, 100 (from 1346).

Adam Occ. 25 Sept. 1188 (*Anc. Chts.*, no. 53).

The next recorded pr., Jordan, occ. Mich. 1228 (*CRR*, XIII, no. 1201).

DORCHESTER (Oxon), St Peter, St Paul and St Birinus (Arrouaisian) f. *c.* 1140

List in *VCH Oxon*, II, 89 (H. E. Salter).

ABBOTS

Alvred Occ. 6 Feb. 1146 (*Reg. Lincoln*, I, no. 286); 1149 (*Ctl. Oseney*, IV, p. 28); 6 July 1163 (*PUE*, III, no. 146); (A.) 1173 × 82 (*Ctl. Eynsham*, I, no. 58).

Eustace Occ. (E.) *c.* 1181 × 5[2] (A. Croke, *A Genealogical Hist. of the Croke Family*, I, 425–6; Baddeley, *Hist. Cirencester*, p. 113); (E.) July 1190 (*Ctl. Oseney*, VI, p. 99); 1186 × 94[3] (*Ctl. Oseney*, IV, p. 442); (E.) 1210 × 11 (*Ctl. Oxford, St Frideswide*, II, p. 246; cf. Cheney, *Inn. III*, no. 871 and n.).

Roger Occ. 1215 +[4] (*Reg. Lincoln*, III, no. 955); 1216 × 17 (*Ctl. Oseney*, IV, p. 228); presumably the abb., unnamed, who res. shortly –1225 (Bracton, *Notebook*, I, 551).

DRAX (Yorks W.), St Nicholas f. 1130 × 9

C.T.C. List in *VCH Yorks*, III, 208.

Norman Occ. *c.* 29 Sept 1178 (Bodl. MS Top. Yorks c. 72, f. 81 v; cf. Burton, *Mon. Ebor.*, p. 114n.).

Alan Occ. 13 Jan. × 3 Feb. 1205 (*Yorks F., John*, p. 93); *c.* 1213 + (Burton, p. 114, citing MS cit. f. 69 v).

Robert Occ. 7 and 14 Jan. 1227 (*Yorks F., 1218–31*, p. 105; Bodl. MS Top. Yorks, c. 72, ff. 81 r–v = 95 v).

DUNMOW, *see* **LITTLE DUNMOW**

DUNSTABLE (Beds), St Peter f. –1125[5]

Lists in *VCH Beds*, I, 377; *Ctl. Dunstable*, ed. G. H. Fowler, p. 16. Basis in *Ann. Dunstable*, on which see C. R. Cheney in *Essays...presented to B. Wilkinson*, pp. 79–98.

Bernard Can. Holy Trinity, Aldgate, brother of Norman, pr. Aldgate (Newburgh, ed. Hearne, III, 695, 697 = *Ctl. London, Aldgate*, pp. 226–31); occ. 1125 (ib., p. 168); (B.) 1148 × 61 (*Ctl. Dunstable*, no. 180).

---

[1] Hamo dean Lincoln (see p. 170 n. 1); Adam abb. Welbeck. [2] J.-d. of Pope Lucius III.

[3] Hugh bp. Lincoln; Stephen chancellor (William de Montibus had succeeded him by 22 Mar. 1193 × 4, *HMC Rutland*, IV, 113–14).

[4] Robert archd. Huntingdon (William of Cornhill was el. bp. Coventry 1214, consec. 25 Jan. 1215).

[5] The foundation cht. was dated 1131 × 2 by G. H. Fowler (*Ctl. Dunstable*, p. 342); but he noted that the house may have existed earlier (he cited a reference in *PR 31 Henry I*, p. 100). There is nothing surprising in a foundation cht. being issued up to ten or fifteen years after the foundation (cf. V. H. Galbraith in *Cambs. Hist. Journ.*, IV (1934), 205). For 1125, see under Bernard.

Cuthbert (Gubert, ? = Hubert) For name, cf. *Ctl. Dunstable*, no. 877. Occ. (Gubert) 1151 × 67 (*HMC Var. Coll.*, VII, 32); –1166 (*Ctl. Dunstable*, no. 165 = *Ctl. Eynsham*, II, p. 157); (H.) 1162¹ × 76 (*HMC Var. Coll.*, VII, 33). H. = Gubert or an unknown pr.: if so unknown to Dunstable tradition since Richard called the 4th pr. (see n. 2).

Thomas[2] –1202 Can. and sacrist of St Bartholomew's (*Wulfric of Haselbury*, pp. 134, 173; *GFL*, no. 236n.); occ. (T.) 1163 × 76 (ib., no. 236, p. 309); 1176 (*EYC*, II, no. 774); 24 Oct. 1185 (*Ctl. Dunstable*, no. 167); 14 Oct. 1200 (*CRR*, I, p. 284); res. 1202 (*Ann. Dunstable*, p. 28), d. 1205 (ib., p. 29).

Richard de Mores 1202–1242 Can. of Merton, el. 1202 (*Ann. Dunstable*, p. 28); occ. 5 Nov. 1202 (*Beds F.*, no. 110); 1227 (*CRR*, XIII, no. 576); 2 × 9 Feb. 1238 (*Derbys F.* (1886), p. 42); d. 9 Apr. 1242 (*Ann. Dunstable*, p. 158). On him see S. Kuttner and E. Rathbone in *Traditio*, VII (1949–51), pp. 327ff., esp. pp. 338–9.

ELSHAM (Lincs), St Mary and St Edmund f. –1166
List in *VCH Lincs*, II, 172.

William Clement Occ. as bp.'s chaplain 1157 × 63 (*DC*, no. 58; cf. Combe); without title 1163 × 6³ (*Ctl. Oseney*, VI, p. 147); as pr. 1160 × 6;[4] prob. 1167 (*Reg. Lincoln*, I, no. 287, cf. note; IV, no. 1293) – all as William Clement; also as William 1170 × 5 (*EYC*, III, no. 1308; see Thornton Curtis); 1173 × 82 (*Ctl. Eynsham*, I, no. 58); late 12th cent. (*DC*, no. 302, with Achard abb. Barlings). He also occ. as William Clement in a fine of 3 Nov. 1208 (*Lincs F.*, PRS LXVII, no. 263), but this gives him a very exceptional span, and the evidence given below suggests his name is an anachronism on the fine.

Henry Can. Elsham, was el. to succeed William Clement, temp. bp. H(ugh) of Lincoln, i.e. 1186 × 1200 or 1209 × 35 (*Reg. Lincoln*, II, no. 353); the earlier date seems proved by his occ. (H.) 2 Sept. 1201 (BM Harl. Cht. 53. D. 10); n.d., but with similar witnesses (ib., 52. E. 48, 54. C. 47); occ. 1213 × 14[5] (York D. and C. Magnum Reg. Album, III, f. 5 v); 25 Nov. 1218 (*Lincs F.*, I, p. 124).

The next recorded pr., William Escrop, can. Elsham, el. 1229 (*Reg. Wells*, III, p. 173).

FELLEY (Notts), St Mary (and St Helena) (Worksop) f. 1152
The Felley Ctl., BM Add. MS 36,872 (16th cent.: the names are on ff. 32–3, 83 v–5, 89, 90, 106), contains various names of prs., for the most part very difficult to date with any precision. *VCH Notts*, II, 112, arranges them in the following order, stated to be conjectural: Walter, prob. first pr.; Adam 'de Nokton' and William de Lovetot, *temp.* Henry II; Henry and Thomas, *temp.* Henry III; Walter, occ. *c.* 1240 (citing *Nottingham Borough Recs.*, I, 38, of 1234 × 41). The first pr. Walter may well be identical with the second (there is no ground for supposing him first pr.); Adam occ. 1252 (ff. 32 v–3); the others may well be later. Thus it is possible that none of these prs. belongs to our period.

GLOUCESTER, St Oswald[6] f. c. 909 (as college); –1153 (priory)
List in *VCH Glos*, II, 87 (R. Graham).

[1] R. pr. Hospitallers in England (Richard Turcus or Ralph de Diva), whose predecessor, Walter, occ. 1162 (BM Lansd. Cht. 679, cited *Ctl.Hospitallers*, I, p. clviii).

[2] *Ann. Dunstable*, Introd., p. xi n. states that the two predecessors of Richard were both named Thomas, but there is no evidence that there were two of the name, save that the 14th-cent. document cited calls Richard the *fourth* prior (p. 410): see above.

[3] If William is the correct name for the dean of Lincoln.

[4] Ralph subdean (*Reg. Lincoln*, VII, p. 203 and n.) and Robert bp. Lincoln.

[5] Nicholas of Tusculum, papal legate (cf. Tillmann, pp. 98–107).

[6] Confusion has arisen because both this house and Nostell were commonly referred to as 'St Oswald'; cf. e.g. *CDF*, nos. 1062, 1388; *York Minster Fasti*, II, p. xiii.

[GLOUCESTER]

Humphrey Can. of Lanthony by Gloucester, occ. 1152 (John of Hexham in *Sim. Dur.*, II, 328).

Ralph Occ. 1163 × 86 (Oxford, Balliol MS 271, f. 112v); *c.* 1170 × 81[1] (*CDF*, no. 29).

William Occ. 1177 (BM Egerton MS 3031, f. 48r–v).

The next recorded pr., William, occ. 19 Mar. 1230 (*HMC, 5th Rep.* App., p. 335).

GREAT BRICETT (Suffolk), St Leonard (Nobiliac) f. 1114 × 19

List in *VCH Suffolk*, II, 95 (from 1312).

Peter Occ. 1187 × 92 (Cambridge, King's Coll., B/9); 1178[2] × 1200 (Bodl. MS Gough, Norfolk 18, f. 11); (P.) 22 Nov. 1206 (CUL Add. MS 4220, ff. 103r–v = 172v–3; PRO DL 42/5, ff. 16v–17; cf. Cheney, *Inn. III*, no. 694. The precise date varies from 19–22 Nov. in the MSS).

H. Occ. 4 May 1218 (Chelmsford, Essex Rec. Office, MS D/DBy Q 19, ff. 35–6).

GRESLEY, *see* CHURCH GRESLEY

GUISBOROUGH (Yorks N.), St Mary f. 1119

C.T.C. Lists in *Ctl. Guisborough*, II, pp. xxxix ff.; *VCH Yorks*, III, 212. Obits ed. F. Wormald, *YAJ*, XXXI (1932–4), 27–8, from BM Add. MS 35,285; also in Bodl. Laud MS Lat. 5, ff. 3 ff. (confirming Cuthbert, Laurence, Roald).

William de Brus Brother of the founder; occ. 6 Oct. 1132 (*Mem. Fountains*, I, 24; cf. p. 10 and n. for day); 1119 × 39 (*Ctl. Whitby*, I, pp. 214–16); d. 3 Aug. (obit) or 1 Aug. (Calendar in *CTG*, IV, 261).

Cuthbert Occ. −1139 (?−1136)[3] (*EYC*, I, no. 375); 1141 (*Sim. Dur.*, II, 311); 1157 × 9 (*PUE*, I, no. 74); (C.) *1160 × 70* (C. occ. in *EYC*, II, no. 693 dated 1160 × 70 by Farrer on grounds not known; also referred to (not necessarily extant) in no. 1061, *1175 × 85*); d. 18 Dec. (obit – *sic* MS; 15 Dec. in Rud, p. 218).

Ralph Occ. 1180 (*PUE*, I, no. 180); −1181 (*Ctl. Guisborough*, II, no. 683); 1186 (Durham D. and C., I. 1. Arch. 8 – cf. St Mary's, York); *1180 × 95* (*EYC*, II, no. 700, cf. nos. 678, 699); d. 8 Dec. (obit). Brother of Pr. Cuthbert (*EYC*, II, no. 699; cf. no. 752).

Roald Occ. 1199 (*Ctl. Guisborough*, II, no. 686c); 1201 × 2 (Durham, Reg. III, ff. 189v–190); (R.) 12 Nov. 1202 (*Ctl. Selby*, II, no. 925); 1199 × 1203 (Raine, *North Durham*, p. 140); *1202 × 11* (*Ctl. Wetheral*, no. 119); d. 20 Sept. (obit).

Laurence Occ. 1204 × 10 (*Bk. Seals*, no. 460); −1212 (*Ctl. Whitby*, I, no. 355); 2 Feb. 1212 (*Ctl. Guisborough*, II, no. 1133); 1203 × 14 (*HMC, 10th Rep.*, IV, 321–2); (L.) 1203 × 17 (*Ctl. Healaugh Park*, p. 224 – for 'J.' read 'L.': so original cht., BM Egerton Cht. 515); res. 1216 × 18.

He resigned the priory into the hands of the legate Guala (according to an act of 1238, *Ctl. Guisborough*, II, p. 358; *Reg. W. Gray*, pp. 80–1); and occ. as 'quondam' 1219 × 23, 1222 × 3 (*Ctl. Whitby*, I, nos., 39, 42); d. 22 Jan. (obit).

Pr. Michael occ. Nov. 1218 (*Ctl. Guisborough*, II, no. 921).

HARTLAND (Devon), St Nectan (Arrouaisian) f. −1066 (Coll.); 1161 × 9 (abbey)[4]

List in Oliver, p. 205.

---

[1] Jeremy, archd. Cleveland; Ralph de Warneville, treasurer of York. Dated 1170 × 5 by Round: cf. p. xxiv – but no evidence is given for these limiting dates. [2] Thomas archd. Norwich.

[3] Prob. earlier than King Stephen's confirmation (*Reg.*, III, no. 942) of Feb. 1136, and witnessed by Archd. Hugh, i.e. Hugh precentor and archd., who prob. d. 4 July 1139 (Clay, in *YAJ*, XXXV (1943), 118).

[4] A prior, John, is known to occ. 29 Sept. 1169 (*CDF*, no. 900 = Morey, p. 147); possibly a claustral pr., or the house may have been a priory in early days. In any case it was presumably regular by 1169.

ABBOTS

B. n.d. (*Ctl. Beauchamp*, p. 58). The name is extended to Benedict by Oliver, pp. 219–20, but apparently without warrant.

?Hugh Oliver, p. 205, places Hugh *temp*. John; no evidence has been found for this and it may well be that the conjectural date is wrong and that this is the Hugh who occ. 6 June 1249 (*Devon F.*, no. 473).

HASTINGS (Sussex), Holy Trinity f. 1189 × 99

List in *VCH Sussex*, II, 77 (L. F. Salzman).

Jonas Occ. 1176 (*HMC De L'Isle & Dudley*, I, 34); 1189 (PRO E326/8901); n.d. (*Robertsbridge Chts.*, no. 3).

A. Occ. ('abbot') 7 × 13 Jan. 1206/7 (Cheney, *Inn. III*, no. 720 and n.).

John Occ. ('abbot') 1215 × 17 (*Ctl. Chichester*, p. 92).

The next recorded pr., Nicholas, occ. *c*. 1232 (case of 1261 × 2, PRO Ass. Roll, 912, m. 16).

HAUGHMOND (Salop), St John the Evangelist f. 1110 or *c*. 1120 (M. Chibnall: see below); the earliest datable document is of June–July 1141 (*Reg.*, III, no. 377).

M.C. Lists in Eyton, *Salop*, VII, 299ff.;[1] *VCH Salop*, forthcoming (M. Chibnall).

PRIOR

Fulk Occ. *c*. 1130 × 48 (?–1138) (Eyton, *Salop*, VII, 285–6; dated *c*. 1130 × 8 by Eyton, because William FitzAlan was driven out of Shropshire in 1138: but it was a temporary exile only. Evidently earlier than the next head, the first abb.).

ABBOTS

?Rouu' (*sic*) Occ. 1129 × 48 (Ctl. Haughmond, Shrewsbury Borough Lib., f. 145).[2]

Alvred Occ. 1163 × 6 or 1170 (Eyton, *Salop*, VII, 290; Henry II at Woodstock, between 1163 and 1173) – *nutricius* of Henry II; 14 May 1172 (*PUE*, I, no. 114); *?c. 1170 × 5* (Eyton, *Salop*, VIII, 27).

Richard Occ. *c*. 1177 × 82 (*Ctl. Chester*, II, p. 302); 1176+, 1186 × 7, 22 Nov. 1192 (Eyton, *Salop*, I, 359; V, 42; VI, 329); 27 Oct. 1194 (*Rot. Cur. Reg.*, I, 103).

?H. Occ. 1204 (Cheney, *Inn. III*, no. 525) – but possibly an error for R.

Ralph Occ. 1204 × 10 (Eyton, *Salop*, X, 336; +1204 if 'H.' above is correct); 1206 (ib., VII, 300); 1203 × 21 (Oxford, Balliol Coll. MS 271, f. 102); *?c. 1210* (*HMC, 10th Rep.*, IV, 437–8).

Osbert Occ. (O.) 1216 × 22 (Eyton, *Salop*, X, 336); 1219+ (Ctl. Haughmond, Shrewsbury Borough Lib., f. 52 = *Trans. Salop Arch. Soc.*, I (1878), 182).

HEMPTON (Fakenham) (Norfolk), St Stephen f. –1135

The list in *VCH Norfolk*, I, 385 is based on Blomefield, *Norfolk*, VII, 101, who lists Simon, 12 Henry II (1165 × 6) and then Richard, 54 Henry III (1269–70) without references.

HEXHAM (Northumberland), St Andrew f. 1113

Lists in *Hist. of N'humberland*, III, 164–5, from Raine, *Hexham Priory*, pp. cxl–clxxxii.

Ansketil 1114–1130 Can. of Huntingdon, first pr.; d. 18 Mar. 1130 (*Sim. Dur.*, II, 247, 284).

---

[1] Also *CTG*, I, 362; *Trans. Salop Arch. Soc.*, I, 175; based on Ctl. Haughmond. Eyton lists Ingenulf (see n. 2); William, occ. 1176 × 82; the other lists give Fulk occ. 1172 × 3, John, 1203 × 4 (al. 1202) – and both place a Nicholas early in the 13th cent. We have found no evidence for any of these.

[2] Eyton includes Ingenulf in his list, from notes based on a Haughmond Ctl. in BM Harl. MS 2188, f.123: 'dedit hanc cartam Ingenulfo abbati'. We have not traced this to its source, but suspect that it is due to confusion with the first abb. Buildwas.

[HEXHAM]

Robert Biseth 1130–1141 Can. and chamberlain of Hexham (ib., II, 284); app. by Abp. Thurstan (Nicholl, *Thurstan*, p. 241); res. 1141 to be m. Clairvaux (John of Hexham in *Sim. Dur.*, II, 311). Occ. 1136×41 (*Reg. Reg. Scot.*, I, no. 18).

Richard 1142– Occ. ?8 Sept. 1141;[1] confirmed 1142 (*Sim. Dur.*, II, 311); occ. 1143×53 (*EYC*, I, no. 450); (R.) 1154×9[2] (ib., I, no. 37); 1162×7 (Howden, II, 70–1 = *Hist. York*, III, 79–81; for date, see Clay, *YAJ*, XXXVI (1944–7), p. 410 and n.). *DNB*.

John Occ. –1174[3] (*EYC*, I, no. 146); late 12th cent. (*Mon.*, V, 284); 1191×4[4] (*EYC*, I, no. 345). Author of ch. 1130–53 (*Sim. Dur.*, II, 284–332).

William Occ. 26 May 1209 (*Yorks F., John*, p. 156); 1215+ (Raine, II, p. clviii, from BM Cott. MS Claud. B. iii, f. 31 (29)).

The next recorded pr., Bernard, occ. 5 Aug. 1226 (ib., ff. 45v–6 (43v–4), cited Raine, II, p. clviii); 1227 (*N'humberland and Durham F.*, no. 84).

HICKLING (Norfolk), St Mary, St Augustine and All Saints   f. 1185 (Oxenedes, p. 433)

List in *VCH Norfolk*, II, 385–6: basis in Ch. Minus of Oxenedes (pp. 433ff.).

Alexander Occ. –1200 (Bodl. Tanner MS 425, f. 38v); 1203 (*Norfolk F.*, PRS LXX, no. 34); d. 1209 (Oxenedes, p. 434): but see below. Perhaps for 1204; or he res. *c.* 1204.

Roger –1232 Dates 1209–32 (res.) in Oxenedes, p. 434; but occ. *c.* 25 Apr. 1204 (Bodl. Tanner MS 425, f. 46v); also occ. 1212 (*CRR*, VI, p. 293); 1217×18 (CUL MS Mm. ii. 20, ff. 30v–31).

HOUGH (Lincs) (Notre Dame du Voeu, Cherbourg)   f. *c.* 1164

List in *VCH Lincs*, II, 243.

William –1228 Occ. 27 Oct. 1208 (*Lincs F.*, PRS LXVII, no. 260); res. 1228 to be abb. of Cherbourg (*Reg. Wells*, III, p. 166).

HUNTINGDON, St Mary   f. –1091; –*c.* 1108(?) (finally Augustinian)

List in *VCH Hunts*, I, 395.

Fredebert Occ. 1114×15 (*Christina of Markyate*, p. 58).

Robert Occ. 15 Aug. 1147 (*PUE*, I, no. 41).

Ger' (?Gerard) Occ. 1164×85 (CUL, Add. MS 3020, f. 114).

William Occ. 1194×9 (*Mon.*, VI, 205); j.d. +13 Dec. 1199 (Peterborough D. and C. MS I, f. 112v = Reg. Fraunceys at Boughton House, f. 215; cf. Cheney, *Inn. III*, no. 170); 1200 (*Beds F.*, no. 71); 18 Nov. 1202 (ib., no. 118).

John –1225 Occ. 1211×12 (*Hunts F.*, p. 4); (J.) 30 Oct. 1219 (*Ctl. Lewes, Norfolk*, pp. 32–3); (J.) 1221 (*HMC Rutland*, IV, 158); res. 1225 (*Reg. Wells*, III, p. 54; Lambeth MS 1106, f.120); d. 1234 (ibid.).

IPSWICH (Suffolk), Holy Trinity   f. *c.* 1133 (–1139: *Reg.*, III, no. 416)

List in *VCH Suffolk*, II, 104.

Alan Occ. 25 Sept. 1188 (*Anc. Chts.*, no. 53).

---

[1] Occ. in cht. dated 8 Sept. 1141 with Ernisius pr. Marton, in Ctl. Hexham, Leeds, Yorks. Arch. Soc. MS 542, ff. 7v–8 (= *CTG*, VI, 42); it is possible that the date is wrong, and since Ernisius occ. as late as 1185+, it is even possible that it is a scribal error for 1161.

[2] John son of Letold, can. York; he was archd. Cleveland by 1159.

[3] William precentor York.

[4] G(eoffrey) abp. York; Simon de Apulia, chancellor of York.

John[1]   Occ. 27 Jan. 1203 (*Suffolk F.*, PRS LXX, no. 400); 13 Oct. 1211 (ib., no. 548); 18 Nov. 1223 (*CRR*, XI, no. 1208).

The next recorded pr., William, occ. (W.) 2 Sept. 1226 (Chelmsford, Essex Rec. Office, MS D/DBy Q 19, f. 34v); 1231 (*CRR*, XIV, no. 1531).

IPSWICH (Suffolk), St Peter and St Paul   f. –1189
List in *VCH Suffolk*, II, 103. Ctl. in Lexington, Kentucky, MS 091–M. 313.[2]

Herbert   Occ. *c.* Easter 1180 (Ctl., f. 13v).

William   Occ. 20 Oct. 1192; (W.) 12 May 1196 (ib., ff. 11v (= *FF.*, PRS XVII, no. 143),[3] 13v). Possibly also the W. pr. 'Irewich' who occ. 1182 × 1201 (Gorham, *St Neots*, Supplement (1824), p. iiij, no. 82 = BM Cott. MS Faust. A. iv, f. 43).

Michael   Occ. 18 Oct. 1198 (*FF.*, PRS XXIV, no. 25); 1 Aug. 1202[4] (*Suffolk F.*, PRS LXX, no. 333); 16 April 1208 (ib., no. 484).

The next recorded pr., Gilbert, formerly subpr., el. 1225 (*CPR, 1216–1225*, p. 519).

IVYCHURCH (Wilts), St Mary   f. –1154 (*KH*, 2nd edn., pp. 141, 161)
List in *VCH Wilts*, III, 295 (D. Styles).

Nicholas   Occ. 1214 (*Sarum Chts.*, p. 78 = *Reg. St Osmund*, I, pp. 236–7).

The next recorded pr., Thomas, occ. 7 Oct. 1221 (*Sarum Chts.*, p. 114).

IXWORTH (Suffolk), St Mary   f. 1170
List in *VCH Suffolk*, II, 106 (from 1338).

Adam   Occ. (A.) Nov. 1206 (CUL, Add. MS 4220, f. 103r–v; cf. Great Bricett); 1207 (*CRR*, V, p. 82); (A.) 1 July 1221 (Chelmsford, Essex Rec. Office, MS D/DBy Q 19, ff. 36v–37v).

The next recorded pr., Gilbert, occ. 1234 × 5 (*Suffolk F.* (Rye), p. 33).

KENILWORTH (Warws), St Mary   f. *c.* 1125
List in *VCH Warws*, II, 89. Fragmentary Ch. in BM Add. MS 35,295, ff. 250ff.

Bernard   Occ. 25 Feb. 1126 (*PUE*, III, no. 14); 1132 (Oxford, Balliol MS 271, f. 88); 1139 × 48 (*Reg. Lincoln*, II, no. 324); 15 July 1147 (*PUE*, III, no. 66); 1148 × 53 (BM Cott. MS Claud. A. viii, f. 121r–v).

Ralph   Occ. 1153 × 5 (*Mon.*, VI, 263).

Hugh   Occ. 1153[5] × 7 (Saltman, p. 363, no. 140).

?Richard   Occ. 1153 × 65[6] – probably for Robert (or Ralph? – Nichols, *Leics*, III, 805).

Robert   Occ. 1158 × 9 (*CDF*, no. 1062; see Nostell); 1164 × 7 (*Anc. Chts.*, no. 37); 1176 (Morey, p. 140; cf. *PUE*, I, no. 141 for date); 30 Mar. 1188 (*PUE*, III, no. 406); 1188 × 98 (*SHC*, VI, i, 12).

Silvester   *c.* 1188–1203 Succeeded Robert in 1186 = 32 Henry II (*sic*); d. 6 Aug. 1203 after 16 years (Ch., f. 250). Occ. (S.) 1196 × 8 (BM Harl. MS 3650, f. 47); ?1196 × 1200[7] (*Ctl. Oseney*, VI, p. 137); 20 Jan. 1202 (BM Add. MS 47,677, f. 240); 1203 (*CRR*, II, p. 226).

Walter   *c.* 1203–1216/17 The account in the ch., ff. 250v–251, is not always easy to follow, but it seems clearly to state that Walter was rightful pr. from 1203 till he d. 1216 or 1217 (1217, last year of King John (!), f. 250). C. 1206 × 7 one William was intruded as pr.,

---

[1] A pr. William occ. with Roger pr. Eye (1202 × 3–1211+) in Chelmsford, Essex Rec. Office, MS D/DBy Q19, ff. 48v–9. But Roger may have survived until 1223+ (or be Roger II, 1230+), and so William may be the pr. of 1226, 1231; alternatively, the references to W., occ. 1182 × 1201 under St Peter and St Paul may be to another William, pr. Holy Trinity.

[2] Photostat in Ipswich Public Reference Library. We owe these references to Dr Greenway: 'r' = left, 'v' = right hand opening.

[3] 'Ipswich', but its presence in the ctl. determines which house is in question.

[4] 'William' pr. in Ctl. version, f. 14.

[5] Ralph de Diceto, archd. Middlesex.   [6] Rotrou, bp. Evreux (*GFL*, p. 538).

[7] Bp. Hugh of Lincoln (–1200); not –1196 if Silvester = S. pr. Stone.

[KENILWORTH]

but dep. by papal delegates in 1208 (ibid.; cf. C. R. and M. G. Cheney, in *BIHR*, XLIV (1971), 99) – see below. The *Ann. Dunstable* (pp. 30, 41) makes the pr. dep. in 1208 *Walter*, and a new pr., formerly subpr. Oseney, el. 1213. In the former case it seems clear that the names were transposed; the latter seems mere confusion (common in *Ann. Dunstable* at that point: see C. R. Cheney in *Essays in Medieval History presented to Bertie Wilkinson*, esp. p. 94).

William Occ. 20 May 1218 (*SHC*, IV, i, 218); probably the intruder, temporarily restored; he d. 2 Sept. 1221 (Ch., f. 251v).

A pr. William (presumably different from the prior of 1218) occ. 7 Mar. 1227 (*Warws F.*, no. 354) and his successor, Henry, formerly subpr., was el. 1227 (*CPR, 1225–32*, p. 142).

KEYNSHAM (Soms) St Mary, St Peter and St Paul   f. 1167×72
    List in *VCH Soms*, II, 131–2.

ABBOTS

William   1167×72–1205 1st abb., occ. 17 Oct. 1173 (*Reg. St Osmund*, I, 254); 1191×7[1] (Bodl. Dugdale MS 12, p. 266); 1199 (*Ad. Dom.*, II, 384; see Bruton); 6×12 June 1205 (*Soms F.*, p. 23); d. 1205 (*Ann. Tewkesbury*, p. 57).

Morgan   Occ. 1206 (Cheney, *Inn. III*, no. 732 and n.).

Richard   1214– Pr. Keynsham, el. 1214 (*CRR*, VII, p. 82; cf. Lambeth MS 1212, f. 110v); occ. 14×20 Jan. 1225 (*Soms F.*, p. 48); 1232 (*CPR, 1225–32*, p. 520).

The next recorded abb., John, pr. of Keynsham, el. 1233 (*CPR, 1232–47*, p. 24).

KIRKHAM (Yorks E.), Holy Trinity   f. *c.* 1122
    C.T.C. List in *VCH Yorks*, III, 222.

William   *c.* 1122–1123 Can. of Nostell (cf. *Ctl. Rievaulx*, p. 264); d. 3 July 1123 (*Mon.*, V, 280).

St Waltheof, Waldef   Son of Simon of Senlis, earl of Northampton and Huntingdon, stepson of King David I of Scotland (cf. Lawrie, *Early Scottish Chts.*, no. 83 and n., pp. 69, 333); sacrist of Nostell (*Vita* in *Acta Sanctorum*, Aug. I, 255). Occ. as 'Waldef filius regine', *c.* 1128 (Lawrie), and as pr. 1141 and 1143 (*Sim. Dur.*, II, 311, 313). Res. to become a Cistercian at Wardon and later at Rievaulx; abb. Melrose 1148–59 (*Vita*; *DNB*; *Ch. Melrose*, ff. 18v–19, pp. 34–5).

Geoffrey   Occ. 1147×53 (*EYC*, II, no. 878); (G.) 1148×53 (*Ctl. Bridlington*, p. 429); n.d., ?*c.* 1150×60 (*EYC*, I, no. 288).

Drogo   Occ. (D.) as j.d. +1188×91: *Ctl. Bridlington*, p. 424; this proves him earlier than Walter, and prob. than Roger. *EYC*, II, no. 1079, in which he appears as Drogo, must therefore be earlier than the date *c.* 1193×1205 assigned by Farrer.

O., pr. occ. in *Ctl. Rievaulx*, p. 171 (so MS, but see ed.'s note). This may be an error for D., and the document is anomalous in form, and possibly spurious.

Roger   Occ. 1181×96 (*Ctl. Brinkburn*, p. 184); (R.) 1189×94 (*EYC*, VI, no. 135 – possibly 1189).

Walter   Occ. (W.) 1196 (*EYC*, II, no. 1177); (Walter) Jan.–Mar. 1201 (Foreville, *S. Gilbert*, pp. 24–5). It is possible that he had res. before writing his letter on Gilbert of Sempringham in 1201.

Andrew   Occ. (A.) 1198×1200 (*Reg. Gray*, p. 50n.); (A.) 1201+ (*EYC*, I, no. 258); (Andrew) 1199×1203 (*Ctl. Guisborough*, II, no. 613); (A.) 27 Apr. 1205 (Cheney, *Inn. III*, no. 619); 1206+ (*YAJ*, VII (1882), 436 (a Ribston cht.) dated by Richard pr. of Warter); 1206×12 (*EYC*, X, no. 13); (A.) *c.* 1213×14 (BM Cott. MS Nero D. iii, f. 57v). The date *1185×95* assigned to *EYC*, I, nos. 390–2 must be too early.

---

[1] Hawise, countess of Gloucester, d. 24 Apr. 1197 (*CP*, V, 688).

William de Muschamp Occ. 22 Feb. 1219, 22 May 1228 (*Yorks F.*, *1218–31*, pp. 30–1, 116); for his name, *Ctl. Rievaulx*, no. 47.

The next pr., Richard, occ. 3 Dec. 1234 (*Yorks F.*, *1232–46*, p. 23).

KYME (Lincs), St Mary f. –1156
List in *VCH Lincs*, II, 173–4.

Lambert Occ. 30 June × 6 July 1177 (BM Cott. MS Vesp. E. xx, f. 95); 8 May 1182 (*Ctl. Bridlington*, pp. 355–6, 434–5); 1182+ (Madox, *Form.*, p. 251 = Nichols, *Leics*, II, i, App. pp. 4–5); late 12th cent. (*c. 1200*–? pal.: *HMC Ancaster*, p. 450).

Roger Occ. (R.) late 12th cent. (*late Henry II*, pal., DC, no. 9); (R.) Jan.–Mar. 1201 (Foreville, *S. Gilbert*, p. 12); 1 July 1202 (*Lincs F.*, PRS LXVII, no. 57).

The next recorded pr., Jordan, res. *c.* 1237 (*Reg. Grosseteste*, p. 11).

LANERCOST (Cumberland), St Mary Magdalene f. *c.* 1166
Simon Occ. 1154 × 86 (*Ctl. Lanercost*, viii, 9); 12 Aug. 1181 (*PUE*, II, 219); 13 Feb. 1185 (ib., no. 234).

John[1] Occ. 1219 × 23 (*Ctl. Holm Cultram*, no. 17); 1223 × 9[2] (*Ctl. Wetheral*, no. 79).

The next recorded pr., S., occ. 1223 × 9 (ib., no. 131).

LANTHONY, see LLANTHONY

LATTON (Essex), St John the Baptist f. –1200
List in *VCH Essex*, II, 154–5 (from 1426).

V. Occ. 1207 (Cheney, *Inn. III*, no. 751).

LAUNCESTON (Cornwall), St Stephen f. 1127
List in Oliver, p. 22.

?Thierry A 16th–17th-cent. hand has written on the verso of a fly-leaf in Ctl. Launceston, Lambeth, MS 719: 'Theoricus Normannus primus prior'.

Robert[3] –1149 Prob. can. of Holy Trinity, London (*Wm. Newb.*, ed. Hearne, III, 697); d. 24 June 1149 (*Ann. Plympton*, UGQ, p. 30).

Osbert Occ. *c.* 1180 × 3 (Morey, p. 158: cf. p. 122).

Walter Occ. 3 × 4 Sept. 1196 (*CDF*, no. 903).

Godfrey Occ. 29 Apr. 1202 (*Cornwall F.*, no. 11).[4]

The next recorded pr., William, occ. 1235 (*Cornwall F.*, no. 59).

LAUNDE (Leics), St John the Baptist f. 1119 × 25
List in *VCH Leics*, II, 12 (R. A. McKinley).

John Occ. 1125 (*London Letter Book C*, pp. 219–20 = *Ctl. London, Aldgate*, no. 871).

Ralph Occ. mid 12th cent. (*SHC*, III, 189); mid-12th cent., ?*c.* 1160 (*DC*, nos. 457–8).

Walkelin Occ. 1186 × 92[5] (BM Cott. MS Vesp. E. xxii, f. 290); prob. 1191 × 3[6] (Madox,

---

[1] In *Ctl. Lanercost*, p. 519 is a reference to 'J.' pr. Lanercost: Mr B. C. Jones, County Archivist of Cumberland and Westmorland, kindly checked the MS for us (17th cent. transcript of lost ctl. in Carlisle, Dean and Chapter Library), and there is no initial or name in the MS: the pr. of Hexham, ibid., is J.

[2] Robert son of William, sheriff of 'Carlisle': see ed.'s note.

[3] 'B'. occ. 1141 × 75 (Reginald, earl of Cornwall) in Oliver, p. 23; this is an error for 'R.'; see *Reg. Bronescombe*, p. 199. For Geoffrey, occ. 1171 in Oliver's list, we have found no evidence.

[4] The editors refer to *Reg. Bronescombe*, p. 290 = *Rot. Lit. Pat.*, p. 153b (1215) as ground for calling him 'de Insula'; but this document refers to a secular clerk of that name.

[5] Robert de Hardres was archd. Huntingdon by 1192 (cf. Cheney, *BRHS*, XXXII, pp. 13, 14; *Reg. Lincoln*, II, no. 338; etc.).

[6] Walter of Coutances apparently acting as chief justiciar (*Handbook*, p. 70).

[LAUNDE]

Form., p. xiv); 1189 × 98[1] (Peterborough D. and C. MS 1, f. 106v); 3 Apr. 1201 (BM Sloane Roll xxxi, 4, m. 1, nos. 1–2).

Adam Occ. 1202 (*Northants Assize Roll*, no. 595).

William of Brompton Occ. 1208 × 9 (Leics F., PRO Transcripts, vol. III).

The next recorded pr., Osbert, occ. early–mid-13th cent.,[2] ?*c.* 1230 (BM Sloane Roll xxxi, 4, m. 1, no. 5).

LEEDS (Kent), St Mary and St Nicholas f. 1119

List in *VCH Kent*, II, 164.

Alexander Professed 1139 × 61 to Abp. Theobald (Saltman, p. 549); occ. 1150 × 61 (ib., pp. 371–2, no. 148).

Robert Occ. 2nd half 12th cent., prob. –1180 (*Arch. Cant.*, VI (1866), facing p. 190 – pal. (see Combwell), and cf. ib., II (1859), 29); 1178 × 88 (*Ctl. Oseney*, VI, p. 171). D. 21 May (BM Arundel MS 68, f. 28).

Nicholas Occ. 29 June 1191 (Maidstone, Kent Archives Office, D. and C. Rochester, DRc T 389/1); 1196[3] × 8 (BM Cott. MS Julius D. ii, f. 100v; also *Ctl. Canterbury, St Augustine*, II, p. 545).

Fulk Occ. 27 Oct. 1205 (*Kent F.*, p. 37); (F.) +17 Feb. 1205 (BM Egerton Cht., no. 382; cf. Cheney, *Inn. III*, no. 601); (F.) 1205 × 14 (*Reg. Rochester*, pp. 52–5); (F.) 1212 (*Essex F.*, p. 48); 1215[4] × 16 (Cheney, *Inn. III*, no. 1170); 1227 (*CRR*, XIII, no. 378); 9 Apr. 1228 (*Kent F.*, p. 106).

The next recorded pr., Roger, occ. 25 Nov. 1231 (*Kent F.*, p. 109).

LEICESTER, St Mary de Prato, Pratis f. 1143

List in *VCH Leics*, II, 18–19 (R. A. McKinley) based on a list in Lambeth MS 585, f. 215 (Wharton transcript) from BM Cott. MS Vitell. F. xvii, f. 46, burnt but mostly legible – all legible for this period; the evidence of the MSS was conflated by Nichols, in *Leics*, I, 275.

ABBOTS

Richard prob. 1143–1167 In list, abb. 24 years from 1144 = 8 Stephen; prob. abb. from f. (cf. *VCH*, II, 18n.). Occ. 1148 × 53 (BM Cott. MS Claud. A. viii, f. 121r–v); 1155 × 9, prob. 1158 × 9[5] (*CDF*, no. 1062); 1164 × 7 (*Anc. Chts.*, no. 37).

William of Calwich ('Kalewyken') 1167–1177/8 In list, abb. 10 years from 1167 = 14 Henry II; see below. Occ. 1176 (Morey, p. 140).

Vacant, in king's hand, 1178–9 (*PR 25 Henry II*, p. 115).

William de Broke 1179–1187 In list, abb. 9 years from 1177 = 23 Henry II (but see above and below); res. to be abb. of Cistercian house (not identified).

Vacant, in the king's hand, 1187–8 (*PR 34 Henry II*, p. 215).

Paul 1188–1204 In list, abb. 19 years from 1186 = 8 Richard I (*sic*). D. 1204 (Ch. Barnwell in *Walt. Cov.*, II, 197). Occ. 1188 × 90 (*Ch. Evesham*, p. 334); 1189 × 94[6] (*Anc. Chts.*, no. 61); 20 Apr. 1204 (*Reg. Lincoln*, I, no. 213); (P. 'tunc' abb.) 1204 (*Rot. Chart.*, p. 124).

---

[1] Hamo dean of Lincoln (not –1189, Diceto, II, 69, nor +1198, *Reg. Lincoln*, II, no. 208).

[2] The MS was written 1237 × *c.* 1256 (Davis, no. 1188A).

[3] Alard archd. London.

[4] *Temp.* Nicholas abb. Faversham. The R. who occ. in a fine 1212 × 13 in PRO Transcripts, Fines, Unknown Counties, must presumably be an error for 'F.'.

[5] See Clay, *Fasti*, II, p. xiii and n.

[6] Hamo dean Lincoln, William de Montibus not yet chancellor (see p. 162 n. 3).

William Pepyn ?1205–1221/2 In list, abb. 19 years from 1205 = 15 John (*sic*). Occ. 26 Feb. 1206 (*Lancs F.*, p. 24); 1212×13 (*Bucks F.*, p. 35); (W.) 14 Jan. 1215 (*Reg. Lincoln*, III, no. 878); Feb. 1218 (ib., no. 875); 1220×1 (*Warws F.*, no. 229). Prob. the abb. William whose obit was kept on 17 Aug. at Lire (*HF*, XXIII, 473); if so 1221 seems more likely than 1222 for his d. – see below.

The next abb., Osbert of Dunton, was el. 1222; royal assent, 22 Aug. (*Rot. Lit. Claus.*, I, p. 508).

LEIGHS (Essex), St Mary and St John the Evangelist f. –1200
　List in *VCH Essex*, II, 156.
William Occ. early 13th cent. (*HMC Rutland*, IV, 40).

LESSNESS (Westwood) (Kent), St Thomas Becket (Arrouaisian) f. 1178
　List in *VCH Kent*, II, 166.

ABBOTS
William Occ. 1182×4 (*Reg. Rochester*, p. 318); cf. *CRR*, V, pp. 145–7.
Fulk –?1208 Occ. 14 Nov. 1197 (*Kent F.*, p. 8); 1205 (*CRR*, III, p. 322). An abb., unnamed (presumably Fulk), d. 1208 (*CRR*, V, p. 157; cf. pp. 145–7).
Mark Prob. previously pr. (*CRR*, III, p. 322); occ. late 1219 (*Essex F.*, p. 55).
The next recorded abb., William, occ. (W.) 15 Feb. 1227 (*Ctl. Chertsey*, I, p. 89).

LILLESHALL (Salop), St Mary (Arrouaisian) f. *c.* 1143 (at Lizard); *c.* 1144 (at Donnington Wood);[1] *c.* 1148 (at Lilleshall)
　M.C. Lists in Eyton, *Salop*, VIII, 224–5; *VCH Salop* (M. Chibnall, forthcoming).

ABBOTS
William Occ. 1148×51 (prob. 1148: *Reg.*, III, no. 461); 1150 (*Ctl. Missenden*, I, p. 73); *c.* 1153×5 (*Reg. Lichfield*, no. 301); 1173 (*HMC, 14th Rep.*, App., VIII, 168 = *Ctl. Oseney*, V, p. 4); prob. 1171×3 (*HMC Hastings*, I, 124; cf. Newstead); d. 5 Nov. (J. C. Dickinson in *TRHS*, 5th Series, I (1951), 83n.).
Walter Occ. –1179[2] (*HMC, 15th Rep.*, X, 68); ?*c. 1177* (Eyton, *Salop*, VIII, 251); ?*c. 1181 or later* (ib., VII, 355); 1186×7 (ib., V, 42); June–Oct. 1200 engaged in a suit but infirm (ib., VIII, 108; cf. *CRR*, I, pp. 196–7); d. 1203 (Eyton, *Salop*, VII, 197).
Ralph Occ. 6 Oct. 1203 (Eyton, *Salop*, VIII, 241); 5 Nov. 1208 (ib., VI, 369); (R.) 6 July 1216 (ib., X, 139).
Alan Succeeded Ralph (ib., X, 248); res. 1226: licence to el. successor 12 Apr. (*CPR*, *1225–32*, p. 26).

LITTLE DUNMOW (Essex), St Mary f. 1104 (Ann. Dunmow: see below; confirmed by BM Harl. MS 662, f. 6)
　List in *VCH Essex*, II, 153. Basis in Ann. Dunmow in *Mon.*, VI, 147, checked by transcripts in BM Cott. MSS Cleop. C. iii, ff. 281–2, Vesp. A. ix, ff. 99ff. and Harl. MS 532, ff. 2ff.
Brihtric (Britricus) 1104–1127 (d.: Ann.).
Augustine 1127–1163 (d.: Ann.).
Robert 1163–1179 (d.: Ann.).
Ralph 1179–?1209 Occ. 1203 (*CRR*, III, p. 38); d. 1208 (Ann.), but occ. 20 Jan. 1209 (*Norfolk F.*, PRS, LXX, no. 138).
Durand ?1209–1217 (1208–17, Ann.: d., Cleop., or res., Vesp. MS.).

---

　[1] Cf. King Stephen's cht. of early 1145 (*Reg.*, III, no. 460).
　[2] Wido sheriff (of Salop).

LLANTHONY PRIMA (Monmouthshire), St John the Baptist f. 1103. Llanthony Secunda was f. 1136, but the two had a single pr., with authority over both, until 1205

List. of prs of Llanthony Secunda in *VCH Glos*, II, 90 (R. Graham), and by J. N. Langston in *BGAS*, LXIII (1942), pp. 1–144. Ch. in BM Cott. MS Julius D. x, ff. 30v–53v, partly printed in *Mon.*, VI, 128ff. (om. preface and contents, carries on to f. 50v. where main hand ends with death of Pr. Clement); extracts in *Arch. Camb.*, I (1846), 202–3, 228–9 (G. Roberts); *AS*, II, 321–2. The ch. ends with Geoffrey, 7th pr. (f. 53v), but the list of contents (f. 32r–v) carries on to Thomas, 14th pr.

Ernisius 1103– 1st pr., formerly chaplain to Queen Matilda (*Mon.*, VI, 129–31).

Robert de Bethune –1131 2nd pr.; consec. bp. Hereford 28 June 1131 (cf. *Mon.*, VI, 131; *Vita* in *AS*, II, 293–321; cf. *GFL*, p. 534); d. 16 Apr. 1148. Occ. *c.* 1123 (1121 × 8: *Anc. Chts.*, no. 11); 1127 (PRO C115 A2 K1/6681, sec. xxii, no. 2); 17 Jan. 1131 (*Glam. Chts.*, I, p. 83). *DNB*.

Robert de Braci *c.* 1131– 3rd pr. (and 1st of Llanthony Secunda); occ. 25 Apr. 1134 (PRO C115 A9 K1/6679, f. 161). He fled with most of the community to Hereford *c.* 1134 to escape Welsh raids; they were maintained by Bp. Robert de Bethune. In 1136 new Llanthony was founded in Gloucester and consecrated; Robert de Braci d. soon after and was buried at Llanthony Secunda (*Mon.*, VI, 132).

William of Wycombe 1137–*c.* 1150 4th pr. (2nd of L. Secunda); prev. can. (occ. 25 Apr. 1134, ut sup.) and chaplain to Robert de Bethune, whose life he wrote (*AS*, II, 293–321; cf. *GFL*, p. 534). Succeeded as pr. 1137 (*Mon.*, VI, 132–3); occ. 30 Apr. 1142, 17 Dec. 1146, 16 July 1147 (*PUE*, I, nos. 26, 35, 39); 1148 × 50 (*Acta Chichester*, no. 38); res. *c.* 1150 (1148 × 52) and retired to Frome (*Mon.*, VI, 133).

Clement *c.* 1150[1]– Can. and sub-pr. of Llanthony, native of Gloucester, el. *c.* 1150 as 5th pr. of Llanthony Prima and 3rd of Llanthony Secunda (*Mon.*, VI, 133); occ. 22 Apr. 1152 (*PUE*, I, no. 53); 10 Jan. 1158 (ib., no. 72); 1167 (*Earldom of Hereford Chts.*, p. 53); prob. 1169 (*MB Epp.* 523; cf. *GFL*, p. 270 n. 3); 1164 × 77[2] (*Berkeley Chts.*, p. 11).

Roger of Norwich Sub-pr. of Llanthony (*AS*, II, 322; cf. *Gir. Camb.*, IV, 82); 6th pr. (4th of Llanthony Secunda); occ. 1174 (PRO C115 A1 K2/6683, sec. viii, no. 10); 28 Feb. × 1 Mar. 1177 (*PUE*, I, nos. 141–2); 14 Apr. 1178 (PRO C115 A1 K2/6683, sec. xvi, nos. 10–11); (R.) 11 Oct. 1184 (Bodl. Lyell MS 15, f. 55r–v); (R.) 1186 × 9 (Gloucester Cath. Reg. A. ff. 86v–7). D. '1191' and succeeded by Geoffrey according to Ann. Winchcombe, BM Cott. MS Faust. B. i, f. 22.

Geoffrey of Henlawe *c.* 1189–1203 (For his name, *AS*, II, 322). 7th pr. (5th of Llanthony Secunda) Can. Llanthony (Ann. Winchcombe, loc. cit.); occ. 27 Mar. 1189 (*Ctl. Oseney*, V, p. 113); 27 Oct. 1189 (ib., p. 114); 1191 (ib., p. 115); 11 July 1197 (PRO C115 A1 K2/6683, sec. i, no. 66).[3] Consec. bp. St Davids, 7 Dec. 1203; d. 1214. On him see *Gir. Camb.*, III, 341–2 (on his medical skill), etc.

Martin *c.* 1203–*c.* 1205 8th pr. (6th of Llanthony Secunda). Occ. 1203 × 5 (Gloucester Cath. Reg. A, ff. 110–11); 1204 × 5 (Selden Soc., LX, p. clxxix).

In 1205 (+ 13 July) a commission of bps. and abbs. set up by Innocent III declared that the two houses were to be separate, each was to have its own pr. and neither was to be subject to the other (*Ctl. Llanthony (Irish)*, p. 211; cf. Cheney, *Inn. III*, no. 570 and n.).

---

1 Langston, art. cit., pp. 16, 25, cites Archd. Furney's notes (Bodl. MS Top. Glouc. c. 5, p. 643) for Clement's succession in 1150: this seems to go back to a marginal note in a Llanthony Chronicle and appears to be of little or no authority. (Possibly the note was once in BM Cott. MS Julius D. x, whose margins have been cut.)

2 Matthew archd. of Gloucester (*GFL*, p. 162n.).

3 Also probably 13 Oct. 1197, ib., sec. iv, no. 120 – but the translation of St Edward could be 18 Feb. or 20 June 1198.

Roger (?de Godestre) *c.* 1205– 9th pr. of Llanthony Prima. Occ. 1209 (*Ctl. St Thomas, Dublin*, p. 351); (R.) 1211 × 13 (*Ctl. Llanthony* (*Irish*), pp. 260–1 with G. pr. of L. Secunda); n.d. (Oxford, Balliol MS 271, ff. 63 v–4).

William 10th pr. of Llanthony Prima. Occ. (W.) *1217 × 24* (*Ctl. Llanthony* (*Irish*), pp. 141–2 with J., pr. of Llanthony Secunda).

The next recorded pr., David, occ. 1242 (*Ctl. Llanthony* (*Irish*), p. 23).

LLANTHONY SECUNDA (Glos), St Mary f. 1136

List in *VCH Glos*, II, 90 (R. Graham).

(For details concerning the first six priors see Llanthony Prima.)

Robert de Braci 1136–*c.* 1137 Pr. of L. Prima from *c.* 1131 and of both houses from 1136 until his death.

William of Wycombe 1137–*c.* 1150

Clement *c.* 1150–1169 +

Roger of Norwich –1174–*c.* 1189

Geoffrey of Henlawe *c.* 1189–1203

Martin *c.* 1203–*c.* 1205

Walter of Monmouth *c.* 1205–*c.* 1207 7th pr. of L. Secunda. Occ. Aug. 1205 (Madox, *Form.*, pp. 25–6, cf. *EHR*, XLVII (1932), 262 (Russell)); 12 Nov. 1207 (*Beds F.*, nos. 163–5).

Gilbert *c.* 1207–*c.* 1216 8th pr. of L. Secunda. ?Occ. (G.) as pr. of Duleek and proctor of L. Secunda from 1188–*c.* 1206 (*Ctl. Llanthony* (*Irish*), p. 65); occ. as pr. 1206 × 12¹ (*Ctl. Dublin, St Thomas*, p. 289); 1211 × 13 with R. pr. of L. Prima (*Ctl. Llanthony* (*Irish*), p. 260); (G.) Mar. 1216 (*Ctl. Malmesbury*, II, p. 7); 3 July 1216 (*Ctl. Oseney*, IV, p. 226).

John of Hempstead[2] *c.* 1217–1240 9th pr. of L. Secunda; occ. (J.) 1217 × 24 with W. pr. of L. Prima (*Ctl. Llanthony* (*Irish*), pp. 141–2); Oct. 1224 (*Ctl. Gloucester*, II, p. 171); 1228 (*Cal. Docts. Ireland*, I, no. 1618); 1234 (ib., no. 2164); d. 29 Dec. 1240 (*Ann. Tewkesbury*, p. 116).

LONDON: HOLY TRINITY, ALDGATE f. 1107 × 8

List in *VCH London*, I, 474; basis in Ann. in *Newburgh*, ed. Hearne, III, 690–707, checked by the MS (Glasgow Univ. Lib., Hunterian U. 2. 6, ff. 1ff.).[3]

Norman 1107/8–1147 1st pr., learned customs at Mont-St-Éloy, can. St Botolph, Colchester (Ann. pp. 696f.; cf. *Anselm, Ep.* 234); app. 5 Apr. 1107 or 1108 (5 Apr. '1107', Ann., p. 704; but f. 1108 in Ann. p. 690; Ann. p. 703: 1132 = 24th yr. of pr. N.). Occ. 1108 × 9 (*Reg.*, II, no. 906); 8 Apr. 1137 (*JL* 7833); 1145 (Gibbs, no. 154). D. 12 Jan. 1147 (Ann. pp. 704f.). Cf. Dunstable.

Ralph 1147–1167 2nd pr., prev. sub-pr.; el. 17 Jan. 1147; d. 14 Oct. 1167 (Ann., p. 707; cf. *GFL*, p. 536). Occ. 26 Oct. 1147 (*JL* 9153 = *Mon.*, VI, 154–5); 1147 × 8 (*Reg.*, III, no. 512); 1150 + (Saltman, p. 386, no. 163).

A vacancy (according to Ann., p. 707) of 2 years, 32 weeks, 1 day, when everything was done in the name of pr. Ed(mund?), 'cum nullus talis creatus extiterat ut patet per litteram testimonialem Gylberti Lond' episcopi scriptam in quanta cum littera B. folio xc°' (lost: see *GFL*, p. 536). Ed(mund) may have been sub-pr., but there is trace of a pr. of that name in Hunterian MS, f. 10, in an extract from rental C (of the 13th cent.).

---

[1] For 1206 see *Ctl. Llanthony* (*Irish*), p. ix. William bp. Glendalough d. –1212.

[2] Two successive prs. named John of Hempstead are thought to have reigned *c.* 1217–40, but it is not known how long the first was in office, see Langston in *BGAS*, LXIII (1942), 40.

[3] And by the edn. of the Ctl. by G. Hodgett (published 1971), who kindly allowed us to consult his MS. Although the 13th-century part of this list has several errors, the 12th-cent. section seems more reliable (cf. the similar, even more curious, case of Bermondsey). F. 1107 or 1108 in Ch.; 1107 confirmed by Ann. Merton (Corpus Christi Coll., Cambridge, MS 59, f. 162).

[LONDON: HOLY TRINITY, ALDGATE]

During this vacancy Master Osbert, pr. Cirencester, was el. (*GFL*, no. 187; cf. *Ctl. Oseney*, v, p. 27); but there is no evidence that he ever accepted office.

?William Occ. 1169 (*MB Epp.* 527); but there is no other record of a pr. of this name (see *GFL*, p. 536).

Stephen 1170–1197 3rd pr., el. 17 May 1170; dep. 2 May 1197, d. 14 Aug. 1198 (Ann., p. 707). Occ. (S.) 1174 × 5 (PRO E 40/13850(6)); 1170 × 80 (*GFL*, nos. 392, 400); (S.) 25 Mar. 1192 (PRO E 40/2383: *Cat. Anc. D.*, II, 72). See *GFL*, p. 536.

Peter of Cornwall 1197–1221 El. 9 May 1197; d. 7 July 1221 (Ann., p. 707); his successor was prob. el. 16 July 1222 (16 July 1223 in Ann., p. 708; but –25 Oct. 1222, *CPR, 1216–25*, p. 342. There are several errors in the dates of 13th cent. prs. in Ann.). Occ. 2 May 1198 (*FF*, PRS XXIII, no. 180); 12 Nov. 1207 (*Yorks F., John*, p. 114); 1221 (*CRR*, X, p. 51). Theologian: see R. W. Hunt in *TRHS*, 4th Series, XIX (1936), 33–4, 38ff.; idem, *Powicke Studies*, pp. 143ff.

LONDON, St Bartholomew f. *c.* March 1123

List in *VCH London*, I, 479–80; basis in *The Book of the Foundation of St Bartholomew's Church in London*, ed. Norman Moore (Early English Text Soc., 1923 – English version of Latin Ch.; henceforth 'ch.'); cf. Norman Moore, I, *passim*.

Rahere 1123–1144 The founder: took up office in *c.* Mar. 1123 (ch., p. 1); d. 20 Sept. after 22 years 6 months (ib., pp. 33–4; cf. Norman Moore, I, 16–23; the date there given, 1145, is corrected in notes to ch. to 1144; this is evidently right: see below). Occ. 1133 (*Reg.*, II, nos. 1761, 1794–5, of doubtful authenticity).

Thomas 1144–1174 Prev. can. St Osyth, el. 1144, 7th indiction (ch., p. 34); d. 17 Jan. 1174, after almost 30 years (ch., p. 34: 17 Jan. 1174, 15 Alexander III, 20 Henry II). Occ. 1145 (Gibbs, no. 154); n.d. (*Ctl. Sandford*, II, nos. 312–13).

Roger Occ. 1185 × 7 (*Ctl. Dunstable*, no. 262); n.d. (–1193:[1] Norman Moore, I, 132–3).

Alan Occ. 1180 × 9[2] (*HMC, 9th Rep.*, I, 50b).

Richard Occ. 1196[3] × 8 (Norman Moore, I, 231–2); 1201 (*CRR*, II, p. 47); 1205 × 6 (*Bucks F.*, p. 29).

G. Can. of Oseney, el. 1213 and res. within a few days (*Ann. Dunstable*, p. 41); became m. Abingdon.

The next recorded pr., John, occ. *c.* Apr. 1226 (*Essex F.*, p. 71); *c.* early *temp.* Henry III (Norman Moore, I, 336–7).

MAIDEN BRADLEY (Wilts), St Mary f. –1164 (hospital); –1201 (priory)

List in *VCH Wilts*, III, 301 (H. F. Chettle and J. L. Kirby).

Andrew Occ. Easter Term 1201 (*CRR*, I, p. 426); 1209 × 15[4] (*Sarum Chts.*, pp. 74–5); 1211 × 12 (FF., Unknown Counties, PRO Transcripts, VII).

The next recorded pr., Hugh, occ. 1225 (*Wilts F.*, p. 13).

MARKBY (Lincs), St Peter f. ? *temp.* Henry II

List in *VCH Lincs*, II, 175.

Osbert Occ. 1148 × 66[5] (Oxford, Bodl. Top. Lincs d. 1, f. 32v); n.d. (*Ctl. Bridlington*, p. 225).

---

[1] Henry FitzAilwin, not mayor of London.

[2] Ralph dean St Paul's; Master David, canon.   [3] Alard archd. London.

[4] Thomas prec. Wells (whose predecessor became dean Wells 1209 × 12, ?1209, before Jocelin bp. Bath went into exile: *Bk. of Fees*, I, p. 82; cf. *HMC Wells*, I, 491; J. A. Robinson (1921), pp. 149ff.); Richard dean of Salisbury (*Ann. Waverley*, p. 282).

[5] Prob. 1150 + : dated mcl... (cut away: ex inf. D. Smith).

Ralph Occ. 1148 × *c.* 1161[1] (E. M. Poynton in *Genealogist*, New Series, xv, 227).

Simon Occ. *late Henry II* (*DC*, no. 153); (S.) 1193 (ib., no. 15); *c. 1200* (pal.: *Reg. Lincoln*, VI, no. 1772); 1202 (*Lincs Assize Roll*, LRS XXII, no. 1079); 1203 × 5 (*HMC Var. Coll.*, 1, 236ff.).

The next recorded pr., Eudo, res. 1228 (*Reg. Wells*, III, p. 166).

MARTON (Yorks N.), St Mary   f. 1135 × 54
C.T.C. List in *VCH Yorks*, III, 225.

Ernisius (Arnisius, Hernisius)   Occ. 8 Sept. 1141 (?: see p. 166, n. 1); *c.* 1150 × 9 (*EYC*, II, no. 1044; cf. Guisborough); 1163 × 6 (ib., no. 333); *c.* 1170 × 86 (*Mowbray*, no. 79); 1185 × 91[2] (*EYC*, II, no. 1141; cf. no. 790).

Henry Occ. 1199 × 1203 (Raine, *North Durham*, App., p. 140); (H.) 1203 (*Ctl. Healaugh Park*, p. 11); *c.* 1213 × 14 (BM Cott. MS Nero D. iii, f. 57v); 14 Dec. 1226 (*Yorks F., 1218–31*, p. 99); 1227 (*CRR*, XIII, no. 134).

MERTON (Surrey), St Mary   f. 1117 (25 Mar. 1117, list; 1117 also in Ann. 1; Ann. Plympton, *UGQ*, p. 27)
Lists in *VCH Surrey*, II, 102; Heales, *passim*. Annals in Eton MS of *Fl. Hist.*, ed. Luard, I, p. lii (Ann. 1, quoted from Luard); BM Cott. MS Faust A. viii, ff. 137–42 (Ann. 2); Cambridge, Corpus Christi College MS 59, ff. 158vff. (Ann. 3; 17th-cent. copy in Lambeth MS 585, pp. 105ff.);[3] list in BM Cott. MS Cleop. C. vii, f. 175.

Robert de Tywe (list)   1117–1150 1st pr., ?can. Holy Trinity, Aldgate, London (Newburgh, ed. Hearne, III, 698; but see St Osyth). Dates: 1117–1150, d. 4 Jan. (Ann. 1, list – ? for 1151; 1150 also in Ann. 3, f. 163v); 1117 in *Ann. Winchester*, p. 45; 4 Jan. 1150, Ann. Plympton, *UGQ*, p. 29. Occ. 1145 (Gibbs, no. 154).

Robert II   1150–1167 2nd pr.; d. 4 Aug. 1167 in his 17th year (Ann. 1), but 9 Apr. 16th year, list; 1167 confirmed by Ann. 3.

William   1167/8–1177 3rd pr.; d. 19 Feb. 1177 in his 11th year (Ann. 1); 24 Feb. 1177 (Ann. 3, f. 165v, list) in his 11th year (list). Occ. 1167 × 70 (*JS Epp.*, ed. Giles, no. 278); June 1174 × June 1175 (PRO E40/13850 (6)).

Stephen   1177 4th pr. 1177 (list, Ann. 1, 3); d. 6 Oct. 1177 (list; cf. Ann. 1).

Robert III   1177–1179/80 5th pr., d. 1180, 13 May (list, over erasure, in '10th' year); Ann. 1 gives 13 May 1179, in 4th year; Ann. 3, f. 166, gives 1186 (but this is the only annal between 1177 and 1188).

Richard   *c.* 1179/80–1197/8 6th pr.; d. 1 Apr. 1198 (list; Ann. 3, f. 168v; 1198 is confirmed by Ann. 1, 2). Occ. (R.) 1184 (Douglas, *Bury*, p. 181, no. 221);[4] 7 Dec. 1194 (*Ctl. Chertsey*, I, no. 134); 13 Aug. 1197 (*FF.*, PRS XX, no. 186).

Walter   1197/8–1218 Entered office 17 May 1198 = Whit Sunday (Ann. 3, f. 168v). 7th pr., res. to become m. Chartreuse in 1218 (Ann. 3, f. 173v; year confirmed by list, Ann. 1, 2;[5] but list and Ann. 2 also give date of accession as 1198, and see below. List gives 1218 as 20th year). Occ. 20 Sept. 1197 (*Beds F.*, no. 19) – which suggests that he was app. 13 Aug. × 20 Sept. 1197, unless there is an error or anachronism in the fine. Also occ. 1202 (*CRR*, II, p. 92); 10 Mar. 1218 (Heales, p. 74).

Licence to el. his successor was given on 2 Oct. 1218 (*CPR, 1216–25*, p. 169). Succeeded 11 Nov., Ann. 3.

---

[1] Baldric de Sigillo, not archd. Leicester (*GFL*, p. 164n).   [2] Dated by Robert de Gant.

[3] There are also Ann. from 1216 in Bodl. Laud MS Misc. 723 (see Heales, facing p. 71).

[4] Printed from an inferior copy in *Reg. Pinchbeck*, I, pp. 423–5, where the pr. is 'D.', and the date 1183.

[5] For his res. see also *CPR, 1216–25*, p. 169; Bodl. Laud MS Misc. 723, f. 1 (Heales, facing p. 71).

MISSENDEN (Bucks), St Mary (Arrouaisian) f. 1133
  Lists in *VCH Bucks*, I, 375; *Ctl. Missenden*, III, p. xxiv (J.G. Jenkins).

ABBOTS
Daniel First abb., occ. 1133 (*Ctl.*, I, no. 30); 27 Jan. 1137 (*PUE*, I, no. 18); 1145 (ib., no. 33); 1149 (*Ctl. Oseney*, IV, p. 28).
Peter Occ. Oct. 1156×April 1158 (*EYC*, IV, no. 30); prob. 1163, 1168+ (*Ctl.*, I, no. 77; III, no. 701; cf. no. 702); 25 July 1163 (Bodl. Dodsworth MS 76, f. 18).
John Occ. 1173 (*Ctl. Oseney*, V, p. 4).
Adam[1] Occ. 1173×7 (*GFL*, no. 420); 26 July 1181 (*PUE*, I, no. 206); 1181×5+ (Baddeley, *Hist. Cirencester*, p. 113); 1191+ (*Ctl. Tutbury*, no. 262); 17×24 Sept. 1197 (*FF.*, PRS XXIII, no. 414); 1212 (*CRR*, VI, p. 220).
The next recorded abb. (since William 'occ. 1217' rests on no known foundation) is Martin, occ. *c*. 20 Oct. 1219 (*Bucks F.*, p. 42).

MOBBERLEY (Cheshire), St Mary and St Wilfrid f. 1198×1204 (cf. *Mon.*, IV, 478; and below); annexed to Rocester 1228×40
Walter First pr. (*Mon.*, IV, 478); occ. 1203×4 (Cheney, *Inn. III*, no. 542).

MOUNTJOY (Haveringland) (Norfolk), St Laurence f. 1189×99 (as cell of Wymond-ham); +1199 (as Augustinian house)
  List in *VCH Norfolk*, II, 388.
?Vincent PRO E40/3013 is a grant to the chapel of St Laurence, Haveringland, and brother Vincent, canon there (late 12th or early 13th cent.). This very probably relates to the period when Mountjoy was being formed as an Augustinian house.

NEWARK (de Novo Loco, etc., Aldbury) (Surrey), St Mary and St Thomas Becket f. *temp.* Henry II; ?*c*. 1169 or later (see below)
  List in *VCH Surrey*, II, 105.
John –1226 D. 1226 after 'sacerdotio functus est' for 57 years; if this is also a reckoning of his priorate, he began *c*. 1169, which may well be the foundation date of the priory (*Ann. Waverley*, p. 302).[2] Occ. 1190×1204[3] (*Mon.*, VI, 383–4); (L.) 1200×2[4] (*Ctl. Chertsey*, I, no. 87 – Aldbury); 1205 (*CRR*, III, p. 262); 1225 (*CRR*, XII, no. 1508).

NEWBURGH (Hood, Coxwold) (Yorks N.), St Mary f. 1142/3 (Hood); 1145 (New-burgh) (*EYC*, IX, pp. 205–6, 248)
  C.T.C. Lists in *EYC*, IX, pp. 248–50 (Sir Charles Clay); *VCH Yorks*, III, 229.
Augustine 1142/3–1154+ First pr. (*EYC*, IX, pp. 206, 248; III, no. 1472, dated, by Clay, *EYC*, IX, p. 248n. to 1142/3); occ. *c*. 1145 (BM Harl. MS 3650, f. 29r-v = Mowbray, no. 177); 1154 (*EYC*, IX, no. 151).
Richard –*c*. 1155–1186 Occ. 1154×*c*. 1155 (Durham D. and C. 3. 1. Pont. 11a); 1154×7 (*EYC*, IX, no. 163); 1175 (ib., II, no. 1230); (R.) 26 Nov. 1181+ (*Ctl. Guisborough*, II, no. 719); (R.) 1186 (Durham D. and C., 1. 1. Arch. 8).

---

[1] The Abb. Christopher in *Ctl. Oseney*, V, p. 36, who might seem to be abb. Missenden, was abb. Bruern (q.v.).
[2] Since both Newark and Waverley are in Surrey, the identification of 'de Novo Loco' does not seem in doubt; the other Newsteads etc. were at a distance, and John's long priorate could not readily be fitted in elsewhere. Prob. the John pr. 'de Nouo Loco' who d. 8 Dec. in Wintney obit (Troke-lowe, ed. Hearne, p. 393). Date of f. *c*. 1189 in *KH*, p. 142; cf. p. 167.
[3] Amicus, archd. Surrey (*Reg. St Osmund*, I, 242–3, before he was archd., cannot be earlier than July 1190; and cf. *Ctl. Peterborough*, no. 496n.).
[4] John sheriff of Surrey temp. M. abb. Chertsey.

Bernard 1186–1199 Can. of Newburgh (Clay, pp. 248–9); occ. 17 Sept. 1186 (papal mandate), and freq. to 1199 (*Gesta Hen. II*, I, 352; *Ctl. Guisborough*, II, no. 686c; cf. Cheney, *Inn. III*, no. 177). Ref. to as 'Benedict' 17 Sept. 1186, presumably in error (*PUE*, III, no. 380). His successor occ. 1199, unless the initial is wrong, in which case Bernard's extreme limit would be 1202. Acted as official of Abp. Geoffrey of York (Clay, p. 249 and n.). The identification of his brother William with William of Newburgh the chronicler cannot be accepted (it was suggested by H. E. Salter, *EHR*, XXII (1907), 510–14; but see R. Jahncke, *Guilelmus Neubrigensis* (Bonn, 1912), pp. 13ff.; C. N. L. Brooke in *EHR*, LXXVII (1962), 554).

M. Occ. 12 June 1199 (papal conf., Cheney, *Inn. III*, no. 136; but see note, ibid., and above).

D. Occ. 12 Nov. 1202 (*Ctl. Selby*, II, no. 925).

Walter Occ. (W.) 27 Apr. 1205 (Cheney, *Inn. III*, no. 619); (W.) –1211 (*Ctl. Wetheral*, no. 119); *c.* 13 May 1212 (*Ctl. Fountains*, II, p. 626); –1214 (*EYC*, VI, no. 136).

The next pr. known, Philip, occ. 1 July 1225 (*Ctl. Kirkstall*, no. 368).

NEWNHAM (Bedford) (Beds), St Paul f. –1086 (secular canons at Bedford); *c.* 1165 (regular canons at Bedford); *c.* 1180 (1178 × 81) (at Newnham). (See *Ctl. Newnham*, pp. ixff.).

Lists in *VCH Beds*, I, 381; cf. *Ctl. Newnham*, pp. x–xiii (J. Godber).

William 1166–*c.* 1170 First pr., app. 1166 or before (*Ctl. Newnham*, I, no. 7; cf. ed.'s note, II, no. 954). Possibly the same as William de Gorham, secular can. of St Paul's, Bedford. D. or res. by 1170 (see below).

Auger Succeeded W. in or shortly before April/May[1] 1170 (ib., I, no. 140); occ. *c.* 1176/7 (ib., II, no. 952); 11 May 1182 (ib., I, no. 8); (A.) 1174 × 98 (*Newington Longeville Chts.*, no. 73).

Ralph Occ.? *c. 1195* (*Ctl. Oseney*, VI, p. 42); 18 Nov. 1198 (*Beds F.*, no. 43); 1199 (*Ctl.*, no. 126); 1205 (*CRR*, III, p. 274); (R.) 23 Feb. 1207 (*Beds F.*, no. 157).

Eustace –1225 Occ. 20 Jan. 1213/14 (*Beds F.*, no. 179); *c. 1220* (*Ctl.*, no. 182); (E.) d. 1225 (*Ann. Dunstable*, p. 93).

NEWSTEAD[2] ('de Novo loco de Sirewda', *HMC Hastings*, I, 123–4; al. outside Nottingham, *Rot. Lit. Pat.*, p. 148) (Notts), St Mary in Sherwood f. *c.* 1163

List in *VCH Notts*, II, 117.

Ansketil Occ. prob. 1171 × 3[3] (*HMC Hastings*, I, 123–4).

Aldred Occ. 1189 × 96 (*Nottingham Borough Recs.*, I, 8); 1192 × 1210 ('Ald'),[4] prob. early 13th cent. (BM Add. MS 36,872, ff. 91, 95r–v).

Eustace Occ. 8 July 1215 (*Rot. Lit. Pat.*, p. 148); 13 Nov. 1226 (*Ctl. Tutbury*, no. 270).

Pr. Thomas occ. 1232 × 3 (*Essex F.*, p. 93). The el. of Robert, prev. canon of Newstead (dioc. York), received royal assent 9 Dec. 1234 (*CPR, 1232–47*, p. 85).

NOCTON PARK (Lincs), St Mary Magdalene f. *temp.* Stephen

List in *VCH Lincs*, II, 169.[5]

R. Occ. *late Henry II* (pal.: *DC*, no. 76).

---

[1] 'iiii^to Maii' (*Ctl.*, I, 140 – *sic* MS); presumably 'kal.', 'non.', or 'id.' is missing.

[2] One of the many houses with similar names which create problems of identification. Ansketil's pr. is precisely identified; Aldred seems to belong to a Notts context as does Eustace.

[3] This is a cht. of Bartholomew, bp. of Exeter, to which John of Salisbury is witness without the title treasurer of Exeter (see *JS Epp.*, II, introd.).

[4] 'Albredo' in one cht., but there seems little doubt that his name was Aldred (Ealdred) not Aubrey.

[5] Includes one Reginald, citing BM Cott. MS Vesp. E. viii (recte xviii), f. 149: but he was an 'abbas' and a layman.

[NOCTON PARK]

Joel Occ. *c.* 1200 (*Reg. Lincoln*, X, no. 1043).

Ivo de Scarla 1230/1– El. 1230/1 (22 Bp. Hugh of Wells); prev. cellarer (*Reg. Wells*, III, p. 195).

NORTHAMPTON (de pratibus iuxta N., etc.), St James f. *c.* 1145 × 50

List in *VCH Northants*, II, 129–30; 15th cent. list in BM Cott. MS Tib. E. v, f. 234, damaged in Cotton fire (list 1); copy made before the fire in Bodl. MS Top. Northants, c. 5 (16622: Bridges' MS), pp. 479–80 (list 2)[1] – list 2 only cited when list 1 is illegible. Cf. J. Bridges, *Hist. Northants*, I (Oxford, 1791), p. 503.

ABBOTS

Ralph ?*c.* 1150–1176 Occ. 7 Aug. 1158 (Bodl. Top. Northants c. 5, p. 301); 1173; d. 14 Jan. 1176 (List 1).[2]

William de Pavily (?Pavilly) *c.* 1176–1180 D. 17 Sept. 1180 (List 1; Ann. Montacute, BM Cott. MS Tib. A. x, f. 165 gives William's d. and Walkelin's succession under 1180).

Walkelin 1180–1206 Occ. –1192 (BM Cott. MS Vesp. E. xvii, ff. 289v–290: see Launde); 2 Dec. 1196 (*FF.*, PRS xx, no. 46); 1200 (*Mon.*, V, 193; cf. p. 191); j.d. +2 Mar. 1202 (*Chts. Luffield*, I, no. 74; cf. Cheney, *Inn. III*, no. 389). D. 28 Jan. 1205 × 6 ('1205', list 1; but 7 John, list 2; 1205 in Ann. Montacute, BM Cott. MS Tib. A. x, f. 166).

Thomas *c.* 1205 × 6–1220 Occ. 1206 × 7 (*Ctl. Cirencester*, II, no. 699 = Cheney, *Inn. III*, no. 1160; see Sulby); 1215 (*Ctl. Cockersand*, II, i, pp. 392–5). D. 13 Oct. 1220 (list 1; for day, list 2).

The next abb., Adam, can. of St James, was el. 1220 (*CPR, 1216–25*, p. 269; cf. list 1).

NORTON (Ches), St Mary and St Bertelinus f. (at Runcorn), *c.* 1115; (at Norton) 1134

List in *Ches. Chts.*, p. 26 (G. Barraclough).

Peter Occ. 1157 × 66 (*EYC*, II, nos. 1109, 1111 = *Bk. Seals*, nos. 515, 517).

Henry Occ. *c.* 1170 × 5, 1172 × 8 (*Ches. Chts.*, pp. 20, 6); 1161 × 82 ('Rancoura': BM Cott. Roll xiii. 6, no. 18); 11 Nov. 1191 (*Ctl. Burscough*, no. 164); 1194+ (Arley Chts., I, 11, cited by Barraclough, p. 26, who points out that the same cht. occ. with wrong initial 'Eg.' in Ormerod, *Hist. Cheshire*, I, 575 and *Ctl. Cockersand*, II, ii, p. 737).

Ranulf Occ. –1203 (*Ches. Chts.*, p. 26); 1211+, 1215 × 23, prob. 1220 +[3] (*Ctl. Whalley*, I, 33, 139).

Andrew was pr. by 1224 × 31[3] (PRO DL 25/273).

NORTON, *see also* COLD NORTON

NOSTELL (Yorks W.), St Oswald f. *c.* 1114

Lists in *York Fasti*, II, pp. xiii, 13–15 (Sir Charles Clay); *VCH Yorks*, III, 234; 15th cent. Ch., used by Burton, *Mon. Eboracense*, p. 310 cited by Clay.

Adelulf[4] –1153 Occ. 1122 (*Reg.*, II, nos. 1319–20); 1118 × 31 (Laurie, no. 82); bp. Carlisle 1133–57, but retained Nostell, res. 1153 (*Ch.*; cf. *EYC*, I, no. 28); d. 1157.

Savard 1153– Can. Nostell (*EYC*, I, no. 28); el. 1153 (*Ch.*); occ. 1153 × 4 (*EYC*, III, no. 1447 = *Reg.*, III, no. 624). Obit, 8 Aug. (Burton).

---

[1] We are grateful to Mr R. G. Parker for help with these lists. The dates are noted by regnal years as well as years of grace: we have assumed that the former were the basis.

[2] The list gives him as first abb., but may only mean first abb. after the move to a new site in 1173.

[3] Ralph of Maidstone, archd. Chester (still archd. Salop prob. 1220 × 1, *Reg. Lichfield*, no. 445; dean Hereford 1231, *Ann. Tewkesbury*, p. 80).

[4] Occ. as Halo in *CDF*, no. 1388: cf. *Reg.*, II, no. 1691n.

Geoffrey Occ. prob. –1159 (*Ctl. Whitby*, I, no. 283, dated by Clay, p. 13). D. 1175 according to *Ch.*; either this is a mistake or there were two Ansketils. Cf. Clay, p. xiii and n. (This is the only case in which a date recorded by Burton from *Ch.* contradicts other evidence).

Ansketil (*or* **Anketil**) Occ. 1158×9 (*CDF*, no. 1062, dated by Clay, p. xiii and n.); 6 June 1163 (*PUE*, III, no. 149); –1181 (*Ctl. Whitby*, I, no. 43, dated by Clay, p. 13); 1186×7 (*EYC*, II, no. 1036); (A.) 1190×6 (ib., no. 1178); 1193×5 (Nichols, *Leics*, III, 865–6); d. 2 Apr. 1196 (*Ch.*).

Robert of Woodkirk –1199 D. 5 Jan. 1199 (*Ch.*). A dispute about his successor's el. was settled on 7 Dec. 1201 following a papal mandate of 10 Mar. 1201, Clay, p. 14, citing PRO Anc. Deed DL 25/1223. Cf. Cheney, *Inn. III*, no. 298.

Ralph of Bedford –1208 Occ. *c.* 22 June 1203 (*Bucks F.*, p. 27); d. 19 July 1208 (*Ch.*).

?Robert Can. Nostell, el. reported ?1208×9 (BM Cott. MS Vesp. E. xix, f. 14v). But this may refer to Robert of Woodkirk (see Clay, p. 14 and n. 2).

John –1209–1237 Occ. 1209, and freq. to 13 Oct. 1236 (BM Cott. MS Vesp. E. xix, f. 166v; *Yorks F., 1232–46*, p. 44). D. 27 Sept. 1237 (*Ch.*).

NOTLEY (Crendon Park, 'de Parco super Thamam') (Bucks), St Mary and St John the Baptist (Arrouaisian) f. –1162
List in *VCH Bucks*, I, 379.

ABBOTS

Osbert Occ. *temp.* Henry II (*Bracton's Note Book*, III, 416).

N. J.d. +1191×7 (*Ctl. Tutbury*, no. 262).

Robert Occ. 1186×94 (*Ctl. Oseney*, IV, p. 442); 1186×94[1] (*Ctl. Dunstable*, no. 100; cf. pp. 263–4); (R.) May 1199+ (*Ctl. Cirencester*, II, nos. 415–16; cf. no. 414n.).

Edward Occ. 14×21 Jan. 1204 (*Bucks F.*, p. 28); 1200×5 (*Newington Longeville Chts.*, no. 38); *c.* 1206 (*Ctl. Sandford*, II, pp. 188–9).

M. Occ. 1210×11 (*Ctl. Oxford, St Frideswide*, II, pp. 246–7; cf. Cheney, *Inn. III*, no. 870 and n.).

Jo. Occ. 1234 (*Bucks F.*, p. 65).

OSENEY (Oxon), St Mary f. 1129 (priory); *c.* 1154 (abbey)
Lists in *VCH Oxon*, II, 93 (H. E. Salter); 13th cent. list in Oxford, Bodl. Rawlinson C. 939, f. 164 = *Ctl. Oseney*, I, p. xiii; basis in list and *Ann. Oseney*.

PRIORS

Ralph 1129–1138 Can. of St Frideswide, el. Jan. 1129 (*Ann. Oseney*, p. 19; list); occ. 1 Dec. 1136 (ed. Andrews, *Antiquaries Journal*, XIV, plate 1); d. 20 May 1138 (*Ann. Oseney*, p. 21; '3' kal. June in list). Pr. 9 years, 5 months (*Ann.*, p. 19; list).

Master Wigod 1138–1154 Pr. and abb. 30 years, 4 months (*Ann.*, p. 33); as pr. 15 years, 7 months (list). Occ. –1148 (*Ctl. Cirencester*, II, no. 646); 1149 ('abb.': *Reg.*, III, no. 455); 17 July 1147, 6 Feb. 1152 (*PUE*, III, nos. 65 ('Euigodo'), 79).

ABBOTS

Wigod 1154–1168 Former pr., occ. as abb. 1160×1 (*Ctl. Oxford, St Frideswide*, I, no. 27); 1154×61, ?1155×58[2] (*Ctl. Cirencester*, II, no. 518); 1 June 1163 (*PUE*, III, no. 146); d. 2 Oct. 1168 (list; *Ann. Oseney*, p. 33). Pr. and abb. 30 years, 4 months (ib.).

---

[1] Master Stephen, chancellor of Lincoln (–1194: cf. *HMC Rutland*, IV, 113–14); Roger of Rolleston not yet archd. Leicester (–1195: see p. 182n.); cf. also *Ctl. Ramsey*, II, p. 180.
[2] Cf. ed.'s note: Roger precentor Lincoln, d. 1160/1.

[OSENEY]

Edward 1168–1183 Dates as *Ann.*, pp. 33, 39; occ. 1173 (*Ctl. Oseney*, V, p. 4); *c.* 1180 (*Ctl. Oseney*, IV, p. 390); d. 22 or 20 Dec. 1183 (list; *Ann.*, p. 39).

Hugh of Buckingham 1184–1205 El. 1184 (ib., p. 40); occ. 1199 (*Bucks F.*, p. 14); d. 20 Apr. 1205 (list; cf. *Ann.*, p. 51; Ann. Winchcombe, BM Cott. MS Faust. B. i, f. 23v).

Clement 1205–1221 Pr. of Oseney,[1] el. 1205 (*Ann.*); occ. 1 June 1209 (*SHC*, III, 174); Oct. 1211 (*Ctl. Oseney*, IV, p. 222); d. 17 Sept. 1221 (list; *Ann.*, p. 62; cf. *CPR*, *1216–25*, p. 301).

OWSTON (Leics), St Andrew f. –1161
List in *VCH Leics*, II, 22 (R. A. McKinley).

ABBOTS

Odo Occ. 1150×61 (Saltman, p. 419, no. 197); –1160 (*DC*, nos. 428–9); –1166 (BM Add. Cht. 6104(1)).

Edward Occ. 1183×4 (BM Campbell Cht. xv, 2; cf. Add. Cht. 6104(2)).

Ralph Occ. ?1199 (prob. 1198×1202: Cheney, *Inn. III*, no. 813; cf. no. 812n.; cf. also Launde); 20 Sept. 1202 (Farnham, *Leics Notes*, III, 106).

Peter Occ. 1208×9 (Leics F., PRO transcripts, III); (P.) 1227 (CUL MS Dd. iii. 87(20), f. 21v); (P.) 24 Feb. 1231 (*Ctl. Cockersand*, II, i, pp. 379–80).

Royal assent for el. of next recorded abb., Richard, 27 June 1236 (*CPR*, *1232–41*, p. 151).

OXFORD, St Frideswide f. 1004 (Secular Canons); 1122 (Augustinian)
List in *VCH Oxon*, II, 100 (H. E. Salter).

Master Wimund (Guimund) 1122–*c.* 1139 First pr., on '19' years (*Ctl. Oxford, St Frideswide*, I, pp. 9–10; cf. *WMGP*, p. 316); but d. –1139 (*Ctl. Oseney*, II, pp. 233–4). Prev. chapl. of Henry I (*Ctl.*, I, pp. 9–10); possibly can. Holy Trinity, Aldgate (*Wm. Newb.*, ed. Hearne, III, 697).[2]

Master Robert of Cricklade Author and scholar (*Collectanea*, Oxford Hist. Soc., II, 160ff.);[3] prev. can. Cirencester (ib., pp. 160–1); occ. ?1140×1;[4] 8 Jan. 1141 (*PUE*, III, no. 35); –1148 (*Ctl. Cirencester*, II, no. 646); 6 Feb. 1152 (*Ctl. Oseney*, II, pp. 217–18); 1174 (ib., II, p. 217).

Philip Occ. 1175×88[5] (*CDF*, no. 436); 4 May 1188 (*Ctl. Eynsham*, I, p. 62); 4 July 1191 (*Ctl. Oseney*, IV, p. 89).

Simon –1228 Occ. 27 Nov. 1195 (*FF.*, PRS XVII, no. 86); (S.) 1197 (*CDF*, no. 145); 13 Oct. 1219 (*Ctl.*, II, p. 220); (S.) 22 May 1225 (ib., II, p. 31); res. 1228 (*CPR*, *1225–32*, p. 194).

PENTNEY (Norfolk), Holy Trinity, St Mary and St Mary Magdalene f. *c.* 1130
List in *VCH Norfolk*, II, 390.

---

[1] Occ. as pr. (C.) 1201, 1202, 1203 (Cheney, *Inn. III*, nos. 279 and n., 445 and n., 513 and n. where the editors correct the readings to 'C.').

[2] But some of the indications in the ch. Holy Trinity are undoubtedly misleading. He has been identified tentatively with Wimund, chapl. Oxford, who occ. 1107×21 (*Reg.*, II, no. 1380); and even more tentatively with 'Wymundus' who occ. in the St Paul's prebendal lists as preb. of Nesden in the early 12th cent. (?+1114×–1129), as dean of Lincoln. But it seems more likely that this is a scribal error for Simon (see Le Neve, *1066–1300*, rev. ed., I, p. 63).

[3] He was the author of an abridgement of Pliny's *Nat. Hist.*, the *Liber de connubio Iob*, and of a lost life of St Thomas Becket (E. Walberg, *La tradition hagiographique de S. Thomas Becket* (Paris, 1929), pp. 25ff.). For his name, see preface to the first of these (*Collectanea*, loc. cit.).

[4] Cht., ed. H. A. Cronne in *Univ. of Birmingham Hist. Journ.*, II (1949–50), 201–7, not certainly genuine, and misdated in the MS '1160', MCLX, but with a witness list consistent with the date 1140, MCXL (1139×42); Cronne suggests Jan. 1141.   [5] Herbert archd. Canterbury.

Geoffrey Occ. 18 Nov. 1167 (*MB Epp.* 334); 29 July 1175 (*Ctl. Coxford, Norfolk Arch.*, XVII (1910), 294, corrected by MS (see Coxford, n. 1), ff. 57v–8; also printed *EHR*, XI (1896), 747–8).

Ralph[1] Occ. 1181 × 96 (*Ctl. Brinkburn*, p. 184).

Simon Occ. 1200 (*CRR*, I, p. 352).

A pr. William occ. n.d. in BM Cott. MS Titus C. viii, f. 51 (13th cent. ctl.).

PLYMPTON (Devon), St Peter and St Paul   f. –909 (College); 24 Aug. 1121 (Augustinian: see Ann., p. 27; list)

List in Oliver, p. 131; transcript of medieval list from lost ctl., in BM Harl. MS 6974, f. 28;[2] Ann. in *UGQ*.

Ralph 1121–1127/8 1st pr. (cf. Ann., p. 27), prob. prev. can. Holy Trinity Aldgate (Newburgh, ed. Hearne, III, 697); dates: 1121–8, i.e. for 7 years, list (cf. Ann., p. 27); but see below.

Geoffrey 1128–1160 2nd pr., ruled 32 years from 1128, list; el. 18 Jan., 'feria quinta', 1128, d. 25 Aug. 1160, Ann., pp. 27, 30. But in 1128 18 Jan. was a Wednesday, and Friday in 1129.

Richard Pilatus 1160–1169 3rd pr.; ruled 8½ years from 1160, list. Occ. 1161 × 9 (BM Cott. MS Tib. D. vi, pt. i, f. 14; *Ctl. Buckland*, no. 224).

John 1169–1176 4th pr., el. 1169; ruled 7 years 2 months, list.

Martin 1176–1188 5th pr., el. 1176; ruled 12½ years, list. Occ. (M.) *c.* 1180 × 4 (Oliver, p. 137; cf. Morey, p. 122).

Joel 1188–1202 6th pr.; ruled 13 years (*sic*, for 23) 8 weeks, list. Occ. 1189 (Oliver, p. 137); 1188 + [3] (*CDF*, no. 1274); 1 July 1201 (*Devon F.*, no. 44); 3 Feb. 1202 (ib., no. 31).

Robert 'Ibslincton' (list) 1202–1214 7th pr., el. 1202; ruled 12 years, list. Occ. 8 June 1208 (*Devon F.*, no. 59).

Anthony 1214–1225 8th pr., el. 1214; ruled 10 years 10 months 15 days, list. Occ. 3 May 1223 (*Reg. Grandisson*, pp. 1579, 1598). 1224 is just possible for his death; but if the arithmetic is correct, 1225 is more likely (but see note 2).

His successor, Pr. Richard de Brugis, was el. 1225 (list).

POUGHLEY (Elenfordesmere) (Berks), St Margaret   f. *c.* 1160 × 78 (see below)

List in *VCH Berks*, I, 86.

Gerelm Occ. 1160 × 78 (27 Jan. 1160, 1161, 1174 or 1178: *JL*, 12980 = Rymer, *Foedera*, I, 43).

Robert Occ. *c.* 20 Apr. 1214 (*Ped. Fin.*, I, 149–50); 13th cent. (PRO C 146/3038; *Cat. Anc. D.*, III, 322; this may refer to the Robert who occ. 1268, *Wilts F.*, p. 58).

The next recorded pr., William, occ. 27 Apr. 1236 (Madox, *Form.*, p. 374).

RANTON (de Sartis, Des Essarz) (Staffs), St Mary   f. mid-12th cent. (–1166: *VCH Staffs*, III, 252)

List in *VCH Staffs*, III, 254[4] (J. C. Dickinson).

O. Occ. ?1198 × 1203 or before (Cheney, *Inn. III*, no. 902).

Alvred Occ. (A.) *c.* 1220 or + (*SHC*, III, 210–11); 22 Sept. 1221 (*Warws F.*, no. 235); 1 Dec. 1240 (*SHC*, IV, i, 236).

---

[1] Geoffrey de Vaux in *VCH* list (and Blomefield, IX, 41) appears to have been a landholder.

[2] Evidently the original list was 15th cent., or an earlier list continued to the 15th cent. It seems possible that the regnal figures included vacancies. If so dates of d. etc. may not be reliable.

[3] See Buckfast.

[4] This list includes Ralph, noting that he was traditionally regarded as first pr., or at least pr. in the founder's lifetime: citing *Mon.*, VI, 257; William Salt Lib. S. MS 237/M, pp. 8, 13 (*VCH Staffs*, III, 254n.). But there seems no contemporary evidence of this.

REPTON (Derbys), Holy Trinity and St Wistan (formerly St Giles and St Wistan, Calke: cf. *Derbys Chts.*, nos. 1939, 1943ff.) f. 1130 × 6 (at Calke);[1] *c.* 1153 × 60 (at Repton) – but the main transfer took place in 1172

    List in *VCH Derbys*, II, 62–3.

Robert (Calke) Occ. prob. 1153 (*Ctl. Chester*, I, p. 232); *c.* 1153[2] (*Ctl. Trentham*, p. 300); 1154[3] × 9 (*Derbys Chts.*, no. 1939).

Nicholas (Calke) Occ. prob. 1171 × 3 (*HMC Hastings*, I, 124; cf. Newstead); 1153 × 96, 1160[4] × 92 (Ctl. Breedon, nos. 47, 56): (Repton) 1163 × 81 (*Derbys Chts.*, no. 1945).

Aldred Occ. (A.) *c.* 1200 (*Derbys Chts.*, no. 1949); 1199 × 1200 (*Hunts F.*, p. 2).

Richard Occ. 15 Nov. 1208 (*Derbys F.* (1885), p. 205); 1200 × 10 (*Ctl. Burton*, no. 45); (R.) 1215 × 16 (*Ches. Chts.*, p. 23).

N[icholas?] Occ. 1215 × 23 (*Derbys Chts.*, no. 1681).

The next recorded pr., John, occ. 24 × 31 May 1220 (*Derbys F.* (1885), p. 214); 19 Apr. × 17 May 1226 (ib. (1886), p. 16).

ROCESTER (Staffs), St Mary f. *c.* 1146

    List in *VCH Staffs*, III, 251 (J. C. Dickinson).

ABBOTS

Thurstan First abb. (*Misc. D. M. Stenton*, p. 26, n. 1; cf. *Mon.*, VI, 410–11).

Ivo Occ. *c.* 1155[5] (*Ctl. Trentham*, p. 301).

Richard Occ. 1155 × 6 (Eyton, *Salop*, VIII, 217: cf. Buildwas); 1161 + (ib., p. 227n. = BM Harl. MS 3868, f. 21).

Henry Occ. 1202 × 3 (N'hants F., PRO transcripts); 28 July 1210 (*HMC Rutland*, IV, 33–4).

W. Occ. 1215 × 23 (*Ctl. Dieulacres*, p. 311); 1216 (*SHC*, 1911, p. 425).

Philip Occ. ?early *temp.* Henry III[6] (*Ctl. Stone*, pp. 11, 17); j.d. +2 Sept. 1239 (BM Cott. MS Calig. A. xiii, ff. 48–50).

ROYSTON ('de Cruce Roisia') (Herts), St John the Baptist and St Thomas Becket. f. 1173 × 9

    List in *VCH Herts*, IV, 440.

Simon Occ. 23 Apr. 1184 (*PUE*, I, no. 219).

Harpin Occ. 1186 × 95[7] (BM Add. MS 46,362, f. 151v).

Gilbert Occ. 5 Feb. 1199 (*FF.*, PRS XXIV, 300).

The next recorded pr., W., occ. Oct. 1229 (*CR, 1227–31*, p. 225).

ST DENYS, Southampton (Hants) f. 1127

    List in *VCH Hants*, II, 163.

?Gerard Prob. 1st pr., occ. 1124 in the foundation cht., described as can. (*Mon.*, VI, 213).

Aelard Occ. 1151 (BM Add. MS 15,314, f. 95; cf. Saltman, pp. 474–5, no. 251).

R. Occ. 1187 × 92[8] (BM Cott. MS Vesp. E. xxiii, f. 9(5) = *Mon.*, VI, 937). A Ruelandus occ. as pr. n.d. – ?12–13th cent. and may = R. (BM Add. MS 15,314, f. 11).

---

[1] *KH*, p. 151; cf. Cheney, *English Bishops' Chanceries*, App. I. For date of transfer, cf. *Ctl. Dale*, pp. 2ff.

[2] Ranulf, earl of Chester (d. Dec. 1153); William, abb. Radmore (see Stoneleigh). This reference has been attributed to Calwich, but 'Calc'' seems much more likely to be Calke.

[3] Hugh earl of Chester's father d. 16 Dec. 1153.

[4] B[aldric] archd. Leicester (*GFL*, p. 164n.).

[5] See Chester.   [6] With Richard, pr. Trentham.

[7] Master Roger of Rolleston (with Hugh, bp. of Lincoln), but not yet archd. of Leicester (Howden, III, 285).

[8] Christopher abb. Waverley; R. archd. Surrey (cf. *Ctl. Peterborough*, p. 169).

John Occ. 1202 × 3 (Hants F., PRO transcripts).

The next recorded pr., Walkelin, can. of St Denys, el. 1220 (*CPR, 1216–25*, p. 230).

ST GERMANS (Cornwall) f. –1184

List in Oliver, p. 2.

William Occ. 1186 × 96[1] (*Mon.*, v, 382).

Auger Occ. 25 June 1201 (*Cornwall F.*, no. 27; *Reg. Bronescombe*, p. 248); 1202 (*HMC Var. Coll.*, IV, 60).

The next recorded pr., Alvred, occ. 1224 and Auger is stated to be his predecessor (*CRR*, XI, no. 1680).

ST OSYTH (Chich) (Essex), St Peter, St Paul and St Osyth f. 1121 (priory); –1161 (abbey: see below).

List in *VCH Essex*, II, 162.

PRIORS

William de Corbeil 1121–1123 1st pr., can. of St Gregory, Canterbury (Hugh the Chanter, p. 50); res. 18 Feb. 1123 to be abp. Canterbury (*WMGP*, p. 146; Gervase, II, 380).

Fulk Occ. 1127 (Eyton, *Salop*, II, 201); 1126 × 8, 1126 × 36 (*Text. Roff.*, ff. 179v–180, 203); 1123 × 38 (*Ctl. Colchester*, I, pp. 230–1); 1139 × 40 (Saltman, pp. 384–5, no. 161).

ABBOTS

Abel Occ. –1161 (*JS Epp.*, I, 120 and n.); 1157 × 62 (PRO E40/5273); (A.) prob. 1169 (*MB Epp.* 525). D. 1184 (*Ralph Cogg.*, p. 20).

Ralph Occ. (R.) 1184 × 94 (Eyton, *Salop*, VII, 366n.); 23 Mar. 1192 (PRO E40/2383); late 1195 (*Essex F.*, p. 9); 1198 × 1205 (Cheney, *Inn. III*, no. 1184). D. 1205 (*Ralph Cogg.*, p. 162).

Richard Occ. 10 Feb. 1207 (*Suffolk F.*, PRS, LXX, no. 472).

David Occ. 1207 × 21 (*Ctl. Lewes*, II, p. 119); 11 Jan. 1221 (*Ctl. Colchester*, II, pp. 532ff.); 26 Oct. 1221 (BM Harl. MS 391, ff. 115v–117); 1229 (*CRR*, XIII, no. 1311); *c.* Apr. 1244 (*Essex F.*, p. 147).

SHELFORD (Notts), St Mary f. temp. Henry II

List in *VCH Notts*, II, 120.

Remigius (?Raymond) Occ. 1173 (Rem' or Reim': *HMC 14th Rep.*, VIII, p. 168 = *Ctl. Oseney*, V, p. 4 = *Ctl. Worcester*, p. 119); definitely as Remigius in *Ctl. Haverholme*, no. 94, which is however only known from the transcript in BM Lansd. MS 207A, ff. 111v–112.

Alexander Occ. *c.* 21 Dec. 1203 (BM Harl. MS 3640, f. 118); n.d. ?*c.* 1200 (*Ctl. Darley*, I, pp. 185–6).

Laurence 1215– El. 1215 (*Rot. Lit. Pat.*, p. 131); occ. 14 June 1220 (*Lincs F.*, I, p. 153).

The next recorded pr., Thomas, occ. 1219 × 23 (*Reg. Lincoln*, VII, no. 2077); 13 Nov. 1226 (*Ctl. Tutbury*, no. 270).

SOUTHWARK (Surrey), St Mary Overy f. 1106

Lists in *VCH London*, I, 484; *VCH Surrey*, II, 111. Basis in BM Cott. MS Faust. A. viii, ff. 119v (14th cent., list 1), 131 vff. (Ann. Southwark); BM Harl. MS 544, f. 100 (list 2).

Algod 1106–1130 Dates as Ann.; d. 6 Jan. 1130. Pr. 24 years, lists 1, 2.

Algar 1130–1132 Dates as Ann.; d. 25 Oct. 1132. Pr. 2 years, lists 1, 2.

Warin (Varinus) *c.* 1132–1142 Dates as Ann.; d. 28 Feb. 1142. Pr. 10 years, list 1, 11 years, list 2.

Gregory 1142–1150 Dates as Ann.; d. 20 Jan. 1150. Pr. 7 years, list 1; 8 years, list 2.

Ralph 1150–1154 Dates as Ann., d. 10 Mar. 1154. Pr. 3 years, list 1; 4 years, list 2.

---

[1] John archd. Exeter (possibly –1189, if Henry II alive).

[SOUTHWARK]

Richard 1154 Succeeded Ralph, Ann.; pr. 1 year, list 2.

Waleran (Valerianus) *c.* 1154/5–1190 D. 1 Apr. 1190, Ann.; pr. 13 years (*sic*), list 1, 36 years, list 2. Occ. 29 Sept. 1174 (*Ctl. Winchester*, pp. 196–7); 1174 × 5 (PRO E40/13850/6); 16 Mar. 1186 (BM Cott. MS Nero E. vi, f. 305 = *Mon.*, VI, 808 ('17 Mar.')).

William of Oxford 1190–1203 Dates as Ann.; d. 10 Nov. 1203. Pr. 12 years, list 1; 14 years, list 2. Occ. 25 Nov. 1198 (*FF.*, PRS XXIV, no. 166); 1201 × 2 (*Cambs F.*, p. 4).

Richard of St Mildred 1203–1205 Dates as Ann., d. 5 Jan. 1205. Pr. 2 years, list 1; 3 years, list 2. Occ. (R.) 13 Oct. 1204 (*Norfolk F.*, PRS LXX, no. 61).

William son of Samarus ?1205 Succeeded Richard, Ann. 1 year, list 2.

Martin ?*c.* 1205–1218 D. 11 June 1218, Ann.; pr. 15 years (*sic*), list 2.

Robert 1218–1223 Prev. pr. Oseney, dates as Ann.; d. 18 Apr. 1223. Pr. 5 years, list 2.

SOUTHWICK (Hants), St Mary   f. 1133 (at Porchester); *c.* 1145 × 53 (at Southwick)
List in *VCH Hants*, II, 168. Ctls. in Hants Rec. Office.

Anselm (Ancelmus or Antelmus) Occ. 14 July × 12 Oct. 1147 (*PUE*, III, no. 72); July 1151 × Oct. 1152 (ib., no. 81).

Walter Occ. Oct. 1162 × June 1163 (ib., no. 143 = Ctl., I, ff. 14v–15).

Philip Occ. 1 Aug. 1177 (ib., f. 3v); 1174 × 88 (*Mon.*, V, 242).

Guy Occ. 15 Mar. 1185 × 7 (Ctl., I, f. 17); 9 Feb. 1186 (*PUE*, III, no. 379); 1199 (*Reg. St Osmund*, I, p. 354); *c.* 8 Mar. 1202 (Cheney, *Inn. III*, no. 394); 5 Feb. 1206 (*Ctl. Chichester*, pp. 48–9). Can. Merton; author of Florilegium in Oxford, St John's Coll. MS 126 – colophon printed in *Letters of Arnulf of Lisieux*, ed. F. Barlow, pp. lxxxvf. and elsewhere; author of treatise on confession (1186 × 98), ed. A. Wilmart, *RTAM*, VII (1935), 337–52. D. 3 Nov. (obit. Wintney, Trokelowe, ed. Hearne, p. 392).

The next recorded pr., Luke, d. 1227 (*CPR 1225–32*, p. 125).

STAFFORD (St Thomas) (Baswich), St Thomas Becket   f. 1173 × 5
List in *VCH Staffs*, III, 266 (J. C. Dickinson).

Walter Occ. *c.* 1174 × *c.* 1181 (*Mon.*, IV, 221–2: see Breedon); *c.* 1174 × 82 (BM Harl. MS 3868, ff. 6v–7); 1184 × 99 (*SHC*, IV, i, 267).

Robert Occ. 2 Oct. 1199 (*Staffs F.* = *SHC*, III, i, 166); 1198 × 1208 (*Ctl. Burscough*, no. 165; *Reg. Lichfield*, no. 144).

?Adam Occ. ?temp. Richard I or John (*SHC*, VIII, i, 129).

Ralph Occ. 1203 (*CRR*, II, p. 223).

The next recorded pr., Philip, occ. 20 Oct. 1221 (*SHC*, IV, i, 220).

STONE (Staffs), St Wulfadus (and St Mary and St Michael) (Kenilworth)   f. *c.* 1135
List in *VCH Staffs*, III, 246 (J. C. Dickinson).

Ralph, brother of Robert son of Odo of Loxley   Occ. ?*c.* 1138 (*c.* 1135 × 54) (*SHC*, II, 215); –1147[1] (*Mon.*, VI, 224); 1151 (BM Add. MS 47,677, f. 252v).

Roger Occ. 1161 × 3, prob. 1162 (*SHC*, II, 252);[2] 31 May 1174 × 6 (*PUE*, I, no. 136).

Henry Occ. n.d. ?late 12th cent. (*SHC*, VI, i, 16, cf. 20).

Silvester Occ. 1194 (*SHC*, II, i, 263); 1188 × 98 (ib., VI, i, 12); (S.) 4 Apr. 1196 (*FF.*, PRS XVII, no. 123); very likely = pr. Kenilworth (occ. –1200).

Richard Occ. prob. 1196 × 8 (*SHC*, VI, i, 12); (R.) n.d. ?*early 13th cent.* (ib., p. 9).

The next pr., Reginald, occ. 3 Nov. 1227 (*SHC*, IV, i, 53).

---

[1] Roger bp. Chester went on Crusade in 1147; d. 1148.

[2] = Madox, no. 78 = PRO E327/78, dated at 'Fissam'. If this is rightly identified as Fécamp, 1162 is the likely date, and it cannot be later than 1163 (see *SHC*, ed.'s note).

STUDLEY (Warws), St Mary f. *c.* 1135 (at Witton); *c.* 1151 (at Studley)
  List in *VCH Warws*, II, 97.
Fromond Occ. 1158×60 (*Mon.*, IV, 115).
Everard Occ. *c.* 1139×50 (*Ctl. Winchcombe*, I, pp. 65–6); 1179 (Evreux, Archives Dépt.
  Eure, II F. 2463, f. 4 – Ctl. Wootton Wawen); 1193×5 (*Ctl. Winchcombe*, I, p. 188).
Roger Occ. (R.) –1199 (Cheney, *Inn. III*, no. 175); 1202×3 (*Warws F.*, no. 88).
Ralph Occ. 1209×10 (ib., no. 197).
The next recorded pr., Nicholas, occ. 1220×1 (ib., no. 291).

TAUNTON (Soms), St Peter and St Paul f. *c.* 1120
  List in *VCH Soms*, II, 144.
William Occ. 14 June 1133 (*EHD*, II, p. 781); 1136×7 (*Ctl. Bath*, I, p. 59).
Stephen Occ. 11 Oct. 1158 (*Ctl. Winchester*, p. 198); 4 Nov. 1159 (*HMC Wells*, I, 27);
  29 Sept. 1169 (*CDF*, no. 900); 8 Nov. 1186 (*Ctl. Buckland*, no. 11); 1189×91 (*HMC
  Wells*, I, 69).
Robert Occ. 1 May 1197 (*Devon F.*, no. 2).
John Occ. 1197×1205 (*HMC Wells*, I, 57); (J.) 5 Oct. 1204 (*Devon F.*, no. 51); 1227×8
  (*Soms F.*, p. 71).
The next recorded pr., Robert, occ. 1235×6 (*Soms F.*, p. 86).

THETFORD (Norfolk), Holy Sepulchre f. +1139
  Lists in *VCH Norfolk*, II, 393; *VCH Suffolk*, II, 110.
Gilbert Occ. mid 12th century – with Constantius, pr. of Thetford, St Mary (Bodl. Gough
  MS, Norfolk, 18, f. 19v).
Herbert Occ. 1196 (*CDF*, no. 677, as pr. of 'Neford', St Sepulchre).
Richard Occ. 3 Nov. 1202 (*Norfolk F.*, PRS LXX, no. 10).

THOBY (Ginges) (Essex), St Leonard (and St Mary) f. 1141×50[1]
  List in *VCH Essex*, II, 163.
Tobias Occ. 1141×1150 (*Cal. Bodl. Chts.*, p. 77; *Mon.*, VI, 554).
Adam Occ. late 12th cent. (*Cal. Bodl. Chts.*, p. 77).
Ralph and H. Occ. in two documents of *c.* 1200 or early 13th cent. – the former with Henry
  pr. Colchester, St Botolph (*Ctl. Colchester*, II, pp. 304–5).
The next recorded pr., William, occ. 1226×7 (PRO Assize Roll 229, m. 13).

THORNHOLME (Lincs), St Mary f. *temp.* Stephen
  List in *VCH Lincs*, II, 168.
Richard Occ. *early Henry II* (pal.: DC, no. 24); 1157×63[2] (ib., no. 312); (R.) 24 May 1163
  (*PUE*, I, no. 95).
Laurence Occ. late 12th cent. (pal.: BM Harl. Cht. 50 I. 4; cf. Newhouse).
Walter[3] Occ. 1201 (BM Lansd. MS 402, ff. 33v–4); 17 June 1202 (*Lincs F.*, PRS LXVII,
  no. 26); 1206 (*CRR*, IV, p. 248); 6 Oct. 1209 (*Yorks F.*, John, p. 159).
Andrew Occ. 1209×23 (*EYC*, VI, no. 107); 1216×18 (BM Cott. MS Claud. D. xi, f. 217r–
  v); 1218 (*Ctl. Peterborough*, no. 522); 6 Oct. 1226 (*Lincs F.*, I, p. 194).
The next recorded pr., Geoffrey, occ. 10 Feb. 1230 (ib., I, p. 225). Alan pr. occ. n.d. in Bodl.
MS Top. Yorks, c. 72, f. 38v.

[1] Dated by Robert bp. of London (so *VCH*).
[2] Walter de Amundeville, sheriff of Lincs.
[3] Possibly Walter Scrop, occ. early 13th cent., with Alan pr. Drax (*Ctl. Selby*, II, no. 1219).

THORNTON (CURTIS) (Lincs), St Mary f. 1139 (1140: see below) (priory); 1148 (abbey)

List in *VCH Lincs*, II, 166; basis in list of abbs. known from Bodl. Tanner MS 166, ff. 4–8, BM Add. MS 6118, ff. 335–6 (Holles transcript); partly corrected in *PUE*, III, p. 24. The list includes copious indications of date, not always reconcilable, and abbatial years which ignore vacancies (i.e. run from one abb.'s death to the next; cf. Fountains). Where no references are given, the details are from the list, though no attempt has been or can be made to reconcile all the dates given. The list is certainly seriously wrong *c.* 1200, but it may well be more correct for the earlier heads.

PRIOR THEN ABBOT

Richard pr. 1140–1148; abb. 1148–1152 First pr. el. 13 Jan. 1140 (4 Stephen, 73 years after the Conquest, Saturday, St Hilary's day);[1] made abb. 1148, on basis of bull of 21 Oct. 1147 (3 Eugenius III, 11th Indiction); d. 16 Nov.[2] 1152 after 12 years, 11 months.

ABBOTS

Philip 1152–1175 Second abb., el. 1152: 15 Ind., 8 Eugenius III, 17 Stephen. The indiction would give a date –1 Sept. 1152; the abbatial years evidently presuppose that Richard d. Nov., either 1151 or 1152. Occ. 1152 × 5 (*Reg. Lincoln*, I, no. 133); 1157 × 63 (*DC*, no. 312 – see Thornholme); 1170[3] × 5 (*EYC*, III, no. 1308). D. 28 July 1175 after 23 years, 8 months, 11 days (8th Indiction, 15 Alexander III, 21 Henry II).

Thomas 1175–1184 Third abb., el. 1175 (8th Indiction – i.e. –1 Sept. – 15 Alexander III, 21 Henry II); occ. (T.) 1180[4] × 4 (*EYC*, III, no. 1310); d. 14 Sept. 1184 in France, on his way to Rome, after 9 years and seven weeks.

John Benton 1184– Fourth abb., el. 1184 (2nd Indiction, 3 Lucius III, 30 Henry II); the list makes him d. 3 Nov. 1203 after 19 years, 7 months, but this must be wrong, as references to Jordan show (see below). A J., who could be John or Jordan, occ. 1193 (*DC*, no. 15); 1191 × 7 (*Ctl. Guisborough*, II, no. 672).

Jordan de Villa Fifth abb., el., according to list, 15 May × 31 Aug. 1203 (6th Indiction, 6 Innocent III, 5 John); but he occ. 1191 × 5[5] (*Ctl. Bridlington*, p. 423): 31 Jan. 1199 (*FF.*, PRS XXIV, no. 268); early 1203 (*CRR*, II, p. 157); 27 Nov. 1203 (*Lincs F.*, PRS LXVII, no. 177): 1205 (*CRR*, III, p. 333); *c.* 20 Oct. 1206 (*Yorks F., John*, p. 109); d. ? 7 Nov. 1223 after 20 years, 4 days. But the next abb., Richard de Villa (el. 1223 in list), occ. 20 Jan. 1222 (6 Henry III: *Lincs F.*, I, p. 162); and an R., former abb. 'Torrington', *nuncius regis*, occ. 1215 (*Rot. Lit. Pat.*, p. 181).

THREMHALL (Essex), St James f. *c.* 1150.

List in *VCH Essex*, II, 164.

Daniel Said to be first pr. in late history of founder's family in *Mon.*, VI, 77.

William Occ. late 1202 (*Essex F.*, p. 27); early 13th cent. (–1208) (*Bk. Seals*, no. 157).

The next recorded pr., John, occ. summer 1231 (*Essex F.*, p. 88).

[1] Correct for 1140; the list makes St Hilary's day fall on a Sunday in 1141 – actually it was a Monday.

[2] The day of St Edmund the abp. The regnal calculations confirm that this was the day, not the alternative feast of St Edmund (the archbishop) in June – it is curious to date the death of a 12th-cent. abbot by the feast of a 13th-cent. archbishop. Cf. below, for the doubt whether the list really meant 1152 or 1151.

[3] It refers to Henry II and his son Henry as kings.

[4] It is a grant of Earl William de Mandeville as successor of Earl William of Aumale, whose daughter and heiress he married in Jan. 1180.

[5] W. archd. Nottingham, Master Simon of Apulia not yet dean of York.

THURGARTON (Notts), St Peter f. 1119 × 39
List in *VCH Notts*, II, 125.
Gilbert Occ. (G.) prob. –1181[1] (*Reg. Master David*, no. 49 = Vat. Lat. MS 6024, f. 148 v, printed Liverani, pp. 600–2); (G.) *c.* 1188 × 91 (*Chts. Newington Longeville*, no. 36); (Gilbert) 1197 × 1205 (BM Egerton MS 2823, f. 99, cf. f. 97 v; *ex inf.* M. Screech).
The pr. was vacant 25 Feb. and 12 Mar. 1205 (*Rot. Lit. Pat.*, pp. 50b, 51b).
Henry Occ. 1208 × 9 (Notts F., PRO transcripts); 6 Oct. 1218 (*Lincs F.*, I, p. 117).
The next recorded pr., Elias, occ. 25 June 1219 (*Lincs F.*, I, pp. 122–3).

TONBRIDGE (Kent), St Mary Magdalene f. –1192
List in *VCH Kent*, II, 168.
John Occ. 2 Jan. 1192 (*PUE*, II, no. 266); 5 Jan. 1202 (Cheney, *Inn. III*, no. 368; cf. nos. 369–71).

TORKSEY (Lincs), St Leonard f. *temp*. Henry II
List in *VCH Lincs*, II, 171.
Absalom Occ. 1201 (BM Lansdowne MS 402, ff. 33 v–34)
The next pr., John, occ. 16 Oct. 1234 (*Lincs F.*, I, p. 261).

TORTINGTON (Sussex), St Mary Magdalene (*Ctl. Boxgrove*, no. 258) f. *c.* 1180
List in *VCH Sussex*, II, 83 (L. F. Salzman).
Nicholas Occ. 1180 × 97[2] (*Ctl. Chichester*, no. 182, p. 43).
Henry Occ. 1218 (*Ctl. Lewes*, II, p. 75 n. 1).
The next recorded pr., Reyner, occ. 1230 (*Sussex F.*, no. 219).

TRENTHAM (Staffs), St Mary and All Saints f. *c.* 1153 × 5
Lists in *Ctl. Trentham*, p. 299; *VCH Staffs*, III, 259–60 (J. C. Dickinson).
John 1155–?1194[3] Occ. *c.* 1155 (BM Harl. MS 3868, f. 34r–v – see Stoneleigh); 12 Oct. 1162 (*PUE*, I, no. 91); 1161 × 72[4] (BM Harl. MS 3868, ff. 34 v–35); 1172 × 81 (*CChR*, II, 310).
Vacant 1203; in charge of Alan canon of Trentham and Henry de Verdun (*Book of Fees*, II, p. 1337). Alan possibly became, or called himself pr.: occ. n.d. (*Ctl. Trentham*, p. 320).
Samson Occ. 1190 × 1211[5] (*Mon.*, VI, 411). Possibly before the vacancy of 1203.
Richard Occ. ?early temp. Henry III (*SHC*, VII, i, 11: +1216; cf. p. 17); 1224 × 38 (ib., p. 19); 25 June 1234 (*Lincs F.*, I, p. 288).

ULVERSCROFT (Leics), St Mary f. 1134
List in *VCH Leics*, II, 20 (R. A. McKinley).
William Occ. 17 Nov. 1174 (*PUE*, I, no. 119).
T. Occ. *temp*. Henry III (pal.: *HMC Hastings*, I, 12).
The next recorded pr., Walter, occ. 1219 × 34, prob. soon after 1219[6] (Nichols, *Leics*, III, 1085).

---

[1] Ref. to an archbp. York, almost certainly Roger.
[2] Matthew dean of Chichester (*Acta Chichester*, p. 211).
[3] Possibly to be identified with John, chaplain to the earl of Chester, who d. 1194 (*Ctl. Trentham*, p. 299; cf. *VCH Staffs*, III, 259n.).
[4] Richard bp. Coventry; Elias archd. Staffs. It is couched in words almost identical with the cht. of *c.* 1155 (Harl. MS 3868, f. 34r–v).
[5] Roger (de Lacy) constable of Chester (*Ches. Chts.*, p. 19); but late in the period 1190 × 1211, because Roger of Mold occ. as seneschal of the earl of Chester.
[6] The widow of Saher, earl of Winchester (d. 1219) has done homage for her inheritance.

WALSINGHAM (Norfolk), St Mary f. *c.* 1153 (J. C. Dickinson, *Walsingham*, pp. 4–7, 132–3).

Lists in ib., pp. 131–4; *VCH Norfolk*, II, 401. 15th-cent. list in BM Cott. Nero E. vii, f. 157v, printed in Dickinson, *Walsingham*, pp. 132–3. The list seems tolerably reliable, but as there is very little control for this period, it must be regarded with some caution.

Ralph *c.* 1153–*c.* 1173 Formerly clerk, 1st regular can. and pr., occ. 1151 × 73[1] (BM Cott. MS Nero E. vii, f. 7r–v); pr. 20 years, list.

Richard *c.* 1173–*c.* 1186 2nd pr.; 13 years, list.

Alexander *c.* 1186–*c.* 1207 3rd pr.; 21 years, list; occ. 1175 × 1214 (BM Cott. MS Nero E. vii, ff. 8v–9).

William *c.* 1207–*c.* 1254 4th pr.; 47 years, list. Occ. morrow St Edward, 19 Henry III, prob. 6 Jan. or 19 Mar. 1235 (BM Cott. Roll, iv, 57, no. 48); *c.* 25 Nov. 1250 (BM Cott. MS Nero E. vii, ff. 48, 96).

WALTHAM (Essex), Holy Cross f. –1060 (secular); 1177 (priory); 1184 (abbey)

List in *VCH Essex*, II, 170–1.

PRIORS

Ralph 1177– Can. Cirencester, app. 1177 (Diceto, I, 420–1). Occ. 21 May 1182 (*PUE*, I, no. 208).

ABBOTS

Master Walter of Ghent 1184–1201 Can. Oseney, app. first abb. 1184 (*Ann. Oseney*, p. 40; *Gesta Hen. II*, I, 317). Occ. 1 × 6 Dec. 1187 (BM Harl. MS 391, ff. 88v–9) and frequently[2] to *c.* 3 Feb. 1201 (Cheney, *Inn. III*, no. 284). D. 2 May 1201 (Howden, IV, 163).

Richard[3] *c.* 1201–1230 Occ. 1203 (*Essex F.*, p. 31); 1204 (*CRR*, III, p. 237); etc.; 27 May 1228 (BM Cott. MS Tib. C. ix, f. 153r–v). He was presumably el. in or very soon after 1201; but his bl. was postponed – no doubt by the interdict – to 120(6 ×)7: 22 March in the 13th year after it fell in 1220 (BM Harl. MS 391, f. 1). D. –22 March 1230 (licence to el. his successor; pr. Henry was el. abb. late Mar., since his el. received royal assent on 1 Apr. 1230: *CPR, 1225–32*, pp. 330–1).

WARTER (Yorks E.), St James f. (priory) *c.* 1132, (Arrouaisian abbey) 1140 × 1, (priory again) 1181 × 92 (*EYC*, X, pp. 110–11)

C.T.C. Lists in *EYC*, X, pp. 140–2 (Sir Charles Clay); *VCH Yorks*, III, 238, 15th-cent. list cited and discussed by Clay, loc. cit.

PRIOR AND ABBOT

Ivo Occ. 1140 × 1 (pr.), 1144 × 6 (abb.) (*EYC*, X, no. 65; I, no. 105 – for date cf. Clay, p. 141).

ABBOT

Richard Occ. 25 Apr. 1178 (papal conf., *EYC*, X, no. 72); abb. (unnamed) occ. 1181 × 5 (papal conf., *EYC*, X, no. 73).

---

[1] Dickinson, p. 5, proposes a date 1152 × 6 for the cht. on the grounds of the style of Roger, earl of Clare: but this was his common title from his succession 1151/3 × 1156 to his death in 1173. A date in or soon after 1153 is quite likely, but cannot be proved.

[2] Esp. as witness to acts of Abp. Hubert Walter. An Abb. Henry occ. by error in 1200 (BM Harl. MS 391, f. 7).

[3] *MPCM*, II, 576, has an Abb. N. (extended by ed. to Nicholas) s.a. 1214; 'N.' was evidently the cipher not a true initial.

PRIORS

Joseph Occ. 1191 × 7 (*Ctl. Guisborough*, II, no. 923, dated by Clay, p. 141); (J.) 1196 (*EYC*, II, no. 1177). Pr. (unnamed) occ. 13 Mar. 1192 (ib.).

Ralph Occ. between Joseph and Nicholas in 15th-cent. list in Ctl. Warter (*Mon.*, VI, 298).

Nicholas Occ. 25 July 1206 (*Yorks F., John*, p. 101).

Richard Occ. 6 Oct. 1209 (ib., p. 159); 1206 × 12 (*EYC*, X, no. 13); 21 May 1212 (Bodl. MS Fairfax 9, f. 34).

The next pr., Thomas, was el. *c.* 1223; cf. list, ut sup., and Clay, pp. 140 n. 4, 142.

WARWICK, Holy Sepulchre (Canons of the Holy Sepulchre) f. *c.* 1119 × 23
List in *VCH Warws*, II, 98–9.

Almer Occ. as Anthony's predecessor (*GFL*, no. 345).

Anthony Occ. as Ralph's predecessor (*GFL*, no. 345).

Ralph Occ. 1157 (Saltman, pp. 501–2); 1158 × 60 (*Mon.*, IV, 115); 1161 × 2 (*GFL*, no. 345); 1162 × 3 (ib., no. 347).

G. Occ. 19 Oct. 1188 (*Ctl. Harrold*, p. 56, no. 69**).

Master Thomas Occ. ?–1184 (BM Harl. MS 3650, f. 21r–v; confirmed by William, earl Warwick, d. 1184: ibid.); 1184 × 1204 (*HMC, 10th Rep.*, VI, 100); 1189 × 91 (BM Harl. Cht., 83. A. 4); *c. 1200* (pal.: *HMC, 14th Rep.*, VIII, 194); (Magister Thomas) 1203 × 8[1] (BM Egerton MS 3033, f. 2 v).

WELLOW (Grimsby) (Lincs), St Augustine and St Olaf f. ?1132
List in *VCH Lincs*, II, 162.

ABBOTS

William Occ. 1148 × 66 (*Mon.*, V, 579–80).

Vacant 1 July 1175 (*Gesta Hen.* II, 1, 91–3).

Thomas El. 1173 × 89, prob. 1175 (*Reg. Lincoln*, I, no. 195).[2]

Richard I Occ. 1189 × 95[3] (BM Harl. MS 391, f. 102); *c.* 1198 (*Ctl. Newnham*, no. 920); *c.* 1200 (*Reg. Lincoln*, IV, no. 1437); 19 June 1202 (*Lincs F.*, PRS LXVII, no. 27).

Richard II 1217– Prev. pr. Snead (Chirbury), el. abb. 1217; royal assent 10 Aug. (*CPR, 1216–25*, p. 83). Occ. until 30 Sept. 1226 (*Lincs F.*, I, p. 182).

WESTACRE (Norfolk), St Mary and All Saints f. *temp.* Henry I (*c.* 1135)
List in *VCH Norfolk*, II, 404.[4]

Oliver First pr., prev. secular priest; occ. early 12th cent.[5] (*Mon.*, VI, 576).

William Occ. 7 Oct. 1198 (*Norfolk F.*, PRS LXV, no. 142); 1198 × 9 (Cheney, *Inn. III*, no. 178); 1200 (*CRR*, I, p. 352).

---

[1] If Walter, pr. 'Chaneturme' (?) = Kenilworth.

[2] An original writ of Henry II, 'Dei gratia rex...' (i.e. +1173). If the place is correctly identified as Brill (Bucks) the dates can be narrowed to 1174 × 88; Foster guessed 1179, following a conjecture of Eyton (*Itinerary*, p. 227) that Henry was at Brill in 1179. The evidence that the abbey was vacant in 1175 suggests a date in that year.

[3] Hamo dean of Lincoln (+1189, cf. Diceto, II, 69, on his predecessor); Roger of Rolleston not yet archd. Leicester (–1195, Howden, III, 285).

[4] Including Richard '*c.* 1193', but citing PRO E40/2907, cf. mid-13th cent. Blomefield, IX, 160, gives Hubert, occ. *c.* 1210; Godwin, late John, and William, 1228; but cites no evidence, and none has been found.

[5] Temp. Ralph de Tosny (the founder) occ. 1086–*c.* 1115, dead by *c.* 1125 (Douglas, *Social Structure*, pp. 254–5, cf. 179).

WIGMORE (Herefs), St James (Victorine) f. 1131 × 5 (at Shobdon); 1172[1] (at Wigmore)
Ann. to 1306 in Manchester, John Rylands Lib., Latin MS 215; Ch. in Wright, *Hist.
Ludlow, Mon.*, VI; now ed. J. C. Dickinson and P. T. Ricketts, *Trans. Woolhope Nat. Field
Club*, XXXIX, 413–45.

PRIOR, THEN ABBOT
Robert Occ. –1148 (Ch. *Wigmore* in Wright, *Hist. Ludlow*, pp. 109–10 = *Mon.*, VI, 345,
cf. 349).

ABBOTS
Andrew of S.-Victor Pr. of S.-Victor; withdrew from Shobdon 1148 × 55; restored 1161 × 3
(*GFL*, no. 138; B. Smalley, in *RTAM*, X (1938), 358–73, esp. pp. 365–6 – based on Ch.).
An eminent biblical scholar; see Smalley, art. cit., and *Study of the Bible in the Middle
Ages* (2nd edn.), pp. 112–85.
Roger Succeeded Andrew, who was called back on Roger's death (Ch. Wigmore; cf.
Smalley (1938), pp. 366–7).
Andrew of S.-Victor 1161 × 3–1175 Restored 1161 × 3 (see above); d. 19 Oct. 1175[2] (year
in Ann., f. 2v, cited Smalley (1938), pp. 369f.; for day, *Obit. Sens*, I, 593). Occ. 1168 × 75
(Lambeth MS 1212, f. 41r–v); 1169 × 75 (*Glam. Chts.*, I, p. 146).
Simon 1175–[2] Pr. Wigmore, el. 1175 and d. before bl. (Ann., f. 2v).
Ranulf 1175/6[2]–1194 Sacrist Wigmore; dates from Ann., ff. 2v, 3v.
Ralph 1194–1216 Dates from Ann., ff. 3v, 4v.

WOMBRIDGE (Salop), St Mary and St Leonard f. 1130 × 5
M.C. Lists in Eyton, *Salop*, VII, 371; *VCH Salop* (M. Chibnall, forthcoming).
Roger Occ. 1183 × 1208 (*Ctl. Wombridge*, in *Trans. Salop Arch. Soc.*, First Series, IX,
317–18); 23 June 1187 (Eyton, *Salop*, VII, 371; cf. p. 364); (R.) 1204, (R.) ?1198 × 1216
(Cheney, *Inn. III*, nos. 525, 1088); 1204 + [3] (Eyton, *Salop*, X, 336); 1207 (*CRR*, V, p. 80).
The next recorded pr., Henry, occ. *c.* 1220 (Eyton, *Salop*, II, 133n.).

WOODBRIDGE (Suffolk), St Mary f. *c.* 1193
List in *VCH Suffolk*, II, 112.
Hugh Occ. ?late 12th cent.[4] (Chelmsford, Essex Rec. Office MS D/DBy Q 19, f. 48v).

WOODKIRK (Yorks W.), St Mary f. –1135
Nicholas Occ. early 13th cent. (*EYC*, XII, no. 80).

WORKSOP (Radford) (Notts), St Mary and St Cuthbert f. +1119
List in *VCH Notts*, II, 129.
William of Huntingdon 1st pr., occ. *c.* 1154[5] (Thompson, *Welbeck Abbey*, p. 14);
(William) –1181 (*EYC*, III, no. 1269; cf. p. 6).
A. Occ. 1188 × 91 (*Newington Longeville Chts.*, no. 36).

---

[1] Ann., f. 2v; the dedication took place in 1179 (ibid.).
[2] Andrew's death, Simon's brief abbacy and Ranulf's accession are all dated 1175 in Ann. The
suspicion that the events of more than one year have been telescoped is increased by the reference to
Cardinal Hugh Pierleone's council of Westminster under the same year. As this fell in 14–19 March
1176 it is often dated '1175' (cf. *Handbook*, p. 550).
[3] If 'H.' was abb. Haughmond in 1204, this document must be later, since Ralph abb. Haughmond
occ. in it.
[4] With T. archdeacon, probably either Thomas of Norwich (1178 × 1199) or Teingrim (Steingrim)
of Norfolk, *c.* 1174–*c.* 1181 × 96.
[5] This is the f. cht. of Welbeck abb.

Stephen Occ. 1194 × 9 (*Mon.*, VI, 205); (S.) *c.* 1200 or + (BM Add. MS 36,872, f. 95r–v); perhaps the same as the S. subpr. who occ. ibid., f. 115v.

Henry Occ. +1200, –1218[1] (*EYC*, III, nos. 1295–6); –1223 (*HMC Var. Coll.*, VII, 249): these probably establish that he was earlier than Robert, i.e. had ceased to be pr. by *c.* 1214.

Robert (?de Pykeburn: R. White, *Dukery Records*, p. 417) Occ. (R.) *c.* 1213 × 14 (BM Cott. MS Nero D. iii, f. 57v); (R.) –1216 (Cheney, *Inn. III*, no. 1148); –1218[2] (*EYC*, III, no. 1288); 18 Nov. 1230 (*Yorks F.*, *1218–31*, pp. 130–1).

The next recorded pr., Walter, occ. 29 Sept. × 6 Oct. 1236 and 3 Feb. 1238 (*Derbys F.* (1886), pp. 38, 42).

WORMSLEY (Pyon) (Hereford), St Leonard and St Mary (Victorine) f. *c.* 1216 (+1200)
List in *Mon.*, VI, 398.

Edwin 'primus heremita',[3] perhaps first pr., occ. BM Harl. MS 3586, f. 91v.

Hugh Occ. prob. *temp.* Henry III (Oxford, Bodl. MS Rawl. B. 329, f. 129).

The next recorded pr., Ralph, occ. 15 Feb. 1222 (BM Harl. MS 3586, f. 84v).

WROXTON (Oxon), St Mary f. *c.* 1217
List in *VCH Oxon*, II, 102 (H. E. Salter).

?Roger called first pr. in *Placita de Quo Warranto*, p. 533.

Geoffrey Occ. first half 13th cent. (pal.: Oxford, New College Archives, Swalcliffe Chts. 127); possibly later than Richard.

The next pr. known, Richard, was el. 1231 × 2 (*Reg. Wells*, II, p. 40).

WYMONDLEY (Herts) St Mary f. –1218
List in *VCH Herts*, IV, 442–3.

William Occ. early 13th cent.[4] (BM Cott. MS Nero E. vi, f. 128r–v); also BM Cott. MS Tib. C. ix, ff. 95v–6.

The next recorded pr., Hugh, occ. 1233 × 4 (*VCH* citing Herts F., 18 Henry III, no. 168).

---

[1] Nos. 1294 and 1295 were evidently of a date, and in 1294 Thomas de Reineville is specified to be steward: Matthew de Eston was steward in 1200 (*EYC*, III, p. 15). No. 1296 was a grant by Gerard de Furnival the younger, who d. 1218 (ib., p. 6 – the elder prob. d. +1219, ib., p. 18) (ex inf. C.T.C.).

[2] Witnessed by Gerard de Furnival, probably the younger, who had an interest in the fee concerned by right of his wife (ex inf. C.T.C.).

[3] Of Pyon, at Pyon early 13th cent.

[4] With Mabel, abbess Elstow (1197 × 1232).

THE
PREMONSTRATENSIAN
CANONS

Of the houses founded before 1216, no name has been found for this period for Cammering-ham, Charlton, Hornby, Kalendar, Newbo, Snelshall and West Ravendale.

N. Backmund, O. Praem., *Monasticon Praemonstratense*, II (Straubing, 1952), has lists for all houses, based on Colvin.

ALNWICK (Northumberland), St Mary   f. 1147 × 8
   List in Colvin, p. 392; also by A. M. Oliver in *Proc. Soc. of Antiquaries of Newcastle*, 3rd
   series, IX (1919–20), 42ff.
Baldwin 1148–1152 First abb.; d. 1152 (dates as *Ch. Melrose*, p. 35, f. 19, confirmed by
   BM Cott. MS Tib. A. x, f. 164). D. 5 Nov. (BM Cott. MS Calig. A. viii, f. 24).
Patrick 1152–1167 Second abb.; d. 1167 (dates as *Ch. Melrose*, pp. 35, 37, ff. 19–20).
Richard 1167– Prev. pr. Alnwick (*Ch. Melrose*, p. 37, f. 20). Occ. 1167 × 84 (*EYC*, I,
   no. 269; cf. no. 268).
Gilbert –1208 Occ. (G.) j.d. +10 May 1197 (*Ctl. Guisborough*, II, p. 50); d. 1208 – 'quon-
   dam', and so perhaps res. earlier (*Ch. Melrose*, p. 53, f. 28).
Adam –1208 Dep. 9 Dec. 1208 (ib., pp. 53–4, f. 28r–v). The *Ch. Melrose* reads: 'Obiit
   Gilebertus quondam abbas de Alnewic cui successit in anno sequenti Galfridus abbas de
   Driburc (Dryburgh)...Adam abbas de Alnewic, depositus est V° Id. Decembris'. Occ.
   20 Nov. 1208 (*Northumberland and Durham F.*, no. 34).
Geoffrey 1209– Prev. abb. Dryburgh, el. 1209 (see above).
Benedict Occ. 1212 (Colvin, citing C. L. Hugo, *Sacrae Antiquitatis Monumenta* (Stivagii,
   1725), pp. 64ff., ep. lxx of Gervase, abb. Prémontré; on whom see C. R. Cheney in
   Bull. John Rylands Lib., XXXIII (1950–1), 25ff.).
The next known abb., Bartholomew, occ. 13 Jan. 1219 (*Northumberland and Durham F.*,
no. 54) and ?1222 (for reference, see Oliver, art. cit., p. 42).

BARLINGS (Oxeney) (Lincs), St Mary   f. 1154 × 5 (cf. Colvin, p. 73)
   Lists in Colvin, p. 394; *VCH Lincs*, II, 204. The order of the first two names is uncertain.
Adam Occ. *c.* 1160 (1154 × 66: Colvin, pp. 340–1).
David Occ. 1154 × 66 (*Reg. Lincoln*, I, no. 306); 1160 × 6[1] (BM Cott. MS Vesp. E. xx, f. 38);
   temp. Henry II (pal.: *DC*, no. 297).
Ralph Occ. 30 June × 6 July 1177 (BM Cott. MS Vesp. E. xx, f. 95); *temp.* Henry II
   (*early temp. Henry II, DC*, no. 282); n.d. (*CDF*, no. 1243).
Achardus, Akarius Occ. –1189 (Colvin, p. 352; cf. p. 329n.); 9 Jan. and Jan.–Mar. 1201
   (Foreville, pp. 12, 24); also *late 12th cent., late Henry II* (pal.: *DC*, nos. 302, 408). D.
   15 Apr. (Newhouse obit, *HMC Ancaster*, p. 482).

[1] Baldric, archd. Leicester and Ralph, subdean Lincoln (*GFL*, p. 164 and n.; *Reg. Lincoln*, IX, p. 115n.,
   cf. VII, p. 203n.).

Robert   Occ. 1203 × 6 (*Reg. Lincoln*, I, nos. 216–18); 1216 (BM Cott. MS Faust. B. i, f. 108r–v); 1221 × 2 (Peterborough, D. and C. MS 5, f. 82 = MS 1, f. 173). D. 6 July (BM Cott. MS Calig. A. viii, f. 16).

BAYHAM (Otham) (Sussex), St Mary and St Laurence   f. 1199 × 1208 (by amalgamation of Brockley, f. –1182, and Otham, f. 1180 × 7)
  Lists in Colvin, p. 395; *VCH Sussex*, II, 88 (L. F. Salzman).

Jordan   Occ ?1200 × 6 and 13 Jan. 1206/7 (Cheney, *Inn. III*, no. 720 and n.; BM Cott. MS Otho A. ii, f. 60); (J.) 13 Dec. 1207 (*HMC De L'Isle and Dudley*, I, 61); 1208 × 11 (abb. Bayham, Colvin, p. 116); 1215[1] (Lambeth MS 1212, f. 106).[2] Cf. Colvin, p. 116 n. 7, for the possibility that he res. to become archd. St Davids.

His successor, Reginald, occ. 1221 (*Sussex F.*, no. 175).

BEAUCHIEF (Derbys), St Mary and St Thomas of Canterbury   f. 1173 × 6
  Lists in Colvin, p. 396; *VCH Derbys*, II, 69. Obits in BM Cott. MS Calig. A. viii (translated in S. O. Addy, *Beauchief Abbey*, pp. 22ff.).

Gilbert   Occ. 1189 × 96 (*Reg. Lincoln*, III, no. 922); (G.)? –1208 (*Reg. Lichfield*, no. 74; see ed.'s note); 1209 × 19 (Colvin, pp. 347–8, cf. Bayham, n. 1). Cf. BM Cott. MS Calig. A. viii, f. 27 (his mother's obit).

He was succeeded either by William or by Stephen. William occ. *early temp. Henry III* (pal.: *Derbys Chts.*, no. 1862); Stephen *early temp. Henry III* (pal.: ibid., no. 1032) and ?1217 × 18 (*Ctl. Darley*, II, p. 372). Obits of Stephen's sister and father occ. in BM Cott. MS Calig. A. viii, ff. 18, 25 v.

BEELEIGH (Parndon, Maldon) (Essex), St Mary and St Nicholas   f. –1172 (at Great Parndon); 1180 (at Beeleigh, near Maldon)
  Lists in Colvin, p. 397; R. C. Fowler, in *Beeleigh Abbey*, pp. 5, 51; and *VCH Essex*, II, 176.

Robert   Occ. 22 Aug. 1172 (*Ctl. Colchester* I, p. 209).

Henry   Occ. 1183 × 9 (BM Wolley Cht., i. 43); Sept.–Oct. 1189 (Colvin, p. 350; cf. p. 136); (H.) 1208 (*CRR*, v, p. 302); (H.) 1209 (*Essex F.*, p. 101); 3 Feb. 1235 (ib., p. 108).

These references can hardly all be to the same man. The next abb., John, first occ. 1247 (Fowler, citing *Cambs F.*, p. 27).

BLANCHLAND (Northumberland), St Mary[3]   f. 1165
  List in Colvin, p. 398.

Alan   1165– App. 1165. Prev. abb. Croxton; first abb. Blanchland (Colvin, p. 346).

Adam (d. 7 Oct.) and **William** (d. 17 Nov.)   occ. in the Beauchief obituary, BM Cott. MS Calig. A. viii, ff. 22, 25, in 13th-cent. hands.

COCKERSAND (de Marisco) (Lancs), St Mary   f. –1190
  Lists in Colvin, pp. 398–9; *VCH Lancs*, II, 158–9. Abbs. 'de Marisco' down to 1205.

---

[1] Refers to the Feast of Purification after the relaxation of the Interdict: i.e. 2 Feb. 1215 (cf. *Councils and Synods*, II, i, 38 and n. 1).

[2] Also occ. 1209 × 19 in the documents printed by Colvin, pp. 345–8. On p. 345 is a mandate addressed by G(ervase) abb. of Prémontré (1209–20) to J. abb. Bayham, among others. In what follows J. abb. Otham acts with R. abb. of L'Île Dieu. If the order of the documents is correct, the letters on pp. 345–8 were written after 1209 but before 1219, when the successor of William abb. of Durford first occ., perhaps before 1218, since G(ilbert) abb. Beauchief (q.v.) wrote one of the documents in the case (pp. 347–8).

[3] Not to be confused with the Premonstratensian house of St Nicholas, Blanchelande (Manche): cf. *CDF*, nos. 859ff.

[COCKERSAND]

Founded as a hospital –1184; Hugh the Hermit, said to be first master, occ. *c.* 1180 × 4: *Ctl. Cockersand*, I, pp. ix–x, xxi; III, i, pp. 758–9.

PRIOR

Henry Occ. as pr. (H.) 6 June 1190 (*PUE*, I, no. 266); (H.) 1186 × 92 (*EYC*, VII, no. 32) and for 'Henry' cf. *Ctl. Cockersand*, III, ii, p. 1054.

ABBOTS

Th(omas) Occ. 1194 × 1205 (*Lancs PR*, p. 339 = *Ctl. Furness*, II, iii, p. 735).

Roger Occ. 1205 × 6 (*Lancaster Hist.*, II, 385–6); (R.) 1209 × 12[1] (Durham Cath. Muniments, 4. 2. 4 Ebor. 4) also early 13th cent. (*Ctl. Cockersand*, III, ii, pp. 1013–14; cf. II, ii, p. 739).

Hereward Occ. prob. 1216 (*Lancaster Hist.*, I, 48–9; cf. 51–2); 13 May 1235 (*Ctl. Cockersand*, I, ii, p. 169). D. 28 Dec. (BM Cott. MS Calig. A. viii, f. 27v).

The next abb., Richard, occ. 15 July 1240 (*Ctl. Cockersand*, II, i, pp. 520–1).

COVERHAM (Yorks N.), St Mary f. (at Swainby) *c.* 1187, (at Coverham) 1197 × 1202 (see below)

C.T.C. List in Colvin, p. 399; *VCH Yorks*, III, 245.

Philip Occ. (P.) *c.* 1197[2] (BM Stowe cht., 504 = *Ctl. Guisborough*, II, p. 41); 29 Nov. 1202 (*Yorks F., John*, p. 72).

Laurence Occ. *c.* 1209 and *c.* 1213 × 14 (BM Cott. MS Nero D. iii, f. 51r–v).

Conan Occ. 17 Apr. 1222, 12 June 1231 (*Yorks F., 1218–31*, pp. 44, 136).

The next abb., John, occ. 1252. An Abb. Robert occ. in 13th cent. addition under 8 Feb. in Beauchief obit., BM Cott. MS Calig. A. viii, f. 6; Abb. Gilbert also occ. at a date unknown: *EYC*, V, no. 132n.

CROXTON KERRIAL (Leics), St John the Evangelist f. 1162

Lists in Colvin, pp. 400–1; *VCH Leics*, II, 31 (R. A. McKinley).

Alan 1162–1165 Res. abb. Blanchland (Colvin, p. 346).

William Occ. 1165 × 74 (*DC*, no. 277); 1171 × 9 (*MB*, II, 218); 10 Jan. 1177 (or 1176)[3] (*DC*, no. 285); d. 20 May (BM Cott. MS Calig. A. viii, f. 13).

Adam Occ. 1202 (*Lincs Assize Roll*, p. 52); 15 Sept. 1221 (BM Add. MS 4934, f. 160; Colvin, pp. 379, 400 and n. citing Belvoir Castle Add. MS 71, f. 47). D. 12 Nov. (BM Cott. MS Calig. A. viii, f. 24v).

The next abb. known, Elias, occ. 20 Dec. 1228 (Nichols, *Leics*, II, i, App., p. 93).

DALE (de Parco Stanley; de Parco iuxta Dereleyam) (Derbys), St Mary f. (as hermitage) *temp.* Stephen; (as Augustinian pr.) 1153 × 8; (as Premonstratensian pr.) ?*c.* 1185–*c.* 1192 and again *c.* 1196; (as abb.) *c.* 1200 (*Ctl. Dale*, pp. 2ff.; cf. Colvin, pp. 170–6)

Lists in *Ctl. Dale*, p. 45; Colvin, p. 402, based on Dale Ch., ed. W. H. St John Hope, *Derbys Arch. Journ.*, V (1883), 1ff.,[4] and medieval list ibid., pp. 81ff.; *VCH Derbys*, II, 75.

PRIORS

Humphrey Occ. 1153 × 8 (Ch., pp. 6, 9f. (30–1)).

Henry D. ?*c.* 1180 (Ch., p. 11 (32)).

---

[1] Henry de Redeman (deputy) sheriff (of Yorks).

[2] J.d. + 30 July 1195 (5 Celestine III); but the decision must be + March 1197 as Robert *de Longchamp* is abb. St Mary's York. [3] Dated 1176.

[4] Now re-edited by A. Saltman, *Derbys Arch. Journ.* LXXXVII (1967), 18–38; page numbers in brackets refer to this edn.

ABBOTS

Walter de Todeni(?) or Senteney[1] c. 1200–1231 Can. of Easby (q.v.) and Newhouse
(31¼ years, list, p. 82; cf. Ch., p. 15 (37; cf. p. 38); Colvin, pp. 175–6). Occ. 4 May 1229
(*Ctl. Dale*, no. 539). His successor was el. abb. Prémontré in 1233 after 2⅓ years as abb.
(*Ann. Dunstable*, p. 135; list, p. 82. If the ed.'s note is correct his promotion took place
10 Oct. 1233).

DEREHAM, *see* WEST DEREHAM

DURFORD (Sussex), St Mary and St John the Baptist f. –1161
Lists in Colvin, pp. 402–3; *VCH Sussex*, II, 91 (L. F. Salzman).
Robert –1183 Occ. –1176 (R.) 1180 × 3 (*Ctl. Boxgrove*, nos. 40, 24); 1179 × 80, 1174 × 80
(*Acta Chichester*, nos. 59–60, 66). Res. to be abb. Leiston (q.v.) 1183.
William[2] c. 1183– El. c. 1183 (cf. Colvin, p. 346); occ. 1199 (Cheney, *Inn. III*, no. 101);
1209 × 19 (Colvin, pp. 346, 348; cf. Bayham, p. 193 n. 2).
Jordan Occ. 1219 (*Sarum Chts.*, pp. 88ff.); 1209 (prob. 1217) × 1228[3] (*Ctl. Sele*, no. 59).

EASBY (St Agatha; Richmond) (Yorks N.), St Agatha f. 1151
C.T.C. Lists in Colvin, p. 404; *EYC*, IV, p. xxvii (Sir Charles Clay); *VCH Yorks*, III, 248–9.
Ch. Dale, *Derbys Arch. Journ.*, V (1883), 15 = LXXXVII (1967), 37–8, asserts that Walter de
Senteney, first abb. of Dale, had previously established the order (*ordinem fundaverat*) at
Easby; cf. Colvin, p. 58. If this means that Walter (who died 1231) was first abb. of Easby,
it is impossible.
Martin Occ. 1157 × 9 (*EYC*, V, no. 236).
Ralph Occ. 15 Oct. 1162 (*EYC*, V, no. 238); 1173 (*Ctl. Rievaulx*, no. 139); 5 June 1191
(*EYC*, V, no. 238n.); 1198 + (ib., IV, no. 115n.).
A. Occ. 1201 × 4 (*EYC*, V, no. 313).
Geoffrey Occ. June × July 1204 (*Yorks F., John*, p. 91); 1209 (*EYC*, V, no. 313n.); (G.)
c. 1213 × 14 (BM Cott. MS Nero D. iii, f. 58).
The next abb., Elias, occ. 12 May 1224 (*Yorks F., 1218–31*, p. 56).

EGGLESTONE (Yorks N.), St John the Baptist f. –1198
C.T.C. List in Colvin, p. 405; by J. F. Hodgson, *YAJ*, XVIII (1905), 175–8; *VCH Yorks*,
III, 251. Baildon, I, 51, includes Ralph de Moleton; an error based on *YAJ*, XI (1891), 185.
William Occ. late 12th cent. and 1197 + (Hodgson, p. 162, citing Curia Regis Roll for
1248).[4]
Nicholas Occ. 1197 × c. 1209 (ibid., pp. 161–2, citing the same).[4]
Stephen Occ. c. 1209 (BM Cott. MS Nero D. iii, f. 52v; Geoffrey, abb. of Easby occ. in
a similar agreement in 1209, BM Egerton MS 2827, f. 289v).
H. Occ. c. 1214 (BM Cott. MS Nero D. iii, f. 52v).
The next abb. in Hodgson's list is Robert, 1216, without ref.: William occ. 1226 (*Yorks F.,
1218–31*, p. 80).

---

[1] See Saltman, art. cit., p. 38: 'Tetenaye' or 'Totenaye' in the better MSS.
[2] Occ. in *Ctl. Chichester*, p. 85, no. 312, dated '1138–' (i.e. 1138 +); but this is a cht. of Henry Hose,
son of Henry Hose, donor of no. 311, i.e. presumably Henry Hose III, late 12th–early 13th cent.;
so 312 can easily be + 1183 (for the Hose family cf. *EYC*, XII, index, s.v. Hose, esp. pp. xii, 135ff.).
[3] Reginald de Braose (restored 1217; d. 1228: Lloyd, II, 652, 666 and n.).
[4] The jurors in 1248 stated that a particular grant had been made to Abb. William, not to his successor,
Abb. Nicholas; the grant (which does not name the abb.) survives, and can be dated 1197 × 1208
(*Reg. palatinum Dunelmense*, ed. T. D. Hardy, RS, II, 1158–9; the dates are those of the donor,
Philip, bp. of Durham).

HAGNABY (Lincs), St Thomas of Canterbury f. (as priory) 1175 × 6; (as abbey) 1250 (BM Cott. MS Vesp. B. xi, f. 24v)

Lists in Colvin, p. 406; *VCH Lincs*, II, 206.

PRIORS

Thomas Occ. *c. 1200* (pal.: *DC*, no. 68).
William of Fultorp, can. of Hagnaby, was made custos of the 'abbey' 1228 (*Reg. Wells*, III, p. 166); and Peter occ. as abb. 1228 × 32 (BM Cott. Cht. xxvii. 65).

LANGDON, or **WEST LANGDON** (Kent), St Mary and St Thomas of Canterbury f. 1189

Lists in Colvin, pp. 407–8; *VCH Kent*, II, 171 (R. C. Fowler).
(In addition to the following the Beauchief obituary, BM Cott. MS Calig. A. viii, f. 22, of the 13th cent. gives Bartholomew, prob. an early abb., and W. Somner, *Antiq. of Canterbury*, I, App. XLI, p. 51, gives John and Robert as abbs. who made profession to Archbp. Hubert after Richard, prob. in error for abbs. who occ. 1248, 1236).

William Bl. by Archbp. Hubert Walter (1193 × 1205: Gervase, II, 410).
Richard Bl. by Archbp. Hubert Walter (ibid.); occ. 20 Jan. 1206 (*Kent F.*, p. 38).

The next abb., Peter, occ. 30 Sept. 1227 (*Kent F.*, p. 89).

LANGLEY (Norfolk), St Mary f. 1195

Lists in Colvin, p. 408; *VCH Norfolk*, II, 421.

Gilbert Occ. 20 Jan. 1202, 6 July 1202 (*Norfolk F.*, PRS LXV, nos. 270, 324); 18 Jan. 1209 (ib., LXX, no. 133).

The next known abb., Hugh, occ. (H.) 21 July 1220 (Chelmsford, Essex Rec. Office D/Dby Q 19, f. 46v); 1223 × 4 (*Norfolk F.* (Rye), p. 39), and up to 1249 – also ref. to as third abb. (BM Add. MS 5948, ff. 3–5).

LAVENDON (Bucks), St John the Baptist f. 1155 × 8

List in Colvin, p. 409; *VCH Bucks*, I, 386.

David First abb. (so obit, 3 Sept., in Beauchief obituary, BM Cott. MS Calig. A. viii, f. 20).
John Occ. 1203 × 4 (Colvin, p. 339).
?W. Occ. ? Oct. 1207 (Cheney, *BHRS*, XXXII (1952), 23).
Ralph Occ. (R.) 1209 × 20 (Colvin, p. 339); (Ralph) 13 May 1218 (*Beds F.*, no. 185).
Augustine occ. 1227 (*Beds Eyre*, no. 85); 1233 × 53 in Ch. Dale, *Derbys Arch. Journ.*, V (1883), 4; cf. p. 100. Abb. William d. 17 Oct., 13th-cent. hand in Beauchief obit (ut sup.), f. 23.

LEISTON (Suffolk), St Mary f. 1183

Lists in Colvin, p. 410; *VCH Suffolk*, II, 119.

Robert 1183–1198+ Prev. abb. Durford (Colvin, pp. 345–8); occ. 1187 × 92[1] (BM Cott. MS Vesp. E. xxiii, f. 9(5) = *Mon.*, VI, 937); 1191 × 8 (*PUE*, I, no. 343); 1198 (*CChR*, I, 426). D. 29 Aug. (BM Cott. MS Calig. A. viii, f. 19v).
Philip Occ. 1198 × 1206, 1199 × 1206 (BM Harl. Chts. 43. I. 18; 44. I. 24); 1206 × 10[2] (BM Cott. MS Vesp. E. xiv, f. 38); 1209 × 19 (Colvin, p. 347; cf. Bayham, n. 2); 7 Nov. 1218 (Chelmsford, Essex Rec. Office, MS D/DBy Q 19, ff. 43–4). Formerly pr.; Robert's successor (Colvin, p. 347). D. 8 Feb. (BM Cott. MS Calig. A. viii, f. 6).

The next abb., Hugh, occ. 1228 × 9 (*Suffolk F.* (Rye), p. 29); but the Beauchief obituary (BM Cott. MS Calig. A. viii, f. 5v) records a Gilbert, 13th cent., d. 29 Jan.

---

[1] See St Denys.
[2] John de Cornheard, sheriff of Norfolk and Suffolk.

NEWHOUSE or **NEWSHAM** (Lincs), St Mary and St Martial f. 1143
Lists in Colvin, p. 412; *VCH Lincs*, II, 201.[1]

Gerlo 1143– First abb. (Ctl. Newhouse, f. 28v, no. 266). Occ. 1143 × 61, ?*c*. 1150 (Stenton, *Feudalism*, pp. 260–2; cf. p. 46n.); 1155 × 66 (*DC*, no. 249);[2] 1156 × 9 (Delisle-Berger, I, no. 204); *c*. 1165 (Colvin, p. 346). D. 26 May (Beauchief obit., BM Cott. MS Calig. A. viii, f. 13v).

David Occ. 18 July 1177; 17 Mar. 1182 × 3 (*PUE*, I, nos. 150, 210); n.d. (–1188: Ctl. Newhouse, f. 65v, no. 689). D. 20 June (BM Cott. MS Calig. A. viii, f. 15).

Gervase Occ. late 12th cent. (pal.: BM Harl. Cht. 50. I. 4).

Robert Occ. 22 Feb. 1193 (*Ctl. Dryburgh*, p. 72); 1194 × 9 (*Mon.*, VI, 205); 1186 × 1200 (BM Harl. Cht. 54. B. 9).

Adam *c*. 1199–*c*. 1200 Prev. abb. Torre; off by 1199 (see Torre; *CAP*, III, p. 141). D. 7 March (BM Cott. MS Calig. A. viii, f. 8). Occ. (A.) 1186 × 1200 (Ctl. Newhouse, f. 6v, no. 54).

Lambert Occ. *c*. 1200 × 1 (Ch. Dale (see Dale), p. 15 (37–8)); ?5 Feb. 1201 (Cheney, *Inn. III*, no. 286); 6 July 1202 (*Lincs F.*, PRS LXVII, no. 77). D. 18 Apr. (BM Cott. MS Calig. A. viii, f. 11).

Geoffrey Occ., called Geoffrey II, 1211[3] (Ctl. Newhouse, f. 30, no. 287; (G.) April 1212 (Ctl. Newhouse, f. 12, no. 107 and see Alnwick); 16 Feb. 1219 (*Lincs F.*, I, p. 123); 13 June 1226 (*Ctl. Dryburgh*, pp. 168–9). The next abb., Osbert, occ. *c*. 28 Sept. 1226 (*Lincs F.*, I, pp. 183–4). And so Geoffrey seems to have d. June × Sept. 1226, and not to be the Pr. Geoffrey who d. 3 May (BM Cott. MS Calig. A. viii, f. 12).

ST RADEGUND'S (Bradsole) (Kent) f. 1193
Lists in Colvin, p. 413; *VCH Kent*, II, 174.

Hugh Bl. by Archbp. Hubert Walter (1193 × 1205: Gervase, II, 410); occ. (H.) 1201 × 3 (Colvin, p. 339); d. before 1219 (ibid., pp. 339–40).
The next abb., Simon, occ. 15 Sept. 1221 (BM Add. MS 4934, f. 160); Richard occ. 20 Jan. 1222 (*Kent F.*, p. 73).

SHAP (Westmorland), St Mary Magdalene f. (Preston Patrick) –1192(?); (Shap) –1201
List in Colvin, p. 414.

Walter Occ. 17 July 1202 (*Ctl. Lanercost*, xiii, 26, p. 499 and n.; cf. Cheney, *Inn. III*, no. 291); 22 Feb. 1209 (?1210: BM Cott. MS Nero D. iii, f. 52v).
The next abb. recorded, Richard, occ. 1231 (*CRR*, XIV, no. 1088).

SULBY (Welford) (Northants), St Mary f. 1155
Lists in Colvin, pp. 414–15; *VCH Northants*, II, 142.

Richard Occ. *c*. 1155 (1155 × 66)[4] (*DC*, no. 253); 1155 × 66 (BM Cott. MS Calig. A. xii, ff. 11v–12); 1165 × 74 (*DC*, no. 277). Prob. d. 1170 × 5: William of Canterbury, *MB*, I, 148, refers to him as 'felicis memorie'; William's *Miracula*, bks. i–v, were written 1172 × 5.[5]

Adam Occ. *c*. 1197 × 1204 (BM Add. Cht. 22,380 = Royal MS 11. B. ix, f. 33r–v);[6] 1206 × 7 (*Ctl. Cirencester*, II, no. 699 = Cheney, *Inn. III*, no. 1160).

---

[1] Amblardus, in *VCH* list, was abb. St Martial, Limoges (Colvin, pp. 51, 337). Ctl. Newhouse (Earl of Yarborough) is deposited in Lincs Archives Office and we are indebted to Dr David Smith for our references to it. [2] Witnesses very similar to no. 253 – see Sulby.

[3] We have found no trace of Geoffrey I, unless he be the pr. Geoffrey who d. 3 May.

[4] An early grant to the first abb.

[5] E. Walberg, *La tradition hagiographique de S. Thomas Becket* (Paris, 1929), p. 73.

[6] Probably contemporary with cht. in Royal MS ff. 31–3, witnessed by Richard of Kent archd. Northampton (see Northampton, St Andrew), and Walkelin abb. St James, Northampton.

[SULBY]

John Occ. 1206 × 7 (Northants F., PRO transcripts); early–mid 13th cent. (pal.: BM Add. Chts. 21,205; 21,278; 22,563).

The next recorded abb., Walter, occ. 1227 (*CPR, 1225–32*, p. 152).

TALLEY (Carmarthen), St Mary, St John the Baptist and (?) St Augustine[1] f. 1184 × 9

Iorwerth (Gervase) –1215 Res. 1215, bp. of St Davids: royal assent to el. 18 June 1215 (*Rot. Lit. Pat.*, p. 143; cf. *Gir. Camb.*, III, 361ff., IV, 150f.), consec. 21 June 1215; d. 1229.

The next recorded abb., Gruffinus, occ. 1239: *Mon.*, IV, 164.

TORRE (Devon), Holy Trinity or St Saviour f. 1196

List in Colvin, p. 416.

Adam 1196–*c.* 1199 First abb., prev. can. Welbeck; entered 25 Mar. 1196; abb. 3½ years, res. to be abb. Newhouse (*CAP*, III, 141; cf. Colvin, p. 153 and n. 5).

Richard Occ. *c.* 1199 (Dublin, Trinity Coll. MS E. 5. 15, f. 56v).[2]

John Occ. 28 Nov. 1200 (*Rot. Chart.*, p. 99); d. 22 June (Beauchief obit., BM Cott. MS Calig. A. viii, f. 15).

The next recorded abb., Robert, occ. 2 June 1223 (*Lincs F.*, I, p. 164).

TUPHOLME (Lincs), St Mary f. 1155 × 66

Lists in Colvin, pp. 417–18; *VCH Lincs*, II, 207.

Ralph Occ. *c. 1175* (pal.: *DC*. no. 10; cf. no. 196); +1177 (BM Cott. MS Vesp. E. xx, f. 95v); 8 May 1182 (*Ctl. Bridlington*, pp. 355–6, 434–5); d. 28 Aug. (BM Cott. MS Calig. A. viii, f. 19v).

Geoffrey[3] Occ. 19 June 1202 (*Lincs F.*, PRS LXVII, no. 28); 1203 × 6 (*Reg. Lincoln*, I, no. 216); 25 Nov. 1218 (*Lincs F.*, I, p. 124); 1230 (*CR, 1227–31*, p. 404).

WELBECK (Notts), St James f. 1153 × 4

Lists in Colvin, p. 418; A. Hamilton Thompson, *Premonstratensian Abb. of Welbeck*, pp. 58ff., 113; *VCH Notts*, II, 138.

Berengar *c.* 1153– First abb. (Colvin, pp. 65ff.); *c. 1155* (1155 × 67: *DC*, no. 248; cf. Sulby); 1154 × 69 (*Acta Chichester*, no. 34); 1159 × 81 (*PUE*, I, no. 186). D. 6 Feb. (Beauchief obit., BM Cott. MS Calig. A. viii, f. 6).

Adam Occ. *c.* 1180 (–1182: Colvin, pp. 342–3); 1183 (ib., pp. 345ff.); 1181 × 5 (*PUE*, I, no. 226); (A.) 6 July 1193 (*DC*, no. 15); prob. 1194+ (Hamilton Thompson, p. 66, citing *Yorks D.*, VII, p. 165, no. 478).

Richard of Southwell El. prob. 1197 (9 Richard I, Ch. Hagnaby, BM Cott. MS Vesp. B. xi, f. 11). For his name see *Ch. Dale*, p. 12. Occ. *c.* 1197 or +[4] (*Mon.*, VI, 924–5); –1197 (BM Harl. MS 391, f. 98r–v); 8 July 1215 (*Rot. Lit. Pat.*, p. 148b); 13 × 20 Jan. 1222 (*Derbys F.* (1885), p. 214); 1217 × 24 (*Ctl. Healaugh Park*, pp. 7–8). D. 24 Oct. (Beauchief obit., BM Cott. MS Calig. A. viii, f. 23).

The next recorded abb., William, occ. *c.* 28 Jan. 1223, 18 Nov. 1223 (BM Harl. MS 3640, ff. 119, 117v); 30 Sept. 1226 (*Derbys F.* (1886), p. 24) and d. 17 Oct. (Calig. A. viii, f. 23).

---

[1] See *Mon.*, IV, 162–3.

[2] Occ. in a document stated to be *temp.* Richard I, and in any case prob. –1202, since William abb. Rufford witnesses.

[3] *VCH* and Colvin list Ivo in the late 12th cent., citing BM Lansd. MS 207C, f. 252; but we have failed to find the source of this reference in the MS.

[4] The f. cht. of Torre abb., or rather the latest of three versions of this: see Colvin, pp. 154–5. The ecclesiastical witnesses from Notts may represent an occasion very shortly after 1196.

WEST DEREHAM (Norfolk), St Mary f. 1188

Lists in Colvin, p. 420; *VCH Norfolk*, II, 418.[1]

Ralph Occ. 1196 × 7 (*PR 9 Richard I*, p. 231).

Henry Occ. 6 July 1202; *c.* 9 May 1204 (BM Add. MS 46,353, ff. 12v, 184v); *c.* 19 Apr. 1209 (*Norfolk F.*, PRS LXX, no. 497).

Ralph Can. of Welbeck and pr. and novice master Durford, occ. 1209 × 19 (Colvin, pp. 345ff.; cf. Bayham); *c.* 24 June 1218 (BM Add. MS 46,353, f. 12v); *c.* 27 Apr. 1225 (*Lincs F.*, I, p. 174). D. 17 May (Beauchief obit, BM Cott. MS Calig. A. viii, f. 13).

The next recorded abb., Angerus, occ. 7 Mar. 1236 (PRO E40/14021).

[1] Includes 'Augustine', first abb., apparently a mistake for 'Angerus', who occ. 1236.

THE GILBERTINE CANONS
AND NUNS

For the houses founded before 1216, no name has been found for this period for Bridge End, Dunstall (or Tunstall), Marlborough, Marmont or Mattersey (for Dunstall, see Haverholme, p. 202 n. 5).

For the Masters of the Order, see under Sempringham.

It is noticeable that in the Gilbertine lists, so far as they can be reconstructed, a few names recur in two or three or more lists; and that these include three exceptionally rare names, Cyprian, Gamel and Torphinus. The repetition of these names strongly suggests that it was a common practice to move priors from one house to another. Though this may seem clear in general, it cannot, in the nature of the case, be proved by identity of name alone in any individual instance. Thus, rather than encumber the lists with cross-references of doubtful value, it seems best to provide an index of the names which occur in the lists: a full index, for convenience, of names appearing more than once, but obviously more significance is likely to attach to Cyprian, Torphinus, Gamel and Vivian and possibly to Adam, Eudo, Martin and Simon, than to the very common names Gilbert, Henry, John and William. In each case only one or two occ. dates have been given: for fuller details, see lists.

Adam: 1164 (Lincoln); 1208 (Sempringham); 1214, 1219 (Malton).

Alan: 1164 (Haverholme); 1226 (Newstead).

Baldwin: 1219, 1220 (York).

Bartholomew: 1201 × 10, 1208 (York).

Cf. B.: 1197 × 9, –c. 1200 (Catley).

Cyprian: 1197 × 9, 1177 × 1212 (Sixhills); 1201, 1204 × 7 (Malton).

Eudo: ?1176 × 1203 (Sixhills); 1195, –1201 (Sempringham).

Gamel: 1202 (Alvingham); 1209 (Bullington).

Geoffrey: 1174 (Alvingham).

Gilbert: (1) St Gilbert, the founder, Master of Sempringham 1131–c. 1188; (2) Other references: 1169 (Malton), 1202 (Lincoln); 1205–25 (Master of Sempringham).

Cf. G.: 1186 × 94, 1197 × 9 (Lincoln).

Henry: 1177, 1199 (Bullington); 1201, 1208 (Haverholme).

Hugh: c. 1150 × 60, 1150 × 64 (Sempringham); 1164, 1174 (Sixhills); –1189 (Lincoln); 1147 × 84, 1188 × 1201 (Bullington).

Cf. H.: late 12th cent. (Catley).

John: late 12th cent. (Newstead); 1204 × 7 (Ellerton); 1206 (Sixhills); (cf. John, Master of Sempringham, 1204–5, d. 11 May 1205); 1214 (York); 1219, 1231 (Ellerton); 1229 (Catley). Apparently at least two in each period.

Martin: c. 1200, –1203 (York); 1201 (Haverholme); 1208 (Alvingham).

Ralph: 1164 (Watton); 1194 (Malton).

Richard: 1164 (Bullington); 1219 (Sempringham); 1219, 1225 (Watton).

Robert: 1164 (Malton); 1199 (Haverholme); 1200, 1202 (Watton); 1210 (York); 1209 × 10, 1212 × 13 (N. Ormsby); 1225 (el. Master of Sempringham).

Roger: 1174, 1178 (Malton); –1188 (el. Master of Sempringham, *c.* 1188–1204); 1178 (Alvingham); evidently two different men.

Cf. R.: 1205 × 23 (Haverholme); 1206 × 9 (Sixhills).

Simon: 1220 (Sixhills); 1223 (Chicksands); 1226 (Haverholme).

Thomas: 1164, 1174, 1182 × 1200 (N. Ormsby); 1199, 1201, 1202, 1204 (Sempringham); 1191 × 1212 (York); 1218 (Alvingham).

Torphinus: 1154 × 8 (Chicksands); 1164 (Sempringham).

Vivian: 1213 (Haverholme); ?(V.) *c.* 1220 (York); 1222 (N. Ormsby); 1225 (Lincoln).

William *c.* 1150 × 60, 1157 × 83 (Watton); *c.* 1200 (Bullington); 1213 (Alvingham); 1216, 1218 (Lincoln); 1219 (Newstead); 1218/19 (Bullington); 1224, 1225, 1234 (Malton); 1224, 1225, 1226 (York); 1226, 1238 (Watton). Clearly at least two in each period.

Cf. W.: ?*c.* 1200 (Bullington).

ALVINGHAM (Lincs), St Mary and St Æthelwold f. 1148 × 54
List in *VCH Lincs*, II, 194 (R. Graham).

Geoffrey Occ. 1174 (Bodl. Laud Misc. MS 642, f. 130v).

Roger Occ. 25 June 1178 (*PUE*, III, no. 249).

Reginald Prob. occ. 23 Feb. 1195 (Laud MS 642, f. 146v).[1]

Gamel Occ. 13 July 1202 (*Lincs F.*, PRS LXVII, no. 127); (G.) 1203 × 5 (*HMC Var. Coll.*, I, 236ff.).

Martin Occ. 4 May 1208 (*Lincs F.*, PRS LXVII, no. 237).

William of Frisby Occ. 1213 (Bodl. Laud Misc. 642, ff. 130v–131); early 13th cent. (pal.: *Gilbertine Chts.*, p. 113).

Thomas Occ. 13 Oct. 1218 (*Lincs F.*, I, p. 116).

The next recorded pr., Roger, occ. 1229 (*CRR*, XIII, no. 2062; Bodl. Laud Misc. MS 642, f. 146v).

BULLINGTON (Lindley)[2] (Lincs), St Mary f. 1148 × 54
List in *VCH Lincs*, II, 192 (R. Graham).

Richard Occ. 1164 (*Ctl. Rievaulx*, no. 246).

Henry Occ. 30 June × 6 July 1177 (BM Cott. MS Vesp. E. xx, f. 95); *temp. Henry II* (pal.: *DC*, no. 60); 17 Oct. 1199 (BM Add. MS 6118, ff. 388v–9).

Hugh Occ. 1147 × 84 (*Gilbertine Chts.*, p. 56); 1188 × 1201[3] (BM Add. MS 6118, f. 438r–v). These dates are clearly incompatible with an orderly succession of Hugh to Henry, but the solution of the difficulty must be left in doubt, since it is possible that one of the datable references to Henry contains a scribal error for Hugh, or *vice versa*; or that there were two Henrys or two Hughs.

W. Occ. ?*temp. Richard I* (pal.: *DC*, no. 8); *c.* 1200 (pal.: *DC*, nos. 18, 55).

Gamel Occ. 4 July 1209 (*Lincs F.*, PRS LXVII, no. 304).

The next recorded pr., William, occ. 15 Nov. 1218, 9 Feb. 1219 (*Lincs F.*, I, pp. 144, 125). No prioress is recorded before the 16th cent.

CATLEY (Lincs), St Mary f. 1148 × 54
List in *VCH Lincs*, II, 197 (from 1245).

H. Occ. ?late 12th cent. (Ctl. Newhouse, Lincs Archives Office transcripts, no. 711).

B. Occ. 1197 × 9[4] (*Reg. Lincoln*, II, no. 637); n.d. – *c.* 1200 (*Gilbertine Chts.*, p. 75).

---

[1] Not named, but prob. Reginald since he is named in the next document.

[2] Cf. *Lincs Domesday* (Lincoln Rec. Soc., XIX (1924), p. lx).

[3] Alexander archd. of Stow (rather than Bedford, since the archd. is presiding over a case on Spridlington, Lincs: cf. *GFL*, p. 246n.; *CRR*, I, p. 442).

[4] William precentor Lincoln (cf. Diceto, II, 150); Laurence archd. Bedford (succeeded by 1199, *Ctl. Wardon*, no. 143).

[CATLEY]

The next recorded pr., John, occ. 10 May 1229 (*Lincs F.*, I, p. 221). No prioress is recorded before Margaret Gastwek in 1538.

CHICKSANDS (Beds), St Mary f. *c.* 1150

List in *VCH Beds*, I, 393.

PRIORS

Torphinus (Thorpinus) Occ. 1154×8^1 (*EYC*, I, no. 158). Cf. Sempringham.

Walter Occ. (G.) 1186 (Gorham, *St Neots*, II, p. lxxiv); –1189 (E. M. Poynton in *Genealogist*, New Series, XV, 222–3); 1188×9 (Cheney, in *BRHS*, XXXII (1952), 14–17); 9 Jan. 1201 (Foreville, *S. Gilbert*, p. 12); 1203 (*CRR*, III, p. 25); 18 Nov. 1211 (*Beds F.*, no. 173).

Simon Occ. 23 Oct. 1223 (*Beds F.*, no. 267).

PRIORESS

Christina Occ. 1201 (Foreville, *S. Gilbert*, p. 52).

ELLERTON (on Spalding Moor, Yorks E.), St Mary and St Laurence f. 1199×1207 (*EYC*, II, no. 1133)[2]

C.T.C. List in *VCH Yorks*, III, 252.

John I Occ. prob. 1204×7 (*EYC*, II, no. 1134; cf. no. 1133).[2]

Ranulf Occ. *c.* 1210×19^3 (*EYC*, II, no. 1263).

John II Occ. 9 Feb. 1219, 30 June 1231 (*Yorks F.*, *1218–31*, pp. 21, 149).

The next recorded pr., Ivo, occ. July 1240 (*Yorks F.*, *1232–46*, pp. 80–1).

HAVERHOLME ('de Insula')[4] (Lincs), St Mary f. 1137 (Cistercian); 1139 (Gilbertine)

List in *VCH Lincs*, II, 188 (R. Graham).

PRIORS

Alan[5] Occ. 1164 (*Ctl. Rievaulx*, no. 246).

Robert Occ. 23 Jan. 1199 (*FF*, PRS XXIV, no. 242).

Martin Occ. 1201 (Notts F., PRO transcripts, vol. v).

Henry Occ. 26 Sept. 1201 (Foreville, *S. Gilbert*, p. 43); 27 Oct. 1208 (*Lincs F.*, PRS LXVII, no. 258).

Vivian Occ. 7 Dec. 1213 (ib., no. 330).

R. Occ. 1205×23 (*Reg. Lincoln*, III, no. 1093).

The next recorded pr., Simon, occ. 15 Sept. 1226 (*Lincs F.*, I, p. 214).

PRIORESSES

Alice Occ. 26 Sept. 1201 (Foreville, *S. Gilbert*, p. 49).

---

[1] Archbp. Roger of York; Osbert archd. (of Richmond: cf. *York Fasti*, I, p. 46: in fact Osbert was probably removed from his archdeaconry *c.* 1157; cf. *JS Epp.*, I, pp. 261–2).

[2] Witnessed by Archbp. Geoffrey, who was last in England in 1207; this is the f. cht. and confirms no. 1134, issued by pr. John. It seems clear, therefore, that John was the first pr.

[3] The witnesses point to a date in 1210s or 1220s; esp. Oliver de Gunby, who d. 1224×8 (*EYC*, XII, p. 45). This seems to establish that Ranulf came between John I (see n. 2 above) and John II.

[4] 'Insulam Hafreholm prius vocatam que nunc Insula sancte Marie appellatur': f. cht. of 1139, BM Lansd. MS 207A, ff. 93ff.; cf. BM Add. MS 6118, f. 422v.

[5] Alan 'de insula'. Several houses were called 'de insula', and Alan has sometimes been identified as pr. Dunstall or Newstead-on-Ancholm. There is, however, no other evidence that these small houses existed as early as 1164 (the same point rules out Mattersey, also called 'de insula', but f. *c.* 1185). Alan appears immediately after the pr. of Sempringham in a document witnessed by virtually all the then priors of the Order; if he was not pr. Haverholme this early and important house seems to be omitted. We therefore reckon Haverholme much the most likely identification.

LINCOLN, St Catherine   f. 1148+
   List in *VCH Lincs*, II, 190–1 (R. Graham).
Adam   Occ. 1164 (*Ctl. Rievaulx*, no. 246).
Hugh   Occ. –1189, possibly well before 1189 (E. M. Poynton in *Genealogist*, New Series, XV, 222–3).
Gilbert   Occ. (G.) 1186×94[1] (*Reg. Lincoln*, III, no. 1096); (G.) 1197×9 (ib., II, no. 637: cf. Catley); 13 July 1202 (*Lincs F.*, PRS LXVII, no. 134).
William   Occ. *?temp. John* (?pal.: *HMC Rutland*, IV, p. 70 (J. H. Round)); 1216 (BM Add. Cht. 20,512); 25 Nov. 1218 (*Lincs F.*, I, p. 133).
The next recorded pr., Vivian, occ. 25 Nov. 1225 (*Lincs F.*, I, p. 180). Cf. Haverholme, North Ormsby, York.

MALTON (Yorks, N.), St Mary   f. 1150
   C.T.C. List in *VCH Yorks*, III, 253–4.
Robert   Occ. 1164 (*Ctl. Rievaulx*, no. 246).
Gilbert   Occ. 30 July 1169 (*PUE*, I, no. 112).
Roger   Occ. 1174 (Bodl. MS Laud Misc. 642, f. 130v); 25 June 1178 (*PUE*, I, no. 154); became Master of the Order –1188 (see Sempringham; cf. Rose Graham, *St Gilbert*, p. 16).
Ralph   Occ. 17 Sept. 1194 (BM Cott. MS Claud. D. xi, f. 222v); (R.) +1197 (*Ctl. Guisborough*, II, no. 673; see Coverham); possibly prev. subpr. (a Ralph occ. 1173, *EYC*, III, no. 1888).
Cyprian   Occ. 27 May 1201 (*Lincs F.*, PRS LXVII, no. 21: 'Christian', but 'Cyprian' in BM Cott. MS Claud. D. xi, f. 210v); (C.) 1199×1203 (*Ctl. Guisborough*, II, no. 1164); 1204×7[2] (BM Cott. MS Claud. D. xi, f. 227); perhaps prev. can. (ib., f. 226).
Adam   Occ. 26 May 1214 (*Yorks F., John*, p. 174); 25 June 1219 (*Lincs F.*, I, p. 133).
The next pr., William, occ. 20 Dec. 1224 and 1 July 1225 (BM Cott. MS Nero D. iii, f. 51r–v); 1234 (*Yorks F., 1232–46*, p. 28). A pr. T. occ. in two documents in BM Cott. MS Claud. D. xi, f. 256v (i.e. –*c.* 1250); one is printed in *EYC*, III, no. 1897, and dated *c. 1190–c. 1200*.

NEWSTEAD-ON-ANCHOLM (Sancta Trinitas de Novo Loco in Lindeseia) (Lincs), Holy Trinity[3]   f. –1173[4]
John   Occ. late 12th cent. (*Gilbertine Chts.*, p. 30).[5]
Paulinus[6]   Occ. 27 Oct. 1210 (*Lincs F.*, PRS LXVII, no. 311).

---

[1] Winemer subdean of Lincoln: certainly off by 1194 (*HMC Rutland*, IV, 113–14, dated 1193, possibly for 1194); he succeeded Savaric as archd. Northampton when the latter became bp. Bath, so a date –1192 is really probable.

[2] Gilbert (II), Master of the Order; R(obert de Hardres) archd. Huntingdon, who d. 1207 (*Ann. Dunstable*, p. 29) and was succeeded by William of Cornhill, who became bp. Coventry in 1214–15.

[3] *Rot. Chart.*, p. 84. These prs. are difficult to distinguish from other Newsteads etc., esp. Newstead by Stamford. William and Alan could not belong to Newstead (Notts.) as Eustace occ. from 1215 to 1226. The Premonstratensian Newhouse was not normally called Novus Locus and Geoffrey fills the period 1211–26. Newark (Surrey) had the phenomenally long-lived John over the whole period. That leaves only Newstead by Stamford as possible alternative.

[4] Founded by Henry II 'in insula de Rucholm in territorio de Cadney quae Novus Locus dicitur' (*Mon.*, VI, ii, 966); dated by Eyton, *Itinerary*, p. 159, July 1171; but it could be as late as 1173, when three of the witnesses became bps.

[5] The identification of the house is probable, though not certain. This is a Lincs Cht.; it is in a Gilbertine collection (Sixhills); Grimblethorpe is about 18 miles S.E. of Newstead-on-Ancholm, but at least 50 miles N. of Newstead by Stamford, the Augustinian house.

[6] 'of the order of Sempringham'.

[NEWSTEAD-ON-ANCHOLM]

William   Occ. 7 Jan. 1219 (*Lincs F.*, I, pp. 131–2).[1]
Alan   Occ. 18 Oct. 1226 (*Lincs F.*, I, p. 195).[2]

NORTH ORMSBY (Nun Ormsby) (Lincs), St Mary   f. 1148 × 54

List in *VCH Lincs*, II, 196 (R. Graham).

Thomas   Occ. 1164 (*Ctl. Rievaulx*, no. 246, p. 183); 1174 (Bodl. Laud Misc. MS 642, f. 130v); 1182 × 1200[3] (*EYC*, I, no. 595; cf. p. 480).
Robert   Occ. 1209 × 10 (*Lincs F.*, PRS LXVII, no. 307); 1212 × 13 (*Lincs F.*, II, p. xxxvii).
Vivian   Occ. 13 Oct. 1222 (*Lincs F.*, I, p. 163).

SEMPRINGHAM (Lincs), St Mary (St Andrew *c.* 1131–9)   f. 1131 (Ch. Sempringham: see below)

List in *VCH Lincs*, II, 186–7 (R. Graham); basis in Ch. Sempringham, PRO 31/9/16, pp. 2–3, transcript from Rome, Vatican, Barberini MS xliii, 74 (2689), flyleaf (ends incomplete in 1364).

MASTERS OF THE ORDER OF SEMPRINGHAM

St Gilbert   1131–*c.* 1188 Founder and Master; res. administration to Roger –1188 (*Vita* in *Mon.*, VI, ii, p. xx*; see below. This seems to reckon Gilbert and Roger joint masters till G.'s death. The Ch. reckons Gilbert master till his death and so gives him 59 years). D. 4 Feb. 1189 (Saturday: *Mon.*, VI, ii, pp. xxii*–xxiii*, xxix*; Howden, II, 354 s.a. 1188; cf. Graham, *St Gilbert*, p. 24). On him, see Graham, ch. I.
Roger   *c.* 1188–1204 2nd Master, given dates 1189–1204, d. 23 Oct. after 25 years (Ch.). Prev. pr. Malton (q.v.: *Mon.*, VI, ii, p. xx*). Occ. 4 July 1188 (*Lincs F.*, II, p. 331); 1193 (*DC*, no. 15); 11 July 1199 (*Lincs F.*, PRS LXVII, no. 2); 1203 (*CRR*, II, p. 295); 9 May 1204 (*Lincs F.*, PRS LXVII, no. 186); 1204 (*Yorks Deeds*, VI, no. 303).
John   1204–1205 3rd Master, 1204–5, d. 11 May after half a year (Ch.).
Gilbert II   1205–1225 4th Master, 1205–25, d. 26 June (Ch.). Occ. –1207 (BM Cott. MS Claud. D. xi, f. 227: see Malton); 27 Apr. 1208 (*Lincs F.*, PRS LXVII, no. 236); 1209 × 23 (*Reg. Lincoln*, II, no. 638).[4]

The next Master, Robert, was el. 1225 (Ch.; *CPR, 1225–32*, p. 31).

PRIORS OF SEMPRINGHAM

Hugh   Occ. *c.* 1150 × 1160[5] (E. M. Poynton in *Genealogist*, New Series, XV, 222); 1150 × 64 (prob. –1159:[6] *Ctl. Haverholme*, no. 13).
Torphinus   Occ. 1164 (*Ctl. Rievaulx*, no. 246). Cf. Chicksands.
Eudo[7]   Occ. 18 Oct. 1195 (*FF.*, PRS XVII, no. 33); mentioned as ex-pr. 26 Sept. 1201 (Foreville, p. 48). Cf. Sixhills.
Thomas   Occ. 1199 (*Rot. Cur. Reg.*, II, 14); 26 Sept. 1201 (Foreville, p. 49); 1201 (*CRR*, II, pp. 35–6); 1202 (*Lincs Ass. Roll*, no. 191); 4 July 1204 (*Lincs F.*, PRS LXVII, no. 188).

---

[1] This cht. concerns land in Blyborough, near Blyton. Blyton lies about 10 miles S.W. of Newstead-on-Ancholm but at least 65 miles from Newstead by Stamford.
[2] This cht. is concerned with a messuage in Lincoln. The difference in mileage is not so great here, but Lincoln is about 20 miles from Ancholm and 46 from Stamford.
[3] Ralph de Clere (ex inf. Sir Charles Clay).
[4] The editor noted that Bp. Hugh did not return to England till 1213 and dated it –1213; but it is not clear that the bp. was in England when it was drawn up.
[5] Humphrey subdean Lincoln (see *Reg. Lincoln*, VII, p. 203 and n.).
[6] Elias abb. Rufford (+1150); Ralph archd. (prob. Cleveland).
[7] He is also mentioned as pr. 20 May 1207 in a protracted law suit (*Lincs F.*, PRS LXVII, nos. 224, 225).

Adam Occ. 27 Apr. 1208 (ib., no. 236).

Richard Occ. 16 Feb. 1219 (*Lincs F.*, I, p. 141). Presumably = Richard of Beverley, occ. 12–13th cent. (*Genealogist*, New Series, XVI, 34–5).

The next recorded pr., Reginald, occ. 13 May 1222 (*Lincs F.*, I, p. 163). No prioresses of Sempringham are recorded before the 14th cent.

SHOULDHAM (Norfolk), Holy Cross and St Mary   f. +1193
   List in *VCH Norfolk*, II, 414 (from 1250).

J. Occ. 1197×9 (*Reg. Lincoln*, II, no. 637; see Catley). Possibly = Jocelin.

Jocelin Occ. 1203 (*CRR*, II, p. 266); 6 Oct. 1204 (*Norfolk F.*, PRS LXX, no. 55).

SIXHILLS (Lincs), St Mary   f. 1148×54
   List in *VCH Lincs*, II, 195 (R. Graham).

Hugh Occ. 1164 (*Ctl. Rievaulx*, no. 246); 1169+ (*Gilbertine Chts.*, p. 41); 1174 (Bodl. Laud Misc. MS 642, f. 130v); *late temp. Henry II* (pal.: *DC*, no. 259).

?Eudo Occ. possibly 1176×1203 (Bodl. Top. Lincs d. 1, f. 8v); but he may be mid-13th cent.; cf. Sempringham.

Cyprian Occ. (C.) 1197×9 (*Reg. Lincoln*, II, no. 637; cf. Catley); (Cyprian) 1177×1212 (*Ctl. Whitby*, I, pp. 220–1).

?Nicholas Occ. *c. 1200* (*pal.*: *Gilbertine Chts.*, p. 18); but possibly the pr. Nicholas who succeeded Simon –1228 (*VCH*).

John Occ. 12 Feb. 1206 (*Lincs F.*, PRS LXVII, no. 207).

R. Occ. 1206×*c.* 1209 (*Reg. Lincoln*, V, no. 1572).

The next recorded pr., Simon, occ. 1220 (*Lincs F.*, I, p. 153).

WATTON (Yorks E.), St Mary   f. 1150
   C.T.C. List in *VCH Yorks*, III, 255.

Ralph Occ. 1164 (*Ctl. Rievaulx*, no. 246; for 'Waltona' read 'Wattona').

William Occ. *c.* 1150×60[1] (E. M. Poynton in *Genealogist*, New Series, XV, 222); 1157×83 (*EYC*, III, no. 1895 – the dates are those of the tenure of William de Vescy). William is given as pr. *c.* 1150 in *DC*, no. 32, but his name (as the editor indicates) does not appear in the original charter.

?Peter Occ. late 12th cent.[2] (*EYC*, II, no. 1233). Perhaps the same as Peter below.

Robert Occ. 28 June 1200, 25 Nov. 1202 (*Yorks F., John*, pp. 4, 67–8); ?1198×1204 (Cheney, *Inn. III*, no. 587); Baildon, I, 215 makes him occur in a fine in 1194, but no such fine has been found.

Peter Occ. Easter term 1205 (*CRR*, III, p. 293); 11 Feb. 1206, 11 Nov. 1208 (*Yorks F., John*, pp. 98, 144).

Richard Occ. 27 Jan. 1219, 20 April 1225 (*Yorks F., 1218–31*, pp. 15, 59).

The next pr., W(illiam), occ. 1 April 1226 (BM Cott. MS Nero D. iii, f. 53v; cf. *VCH*).

YORK, St Andrew   f. *c.* 1200 or before (–1202, *Mon.*, VI, 962)
   C.T.C. List in *VCH Yorks*, III, 256.

Martin Occ. *c.* 1200 (*EYC*, III, no. 1614, a cht. whose grantor occ. 1196, 1208, ibid., p. 274); –1203 (as M.) (*EYC*, IX, no. 31).

Thomas Occ. 1191×1212, perhaps before Martin (*EYC*, II, no. 1122, with Robert pr. Holy Trinity, York, who occ. 1206, 1208, and Hugh of Silkstone, dean of Doncaster, who occ. *c.* 1170×7, before 1177, *EYC*, I, no. 584).

---

[1] Humphrey subdean Lincoln (see p. 204).

[2] Dated by Farrer *c.* 1170×*c.* 1179; but the grounds for this are not known (for Master Henry de Willerby, perhaps cf. *EYC*, II, nos. 1224, 1228).

[YORK]

Bartholomew   Occ. 12 Nov. 1208 (*Yorks F., John*, p. 147); (B.) 1201 × 10 (*York Fasti*, II, no. 75).

Robert   Occ. 20 Jan. 1210 (*Yorks F., John*, p. 162).

John   Occ. 14 Aug. 1214 (*Ctl. Furness*, II, ii, p. 313); (J.) *c.* 1213 × 14 (BM Cott. MS Nero D. iii, f. 53v).

Baldwin   Occ. 27 Jan. 1219 (*Yorks F., 1218–31*, p. 12); (B.) 9 Oct. 1220 (*Ctl. St Bees*, p. 142, no. 104).

A 'V.' occ. *c.* 1220 (j.d. + 5 March 1220) (*Ctl. Bridlington*, p. 270) – ?for Vivian (see p. 201) – and William (perhaps the same) j.d. + 20 Dec. 1224 (BM Egerton MS 2823, f. 93); 1 July 1225 (*Ctl. Kirkstall*, no. 368) and 25 Nov. 1226 (*Yorks F., 1218–31*, p. 82).

THE NUNS

The houses of nuns are listed here in a single alphabetical list, not divided among the orders, as in *KH*. No lists are included for the following, founded before 1216, but yielding no names: Aconbury, Armathwaite, Arthington, Barrow Gurney, Blithbury, Bretford, Brewood Black Ladies, Broomhall, Cannington, Catesby, Cheshunt, Chester, Chichester, Cook Hill, Ellerton, Esholt, Farewell, Foukeholme, Gokewell, Guyzaunce, Hampole, Henwood, Heynings, Holystone, Kirklees, Lambley, Langley, Limebrook, Llanllyr, Llansaintffraed in Elvel, Lyminster, Moxby, Neasham, Newcastle upon Tyne, Nun Appleton, Nunkeeling, Pinley, Polsloe, Ramestede, Rosedale, Rowney, Rusper, St Margaret's, Seton, Sewardsley, Stone, Swaffham Bulbeck, Wallingwells, Wilberfoss, Wothorpe. See **Addendum**, p. 238.

AMESBURY (Wilts), St Mary and St Mellor. Benedictine abb. and Fontevrault pr. f. *c.* 979 (Ben. abb.); 1177 (pr. of Fontevrault)
List in *VCH Wilts*, III, 258, cf. 243 (R. B. Pugh).
Heahfled   Occ. 978 × 1016 (*VCH Wilts*, III, 243, 258, citing 15th-cent. Exchequer suit in the PRO – 'Heahpled'); referred to in *Roul. Morts*, p. 189 (roll of 1113: 'Hehahfleda').
Rachenilda   Probably 11th cent. (referred to ibid.).
Beatrice   –1177 Pensioned off 1177: last abb. of old foundation (*PR 23 Henry II*, p. 166 (half year) to *29 Henry II*, p. 141 (half year): i.e. *c.* Easter 1177–*c.* Easter 1183).

PRIORESSES
Joan D'Osmont   1177– Traditionally 1st prs. (see *VCH*). Occ. late 12th cent. (pal.: *DC*, no. 329; see Nuneaton).
Emeline   Occ. 1208 (*Ped. Fin.*, I, 145); *c.* 1215 × 20 (*Ctl. Oseney*, I, pp. 246–7); 1221 (BM Stowe MS 882, f. 39).
The next recorded prs., Felicia, occ. *c.* 27 June 1227 (*Wilts F.*, p. 18); Aug. 1228 (*CChR*, I, 80).

PRIORS
John   Occ. 1194 (*Roll of King's Court*, PRS XIV, 24).
Robert   Occ. 12 Apr. 1198 (*Rot. Cur. Reg.*, I, 144; *Abb. Plac.*, p. 21).
John de Vinci   Occ. *c.* 1215 × 20 (*Ctl. Oseney*, I, pp. 246–7); 7 Oct. 1221 (*Sarum Chts.*, p. 114); (John de Vinci) 29 Sept. 1229 (T. F. Kirby in *Archaeologia*, LIX, i (1904), 77).

ANKERWYKE (Bucks), St Mary Magdalene. Benedictine pr.   f. *c.* 1160
List in *VCH Bucks*, I, 357.
Lettice (Lecia)   Occ. (L.) 1189 × 98[1] (*CRR*, V, p. 185); 1194 (BM Campbell Chts., X, 7); 1203 (*Essex F.*, p. 33).
The next recorded prs., Emma, occ. 1236 (*Mon.*, IV, 230).

ARDEN (Yorks N.), St Andrew. Benedictine pr.   f. –1147(?)
List in *VCH Yorks*, III, 115.
Muriel   Occ. (M.) 3 Nov. 1187 (BM Egerton MS. 2823, f. 31 v); 1189 (*Mon.*, IV, 285–6).

[1] Hamo, dean Lincoln (cf. Diceto, II, 69); Roger of Rolleston archd. Leicester (dean by 1198, *Reg. Lincoln*, VII, no. 2068).

BARKING (Essex), St Mary and St Ethelburga. Benedictine abb.   ref. –975[1]
List in *VCH Essex*, II, 120: medieval lists, of no value, in *Mon.*, I, 441–2.

St Wulfhild   *WMGP*, p. 143, in a somewhat obscure sentence, places her in, or a short while before, Edgar's reign; Florence, I, 33–4, in Edgar's reign. These may be based on Gocelin's *Vita S. Vulfildae*, which describes her as a nun of Wilton, who was carried off by Edgar and subsequently made abb. Barking; later expelled for 20 years by Queen Ælfthryth – years spent by W. at Horton – and later restored. She died 10 Sept. 996+ (*Vita*, ed. M. Esposito, in *Analecta Bollandiana*, XXXII (1913), 14ff., esp. 14, 17, 21–2, 22n.). Cf. Horton.

St Edith   –984 (see Winchester, Nunminster).

Ælfgyva(?)   Occ. (A.) 1066 × 87 (*CChR*, V, 284 = *Reg.*, I, no. 240); perhaps the Ælfgyva whose death was noted in the roll of 1122, *Roul. Morts*, p. 315, and whose obit occ. 11 May in BM Cott. MS Vitell. C. xii, f. 128v.

Agnes   App. 1114 × 22 (?1121) (*CChR*, V, 284–5 = *Reg.*, II, no. 1242).

Alice   Occ. –1133 (?1126) (*CChR*, V, 285 = *Reg.*, II, no. 1453). There may have been one or two of the name, since Abb. Alice's appointment was made or confirmed 1136 × 8 (*CChR*, V, 283–4 = *Reg.*, III, no. 32);[2] she occ. +1156 (Osbert de Clare, *Ep.* 42: see *JS Epp.*, I, p. 111 and n.). D. 25 Jan. 1166 (for day, BM Cott. MS Vitell. C. xii, f. 117; for the year see below).

Vacant 1166–73. Cf. *PR 15 Henry II*, p. 135 – account for 3¾ years to Michaelmas 1169; *PR 18 Henry II*, p. 45 – account for 2 years to Michaelmas 1172; see below.

Mary   1173– Sister of St Thomas Becket; app. 1173 (Gervase, I, 242; *CChR*, V, 285); d. 21 Jan. (BM Cott. MS Nero C. ix, f. 4).

Matilda   Daughter of Henry II, app. 1175 × 9; occ. 1179 (*CChR*, V, 286; cf. *GFL*, p. 401n.); ?1176 × 81 (*Ctl. Clerkenwell*, nos. 90, 146); 1198 (*Essex F.*, p. 13); (M.) 3 Feb. 1198 (*FF.*, PRS XXIII, p. 97, no. 133). D. 17 Aug. (BM Cott. MS Otho A. v, f. 2v).

Christina de Valognes   Occ. *c.* Michaelmas 1202 (*Essex F.*, p. 26); 13 Oct. 1204 (*Beds F.*, no. 131); *c.* Michaelmas 1205 (*Essex F.*, p. 36). An abbess unnamed, possibly Christina, d. 1213/14 (*Ann. Dunstable*, p. 41, s.a. 1213, but apparently ref. to 1214).

Sibyl   1215– Royal assent to el. 24 June 1215, previously prioress Barking (*Rot. Lit. Pat.*, p. 144); res. the same year (see below).

Mabel of Bosham   1215–1247 Royal assent to el. 31 Aug. 1215 (*Rot. Lit. Pat.*, p. 154). Occ. 25 June 1220 (*CRR*, IX, p. 140); 14 Jan. 1228 (*Beds F.*, no. 285); d. 1247 (cf. *CPR, 1232–47*, pp. 505–7).

BAYSDALE (Yorks N.), St Mary. Cistercian pr.   f. (at Hutton) *c.* 1162, (at Nunthorpe) *c.* 1167 (?), (at Baysdale) *c.* 1189
C.T.C. List in *VCH Yorks*, III, 160.

Isabella   Occ. 1197 × 1211 (*EYC*, I, no. 564).
The next name, Susanna, occ. 1229 × 45 (*Ctl. Whitby*, I, no. 292).

BERKELEY (Glos). Benedictine abb.   f.?; suppressed –1051 (Freeman, *NC*, II, 545ff.; C. S. Taylor in *BGAS*, XIX (1894–5), 80–1; B. R. Kemp, 'The Churches of Berkeley Hernesse' *Trans. Bristol and Glos. Arch. Soc.*, LXXXVII (1968), 96–110, for old nunnery pp. 98ff.)

Ælfthryth   Occ. 10th–11th cent. (*LVH*, p. 58).

BLACKBOROUGH (Norfolk), St Mary and St Catherine. Benedictine pr.   f. mid-12th cent. (monks); *c.* 1170 (monks and nuns); *c.* 1200 (nuns).

---

[1] A religious foundation of some kind, dedicated to St Mary, existed 946 × *c.* 951 (*AS Wills*, no. 2).
[2] The grant of custody to the queen in 1136 × 7 (*Reg.*, III, no. 31) also perhaps suggests that there was a vacancy at this stage.

List in *VCH Norfolk*, II, 351.

?**Avelina** Occ. n.d. (*VCH* cites *Mon.*, IV, 207, *recte* 204, for the date *c.* 1200 for Avelina. The source is BM Egerton MS 3137, ff. 33 v, 41 v, 74 v – n.d. but presumably 13th cent., and possibly early 13th cent.).

Margaret Occ. 15 Sept. 1222, 6 Nov. 1223, 8 July 1228 (ib., ff. 65, 117 v, 190, 50 v).

BREWOOD WHITE LADIES (Salop, near Boscobel), St Leonard. Augustinian pr. f. *c.* 1199(?)

List in *VCH Salop* (M. Chibnall, forthcoming).

Alditha Occ. early 13th cent.(?): *c. 1225* (Eyton, *Salop*, I, 361 from Ctl. Salop, Aberystwyth, Nat. Lib. Wales, MS 7851D, p. 339).

Cecilia Occ. ibid. (pp. 339–40) of about the same date.

The identification of the house is not certain.

BRISTOL (Glos), St Mary Magdalene. Augustinian pr. f. *c.* 1173

List in *VCH Glos*, II, 93 (R. Graham).

Eva widow of Robert FitzHarding, is said to have f. the house and become prioress there after her husband's death (5 Feb. 1170), and herself to have died 13 March 1173 'or neer thereabouts' (J. Smyth, *Lives of the Berkeleys*, ed. Maclean, I, 44, 59, ff. 54, 71).

BROADHOLME (Notts), St Mary. Premonstratensian pr. f. –1154

Lists in Colvin, p. 421; *VCH Notts*, II, 140 (from 1326).

Avice of Grimsby n.d.: obit 17 April (Newhouse obit, *HMC Ancaster*, p. 483).

Thomasina Occ. 1201 × 2 (Notts F., PRO transcripts, v). Possibly earlier than Avice.

BUCKLAND (Soms), St John the Baptist. Hospitallers pr. f. *c.* 1166 (Augustinian Canons – q.v.); *c.* 1180 (Sisters of the Order of St John of Jerusalem: Hospitallers)

Lists in *VCH Somerset*, II, 150; *Ctl. Buckland*, p. xxvii.

Fina Said to be first prioress, on for 60 years, in 15th-cent. list of prs. of the Hospital (BM Cott. MS Nero E. vi, f. 467 v), not of much authority or precise accuracy, which makes her a contemporary of the prs. from Garnier of Nablus[1] of the 1180s to Hugh d'Aunay (occ. 1216, 1221, 1225 × 9[2]): Robert the treasurer, who occ. 1204, is the last on the list, but Hugh was in fact later than he. It does not make her contemporary with Terric de Bussard who occ. 1237.

BUNGAY (Suffolk), St Mary and Holy Cross. Benedictine pr. f. 1183

List in *VCH Suffolk*, II, 82.

Anastasia First prs. occ. 7 Aug. 1183 at foundation (Oxenedes, p. 69).

The next recorded prs., Mary of Huntingfield, occ. early 13th cent. in BM Topham Cht. no. 13.

CAMBRIDGE (St Radegund 'de Grenecroft'), St Mary and St Radegund. Benedictine pr. f. *c.* 1133 × 8

List in *VCH Cambs*, II, 219.

E. Occ. –1214 (Le Keux, *Memorials of Cambridge*, All Saints, p. 11 n., from BM Add. MS 5804, f. 69 v).

The next recorded prioress, Lettice, occ. 1228 × 9 (*Cambs F.*, p. 14).

CAMPSEY ASH (Suffolk), St Mary. Augustinian pr. f. *c.* 1195

List in *VCH Suffolk*, II, 115.

---

[1] On the prs., see J. Delaville Le Roulx, in *Mélanges d'archéologie et d'histoire, École Française de Rome*, I (1881), 373 ff., VII (1887), 59. Garnier ceased to be pr. in 1189/90 (art. cit. I, 373).

[2] Art. cit. I, 375, VII, 59; for the other prs. see esp. I, 373–5.

[CAMPSEY ASH]

Joan de Valognes Sister of founder and first prioress.[1] Occ. 18 Oct. 1211 (*Norfolk F.*, PRS LXX, no. 259); 1220 × 1 (*Norfolk F.* (Rye), p. 37).

The second prioress, Agnes de Valognes, sister of Joan, occ. 11 Nov. 1232 (*CRR*, XIV, no. 2248).

CANTERBURY (Kent), Holy Sepulchre. Benedictine pr.   f. *c.* 1100

List in *VCH Kent*, II, 143.

Juliana Occ. late 12th cent. (Urry, pp. 418–19); ?1184: 'Iuliana tunc priorissa et Cristina tunc priorissa' (*Ctl. St Augustine's Canterbury*, II, p. 542): *sic* MS – perhaps Christina was subprioress.

?Christina ? occ. 1184: see above.

A prioress Juliana, presumably distinct from the above, occ. ?1227 (*Mon.*, IV, 413 – source untraced); 1236, 1244 (*Kent F.*, pp. 132, 181); d. 1258 (Gervase, II, 208).

CARROW, see NORWICH, Carrow

CASTLE HEDINGHAM (Essex), Holy Cross, St Mary and St James. Benedictine pr.   f. –1191

List in *VCH Essex*, II, 123.

Lucy de Vere Foundress and 1st prioress[2] (*VCH Essex*, II, 122); occ. 7 Nov. 1198 (*FF.*, PRS XXIV, no. 98).

Agnes 2nd prioress, occ. in Bede Roll of prs. Lucy (*HMC, 5th Rep.*, p. 321 = BM Egerton MS 2849).

Agnes Occ. 1243, 27 Jan. 1248 (*Essex F.*, pp. 145, 161). Possibly the same as the above.

A Christiana occ. 12th–13th cent. (BM Cott. MS Claud. D. xi, f. 171).

CHATTERIS (Cambs), St Mary (and All Saints).[3] Benedictine abb.   f. 1006 × 16

List in *VCH Cambs*, II, 222 (Dorothy M. B. Ellis and L. F. Salzman). The following names, prob. early or mid-thirteenth cent., occ. in the Ctl. Chatteris (BM Cott. MS Julius A. i) without clear indication of date.

A. de Rouen Ctl., f. 103r–v.

Albreda Ctl., f. 137.

Mabel de Bancis Ctl., f. 124.

Mary de St Clare Ctl., ff. 89, 95v, 106, 117v, 126v.

CRABHOUSE (Crabb's Abbey in Wiggenhall, St Mary Magdalene) (Norfolk), St Mary and St John the Evangelist. Augustinian pr.   f. *c.* 1181

List in *VCH Norfolk*, II, 410.

Catherine Occ. n.d., prob. early 13th cent. (*Norfolk Arch.*, XI (1892), 16); and see below.

Cecily Occ. 1250; Catherine her predecessor (PRO Assize Roll 560, m. 31d).

DAVINGTON (Kent), St Mary Magdalene. Benedictine pr.   f. 1153

List in *VCH Kent*, II, 145.

In BM Cott. MS Faust. B. vi, f. 101v, are late obits of Prioresses Beatrice (15 Mar.), and Gunnora (15 Feb.); their date is quite uncertain, but they were presumably prioresses of Davington (wrongly attributed to Minster in Sheppey by *VCH Kent*, II, 150). Gunnora may be the 'abbess Keneyare' who d. 12 Feb. (BM Arundel MS 68, f. 15r–v).

Prioress Matilda occ. 9 May 1232 (*Kent F.*, p. 117).

---

[1] On 28 Jan. 1204 King John confirmed the grant for the foundation by Theobald de Valognes to his sisters Joan and Agnes (*Rot. Cht.*, p. 116).

[2] Wrongly identified as wife of first earl of Oxford (*VCH Essex*, II, 122; cf. *CP*, X, 207n.).

[3] Ctl. ff. 90v, 105.

DE LA PRÉ, DELAPRE, *see* NORTHAMPTON, DE LA PRÉ

DERBY, KINGSMEAD (de Pratis), St Mary. Benedictine pr.   f. 1149 × 59
List in *VCH Derbys*, II, 44.

PRIORESSES
Margaret   Occ. 1201[1] × 10 (*Derbys Chts.*, no. 2383; cf. R. R. Darlington, *Ctl. Darley*, I, p. 121).
Emma[2]   Occ. –1210 (*Derbys Chts.*, no. 2382); *c.* 1220 (*Ctl. Darley*, I, p. 121); 4 Sept. 1230 (*Derbys F.* (1886), p. 27).
The next prs., Rametta, occ. 29 Sept. × 6 Oct. 1236 (ib., p. 35).

MASTER
William   Pr. of Hospital of St Helen's, Derby (Aug.), occ. 1201 × 10 (*Derbys Chts.*, no. 2383).

ELSTOW (Beds), Holy Trinity, St Mary and St Helen. Benedictine abb.   f. *c.* 1078
List in *VCH Beds*, I, 357.
Cecily   Occ. 1174 × 81 (*Ctl. Dunstable*, no. 155; see p. 286); 1178+ (*c.* 1180+) (*Ctl. Newnham*, I, no. 149: cf. p. x); 9 Oct. 1197 (*FF.*, PRS XXIII, no. 37).
Mabel I   –1213 Occ. 1202 (*Beds. Eyre*, BHRS, I, no. 113); an unnamed abbess d. 1213 (*Ann. Dunstable*, p. 41).
Mabel II   1213–1232 A successor's el. noted s.a. 1213 (ib., p. 42); occ. April 1222 (*Oxford F.*, p. 66); 1227 (*CRR*, XIII, no. 381); d. 1232 (*CPR, 1232–47*, p. 7: –*c.* Jan. 1233).

EXETER (Devon), St Peter(?). Benedictine abb.   f. 968 (Florence, I, 141): suppressed 1050 and converted into secular Cathedral. Probably two houses at first, one of monks, one of nuns: *WMGP*, p. 201; cf. *AS Chts.*, p. 344. But it is not certain that the house of nuns was at Exeter. See p. 48.

ABBESS
?Eadgyfu (see above)   Occ. with Abb. Leofric, i.e. prob. 973 × 93 (*AS Chts.*, no. 47; cf. p. 344).

FLAMSTEAD (St Giles in the Wood, Woodchurch) (Herts), St Giles. Benedictine pr. f. *c.* 1150
List in *VCH Herts*, IV, 433 (from 1244).
Alice (Aliz)   Occ. ?early 13th cent. (pal.: St Paul's Cathedral, A25/1109 = *HMC 9th Rep.*, p. 27b).
Alice presumably preceded Agnes, who occ. 25 June 1244 (*Bucks F.*, p. 83).

FOSSE (Lincs, by Torksey), St Mary and St Nicholas. Cistercian pr.   f. –1184 (see below)
List in *VCH Lincs*, II, 159.
Siderida   Occ. 'quondam' in 1184 (BM Cott. Vesp. E. xviii, f. 214v).
Beatrice   Occ. 1225 × 6 (*Rot. Lit. Claus.*, II, p. 149).

GODSTOW (Oxon), St Mary and St John the Baptist. Benedictine abb.   f. *c.* Easter 1133
List in *VCH Oxon*, II, 74–5.
Edith Lancelene (Ediva)   1133– First abb. (*Ctl. Godstow*, I, p. 27); occ. (?or Edith II)

---

[1] William de Muschamp, archd. Derby, +28 Dec. 1201 (when his predecessor became bp. Coutances (*Rot. Lit. Pat.*, p. 4)).
[2] The *VCH* shows another Emma for *c.* 1160 (citing the MS of the *Ctl. Darley*) but Darlington shows that there was only one (*Ctl. Darley*, I, p. 121n.) and that Cox dated the cht. wrongly.

[GODSTOW]

1145 (*PUE*, I, no. 32); named and said to have ruled 51 years in 15th cent. note in Ctl., PRO E164/20, cited *PUE*, I, p. 41 – which is impossible.[1]

?Edith II Occ. 1167[2] as 'E. secunda' (*Ctl. Godstow*, I, p. 162); presumably the abb., not named, who d. *c.* 1182 (14 years before 1195); *Visio monachi Eynsham*, in *Ctl. Eynsham*, II, p. 361 and n.

Agnes Occ. prob. 1186 × 93[3] (PRO E164/20, f. 140); presumably the abb., not named, who d. 1195 × 6 (*Visio, Ctl. Eynsham*, II, p. 354; cf. 354n., 285 for date; pp. 258–9 for discussion).

Juliana Occ. 14 June 1197 (*Ctl.*, I, pp. 229–30); 1213 × 19 (*Reg. Lincoln*, III, no. 657).

Alice Occ. 6 Oct. 1220 (*Soms F.*, p. 41).

The next recorded abb., Felicia (Philicia) of Bath, occ.? *c.* 1220 (*Ctl. Sandford*, I, p. 46, cf. n. 1); 3 Feb. 1223 (*Bucks F.*, p. 49).

GORING (Oxon), St Mary. Augustinian pr. f. *temp.* Henry I

Lists in *VCH Oxon*, II, 104; *Goring Chts.*, I, p. xix.

Margaret or **Margery** Occ. June 1200, April 1203 (*Bucks F.*, pp. 19, 22); 1205 × 21 (*Ctl. Oseney*, IV, no. 349, pp. 391–2).

The next recorded prioress, Matilda, occ. 1227 (*Goring Chts.*, I, p. xix).

GREENFIELD (Lincs), St Mary. Cistercian pr. f. –1153

List in *VCH Lincs*, II, 155–6.

PRIORESSES

Matilda Occ. 1195 × 1223 (BM Lansd. MS 207A, f. 116: see Stixwould).

Agnes and **Sarah** are given without dates. An **Agnes**, possibly the same, occ. 1230 (*CPR*, *1225–32*, p. 353).

MASTERS

Thori Occ. *temp.* Henry II (pal.) as pr. (*DC*, no. 143); as master (ib., no. 125).

William Occ. *temp.* Henry II (pal.) and +1160[4] as pr. and *custos* (ib., nos. 145–6).

GRIMSBY (Lincs), St Leonard. Augustinian pr. f. –1184

The list in *VCH Lincs*, II, 179 gives Emma and cites BM Lansd. MS 207 B, f. 216v, but this is a wrong reference and we have not been able to trace the source of the entry.

HANDALE (Grendale: cf. A. H. Smith, *Place-names of Yorks N.*, pp. 140–1) (Yorks N.), St Mary. Cistercian pr. f. 1133

List in *VCH Yorks*, III, 166.

Beleisur Occ. 12 Nov. 1208 (*Yorks F., John*, p. 148).

The next name, Bella, occ. 17 June 1240 (*Yorks F., 1232–46*, pp. 58–9).

HARROLD (Beds), St Peter. Augustinian pr. f. *c.* 1136 × 8 (Arrouaisian); *c.* 1188 (independent). See *Ctl. Harrold*, p. 8

---

[1] If the reading of *Ctl.*, I, p. 162, is incorrect, and there was only one Edith, she would, however, have reigned 48–9 years. This seems very improbable.

[2] Dated by the coming of the cardinals to try and reconcile Henry II and Becket – this must refer to the legation of 1167.

[3] Master Roger of Rolleston, evidently bishop's clerk not archd. Leicester; so prob. after St Hugh's accession (1186); Roger occ. as archd. by 1195 (Howden, III, 285; cf. *MVH*, iii, 8, ed. Douie and Farmer, I, 112–13).

[4] *temp.* Ralph sub-dean Lincoln (see p. 192).

Lists in *VCH Beds*, I, 389–90; *Ctl. Harrold*, pp. 13–14.

Gila Occ. 19 Oct. 1188 (*Ctl. Harrold*, p. 56); canoness of Maroeuil (ib., pp. 58–9).

Jelita[1] Canoness of Boulogne (*Ctl. Harrold*, pp. 58–9); occ. *c.* 1200 × 10 (ib., p. 25).

The next recorded prioress, Agnes, occ. 1227 (*Beds Eyre*, BHRS, III, 35).

HEDINGHAM, *see* CASTLE HEDINGHAM

HIGHAM (Lillechurch) (Kent), St Mary. Benedictine pr. (S. Sulpice, Rennes) f. (?) 1148
List in *VCH Kent*, II, 146.

Mary First prioress, d. of King Stephen (*Mon.*, IV, 381).

Juliana Occ. *c.* 1179 × 1180[2] (*Ctl. Colchester*, II, pp. 525–6).

Royal assent given to the el. of the next recorded prioress, Joan de Meriston, nun of Lillechurch, 24 Nov. 1247 (*CPR, 1247–58*, p. 2).

HORTON (Dorset). Benedictine abb. f. ?10th cent. as abbey of nuns; ref. *c.* 1050 (1033 × 61) as abb. of monks (*EHR*, LVIII (1943), 195); 1122 × 39 (priory subject to Sherborne). See p. 53.

ABBESSES

(St) Wulfhild according to Gocelin's *Vita* (see Barking), spent 20 years at Horton when expelled from Barking by Queen Ælfthryth – i.e. very roughly *c.* 970–*c.* 990. She may be the Wulfhild abb. of Horton ('Hortun') who occ. in *LVH*, p. 57; or Gocelin may have made a false identification of the Saint with an abbess of the same name.

ICKLETON (Cambs), St Mary Magdalene. Benedictine pr. f. –1154(?)
List in *VCH Cambs*, II, 226 (D. M. B. Ellis and L. F. Salzman).

Eufemia Occ. 1206 × 15 (j.d. decision +24 Apr. 1206: BM Add. MS 46,353, f. 294; cf. Cheney, *Inn. III*, no. 705).

The next prioress recorded, Ellen, occ. 1232 (*VCH*, citing PRO E326/11550).

IRFORD, *see* ORFORD

KELDHOLME (Yorks N.), St Mary. Cistercian pr. f. –1143
C.T.C. List in *VCH Yorks*, III, 169–70.

(K. occ. 1208 × 9, according to Baildon, I, 98, citing a fine which cannot be found; possibly a confusion with Basilia.)

Basilia Occ. 19 Nov. 1208 (*Yorks F., John*, p. 152).

Sibyl Occ. 1224 × 69 (*EYC*, X, p. 93, correcting Burton, *Mon. Ebor.*, p. 380n., and other authorities).

KILBURN (Middlesex), St John Baptist. Benedictine pr. f. 1139
List in *VCH Middlesex*, I, 181–2 (J. L. Kirby).

Alice Occ. 1207 × 8 (*London and Middlesex F.*, p. 10).

The next recorded prioress, Margery, occ. 1232 (*VCH Surrey*, III, 147). An Adelina occ. n.d., in Oxford, New Coll. Reg. Secundum, f. 2 v; and Sabina n.d. in London, St Bartholomew's Hospital, Cok's Ctl., f. 226.

KINGTON ST MICHAEL (Wilts), St Mary. Benedictine pr. f. –1155
List in *VCH Wilts*, III, 261 (J. L. Kirby).

No early evidence; but the 15th-cent. obituary in CUL MS Dd. viii. 2, ff. 11–20 v, gives two

---

[1] Juliana, who occ. in no. 15 in the cartulary should be Jelita as in the original (*Ctl. Harrold*, p. 13). Probably contemporary with *GFL*, p. 409, no. 360 = *Ctl. Colchester*, II, pp. 526–7.

[KINGTON ST MICHAEL]

names which may be of this period – Susanna, 19 Mar. (f. 13v), Edith 26 and/or 27 Dec. (f. 20v). The other names in the obituary, cited in *VCH* from J. E. Jackson, 'Kington St Michael', *Wilts Arch. Magazine*, IV (1858), 54–5, all seem to be mid-13th cent. or later.

LEGBOURNE (Lincs), St Mary. Cistercian pr. f. 1150+
List in *VCH Lincs*, II, 155.

PRIORESSES
Mabel Occ. 25 June 1219 (*Lincs F.*, I, p. 133).
The next recorded prioress, Beatrice, occ. 30 Sept. 1226 (ib., I, p. 216).

PRIORS
Robert Occ. ? late 12th cent. (pal.: Harl. Cht. 47. F. 49 = *DC*, no. 478); 1202 (*Lincs Ass. Roll*, no. 1152); 1203 (*CRR*, II, p. 280); 6 Oct. 1208 (*Lincs F.*, PRS LXVII, no. 197); 1228 Master of the nuns (*CPR, 1225–32*, p. 209); 12 July 1231 (*Lincs F.*, I, p. 245).

LEOMINSTER (Herefs). Benedictine abb. f. ?; suppressed 1046 (on this house, see B. R. Kemp, 'The Foundation of Reading Abbey'; idem, *EHR*, LXXXIII (1968), 505ff.)
Eadgifu –1046 Dep. and house probably dissolved after she had been carried off for a time by Earl Swein in 1046 (*ASC*, C; Florence, I, 201–2 (s.a. 1049); cf. Freeman, *NC*, II, 89, 545ff.).

LITTLE MARLOW (Bucks), St Mary. Benedictine pr. f. –1218
List in *VCH Bucks*, I, 360.
Margaret Occ. –c. 1220[1] (BM Harl. MS 391, ff. 103v–4v).
The next recorded prioress, A., d. 1230 (*Reg. Wells*, II, p. 33).

LITTLEMORE (Sandford) (Oxon), St Mary, St Nicholas and St Edmund.[2] Benedictine pr. f. 1135 × 54
List in *VCH Oxon*, II, 77 (H. E. Salter).
Matilda Occ. 1150 × 61 (Saltman, p. 384, no. 160).
Amice Occ. 1219 (*Cambs F.*, p. 10); +1221 (*Cal. Bodl. Chts.*, p. 295).
The next recorded prs., Isabel de Henred, was el. 1230 (*Reg. Wells*, II, p. 32).

LONDON, CLERKENWELL, St Mary de Fonte. Augustinian pr. f. *c.* 1144 (cf. J. H. Round in *Archaeologia*, LVI, ii (1899), 223–8)
Lists in *Ctl. Clerkenwell*, ed. W. O. Hassall, pp. 281ff. based on a medieval list, ib., p. 270; *VCH Middlesex*, I, 174 (J. L. Kirby).
Christina First prs., occ. *c.* 1144 (?1143 × 4, '9 Stephen' in a late entry in *Ctl. Clerkenwell*, p. 270); 1152 × 61 (Saltman, pp. 296–7, no. 72); ?*c.* 1160 × 70 (*Ctl. Clerkenwell*, no. 310).[3]
Ermengarde Occ. 19 Oct. 1186 (W. O. Hassall in *EHR*, LVII (1942), pp. 98ff.); 2 March 1197 (*FF.*, PRS XX, no. 101); 10 Feb. 1199 (*Ped. Fin.*, II, 75).
Isabel Occ. 1206 (Norman Moore, I, 121–2).
In 1208 the priory was in the king's hand (*CRR*, V, p. 199).
Alice Occ. 1216 × 20 (*Ctl. Clerkenwell*, no. 286); 29 June 1220 (ib., no. 287); 1221 × 2 (*Roll of the Justices in Eyre*, Selden Soc., LIX (1940), p. 24, cf. pp. 85–6); 1221 (*CRR*, X, p. 2).
The next recorded prs., Eleanor, occ. –1223 (*Ctl. Clerkenwell*, no. 278).

[1] Date of MS (Davis, no. 989). [2] Cf. *Cal. Bodl. Chts.*, p. 297.
[3] Dated by the editor ?1186 because it concerns a purchase not included in the confirmations of 1181 × 2 and 1186; but this cannot be regarded as cogent evidence of date, especially as Ermengarde was prs. by the time of the second confirmation.

LONDON, HALIWELL, St John the Baptist. Augustinian pr.   f. –1127
  List in *VCH Middlesex*, I, 178 (J. L. Kirby).
Clementia   Occ. 1193 × 4 (Gibbs, no. 110); *c*. Easter 1201 (*Essex F.*, p. 22); 1203 (*CRR*, II, p. 146).
?Magdalena   Occ. ?early 13th cent. (*Ctl. Missenden*, III, no. 749); also BM Cotton MS Vitell. F. viii, f. 85 v, cited *VCH Middlesex*, where it is dated ?*c*. 1185 or +1203.
The next recorded prioress, Matilda, occ. 1224 (*Surrey F.*, p. 12).

LONDON (St Helen's, Bishopsgate), St Helen and Holy Cross. Benedictine pr.   f. –1216
  List in *VCH London*, I, 460–1.
D.   Occ. 1212 × 16[1] (*HMC 9th Rep.*, App. I, 57); –1216 (BM Cotton cht. v. 6 (2)).
Matilda   Occ. early 13th cent.: a grant of hers is witnessed by William FitzAlice and John Travers[2] (Glasgow U.L. Hunterian U. 2. 6, ff. 66 v–67 = *Ctl. London, Aldgate*, no. 336).
The next recorded prioress, Helen, occ. 1229 × 30 (*London and Middlesex F.*, p. 18).

MALLING (Kent), St Mary and St Andrew. Benedictine abb.   f. *c*. 1090
  List in *VCH Kent*, II, 148.
No abbess was appointed until Bp. Gundulf, the founder, was on his deathbed (*PL*, CLIX, 829–33; cf. R. A. L. Smith, *Collected Papers*, pp. 96–7). He d. 7 Mar. 1108.
Avice   First abb. (*Mon.*, III, 384); app. early 1108 (cf. *Vita Gundulfi*, *PL*, CLIX, 833, cf. *Text. Roff.*, f. 198); occ. (A.) 1108 × 14 (*Reg.*, II, nos. 943, 1081).
Ermelina   Occ. 1145 × 50 or 1159 × 60, prob. late (Saltman, p. 398; for date cf. *GFL*, p. 506).
The next recorded abbess, Regina, occ. 13 Oct. 1227 (*Kent F.*, p. 96).

MARKYATE (Caddendon, Cella, de Bosco) (Herts, formerly Beds), Holy Trinity. Benedictine pr.   f. 1145
  Lists in *VCH Beds*, I, 360–1; on origin see *Life of Christina of Markyate*, ed. C. H. Talbot.
Christina I   Occ. 1145 (Gibbs, nos. 154, 156); d. 8 Dec. *c*. 1155 × 66 (*St Albans Psalter*, p. 27 and pl. 13; *Christina*, p. 15; cf. pp. 9–10; *GASA*, I, 127).
Christina II   Occ. 1202 × 3 (*Warws F.*, no. 116). Cf. p. 228.
Joan   Occ. 1212 (*Mon.*, III, 368).[3]
B.   Occ. 1214 (*CRR*, VII, p. 103).
Isabel I   Occ. early 13th cent. (pal.: BM Cott. Cht. xxi, 5); (Isabel I or II)1220, 1230 (*Warws F.*, nos. 290, 438).
Isabel II   Subprioress, succeeded Isabel, deceased (Gibbs, no. 155. This cht. is in St Paul's, Liber A, original section, written 1241 × 2).

MARLOW, *see* **LITTLE MARLOW**

MARRICK (Yorks N.), St Mary and St Andrew. Benedictine pr.   f. 1154 × 8
  List in *VCH Yorks*, III, 118.
Agnes   Occ. *c*. end of 12th cent. and prob. *c*. 1211 (*Ctl. Rievaulx*, no. 361 – cf. *EYC*, II, no. 962n. for date; BM Cott. MS Nero D. iii, f. 22).
The next recorded prioress, Isabel, occ. 27 July 1240 (*Yorks F., 1232–46*, p. 86).

MINSTER IN SHEPPEY (Kent), St Mary and St Sexburga. ?Benedictine pr.   f. *c*. 670; ref. –1186 (after a complex history in the 11th–12th cents).
  List in *VCH Kent*, II, 150 (cf. Davington).

---

  [1] W(illiam) archd. and A(lard) dean London.
  [2] Occ. 1224, 1230 (G. Williams, *Medieval London*, London, 1963, p. 64).
  [3] ? The I. (extended Isabel) of Gibbs, no. 236, who succeeded Christina.

[MINSTER IN SHEPPEY]

PRIORESS
Agnes Occ. 1186 (Thorne, p. 1839); (A.) 1187 (Urry, p. 427; cf. p. 429).

PRIOR
A Simon pr. Sheppey d. 22 Dec. (BM Cott. MS Faust. B. vi, f. 106v).

MINSTER IN THANET (Kent), St Mildred. Benedictine abb. f. *c.* 670; deserted ?1011 (*KH*, 1st edn., p. 71)
List in *VCH Kent*, II, 151.

Leofrun was taken captive by the Danes in 1011 (*ASC* C, D; Florence, I, 164; Thorne, p. 1908); possibly to be identified with the Liofrun who occ. *c.* 990 × 2 (*AS Chts.*, no. 66); but see Reading.

NORTHAMPTON, DE LA PRÉ (Delapre), St Mary. Cluniac abb. f. *c.* 1141 (at Fotheringay); *c.* 1145 (–1153,[1] at Northampton)
List in *VCH Northants*, II, 115–16.

Azelina First abbess, *temp.* Stephen (*Mon.*, V, 208).

Odierda Mentioned in 1219 as having been abbess *temp.* Henry II (*CRR*, VIII, p. 104).

The election of the next recorded abbess, Cecilia of Daventry, nun of de la Pré, received royal assent 7 Nov. 1220 (*CPR*, *1216–1225*, p. 270).

NORWICH (Norfolk), Carrow, St Mary. Benedictine pr. f. 1146[2]
List in *VCH Norfolk*, II, 354.

Matilda[3] Occ. 26 Oct. 1198 (*Norfolk F.*, PRS, LXV, no. 189); 6 Aug. 1206 (*Norfolk F.*, PRS, LXX, no. 92).

The next recorded prs., Agnes de Monte Caenesi, occ. early 13th cent. (*Norfolk Arch. Misc.*, II, 496).

NUNBURNHOLME (Yorks E.), St Mary. Benedictine pr. f. *temp.* Henry II
List in *VCH Yorks*, III, 119.

Millicent Occ. 25 July 1206 (*Yorks F.*, *John*, p. 101).

NUN COTHAM (Lincs), St Mary. Cistercian pr. f. 1147 × 53
List in *VCH Lincs*, II, 153.

PRIORESSES
Matilda Occ. 1153 × 4, 1168 × 77 (*PUE*, III, nos. 95, 236).

The next recorded prs., Alice, occ. 25 Nov. 1218 (*Lincs F.*, I, p. 144).

PRIOR
An S. prior apparently occ. 1176 × 1203 (Bodl. MS Top. Lincs d. 1, f. 8v; but this may be mid-13th-cent.).

NUNEATON (Warws), St Mary. Fontevrault pr. f. +1147 (at Kintbury); *c.* 1155 (at Nuneaton)
List in *VCH Warws*, II, 69–70.

---

1 See Northampton, St Andrew, n. 1.

2 W. Rye, in *Norfolk Arch. Misc.*, II (1883), 465ff., esp. p. 497; *Carrow Abbey* (Norwich, 1889), App. p. i, printed an extract from the lost ctl. which ascribes the f. to 1146 = 10 Stephen (1145 × 6) = 2 Bp. William of Norwich (1147 × 8), and to two nuns Seyna and Lescelina, of the hospital of St Mary and St John in Norwich. The latter was f. by 1136 × 7, when it received a cht. from King Stephen (*Reg.*, III, no. 615).

3 Called Le Strange by Blomefield (*Norfolk*, IV, 525; no reference, but date 1198, presumably from the fine).

PRIORESSES

Agnes Occ. *c.* 1160[1] (*DC*, no. 336); ?late 12th cent. (BM Add. Cht. 47,854).[2] With Pr. William in the first and Pr. Hugh in the second; if this is reliable, it seems probable from the overlapping of prs. and prioresses that the order of prioresses was Agnes, Alice, Juliana, and of prs. William (with Agnes), Hugh (with Agnes, Alice), Berengar (with Alice), Vitalis (with Juliana) – and this is confirmed by the pal. evidence of *DC*, nos. 336 (Agnes and William) and 329 (Juliana and Vitalis).

Alice Occ. 1167×86 (*DC*, no. 320); (A.) 1186 (BM Add. Cht. 47,638); (A.) 1185+ (*CRR*, VII, p. 260; IX, p. 217); 1188×98 (BM Add. Cht. 49,118); also Add. Chts. 47,483,[3] 47,954, 49,117.

Juliana Occ. late 12th cent. (pal.: *DC*, no. 329, dated by ed. 'late Henry II').

?Mabel Occ. Michaelmas 1202 (*Warws F.*, no. 122).

Emma Occ. 1 July 1206 (*Suffolk F.*, PRS LXX, no. 464); (E.) prob. 1206×7[4] (BM Add. Cht. 47,646).

Mabel Occ. 1213×14 (*Warws F.*, no. 210); (M.) early 13th cent. (pal.: BM Add. Chts. 47,484, 48,145). Possibly M. was different from Mabel: see below under prs.

Ida Occ. 6 Oct. 1214, 18 Nov. 1226 (BM Add. Chts, 47,958, 49,068).

The next recorded prioress, Sibyl, occ. 1227 (*CPR, 1225–32*, p. 165); 1227×8[5] (PRO E40/5785 = *Cat. Anc. D.*, III, 223).

PRIORS (for the order of the first four, see above)

William Occ. *c.* 1160 (*DC*, no. 336).

Hugh Occ. *c.* 1160×80 (BM Add. Chts. 47,854, 47,483).

Berengar Occ. 1167×86 (*DC*, no. 320); late 12th cent. (pal.: *DC*, no. 330, dated by ed. 'late Henry II').

Vitalis Occ. late 12th cent. (pal.: *DC*, no. 329 – cf. prioress Juliana). ? = Vitalis, pr. of Grovebury.

N. Prob. 1213×14 (see Emma). The order of the next three prs. is conjectural; and perhaps suspicious, since it is tempting to equate N. and Nicholas.

A. Occ. early 13th cent. (BM Add. Cht. 47,645 – pal. – and 48,145: see Mabel). A. and G. both coincide with M(abel) in Chts., and are therefore placed later than N.; but one or other (or even both) may have been contemporary with the earlier Mabel, occ. 1202.

G. Occ. early 13th cent. (BM Add. Cht. 47,484).

Nicholas Occ. 17 Nov. 1221 (*CRR*, X, p. 247).

The next recorded pr. was Robert,[6] occ. 1227×8 (PRO E40/5785: see above).

NUN MONKTON (Yorks W.), St Mary. Benedictine pr. f. –1153
List in *VCH Yorks*, III, 123.

[1] Pal., but confirmed by evidence of Agnes's date: see below.
[2] This is one of a series of 'originals', Add. Chts. 47,629, 47,631, 47,640 and 47,854 concerning Nuneaton pr.'s rights in Catherington Church, which appear (as Dr G. R. C. Davis has pointed out to us) of dubious authenticity. This cht. is ruled on the back, and written in a 13th-cent. hand. In the light of this, a certain caution should be attached to the evidence of Nuneaton chts.; but it may well be that the names even in these four chts. are based on genuine documents.
[3] With Hugh Barre, possibly the same man who was archd. Leicester *c.* 1148–*c.* 1160 (between Robert de Chesney and Baldric de Sigillo: *GFL*, pp. 535, 164n.). *CDF*, no. 1062 (the f. cht. of Nuneaton pr.) may indicate that he *res.* the archdeaconry *c.* 1159 and so the cht. could be later, perhaps much later; a date before 1148/9 is impossible.
[4] Refers to agreements made at Michaelmas after the interdict (*post interdictum Anglie* – presumably its start).
[5] William de Stuteville sheriff of Warws and Leics; confirmed in a cht. dated 1 Pope Gregory IX.
[6] 'Richard' in the later copy of this document in BM Add. Cht. 48,490.

[NUN MONKTON]

(?) **Matilda de Arches**   ?Prs. occ. 1147 × 53 (*EYC*, I, no. 535 and n.).[1]
Agnes   Occ. 28 Apr. 1224, 1 Dec. 1226 (*Yorks F., 1218–31*, pp. 55, 86).

ORFORD or **IRFORD** (Lincs), St Mary. Premonstratensian pr.   f. *c.* 1155 × 60
  Lists in Colvin, p. 422; *VCH Lincs*, II, 209.
Eda   Occ. early 13th cent. (*Reg. Lincoln*, VIII, no. 2277).
?Matilda of Borwell   d. 17 Apr. (Newhouse obit., *HMC Ancaster*, p. 483). Probably later.

PRIORS
Thomas   Occ. 1228 × 32 (*Gilbertine Chts.*, p. 11).

POLESWORTH (Warws), St Edith (BM Harl. Cht. 45. G. 25). Benedictine abb.   ref.
c. 980(?) (Polesworth); 1066 × 70 (priory at Oldbury); *c.* 1130 (abbey at Polesworth).
  List in *VCH Warws*, II, 64.

ABBESSES
Osanna   Occ. prob. 1171 × 4[2] (*MB*, I, 287).
The next recorded abbess, Muriel, occ. 1220 × 1 (*Warws F.*, I, no. 242).

READING (Berks). Benedictine abb.   f. ?; dissolved ?1006
Leofrun   Occ. *LVH*, p. 58; probably to be identified with Liofrun who occ. *c.* 990 × 2
  (*AS Chts.*, no. 66, cf. p. 381; more likely Reading than Minster from the context).
?Leveva   See Shaftesbury.

REDLINGFIELD (Suffolk), St Andrew and St Mary. Benedictine pr.   f. 1120
  List in *VCH Suffolk*, II, 85.
The *VCH* list includes Emma, conjecturally a relative of the founder (the Count of Guînes,
whose wife was called Emma), and Alice Davolers, *temp.* Henry III, citing BM Add. MS
19,099, f. 70 v; the reference is evidently to Add. MS 19,090, f. 70 v, where there is a modern
list, without precise references, based on 'T. Martin, *Church Notes*' (evidently a MS). These
prs. come from 'two deeds without date', and the *VCH* date, and the link with the founder
(already hinted in the MS) are evidently quite conjectural.

ROMSEY (Hants), St Mary and St Æthelfleda.[3] Benedictine abb.   ref. 967 (Florence, I,
141; on early history, see *Romsey Records*, pp. 11f.)
  List in *VCH Hants*, II, 132.
St Merewenna (Merwynn)   App. 967 (Florence, I, 141); occ. 967 × 75 (Birch, no. 1187, if
  trustworthy; also occ. in spurious Birch, nos. 1178–9 of ?966); she and her two succes-
  sors occ. in the *Vita* of Æthelfleda and Merewenna in *Romsey Records*, pp. 19ff., from
  BM Lansdowne MS 436, ff. 43 v–45 v. Occ. in *LVH*, p. 58.
Elwina   fled to Winchester during the period of the second Danish invasions (in the time
  of Swein: ?990s).
Æthelflæd   daughter of Ethelwold, born *c.* 962 or before; nun of Romsey; abb. ?990s (*Vita*,
  loc. cit.), died 23 Oct. (*Romsey Records*, pp. 25, 27). Occ. in *LVH*, p. 58.
Wulf(w)ynn   prob. 11th cent. (*LVH*, p. 62).
Ælfgyfu   prob. 11th cent. (ibid.).

[1] Abp. Henry Murdac confirms a gift by William de Arches and Juetta his wife to their daughter
  Matilda and the nuns of Monkton: Matilda is not called prioress, but her name is placed as if she
  was. Prob. 1151 × 3 (see p. 146 n. 4).
[2] Cf. E. Walberg, *La tradition hagiographique de S. Thomas Becket*, p. 73.
[3] St Mary at first; *Romsey Records*, p. 68, shows the double dedication in 1266, but it may be recorded
  earlier.

(**Christina**   sister of St Margaret, queen of Scotland, was a nun at Romsey and Wilton(?); Eadmer, *HN*, pp. 122–3, puts Matilda, her niece, later queen, 'sub ... virga' of Christina. This seems the only evidence that she was abbess. Orderic, III, 399 calls her a nun of Romsey; as do *ASC* E, s.a. 1086 ('1085'); Florence, II, 19; *WMGR*, I, 278; *Ann. Winchester*, p. 34; Eadmer alone places her – by implication – at Wilton.)

Athelitz   Occ. prob. –1102 (Anselm, *Ep.*, 237; see ed.'s note).

Matilda   –1155 D. 1155 (*Ann. Winchester*, p. 55).

Mary of Blois   Daughter of King Stephen; on death of her brother, William, count of Boulogne and earl of Warenne (Surrey) in Oct. 1159 she became sole survivor of Stephen's children. In 1160 she res., was brought out of the cloister, and married the count of Flanders, taking the county of Boulogne with her (cf. *Ann. Waverley*, p. 238; Ann. Southwark, BM Cott. MS Faust. A. viii, f. 134). D. 1182.

Juliana   Occ. n.d. (*Ctl. Winchester*, pp. 213–14, nos. 502–3); d. Feb. 1199 (*Ann. Winchester*, p. 71).

Matilda Patriz   1199–1230 Sister of Walter Walerand, el. 3 June 1199 (*Ann. Winchester*, p. 72). Presumably the Matilda who d. –14 Dec. 1230 when royal licence was given for her successor's el.; assent to the el. of Matilda de Barbefle was given on 19 Jan. 1231 (*CPR, 1225–32*, pp. 418, 420). Occ. late 1228 (*CRR*, XIII, no. 1222).

SHAFTESBURY (Dorset), St Mary and St Edward. Benedictine abb.   f. *c.* 888
   List in *VCH Dorset*, II, 79.

(**Æthelgeofu**   First abb., daughter of Alfred, *c.* 888–: Asser, ed. W. H. Stevenson, *c.* 98).

?Ælfthryth   Occ. 948 (Birch, no. 868). A religious: not called abbess.

Herelufu (Hereluva)   –982 D. 982 (*ASC*; Florence, I, 147); occ. *LVH*, p. 58.

Leveva (?Leofgifu)   Occ. –1066 (*DB*, I, 60, III, 176; Freeman, *NC*, IV, 40n. The first reference is to a holding in Reading, the second to a holding of the abb. of Shaftesbury. It is just possible that L. was abb. Reading q.v.).

Eulalia   1074– App. 1074 (*Ann. Winchester*, p. 30); occ. 1103 + (?*c.* 1104), +Aug. 1106 (Anselm, *Epp.* 336, 403); referred to in 1136, evidently as former abb. (*Reg.*, III, no. 818).

Cecily   App. +1107 by Henry I; daughter of Robert FitzHamon (*Mon.*, II, 60; cf. Wilton).

Emma   Occ. 1136 (?former abb.: *Reg.*, III, no. 818); also referred to as former in 1201 (*CRR*, II, p. 64).

Mary   Half-sister of Henry II, occ. 1174 × 88,[1] and frequently to 1215 × 16 (see J. C. Fox in *EHR*, xxv (1910), 303–6; xxvi (1911), 317–26; esp. p. 322 for first occ.; for later occ. p. 319 and *Rot. Cht.*, p. 150a: 23 May 1205; *EHR*, xxv, 305, 1215 × 16). She was dead by 5 Sept. 1216 (*Rot. Lit. Claus.*, I, 286b; cf. *Rot. Lit. Pat.*, p. 197). J. C. Fox, loc. cit., tried to identify her with Marie de France, the poetess; this is not now accepted.

Her successor, J(oan), subprioress, was el. –29 Nov. 1216 (*CPR, 1216–25*, p. 7); occ. 1220 × 1 (*Sussex F.*, no. 171); the el. of Joan's successor, Amicia Russell, nun of Shaftesbury, received the royal assent on 3 July 1223 (*CPR, 1216–25*, p. 376).

SINNINGTHWAITE (Yorks W.), St Mary. Cistercian pr.   f. *c.* 1155 (*Mon.*, V, 468)[2]
   C.T.C. List in *VCH Yorks*, III, 178.

Christina   Occ. 18 Dec. 1172 (*EYC*, I, no. 200).

Agnes   Occ. 29 Nov. 1184 (*Mon.*, V, 466–7).

The next prioress, Euphemia, occ. 18 Feb. (not 19 Feb., as ed.), *Yorks F., 1218–31*, p. 26: 'Euferia', 'Eufemia' in Index. As Euphemia *Haget* in *Ctl. Healaugh Park*, p. 1.

---

[1] Dated 1181 by Eyton, *Itinerary*, p. 244, perhaps rightly; but it can only be proved to be during one of Henry II's visits to England between 1173 ('Dei gratia', confirmed by the witnesses) and 1189, i.e. 1174 × 88.   [2] Cf. Eyton, *Itinerary*, pp. 10–11 (ex inf. D. Greenway).

SOPWELL (Herts), St Mary. Benedictine pr. f. 1140
  List in *VCH Herts*, IV, 425 (from 1233).
Avice Occ. 12th cent.: her obit is in a mid-twelfth cent. hand (+1155) in *The St Albans Psalter*, p. 28 and pl. 4, under 20 March.

STAINFIELD (Lincs), St Mary and St Andrew. Benedictine pr. f. c. 1154
  List in *VCH Lincs*, II, 132.

PRIORESSES
Margaret Occ. prob. –1168 (Lincoln D. and C., Dij/74/1/1); 1197 × 1203[1] (*Mon.*, I, 633–4).
Petronilla D. 16 × 17 April 1209 × 25[2] (*Mon.*, IV, 309–10; cf. Newhouse obit., *HMC Ancaster*, p. 483).
Constance (Custancia) Succeeded Petronilla (*Mon.*, IV, 308) and occ. 1225 (*CPR, 1225–32*, p. 72); 20 Aug. 1226 (*Mon.*, IV, 309).

MASTERS
William of Appleby Mentioned 1225 as former master (*CPR*, ut supra).
Robert de Sammar' M. Whitby, installed 4 April 1223 (*Reg. Wells*, III, 126); occ. 1226 (*CRR*, XII, no. 2611); (R.) 20 Aug. 1226 (*Mon.*, IV, 309).

STAMFORD (Northants), St Mary and St Michael. Benedictine pr. f. c. 1155
  List in *VCH Northants*, II, 100–1.

PRIORESSES
A. Occ. 1174 × 81 (London, Soc. of Antiquaries, MS 60 f. 154r–v).
Agnes de Boby N. of Stamford, confirmed by the bp. of Lincoln, Hugh of Wells ?1219 × 20 (*Reg. Wells*, III, p. 107).
Alice Occ. 1225 × 9 (*Ctl. Peterborough*, no. 391); 30 Sept. × 20 Oct. 1230 (*Bucks F.*, p. 59); also 1230 in *Reg. Wells*, II, p. 79. See *Ctl. Peterborough*, no. 391n. D. +1235 and succeeded by Petronilla of Stamford (Soc. of Antiquaries, MS 60, f. 208). See *Ctl. Peterborough*, no. 391n.

PRIORS
Henry of Fiskerton The first known, was pr. 1225–9 (*Reg. Wells*, III, pp. 142, 173; cf. *Ctl. Peterborough*, no. 391n.).

STIXWOULD (Lincs), St Mary. Cistercian pr. f. c. 1135
  List in *VCH Lincs*, II, 149.

PRIORESSES
L. Occ. 1184 (*Reg. Pinchbeck*, I, 424–5; cf. 423–4, and, for the date, Douglas, *Bury*, no. 221, pp. 181–2).
Matilda Occ. late 12th cent. (*Ctl. Haverholme*, no. 121); 1209 × 35, prob. –1227 (*Reg. Lincoln*, VI, no. 1943); res. or d. –1236 when an unnamed prs. el. (*Reg. Grosseteste*, p. 11).

MASTERS
Simon Occ. c. 1150 × 60 (E. M. Poynton in *Genealogist*, New Series, XV, 222; see Sempringham).

---

[1] Master William, precentor Lincoln (Diceto, II, 150; cf. *Ann. Tewkesbury*, p. 57).
[2] With H., bp. Lincoln and Richard de Percy: the latter (d. 1244: *EYC*, XI, p. 7; cf. p. 60) confirms that the former is Hugh of Wells, 1209–35. Petronilla's successor occ. 1225.

Hugh   Occ. 1191 (BM Cott. MS Vesp. E. xviii, f. 147); –1198 (*Reg. Lincoln*, VI, no. 1860); 1202 (*Lincs Assize Roll*, no. 98); 24 Apr. 1205 (*Lincs F.*, PRS LXVII, no. 198); 1195 × 1223[1] (BM Lansd. MS 207A, f. 116).

Matthew   Occ. 1209 × 35, prob. –1227 (*Reg. Lincoln*, VI, no. 1943).

The next recorded master, Geoffrey, occ. 1227 (*CPR, 1225–32*, p. 165).

STRATFORD-AT-BOW (Middlesex), St Leonard. Benedictine pr.   f. –1122
 List in *VCH Middlesex*, I, 159 (H. P. F. King; from 1264).

Lettice   Occ. *c.* 15 June 1203 (*CRR*, II, p. 277).

The next recorded prs., Catherine, occ. 1245 (*Essex F.*, p. 151).

STUDLEY (Oxon), St Mary. Benedictine pr.   f. *c.* 1176
 List in *VCH Oxon*, II, 79.

Petronilla   Occ. 27 Jan. 1200 (*Oxford F.*, p. 15); 7 March 1227 (ib., p. 82).

The next recorded prs., Juliana, occ. 11 Nov. 1230 (*CRR*, XIV, no. 864) and another Petronilla 19 × 25 May 1231 (*Bucks F.*, p. 60).

SWINE (Yorks E.), St Mary. Cistercian[2] pr.   f. –1153
 List in *VCH Yorks*, III, 182.

PRIORESS: the first known is
Helewise   Occ. 14 Dec. 1226 (*Yorks F., 1218–31*, p. 97).

?PRIOR
Master Robert   Occ. 1170 × 5 (*EYC*, III, no. 1308; cf. Thornton).

THETFORD (Norfolk), St George and St Gregory. Benedictine pr.   f. ?(at Ling); *c.* 1160 (at Thetford)
 Lists in *VCH Norfolk*, II, 355–6; *VCH Suffolk*, II, 86.

Cecilia   Occ. 1163[3] (BM Harl. MS 743, ff. 271v–272v).

THICKET (Yorks E.), St Mary. Benedictine pr.   f. –1180
 List in *VCH Yorks*, III, 125.

Sibyl   Occ. 16 Feb. 1219 (*Yorks F., 1218–31*, p. 24; also '1214' in Baildon, I, 208, without reference).

The next recorded prs., Eva, occ. 12 June 1231 (ibid., pp. 135–6).

WAREHAM (Dorset), Benedictine abb.   f. *c.* 672 (*KH*, new edn, p. 484); –876 (Asser, c. 49)
Wulfwyn   D. 982 (*ASC* C; Florence, I, 147). Cf. Appendix I.

WESTWOOD (Worcs), St Mary. Fontevrault pr.   f. *temp.* Henry II
 List in *VCH Worcs*, II, 151.

No prioresses are recorded earlier than the 14th cent.

PRIOR
Elias   Occ. *c.* 27 Oct. 1207 (*CRR*, V, p. 58).

---

[1] R(oger) dean Lincoln (see pp. 92 n. 6, 207, 212 n. 3).

[2] The community was apparently partly Cistercian nuns and lay brothers, partly Premonstratensian canons (so *KH*, p. 276).

[3] Geoffrey archd. Canterbury; William de Chesney sheriff of Norfolk and Suffolk (but prob. a later record: e.g. William bp. Norwich is 'venerabilis memorie').

WHERWELL (Hants), Holy Cross and St Peter. Benedictine abb. f. ?c. 960 or before (see below)

List in *VCH Hants*, II, 137.

?Wenfleda   Occ. *c.* 960 in *Vita S. Wulfhilde* (*AB*, XXXII (1913), 10ff.; cf. Barlow in *Life of King Edward*, p. 96).

Ælstrita   D. –1113 (*Roul. Morts*, p. 188); presumably = 'Elstrudis' noted as foundress in BM Egerton MS 2104, f. 43, where she is called King Edgar's widow and said to d. 17 Nov. 1002.[1] Either the spellings are late variants of Queen Ælfthryth's name, or the queen and an abbess have been confused.

Heahfled   Occ. 1002 (Kemble, no. 707), possibly the abb. Heahflæde who d. 6 May (*LVH*, p. 270).

—   An abb. unnamed, sister of Edward the Confessor, occ. 1051 (*ASC* E, s.a. 1048).

Matilda   d. –1113 (*Roul. Morts*, p. 188).

Aubrey (Alberéda)   d. –1113 (ib.).

Matilda   Occ. 7 Sept. 1198 (BM Egerton MS 2104, ff. 16v–17); (M.) 21 May 1194 (*PUE*, I, no. 318); 21 March 1201 (BM Egerton MS 2104, ff. 98r–v, 200); 25 Oct. 1207 (*Rot. Cht.*, p. 171); d. 26 April (BM Egerton MS 2104, f. 44v).

The next recorded abbess, Euphemia, occ. 1254 (BM Egerton MS 2104, f. 43v) and d. 26 April 1257 after 40 years as a nun at Wherwell (ib., ff. 24v–25).

WILTON (Wilts), St Mary, St Bartholomew and St Edith. Benedictine abb. f. 890

List in *VCH Wilts*, III, 241 (E. Crittall; cf. F. Barlow in *Life of King Edward*, pp. 94ff.; J. E. Nightingale, *Memorials of Wilton...*, Devizes, 1906, pp. 14ff.).

Ælfgyth, Ælfgith I and II   occ. 944 (called 'monialis femina'), 955 (Birch, nos. 795, 903, 917).

St Wulfthryth   *c.* 965–1000 Educated as a secular at Wilton; King Edgar's concubine and mother of St Edith (see Barking, Winchester, New Minster) *c.* 960; then abb. Wilton (*Vita S. Wulfhilde* and *Vita S. Edithe*, *AB*, XXXII (1913), 10ff. (M. Esposito); *AB*, LVI (1938), 34ff., 275 and n. (A. Wilmart)). Occ. ?974 (Birch, no. 1304). D. 21 Sept. 1000 (*AB*, LVI, 275 and n.). Obit (21 Sept.) in BM Cott. MS Titus D. xxvii, omitted in *LVH*, p. 272.

Brihtgifu (Brihtwitha, Brihtiva)   followed after two abbesses not named and d. *c.* 1065 (*AB*, LVI, pp. 99, 295–6).

Ælfgifu (Ælviva)   1065–1067 (d.) (ib.).

Godgifu (Godyva)   sister of Ælviva, *c.* 1067 (ib., pp. 36, 36–7n., 296).

Matilda   Occ. 1093×9 (?1094: Anselm, *Ep.* 185).

Hawise   Occ. 1160×79[2] (*HMC*, *9th Rep.*, App. II, 397b). According to Tewkesbury tradition she was daughter of Robert Fitz Hamon (d. 1107: *Mon.*, II, 60;[3] Leland, *Itin.* (ed. Toulmin Smith), IV, 139, 153).

The abbey was vacant, in the king's hand, in or shortly before 1179–80 (*PR 26 Henry II*, p. 122).

Alice   Occ. ?c. 1191 (*Sarum Chts.*, p. 52; cf. note citing cht. of 3 Richard I, 1191–2); 1192 (*VCH* citing Wilton House MSS, chts., no. 3).

Mary   Occ. 1194 (Wilton House cht. no. 78); 10 July 1195 (*HMC 9th Rep.*, App. II, 379b); 1195×6 (*Cambs F.*, p. 1); 4 Feb. 1198, 29 June 1200 (*Wilts F.*, pp. 3, 5); D. 2 or 3 Aug. (2: Exeter Cath. Lib. MS 3518, *sub die*; Lire (Wareham) obit., *HF*, XXIII, 473 – 'Winton').

---

[1]   The year is approximately correct, and the day confirmed by *LVH*, p. 272.

[2]   Richard, sheriff Wilts.

[3]   Wyntoniae, *Mon.*, but Wilton (*bis*) in Leland.

Ascelina[1] Occ. July 1206, *c.* 15 July 1208 (*Wilts F.*, pp. 9–10).

Margaret Occ. 30 June 1216 (*Rot. Chart.*, p. 223). D. –12 Feb. 1222 (*CPR, 1216–25*, p. 326).

WINCHESTER (Hants), NUNMINSTER, St Mary. Benedictine abb.   ref. 963[2]
List in *VCH Hants*, II, 126.

Æthelthryth First abbess, app. by St Æthelwold (cf. Ælfric's *Vita Ethelwoldi, Ch. Abingdon*, II, 261, with Wulfstan's, *PL*, CXXXVII, 92).

Eadgifu Her name seems to be established by *AS Chts.*, no. 49 (964 × 75, but to be dated *c.* 975 unless E. became abb. as a small child; cf. however, ib., p. 348); very likely the E. who occ. 990 × 2 (*AS Chts.*, no. 66; cf. p. 381). According to the *Vita S. Edithe* (*AB*, LVI (1938), 34ff., esp. pp. 76–7) by Goscelin, 'Edith' was daughter of Edgar by Wulfthryth (see Wilton), and was brought up at Wilton as a nun and made abbess in her father's lifetime of three abbs., Barking, Nunminster and another not named, by St Æthelwold; she d. 16 Sept. 984 (cf. ib., pp. 40n., 94n., 94ff.), aged 23. But Edith (Eadgyth) and Eadgifu cannot be the same name, yet could easily have been confused by Goscelin,[3] esp. if there was a tradition (represented by the 12th-cent. Cod. Wintoniensis, BM Add. MS 15,350, source of *AS Chts.*, no. 49) that Eadgifu was Edgar's daughter.

Beatrice –1084 D. 1084 (*Ann. Winchester*, p. 34).

Alice (Athelits) 1084– App. 1084 (ibid. – Alicia). Occ. 1102 + : *c.* 1102 × 3 (Anselm, *Ep.* 276 – Athelits).

?Hawise See Wilton, p. 222 n. 3.

Lucy Occ. +1142 (*Ctl. Lewes*, II, p. 79).

Emma Occ. 1159 × 81 (*JL*, 14,033) – prob. –1173; see below.

Abbey vacant 1172 × 3 (*PR 19 Henry II*, p. 201).

Claricia 1174– App. 1174, previously nun of Wilton (Diceto, I, 396).

Isabel Occ. 6 Oct. 1230 (*CRR*, XIV, no. 546).

WINTNEY (Hants), Sts Mary, Mary Magdalene and John the Baptist. Cistercian pr. f.–1200[4]
List in *VCH Hants*, II, 151. This is based on the late 13th-cent. obituary in BM Cott. MS Claud. D. iii, ff. 140vff., ed. Hearne in Trokelowe, ed. Hearne, pp. 384–93. We give the names in the order of their obits: their chronological order seems irrecoverable, save that Roisa, whose obit occ. in red, may have been the first pr., Lucy II is an addition to the list and so possibly of the late 13th cent., and a Lucy, presumably Lucy I, occ. 1223 × 4 (see below).

Emma d. 7 Jan. (Hearne, p. 384).

Sabina d. 14 Apr. (p. 387).

Isilia(?) d. 30 Apr. (p. 387).

Claricia d. 5 May (ib.).

Lucy I d. 20 June (p. 389); presumably the Lucy who occ. 1223 × 4 (*L. and M'sex F.*, p. 215).

---

[1] Probably the date 1197 assigned to her in *VCH* is a few years too early. (Miss E. Crittall has kindly helped us on this point.)

[2] *WMGR*, I, 137, names two daughters of Edward the Elder who were nuns: Eadburh (Edburga), nun of Winchester, and Eadflæd (Edfleda), of a community not named. Later legend (Rudborne in Leland, *Collectanea*, I, ii (ed. Hearne, 1715), 413 – not in Wharton's edn., *AS*, I, 207–8; *Romsey Records*, pp. 11ff.) made them foundresses of Nunminster and of Romsey: for this there is no early evidence.

[3] The identification of Eadgyth, Edgar's daughter, with the abbess is also made e.g. by a late hand in *LVH*, p. 57.

[4] By Geoffrey FitzPeter – Hearne, op. cit., p. 387 – whose *floruit* was from 1190 (or a little before) to his death in 1213.

[WINTNEY]
Juliana   d. 15 Aug. (p. 390).
Alice   d. 21 Aug. (ib.).
Lucy II   d. 23 Aug. (ib., but see above).
Hawise (Hauuisa)   d. 2 Sept. (ib.).
Cecily   d. 10 Sept. (ib.).
Roisa (Rose)   d. 29 Sept. (p. 391).

WIX (Sopwick) (Essex), St Mary. Benedictine pr.   f. ?1123 × 33
   List in *VCH Essex*, II, 124–5.
Idonia   Occ. 14 Oct. 1198 (*FF.*, PRS XXIV, no. 6; cf. *Misc. D. M. Stenton*, p. 56); 18 Nov. 1202 (*CRR*, II, p. 119).
Christina   Occ. early 13th cent., n.d. (PRO E40/3357, 3529, 3706, 8897: *Cat. Anc. D.*, II, 183, 200, 217; IV, 371–2).
The next recorded prs., Constance, occ. 20 Jan. 1235 (PRO E40/3316; *Cat. Anc. D.*, II, 178).

WROXALL (Warws), St Leonard. Benedictine pr.   f. *c.* 1135(?)
   List in *VCH Warws*, II, 72–3, based on a list cited in Dugdale, *Warws*, II, 649, from 'Chron. MS. Priorat. de Wroxhal penes Joh. Burgoyn Bar. f. 5b'. This, or an antiquarian account in English based upon it, was printed in *Mon.* and the following list of early prioresses is embedded in it (IV, 91):
   Ernborow, Helin, Sabin, Helin, Mawd, Emme, Mawd, Cecelie, Ide, Amice, Abtot (*sic*), Annis and Sibill Abtot (with date 1284 and reference to the *Reg. Godfrey Giffard*).
   The list in Dugdale, *Warws*, is virtually identical, but in Latin: Erneburga, Helena, Sabina, Helena, Matilda, Emma, Matilda, Cecelia, Ida, Amicia, Sibilia d'Abetot.
   There appears to be some repetition (and possibly confusion) in this list, and it cannot be checked in detail. The only prioresses otherwise known are:
Sabina   Occ. 10 June 1163 (*PUE*, I, no. 97).
Helena   Occ. 3 Feb. 1229 (*CRR*, XIII, no. 1540); 1235 × 6 (*Warws F.*, no. 518).

WYKEHAM (Yorks N.), St Mary and St Michael. Cistercian pr.   f. *c.* 1153
   List in *VCH Yorks*, III, 184.

PRIORESSES
The first recorded prioress, Eva, occ. 18 Nov. 1234 (*Yorks F., 1232–46*, p. 14).
MASTERS
Simon   Occ. 1203 × 14 (*HMC, 10th Rep.*, App., IV, 321–2).

YEDINGHAM (Little Mareis) (Yorks E.), St Mary. Benedictine pr.   f. –1163
   C.T.C. List in *VCH Yorks*, III, 128.
Beatrice   Occ. 1182 × 1200[1] (*EYC*, I, no. 597).
Christina   Occ. 12th or 13th cent. (BM Cott. MS Claud. D. xi, f. 171: the MS is mid-13th cent.).
Sibyl   Occ. 3 Feb. 1219 (*Yorks F., 1218–31*, p. 18).

YORK, St Clement. Benedictine pr.   f. *c.* 1130
   C.T.C. List in *VCH Yorks*, III, 130–1.
Alice   Occ. 1192 (*Gesta Henrici II*, II, 240).
Ascelina   Occ. 20 Oct. 1221 (*Yorks F., 1218–31*, p. 40).
The next prioress, Agnes, occ. 1234 (*Yorks F., 1232–46*, p. 16).

---

[1] Probable dates of tenure of Ralph de Clere I, donor of no. 596, and witness of no. 597 (which confirms no. 596): this is based on information supplied by Sir Charles Clay.

APPENDIX I

UNIDENTIFIED PRE-CONQUEST ABBOTS AND ABBESSES

See above, pp. 12–16. In a sense all abbs. who sign most Pre-Conquest charters are un-identified, in that normally their house is not named. But where a reasonably probable identification (or choice of identification) can be made, an abb. is not included in the following list.

Names in brackets only occur in charters of doubtful authenticity, and may be fictitious – not (most probably) in the sense that the forger, or some copyist, invented them, but that they have either been imported from a different period or context to embellish a list of signatories, or are seriously corrupt.

Ægfridus   occ. in Ely Calendar (Cambridge, Trinity Coll. MS O.2.1, f. K10v) under 28 Oct. See Ely, St Albans.

Ælfhere, Æluere   occ. ?1018, ?1019, 1019, ?1022, 1023, ?1026, 1031 (Kemble, nos. 728–30 (cf. *OS Facs.*, II, Exeter no. 10); *EHD*, I, 553ff.; Kemble, nos. 734, 739, 743, 744). See Bath.

Ælfnoth   occ. 974 (Birch, nos. 1303–4).

Ælfnoth, Æthelnoth (presumably different from above)   occ. 999, 1002, 1005, 1007, 1014, ?1019 (Kemble, nos. 703, 707, 714, 1303, 1309, 730; cf. 729: 'Filnoth'). Cf. Muchelney, Winchester, New Minster.

(Ælfred   occ. 994 in Kemble, no. 686, but the earliest MS reads Ælfweard.)

Ælfsige, Æthelsige   occ. (Æthel–) 974, 988, (Æl–) 990(× 1) (two of the name), 994 (Birch, no. 1303; Kemble, nos. 664, 712, 686 – see p. 232 n. 3) – and see Ely, to which one of the pair probably belonged. Later references to pairs (999–1012) are probably to Ely and Win-chester, New Minster, or Peterborough: but in MS 1 of Kemble, no. 703 (see Appendix III) one Ælfsige is identified as abb. 'Ceas'', the other as of Ely.

(Ælfstan   occ. ?1019 (Kemble, nos. 729–30): cf. Brihtrig below, and Canterbury, St Augustine.)

Ælfwig   Two Æs. occ. ?1033, 1035, ?1044, and an Æ. and an Æthelwig occ. in 1045 (Kemble, nos. 1318, 1322, 772, 778). For the other, see Bath; cf. also Westminster.

(Ælfwine   occ. ?995 in *Mon.*, VI, 1443–6).

(Ælfwold: *see* Winchcombe.)

Æthel-:   *See also* Æl-

?Æthelstan: occ. ?963 (*Ctl. Muchelney*, no. 3) – but perhaps = Ælfstan, Glastonbury.

Æthelweard: two of the name sign in 982 (Kemble, no. 632): see Malmesbury (and Athelney).

Æthelwig   occ. ?1033, 1035, ?1044 ('Æthelwi'), 1045 (Kemble, nos. 1318, 1322, 772, 778). Cf. Ælfwig (Æ. occ. with two Ælfwigs in all four cases).

Æthelwin, Ægelwin   occ. 1061, 1062 × 6, and in spurious cht. dated 28 Dec. 1065 (Kemble, nos. 811, 823–4). These references might be to Æthelwig of Evesham, or even, one or two of them, to Ælfwine of Ramsey.

Alhhard   occ. prob. 970 × 5 (*AS Chts.*, no. 50).

Aua (Aeua, Afa)   occ. 1017, ?1019, 1016 × 23, ?early 11th cent. (Kemble, nos. 1313, 729;

AS Chts., no. 81; N. R. Ker in *Powicke Studies*, p. 75 – 'abbot of Exeter' is a slip). Possibly the same as 'Anna' in the dubious Kemble, no. 1317, where he is attributed to St Oswald's, Gloucester: see p. 52 n. 1. Kemble, no. 1313, is a good text of a cht. of Abp. Wulfstan (as Professor Whitelock has pointed out to us), and so Gloucester would be a plausible home for Aua – if it existed.

Brihstan   occ. 1012 (Kemble, no. 719).

Brihteah, Brihteh, Byrhteh'   occ. 970, 972, 974 (Birch, nos. 1269, 1282,[1] 1284, 1303–4).

Brihtnoth, Brichtnoth   occ. ?1019 (Kemble, no. 730).

Brihtrig   occ. ?1018 (*OS Facs.*, II, Exeter, no. 10); ?1019 (Kemble, no. 729 – but the signatures are doubtful and cf. Burton). In Kemble, no. 728, Brihtrig is an error for Brihtwig (Glastonbury).

Brihtwig, Brithwi   occ. 1024 × 32 (Kemble, no. 1324); cf. Glastonbury.

Brihtwold: *see* Malmesbury, Winchester, New Minster. Also occ. 1019 (*EHD*, I, 553ff.).

Clement   occ. 958 × 9 (Birch, no. 1030).

Eadnoth   occ. 1021 × 3 (Kemble, no. 736). Cf. Ramsey.

Eadred   occ. 1004: see Milton, p. 56 n. 3.

Eadric   d. 15 May (Cambridge, Trinity Coll. MS O.9.25, f. 158v) – possibly St Albans, of the old foundation.

Ealdred   occ. 949, 958, 959, 964, 968, ?969, 970, 982, 983 (Birch, nos. 883 – 'Aldredus' not called abb., but among them – 1042, 1046 (cf. no. 1047); *Ctl. Muchelney*, no. 3; *Mon.*, II, 323–4 (cf. *AS Chts.*, no. 45); Birch, nos. 1264 (spurious), 1266; Kemble, nos. 633, 636).

(Folcmerus   occ. in spurious Westminster cht. dated 969: Birch, nos. 1228 = 1264).

Freothegar   occ. 972 × 4 (Birch, no. 1283).

Godwine   occ. 970, 972, 974, 968 × 74, 975, 980, 982, 983, 25 July 997, 998, 1001, 1002 – very likely more than one man; very likely one or other of or both the Gs. who were bps. Rochester in the years following 995 (Birch, nos. 1257, 1269, 1282,[1] 1284, 1303–4, 1302, 1316; Kemble, nos. 624, 632–3,[2] 1279; *OS Facs.*, III, no. 35; Kemble, nos. 701, 706, 1297; *Gilbert Crispin*, pp. 167–8). Also occ. in spurious chts. dated 969 (Birch, nos. 1228 = 1264).

(Leofl'   occ. in spurious cht. dated 969: *Crawford Chts.*, no. 6 = Birch, no. 1264, who reads 'Leofric'. Cf. Birch, no. 1228. Cf. Exeter.)

Leofnoth, Lyfnoth   occ. 1046 (Matthew, pp. 143–5).

Leofsige (1)   occ. 986, 16 Apr. 988 (Kemble, no. 655; *Liber de Hyda*, pp. 238–42).

Leofsige (2)   occ. 1053 × 5 – two Ls. sign *AS Chts.*, no. 115; one may be Ely, but L. abb. Ely prob. d. 1044; one may be for Leofsine, Thorney, q.v.

Leofwine   occ. 1020, 1021 × 3, ?1022, 1022 × 3: see Ely, Thorney.

(Luxihs (*sic*)   occ. ?1019, Kemble, no. 729 – presumably a corrupt reading.)

Martin   occ. 970 (Birch, no. 1266).

Sifrith, Siferth   occ. 964, 968, 969, 970 (*Ctl. Muchelney*, no. 3; *Mon.*, II, 323–4; Birch, nos. 1212, 1230, 1266); possibly bp. Lindsey (Sigefrith), who occ. 997, 1004.

Siward   occ. 1042 × 4, 1045, 1045 × 7; bp. Rochester 1058–75. See Chertsey.

(Somer   occ. in spurious Westminster cht. dated ?969 (Birch, no. 1228) ?for Wymer in virtually identical no. 1264.)

Wighard, Wigard   occ. '1006' (?for 1002), ?*c.* 1004 × 14 in spurious witness list (Kemble, no. 715; *AS Wills*, no. 22, cf. pp. 175–6).

Wigstan   occ. 949 (Birch, no. 883).

[1] = BM Cott. Aug. ii. 6: the name is legible under Ultra Violet light.
[2] In one MS there are two Godwines.

('Willnoth'   occ. 1002 in Kemble, no. 707 – a scribal error: see p. 232 n. 6.)

(Wlfredus   occ. 1022 × 3 in the dubious Kemble, no. 735.)

Wulfgeat   occ. 1066, 1068 (Kemble, no. 897; *Reg.*, I, no. 23).[1]

Wulfsige   occ. 1042, 1043, 1045: see Chertsey.

(Wulfstan   occ. 1002 in Kemble, no. 707, but this is an error for Wulfgar, of Abingdon.)

Wulfward   occ. 1042 × 4, 1044, 1045, 1050, *c.* 1053 (Kemble, no. 769; *OS Facs.*, II, Exeter 12; Kemble, nos. 778, 792–3, cf. no. 800; *BM Facs.*, IV, no. 32).

(Wulwina   'Mercamensis abbas' occ. in spurious Crowland cht. dated 966: Birch no. 1179. ?Wulfwyn abb. Wareham.)

(Wymer   occ. in spurious Westminster cht. dated 969: Birch, no. 1264. See Somer.)

---

[1] Miss Robertson, *AS Chts.*, p. 488, suggests that he may have been abb. Athelney, which seems a likely possibility (cf. also abb. Crowland).

APPENDIX II

UNIDENTIFIED ABBOTS AND PRIORS, AFTER 1066

Where ghosts have been laid or uncertain identifications made in the lists in the main body of the book, they are not included here, though in every case the doubtful form of a house is given in the Index. 'Abbas' was a common surname for laymen in the twelfth century: we make no attempt to list the numerous examples which have led to confusion here; nor the cases where 'pr(esbyter)' has been read as 'pr(ior)'.

Car' 'A. priore Car'' occ. in a very corrupt cht. of ?*1161 × 8* in *CDF*, no. 1380.

Cotes Ralph pr. occ. prob. 1163 × 86[1] (PRO C115 A1 K2/6683, sec. x, no. 9). Perhaps the Hospital (Cotes, Northants).

Denedan Hugh pr. St Augustine's, occ. 1204 × 5 (Northants F., PRO transcripts): evidently corrupt. Possibly Daventry (see p. 117).

Holen Adam pr. occ. *c.* 1170+ (*Ctl. Montacute*, no. 110; see Monk Sherborne).

Llwythlawr Gwrgenau abb. d. 1168 (*Brut, Peniarth*, p. 65; *Red Book*, p. 149); a suggested identification with Ludlow seems very unlikely: more probably the lay abbot of a *clas* church.[2]

Neop' John pr. of, occ. twice, mid-twelfth cent. (+1153, with Isabel, countess of Northampton, evidently wife of Gervase Paynel: cf. *CP*, VI, 643; *HMC Rutland*, IV, 165, from Belvoir ctl.).

Neuham Hugh pr. occ. 1139 × 41 (Stenton, *Eng. Feudalism*, 2nd edn, p. 265, from PRO E40/14,208 (original)).

St Pernit Cristina prs., occ. 1204 × 5 (Northants F., PRO transcripts); possibly Markyate (St Trinity).

---

[1] Robert, bp. Hereford, prob. de Melun (1163 × 7) or Foliot (1173/4 × 86) rather than de Bethune (1131 × 48), since David, can. of Hereford (see *GF*, p. 268) and a m. Wardon (f. 1136, but usually 'de Sartis' in early chts.) also witness.

[2] We are grateful to Professor Melville Richards for advice on this.

APPENDIX III

LIST OF PRE-CONQUEST CHARTERS USED

See pp. 12–16. They are arranged in four groups: those in Birch, those in Kemble, those in *AS Chts.*, *Wills* or *Writs*, those in none of these collections – the fourth in their order in Sawyer.

In a majority of cases in the first two groups we have checked abbots' names and other signatories against one or more MSS or a modern edition. The number(s) in brackets after the number in Sawyer in groups I, II and IV in each case indicates the MS(S) in his list which have been consulted.

I

Birch no.	Sawyer no. and MS consulted	Date	Comment
868	534 (1)	948	Ss. consistent, but few: no grounds for suspicion.
880	546 (1, 2)	949	Two contemporary or near contemporary copies survive and ss. consistent; but has been supposed a forgery
883	544 (2, 3)	959	Genuine. Ss. consistent.
890	557 (1)	951	As 883.
893	556[1]	951	Prob. authentic.
919	607 (1, 2)	13 Feb. 956	Doubtful. Ss. consistent.
924	605 (2, 3, 4)	956	Ss. consistent.
933	625[2]	956	?Interpolated: ss. possible, but only three.
941, 949	597 (1, 2)	956	Ss. consistent.
1030	586 (1)	958 × 9	Possibly genuine, but doubtful: ss. consistent.[3]
1042	675 (1)	958	?Genuine, but ss. doubtful.[4]
1045	660	959	Doubtful in form, though believed genuine by some scholars; ss. consistent,[5] but not numerous.
1046	658 (1, 2)	959	Doubtful; ss. as 1030, 1045.
1047	673 (1, 2)	prob. 959	Doubtful; dated '958', but ss. virtually as 1046, except that MS 1 has Abp. Oda (d. 958 or 959).

[1] The text used is that in Hart (1966), pp. 155–6; only a fragment in Birch; Hart's text gives abbs. Eadhelm (Canterbury, St Augustine's) and Dunstan. The MS reads 'Lyneweard' for Cyneweard abb.

[2] Text checked by *Ctl. Glastonbury*, III, no. 1199.

[3] If we accept two bps. Beorthhelm. Prof. Whitelock, in an unpublished study, has shown that it is probable that one B. was bp. of Sherborne and Wells (and Canterbury for a time in 958–9), the other of Winchester (a third, of London, was presumably dead by this date).

[4] Because of Bp. Leofric, and because bps. Leofwine and Oscytel (of Dorchester) both sign.

[5] If Beorhthelm became bp. Winchester in 958 or 959.

Birch no.	Sawyer no. and MS consulted	Date	Comment
1101	717 (1)	963	Authentic: ss. consistent.
1120	719 (1)	963	?Genuine; ss. consistent.
1124	708 (1, 2)	963	Ss. as 1120.
1135	731 (1)	964	Controversial, but agreed to be spurious in its present form; ss. consistent.[1]
1143	725 (1)	964	?Suspicious. Ss. consistent, if Ælfthryth queen in 964.
1145	668 (1)	?972	Possibly genuine. Dated 922, perhaps for 972: ss. consistent with 964 × 74.
1164	735 (1)	965	?Genuine: ss. consistent.
1169	734 (1, 2)	965	Ss. consistent, but relatively few.
1175	739 (1)	966	?Genuine. Ss. consistent, but not numerous.
1176	738 (1,2)	966	Original. Ss. consistent.
1178	741 (1)	966	Spurious, but ss. consistent.
1179	1294 (1)	966	Spurious; ss. not consistent.
1187	812 (1)	?967 × 75	Suspicious; no. ss.
1189	737 (1)	966	Ss. consistent.
1190	745 (1)	966	Original. Ss. consistent.
1212	1215 (1)	968	Original. Ss. consistent, but very few can be checked.
1216	767 (1)	968	?Genuine. Ss. consistent.
1217	763 (1)	968	Ss. consistent.
1228, see 1264			
1230	771 (1)	969	?Genuine. Ss. consistent.
1243	1321 (1)	969	Early copy; but doubtful (J. A. Robinson (1919), pp. 34–7). No. ss.
1257	777 (1)	970	Prob. genuine; s.s consistent (see n. 1).
1264	774	?969	Spurious (Westminster). Ss. inconsistent.
= Crawford Chts. no. 6 (virtually = Birch, no. 1228)			
1266	779[2]	970	Prob. spurious. Ss. consistent, except for a Bp. 'Ælric'; see n. 1.
1268	780	970	Prob. authentic: ss. consistent.
1269	781	970	Prob. authentic: ss. consistent (see n. 1).
1282	786 (1)	972	Very early copy; but suspicious. Ss. would be consistent if Kinsige = Wynsige (bp. Lichfield); see Birch, no. 1284.
1283	749 (1)	'967'[3] (972)	Ss. consistent with 972 × 4 (if Oswald correctly abp.), but few. Prob. to be dated 972, and genuine.

[1] If Bp. Wulfric is accepted, and if Ælfthryth was queen by 28 Dec. 964. Bp. Wulfric's see cannot be certainly identified, but he seems evidently to have existed, and Prof. Whitelock tells us there is evidence to suggest he was bp. Hereford. The presence of this rare name confirms that the list itself is based on a genuine original. W. occ. in Birch, nos. 1040 (958), 1121 (963), 1164 (965), 1211 (968), 1257, 1266, 1269 (970); but in Kemble, no. 629 (981) one should read Wulfsige (see Finberg in EHR, LVIII (1943), 200). Cf. Searle (1899), pp. 221–2.

[2] The texts of nos. 1266, 1268–9 have been checked by Lib. El., pp. 76–8, 81–2, 112–13.

[3] Dated 967 in text, 966 in rubric, MS 1.

Birch no.	Sawyer no. and MS consulted	Date	Comment
1284	788[1]	972	Spurious, but ss. identical with Birch, no. 1282 (whose lacunae it fills) to end of *duces* (no *ministri*).
1298	1329 (1)	974	?Doubtful; no ss. but early 11th-cent. text.
1301	796 (1)	974	Doubtful: ss. consistent, apart from three Æthelwolds (?a scribal error).
1302	807 (1)	968 × 74[2] ('984')	Has been doubted; ss. consistent.
1303	795 (1)	974	Prob. original. Ss. consistent.
1304	799 (1)	974	?Spurious. Ss. consistent.[3]
1305	794	974	Genuine.
1309	805 (no MS)	970 × 2[4]	Ss. consistent.
1312	801 (1)	975	Survives in early copy, almost certainly genuine; ss. consistent.
1313	804 (1)	975	Doubtful; ss. consistent, but few.
1315	802 (1)	975	Ss. mostly abbs.; they include Sigeric, ?the abb. St Augustine's, Canterbury, 980–8; the rest are possible for 975.
1316	800 (1)	975	Ss. consistent.

II

Kemble no.	Sawyer no. and MS consulted	Date	Comment
621	834 (1)	979	Prob. genuine: ss. consistent.
622	835 (1)	979	Prob. genuine: ss. consistent.
624	837 (1)	980	Ss. consistent.
629	838[5]	981	Prob. genuine; ss. consistent.
632	841 (1)	982	Ss. consistent (?re-touched: A. Watkin in *VCH Wilts*, III, 229, n. 45).
633	840 (1, 2)	982	Ss. consistent.[6]
636	848 (1)	983	Ss. consistent.
648	856 (1)	985	Ss. consistent.
650	860 (1)	985	Ss. consistent (very similar to Kemble, no. 648).
655	861 (1)	986	Ss. consistent.
657	864 (1)	987	Prob. original. Ss. consistent.
660	1353 (1)	987	Prob. genuine; early 11th-cent. text.
661	1354 (1)	987	As 660.
663	872[7]	988	Ss. consistent.[7]

[1] Text checked by Smith, *Bede* (ed. of 1722, cited Sawyer), pp. 775–7 from lost MS 1; MS 2 only a brief summary.

[2] Dated by abbs. Sideman and Cyneweard (see Exeter, Milton).

[3] But MS 1 reads 'Lyneweard' for abb. 'Cyneweard' (Milton: MS BM Harl. 436, ff. 87v–91v).

[4] Three bps. Ælfstan, two bps. Ælfwold.

[5] We have used the text ed. H. P. R. Finberg, *EHR*, LVIII (1943), 198–200.

[6] Godwine *dux* appears as abb. in MS 1; MS 2 adds second Abb. Æthelweard (as Kemble, no. 632).

[7] Cf. Barker (1949), pp. 103–9. Ss. consistent if Æthelstan bp. = Ælfstan and Æthelwold = Ælfwold.

8-3

Kemble no.	Sawyer no. and MS consulted	Date	Comment
664	868 (1)	988	Ss. consistent.
665	870 (1)	988	Ss. consistent.
673	874 (1)	990	Ss. consistent.[1]
677	1364 (1)	991	As 660.
678	1365 (1)	991	As 660.
684	876 (1)	993	Prob. original. Ss. consistent, but raise certain difficulties.[2]
686	880 (1)	994	Original. Ss. consistent.[3]
687	881 (1)	994	Prob. genuine basis at least; ss. consistent.
692	886 (1)	995	Genuine.[4]
695	1381 (1)	996	Prob. authentic.
696	888 (2, 3)	996	Ss. consistent.
698	819 (1)	997	Ss. consistent.
700	893 (1, 2)	998	Ss. consistent.
701	895 (1)	998	Ss. consistent; otherwise dubious.
703	896 (1, 2)	999	Ss. consistent.
705	898 (1)	1001	Ss. consistent; prob. original.
706	899 (1)	1001	Ss. corrupt,[5] but not unrecognizable; prob. basically authentic.
707	904 (1)	1002	Ss. consistent, in MS 1.[6]
710	906 (1, 2)	1004	MS 1 not original, but possibly cht. genuine; ss. consistent.[7]
712	942 (1)	990 × 1[8]	Ss. consistent (990 if Eadwin abb. Abingdon); no ground for suspicion.
714	911[9]	1005	Ss. consistent; prob. authentic.
715	914 (3)	'1006'	?for 1002; prob. spurious.
719	926 (1)	1012	Ss. consistent; prob. authentic.
724	1388	1016	Prob. genuine.
728	951 (1)[10]	?1018	Ss. consistent (allowing Bp. Brihtwine: see p. 15); but prob. not authentic.

[1] Assuming one of the Bps. Æthelsige = Ælfsige of Chester-le-Street.
[2] See Cholsey, Ramsey, Winchcombe.   [3] In MS 1, for Abb. Ælfric, read Ælfsie.
[4] Cf. Robinson (1923), p. 37.
[5] E.g. Ælfstan, for Ælfheah, bp. Winchester.
[6] In Kemble occ. Bps. Saxwulf, Ælfstan (Ælfgar in MS 1), Brihtric and Ecgwin who cannot be identified for 1002; but the bps. in MS 1 (who include Athulf, Lyvingc and Æscwig, not in Kemble) are consistent, if Æthelric Sherborne (1002 +) was contemporary with Æscwig of Dorchester and Eadwulf of York (d. 1002). The abbs. appear to be identifiable as follows: Ælfweard (Glastonbury), Wulfgar (not Wulfstan, as Kemble, Abingdon), two Ælfsiges (Ely and Winchester, New Minster), Ælfuere (Bath, 'Alfuese' – Kemble omits), Coenwulf ('Keanulf', Peterborough), Ælfwold (Winchcombe), Godman (Thorney – 'Godwin', Kemble), Wulfric (Canterbury, St Augustine), Ælfgar (Evesham), Æthelnoth (unidentified, see Appendix 1; 'Willnoth', Kemble), Ælfric (Malmesbury), Leofric (Muchelney or St Albans). The first dux, Ælfric, is Ælsie in Kemble. Kemble's text comes from MS 2 (Charter Roll), via *Mon.*
[7] Wulfheah abb. among *ministri* in Kemble should be *minister.*
[8] Ealdorman Brihtnoth d. 991 (at Maldon).
[9] Checked by MSS 1 (no ss.), 11 (= *Ctl. Eynsham*, facing p. xxxii: 1, pp. 19–28).
[10] MS 1 has Abb. Brihtwig (Glastonbury) for Brihtrig (Kemble).

Kemble no.	Sawyer no. and MS consulted	Date	Comment
729	954 (2)	?1019	Spurious, though ss. mainly consistent; but see Ely.[1]
730	955 (1)	?1019	Ss. doubtful.[2]
734	958[3]	?1022	Ss. seem consistent,[4] but authenticity not certain.
735	980 (1)[5]	1022 × 3	Dubious.
736	977 (1)	1021 × 3	Ss. consistent; prob. original.
739	960 (1)	1023	Prob. genuine; ss. consistent.
741	961 (1)	1024	Prob. original; ss. consistent.
743	962 (1)	?1026	Doubtful: grant to Bp. Lyfing, app. 1027; ss. consistent with 1027.
744	963 (1)	1031	Prob. original, though it confuses Canterbury and York – ss. otherwise consistent.
746	964 (1, 2)	1032	Ss. consistent.
748	965 (1)	?1032	Spurious.
751	967 (1)	1033	Ss. consistent.
762	993 (1)	1042	Dubious, but ss. consistent.
763	994 (1)	1042	Prob. original. Ss. consistent.
764	1396[6]	1041 × 2	Ss. consistent.
767	999 (1)	1043	Ss. consistent.
769	1044 (1)	1042 × 4	Possibly original; ss. consistent.
771	1002	?1044	Spurious. Ss. not consistent.[7]
772	1004 (1)	?1044	Doubtful: a supposed original, but ss. inconsistent.[8]
774	1006 (1)	1044	Possibly genuine; ss. consistent.
776	1012 (1)	1045	Prob. genuine. Ss. consistent.
777	1397[9]	1045	No obviously objectionable features.
778	1010 (1)	1045	Ss. consistent.
779	1011 (1)	?1045	Spurious, but ss. seem prob. consistent, if Ægelricus = Æthelric of Durham.
781	1008 (1, 2)	1045[10]	Prob. genuine; ss. consistent.
784	1014 (1)	1046	Prob. genuine; ss. consistent.
785	1055 (1,[11] 2)	?1047	Prob. spurious; but ss. consistent with 1047,[12] apart from 'Godric', abb. Evesham, q.v.

[1] In Kemble Æthelfred bp. is for Æthelstan of Hereford (Æthelstan in MS 2), the two called Brichtwolf for Brithwold of Ramsbury and Cornwall. We have ignored impossible forms: e.g. Abb. Luxihs; Filnoth possibly = Eilnoth, Ælfnoth (see p. 225).

[2] Wine bp. perhaps = Eadnoth of Crediton (cf. *WMGP*, p. 200); Ælfstan abb. is only known from Kemble, no. 729. For Bp. Brihtwine, see p. 15.　　　[3] Text used, *Lib. El.*, pp. 150–1.

[4] For Bp. Brihtwine, see p. 15; Eadric bp. may be Ætheric of Dorchester.

[5] MS omits bps. Ælfwinus and Brihtwaldus, and rearranges abbs., replacing Ælfuine by Ælfsius.

[6] No MS: text of Kemble, nos. 764, 777, checked by Smith, *Bede* (1722, for references see Sawyer).

[7] Though only Bp. Wulfstan of Worcester seems clearly anachronistic.

[8] Bps. Ælfwold (Sherborne from 1045) and Ealdred seem anachronistic; but on Ealdred see Tavistock.

[9] See n. 6.　　　　[10] In MS 2 the three abbs. are *duces*; abbs. in MS 1.　　　[11] No ss.

[12] Save that Æthelmær bp. 'Thetford' (Elmham) appears with Ælfwine bp. Winchester, but the former succeeded on Stigand's translation which followed Ælfwine's death.

Kemble no.	Sawyer no. and MS consulted	Date	Comment
787	1019 (1)	1049	Prob. original; ss. consistent.
791	1021 (1)	1050[1]	Prob. original; ss. consistent.
792	1020 (1)	1050[1]	Ss. consistent, apart from Abb. Ordric (Abingdon).
793	1022 (1)	1050[1]	Ss. consistent.
794	1049 (1)	?1045 × 50	Spurious.
795	1230 (2)	?1051	Spurious.
796	1023 (1, 2)	?1052[1]	Ss. prob. consistent.
797	1058 (1)	1044 × 51	Dubious; ss. consistent.[2]
800	1025 (1, 2)[3]	?1054	Doubtful; ss. include Archbp. Eadsige and are consistent with 1049 × 50.[1]
801	1026 (2)[4]	?1055	Spurious; ss. inconsistent.
807	1475 (1)	1051 × 3	Ss. consistent (not numerous); but cht. doubtful.
810	1033 (1)	1061	Prob. authentic basis; ss. consistent.
811	1034 (1)	1061	Prob. authentic base; ss. consistent.
812	1035 (1)	1062	Spurious, but ss. consistent.
813	1036 (1)	?1062	Spurious; ss. not consistent.
815	—	?1065	Spurious: see Winchester, New Minster.
817	1038 (1)	?1065	Doubtful; ss. few but not definitely inconsistent.
823	1480 (1)	1062 × 6	Doubtful; ss. consistent.
824	1043 (1)[5]	?28 Dec. 1065	Spurious, but ss. consistent.
825	1041 (2)	?1065	Spurious, but ss. nearly consistent.[6]
897	—	—	A note apparently genuine.
912	1057 (1)	?1044 × 58	Spurious; ss. not consistent.
916	1000 (1, 4)	?1043	Spurious; ss. corrupt and prob. inconsistent.[7]
939	1226 (1–3, 5)	?1046 × 50	Spurious; ss. few but prob. consistent.
964	1479 (1)	1061 × 2	Dubious; ss. few but seem consistent.
1277	829 (1, 2)	975 × 8	Ss. not numerous; consistent with 975 × 8, not 965 as dated.
1278	839 (1)	982	Ss. consistent.
1279	843 (1)	983	Ss. consistent.
1282	855 (1)	984	Ss. consistent.
1283	858 (1)	985	Ss. consistent.
1289	883 (1)	992 × 5 (prob. –994)	Prob. authentic: see *EHD*, 1, p. 525. Ss. consistent.

[1] On the *signa* and dates of Kemble, nos. 791–3, 796, 800 see Barlow (1963), pp. 154–5: it seems that all the ss. are based on lists of 1050, in spite of the dates attached to 796 and 800, and that Abb. Ordric's appearance in 792, 796 and 800 is prob. an anachronism: they are chts. for Abingdon, of which he was abb. 1052–66.   [2] Abb. Earwini evidently = Earnwig of Peterborough.
[3] MS 2 has Abb. Alfward' for Wulfwardus in MS 1 and Kemble.
[4] Adding bps. William and Leofwine before Wulfstan. Ss. as in p. 233 n. 7.
[5] Lacking Bp. Wulfwine, but the MS is burnt.   [6] Apart from Bp. Godwine, d. 1061.
[7] For Abb. Manwig (Manni) see Evesham; for Bp. Ealdred, however, see Tavistock.

Kemble no.	Sawyer no. and MS consulted	Date	Comment
1292	887 (1)	996	Ss. consistent.
1295	901 (1, 2)	1002	Ss. almost consistent, but Bp. Ælfhelm signs as well as Æscwig (of Dorchester).
1297	900 (1, 2)	1002	Ss. consistent.
1299	1664 (1)	1003	Ss. consistent, but few.
1301	910 (1)	1005	Ss. consistent; prob. genuine.
1303	915 (1)	1007	Ss. consistent.
1304	916	1007	Prob. genuine. Ss. consistent.
(= Crawford Chts., no. 11)			
1305	918 (1)	1008	Ss. consistent, if Bp. Osbriht = Ordbriht, Selsey.
1306	921	1009	Ss. consistent, prob. genuine.
1307	927 (1–3)	?1012[1]	Ss. consistent, but Bp. Lyfing ?1013+
1308	931 (1)[2]	1013	Ss. difficult;[3] but prob. genuine base.
1309	933 (1)	1014	Ss. consistent; prob. genuine.
1313	1384 (1)	1017	Ss. consistent, but few; prob. genuine.
1316	957 (1)	1020	Spurious, but ss. consistent.
1317	1424 (1)	c. 1022	Doubtful.
1318	969 (2)	?1033	Ss. nearly consistent;[4] prob. genuine.
1322	975 (1)	1035	Ss. consistent; prob. genuine.
1324	979	1024[5] × 32	Ss. few, but consistent, if Æthelwold, archbp. Canterbury = Æthelnoth.
1351	—	—	Manumission, prob. genuine.

III

As Chts., No.	Sawyer no. (MSS not consulted)	Date	Comment
23	391	?934	Dubious, but ss. consistent.
32	1506	Prob. 958	Prob. original.
40	—	(963 × 92)	A series of transactions.
45	806	'978' (?for 968)	Prob. authentic base: ss. doubtful.
47	1452	See Exeter (pp. 48, 211)	Prob. genuine.
49	1449	964 × 75	Prob. genuine.
50	813	Prob. 970 × 5	Ss. spurious.
55–8	1332, 1373–4, 1372	977, 975 × 8	Prob. genuine.
61	1369	983 × 5[6]	Prob. genuine.

[1] Dated June, MS 1; July, MSS 2–3.
[2] Cf. Hart (1966), pp. 193–4; ss. discussed pp. 195–6. The abbs. are German, Brihtred, Godeman, Ælfsige, Brihtmer, Wulgar.
[3] Consistent if Æthulf bp. is for Æthelwold of Winchester; and Ælfsige for Æthelsige of Sherborne.
[4] All consistent with 1032, when Ælfmaer bp. Selsey seems to have d.
[5] Accepting the date in J. A. Robinson (1918) for Brihtric bp. Wells.
[6] Ælfric, ealdorman of Mercia.

As Chts., No.	Sawyer no. (MSS not consulted)	Date	Comment
63	877	989 × 90 (MS 993)	Prob. genuine; ss. consistent.
64–5	1363, 1362	990	Prob. genuine.
66	1454	990 × 2	Prob. original.
67	1366	991	Prob. genuine.
69	1456	995 × 1006	Prob. genuine.
70	1420	995 × 1006	Ss. consistent, but few.
74	1422	1012	Prob. genuine.
75	1220	1013 × 20	Possibly original.
76	1459	c. 1014 × 16	Authentic.
77	1461	1016 × 20	Authentic.
81	1423	1016 × 23	Prob. genuine.
82	959	1023	Ss. consistent; authentic base at least.
85	981	—	Spurious.
86	1465	?1032	Presumably genuine.
94	1394	1042	Prob. original.
97	1468	1043 × 4	Prob. genuine.
101	1471	1045 × 7	Prob. original.
103	1473	1044 × 8	Prob. original.
105	1474	1045 × 6	Prob. genuine.
107	1403	1047 × 52	Prob. genuine.
112	1406	1046 × 56 (?1051 × 2)	Prob. genuine.
114	1476	?c. 1053	Very likely an early forgery; but possibly genuine.[1]
115	1478	1053 × 5	Authentic.
116	1234	1052 × 70 (?1054)	Prob. genuine.
117	1426	1061 × 5	Prob. genuine.

AS Wills

As Chts., No.	Sawyer no. (MSS not consulted)	Date	Comment
16 (2)	— (cf. 1501)	995 × 9	Genuine (ss. few, but consistent).
18	1488	Prob. 1003 × 4 (1002 × 5)	Genuine.
20	1503	1015	Genuine.
22	1495	?c. 1004 × 14	Prob. basically genuine, though ss. inconsistent.
31	1531	1043 × 5	Genuine.

AS Writs

As Chts., No.	Sawyer no. (MSS not consulted)	Date	Comment
62	1110	—	Spurious.
71	1163	1066	Authentic.

[1] Cf. evidence cited *AS Chts.*, p. 462.

IV

Charters not in Birch, Kemble, etc.

Sawyer no.	Source used	Date	Comment
729	*Ctl. Muchelney*, no. 3.	964	Doubtful; ss. consistent for 964 × 70.[1]
766 (1)	*Mon.*, II, 323–4 (and MS 1).	968	Ss. consistent; possibly authentic.
865	*Liber de Hyda*, pp. 231–6.	987	Ss. consistent.
869	*Liber de Hyda*, pp. 238–42.	16 Apr. 988	Ss. consistent.
879 (2)	MS 2: Aberystwyth, Nat. Lib. Wales, Peniarth MS 390, p. 357.	?996[2]	Ss. consistent for 996.
890 (1)	*OS Facs.*, III, no. 35.	25 July 997	Ss. consistent; prob. original.[3]
903	*Gilbert Crispin*, pp. 167–8.	1002	Ss. consistent, if Bp. Ælfstan = Lyfing (Wells).[4]
920 (1)	MS 1: as 879, pp. 363–4.[5]	1008	Ss. consistent.
930 (1)	MS 1: as 879, p. 366.	?1012	Ss. mostly consistent.[6]
950 (1)	*OS Facs.*, III, no. 39.	1018	Ss. consistent; prob. original.[7]
953 (1)	*OS Facs.*, II, Exeter, no. 10	?1018	Ss. consistent, but 'original' a forgery.
956 (1)	*OS Facs.*, II, Winchester Coll. no. 4; *EHD*, I, 553–5.	1019	Prob. original.
971 (1)	*OS Facs.*, II, Exeter, no. 11.	1031 (not 1033)	Ss. consistent; prob. original.
973 (1)	*Ch. Abingdon*, I, 434–5 (and MS 1).	1034	Ss. mostly omitted in MS; if not genuine, represents Abingdon tradition.
974 (1)	*OS Facs.*, III, no. 42.	1035	Ss. consistent; MS seems to be original.
1003 (1)	*OS Facs.*, II, Exeter, no. 12.	1044	Ss. consistent; possibly genuine.
1015	Matthew, pp. 143–5.	1046	Ss. consistent; prob. genuine.
1017 (1)	MS 1: as 879, p. 368.	1048	Ss. consistent.
1027 (1)	*OS Facs.*, II, Exeter, no. 14; Earle, pp. 300–2.	?1059	Ss. consistent with 1058.[8]
1218	Hart (1957), p. 19.	995 × 9	Ss. consistent.

[1] But Adhelstan bp. – ?for Ælfstan; and we assume that Abb. Ælfstan was of Glastonbury (964 × 70).

[2] Dated 993, indiction 9. The two archbps. enforce a date +995, Wulfstan, bp. London 996+; Brihtnoth, abb. (Ely) –999. The 9th indiction would fit 995 × 6, and all ss. would be consistent with 996.

[3] Apart from Bp. Ælfstan – ?for Athelstan Elmham (the Ælfstans of Rochester and London seem certainly to have been off by 997).

[4] Cf. *WMGP*, p. 194; Florence, I, 158 (Athelstan).

[5] Cf. Shaw, *Staffs*, I, 28.

[6] The last two bps. Æscwig (?Dorchester, d. 1002) and Sigegar (?Wells, d. *c.* 997) are impossible, but were perhaps added.

[7] See p. 15 (bp. Brihtwine).   [8] When Ælfwold bp. Sherborne d.

Sawyer no.	Source used	Date	Comment
1380	*Mon.*, VI, 1443–6.	?995[1]	Doubtful, but prob. a genuine base.
1405 (1)	*BM Facs.*, IV, no. 38; Earle, pp. 247–8.	1058	Prob. original.
1407 (1)	*BM Facs.*, IV, no. 32.	*c.* 1053[2]	Prob. original.
1773, 1775, 1780	*WMAG*, pp. 85, 87, 101.	965, 1000, 979 × 97	References only; and the dates are very doubtful (see Glastonbury).
1860	Ker in *Studies...presented to F. M. Powicke*, p. 75.	?early 11th cent.	A Worcester fragment: no grounds for suspicion.

[1] Archbp. Sigeric prob. d. in Oct. 994, and Ealdwulf of York and Godwine of Rochester prob. succeeded in 995. Otherwise ss. consistent with 995, but cht. dated 996. On other grounds doubtful.

[2] Earl Harold without Godwine may suggest a date +1053; but Abb. Brihtwold, presumably of Malmesbury, apparently d. before Godwine.

ADDENDUM

HINCHINGBROOKE (Hunts: previously at Papley in Eltisley, Cambs), St James. Benedictine pr.   f. –1087

List in *VCH Hunts*, I, 390.

Lettice   Occ. *c.* 1160 × May 1169 (Mowbray, no. 168, ex inf. D. E. Greenway).

INDEX OF HEADS

This index is solely a list of heads, the information being kept to a minimum for convenience in use. The order is based on Christian names, with abbots before priors, abbesses before prioresses, and in alphabetical order of their houses: surnames are always in parentheses and ignored in the order. As in the large majority of documentary references to medieval heads Christian names alone occur, it is hoped that this system will be helpful and save confusion. The arrangement means that heads who moved from house to house occur twice: thus Adam, pr. Bermondsey, later abb. Evesham, appears under each, but with a cross-reference. Square brackets enclosing the name of a house indicate that the head moved to it later than 1216 and his name is not, therefore, to be found in the list for that house. Names occurring in earlier printed lists which we have eliminated are in italics; names due to scribal error are in inverted commas (with cross-reference to the correct form); and names queried in the lists are queried here.

Adam, pr. Monks Horton, 120
Adam (Sortes), Master, pr. Penwortham, 94
Adam, pr. Pontefract (pr. Monk Bretton), 120, 124
Adam, pr. Sempringham, 205
?Adam, pr. Stafford, 184
Adam, pr. Thoby, 185
Adam, pr. Weedon Lois, 112
Adam (de Subiria), pr. Wilsford, 112
Adebold, Adelulf, pr. Bridlington, 154 n. 3
Adelelm, abb. Abingdon, 24
Adelina, prs. Kilburn, 213
Adelulf, pr. Nostell (bp. Carlisle), 178
Ademarus, pr. Lewes, see Aimarus, 119
'Adolphus', pr. Freiston, see Ralph Simplex, 90 n. 2
Ædwi, pr. Worcester, 82
Ægelric, abb. Crowland (2), 41
Ægelric, abb. Milton, 56
Ægelsige, Ægelsie, pr. Worcester, 83
Ægelward, pr. Sherborne, 70
Ægelweard, abb. Glastonbury, see Æthelweard, 51
Ægelwin, abb. see Æthelwin, 225
Ægelwine, pr. Worcester, 83
Ægfridus, abb. 225
Æiricus, pr. Hurley, 92
Ælard, pr. St Denys, Southampton, 182
Ælfgar, abb. Evesham, 46
Ælfgifu, abb. Wilton, 222
Ælfgith, abb. Wilton, see Ælfgyth, 222
Ælfgyfu, abb. Romsey, 218
Ælfgyth, abb. Wilton (2), 222
Ælfgyva, abb. Barking, 208
Ælfheah, St, abb. Bath (bp. Winchester, archbp. Canterbury), 27, 28
?Ælfheah, St, abb. Deerhurst, 102
Ælfhere, abb., 225
Ælfhere, abb. Bath, 28
Ælfhun, Ælfhim, abb. Milton, 56
Ælfmaer, abb. Canterbury, St Augustine (bp. Sherborne), 35
Ælfmaer, abb. Tavistock (? bp. Selsey), 71
Ælfnoth, abb. (2), 225
Ælfnoth, abb. Winchester, New Minster, 81
Ælfred, abb., 225
Ælfric, abb. Abingdon, 24 n. 1
Ælfric, abb. Athelney, 26
Ælfric, abb. Canterbury, St Augustine, 35
Ælfric (Puttoc), ? abb. Cerne, 37 and n. 1
Ælfric, abb. Evesham, 46
Ælfric, abb. Eynsham, 48
?Ælfric, abb. Glastonbury, 50
Ælfric, abb. Malmesbury, 54
Ælfric, abb. Malmesbury (bp. Crediton), 54
Ælfric, abb. Milton, see Eadred, 56
Ælfric, abb. Pershore, 58
Ælfric, abb. St Albans, 65

Ælfric, abb. St Albans (? bp. Ramsbury, archbp. Canterbury), 65
Ælfric, pr. Sherborne, 70
Ælfric (Puttoc), pr. Winchester, St Swithun (archbp. York), 80
Ælfsie, abb. Canterbury, St Augustine, see Æthelsige, 36
Ælfsige, abb. 225
Ælfsige, abb. Bath, 28
Ælfsige, abb. Ely, 44
Ælfsige, abb. Peterborough, 59
Ælfsige, abb. Ramsey (abb. Canterbury, St Augustine), 35, 62
Ælfsige, abb. St Benet of Hulme, 67
Ælfsige, abb. Winchester, New Minster, 81
?Ælfstan, abb., 225
Ælfstan, abb. Canterbury, St Augustine, 35
Ælfstan, abb. Chertsey, see Lyfing, 38
Ælfstan, abb. Glastonbury (? bp. Ramsbury), 50
Ælfstan, pr. Worcester, 83
Ælfthryth, abb. Berkeley, 208
?Ælfthryth, abb. Shaftesbury, 219
Ælfuere, abb. Bath, see Ælfhere, 28
Ælfweard, abb., 225
Ælfweard, abb. Evesham (bp. London), 47
Ælfweard, abb. Glastonbury, 51
Ælfwig, abb., 225
Ælfwig, abb. Bath, 28
Ælfwig, abb. Westminster, 76
Ælfwig, abb. Winchester, New Minster, 81
Ælfwine, abb., 225
Ælfwine, abb. Buckfast, 128
Ælfwine, abb. Malmesbury, 54
Ælfwine, abb. Ramsey, 61
Ælfwine, abb. Winchester, New Minster, 81
Ælfwine, Alfwinus, pr. Canterbury, Christ Church, 33
Ælfwold, abb., 225
Ælfwold, abb. Muchelney, 56
Ælfwold, abb. St Benet of Hulme, 67
?Ælfwold, abb. Winchcombe, 78
Ælfwy, abb. Winchester, New Minster, see Ælfwig, 81
Ælsi, abb. Bath, see Ælfsige, 28
Ælsi, abb. Ramsey, see Ælfsige, 62
Ælstrita, abb. Wherwell, 222
Æluere, abb., 225
Ælviva, abb. Wilton, see Ælfgifu, 222
Æscwig, abb. Bath (? bp. Dorchester), 28
Æsuuerdus, abb. Abbotsbury, 23
Æthelflaed, abb. Romsey, 218
Æthelgar, abb. Winchester, New Minster (bp. Selsey, archbp. Canterbury), 80
?Æthelgeofu, abb. Shaftesbury, 219
Æthelnoth, abb., 225
Æthelnoth, abb. Canterbury, St Augustine, 35
Æthelnoth, abb. Glastonbury, 51
Æthelnoth, abb. Winchester, New Minster, 81

Austorgius, pr. Horsham St Faith, *see* Eustorgius, 104
?Avelina, prs. Blackborough, 209
Avice, abb. Malling, 215
Avice (of Grimsby), prs. Broadholme, 209
Avice, prs. Sopwell, 220
Aymerius, pr. Totnes, 110
Azelina, abb. Northampton de la Pré, 216

B., abb. Hartland, 165
B., pr. Catley, 201
B., pr. Ely, 46 and n. 2
B., pr. Launceston, 169 n.
B., prs. Markyate, 215
Baldwin, abb. Alnwick, 192
Baldwin, abb. Bourne, 153
Baldwin, abb. Bury St Edmunds (pr. Deerhurst), 32, 102
Baldwin, abb. Forde, (bp. Worcester, archbp. Canterbury), 132
Baldwin, abb. Tavistock, 72
Baldwin, pr. Axmouth, 100
Baldwin, pr. Deerhurst (abb. Bury St Edmunds), 32, 102
Baldwin, pr. Loders, 105
Baldwin, pr. Monks Kirby, 106
Baldwin, pr. Tywardreath, 111
Baldwin, pr. York, St Andrew, 206
Bartholomew, abb. Alnwick, 192
Bartholomew, abb. Langdon, 196
Bartholomew, pr. Carlisle, 158
Bartholomew, pr. Tutbury, 111
Bartholomew, pr. York, St Andrew, 206
Basilia, prs. Keldholme, 213
Basset, William, abb. St Benet of Hulme, *see* William, 68
Beatrice, abb. Amesbury, 207
Beatrice, abb. Winchester, Nunminster, 223
Beatrice, prs. Davington, 210
Beatrice, prs. Fosse, 211
Beatrice, prs. Legbourne, 214
Beatrice, prs. Yedingham, 224
Beleisur, prs. Handale, 212
Bella, prs. Handale, 212
Benedict, abb. Alnwick, 192
Benedict, abb. Athelney (2), 27
Benedict (of Stratford), abb. Coggeshall (abb. Stratford Langthorne), 130, 144
?Benedict, abb. Hartland, 165
Benedict, abb. Peterborough (pr. Canterbury, Christ Church), 34, 61
Benedict, abb. Sallay, 141
Benedict, abb. Selby, 69
Benedict, abb. Stratford Langthorne (abb. Coggeshall), 130, 144
Benedict, abb. Tewkesbury, 73
Benedict, abb. Whitby, 78
Benedict, pr. Bath, 28

Benedict, pr. Burscough, 156
Benedict, pr. Canterbury, Christ Church (abb. Peterborough), 34, 61
Benedict, pr. Daventry, 117
Benedict, pr. Exeter, St Nicholas, 89
'Benedict', pr. Newburgh, *see* Bernard, 177
Benedict, pr. Swavesey, 110
Benton, John, abb. Thornton Curtis, *see*, John, 186
Beorhtred, abb. Glastonbury, *see* Brihtred, 51
Berengar, abb. Welbeck, 198
Berengar, pr. Nuneaton, 217
Bernard, abb. Burton (abb. Cerne), 31, 37
Bernard, Master, abb. Cerne (abb. Burton), 31, 37
Bernard (of St Albans), abb. Ramsey, 62
Bernard, abb. Tewkesbury, 73
Bernard, pr. Bermondsey, 116
Bernard, pr. Bridlington, 154
Bernard, pr. Burwell, 101
Bernard, pr. Dunstable, 162
Bernard, pr. Hexham, 166
Bernard, pr. Kenilworth, 167
Bernard, ? Benedict, pr. Newburgh, 177
Bernard, pr. Tickford, 110
Bernard, pr. York, Holy Trinity, 113
Bertram, abb. Chertsey (pr. Horsham, St Faith), 38, 104
Bertram, pr. Bermondsey, 115
Bertram, pr. Durham, 43
Bertram, pr. Ewenny, 89
Bertram, pr. Pontefract, 124
Bertrand (Bertram), pr. Horsham St Faith (abb. Chertsey), 38, 104
Biseth, Robert, pr. Hexham, *see* Robert, 166
Blakere, pr. Rumburgh, 95
Blanchard, Robert, abb. Battle, *see* Robert, 29
Blont, Henry, abb. Gloucester, *see* Henry, 53
Bovo, pr. Witham, 149
Brand, abb. Peterborough, 60
Brian, pr. Rochester, 64
Brientius, pr. Belvoir, 85
Brihstan, abb., 226
Brihteah, Brihteh, abb., 226
Brihteah, abb. Pershore (bp. Worcester), 58
Brihtgifu, abb. Wilton, 222
Brihthelm, abb. Exeter, St Peter, 48
Brihthelm, abb. Malmesbury, 54
Brihtiva, abb. Wilton, *see* Brihtgifu, 222
Brihtmær, abb. Crowland, 42
Brihtmær (Brithmar), abb. Evesham, 46
Brihtmær, abb. Winchester, New Minster, 81
Brihtnoth, Brichtnoth, abb., 226
Brihtnoth, abb. Ely, pr. Winchester, St Swithun, 44, 79
Brihtred, abb. Glastonbury, 51
Brihtric, abb. Burton, 30
Brihtric, abb. Burton, abb. Malmesbury, 31, 55
Brihtric, Britricus, pr. Little Dunmow, 171

Fulk, pr. Bicknacre, 151
Fulk, pr. Haughmond, 165
Fulk, pr. Lapley, 105
Fulk, pr. Leeds, 170
Fulk, pr. Pembroke, 107
Fulk, pr. Pontefract, 124
Fulk, pr. St Osyth, 183
Fulk, pr. Tutbury, 111

G., abb. Calder II, 130
G., abb. Sherborne, 70 n. 3
G., abb. Strata Marcella, 144
G., pr. Chicksands, *see* Walter, 202
G., pr. Ely, 46
G., pr. London, St Bartholomew, 174
G., pr. Montacute, 122
G., pr. Nuneaton, 217
? G., pr. Sporle, 109
G., pr. Stogursey, 110
G., pr. Stoke by Clare, 110
G., pr. Warwick, St Sepulchre, 189
Gabriel, William, pr. Llangennith, *see* William, 105
Galandus, Galannus, abb. Winchcombe, 79
Galyenus, pr. Wymondham, 98
Gamel, abb. Rufford, 141
Gamel, pr. Alvingham, 201
Gamel, pr. Bullington, 201
Gardinus, pr. Breamore, 153
Garinus, pr. Spalding, 109
Gastwek, Margaret, prs. Catley, *see* Margaret, 202
Gausbert, abb. Battle, 29
Gauselinus, Gaulenus, Zolinus, pr. Eye, 102
Geoffrey, abb. Abbotsbury (2), 23
Geoffrey, abb. Alnwick (abb. Dryburgh), 192
Geoffrey, abb. Bruern, 128
Geoffrey, abb. Burton (pr. Winchester, St Swithun), 31, 80
Geoffrey (de Mala Terra), abb. Burton, 31
Geoffrey, abb. Chester, 39
Geoffrey, abb. Combermere, 130
Geoffrey (d'Orleans), abb. Crowland, 42
Geoffrey, abb. Easby, 195
Geoffrey, abb. Newhouse, 197
Geoffrey, abb. Newminster, 138
Geoffrey, abb. Pipewell, 139
Geoffrey, abb. Rievaulx, 140
Geoffrey (de Gorron), abb. St Albans, 67
Geoffrey, abb. Sallay, 142
Geoffrey, abb. Swineshead, 144
Geoffrey, abb. Tavistock, 72
Geoffrey, abb. Tupholme, 198
Geoffrey, abb. Westminster, 76
Geoffrey, abb. Winchester, Hyde, 82
Geoffrey, abb. York, St Mary, 84
Geoffrey, master of Stixwould, 221
Geoffrey, pr. Alvingham, 201

? Geoffrey, pr. Barlinch, 150
Geoffrey (of Huntingdon), pr. Barnwell, 150
Geoffrey, pr. Bermondsey, 115
Geoffrey, pr. Binham, 86
Geoffrey, pr. Bolton, 152
Geoffrey, pr. Boxgrove, 101
Geoffrey, pr. Bradenstoke, 153
Geoffrey, pr. Brinkburn, 154
Geoffrey, pr. Burscough, 156
Geoffrey, pr. Canterbury, Christ Church, 34
Geoffrey, pr. Canterbury, Christ Church (abb. Dunfermline), 33
Geoffrey, pr. Covenham, 101
Geoffrey, pr. Coventry, 41
Geoffrey, pr. Exeter, St Nicholas, 89
Geoffrey, pr. Hamble, 103
Geoffrey, pr. Kirkham, 168
Geoffrey, pr. Lancaster, 104
Geoffrey (of Henlawe), pr. Llanthony I and II (bp. St Davids), 172, 173
Geoffrey, pr. Launceston, 169 n. 3
Geoffrey (Parvus), pr. Monmouth, 106
Geoffrey, pr. Nostell, 179
Geoffrey, pr. Pentney, 181
Geoffrey (de Vaux), pr. Pentney, 181 n. 1
Geoffrey, pr. Plympton, 181
Geoffrey, pr. St Neots, 108
Geoffrey, pr. Spalding, 109
Geoffrey, pr. Stogursey, 110
Geoffrey, pr. Stoke by Clare, 110
Geoffrey, pr. Thornholme, 185
Geoffrey, pr. Tynemouth, 96
Geoffrey, pr. Winchester, St Swithun (2), 80
Geoffrey, pr. Winchester, St Swithun (abb. Burton), 31, 80
Geoffrey, pr. Wroxton, 191
Ger', pr. Huntingdon, 166
Gerald, abb. Byland, 129
Gerald (of Avranches), abb. Cranborne and Tewkesbury, 73, 87
Gerard, abb. Furness, 134
Gerard, pr. Barnwell, 150
Gerard, pr. Norwich, 58
? Gerard, pr. St Denys, Southampton, 182
Gerard, pr. Wootton Wawen, 113
Gerelm, pr. Poughley, 181
Gerin (d'Alencon), pr. Stogursey, 109 n. 6
Gerlo, abb. Newhouse, 197
German, abb. Selby (pr. Tynemouth), 69, 96
German, pr. Belvoir, 85
German, pr. Coventry, 40
German, pr. Durham, 43
German, pr. Tynemouth (abb. Selby), 69, 96
Germanus, abb. Cholsey (?abb. Winchcombe), 39, 78
? Germanus, abb. Ramsey (abb. Cholsey), 39, 61
Germanus, abb. Winchcombe, pr. Westbury-on-Trym, 78, 97

INDEX OF RELIGIOUS HOUSES

Houses noted on pp. 114, 126, 150, 192, 200, 207 as having no lists are none the less included in the Index for convenience.

Abbreviations for Orders, etc.

The abbreviations used in this Index are identical with those in *KH*.

A	Augustinian Canons
B	Black Monks, Benedictine
BC	Cluniac
BF	of Fontevrault
BT	of Tiron
C	Cistercian Monks
CA	Carthusian Monks
G	Gilbertine Canons
NA	Augustinian Canonesses
NB	Benedictine Nuns
NBC	Cluniac Nuns
NBF	Fontevrault (Double Order)
NC	Cistercian Nuns
NG	Gilbertine (Double Order)
NK	Sisters of St John of Jerusalem
NP	Premonstratensian Canonesses
P	Premonstratensian Canons

a (as suffix)   Alien
(a) (as suffix)   Alien, but later Denizen (not given in Orders of Cluny and Fontevrault)
Alternative names are shown in brackets.